# Marketing Management Casebook

# Marketing Management Casebook

Edited by

**HARPER W. BOYD, JR.,** Ph.D.
Robert A. and Vivian Young Distinguished
Professor of Business Administration
College of Business Administration
University of Arkansas (Fayetteville)

and

**ROBERT T. DAVIS,** D.C.S.
Sebastian S. Kresge Professor of Marketing
Graduate School of Business
Stanford University

 1976    Revised Edition

**RICHARD D. IRWIN, INC.**    Homewood, Illinois    60430
Irwin-Dorsey International    Arundel, Sussex    BN18 9AB
Irwin-Dorsey Limited    Georgetown, Ontario    L7G 4B3

Revised Edition

*First Printing, April 1976*

ISBN 0-256-01837-5
Library of Congress Catalog Card No. 75–43159
*Printed in the United States of America*

# Preface

The effective life of most casebooks is relatively short, and this is particularly true of one in marketing given the dynamics of the subject area. It has been more than four years since the publication of the first edition so the time has come for this revision. As before, our goal is to provide teachers of marketing management with a selection of cases designed to cover in considerable depth a variety of marketing subjects. This revision contains a total of 46 cases, of which 22 are totally new. Two "old" ones have been revised, and 22 are continued from the previous edition. Sixteen cases deal with consumer goods, 17 are industrial, 8 are service-oriented, and 5 cover the public sector. A number can or do involve the use of a decision model.

The cases included are classified by nine subject areas—one more than before. The new section is on marketing strategy—a subject which has grown substantially in importance over the past several years. Of the seven cases on this subject, six are new. The other sections are the same as before—the role of the marketplace, product and product line, price, channels of distribution, personal selling, organization, development of marketing plans, and control and reappraisal. All the cases are designed to challenge both the conceptual and analytical skills of students. All have been tested in the classroom.

Inevitably we are greatly indebted to a great many different people. First, we acknowledge with deep gratitude the contributions of the firms that made these cases possible. Many executives gave substantial amounts of time to help in developing the needed information. In many cases both the company and its executives remain anonymous because, for a variety of reasons, it was necessary to use fictitious names.

We are immensely grateful for the use of case material written by our colleagues: Professors Henry J. Claycamp, George S. Day, Gerald J. Eskin, Richard T. Johnson, William F. Massy, David B. Montgomery, Joseph W. Newman, Carlton A. Pederson, David L. Rados, Michael Ray, Sterling D. Sessions, and David Weinstein. We especially want to thank

v

Thomas J. Perkins of Kleiner & Perkins for his help in developing the marketing strategy section. INSEAD (The European Institute for Business Administration, Fontainebleau, France) gave us permission to use several of their cases, for which we are are most grateful.

*April 1976*                                        HARPER W. BOYD, JR.
                                                   ROBERT T. DAVIS

# Contents

# SECTION IV

## PRICE

# SECTION V

## CHANNELS OF DISTRIBUTION

# SECTION VI

## PERSONAL SELLING AND ADVERTISING

# SECTION VII

## ORGANIZATION

SECTION **VIII**

DEVELOPMENT OF MARKETING PLANS

SECTION **IX**

CONTROL AND REAPPRAISAL

# SECTION I

## ROLE OF THE MARKETPLACE

# Custom Furniture Rental Corporation

## STRATEGY FOR A SERVICE COMPANY

In February 1972 Mr. Donald Bjorklund, founder and president of Custom Furniture Rental Corporation (CFRC), was reviewing his company's progress. Sales and profits had grown nicely during the company's history, but current economic prospects were shaky, and Mr. Bjorklund wanted to be certain that his firm's position was sound.

### Company History

The idea of renting home furnishings to householders occurred to Mr. Bjorklund while he was running a retail furniture store in Seaside, Oregon. He noted that many young adults, high mobiles (e.g., stewardesses), and certain senior citizens whose children had left home shared a need for inexpensive but appropriate furnishings for their new and often temporary households. Although there had long been the option of renting furnished apartments, direct rental of furniture was not readily available.

There were two apparent alternative approaches—direct to tenant and through apartment house owners and managers. For both targets there seemed to be legitimate potential need for rental. The challenge was to switch the tenant from "purchase on time" to rental and to switch the owner-manager from investing his funds in a depreciating asset to rental. The challenge appealed to Mr. Bjorklund.

Thus, in May 1963 he launched his new business, operating from an existing store in Portland. There were few employees, and deliveries were made in one old truck. By 1965 the firm had been incorporated and operated branches in the San Francisco Bay area including Sunnyvale,

This case originally appeared as "Grantee Furniture Rental Corporation." Reprinted from *Stanford Business Cases 1975* with the permission of the publisher, Graduate School of Business, Stanford University. Copyright © 1975 by the Board of Trustees of the Leland Stanford Junior University.

San Mateo, Burlingame, San Francisco, and the East Bay—all areas with high apartment growth rates. Early sales were modest but encouraging, as indicated in Exhibit 1.

In subsequent years CFRC acquired two local rental firms with strong managers (a rarity in this business) and by the end of 1971 had 24 domestic showrooms, 1 Canadian showroom, 12 warehouses, and 6 used furniture outlets. Expansion had been limited to the West Coast and included Vancouver, Seattle, Edmonds, Bellevue, Portland, Beaverton, Corvallis, Eugene, Oakland, San Leandro, Walnut Creek, San Francisco, Burlingame, San Carlos, Sunnyvale, San Jose, Hollywood, Mira Loma, La Habra, Anaheim, Costa Mesa, and San Diego. Sales had climbed to over $5 million.

Although Exhibit 1 reveals a healthy growth in volume and profits, Mr. Bjorklund wondered if success was not due, in part at least, to a countercyclical aspect of the business—did furniture leasing thrive in hard times? Regardless of the explanation, faster growth was limited by capital requirements. The investment in furniture both in stocks and on lease was substantial.

To relieve the financial strain, Custom Furniture Rental Corporation merged in July 1971 with a Portland financial institution, Granning and Treece (a family-owned business which specialized in loans). Mr. Bjorklund remained president of the furniture rental operation; two other executives ran smaller but profitable consumer finance and equipment leasing divisions. Walker Treece continued as chairman of the surviving company.

The furniture industry consisted of 5,300 companies making wood, metal, or upholstered furniture for home and contract (industrial) markets. Most manufacturers were small and specialized by raw material or type of furniture. Only Bassett Furniture and Kroehler Manufacturing had sales exceeding $100 million per year. After 1960, however, there had been a trend toward large manufacturers diversifying into the furniture business by acquisition. Examples of these "newcomers" include Mohasco Industries, Armstrong Cork, Litton Industries, U.S. Plywood, Sperry Rand, and Beatrice Foods. Some of these companies had experience in closely allied businesses (Simmons, Magnavox) while others were novices.

By far the majority of the furniture manufacturers were small, family-owned, tradition-bound outfits concentrated in North Carolina, Virginia, New York, Illinois, Indiana, and California, all close to sources of raw material and low labor costs. They have been described by *Fortune* as "insignificant in size, inbred in management, inefficient in production, and inherently opposed to technological change."

In recent years, however, automation and new technologies have altered the labor cost situation in case goods (i.e., wood furniture) operations. Upholstered furniture, on the other hand, was not as adaptable to these innovations and has remained largely a custom, handcraft business. In the future, when synthetics and more efficient machinery gain acceptability, productivity is expected to improve considerably. This will presumably attract more large-scale manufacturers into the industry and have significant impact on marketing and manufacturing.

## Distribution

Furniture distribution was as inefficient as production. The major structure was as follows:

Manufacturers
(5,300)

| Furniture | Manufacturers |
|---|---|
| Market | Agents |
| (few) | (hundreds) |
| Furniture | Decorators |
| Rental | (thousands) |
| (60) | Retailers |
| Wholesalers | (35,000) |
| (3,400) | |

Despite the profusion of intermediaries 80% of the volume went direct from manufacturer to retailer. The retailers, both chain and independent, could be classified by *type* and by *function:*

### By Type

1. Specialty furniture stores.
2. Department stores.
3. Mail order houses.
4. Premium houses.
5. Catalog offices.
6. Dealers in office furniture.
7. "Wholesale showrooms" (a misnomer since these were actually retailers selling to the ultimate user).
8. Warehouse showrooms—e.g., Levitz Furniture Company.
9. Interior designers.
10. Discounters.

### By Function

1. Deluxers—uncrate, assemble, check for damage and repair; usually more expensive than prepackers.
2. Prepackers—reship to buyer in original crate.

The remaining major intermediaries were wholesalers, interior designers, and rental firms. The *wholesaler* was classified either as service or drop shipper. The former was a traditional operator who performed many services for the retailer, manufacturers, and customer—such as buying, warehousing, credit extension, delivery, merchandising, promotion, and financial assistance. The drop shipper usually limited his functions to buying and selling; he took title but not physical possession because the manufacturer shipped direct to the retailer. Some wholesalers limited their selling efforts to the showroom (and were therefore called "showroom wholesalers"), while others, the "road-sellers," sent salesmen into the field.

*Interior designers* were a varied group, sometimes retailers, sometimes not. Their format ranged from high-priced specialty shops to semi-amateurs. Some concentrated on contract custom designing (as for hotels, apartment complexes and institutions) while others provided guidance, for a fee, to individual customers. Some maintained showrooms while others used the facilities of manufacturers, wholesalers, or retailers.

*The furniture rental firms* were few in number, perhaps 60 in 1972. Most were offshoots of retail stores and concentrated on the East and West Coasts. Custom Furniture Rental Corporation was the leader; the second largest was two-thirds the size of CFRC. Competition was generally local and restricted to a single outlet. Most competitors were small, inefficient mom and pop operators. Service was limited. The major competitive tactic was price-cutting, and advertising was confined to the classified ads, the yellow pages, and occasional display ads in local newspapers. There were no data on share of market, though the recent establishment of the Furniture Rental Association of America augured well for the infant industry.

Purchase of used furniture was an important alternative to furniture rental. Competition in used furniture was keen. In addition to used furniture outlets there were garage sales, householder sales, and institutional outlets such as Goodwill and the Salvation Army.

Leasing in general seemed to be popular. There were obvious financial and tax advantages for a company in leasing rather than owning, including protection against obsolescence, rising property taxes, and "tied-up" capital. And for the individual tenant there likewise appeared to be a favorable climate.

The socioeconomic and cultural changes that had taken place since World War II had altered the value systems and life-styles of many people. Diminished was the Puritan ethic of "pay-as-you-go"; it was no longer considered a sin to buy on credit. Particularly for young adults a lease provided the convenience of product use without the obligation of ownership.

The advantages of furniture rental described in a brochure distributed by CFRC salesmen were these:

Have the furniture you want and need now at a low cost.

Select the furniture yourself.

Immediate delivery.

No large investment.

No personal property taxes.

No moving expenses.

No maintenance costs.

Saves time and expense of shopping for furniture.

Flexibility of style and need through easy exchange privileges—an ideal arrangement for persons who require frequent moves or are in an area on a temporary basis.

Robert C. Hampton, executive director of the Furniture Rental Association, stated that "in 1969 for the fifth consecutive year furniture rental volume in America grew more than 30%. Several companies, CFRC for one, have seen rental volume nearly doubling annually during this period." He predicted that in the 1970's at least 10% of the apartments in the United States would be furnished with some item acquired on lease.

## INDUSTRY PROBLEMS

Whereas the rental segment of the furniture business seemed to offer potential promise, the traditional furniture industry had many problems. Retailers dominated the channels, a phenomenon which had diminished the effectiveness of distribution. These retailers had not been capable "channel captains" due to a lack of marketing or distribution skill and their preoccupation with other tasks. In most other industries manufacturers were channel captains.

The major problem of the industry was product damage incurred either in materials handling or during shipment. Case goods were the most vulnerable and required great care by shippers and packers. The high incidence of damage meant the maintenance of repair and refinishing facilities along the channels. In some instances damaged goods had to be disposed of at markdown prices.

Slow delivery was another vexing problem, particularly for retailers and their customers. Orders received by manufacturers were usually limited to a single consumer order, frequently for individual units. Typically, the manufacturers held these small orders until a sufficient number in one geographical destination had been accumulated, thereby avoiding the higher LCL and LTL shipping rates. Inevitably, the delay often inhibited purchase.

In merchandising the major problems revolved around inadequate brand promotion and cooperative advertising. Except for a few national labels most advertising was store-oriented. Little assistance was provided by manufacturers to dealers in regard to promotion, display, sales training, or general management practices.

The retail furniture markets were highly competitive. Price competition was rife, as illustrated by many markdowns, special sales, cash-and-carry sales, and discounts to certain "club members." Nonprice competition was primarily advertising, done only by the largest firms.

The most exciting competitive development of the early 1970's was warehouse-showroom marketing, best illustrated by Levitz Furniture

Company. Practically unheard of a few years earlier, the warehouse-showroom format obtained annual sales of nearly $400 million by 1972, about 4% of the total furniture sales volume in the United States. It was expected to capture a 15% share by 1975. The full import of this new competition was uncertain, but the prime targets for warehouse show-rooms were young householders and bargain hunters, all important potential subscribers to furniture leasing.

Competition from foreign manufacturers was a further important threat. The popularity of Scandinavian furniture was a case in point. Such imports were less a problem for the furniture retailer than the manufacturer, except for the long delivery time involved and the concomitant need for the retailer to carry larger inventories.

## THE MARKETS FOR RENTAL FURNITURE

Data on rental furniture penetration among households were scarce. One broad estimate was that 5% of total consumer expenditures in 1972 were for furniture and appliances, either purchased or rented. Executives in CFRC reasoned that rentals were primarily found among apartment renters. It was their considered judgment that for every 100 apartment units in 1972 in the West Coast markets:

Seventy-five were furnished by the tenants with their own furniture.

Twenty-five were furnished with rented furniture.

One or 2 of the 25 were furnished with items rented from such firms as CFRC—the rest furnished by the owner-builder.[1]

The ultimate rental consumers, whether dealing direct with a CFRC or through an owner/manager, were described by one CFRC executive as:

Young marrieds, the transferred executives, ball players, stewardesses. Many of our customers are young persons who formerly rented furnished apartments and homes. High interest rates make young people unwilling to take long-term financial obligations unless they are definitely ready to commit themselves to a particular style of furniture.

Another major segment of our market is the mobile element of our society. These are people of all ages; people who want "instant living," who don't want to buy furniture until they finally select their permanent home.

Income brackets of people who rent furniture are mixed—high-income families rent for convenience while the "economy class" rents to spread a limited budget.

Mr. Bjorklund felt that there were two separate segments of consumers, the buyers and the renters. He saw little evidence that consumers switched readily from one group to the other.

---

[1] The percentage of "furnished" apartments on the East Coast seemed to be much lower. The West Coast had the highest percentage regionally in the United States. Seventy percent of the apartments in Phoenix, for example, were furnished.

An important factor in the demand for home furnishings (either purchase or rental) was the degree of population mobility. U.S. population studies indicated that each year about 20% of the people changed residence. Of these relocations about two-thirds moved within the same county and one-third moved to other counties. The most mobile segment of the population was the 18–34 group. The mobiles were young, well-educated, held higher status occupations, had above average incomes, tended to be socially active and generally needed to revise their household inventories to suit the new living quarters. Mobiles represented a unique opportunity for furniture marketers.

The reasons for migration, as discussed recently among psychologists, had potential marketing relevance. Human dignity was frequently an important factor in the change of surroundings. A new environment was perceived as giving one a new and better chance for success. Voluntary relocations might be perceived as a way of destroying the past or of moving up. Many people relocated to achieve social and personal growth. Others looked for economic gain.

Mr. Bjorklund, in describing the prime markets, reasoned that there were several bases for segmentation:

1. *Demography*—geography, family composition and size, educational attainments of the family head, occupation, income, ethnic origin, race, home ownership, marital status, and number of wage earners in the household.
2. *Physical characteristics*—age, health, sex, height, weight.
3. *Psychological traits*—personality, intelligence level, avocational interests, political bias, psychological needs and preferences.
4. *Behavioral patterns* (with respect to the product)—i.e., product use, product loyalty, brand use, brand preference, buying habits, buying behavior.
5. *The commercial market*—which accounted for 40% of CFRC's revenues; mainly apartment owners, and institutional customers.

CFRC considered the owners of furnished apartments to be strong competitors, not other rental companies. Apartment house owners needed furnished apartments primarily to help rent their units. Prospective tenants without furniture, unless they knew about direct renting, would shy away from unfurnished quarters, or, if they favored a particular apartment, might not return if they had to leave to rent furniture and thus be potentially exposed to other apartment alternatives.

Why so many owners continued to supply their own furniture in rental units was presumably because of inadequate knowledge on the part of their own furniture salesmen and inadequate knowledge about the existence of rental firms. In many ways the apartment owners were not as strong competitors in fact as in theory. They rarely gave much service to the tenants. Furniture ownership was a traditional necessity and an expensive one at that. The typical owner invested between $600–$1,000 per one-bedroom apartment and had to assume the costs of storage, maintenance, theft, damage, replacement, tied-up capital, diversionary use of the apartment manager's time, and an asset that dwindled to zero after five years.

The reasons why the apartment owner should rent furniture were summarized in an April 16, 1972, article in the *Los Angeles Times:*

Apartment owners look to furniture rental organizations for home furnishings. In essence these organizations are helping apartment owners to solve a serious problem. Orange County apartment owners are faced with a dilemma. Southern California by nature is comprised of people on the move. Executives are transferred here for one or two years and then transferred again. Young marrieds, students, the military, single adults, various government employees— all apartment hoppers, moving from apartment to apartment every few years. They demand furnished apartments.

Vacancies are growing higher and higher every year. In order to attract the prospective tenants and lower the vacancy factor, the apartment owner must invest in furniture. This is where his many problems begin.

The owner must provide furnishings that are stylish and appealing to the apartment dweller. Furniture is expensive, both in time and money. The owner must now spend valuable cash or finance at today's high interest rates. The furniture must be delivered and installed; more money and time is required for this labor.

Once the furniture is installed, the apartment must be rented before the owner can begin to recover his investment. Often a unit must be moved to satisfy a new tenant, or twin beds are needed instead of the double provided —more expense to move the unit and for the bed exchange. The furniture becomes worn and damaged; repair and replacement costs are incurred to prevent the new building down the street from luring away your present tenants and prospective tenants.

After three years you have a small unprofitable return on your investment. The furniture is now old and worn, the salvage value is 20% of its original cost. You have paid the principal and interest, the taxes, and management costs of furniture ownership.

Vacancies are rising because your building is downgraded by the old and shabby furniture; your apartments no longer appeal to our southern California transient market. What does it add up to? You must start all over again, more time and more money to refurnish your apartments.

The furniture rental organization offers a simple solution to this dilemma. They procure apartment furnishings in a wide selection of styles that appeal to the apartment dweller. Prompt delivery and installation are provided by their trained personnel; all service is performed by the rental company. All costs of procurement, delivery, installation, repair, and replacement are borne by the furniture rental organization.

. . . To the apartment owner it is the most economical approach to the dilemma of furnished or unfurnished apartments.

## CFRC Marketing Strategy

CFRC leased home furnishings for one month or longer, the typical commercial contract being of longer initial duration than the direct-to-tenant. During 1971 CFRC rented furniture to 13,000 customers in the United States and 700 in Canada. Sixty percent of the rentals were to individual tenants and could be canceled by the customer on 30 days prior written notice. The average term of rental agreement was nine months.

On direct-to-tenant business the firm realized a nine-month payback (i.e., 11% per month of the purchase price) but 20 months 15% on commercial. The commercial rentals had the offsetting benefits of less physical handling, larger unit transactions, and, hopefully, a more responsible lessee. The latter assumption, however, was tenuous.

The owner included the tenant's furniture rental in a single figure for the "furnished apartment." He then paid CFRC but often after a five-month delay. CFRC picked up the rental on its books as income as soon as the tenant signed the apartment lease. If a builder went broke, CFRC would find itself with five or six months of income write-off; in fact, in one case the bankrupt builder sold the CFRC furniture as if it were his own. Although commercial failures were not all that frequent, it was difficult for Mr. Bjorklund to know which business—tenant or commercial—was the more profitable. It was his opinion that both markets were equally attractive.

CFRC let the tenant or lessee select any one item (or coordinated group of items) from a wide assortment of styles. Delivery and installation of the selection was made within 24 hours after the lease was signed. Rental rates, which required a monthly advance, depended upon the selections. The average charge was $30 per month, which covered furnishings for a living room, dinette, and bedroom. The company's rental fees were competitive with the time payments on purchased furniture; in some cases CFRC's prices were lower than either monthly payments due on purchased furniture or on rental rates charged by competing firms. In the San Jose area, for example, CFRC's rate for a minimum group was $22.50 per month—local competitors charged $25–$30. CFRC also offered a much wider selection and generally higher quality furniture than its rental competitors.

A deposit of $35 was required for each account and was returned if the lease was in effect at least 12 months. This fee covered the cost of delivery and installation. Customers could make additions, deletions, or changes of items, but there was a $15 charge for each such order. The rate was in effect a delivery charge and applied to any or all pieces of furniture involved in the service call.

If the lessee moved, there was a $20 charge to shift the furniture. If a customer transferred to another geographical area serviced by CFRC, the lessee could return the furniture and ask for delivery at the new location. The company required 30 days written notice of this change of address.

CFRC's customers had the option of buying part or all of the rented furniture. The purchase price amounted to 25 times the monthly rental fee. A selection of furniture carrying a monthly rental of $30 would bear, therefore, a total purchase price of $750. The purchase option offered provided that credit toward the total purchase price be given as follows:

100% for the first year's rent;
75% of the second year's rent;
50% of the third year's rent; or
80% of this credit could be applied to the purchase of a similar piece of new furniture.

Using the example of a $30-per-month rental and a $750-purchase price, the customer, having paid the first year's rental fees, would be given a credit of $360 and would pay the balance of $390 to complete the purchase. The customer who had completed making rental payments for two years would be given credit of $630 (100% of $360 plus 75% of $360) toward the $750 purchase price, leaving a balance of $120.

Persons opting to buy their rented furniture generally did so after the first year and certainly not beyond the second year. In 1971 there were 1,400 customers who decided to purchase one or more pieces of rented furniture. Gross receipts from those sales were $330,000. However, less than 8% of the total customer base exercised their buying option.

Used furniture was sent out for rental "like new," but the company openly invited all of its customers to return any piece that failed to meet the "like new" test. In the words of Mr. Bjorklund, "We sell service, and there's no sense trying to pass off shabby merchandise on the renter. It is in this quality control that we have a big advantage over most of our competition."

*Used Furniture Sales.* Reporting to the local rental managers were six used furniture stores in the major CFRC markets. Furniture that was considered unusable for rental was disposed of on an "as is" basis at bargain cash prices. Sales volume in these stores by 1972 approximated $1.5 million per year, but the profit or loss was not clear. It was estimated that losses were about $250,000 each year. Although a significant portion of the original buying price was recovered in the used sale, there was no clear-cut policy about where to set the used furniture selling price in terms of depreciated value and selling costs of disposal. At these six used furniture stores some new furniture was sold (less than 10% in 1971) in order to highlight the "good values" on the used. Mr. Bjorklund thought that the new furniture sales were profitable. Used furniture employees were typically ex-warehousemen and drivers who wanted to sell. Being in the used furniture business was considered a necessary evil to being in the rental business.

*The Product Mix.* An important aspect of the company's marketing mix was the product line which had been carefully selected by company personnel highly knowledgeable about furniture buying. The line was under constant review for style and compatibility with consumer preferences and demand.

CFRC's product line included the following:

| | |
|---|---|
| Davenports | Dining chairs |
| Chairs (living room) | Beds |
| Table lamps | Mattresses |
| Stereo systems | Pictures |
| Bars | Love seats |
| Dinette sets | Cocktail tables |
| Headboards | Television sets |
| Box springs | Bookcases |
| Rugs | Dining tables |
| Sofas and sofa-beds | Buffets |
| End tables | Bed frames |
| Floor lamps | Night stands and lamps |
| Room dividers | Refrigerators |
| Bar stools | |

In terms of decor the firm offered 12 living room and 3 bedroom choices in 1972, a significant increase over the past three years. The quality of the furniture had likewise been upgraded as evidenced by the steadily increasing "average monthly rental charge."

Custom Furniture acquired 90% of its furniture from about 25 major suppliers, mostly located in the West in order to minimize inventory requirements. It was considered prudent to have duplicate suppliers (there were three, for example, for upholstered furniture) in order to guarantee merchandise in the case of emergencies. Another 75 companies supplied CFRC with the remaining 10% of its needs, mostly in knickknacks, lamps, and small specialty items. Because of its size and importance CFRC had considerable leverage with its suppliers.

*The Promotion Mix.* The major components of the CFRC's promotion mix were: (1) personal selling; (2) advertising; (3) sales promotion; (4) publicity and public relations; and (5) miscellaneous promotions. The total marketing budget came to between 10% and 12% of net sales and most of that was reflected in costs attributed to personal selling. Advertising was concentrated in telephone directories (yellow pages) and occasionally-placed newspaper display advertisements for special events. Media advertising accounted for about 2.5% of new sales.

It was estimated that 50% of the direct-to-tenant sales came from recommendations by owners/managers. The other half came from the yellow pages, friends, and customers.

*The Sales Forces.* There were three distinct kinds of salesmen in CFRC, reflecting three sales approaches. First, there were the showroom salesmen who waited on those customers who came into the showroom.

These salesmen did not customarily make any sales off the premises. Second were the sales and service representatives who worked in the field, calling on apartment managers and owners. They did not make actual sales but paved the way for future sales by making known CFRC's service for the apartment tenants. (Given apartment vacancy rates of 10–15%, the owners and managers were anxious to gain a competitive edge and thus represented a fairly responsive market segment.) The third kind of salesman attempted to make contracts with large commercial accounts. Typically these were the veteran salesmen or sales managers.

*Sales Management Duties.*  In addition to selling commercial accounts, sales managers were responsible for recruiting, selecting, and training new salesmen. They were also expected to assist top management in the development of sales plans and strategies. They were judged on their ability to supervise, stimulate, evaluate, and control the salesmen in their respective jurisdictions.

*Recruiting and Selecting Salesmen.*  CFRC recruited most of its salesmen from employment agencies but occasionally used referrals from customers and other employees.

*Orientation and Training.*  Immediately after being hired, the new salesman was given an orientation to the firm's policies and practices. The orientation was handled by the sales manager and administration manager. Following the indoctrination, the new employee received on-the-job training for about one week. He or she was then assigned as a showroom sales person. Field selling assignments were earned only after the sales person was considered well-informed on company policy, product line, lease agreements, and selling techniques.

*Compensation.*  Sales compensation was straight salary. Reimbursement was made for travel expense at the rate of 12 cents per mile. The employees also received a number of fringe benefits such as discounts on furniture, nine paid holidays and vacation pay (one week's pay for one year's service), sick pay, health insurance, and life insurance (the company's share of the premium was two-thirds while employees paid one-third). The firm had a profit-sharing plan. Furthermore, salesmen participated in prize contests and could earn P.M.'s for good performance.[2] The compensation plan applied to each type of salesman.

*Selling Tasks.*  An insight into the nature of the CFRC selling job is helpful. The following list of salesmen's tasks was included in company sales material:

*Preparation of showroom for customers.*
   See to it that windows and doors are clean and showroom is tidy.
   Check to see that all furniture on the floor is properly tagged.
   Keep display groups according to plan.
   Replace items sold and taken off the floor with other items.

---

[2] Premium Money—sometimes called "push money."

*Prospecting.*
   Develop and maintain a good prospect list from sources such as referrals, telephone canvas, prospecting in person.

*Selling.*
   Waiting on customers entering the showroom.
   Calling on prospective buyers—i.e., follow-ups.
   Performing those selling techniques that will get sign-ups.

*Public relations.*
   Thanking apartment managers and owners for referrals.
   Behave on the job to reflect favorably upon yourself and the company.
   Participating in branch sales meetings.
   Preparation of lease contracts and other required reports.

**Advertising.** CFRC made limited use of mass media advertising and relied primarily on the yellow pages. Classified ads in local newspapers were used occasionally. Mr. Bjorklund recalled that the company had tried a radio campaign but that it was unproductive and had been discontinued. Advertising was handled by CFRC personnel, and there were plans to establish an in-house agency to handle this function in the future.

The company favored use of four-color brochures displaying the product lines available to potential renters. It also believed that advertising specialties such as ball point pens, bumper stickers, book matches, four-foot rulers, and the like were good promotional tools. Mr. Bjorklund expressed the opinion that word-of-mouth advertising was very effective, as was the development and maintenance of a good corporate and product image.

**In-Store Display.** In-store (showroom) display appeared to be important in the marketing of furniture, either rented or purchased. A study made in May 1968 by the research department of Fairchild Publications throws some light on the effectiveness of various promotional devices:

**Sources Perceived by Residents as Most Helpful in Selection of Furniture and Bedding**

| *Source* | *Furniture* | *Bedding* |
|---|---|---|
| Discussion with family, friends, neighbors | 47% | 49% |
| Discussion with professional designers and/or interior decorators | 8 | 3 |
| Seeing other homes | 27 | 9 |
| Visiting model homes | 12 | 1 |
| Window shopping | 43 | 21 |
| Newspaper ads | 28 | 46 |
| Home shows | 2 | 1 |
| Magazine articles | 21 | 20 |
| Magazine ads | 30 | 17 |
| Manufacturers' booklets/mailing pieces | 8 | 8 |
| TV programs and/or commercials | 3 | 11 |
| "Know what I want" | 3 | 7 |
| Catalog | 2 | 3 |

## Organization

When CFRC was first established and during its formative years, the organization was highly centralized. Like many entrepreneurs Mr. Bjorklund was largely a one-man show. As the firm expanded, Mr. Bjorklund recognized the need to formalize and decentralize his organization. It was his intention to shove the operating decisions down to the district managers while reserving the strategic and policy matters for himself. The "theoretical" organization chart of 1972 appears as Exhibit 2.

The company maintained showrooms and warehouses in Washington, Oregon, California, and Vancouver, B.C. Each branch was manned by sales and warehouse personnel. Personal selling, the major element in the CFRC promotional mix, was handled both in the showroom and by field operations. Each branch maintained facilities for repairing, cleaning, fumigating, assembling, servicing, and installing. The deliverymen played a key role in the development and maintenance of a favorable company image.

## Growth Alternatives

Mr. Bjorklund's main line of attack had been first to blanket the Western apartment market before turning to geographic expansion, the penetration of new markets such as commercial offices, or vertical integration back into manufacturing.

Coverage of the West was attained by internal growth (i.e., establishing company units in new locations) and by acquisition. It was not easy, however, to decide when a particular market had been satisfactorily penetrated.

When asked how he measured penetration, Mr. Bjorklund stated that a reasonable penetration rate for a single company seemed to be 5% of the total apartment units.[3] The total obviously included a large number of low-income apartments for which the rental of furniture was practically out of the question. Thus, Mr. Bjorklund was pleased with his firm's 5% penetration in Portland and Eugene but not with the 1% in San Francisco. Confirmation of the reasonableness of the 5% target figure came from a study of market penetration elsewhere. In Washington, D.C., for example, the penetration rate was 25%, but the business was shared by three strong competitors and several smaller concerns. Similarly, in Houston there was a high penetration rate (20%), but no single firm had more than 6%.

The company's long-range plans called for expansion by entering additional market areas. The normal procedure for breaking a new market was to open a warehouse with attached showroom and trucks. Later addi-

---

[3] The count of apartment units was purchased from the federal government which maintained a Post Office Mail Carrier Survey.

tional showrooms were added closer to the prime apartment areas. Finally, after a critical mass of furniture was on rental (probably two to three years), a used furniture store was opened.

Before making a decision to enter any given market, the company made a series of market studies. The investigations produced a "census" of existing multiple housing units, housing under construction, and plans for future construction. Market profiles were prepared with emphasis on classes of people and their life styles. Demographic data were included. These surveys and analyses were made by CFRC district managers and reviewed by Mr. Bjorklund and the executive vice president. In addition the proposed market was traversed by automobile and airplane for observation of its physical characteristics.

The typical requirements for an attractive market were a high mobility rate (such as a political center) and active apartment construction. Sacramento and Phoenix, for example, were prime targets, whereas Bakersfield and Fresno were less attractive in the short run.

The company's marketing effectiveness in the past two years had been improved significantly by the use of several strategies. One of these was the relocation of showrooms/salesrooms from back streets to high traffic streets. Another was the establishment of used furniture outlets in six major areas.

## The Future

The socioeconomic climate expected in the 1970's appeared to be favorable for the home furnishings industry. Prospective growth was estimated at 7% to 7½% annually, reflecting the following trends:

1. *New Family Formations and New Households.* More new families and more newly established households (for couples and singles) were predicted by the Census Bureau (see Exhibit 3). In 1970 there were 62,872,000 households in the United States; by 1975 this figure would reach 70,036,000. Significant also was the prediction that the 1975 total would include 50 million persons in the 20–34 year age bracket. This group represented an important target market for furniture and furnishings.

2. *Increased Housing Construction.* Construction of housing was in a slump during 1969–70 but began to recover strongly after mid-1970. It was expected that close to 2.5 million housing units would be completed in 1972.

3. *Growing Affluence.* Disposable income grew from $591 billion in 1969 to $678.8 billion in 1970. Government sources indicated that disposable income would continue to rise at the same or even greater rate in the near future.

4. *New Consciousness of Style and Decor in the Household.* Americans were becoming more sophisticated. In addition they seemed to

seek and accept change more readily, which was expected to generate additional demand for freshly styled furniture. Motivation research disclosed that such furniture had more than functional value (see Exhibits 4 and 5). Furniture reflected directly the personality and the tastes of the user. It also reflected the status of the family. Many people, particularly the young adults, were no longer willing to keep the same furniture for their lifetimes.

5. *More Aggressive Marketing.*   As one furniture executive stated recently, "This is a new ball game. We are slowly but surely coming out of the traditionbound, family-oriented, pokey-slow method of operations into a dynamic, highly competitive environment." Warehouse showrooms and mass merchandising by department stores, discount houses, and even furniture specialty stores triggered an aggressive marketing era for the industry. Observers expected that marketing would be characterized by hard-hitting promotion, not only by big-name firms, but by small firms as well.

### The Issue

Mr. Bjorklund, as stated earlier, was not displeased with his firm's progress, but he had the uneasy feeling that he wasn't sure about the best strategy. His company was still small, and there was little real evidence that there was a realizable market potential.

**EXHIBIT 1**

**Summary of Growth and Profit**
**Custom Furniture Rental Corporation**
**1965–1972**

|  | *Original* | |
| --- | --- | --- |
|  | *Revenues* | *Net Income* |
| June 30, 1965– | | |
| February 28, 1966. . . . . . . . . . . . . . . | $   178,507 | $   18,824 |
| FYE February 28, 1967. . . . . . . . . . . | 597,514 | 46,304 |
| FYE February 29, 1968. . . . . . . . . . . | 1,046,045 | 71,236 |
| FYE February 28, 1969. . . . . . . . . . . | 1,922,171 | 80,591 |
| FYE February 28, 1970. . . . . . . . . . . | 4,239,987 | 216,352 |
| FYE February 28, 1971. . . . . . . . . . . | 5,358,286 | 275,212 |
| FYE February 29, 1972. . . . . . . . . . . | 6,090,562 | 397,993 |

# EXHIBIT 2

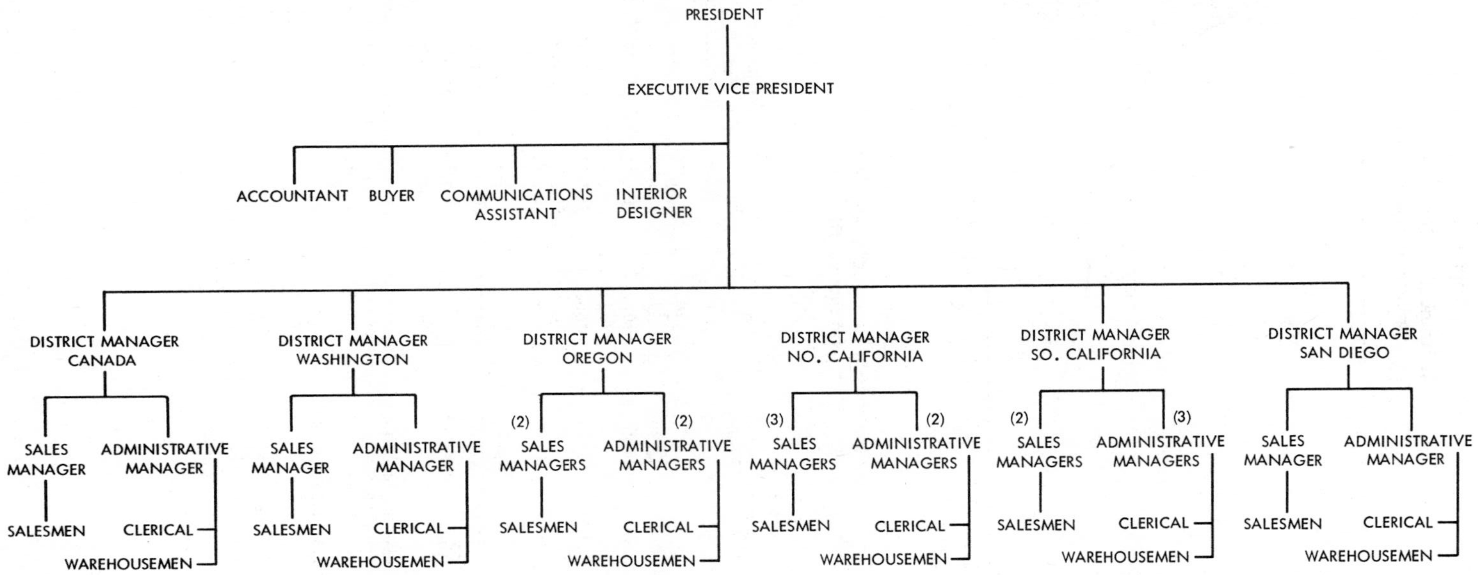

Organization chart. President — Executive Vice President, with staff positions: Accountant, Buyer, Communications Assistant, Interior Designer.

District Managers reporting to Executive Vice President:

- **District Manager, Canada** — Sales Manager (Salesmen), Administrative Manager (Clerical, Warehousemen)
- **District Manager, Washington** — Sales Manager (Salesmen), Administrative Manager (Clerical, Warehousemen)
- **District Manager, Oregon** — Sales Managers (2) (Salesmen), Administrative Managers (2) (Clerical, Warehousemen)
- **District Manager, No. California** — Sales Managers (3) (Salesmen), Administrative Managers (2) (Clerical, Warehousemen)
- **District Manager, So. California** — Sales Managers (2) (Salesmen), Administrative Managers (3) (Clerical, Warehousemen)
- **District Manager, San Diego** — Sales Manager (Salesmen), Administrative Manager (Clerical, Warehousemen)

## EXHIBIT 3

### A. Number of Households
### (million units)

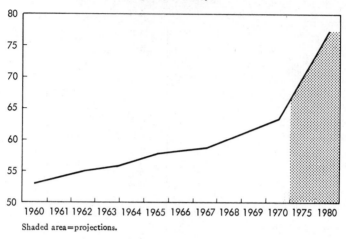

Shaded area=projections.

### B. Number of Household and Family Units
### (in thousands)

| | Projections | | | Households | | |
|---|---|---|---|---|---|---|
| | Total Households | Family Units | | Total | Urban and Rural Nonfarm | Rural Farm | Primary Family Units |
| 1980: | | | 1970....... | 62,874 | 60,150 | 2,724 | 51,110 |
| Highest....... | 76,494 | 62,967 | 1969....... | 61,805 | 58,935 | 2,870 | 50,416 |
| Lowest........ | 73,601 | 61,977 | 1968....... | 60,444 | 57,501 | 2,944 | 49,734 |
| | | | 1967....... | 58,845 | 55,910 | 2,934 | 48,791 |
| | | | 1966....... | 58,092 | 54,875 | 3,214 | 48,169 |
| | | | 1965....... | 57,251 | 53,899 | 3,350 | 47,720 |
| | | | 1964....... | 55,996 | 52,651 | 3,345 | 47,278 |
| 1975: | | | | | | | |
| Highest....... | 70,036 | 57,670 | 1963....... | 55,189 | 51,725 | 3,464 | 46,813 |
| Lowest........ | 67,730 | 56,865 | 1962....... | 54,652 | 50,890 | 3,762 | 46,185 |
| | | | 1961....... | 53,464 | 49,115 | 3,749 | 45,299 |

Note: All years as of March; projections are as of July. A household includes all of the persons who occupy a house, an apartment, or other group of rooms, or a room that constitutes a dwelling or housing unit. The term "family" as used here refers to a group of two or more persons related by blood, marriage, or adoption and residing together, all such persons considered as members of one family.

Source: U.S. Department of Commerce.

## EXHIBIT 4

### Some Conclusions and Recommendations of the Kroehler Report

1. Furniture buying in many cases is approached with a feeling of uneasiness.
2. The traditional American conception of the home as a symbol of "family relationship" should be stressed in promotion of furniture.
3. Furniture merchandising should stress an association of furniture in use with people.
4. Pleasure and respect should be stressed in connection with furniture images.
5. Promotion should provide direction, definition, and reassurance relating to many diverse elements such as taste, style, price, quality, and integration into the home.
6. The retail salesman could benefit by knowing the human elements making up his market as well as by having a better knowledge of his product.
7. Presently owned furniture should not be ridiculed because often an insult to her present furniture may be considered by the customer as an insult to herself.
8. Furniture should be displayed in a surrounding or setting similar to its end use and not in a massed display.

Source: Ralph Westfall and Harper W. Boyd, Jr., *Cases in Marketing Management* (Homewood, Ill.: Richard D. Irwin, 1961), p. 53.

## EXHIBIT 5

### Some Random Notes On the Psychology of Home Furnishings

When we visit each other, we are curious to find out how the other person has arranged his dwelling place.

The home provides security—even to the extent of how the home is organized on the inside.

### BEDS:

Beds have a symbolic meaning . . . "It is a refuge—sort of womb to which one can return, providing a feeling of security and protection." This explains the importance of sleeping in one's own bed and the difficulty many people have in sleeping in strange beds. They do not feel secure, cannot relax.

### CARPETS:

People have an emotional investment in carpets. A carpet belongs to an individual and has a major value. It is personal—a showing of one's personality in choosing a carpet. Carpets are really the things that pull the home together—they establish a relationship between the pieces of furniture. Carpets are a token of unity and continuity of a home. They are symbolic and the thicker the carpet the higher the surface status. Carpets are "warm" whereas bare floors and linoleum give one an impression of coldness.

**EXHIBIT 5 (Continued)**

## FURNITURE:

Furniture represents the movable parts of the home and thus is capable of expressing the personality and the emotion of the inhabitants.

Furniture is no longer bought for lifelong periods but just for a few years.

People have become more sure of themselves as far as taste is concerned and buy to satisfy the "inner Jones" rather than to impress other people. Gone is the taboo of mixing too many period pieces. There is now a greater flexibility and movability in both a physical and psychological sense.

Furniture is like clothing. Some people "go well" with certain types of furniture, others don't.

Many pieces of furniture have the quality of protecting. In a deep easy chair you are returning to the womb; you may curl up and feel surrounded. You can escape into it and feel removed from the troubles and tribulations of everyday life.

There is moral and immoral furniture. It can be puritanical and punishing or luxurious, sensuous. Furniture can be expression of a person's weltenschaunig (philosophy or view).

### Some Suggestions for Furniture Advertising

Use very few of the available appeals. Furniture is a *permanent* expression of a person. A person's life really begins with furniture—the crib or bassinet. Therefore, buying furniture is very important—a major decision; yet most furniture advertising is rather a static display without introducing the human element. One should stress the fact that the choice of furniture is a very important decision in a person's life. Therefore, this choice should be made a major topic of the ad.

Memories of furniture are common to all of us. These memories should be turned into important testimonial appeals in furniture advertising such as a nostalgic reminder of the pleasant past.

SOURCE: Reported in Ernst Dichter, *Handbook of Consumer Motivations* (New York: McGraw-Hill Book Co., 1964), pp. 117–54.

# The College of Business Administration of the University of Arkansas

The University of Arkansas, a state land grant institution, is presently comprised of four campuses—Fayetteville (11,184 students), Little Rock (6,144 students), Monticello (1,646 students) and Pine Bluff (2,016).[1] The main campus, located at Fayetteville, offers 99 bachelor, 67 master, and 124 doctoral level degree programs. The College of Business Administration, one of the largest schools within the university, was founded in 1926 and is the fifth oldest of the colleges comprising the university. In 1975, faced with declining enrollment projections over the next several years, the school was considering whether to introduce a night school program designed to attract local residents.

The college currently offers an extensive undergraduate degree curriculum along with graduate degree programs which include a Master of Business Administration, a Master's degree in Economics, a Master's degree in Accounting, a Doctor of Philosophy in Business Administration, and a Doctor of Philosophy in Economics. The faculty of the college consists of 88 full-time faculty equivalents of whom about 90% hold doctoral degrees. The college is accredited by the American Association of Collegiate Schools of Business.

The University of Arkansas at Fayetteville had experienced enrollment declines in recent years in much the same pattern as had been experienced by many institutions of higher learning through the nation. During the 1960's the university's enrollment doubled while that of the College of

The text of this case is excerpted from a 1974 study on "Night School Demand" by John E. McCain, Assistant Professor, Department of Economics, University of Arkansas (Fayetteville).

[1] Figures are for the 1974–75 academic year. Note: The Medical Center (Little Rock) is treated as a separate campus.

Business increased by about 90%. Enrollment for the college was, in 1975, about 2,100 of which some 90% represented undergraduates. Enrollment decline began in 1970 for both the university and the business school. Further reductions in day school enrollment are projected in the 1980's. One source predicts a decline in the undergraduate enrollment of the school by 1980 of 14.1% from the fall 1974 level.

## ENROLLMENT TRENDS FOR U.S. HIGHER EDUCATION INDUSTRY

The U.S. Office of Education reported 10,137,065 students had enrolled on the nation's 3,000 university, college, and junior college campuses in the fall of 1974. This was an increase of 5.5% over the previous year's enrollment and came after several years when the rate of increase in aggregate student enrollment had been declining. In fact, the upturn came at a time when most colleges were predicting absolute enrollment declines over the next decade. A number of knowledgeable observers believe this change may be a short-term phenomenon brought about by a deteriorating job market and intensive recruiting drives undertaken to attract more women and part-time students onto college campuses. The increasing availability of tuition loans and grants in some states and the relatively recent expansion of low-cost junior colleges might also explain the short-run increases. Enrollment at junior colleges was up 11.6% in 1974. Yet, since 1969 the percentage of 18- and 19-year-olds attending college, had declined from 50.3% to 43%, and it is this traditional age group that higher institutions rely upon to fill undergraduate classroom vacancies. While it is too early to tell whether the secular enrollment downtrend has been reversed based on 1974 enrollments only, many experts are still predicting large-scale closings of private colleges and consolidation of public campuses throughout the 1980's.

In the 1960's higher education could not expand rapidly enough to meet the demand for student spaces. This was due in great measure to the influx of postwar babies, reinforced by an increase in demand for a college degree associated with expanded job opportunities. Rising incomes, complementing an expanding economy, put the cost of a college education within the reach of more U.S. residents. Based on current predictions, the boom may be over. A number of reasons are cited to support a continuing student enrollment decline. These include ending of the draft, youth disillusionment with formal education, rising costs associated with the recent inflation, and availability of alternatives in the form of noncollege technical training. Population trends are expected to aggravate the problem even further. The decline in the number of annual births, extending back to 1962, is expected to continue into the future and result in a national zero population growth which will reduce the aggregate supply of students available for higher education. If the enrollment ratio (proportion of 18–21-year-olds entering college) reverses its decline, and this ratio has been declining since 1929, it would still have to increase substantially to offset the decline in birth rates.

Many colleges have also been faced with a cost-price squeeze. Inflation of the 1970's has escalated operating and maintenance expenses, and capital construction projects are continually being bid in at figures much higher than original estimates. This situation has become increasingly intolerable at institutions which have, at the same time, suffered declining student enrollments with accompanying reduced revenues from tuition and fee payments.

## RESPONSE OF COLLEGES TO DECLINING ENROLLMENT

In an effort to counteract the financial dilemma, many universities have engaged in extensive campaigns to attract students. Radio and television commercials, newspaper ads, and direct mailings are being used to entice potential applicants. Mobile recruiting booths have been set up in shopping centers and high schools so students can be signed up on the spot. Some higher educational institutions have hired professional recruiting firms to search for students. Herbert Livesay, admissions director of New York University, reported on a recruiting technique which seems somewhat questionable. An applicant for admission wrote to explain that he had chosen another college over NYU because it had offered him $100.00 for every student he brought with him.[2]

In an effort to attract students a number of colleges are offering a variety of "no-need" scholarships and other forms of financial aid. For example, a school that costs $3,000 per year to attend may give a student a $1,000 scholarship in order to get the remaining $2,000 which more than covers the marginal cost of adding that person to the student body. Lowering admission standards is another device used to attract students. One private institution indicated that its entrance requirements have dropped from a C average to a D plus. To retain poor students, some universities have changed their "drop course" rules to reduce failure rates. Under this arrangement failing students can drop a course shortly before the end of the semester and thereby avoid an "F" grade.

Some universities have taken a different approach to the problem by searching for new markets which can use their resources; for example, adult continuing education. Such programs can be offered on-campus and are intended to reach the part-time student. Some colleges have found enrollments in this area far exceeding their expectations. The University of Arkansas at Little Rock, for example, is offering 26 off-campus courses for the 1975 spring semester. These courses are being taught at 17 separate geographical locations in an effort to make "learning" more convenient for persons living some distance from the UALR campus.

St. Louis University provides yet another example of a school seeking

---

[2] *U.S. News & World Report,* "Campus Scene: Now It's Buyer Choice" (April 15, 1974), p. 54.

to capitalize on adult education programs. They determined that there were 356,000 high school graduates, 25 years old and over, residing in their service area who had already completed one to three years of college. They had been offering noncredit courses through their Metropolitan College division for the past ten years. Starting in the fall of 1973, this division instituted three full degree programs: a Bachelor of Business Studies, Bachelor of Liberal Studies, and a Bachelor of Urban Affairs and Community Service—all designed to meet the needs of adults. Classes are held on weekends and in the evening. A high school diploma or educationally related work is being accepted for admission to these programs. Students may even transfer up to 90 hours of credit which they have completed at other colleges in prior years.

Specialized training courses designed to improve the skill level of full-time workers were thought to be yet another area which promised significant new enrollment potential. Rensselear Polytechnic Institute's program is typical of this form of continuing education. RPI offers a variety of courses for employees of a specific company or group of business firms. The university works closely with businesses to design courses tailored to the objectives of one or several companies with similar needs. If there are not enough individuals available in one company to justify a course, RPI will pool employees from firms having a common interest. Many students enrolled in these specialized courses are not interested in completing a full degree, so the school generally provides these courses on a noncredit basis.

Recently a nationwide study was undertaken to examine the business schools' role in providing continuing education for middle managers.[3] Due to the dynamic nature of middle manager work it was generally agreed by business enterprises that managers must continue to up-date their skills in supervision, human relations, and quantitative aspects of modern management. Business leaders and executives of trade and professional associations were asked to rate the effectiveness of various sources providing manager enhancement programs. Respondents to the survey generally rated collegiate business schools first or second as the most effective source of middle manager development.

## UNIVERSITY OF ARKANSAS (FAYETTEVILLE) ADULT EDUCATION PROGRAMS

The Division of Continuing Education at the university undertakes a broad range of activities to meet the needs of off-campus students, part-time students, and adults whose education has been interrupted. This division, initially emphasizing the extension concept, has been a part of

[3] Gerald L. Richards and Gordon C. Inskeep, "The Middle Manager—His Continuing Education and the Business School," *Collegiate News and Views* (Spring 1974), pp. 5–8.

the University of Arkansas since 1893. The various programs make contact with every county in the state, every state in the union, and with 26 foreign countries. A variety of conferences, institutes, short courses, and other programs are conducted by the division both on and off the main campus. The major activity in terms of degree offerings is administered by the Department of Independent Study. Correspondence study is offered in 134 college level courses and in 50 high school level courses. As of June 30, 1973, 12,033 students were actively enrolled in these correspondence courses with approximately 8,000 of them engaged at the college level. At the present time very few on-campus evening courses are taught by this division or by other divisions or colleges on the Fayetteville campus.

The College of Business Administration conducts its own continuing education program chiefly administered by the Industrial Research and Extension Center (IREC), headquartered in Little Rock. This center's activities consist of seminars, workshops, and conferences designed to assist in upgrading and developing the professional skills of persons working in both public and private sectors. The IREC offers four major types of education services which include: executive level programs, middle management and staff specialist conferences, first-line supervisory programs, and business development seminars. A number of regular faculty members in the College of Business Administration regularly serve as moderators in programs.

Starting in the 1974 fall semester, the College of Business Administration began offering one evening course in Principles of Management. This undergraduate course was made available to test the market for an expanded selection of evening course offerings. Thirty-seven students, primarily working adults, were enrolled in this course. The response was favorable enough so that the college has decided to offer four courses in the 1975 spring semester—Principles of Management, Principles of Accounting, Principles of Economics, and a graduate course in Accounting.

In attempting to assess the demand for an evening program the College of Business defined its market as consisting essentially of two counties—Washington and Benton, which are located in the northwest corner of the state. The University at Fayetteville is situated close to the center of Washington County (see Exhibit 1).[4] The 1974 population of Washington County was estimated at 85,000 while that of Benton County was 56,000 residents. The other counties surrounding the University of Arkansas were eliminated from the university night school service area on the basis of travel time and low population density.

The economic base of this two-county area is made up of agriculture, light manufacturing, leisure industries, and higher education. The num-

---

[4] Only one other educational institution was located in the area, and it did not conduct night classes.

ber of people employed in farming has become relatively stable after the declines of the 1950's and 1960's. The main agricultural activities are in beef cattle, hogs, poultry, milk production, and apple orchards. Industrial and commercial activity in the area has expanded considerably during the decade of the 1960's. For the most part these businesses are located in the urban centers of Fayetteville and Springdale of Washington County, and Rogers, Bentonville, and Siloam Springs of Benton County. While per capita income doubled during the 1960's, income levels remain at approximately 50% of the national average. Food processing, wood products, apparel, electrical and plastic manufacturing are the major industries. It is not unusual to find persons commuting 20 to 30 miles to reach their work location among the cities in this area.

In late 1974 the College of Business undertook research to attempt to determine the demand for an evening program. From information obtained from schools located in Arkansas and nearby states, the following was determined:

### Selected Statistical Data on Night School Programs at Neighboring Universities and Colleges

| Item Number and Description | Statistic |
|---|---|
| 1. Institutions with night school programs | 80% |
| 2. Business courses in their night school program | 87% |
| 3. Schools offering a business night school program which report increasing attendance over past five years | 97% |
| 4. Schools offering business courses both on and off campus | 38% |
| 5. Students taking business courses who are not considered full-time students in the day school program | 52% |
| 6. Ratio of nonday school business students (expressed as a percent) to total enrollment of all universities in sample | 5% |
| 7. Schools which offer the business night school program where students are unable to complete a degree program by attending night school exclusively | 31% |
| 8. Schools offering a business night school program which enables a student to complete a graduate and/or undergraduate degree by exclusive night school attendance | 56% |
| 9. Schools offering a business night school program which enables a student to complete the undergraduate degree only by exclusive night school attendance | 16% |
| 10. Average number of business courses offered in the night school program each semester | 30 |
| 11. Percentage of schools which offer extra compensation for night school teaching and/or adjust daytime teaching loads | 41% |

Note: All statistics relate to 32 schools which provided enough detail to make the necessary compilation with the exception of item 1 (40 schools) and item 5 (21 schools).

This same survey revealed that schools with a market potential about the same size of that of the University of Arkansas had a smaller number of "new" students enrolled in evening business courses than did more urban schools. This worked out to 3.5% of the day student population versus 18.9%. Not surprisingly the "rural" schools offered an average of 16 business courses per semester while the "urban" schools offered 48.

A survey among business firms located in the two-county area revealed that 71% had some program or policy designed to encourage employees to take college courses. Further, some 60% indicated that they provided some form of financial support for such personnel, provided the courses were job related and the work was completed satisfactorily. Better than 80% stated they hoped the university would offer courses of a noncredit nature which would be aimed at key personnel involved in management decision making. It was estimated that the potential number of managers for these short courses was in excess of 3,000.

Yet another study revealed that of the 54,297 working persons residing in the two-county market area about 46,000 were eligible for college level courses. A sample of these people showed that better than 11% assessed the probability of enrolling in night business courses to earn a degree—if such were available—as "very likely." A total of 29% indicated the probability as "likely" while the remainder replied "not likely." Considering only the "very likely" category as representing the potential and applying the proportion here to the eligible population of 46,295 yielded a potential of better than 5,000 students. If each student enrolled in one course, then this would represent a full-time equivalent of some 1,300 students.

This same study showed that a night school program would have its greatest appeal to persons under 30 years of age. Approximately 50% of these individuals indicated that it was very likely or likely that they would enroll in evening business classes if they were offered. Management, general business, and accounting were the subject areas indicated to be of the greatest interest.

If the College of Business were to undertake an evening undergraduate program, it would be necessary to offer a variety of basic and advanced courses with sufficient frequency to enable students to progress towards their degree with a minimum of scheduling delays. Further, the number of course offerings would increase over time as students advanced through the curriculum. Graduate work posed a special problem because of the inevitability of small enrollments beyond the "basics."

It was not thought that at the outset the college could receive special funding to hire the additional faculty and staff required to man this program. Thus, since the faculty was fully utilized in the day program, it would be necessary to divert faculty. This would mainly have to be done by increasing the average class size, and/or offering courses less frequently; e.g., once every other semester rather than every semester. The college's average class size was thought to be "about right," and it was feared that any substantial change in the size and frequency of offering might have a negative impact on day enrollments.

Nor was it clear just how many faculty would be involved in an evening division program. Much would depend upon how fast the market responded as well as the numbers involved. There was also the fear that the number of dropouts would be substantial—perhaps as high as 20–30%. In any event it was thought that initially a minimum of some six–eight full-time faculty equivalents would be required and that this would increase over time if the program was successful. Students would pay the same tuition as day students or per course.

What action should the College of Business take with regard to evening classes? If it decides to offer courses how should it market them?

## EXHIBIT 1

### Primary Market for Evening College of Business Program

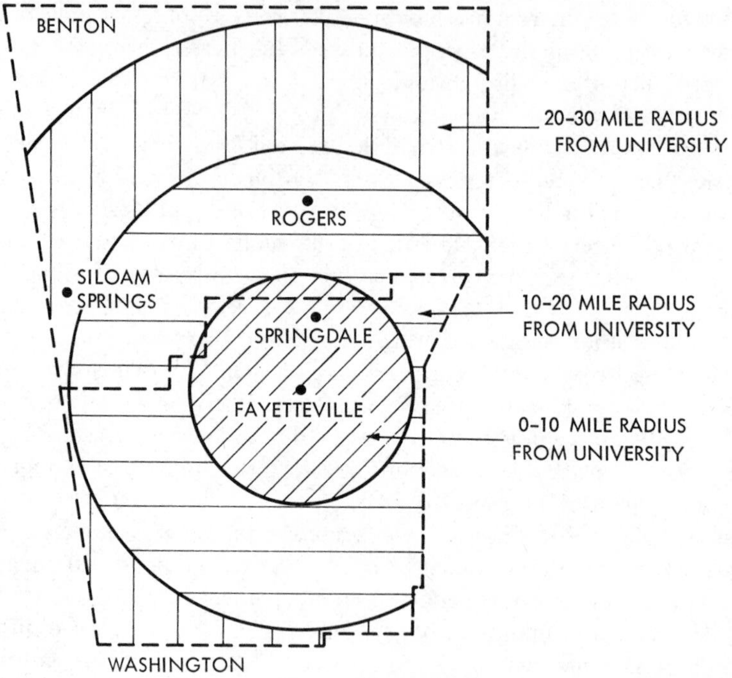

# Marchand (Canada) Ltd.

### QUESTIONS TO CONSIDER

1. Which influences and developments, inside and outside the company organization, were the most important to the final purchase decision? What are the implications of this analysis to the marketing programs of: the companies involved in this particular situation and all companies selling industrial products?

2. How effective was the decision-making process in this purchase? What, if anything, would you do to improve it?

3. How would you define the duties of the Marchand purchasing department? What criteria would you use to appraise the performance of these duties?

In 1961 the razor blade division of Marchand (Canada) Ltd., the wholly-owned subsidiary of Marchand Corp., was the largest manufacturer of safety razors and razor blades in Canada. During April 1961, division executives completed the arrangements for the first blister package to be used in the Canadian company (see Appendix A). The investigation of this packaging medium and discussions with related equipment and material suppliers had extended over a period of 17 months. The following discussion traces the chronological sequence of events and the process by which the necessary decisions were made within the organization.

### COMPANY BACKGROUND

The razor blade division was the largest and most profitable of the four Canadian divisions. The other divisions produced a complex variety of high volume, heavily promoted, consumer durable and nondurable goods. All manufacturing facilities and the head office were located in Windsor, Ontario.

Copyright by the University of Western Ontario. This case was prepared by George S. Day under the direction of Professor David S. R. Leighton. Reproduced by permission.

The company's dominant position in the razor blade market was the result of advanced and sophisticated manufacturing skills and aggressive sales and promotion policies. A major marketing strength was the extremely broad distribution pattern. Wholesale drug distributors, who covered drugstores, tobacconists, and other small stores, provided 75% of the company's sales. The remaining 25% of sales were made direct to chain retailers. In 1960 the company was estimated to have 35% of the total shaving market: electric shavers had 50% of the market, and four other razor blade manufacturers held the remaining 15%. The most severe competition was felt from electric razor manufacturers, who had rapidly expanded their market share between 1948 and 1953.

The division also manufactured and marketed five razor sets, ranging from an inexpensive three-piece model to an expensive gold-plated, one-piece prestige set. All sets were manufactured to extremely high tolerances. Razors had traditionally been a loss item, although as a result of automation some profits were being incurred. A strong justification for the emphasis of razor sets was the high degree of correlation between Marchand razor ownership and the usage of Marchand blades.

## PURCHASING DEPARTMENT ORGANIZATION AND RESPONSIBILITIES

In 1956 the rapid growth of the Canadian subsidiary necessitated a major revision of the organization into separate and distinct divisional units (see Exhibit 1). However, the purchasing department, directed by John Reid, continued to serve all divisions. In common with purchasing departments in similar companies, its basic responsibility was to select from among various possible sources of supply. Exceptions to this included the choice of advertising media and salesmen's cars, which were handled in other departments.

The buyers in the purchasing department issued approximately 40 purchase orders each working day. Each order ranged in purchase value from $5.00 to $30,000 with an average of $2,500. Each order was usually the result of three or four separate purchase requisitions issued by other departments. They were grouped either for convenience, or to take advantage of quantity discounts. Bruce Lee, the packaging buyer, issued 20 or more purchase orders each day, since he did the more routine ordering. Lee also did the buying for the purchasing engineer, Jack Hughes. However, most of the activity in the department was nonroutine and related to changes in materials, specifications, and vendors. These changes usually required considerable time and analytic work. Consequently the manager of the purchasing department, John Reid, seldom issued more than two purchase orders per day. The other buyers, Palmer and Myers, might account for 8 or 10 orders per day.

**John Reid—Purchasing Department Manager**

To elaborate on his department's role, John Reid said,

In our company, over 50% of the sales dollar goes for purchases of raw materials that we process further, and finished products for our own use or resale. In some areas, such as raw materials, we have undisputed decision-making powers, subject to the usual controls by top management concerning large expenditures. In other areas we act as the co-ordinator for the points of view of all the people who are interested in the purchase such as production, industrial engineering, warehousing, and so on. . . . We seem to be in the best position to assess and summarize the pertinent cost factors. Accountants are good on plant costs but don't understand the total cost picture which considers demurrage, damage, returns, and so on. . . . In either kind of purchase, however, the decision almost always becomes apparent once the significant factors have been defined and quantified. The most indeterminate and difficult part is appraising the long-run performance. For example, what is the sacrifice that a cost-cutter makes to get our business? If it's in quality control, what is the cost to us in the final analysis? That's why good working relationships are so important. In case of doubt you go to the company where you know the people, the equipment, the potential, and their weaknesses—and they understand your needs.

Concerning equipment selection specifically, John Reid made the following comment:

The responsibility for specification sometimes falls in a gray zone between our department and engineering, when their specification can only be met by one source. Our attitude is that this is either laziness or expediency. By and large, few pieces of equipment are so special that they can't be reduced to blueprints.

John Reid defined his own job as head of the purchasing department as follows;

Besides some responsibility for major purchases of commodities, such as steel and plastic films, my job is primarily to keep my people fully aware of the long-range implications of their actions. Sometimes they are prone to get carried away with immediate problems and pressures, such as processing requisitions, and neglect to make complete investigations. . . . At all times we're concerned with cost reductions, and I expect my people to initiate many opportunities.

John Reid was regarded by people inside and outside the company as an "enlightened" purchasing agent. A university graduate in science, with 16 years service with Marchand, he was active in a number of community affairs as well as the national executive of the Canadian Association of Purchasing Agents.

He was vitally interested in learning as much as possible about the industry and suppliers he dealt with. To this end he read *The Financial Post* and *Canadian Business* magazine closely and scanned articles of interest in the seven major Canadian and U.S. purchasing, packaging, and plastics magazines. He found direct mail advertising and institutional material such as internal house organs, employee papers, and company trade papers such as Dupont's *Packaging Patter*, to be more meaningful than normal trade magazine advertisements in developing a good supplier image and "keeping their name in front of me."

In 10 years' time John Reid's relations with salesmen had changed substantially as the purchasing department grew from one to five men. Originally, he saw an average of 10 salesmen a day. By 1961, the increasingly technical and longer term nature of his buying decisions meant he saw about two salesmen or groups of salesmen a day, usually by previous appointment or at his request. He preferred technical forums once or twice a year where key supplier people and Marchand technical people met for half a day to review all outstanding problems and plan for the coming period. In this situation he saw his job as ensuring that both parties understood each other completely. For the rest of the time, close telephone and mail contact sufficed.

John Reid was very positive about the key role of the salesman in providing service by communicating information quickly and representing the customer's interest to the supplier. "We're a marketing-oriented company, and the need to get promotions set up and into the market in a matter of days creates a real pressure for speed. The supplier must recognize this fact and do a conscientious job of meeting our needs, following up quickly on problems, and keeping us fully informed of the situation . . . one thing we don't need is a bunch of alibis."

### Jack Hughes—Packaging Engineer

For historical and other reasons, within the Canadian subsidiary, the purchasing department also included a packaging engineer (see Exhibit 1), who kept in touch with packaging problems in every division. The packaging engineer, Jack Hughes, was a graduate engineer with seven years experience in industrial engineering and product supervision and three years in his present position.

His view of his job was,

. . . . primarily to co-ordinate the development of new packages for the Canadian company—right from the idea stage to the details of the specifications and the placing of the first order. Some of the ideas I initiate myself to achieve cost reductions. This includes reducing the overlap in our 2,500 different packages. Other ideas stem from marketing innovations or from the production department's desire to change a process. . . . In the future I'm planning to do a lot in getting more uniformity in our suppliers' packages.

Although I pretty well run my own show, I find some real advantages in being part of the purchasing department. It provides a flexibility that our parent, with separate groups, certainly doesn't have. Of course they have more factories, people, and other variables to co-ordinate. It may take them a year to make a change that would only involve us for a month or so.

At present I'm too involved in the actual purchasing process, although Bruce Lee (the packaging buyer) handles the repeat orders, my requests for quotations and does the printing buying. The only way I can cut it down is to give Bruce detailed specifications at an earlier stage. This is difficult to do, because the requirements usually remain in a state of flux for too long.

Bruce also acts as a screen for packaging salesmen, so that I just talk to those whom I've asked in for a specific purpose or who have something new that I can use immediately. Normally when I have a specific requirement I use catalogues and other trade listings to give me leads on possible suppliers. I read all the major U.S. and Canadian packaging and plastics magazines and attend four or five trade shows each year, mainly as a source of new ideas. In these ways I've collected a lot of data, although I'm still finding it hard to keep up to date on all the changes in packaging technology.

### Edward Palmer—Purchasing Engineer

Essentially the purchasing engineer's job was to act as the buyer and a screen against salesmen for the engineering and maintenance departments. Ed Palmer, a graduate engineer, was well suited for this job, having spent 12 years as a project engineer in the engineering department before taking his present job in 1958.

Although most of the requirements were defined by the engineering department, Ed Palmer reviewed 10 magazines a month, on topics such as materials handling, design engineering, equipment selection, and purchasing, in search of new ideas or improvements that might be pursued. In describing the process of selecting possible suppliers, he said, "The big trade directories (Fraser for Canada and Thomas for the U.S.) handle about 90% of my problems. In the more difficult situations I'll depend on manufacturer and distributor catalogues and my knowledge of suppliers' capabilities . . . . direct mail is of very little use, since the information is limited and seldom comes when I'm interested in buying something."

Ed Palmer concluded, when he looked at the influence of salesmen on his decisions:

. . . In most cases we could do without them. Ideally the supplier should have a good office that is readily accessible by telephone when I have a problem, will keep me stocked with good literature and prices, and has technically competent salesmen who can advise me in case of problems. . . . In my experience, most salesmen don't know much about technical details, and fewer are of any use in following up orders, keeping us informed about the status of orders, or solving problems quickly.

On some days I will see as many as six or eight men, for visits of 20 minutes to over an hour (if, for example, they've been called in to talk with engineering also). About a third are suppliers who already have good relations with us and are calling to service orders or show new products. Another half are people who have never sold to us and seldom call. Sometimes they have a new product and can't understand why we won't try them out. As far as we're concerned, if the product doesn't have immediate application, then we don't have time to try it. The remainder of my callers are various agents and distributors who sell staples like bolts, ball bearings, etc., and can only offer service. There are a lot of these around; particularly now that they're coming from as far away as Toronto.

Over the long term, Ed Palmer expected to see the scope of his job expand substantially. "It will mean eliminating the routine of ordering, pricing orders, and grouping orders to save money, that any clerk can do, in favor of more special work. . . . I feel I have as much opportunity as anyone in the company to save money, by spending more time on negotiation with suppliers, arranging equipment trials, following new products, and developing Canadian sources of supply."

### Sequence of Events

*Need for New Package.*   As early as 1950 Canadian marketing executives had been unhappy with the alternatives for packaging inexpensive razors (those costing between $0.80 and $1.50). The most frequently used package, essentially a formed rigid plexiglass box, was felt to lack eye appeal and consumer interest. Consequently, between 1955 and 1958 the newly-developed techniques of blister and skin packaging (Appendix A) were examined. The chief attraction, in addition to improved product visibility, was the possibility of multiple packaging of blades with razors. During this period these advantages did not appear to overcome the high cost of materials, forming blisters, and sealing blisters to cards.

*Initiation of Informal Packaging Project.*   The first serious investigation of blister packaging was started in December, 1959. Ray Lewis, assistant marketing manager, had seen a new and inexpensive sealing machine[1] demonstrated at the annual Canadian Packaging Show. He returned to Windsor, very enthusiastic about the possibilities for the machine at Marchand. The marketing manager, Bert Crofts, agreed and suggested that the company packaging engineer conduct an informal investigation of blister packs in general.

In the early stages of the investigation Jack Hughes confined himself to collecting a firm quotation on the Melville Engineering sealing machine, seen by Lewis, and competitive quotations from blister and card suppliers. For these latter quotations he used sizes and order volumes typical of most of the existing razor packages. Hughes also submitted the published literature on the Melville Engineering sealing machine to the division industrial engineer for an estimate of the sealing and packing time per razor.

After consultation with the purchasing agent, John Reid, Hughes chose

---

[1] A Melville Engineering Corporation Model A 10 distributed in Canada by Clement Equipment of Canada. See Appendix A for a summary of the manufacturers' literature.

Multi-Pak Limited of Guelph, and Service Packaging of Toronto, as the best sources of quotes for blisters. Service Packaging was an easy choice; they had done excellent custom packaging work for Marchand for more than 10 years, they were known to be technically competent, and their salesman made a point of calling four or five times a year. As John Reid summarized, "We always think of them in this connection."

Multi-Pak was chosen for different reasons. John Reid had been aware for several years that they were one of the first companies in Canada to attempt skin and blister packaging at a time when the technology was still changing very rapidly. He had also not heard anything unfavourable about other custom packaging jobs they had undertaken. Consequently he thought that they could probably provide a good quality of formed blisters. Rather than depend on hearsay he asked the opinion of a salesman whom he trusted from long previous association. The salesman, John Doyle of Fairmont Chemical, currently the major supplier to Marchand of polyethylene and cellulose acetate packaging films, had developed a strong personal interest in packaging technology in order to sell more packaging film. Doyle was acquainted with Multi-Pak and judged them to be one of the leading companies in blister packaging.

Hewson Printers and K. J. Cowan and Sons were chosen as sources of quotes for printed and coated backing cards. These two printing houses had been doing most of Marchand's printing, and the relatively small requirement precluded asking for quotes from any other suppliers.

On January 25, Jack Hughes asked Bruce Lee, the packaging buyer, to contact the chosen suppliers and request quotations. Since there was no urgency to the request, the letters were not sent until February 19. All replies were received between February 25 and March 12. Jack Hughes summarized the lowest material quotations, the machine quote and the estimated packing time, and asked the divisional controller to ". . . establish and report the cost of this package, so it can be used as a guide to compare with other methods of packaging." Based on these costs[2] and normal depreciation and overhead charges, it appeared there would be a 15% to 25% premium for blister packages.[3]

Crofts and Lewis found these results, "interesting but speculative." No action was taken however, as other more pressing projects had to be given priority. As far as Hughes was concerned the project had died. This situation continued until the middle of June, when John Eadie, the division manager, sent a copy of a recent article on skin and blister packaging to John Reid and asked what the company was doing to evaluate these pack-

---

[2] The sealing machine was quoted as $1,733 plus $150 for the required tooling. The lowest blister quote was $15.80 per thousand for 100,000 units (from Multi-Pak). The lowest card quote was $11.35 per thousand for 100,000 units (Hewson Printers).

[3] This comparison applied to typical volumes and sizes of packages. (Total package cost figures have not been included because of the complexity of the overhead allocation procedure.)

ages. This enquiry was handed on to Jack Hughes. He, in turn, checked with Ray Lewis and found that there had been no concrete thinking on appropriate applications.

It was finally decided that the same two companies should be asked to requote on the costs of blisters, and also on skin packaging, for one of the smaller razor sets. This was done as before by Bruce Lee. The quotes were received from both Multi-Pak and Service Packaging by the end of July. Also, during July, Jack Hughes arranged to have some of the company products blister packed by Clement Equipment during a demonstration of the Melville Engineering heat sealer in Toronto. Several skin packages were also made for the same products.

The new cost information, plus the standard samples, was ready by the end of August. Skin packaging was immediately eliminated from consideration because of poor display appearance. The cost summary did show that blister packaging became appreciably more attractive as the package size diminished.

The razor marketing group responded quickly to the favourable cost summary and on September 5, Ray Lewis wrote to Bert Crofts:

We are writing to recommend that as a further step in our investigation we arrange, if possible, the loan or trial installation of a blister sealing unit from Clement Equipment, and also that we procure samples of blisters and cards for further in-plant investigation of this project. The blister samples and cards will be a standard item available from Clement Equipment at a nominal cost (to be confirmed by Jack Hughes). The trial installation would give us more accurate industrial engineering times for further costing.

May we refer you to the preliminary estimate prepared on March 21 by the cost department. You will note on this study that the blister pack compares favourably with our standard display pack. It is on the basis of this original cost study and our recent confirmation of these costs by Jack that we recommend the procurement, on a trial basis, of the necessary equipment.

### Formal Packaging Project T-145

As a consequence of Lewis' letter, Bert Crofts and John Eadie decided that a formal packaging project designed to study specific alternatives was desirable and necessary. The project was to cover two promotional items that were suffering from packaging limitations. One was a projected "deal" combining 15 blades with a safety razor for a dollar. It was further suggested that at least 100 units be packed on the Melville Engineering equipment to gain some operating experience.

As a routine measure, Ray Lewis reported the keen interest in blister packaging to the regular semimonthly meeting of the razor division packaging committee on September 15. This committee, chaired by Jack Hughes, met primarily to keep members informed about current packaging projects, manufacturing and marketing problems, and new products within the division (see Exhibit 1 for the actual committee membership). The meetings usually lasted less than an hour and covered 12 to 20 separate items.

The consequences of Lewis' report to the meeting were immediate and rather unexpected. It transpired that this was the first time the production department had been informed about the interest in the packaging machine and the recommendation for a trial purchase. Jim Murphy, the production superintendent, reacted to the report from his representatives on the packaging committee by immediately calling Bert Crofts. Murphy accused the marketing people of ". . . not consulting or informing the production people . . . making all sorts of unfounded assumptions without establishing a proper need." He concluded by saying that he wouldn't have anything to do with the blister sealer until he knew exactly what the machine would be doing, how it would affect his production rates, and that it was the best available piece of equipment from the standpoint of quality control, maintenance, and flexibility of output.

The reaction of Crofts and Lewis was one of surprise, since their attitude was primarily, ". . . We're not really specifying a piece of equipment, all we want are some costs." Although they did confess to having made a "faux-pas over communications," there was a strongly implied feeling that, "Jim Murphy is somewhat against change in general, because he has everything going so smoothly right now."

According to Ray Lewis, "For the next week, there was a lot of pussy-footing around; no one was quite sure what to do or wanted to take the responsibility for a decision." Finally Crofts got the production and industrial engineering groups to agree to an in-plant trial where a number of samples could be prepared and the necessary equipment evaluations could be made. The trial was conducted soon afterward, and all concerned pronounced themselves well satisfied with the construction and performance of the Melville Engineering equipment.

The successful demonstration convinced Crofts and Lewis that the Melville Engineering sealer was ideally suited to their needs. Furthermore, ". . . we've been looking at this machine for eight months now, why should we delay any longer?" This attitude led to further resistance from the production department, who contended that no specific requirements concerning output, size, and so on had been decided. It also resulted in a negative reaction from the purchasing department. John Reid, who until that time had not been directly concerned, questioned the advisability of an immediate purchase in a memo dated September 27 directed to Bert Crofts (see following). Reid's contention was, "It may be their dollars they're spending, but it's the responsibility of this department to recommend how it should be spent." His memo read:

I am sending this memo as a cautionary note with respect to Project T-145. The memos received to date seem to be strongly oriented towards the purchase of a blister sealing machine without a complete understanding of (*a*) the customer acceptance of our product packaged in blister, and (*b*) a full definition of our requirements. We may well find ourselves with a machine that either we don't need, after a period of a year, or we may find that it has too limited an output. Our basic interest in expediency now may result in buying a machine with much too limited an output, based on actual market acceptance of a blister pack.

We intend to investigate this project from the standpoint of custom packaging which would enable us to test market this package without an investment in equipment, as well as to explore, to a somewhat limited degree, the cost of blister sealing equipment and the cost of blisters from different sources.

If the blister package is completely acceptable to our customers and more than exceeds your honest expectation, it may well be that our strength would lie in having a completely integrated line for blister forming, loading, and blister sealing.

Should not then our main thrust be directed toward custom packaging and test marketing of these packages and, as a secondary objective, canvassing the market for prices of blisters and packaging equipment?"

### Formal Packaging Project T-153

The marketing department, faced with these arguments, agreed to redefine packaging project T-145 by prescribing exact requirements and a target date for distribution of January 2, 1961. The new project, number T-153, was issued on October 10, based on an estimated demand per order of 96,000 units of the razor-plus-15-razor-blades deal. This amount was roughly six months' normal demand for the cheapest razor set.

Most of the information needed for the new project had been submitted by Multi-Pak and Service Packaging by October 9 in response to a previous request for quotes. Because of confusion over who would pay die costs, Jack Hughes was unable to compare the suppliers on an equal basis until November 10. His results, as forwarded to the controller's department on November 12, showed:

1) Custom packaging charges of $34.00 per thousand for quantities of 100,000 (based on Multi-Pak supplying backing cards, blisters, equipment time, and packing labor).
2) Material costs of $8.28 per thousand for blisters (from Multi-Pak) and $12.75 per thousand for the coated backing board (from Hewson Printers). Packing times and the machine cost (of $1,883) had been submitted previously to the controller's department. It was then up to the marketing department and the division manager to make the key decision authorizing the blister packed deal by balancing market acceptance against any additional costs. Only after this decision was made did the purchasing department have the authority to select suppliers.

At this time John Eadie, the division manager, was asked about the alternative of custom packaging that had been suggested earlier by the purchasing department to give the whole project more flexibility and avoid an undesirable equipment purchase. According to Eadie, ". . . there are just too many production problems for us to be able to do this. However, it does give us an interesting comparison with our own costs. Production people have always taken a very dim view of work being taken away from their people. And it's hard to explain but people on the line really feel it is a slap in the face. Equally important is the effect on union relations. This issue has never come up, but there is always the possibility."

In early December Ray Lewis queried the controller's department to find out what had happened to the final cost summary, only to find that the cost accountant was overloaded with more urgent projects. Several days later some unexpected price cutting by Marchand's largest competitor demanded the full-time attention of the whole razor blade marketing group. It was decided that it was neither feasible nor desirable to put the new package into the market during January or February.

### New Sources of Supply

With his report of November 5, Jack Hughes had no further authority or pressure to go further in his examination of blister packaging for the razor deal. However, he did continue to keep himself informed, in anticipation of the decision to go ahead.

Since he was in close contact with the U.S. head office packaging department on several problems each week and depended on the head office for technical assistance on various packages being developed in Canada, he requested comments on U.S. experience with blister packaging for low price deals. The reply, dated November 15, dealt mainly with technical matters of board quality, blister material, and quality control. The end of the letter, dealing with equipment recommendations and comments on the usefulness of blister packaging, read:

We have an old vacuum-forming machine, known as an Abbott, which we have had at our main plant for probably six or eight years. While this machine is certainly not the greatest piece of equipment, it has done a job for us in adequate style. I would suggest, however, that if you are entertaining the idea of buying a vacuum former you contact someone like the Vacuum Equipment Company at Chicago. I do not know whether they have a Canadian plant, but I do know they are well established along these lines and produce an excellent piece of equipment for almost any vacuum or pressure forming operation you might be interested in.

In answer to your last question, I believe the most used comment on blister packaging that we have is that generally speaking it is quite expensive, and while we have used blister packing on a number of the kinds of items you are interested in, we usually end up with some other package that is less expensive and sooner or later drop the use of the blister.

I do believe the blister package does a good job and is a popular package on today's market. However, as for the product you have suggested, we feel we have not found that the blister has actually added to sales and consequently we find no reason to pay a premium to use a blister package.

Also during November, Jack Hughes followed up on some reports that the purchasing department had received about a Berwin blister sealer. They came from John Mason, a new salesman for Johnson Printers. According to John Reid:

Although Mason has only called on us a few times, and we really haven't had very good experience with his firm in the past, he has a fresh approach that is very worthwhile. Not only is he enthusiastic, but he has developed a strong technical orientation toward blister packaging—apparently as a hobby. He feels that he can ultimately sell printing by first selling the blister pack idea or at least being in a position to offer good technical assistance. One step he has taken is to ally himself with the Berwin people so he can offer a complete system. This is good for Berwin too, since it increases their sales representation. In this particular instance it's not going to work, because the backing-card requirement really isn't big enough to justify quotes from more than two printing houses. However in our eyes he has definitely overcome the past inertia of Johnson Printers and will be well received in the future.

At Mason's request Ken Murray, a manufacturers' agent representing Berwin in the Windsor-London area, submitted literature and a quotation for a blister sealing machine and also offered a 30-day in-plant trial. The machine chosen for quotation was designed to handle smaller volumes than the Melville Engineering sealer and lacked an automatic indexing mechanism to move the blisters in and out of the sealing area. It was priced at $1,050, compared with $1,700 for the Melville Engineering sealer.

Up to this point Jack Hughes had co-ordinated the contacts with the equipment suppliers. This constituted a minor precedent, since the engineering department, by virtue of its responsibility for equipment specification, was usually involved in equipment supplier contact at an early stage in the purchase decision. However, due to the nature of the purchase and a heavy work load, the engineering department had declared that it wasn't interested in participating in setting specifications on equipment that might not be purchased. Had the usual situation been true, Ed Palmer would have handled the supplier contacts for the equipment.

John Mason also supplied the lead on a new adhesive-coated blister being supplied by Remco Industries, a small plastics fabricator in Chicago. This represented a considerable innovation and potential cost-saving, as it meant that the backing board didn't have to be coated. At Mason's request, Remco submitted a quotation that proved competitive with Multi-Pak and also supplied a number of high-quality samples of their work. Jack Hughes commented, "At the moment I don't know anything about them, although since it's not a critical item, I suspect we can take a chance and not get into trouble. If I have time I'm going to try and visit them in Chicago. . . . The big reservation is that buying from them goes against my principle of using Canadian sources of supply wherever possible."

## Top Management Approval of Blister Package

The razor blade marketing department received the necessary cost data from the divisional controller on December 14, 1960. It was used to prepare a formal "Request for Addition to Stock"[4] which was duly approved by Messrs. Eadie and Hilson. In view of the changed circumstances in the market, volume per order was reduced from 96,000 to 72,000 units, and the target date for the completion of the packages and display racks was advanced to March 31, 1961.

On January 10, 1961, Jack Hughes received his copy of the approved "Request for Addition to Stock." This was his authority to obtain a final set of quotes based on the exact quantity required and decided on the source of supply for the blisters and backing cards. The only change from the earlier list of suppliers was the decision to have Johnson Printers' quote on the printed backing board. Simultaneously, the engineering department was authorized to prepare machine specifications for Ed Palmer and thereby initiate the purchase process for this piece of equipment. Ed Palmer anticipated the receipt of the specifications and asked Ken Murray to supply a Berwin sealing machine for an in-plant trial during February.

Ed Palmer reported on February 5 that he hadn't yet received the approved specifications.[5] "When I do, I'll send 'requests for quotations' to four or five suppliers that are listed in Fraser's trade directory. I expect there should be quite a number of suppliers, although I haven't looked yet. Actually I don't have much of a feel for the packaging machine market. We seldom buy this kind of equipment, preferring to build most of it ourselves. Also, I don't know when a packaging equipment salesman has been in to see me. I guess they are just too busy calling on the big buyers who are always in the market for more equipment."

A follow-up by Jack Hughes, after the normal two-week time allowance for projects of this nature, revealed that the assigned engineer had been tied up with other projects, then took sick. The upshot was the decision on February 10 to restrict the consideration of sealing machines to those made by Melville Engineering and Berwin and go with the cheaper Berwin machine if the in-plant trial was satisfactory. Jack Hughes commented, "Because of the pressures of time we won't be able to canvass other manufacturers or find out if any other divisions could use blister packaging. If we choose the Berwin machine we'll probably scrap it or

---

[4] Approval meant that the sale of new product or package was authorized, and purchase orders for necessary supplies and equipment could be initiated.

[5] Specifications included: maximum size of blister, cycle time, air pressure and electrical power requirements, and a limit on the price.

trade it for a bigger machine in one or two years as our requirements become clearer."

In the meantime the quotes on the blisters had been received, and an order placed with Multi-Pak, the low bidder. Jack Hughes said about Remco Industries, "After we get going with the initial order we'll get 150 or 200 of the new coated blisters and test them in the lab. If this blister is as good as it is supposed to be, there will probably be a Canadian company supplying it fairly soon."

The selection of a printed backing card supplier was delayed by a decision to completely revise the art work. It was March 15 before a sample card was finished by the art department and sent out for quotations. Quotes on the original card had been received from the three printing houses before February, so the two lowest were given the opportunity to requote. The lowest by far was Johnson Printers at $9.00 per thousand, although Jack Hughes suspected that they were either sacrificing something to get established with Marchand or had overlooked some costs. The next lowest was Hewson Printers at $12.10 per thousand. This was a large company with a number of printing plants across the country and considerable experience in this type of work. The highest quote was K. J. Cowan and Sons, a smaller local supplier. Their price of $18.00 per thousand reflected their inexperience in printing on this medium and the inconvenience of a small order of this sort. Johnson Printers were still the lowest by a wide margin on the second set of quotes and were awarded the job on April 6.

The Berwin blister sealing machine trial was concluded at the end of February with high marks in output, construction, and durability. A meeting of engineering, production, industrial engineering, and purchasing decided that there was no immediate advantage of speed of output or flexibility of the Melville Engineering sealer, that justified an extra $650. During the period previous to the decision Ed Palmer had one contact with Ken Murray to arrange a demonstration, and had heard nothing from Clement Equipment, the distributor of the Melville Engineering sealer, since the in-plant trial on September 1960.

The blister sealing machine was on hand, and all material deliveries completed by April 28. The sealing and packing operations were finished by May 12, 1961 in time for a June 1 introductory campaign. Further material orders from Johnson Printers and Multi-Pak would be contingent on market acceptance of the blister package.

**EXHIBIT 1**

**Organization Chart**

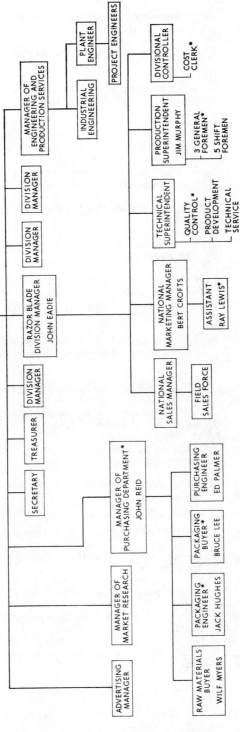

NOTE: Each * represents one member of the razor packaging committee.

SOURCE: Company records and personnel.

## EXHIBIT 2

### Chronological Summary of Events

*1959*

December 14 — Ray Lewis attended Canadian Packaging Show in Toronto.

*1960*

January — Jack Hughes selected five suppliers and requested quotations on blisters, backing cards, and a sealing machine for a representative size of package.

March 15 — Quotations were summarized and submitted to the divisional controller for cost analysis.

March 30 — Razor blade marketing department received cost comparisons of a representative blister package against the present package.

June 15 — John Eadie queried the status of blister and skin packaging in the company.

June 30 — Backing card and blister suppliers were asked to requote on a small razor set package.

August 28 — Second set of costs, plus sample packages, submitted to the marketing department for consideration.

September 10 — Packaging project T-145 issued.

September 15 — Backing card and blister suppliers were asked to requote on a projected "deal" comprising 15 blades with a safety razor for one dollar.

September 23–25 — In-plant trial of Melville Engineering blister sealing machine.

October 10 — Packaging project T-153 issued, defining exact volume requirements and a target date of January 2, 1961.

November 12 — Quotations, based on requirements of project T-153, were summarized and submitted to the divisional controller.

December 20 — Blister packaging of razor plus razor blades deal approved by top management.

*1961*

January 10 — Jack Hughes authorized to obtain final blister and backing card quotes based on revised volume requirements, and select a final supplier. Engineering department authorized to establish machine specifications.

February 2 — Multi-Pak chosen as blister supplier.

February 10 — Choice of blister sealing machines limited to Berwin and Melville Engineering due to lack of time.

February 27 — Berwin blister sealing machine chosen after successful in-plant trial.

March 15 — Revised backing card sent out for quotations.

April 6 — Johnson Printers chosen as backing card supplier.

**EXHIBIT 2 (Continued)**

| | |
|---|---|
| April 28 | —All material deliveries completed, and blister sealing machine installed. |
| May 12 | —Sealing and packing operations completed. |

## APPENDIX A:—DESCRIPTIVE NOTE ON BLISTER AND SKIN PACKAGING

The following has been extracted from an article entitled "Thermo-formed Plastics" that appeared in the February 1958 *Modern Packaging* magazine, and literature supplied by the Melville Engineering Corporation.

### Introduction

To understand thermoforming it is necessary to keep in mind that this process is confined to plastics in sheet or film form. In packaging terminology, sheet plastic is any gauge more than 3 mils in thickness; anything under 3 mils is classed as film. For the purposes of this discussion, "sheet" will be used as covering the entire range of plastics for thermoforming, although many skin packs now use thin film on a backing board.

In the thermoforming equipment, the sheet is softened with heat, while pressure forms it to the contours either of a die or mold, or of the actual product to be contained. Such mechanical assists as plugs, rings, and clamps are often used.

The simplest type of equipment employs atmospheric or vacuum pressure at about 15 lbs. per square inch. This is vacuum forming. Although the method is basically easy, for high speed and accuracy, very complex machines are needed and have been developed. Vacuum forming's forte is versatility in handling different materials, gauges, and forming requirements with minimum cost in dies and change-over time.

Where greater force is needed for higher speed and more precision, air or hydraulic pressures (up to 200 p.s.i.) are used. This is pressure forming.

### The Package

These are the distinguishing features of the three basic types of thermo-formed packages:

1. The skin pack uses thin sheet or film which is thermoformed directly about the product and seals it, usually onto a backing—eliminating mold costs and providing the skintight fit which gives the package its name. Skin packaging is done only by vacuum forming.

2. The contour pack is related to the skin pack only in the sense that it conforms closely to the contours of the product. It is preformed, often in multiples, over a mold or die rather than the product itself, and it generally uses heavier, semirigid sheet stock.

3. The blister or dome pack differs from the contour pack in that the blister is a simple curved or angular shape, not conformed to the shape of the product, and hence is applicable to many different products within a given size range.

Contour and blister packages can be made by either vacuum or pressure forming.

*Advantages*

1. Transparency and sparkle—to display the product and attract sales. Colour, opacity, and printing are available.

2. Conformability—thermoformed sheet plastics are supreme in this characteristic. Few limitations are imposed on size, shape, or detail; the packager has a freedom in blister and contour thermoforming not found in any other type of rigid packaging.

3. Flexural strength—this characteristic is like a built-in muscle. It means that all sorts of working and gripping features can be devised. Thermoformed plastic sheet can be made to hold a product or to provide such dispensing features as slide tracks, snap locks, and hinges.

4. Adaptability—the choice of materials is wide and growing wider. Because of this and the protective properties inherent to plastics, thermoformed packs are among the most versatile packages you can find.

5. Economy—the equipment, the dies (if any), and the process are relatively low in cost. Some blister and skin packs cost as little as two cents apiece. Even elaborate, high-cost thermoformed containers as used for instruments, gifts, and personal products are competitive and economical for their purpose.

6. Sales appeal and dealer convenience. The thermoform neatly combines the features most essential in packaging for today's merchandising requirements. It secures the product so that it cannot be lost or damaged, yet puts it fully on view for close examination by the shopper. The backing card or folder usually used with the thermoform provides a billboard for promotional and informational copy that can be taken in at a glance along with the product itself —and it has the very important advantage to the dealer of giving manageable size to items which would otherwise have to be stowed out of sight in bulk and in bins, to be sold only—and often unprofitably—by clerk service. The latter advantage explains why thermoforms have swept so prominently into hardware stores. Many carded packs are perforated for display on wire racks.

*Blister Sealing* (extract from Williams Engineering product literature)

Williams Engineering machines can seal one blister in just 1½ seconds and can be handled by a single inexperienced operator. Efficient two-station indexing table rotates automatically as each blister is sealed. Tooling is an inexpensive operation and can be done in your own plant. Changeover from one package size to another can be made in less than five minutes. The sealing area (up to 10″ × 9″ × 3″ deep) is generous enough to accommodate virtually any small product. Each machine comes complete. Simply connect to 50–60 p.s.i. air supply, standard electrical supply, and operate. There's nothing else to buy.

# Austin Company

Bergen Equipment Company, a manufacturer of heavy cranes, materials-handling equipment, and earth-moving equipment, developed a special paste solder for use in its own plants to seal joints in air, fuel, and hydraulic lines. Over a period of several years a significant external demand developed, a separate company was formed, and by 1965 it was apparent that major decisions would have to be made on the general sales program.

The new solder had a definite advantage in that it could be applied before a joint was assembled. If heat were applied to the joint after assembly, the solder would make a permanent bond, completely sealing the joint. At the time Bergen developed the solder, the company was manufacturing equipment for the Navy and presented the product to the Navy Department for approval. The Navy liked the item and saw other applications for it. Within a short time, Bergen had received several large orders for its solder. To fill these, it purchased a plant in Austin, Minnesota, and set up a separate division, the Austin Company, to handle production and distribution. In subsequent years Austin started producing a fairly complete line of solid and liquid solders so as not to be dependent on one product. By 1965 the special paste solder accounted for about 40 per cent of all sales. By this time, competitors had developed products comparable to it.

During the Korean War there was no sales problem—demand exceeded supply and distribution was a matter of allocation according to priority. This situation prevailed to some extent until the late 1950's. After that, however, the Austin management began work on a sales and distribution organization, looking forward to the time when the market would be more competitive. But the management of Bergen Equipment, the parent company, refused to allocate funds for the development or expansion of this division. As a result, little was accomplished.

This attitude changed in 1965, after Austin's sales and profits declined from their record high in 1960. The management of Austin was able to convince the parent company that the solder business still had a bright future but that substantial revisions in marketing were needed. In 1965 Austin was given permission to submit an action plan with respect to its selling activities.

At that time Austin had 135 distributors in seventeen sales districts in the United States and also had outlets through the parent company in Europe, South America, and Canada. The districts were the same as those maintained by the parent company. A salesman was maintained in each district to work with the distributors and to solicit business directly from large users. These salesmen were specialists who furnished technical advice both to direct customers and to customers of distributors. They worked out of the Bergen district offices but sold only Austin products.

TABLE 1

Total Industry and Austin Sales of Solder by End Use: 1964
(millions of pounds)

| End Use | Total Industry Sales | Austin Sales | Austin Per Cent of Market |
|---|---|---|---|
| Manufacturing | | | |
| Industry................. | 354 | 31.9 | 9.0 |
| Electrical equipment | | | |
| and machinery........... | 42 | 7.2 | 17.2 |
| Fabricated metal | | | |
| products................ | 58 | 8.4 | 14.6 |
| Machinery (except | | | |
| electrical).............. | 96 | 7.6 | 8.0 |
| Primary metals............ | 11 | 0.7 | 6.3 |
| Transportation | | | |
| equipment.............. | 103 | 6.3 | 6.1 |
| All other................. | 44 | 1.7 | 3.9 |
| Nonmanufacturing | | | |
| Industry................. | 157 | 10.6 | 6.8 |
| Construction.............. | 39 | 3.7 | 9.5 |
| Utilities.................. | 22 | 0.6 | 6.6 |
| Metal working shops........ | 49 | 1.2 | 2.4 |
| Transportation............ | 25 | 0.3 | 1.1 |
| All other................. | 22 | 4.8 | 21.8 |
| Total Market.......... | 511 | 42.5 | 8.3 |

From industry publications the sales staff developed data on the total market for solder. These data were compared with their own sales figures, and it was found that Austin's pattern of solder sales by end use varied considerably from the industry (Table 1). The company's market share was higher among manufacturing users than among nonmanufacturing users. Among manufacturers, Austin's sales were highest in the electrical equipment, machinery, and fabricated metal products segments. In the nonmanufacturing markets the company was strong in the construction and "all other" segments.

Total industry sales were broken down geographically and compared with Austin's geographic sales pattern (Table 2). Again it was found that Austin's geographic sales pattern differed substantially from that of the industry. Three of the seventeen Austin sales districts accounted for nearly half the total solder industry market. Part of the variation was the result of shipping to warehouse stocks. Austin maintained a warehouse in each of the four districts—Norfolk, Kansas City, Milwaukee, and Dallas—to

**TABLE 2**

**Austin and Industry Sales by Austin Sales Districts: 1964**
**(millions of pounds)**

| | Total Industry Sales | Austin Sales | Austin Per Cent of Market |
|---|---|---|---|
| Detroit | 87 | 6.2 | 7 |
| Pittsburgh | 74 | 5.9 | 5 |
| Chicago | 64 | 2.5 | 4 |
| Boston | 41 | 2.7 | 7 |
| Los Angeles | 36 | 2.7 | 7.5 |
| New York | 35 | 0.8 | 2 |
| Philadelphia | 26 | 5.0 | 19 |
| Kansas City | 25 | 1.8* | 7.5 |
| Milwaukee | 20 | 3.5* | 17 |
| St. Louis | 18 | 2.0 | 11 |
| Minneapolis | 17.5 | 3.0 | 17 |
| Seattle | 17 | 1.3 | 8 |
| San Francisco | 14 | 2.9 | 21 |
| Denver | 11 | 0.7 | 6.5 |
| Norfolk | 10 | 1.9* | 19 |
| Dallas | 7 | 0.8* | 11 |
| Washington, D.C. | 7 | 0.5 | 8 |
| Total† | 509.5 | 44.2 | 8.3 |

\* Includes shipments to warehouse stocks.
† Totals do not agree with those in Table 1 because of different sources and the inclusion of shipments to warehouse stocks.

serve areas where distributors were not really available. Shipments to these warehouses were recorded as sales. The penetration of individual sales districts had been determined primarily by allocation to customers up to 1958. The sales pattern still reflected much of this practice.

Industry data showed that 54 per cent of all sales were made through distributors, while 46 per cent were made direct to end users. Austin's pattern was almost the same, 56 per cent through distributors and 44 per cent direct. Austin's policy was to attempt to sell direct to end users who purchased 50,000 pounds or more annually, even though in many cases this volume was bought from several suppliers. The percentage sold through distributors was exaggerated in those districts where shipments of solder were made to warehouse stocks, because these shipments were recorded as sales to distributors, although much of the warehouse sales were made direct to small users in the area. Actually, the warehouses were essentially sales branches. Sales analysis showed further that 81 per cent of the total tonnage of solder sold direct by Austin went to eighty-nine accounts buying 50,000 pounds or more. These eighty-nine accounts represented only 13 per cent of the total direct accounts. The same pattern existed in sales to distributors where 82 per cent of the company's shipments went to 21 per cent of the distributors, all of whom purchased 100,-000 pounds or more annually. Solder prices averaged about 10 cents a pound, so that a distributor handling less than 100,000 pounds accounted for less than $10,000 in sales. Table 3 shows the direct and distributor sales patterns.

### TABLE 3
**Austin Shipments Direct and to Distributors by Size of Account: 1964**

| | Accounts | | Shipments | |
|---|---|---|---|---|
| | No. | Per Cent | Millions of lbs. | Per Cent |
| Direct Sales | | | | |
| Under 1,000 lbs.............. | 302 | 44 | 0.056 | 0.3 |
| 1,000–1,999................. | 129 | 19 | 0.374 | 2 |
| 5,000–9,999................. | 44 | 6 | 0.374 | 2 |
| 10,000–19,999.............. | 48 | 7 | 0.561 | 3 |
| 20,000–49,999.............. | 68 | 10 | 2.151 | 11.5 |
| 50,000–99,999.............. | 42 | 6 | 2.618 | 14 |
| Over 100,000................ | 47 | 7 | 12.529 | 67 |
| Sales to distributors | | | | |
| Under 20,000 lbs............ | 122 | 52 | 0.714 | 3 |
| 20,000–49,999.............. | 42 | 18 | 1.666 | 7 |
| 50,000–99,999.............. | 22 | 9 | 1.904 | 8 |
| 100,000–249,999............ | 24 | 10 | 4.403 | 18.5 |
| 250,000–499,999............ | 17 | 7 | 7.616 | 32 |
| Over 500,000................ | 8 | 3.4 | 7.378 | 31 |

Data on the sales of solder to different types and sizes of firms were obtained from trade publications and from Austin's own sales records. From these data, estimates were made of the potential sales of solder to different types of firms according to their sales volumes. With these estimates and with data on the distribution of manufacturers in the United States from the Census of Manufacturers, the sales staff established sales potentials by district for both direct and distributor sales. All firms with an annual potential of 50,000 pounds or more were classified in the direct-sales group. The others were put in the distributor-sales group. The total was adjusted to make the total potential approximately equal the industry's total sales volume. Table 4 shows the breakdown of potential by sales district and the number of prospects for direct sales in each district.

A survey was made among solder users to determine future trends, but the results brought a different problem to the attention of the company. Although Austin accounted for 8.3 per cent of the total sales of solder,

## TABLE 4
### Number of Direct Sales Prospects and Potentials for Direct Sales and Distributor Sales by Sales District
(millions of pounds)

| Sales District | Number of Direct Sales Prospects | Direct Sales | | | Distributor Sales | | |
|---|---|---|---|---|---|---|---|
| | | Est. Potential | Austin | Austin Per Cent of Potential | Est. Potential | Austin | Austin Per Cent of Potential |
| New York | 127 | 16.3 | 0.4 | 2.4 | 18.8 | 0.4 | 2.1 |
| Boston | 195 | 18.9 | 1.1 | 5.8 | 21.8 | 1.6 | 7.3 |
| Los Angeles | 211 | 16.8 | 2.2 | 13.1 | 19.5 | 0.5 | 2.6 |
| Detroit | 271 | 40.5 | 2.3 | 5.7 | 46.9 | 3.9 | 8.3 |
| Pittsburgh | 297 | 34.1 | 2.6 | 7.6 | 39.4 | 1.3 | 3.3 |
| Chicago | 150 | 29.6 | 1.2 | 4.1 | 34.4 | 1.4 | 4.1 |
| Minneapolis | 86 | 8.1 | 1.9 | 23.5 | 9.4 | 1.1 | 11.7 |
| Dallas | 25 | 3.2 | 0.2 | 6.2 | 3.8 | 0.6 | 15.8 |
| San Francisco | 36 | 6.3 | 2.4 | 38.1 | 7.4 | 0.5 | 6.8 |
| Seattle | 19 | 7.9 | 0.1 | 12.7 | 9.2 | 1.2 | 13.0 |
| St. Louis | 33 | 8.5 | 1.6 | 18.8 | 9.9 | 0.5 | 5.1 |
| Philadelphia | 85 | 12.1 | 1.6 | 13.2 | 13.9 | 3.5 | 25.2 |
| Milwaukee | 28 | 9.4 | 0.4 | 4.2 | 10.9 | 3.1 | 28.4 |
| Washington, D.C. | 9 | 3.2 | 0.3 | 9.4 | 3.7 | 0.2 | 5.4 |
| Norfolk | 12 | 4.6 | 0.2 | 4.3 | 5.3 | 1.7 | 32.1 |
| Denver | 25 | 5.0 | 0.3 | 6.0 | 5.8 | 0.4 | 6.9 |
| Kansas City | 33 | 11.5 | ... | ... | 13.3 | 1.8 | 13.5 |
| Total U.S. | 1,665 | 236.0 | 18.8 | 8.0 | 273.4 | 23.7 | 8.7 |

the survey showed that only 1.9 per cent of the users expressed a preference for Austin products when asked which brand of solder they preferred. Jansen solder had outstanding preference, with four to six times the percentage preferring it as preferred to the next highest ranking brand. Jansen was the leading brand in the field and probably accounted for one-third of the industry's sales. Table 5 shows the relative preference ratings for all major brands of solder. There were no technical reasons expressed for preferring a particular brand, although each respondent was asked the reasons for his preference. Most respondents gave noncommittal replies, such as, "We've always dealt with them" or "We just like them better."

An executive committee was appointed to evaluate the information given in Table 5 and recommend specific steps to be taken, as follows:

### TABLE 5

#### Brand of Solder Preferred by Users

| | | | |
|---|---|---|---|
| Jansen | 32.3% | Austin | 1.9% |
| A & T | 5.1 | A. A. Metal | 1.6 |
| Harley | 4.6 | Bondex | 1.3 |
| Mueller | 4.5 | Fastet | 0.8 |
| Hobert | 3.8 | All others | 4.0 |
| Permafix | 3.5 | No preference | 10.0 |
| Metal Products | 2.3 | Don't know | 22.2 |
| Solderall | 2.2 | | |
| Total | | | 100.0% |

(1) build Austin product preference, (2) set sales goals and quotas for direct and dealer sales, and (3) realign sales districts. In addition, the committee was to study the future trends of the solder market.

To build Austin product preference, the committee made the following recommendations: (1) distribute the facts of the market situation to the Austin sales organization; (2) give strong support to the sales organization through advertising and publicity; and (3) make a survey of present users to serve as a guide to future product improvement.

Another recommendation was that the company establish a goal in terms of the total tonnage of solder Austin should sell in 1965. Austin's market share was estimated at 8.3 per cent in 1964; 10 per cent was recommended as a reasonable and practical goal. The goal would be distributed among the sales districts in proportion to potential; e.g., if Detroit had 8.7 per cent of the industry potential, it would have 8.7 per cent of the Austin sales goal. The breakdown based on industry sales of 509.4 million pounds is shown in Table 6.

If there were any reason why a sales district should not have a goal relative to its potential, it would be given special consideration. The goal for each district should be divided into two parts, a goal for direct sales and a goal for distributor sales (Table 7). This division was based on the national sales pattern of 54 per cent through distributors and 46 per cent direct. Both these markets were to be developed equally. In many outlying territories large accounts were being sold by distributors. It was recommended that a policy be established for direct solicitation of all prospective customers whose total solder purchases exceeded 50,000 pounds and that smaller accounts be left exclusively to distributors.

Many of the districts would be unable to attain their goals immediately, so each year quotas would be set that would permit them to move at a

### TABLE 6

|  | Sales (Millions of Pounds) | Per Cent |
|---|---|---|
| Austin total goal | 50.9 | 100 |
| Detroit | 8.7 | 17 |
| Pittsburgh | 7.3 | 15 |
| Chicago | 6.4 | 13 |

### TABLE 7

|  | Sales (Millions of Pounds) | | |
|---|---|---|---|
|  | District Total | Direct | Distributors |
| Total company | 50.9 | 23.4 | 27.5 |
| Detroit | 8.7 | 4.0 | 4.7 |
| Pittsburgh | 7.3 | 3.4 | 3.9 |
| Chicago | 6.4 | 3.0 | 3.4 |

reasonable rate toward their goals. Some districts were already over the 10 per cent goal and would require quotas higher than their goals. An analysis of each individual district would be necessary in setting the quota to determine the district potential, the areas within the district that needed further development, and manpower requirements. The Chicago sales district was analyzed as an example (Table 8).

It was recommended that each area be further analyzed by class of user so that the company could tell more precisely the industries from which additional business should come. The company could provide each district with a detailed list of accounts that should be solicited. The committee further recommended that in the future a refinement of the market analysis be worked out on the basis of type of solder used. It also recommended that the company consider methods of realigning sales districts so that all would be approximately equal. The committee believed that it

**TABLE 8**

**Example of Breakdown of Sales Goals in Chicago District**

**(millions of pounds)**

| | Industry Total | Direct Sales | | | Distributor Sales | | |
|---|---|---|---|---|---|---|---|
| | | Industry | Austin Goal | Austin 1956 Shipments | Industry | Austin Goal | Austin 1956 Shipments |
| Total district | 63.9 | 29.3 | 2.93 | 1.2 | 34.6 | 3.46 | 1.36 |
| Chicago | 41.9 | 19.2 | 1.90 | 1.1 | 22.7 | 2.27 | 0.83 |
| Gary | 7.2 | 3.3 | 0.30 | 0.1 | 3.9 | 0.39 | 0.41 |
| Hammond | 3.3 | 1.5 | 0.15 | ... | 1.8 | 0.18 | ... |
| Waukegan | 3.2 | 1.5 | 0.15 | ... | 1.7 | 0.17 | ... |
| Rockford | 2.7 | 1.2 | 0.12 | ... | 1.5 | 0.15 | 0.01 |
| Aurora | 2.0 | 0.9 | 0.01 | ... | 1.1 | 0.11 | ... |
| Peoria | 1.4 | 0.7 | 0.07 | ... | 0.7 | 0.07 | 0.05 |
| Springfield | 0.8 | 0.4 | 0.04 | ... | 0.4 | 0.04 | 0.01 |
| Elgin | 0.7 | 0.3 | 0.03 | ... | 0.4 | 0.04 | 0.04 |
| Other areas | 0.7 | 0.3 | 0.03 | ... | 0.4 | 0.04 | 0.01 |

was desirable to divide the sales districts so that each would have a sales goal of between 2 and 3 million pounds annually.

The conclusion was reached that in the long term the demand for solder would remain fairly constant, with possibly a slight downward trend. New materials, such as plastic pipe, and new methods, such as printed circuits in the electric industry, would have a noticeable effect on the solder market, but little change was expected in the next ten years. The demand for solder was closely tied to the demand for durable goods, which was expected to have a long-term upward trend. This trend would offset any loss resulting from new innovations during the next ten years.

## Questions

1. Are the committee's recommendations sound?
2. Are the sales goals and quotas valid and useful?

# California Office of Consumer Counsel

Mr. Jerry Miner, senior staff member of the Committee for the Assessment of Government Efficiency (CAGE)[1] was reviewing his notes for a report to CAGE on the California Office of Consumer Counsel (COCC). CAGE was a nonpartisan group of concerned citizens whose ongoing examination of the Government of California had been the basis for many changes initiated by both the Governor's Office and the State Legislature. Many of its recommendations had been adopted by several other states as well. It was expected that the CAGE report on the COCC would have an important bearing on the future structure and functioning of this institution.

In 1959 the California legislature created the position of Consumer Counsel in the Office of the Governor and authorized the Governor to appoint such assistants and employees for the Consumer Counsel as he found necessary. Two primary duties were given to the Consumer Counsel: to advise the Governor on "all matters affecting the interests of the people as consumers," and to "recommend to the Governor and the Legislature the enactment of such legislation as he deems necessary to protect and promote the interests of the people as consumers." To fulfill these duties the Consumer Counsel was directed to conduct studies and to report the results of such studies to the people of the state. The law also authorized the Consumer Counsel to "appear before governmental commissions, departments, and agencies to represent and be heard on behalf of consumers' interests," and to "cooperate and contract with public and private agencies" to obtain and publish statistical and economic information as necessary. Finally, "each agency, officer, and employee of the

Reprinted from *Stanford Business Cases 1970* with the permission of the publisher, Graduate School of Business, Stanford University. Copyright © 1970 by the Board of Trustees of the Leland Stanford Junior University.

[1] The Committee for the Assessment of Government Efficiency and its staff are fictitious. All other persons and organizations referred to in this case are real.

State" was ordered to cooperate with the Consumer Counsel in carrying out these duties. In the first ten years of existence of this law, only two people served as Consumer Counsel, but their respective interpretations of their responsibilities under this legislation reflect quite different approaches to providing consumer protection.

Serving from 1959 to 1967, under Governor Edmund Brown, Mrs. Helen Ewing Nelson was the first Consumer Counsel. In Mrs. Nelson's view: "The consumer is alone. Business likes him that way—alone, impotent, submissive, uninformed. He's easier to deal with that way." Speaking of the legislation creating her position, she said, "The intent of it clearly was that the Consumer Counsel should speak for the consumer." As spokesman for such a hapless constituency, Mrs. Nelson sought to buffer the power and influence of business by aggressively voicing the consumer's position before the Legislature, and the administrative and regulatory agencies: ". . . all the other interest groups have the lawmaker's ear. The pressure should be equalized. Legislators should hear the consumer view put to them often and competently." Her active lobbying for consumer interests created many enemies in the Legislature, but she dismissed this:

Certainly they resented me, and understandably so. My office caused a great deal of embarrassment. Legislators were faced with a dilemma caused by the fact that consumers can't give great blocks of money to finance reelection campaigns—while interest groups can. There were a great many pressures on the legislators not visible in the hearing room.

Mrs. Nelson's vigorous advocacy of consumer interests, often focused (by legislative lobbying or administrative agency hearing) against specific industry representatives, seemed to lead to a characterization of the Office of Consumer Counsel as an adversary of the business community. Having adopted an adversary role, the Office, under Mrs. Nelson, tended to respond to consumer complaints with a legalistic approach. Solutions to consumer problems were either found through encouraging the use of existing legal remedies, or they were sought by proposing and lobbying for new legislation in the area of the complaint. This approach is reflected in several extracts from correspondence from the Office during Mrs. Nelson's incumbency.

The following extracts are from responses to consumers who had written to complain of misleading advertising:

I can certainly understand your concern for the techniques employed. Information such as you have provided is extremely useful to our program and can be used to advise the Governor and the Legislature on specific problems of consumer concern.

The type of problem you describe is a very difficult one to resolve. Unfortunately, there is no government agency with authority to assist you directly. If you can prove that the [product] was misrepresented, you would likely have legal grounds for an adjustment. However, you will need legal advice to make this determination. Therefore, I would suggest that you consult with an attorney on this matter.

California has laws prohibiting false and misleading advertising (Section 17,500 of the California Business and Professions Code). It is the responsibility of the district attorney in each county to interpret these laws. Therefore, you should call this matter to the attention of your local district attorney.

I am forwarding your recent letter and its enclosures to the California Bureau of Weights and Measures. This matter comes under the jurisdiction of that state agency. The Bureau will advise you of its findings.

The matter described in your letter does not come under my jurisdiction. However, I am taking the liberty of forwarding a copy of your letter to the Federal Trade Commission in San Francisco. That Federal Agency is very much interested in the type of situation you describe.

I am sending a copy of your letter to the [X] Corporation and to the [Y] Corporation, because I think that they will be interested to know how their brand names are being used. If their names are registered, as I believe they are, the companies will want to stop this practice.

If you feel you are personally entitled to a refund, I would suggest you consider taking action in the Small Claims Court to recover the amount of money in question. The enclosed brochure explains how to use the Small Claims Court.

During Mrs. Nelson's incumbency, California was swept by a referral selling scheme (customers charged exorbitant prices but promised large cash rebates for providing names of others who subsequently became purchasers) for aluminum house siding. The progress of attempts to halt these operations is revealed in letters which contain, in substance, the following kinds of comments:

Interpreting your contract is a legal matter, and as a state officer I cannot give legal advice. I recommend that you consult an attorney.

Thank you for your letter, which I will add to our file on aluminum siding in preparing support for legislation soon to be proposed.

Copies of pending legislation in regard to aluminum siding are attached for your information.

Your letter has been referred to the Consumer Fraud Unit of the Attorney General's Office for action.

A similar file on usury contains responses of the same type recorded above, enclosing brochures on the cost of credit and the maximum credit charges allowed by California law, and pointing out the California laws regulating pawnbrokers and encouraging consultation with the local district attorney to seek enforcement.

With an aggressive legislative program, an active information program that consisted primarily of the preparation and distribution of reprints and special pamphlets of general interest to the consumer, and a close involvement with other state sponsored programs directed toward specific population groups, the Office staff grew to eight persons and the operating budget rose to $119,000 per year during Mrs. Nelson's term in office.

In 1967, following a two-month study of the Office of Consumer Counsel for the newly elected Governor Ronald Reagan, Mrs. Kay Valory was appointed Consumer Counsel and asked to implement the recommendations of her investigation. One of her first actions was to reduce her staff to one secretary and her budget to $33,000. Mrs. Valory's approach to her position stands in vivid contrast to the activities of the Office of Consumer Counsel under Mrs. Nelson. Summarizing her first two years in office, a report to the Governor contained the following description of the job of Consumer Counsel:

Mrs. Valory views her role as that of educator and catalyst in the consumer-business-government relationship. Working as a clearinghouse for individual consumer complaints, the Consumer Counsel initially channels them to the business or professional association traditionally responsible for maintaining ethical standards in that area of commerce. When necessary, these complaints are referred to the appropriate regulatory and law enforcement agencies. The Consumer Counsel encourages these authorities to act vigorously, but responsibly; bringing to justice those who would defraud the consumer, but bringing to bear the full weight of the law only in cases of criminal activity or when business fails in its responsibility to police itself.

This catalyst's role differs in several important respects from Mrs. Nelson's role as advocate or spokesman. First, it implies neutrality in the consumer-business-government relationship rather than identification with consumer interests in an adversary posture toward business. This neutrality is expressed by Mrs. Valory's opinion that most consumer-business problems reflect misunderstanding; a communication gap between the consumer's wishes and demands and the sizable contributions business is currently making for the consumer's benefit. A national news magazine recently characterized Mrs. Valory's incumbency as follows:

California's Kay Valory, consumer counsel to Governor Ronald Reagan, has not testified in three years before any committee considering consumer legislation. She recently made the extraordinary recommendation that buyers shun the "very narrow" testing reports of Consumers Union in favor of the handbook of the National Association of Manufacturers.

Mrs. Valory contends that her practice of seeking to bridge this gap by bringing consumer complaints directly to the business or industry concerned has been successful in all but a small percentage of cases, which demonstrates that consumers and business need not be considered implacable enemies. Mrs. Valory's neutrality is also manifested by her absence from active lobbying; her conception of her role as a catalyst leads her to research all aspects of a given problem so that her office can be used as a legislative resource rather than an advocate in the legislative process.

Responding to a consumer complaint about confusing billing statements from a finance company, Mrs. Valory writes:

Thank you for your letter concerning the new truth-in-lending law and [X] Company statements. Such letters are extremely helpful to this office as they provide us with firsthand information on consumer concerns.

We are enclosing a brief summary of the law which we thought might be of interest to you. We are also taking the liberty of forwarding a copy of your letter to [X] Company for their comments.

Copies of the letter were sent not only to the [X] Company, but also to the California Retailers Association.

Another consumer wrote directly to the offending company and sent Mrs. Valory a copy of that correspondence along with a further explanation. Her reply:

Although this office does not have regulatory or enforcement authority, we have had some success in enlisting the cooperation of business and industry in solving individual consumer complaints. If you do not receive a satisfactory response to your letter to [X] Company in a reasonable time, please let us know and we will attempt to assist you.

Letters such as yours are extremely helpful to this office for advising the Governor and the Legislature on matters of concern to consumers. Thanks for writing.

Occasionally Mrs. Valory has sought to enlist the assistance of her counterparts in other states, rather than seeking either federal intervention or dealing directly with the firm herself. This is a letter to the Consumers' Council of Massachusetts:

Gentlemen:

Enclosed are copies of correspondence from Mr. [X] concerning a transaction with a Massachusetts firm. Will you please take whatever action you can to assist Mr. [X] with his problem.

The most characteristic method of dealing with consumer complaints has been direct correspondence with the company against whom the complaint has been lodged. A typical letter follows:

Enclosed is a copy of a letter from Mr. [Y] of [Z], California, concerning a complaint against your company.

It is the responsibility of the California Consumer Counsel to advise the Governor and the Legislature on matters of interest to consumers and to recommend any needed legislation or regulation.

In carrying out this responsibility, it is our policy to encourage business to take the initiative in solving consumer problems without further legislation or regulation.

In view of this policy, we would appreciate receiving your comments on the enclosed letter and your advice as to what action Mr. [Y] should take.

If this letter failed to induce a response which satisfies the complaining consumer and/or brings the company's operating practices within the bounds of existing regulations, Mrs. Valory then referred the entire file of correspondence to the state agency or local district attorney with the jurisdiction and authority to further pursue the complaint.

In some aspects the catalytic role is the more active one in the resolution of consumer problems. Mrs. Nelson's adversary position generally led to either: (1) presentation and definition of a disputed problem before a legislative or administrative body, with the responsibility for formulating solutions to the problem remaining with that body; or (2) referral of the problem to an appropriate legal enforcement mechanism for resolution. Mrs. Valory's catalytic role often results in the use of her position to resolve the problem directly through either: (1) bridging an actual communication gap between the businessman and consumer involved; or (2) applying a subtle moral persuasion on the businessman by catching him in an unfavorable position; or (3) presenting an implied threat of governmental intervention if he doesn't get his affairs straightened out.

Perhaps the greatest difference in the approach taken by the two Consumer Counsels involves the question of consumer education. In a speech given July 9, 1969, Mrs. Valory commented:

Acting from my conviction that the best protected consumer is the aware and informed consumer, I have focused my strongest efforts on educating and informing the buying public, for I believe that a thoroughly informed society of consumers is a far more effective and less expensive deterrent to dishonesty, fraud, and misrepresentation than the enactment of sometimes costly, sometimes ineffective new "consumer protection" laws.

Mrs. Valory's legislative research on consumer interest topics is a reflection on this view. Also consistent with this attitude is an active attempt to prepare special consumer education films to be presented on television, and even public service "spot commercials" of consumer advice.

Mrs. Nelson, from her subsequent position with the Illinois Federation of Consumers, has been particularly critical of this portion of Mrs. Valory's program: "There is no excuse for anyone in the Governor's office taking a chiefly educational role." One of the sources of this criticism is undoubtedly a sharp disagreement about the nature of the "consumer revolution." Returning to the origins of this movement, recall that the initial consumer protection measures arose to counteract the impact of the doctrine of *caveat emptor* in a marketplace where the buyer had become incapable of attaining equality of bargaining power with the seller. Miner thought that Mrs. Valory's educational goal seems to tacitly accept *caveat emptor*, but attempts to attain bargaining equality by educating the buyer. Speaking of a federal study describing deception in gasoline and supermarket games, Mrs. Valory observed: "I am not sure it is the government's place to legislate in areas of this sort. I think it may be enough for the government to warn that deceptions may exist." Miner saw Mrs. Nelson's aggressive advocacy of the consumer interest can be seen as an attack on *caveat emptor* itself, accompanied by a conviction that the only practical, sure way to attain bargaining equality for all consumers is not to rely on education of the buyer, but rather to limit or restrict the powers of the seller.

Mr. Miner had also referred to the note on "The History of Government and Consumer Protection." This note, which had been prepared for him by his assistant, Miss Marion Arnold, a law student, appears as Appendix A.

In preparing his report, Miner had discovered that there are many other state agencies that guard the consumer's interests. Most of these agencies had been in existence long before the COCC was formed and many had functions that overlapped those of the COCC, particularly under Mrs. Nelson. Appendix B lists those agencies.

He reflected upon a recent speech about the respective roles of business, government and consumer. The following excerpt was particularly important to Mr. Miner:

Business and government must work together to solve problems posed by the knowledge explosion and the population explosion. But there must be a clear definition of which functions belong to government and which to business.
. . . As it happens there are few major problems that can be solved by government alone without business or by business alone without government. As government and business both respond to the major problems of our day, as each of them enlarges the scope of its responsibilities to the public, they inevitably move into the no-man's-land where functions overlap and boundaries are ill defined, so the real question is which of them should do what.

Miner thought that the relationship between the individual citizen in his role as a consumer in the American marketplace and the businessman who provides the goods and services offered in that marketplace has become one of those areas of overlapping functions and ill defined boundaries. He was concerned about where does government, as a representative of the citizenry as a whole, fit into this relationship between consumer and business?

Before he drafted his report to CAGE, Miner was particularly concerned then with two major issues. First, what ends should the COCC serve; and second, how should it be organized to do so.

## APPENDIX A: REPORT ON CONSUMER PROTECTION FOR THE COMMITTEE FOR THE ASSESSMENT OF GOVERNMENT EFFICIENCY

*prepared by M. L. Arnold*

### The Beginnings of Consumer Protection

During the Middle Ages there was a clear answer to the question of consumer protection. In that society the equality of bargaining position between buyer and seller was complete: First, all goods (grain, vegetables, cloth) were displayed on the open market and could be examined thoroughly for defects. Secondly, a man bargained almost exclusively with his neighbors, who cheated him only at the risk of severe social repercussions in the community. Government had no place in this relationship, and the legal doctrine *caveat emptor* (let the buyer beware) evolved.

The expansion of trade, and improved transportation systems which made new markets available to distant producers, eroded the equality of bargaining position by increasing the distance between buyer and seller. Their relationship was no longer marked by personal knowledge and mutual responsibilities in a common community, but by an impersonal marketplace where the buyer had to rely on the assurances of an occasionally irresponsible seller. As this void between buyer and seller began to open, government (and its legal institutions) began to act to protect the trusting buyer from those sellers who sought to exploit their freedom from the informal sanctions of the buyer's community. If a seller had made a definite statement about an article (a warranty), in a case where a defect could not easily be seen, the medieval courts ignored *caveat emptor* and gave the buyer legal recourse against the seller. Similarly, doctrines protecting the buyer from fraud or misrepresentation by the seller were developed and later codified.

In the late nineteenth and early twentieth centuries the pace of government intervention into business activities quickened. Much of this early activity was directed toward protecting the businessmen themselves from their overzealous competitors. But such activities as "trust-busting" (the Sherman and Clayton Acts), prevention of unfair trade practices (formation of the Federal Trade Commission), and regulation of the transportation, utility, communications, and securities industries (creation of the ICC and CAB, FPC, FCC, SEC, etc.) have all produced indirect benefits to consumers by ensuring orderly industrial growth and adequate and fairly priced goods and services in markets relatively free from fraud and deception.

Protection was provided directly to the consumer only in those areas where his health or safety was jeopardized by the seller's products. Publication of Upton Sinclair's *The Jungle* in 1906 shocked the country with its accounts of the unsanitary conditions in Chicago's meat-packing houses, and the government responded with the Food and Drug Act of 1906 and the Meat Inspection Act in 1907. Similar exposés have resulted in such additional governmental action as: expansion and tightening of the food and drug laws in 1938 and 1962; the Flammable Fabrics Act in 1953; and recent developments in automobile safety, gas pipeline safety, control of environmental pollution, further tightening of meat inspection standards, and the extended debate over the health hazards of cigarette smoking.

### Consumer Protection in the 1960's

Much of the legislation directed toward consumer protection has been enacted during the decade of the sixties, including the initial efforts to break away from the limitations of health and safety protection. The "truth-in-packaging" and "truth-in-lending" bills, enacted in 1966 and 1967, represent a movement toward economic protection of the consumer, and this move has excited the questioning of the relative roles of business, government, and the consumer.

Critics of this expansion of the boundary of government action argue primarily along two lines. In 1968, 33 federal departments devoted 64,714 employees and nearly a billion dollars to consumer protection activities. Most of the states have bodies which parallel the activities of at least some of these federal departments, further increasing the total tax bill for consumer protection. It is argued that these costs, to support the administrative machinery required to implement consumer legislation, have risen beyond the point where further legislative proliferation can be justified.

The second common line of criticism is that economic protection of the consumer constitutes an interference with our overall economic structure and poses a threat to the capitalistic system on which our country has risen to its present state of economic well-being:

When protecting the consumer is used as a base for launching antibusiness missiles, it does the consumer more harm than good. It undermines the foundation on which our competitive system rests.

. . . . .

The crucial question is: To what extent can the government continue to castigate the business community and deprecate business in the public's eyes without completely undermining public confidence, jeopardizing our free enterprise system, and creating a class society?

Two advocates of further expansion of governmental consumer protection activities respond as follows:

The trouble is not in the precepts of the American economy, but in its practices. No fundamental weakness in capitalism or the profit system has been identified, and none is suggested here. There can be no doubt that this nation's industrial revolution has created the most productive and rewarding economic system in history. But the robber barons who created it handed down as part of their legacy a system and an attitude with monstrous flaws. The ills they inflicted upon the society are such a part of the American scene that some, such as water and air pollution, may already be impossible to eliminate. Others are correctable, but the lengthy and often vicious battles over impure meat, dangerous drugs, or hidden installment costs amply demonstrate how difficult they are to identify, fix, and eliminate.

The modern businessman cannot be blamed for creating the industrial system. Nevertheless, he can be blamed for preserving it in its original form. He defends the status quo with all his strength and warns that any change, any governmental intrusion, any adjustment not of his own making, will lead to disaster. To an extent, he is right. Wanton disregard of the realities of American business could seriously disrupt the nation's economy. Revolutionary schemes such as nationalization or decentralization could very well end in disaster. But such an attack has never been mounted or even intended.

It would not succeed if it were. For all its serious flaws, the system built by the Morgans and the Rockefellers at least has permanence. Indeed, the edifice created by the American industrial revolution has such structural rigidity that it has proved and is still proving to be incredibly resistant to change. But is it change that the consumerists want—not a revolution in economics, but a revolutionary change in the attitude of its practitioners.

The change in attitude these advocates seek would include a willingness on the part of manufacturers, distributors, and sellers to adopt a greater sense of responsibility toward the consumer. They ask that more complete product information be provided to the buyer so that he can make his consumption choices in a marketplace of known qualities and values, and they insist that unnecessarily dangerous, harmful, or deleterious products be kept from the marketplace.

The consumerist advocates argue that these conditions are necessary to facilitate a return of equality of bargaining position to the American marketplace. Since this equality is also believed to be a minimum requirement for attaining the "quality of life" this country assures its citizens, the consumerists insist that, if the business community fails to meet its responsibility here, government intervention is not only appropriate but should be pursued regardless of cost.

### Governmental Organization for Consumer Protection

One point should be apparent from this brief account of the history of consumer protection: governmental intervention into the relationship between the consumer and business is a deeply ingrained fact of the American marketplace. It is highly unlikely that this intervention, particularly the protection of the consumer's health and safety, will be discontinued no matter how the conflict described above is resolved. Granting, then, that government will remain involved in consumer protection, three practical problems are posed:

1. What levels of government should be involved?
2. How should the governmental consumer protection efforts be organized?
3. Is there a preferred approach which the principal overseer of governmental consumer protection activities should take?

## What Government?

The massive involvement of the federal government has been indicated previously, and it is clear that in many areas the adoption of uniform standards and the need for consistency in regulatory action require formulation and enforcement of laws on a national scale. (Imagine the chaos confronting a national marketer of consumer products if each of the 50 states had its own labelling and packaging laws!) But many of the deceptive or fraudulent activities of unscrupulous operators are outside the reach of federal authority, or they may employ a "hit-and-run" tactic that an often ponderous and slow federal mechanism cannot react to quickly enough. Paul Rand Dixon, Chairman of the Federal Trade Commission (1961–69), has stated: "By stopping such practices before they grow into problems of interstate proportions, the need for federal action will be minimized, and the people most directly affected will have a telling voice in deciding what constitutes unfairness and deception."

The limitations to the effectiveness of national action are not restricted to regulatory or enforcement activities. After seventeen months as the Special Assistant to the President for Consumer Affairs, Mrs. Esther Peterson remarked:

The letters that pour into us, the requests from agencies, indicate that the place where the real consumer protection is needed and where the action is needed is at the state and local level where the people are. One thing has become very clear—consumer representation at the federal level is not enough. The consumer must also receive representation at the state level and also at the local level.

## What Organization?

The great volume of existing consumer protection legislation has already defined some of the organizational parameters of governmental activity in the field. It seems reasonably clear that the administration and enforcement of the technical requirements of various laws are best left to those executive departments and administrative agencies with special expertise in the subject of the regulation. Thus administration of automobile safety standards is entrusted to the Department of Transportation, the Civil Aeronautics Board and Federal Aviation Administration ensure safe operating practices for the nation's airlines, harmful drugs are kept off the market by the Food and Drug Administration, etc. This pattern of technical agencies responsible for administering consumer legislation is also prevalent at the state and local levels.

Where legislation has established specific standards of compliance or provided for criminal or other sanctions for actions in violation of the laws, responsibility for enforcement is commonly vested in the appropriate prosecutorial agency: the U.S. Department of Justice, state attorney general, or local district attorney. These local bodies also enforce the more general laws against fraud and misrepresentation in their jurisdictions. As the consumer movement has grown, many of these agencies have formed special units to coordinate their enforcement efforts in areas of special consumer interest.

Legislative bodies have, themselves, acknowledged the growth of consumerism by establishing committees and subcommittees to investigate, propose, and screen potential legislation of interest to the consumer. In addition to fulfilling an important legislative function, these committees also provide an invaluable forum for the presentation and discussion of the many different views toward consumer protection.

As these diverse interests and multiple agencies have proliferated, the need for some form of central coordinating group has arisen. There are, however, wide differences of opinion over the form and scope of duties such a group should have. The most common structure has been the special adviser to the chief executive, a form which has been justified on the national level as follows:

To coordinate and catalyze action on the part of the consumer, the simplest and best idea seems to be to have an office in the White House separate from the cabinet empires. This office can act as an executive oversight agency and exert its influence through the President directly and through interdepartmental meetings. . . . The Presidential adviser . . . acts as the cutting edge of the movement, listening to the consumer's complaints and industry's responses, proposing, suggesting, cajoling, and recommending legislation to the President if need be.

More vigorous consumer advocates have proposed a cabinet level Department of Consumer Affairs, contending:

You need a large number of people—lawyers, economists, scientists—to deal with consumer problems in a continuous way. . . . You need cabinet status to give the whole thing the prestige to compete with other government power centers.

These active consumerists seek, at the very least, a formal Office of Consumer Affairs with specified duties and responsibilities, rather than the informal "special adviser" type of organization.

## APPENDIX B: STATE OF CALIFORNIA AGENCIES
## SAFEGUARDING CONSUMERS

Bureau of Food and Drug Inspection, State Department of Health
Bureau of Meat Inspection, Division of Animal Industry
Deputy Attorney General in Charge, Consumer Fraud Section (Fraud and
  Deceptive Practices)
Bureau of Weights and Measures
State Insurance Commissioner
Bureau of Air Sanitation, State Department of Public Health
State of California Air Resources Board
State Water Resources Control Board
Bureau of Field Crops and Agricultural Chemicals, State Department of
  Agriculture (Pesticide Control)
Public Utilities Commission
California Office of Consumer Counsel

SECTION **II**

# DEVELOPMENT OF
# MARKETING STRATEGY

# The Leisure Group (A)

On a late afternoon in May of 1969 Merle Banta walked into his office, closed the door, and gazed at the Los Angeles sunset while reflecting on his previous five years at The Leisure Group. In 1964 The Leisure Group had been incorporated in Los Angeles with the expressed corporate goal of building a major business enterprise engaged in the manufacture and marketing of leisure time products. As a result of his efforts Mr. Banta, in partnership with Stephen Hinchliffe, Jr., had seen TLG grow from a company with slightly over $1 million in sales in 1964 to a company with sales of $39 million at the end of 1969.

During this five-year period of rapid growth at TLG the industry itself had been going through significant structural changes in the marketing of its products. Cognizant of the dynamic growth characteristics of companies related to leisure time and the markets they served, Mr. Banta was concerned with how TLG was structured in order to capitalize on the many opportunities that this industry afforded. Standing, in a sense, on the threshold of a new decade, Mr. Banta was deep in thought, attempting to project what the coming ten years would hold for his company and, at the same time, questioning how TLG would be able to respond. Among the more pertinent challenges that Mr. Banta perceived were: (1) further expansion of TLG's product lines, both externally through acquisition and internally through new product development; (2) possible changes in the approach taken to market segmentation within the product lines themselves; (3) the extent to which TLG will be identified to both the trade and the consumer in advertising and packaging TLG's various product lines; and (4) since TLG had operated under a very informal organizational structure, Mr. Banta wondered if this organizational policy would be sufficient for TLG to be able to continue to grow as it had during its five years of existence.

This case was prepared by Sterling B. Sessions. Reprinted from *Stanford Business Cases 1970* with the permission of the publisher, Graduate School of Business, Stanford University. Copyright © 1970 by the Board of Trustees of the Leland Stanford Junior University.

73

## BACKGROUND OF THE LEISURE GROUP

The Leisure Group had been founded to participate in the growing leisure time goods market. In the 1960's this market had expanded rapidly as a result of the increase both of disposable income in the hands of more affluent consumers and of time available for leisure activities. Leisure time products were defined by the company's co-founders to include those products which would be used for sporting or leisure purposes or would be used during the leisure hours of the day. In establishing the company's operating objectives, Banta and Hinchliffe had framed four aggressive and ambitious goals:

1. A 15% annual sales increase, beginning one year after acquisition for each new company acquired. This would be considered as an internal growth objective.
2. A 50% annual corporate sales increase through acquisition of companies engaged in leisure time activities.
3. The maintenance of a 6% net profit margin after taxes on sales.
4. A minimum annual increase in corporate earnings per share of 25%.

During the period from 1965–1969, sales had increased at an average annual rate of 40%, with an accompanying net earnings increase of 108% and an earnings per share growth rate of 64% annually. (See Exhibits 1 and 2 for the company's financial and operating statements.)

To achieve these financial goals, TLG adopted three basic business strategies: (1) concentrating and expanding TLG's activities within the leisure time market; (2) capitalizing on the changing pattern of distribution channels for leisure time products; and (3) applying professional management techniques to the operation of all phases of the business. In satisfying the first strategy, TLG was involved in bringing out new products within the existing brand names in the company and acquiring new companies that would take them into new areas. The introduction of the Classic Crossbow in December of 1969 illustrated a new product concept which was realized by combining the technology and manufacturing capabilities of High Standard and Ben Pearson, two TLG product lines.

During the last ten years the impact of the mass merchandiser such as Sears, Penney's, and the mushrooming number of discount houses had produced a basic structural change in the marketing of leisure time products. Many small sporting goods and hardware outlets had yielded to the large discount type operations which sold in greater volume because of lower prices and entirely new merchandising methods. The mass merchandiser needed products of several different qualities to meet his own pricing requirements.

According to a corporate vice president TLG anticipated these needs by offering effective packaging, point-of-purchase information pieces, providing sales training support, and servicing retail stores in regard to display and inventory control. In many cases such help made it possible for TLG to gain firm positions in many mass merchandising firms, thereby outmaneuvering its competition.

During the five years of its existence, TLG had acquired 12 companies in various segments of the leisure time industry:

1. *Thompson Manufacturing Company*, a manufacturer of lawn and garden sprinklers, provided the core of TLG and took the company initially into the home and yard care product areas.

2. *Hayes Spray Gun Company* pioneered the development of water-hose-ended garden sprayers for the application of liquid insecticides and fertilizers for use on both lawns and gardens.

3. *Ben Pearson, Inc.*, took TLG into the sporting goods market with the leading line of archery equipment in the United States.

4. *S. L. Allen & Company, Inc.*, took the company into the children's market of sporting equipment with the well-known "Flexible Flyer" and "Yankee Clipper" lines of sleds. Allen also manufactured and distributed a line of farm tools which did not blend well with TLG's existing lawn and garden product line.

5. *Rain Spray Division* provided TLG with a line of inexpensive underground lawn and garden sprinklers. This product line was integrated into TLG's lawn and garden line as a means of expanding and diversifying Thompson's product line.

6. *Black Magic, Inc.*, manufactured a broad line of horticultural products for the care of indoor plants and flowers.

7. *The High Standard Manufacturing Corporation* moved TLG into another new field, that of sporting firearms. High Standard manufactured· and distributed a broad line of shotguns, .22 caliber rifles, and hand guns with special emphasis on high-quality target pistols.

8. *Werlich Industries, Ltd.*, with its line of wood and metal toboggans, provided additional expansion into the growing sporting goods market, as well as opening a new market in Canada for TLG's other product lines.

9. *Sierra Bullets*, regarded as the leading manufacturer of ammunition for sportsmen who reloaded their own cartridges, blended in well with the existing line of firearms.

10. *Lyman Co.* manufactured accessories for cleaning and servicing firearms and provided a close fit with Sierra Bullets and High Standard in the shooting sports group.

11. *Blazon Co.*, one of the leading producers of outdoor gym equipment for the backyard, further expanded TLG's participation in the youth recreation field. The company also marketed a line of snow toys and hobby horses.

12. *Mascon Industries* expanded TLG's youth recreation group activities with a line of toy telephones and pull toys.

As a result of these acquisitions, the following three general product groups were established:

1. *Lawn and garden*
   a. Thompson Manufacturing.
   b. Hayes Spray Gun.
   c. Rain Spray.
   d. Black Magic.
2. *Youth recreation*
   a. S. L. Allen.
   b. Blazon.
   c. Mascon.
3. *Sporting goods*
   Shooting sports
   a. High Standard.
   b. Sierra Bullet.
   c. Lyman Company.
   Outdoor activity
   a. Ben Pearson.
   b. Werlich Industries, Ltd.

During the period of these acquisitions a policy was developed for evaluating possible acquisition candidates. Reid Calcott, vice president of sporting goods, in describing this policy said, "There is largely a ratchet effect at work in bringing an acquisition into the company. Although suggestions for possible acquisitions can be brought in at both the highest level in the organization and at the product manager level, it is easier for ideas to move down through the organization than up through it in cases of a difference of opinion."

Veto power, in regard to new acquisitions, rested firmly in the hands of the company chief executive officers. However, in practice, corporate vice presidents, product group vice presidents, marketing managers, product managers, and operations managers were all involved in various stages of all acquisitions, and their various recommendations were given great weight. In fact, Rick Berthold, a corporate vice president said, "I know of no decision where an acquisition candidate has been abandoned or an acquisition made which overrode strong recommendations to the contrary made by one of the operating managers."

## ACQUISITION POLICIES

Since The Leisure Group was organized, it had followed specific criteria for growth by acquisition. These criteria were divided into four major areas.

## Distribution

Compatible integration of acquired product lines into TLG's distribution system was a basic requirement, since TLG consolidated marketing with a single nationwide sales force handling all products. The company's concept was to concentrate largely on fast-growing mass merchandisers, servicing them at all levels from major buyers to retail store managers.

While all product lines continued to be sold through traditional retail outlets, the bulk of the marketing effort was aimed at large retail chains. The objective was to upgrade sales of acquired lines by professional marketing oriented to large-volume operations.

## Products

TLG looked for products with strong brand recognition, because a well-established consumer franchise was essential in mass merchandising.

If a product did not enjoy strong identity, then at least it should have easily lent itself to being marketed under a TLG brand name. An example of the latter was Werlich toboggans, a name associated with quality and well known in Canada but not in the United States. These products, however, were being sold successfully under TLG's popular Flexible Flyer name.

In addition to brand recognition, TLG looked for other desirable product characteristics: patent coverage, specialized machinery to manufacture the product competitively and technological know-how. The reason for the last two requirements was to avoid extreme price competition, particularly over products easily copied or sold as commodities.

## Industry Position

Size of acquired firms was less important than their relative position of leadership. TLG's strategy was to move into markets only with a lead product. This did not necessarily mean the acquired product line must have had the largest share of the market, but it did require a leadership brand image. TLG's Ben Pearson archery line, for example, achieved stature in the field in terms of both size and product quality, whereas Flexible Flyer, while not the largest, enjoyed a long-standing position of leadership.

Once TLG had established major leadership positions in specific markets, it applied a second set of acquisition criteria. These related to accessory products. One example was sporting firearms. With a basic leadership position established by the High Standard line, TLG could add companion products such as the recently acquired Sierra line of reloading ammunition. Similarly, the Black Magic line of indoor plant care products was added to TLG's established lines of lawn and garden products, whereas the same line would not have been acquired on its own.

## Operational Characteristics

In analyzing operations of potential acquisitions, TLG concentrated on three major areas: cost of goods sold, manufacturing methods and technologies that capitalized on the company's design know-how. These areas were particularly pertinent because of TLG's policy of total integration of acquired companies. Because of this policy, earnings history was not relevant as an acquisition criterion.

*Cost of Goods Sold.* TLG preferred operations that exhibited a high manufacturing overhead and a high labor content as they represented the greatest potential for improved gross margin.

*Manufacturing Methods.* Acquisition prospects which had not applied professional management techniques in the areas of inventory control, production planning, work simplification, and value engineering provided the best opportunity for TLG to make significant improvement.

*Design and Manufacturing Technologies.* Inasmuch as each acquired plant was considered a center of specific manufacturing capability instead of a producer of specific products, TLG was always interested in acquiring new technologies that might subsequently be applied to existing product lines.

## HOW TLG WAS ORGANIZED

Consistent with The Leisure Group's concentration of effort in specific market areas, the company was organized along product line groupings, with certain functional activities operating on a centralized basis for greater efficiencies.

Responsibility for product groups was assigned to two corporate vice presidents who shared general management type problems. Since these men reviewed and approved sales forecasts and budgets, there was a strong profit orientation at work. Each product group, in turn, was organized along traditional functional lines, with marketing and operations responsibilities reporting to a product group vice president. Each of the three TLG product vice presidents was responsible for a group of product lines. His mission was to achieve targeted goals in marketing, manufacturing, and overall profit contributions for all his product lines; motivate and develop marketing managers and managers of operations; and integrate newly acquired product lines assigned to his group. (See Exhibit 3 for an approximate idea of the TLG organization.)

In addition, the functional areas of sales, product development and control were centralized. Their activities were coordinated with those of product groups to achieve corporate goals.

Within each functional area, professional management techniques were applied, with particular emphasis on data analysis, planning, establishing objectives, and monitoring results. Performance targets were a key element in this management cycle, and each individual's compensation depended heavily on his ability to meet specific objectives.

## Marketing Management

The company's marketing programs were directed to identification of consumer needs and development of products and programs to satisfy those needs.

Marketing managers for each of TLG's major product areas were responsible for researching and analyzing markets and product lines; developing long- and short-term marketing plans; and implementing these plans. They directed product managers for each product line, coordinated their activities with other departments, preparing budgets and controlling expenses.

Market research was used as a key marketing tool to determine market sizes, structures, and growth potentials. Research also analyzed consumer preferences, habits, and attitudes.

Research data were used in the development of new products, product modification, or acquisition of related product lines. Research results also aided in the planning for manufacturing and merchandising.

## Marketing Programs

These programs were derived from a series of five major interrelated marketing plans which were implemented by marketing managers through their product managers. The TLG marketing managers were responsible for achieving targeted goals for all product lines. They controlled planning for annual sales and profit increases and were responsible for directing and developing product and assistant product managers under their supervision.

The first report was the annual product plan. This established long- and short-term profit, market share, and sales goals by specific product groups. It also specified strategy and the action needed to achieve goals.

The second plan in the cycle was the product line introduction report. Prepared annually, this report detailed every product in the line, along with selling prices, cost factors, and the resulting "merchandising profit."

The sales forecast was prepared for individual products. It set unit sales estimates and provided specific targets against which all other departments coordinated their programs.

The annual budget listed all expenditures to be made to support the product line. It provided detail on specific promotions, advertising, publicity, packaging, research, advertising allowances, and related expenses.

Finally, there was the annual promotion plan. It supplied extensive detail on actions to be taken throughout the year and described timing, theme, strategy, and implementation of each program.

Each product manager worked closely with his counterpart in operations to produce and market a particular product line. This joint responsibility resulted in a project orientation throughout the organization with both the marketing and operations managers held mutually accountable for the solution of problems which affected their product line.

The product managers had profit and loss responsibility for their lines and were expected to research and analyze their markets, develop both a long- and short-term marketing plan, and prepare budgets to implement the plans. The product and operations managers were evaluated jointly on their ability to implement these plans.

The product managers also had to encourage the general sales force to emphasize their particular product or promotions. Since each salesman handled every product in the rapidly expanding TLG line, all the product managers were in competition with each other to obtain more of the salesman's selling effort. Although this had not been a hindrance to TLG's early development because of the limited product lines its salesmen carried, the company's rapid growth had increasingly strained the sales force since it had to become knowledgeable about an expanding number of products.

By applying advanced marketing techniques and capitalizing on the distribution evolution, TLG had been successful in expanding market shares and increasing significantly the sales of all acquired product categories. These increases are illustrated in the following table:

| | Sales (millions of dollars)* | | Annual Growth Rate (percentage) | |
|---|---|---|---|---|
| | Last Audited Fiscal Year Prior to Acquisition | Fiscal 1969 | Prior to Acquisition† | Since Acquisition‡ |
| Lawn and garden.......... | $ 4.4 | $ 7.1 | 0.7 | 19.2 |
| Sporting goods............ | 11.6 | 14.1 | 7.4 | 8.6 |
| Youth recreation§........ | N.A. | N.A. | −4.1 | 37.1 |
| Average............... | — | — | 4.5 | 14.6 |

  * Included only product lines owned as of November 1968.
  † Average over three to six years prior to acquisition depending upon availability of data.
  ‡ Compounded relative to last audited fiscal year prior to acquisition and weighted by sales volume and years owned.
  § For competitive reasons, dollar figures on the sales of sleds and toboggans were omitted.

### The TLG Selling Effort

These efforts concentrated on obtaining distribution of the company's products and on supplying professional assistance to retailers and distributors. To achieve these goals, the TLG sales department offered a broad line of products, packaged for self selling. Buyers also were offered special promotions, private labeling, and the benefits of TLG research results.

TLG support at the retail level included counseling on inventory and the training of store personnel, as well as the customary merchandising aids. Responsibility for managing this program rested with TLG's vice president of sales. He worked closely with buyers, helped product managers prepare the sales forecast, and also was responsible for the organization, development, recruitment, training, motivation, and supervision of the sales force.

TLG's sales force was organized into two key groups—a product sales force and a merchandising sales force. The product sales force, composed of specialists in each of the product categories, was responsible for developing and presenting sales programs for individual product lines to major accounts. The merchandising sales group was organized along geographic territory lines to implement sales programs at the retail level and for all product lines.

TLG had decided to operate with one sales force which would handle all of the company's product lines because of the high cost of fielding a sales force for each basic product line. This had not been difficult in the beginning, due to the limited number of product lines TLG carried, but, with the firm's rapid expansion into many new types of products, increasing work loads were placed on the sales force. Not only were there more products, but several of TLG's acquisitions had been companies with technically complicated products which required a considerable amount of knowledge to sell. This was particularly true of the High Standard, Sierra, and Lyman product lines.

The zone sales manager, the national sales manager, and a staff group reported to the vice president of sales. The position of zone sales manager had been created initially when TLG contemplated dividing the country into regional zones. Currently, however, the sales force was not large enough to warrant more than one zone manager.

Five district managers reported to the zone manager, and each district manager had several salesmen working for him. It was the responsibility of the district salesman to call on all accounts which were large enough in terms of sales volume to warrant a call. Many of the small-volume specialty outlets, on the contrary, were serviced by mail due to the small size of the field selling staff. Each salesman was expected to fill out complete call reports at the end of the day summarizing the success or difficulties which he had experienced. This information was then transmitted back through sales administration personnel to product managers to detect any problems that might be cropping up within individual products.

A responsibility of the national sales manager was to develop specialists who could provide expert advice and information to the retailer on technical product characteristics. The product specialists (often with the district manager of that particular area) would make their own sales calls on key accounts with large-volume sales. Many of these sales calls would be made to house accounts such as Sears or Wards for the purpose of getting a product into distribution or introducing a new product.

Each retail buyer was assigned to a specific TLG salesman for sales calls and service. Similarly, in larger firms such as Sears, a TLG product specialist was assigned to a specific buyer, such as a sporting goods specialist contacting a particular sporting goods buyer.

Both a district salesman and a product specialist received credit for all products shipped into their territory. The credit was apportioned on the basis of separate quota arrangements. This was a TLG policy designed to avoid controversy over who should receive credit for a sale and to encourage a district salesman to service the account as far as the functions of display and inventory availability were concerned.

Another interesting aspect of the sales system allowed a customer to decide whether to receive his product through distributors or by direct shipment from TLG. The management of TLG thought that this offered maximum penetration and coverage of a sales territory while offering convenience to the customer in giving him an option as to how he wished to receive the product.

District salesmen were paid an annual salary of about $9,000, provided with a car, and received reimbursement for all selling expenses. Additionally the salesmen received a bonus based on all shipments in their territory as follows:

| Percentage of Quota | Bonus |
|---|---|
| 90% | $1,800 |
| 100 | 2,400 |
| 110 | 3,600 |

Account managers and district sales managers received an annual salary of about $13,000, a car, and selling expenses, and the following bonus:

| Percentage of Quota | Bonus |
|---|---|
| 90% | $2,700 |
| 100 | 3,600 |
| 110 | 5,400 |

Product sales managers received an annual salary of $16,000, a car, and selling expenses, and a bonus similar to that of account managers with the exception of a $5,000 ceiling for exceeding quota by 110%. Also, product sales managers could earn an additional $400 annually for obtaining certain objectives outlined by top management.

Sales quotas were developed "from the top down" on the basis of previous sales by product line and district and "from the bottom up" by analyzing individual accounts. Additional modifications of the quota were made on the basis of new acquisitions, expansion of existing product lines, competition, and general economic conditions.

The vice president of sales also had a staff group reporting to him composed of the sales merchandising manager, the international sales manager, and the military-premium sales manager. The total size of this selling organization, exclusive of representation and distributors, had been reduced from 64 earlier in the year to 59 in December 1969. TLG was able to service approximately 4–5,000 accounts, with varying degrees of call frequency, with these 59 salesmen and the mail order department.

### Operations Management

An operations manager worked in close conjunction with his counterpart, the product manager, to produce production plans and operating strategy. The company's marketing plans and profit goals were the basic constraints on his performance. In this sense both operations managers and product managers shared the responsibility of meeting the profit goals established under the direction of each product group vice president. Naturally, an operations manager's effectiveness was measured in terms of quality control, customer service, labor relations, and certain critical financial indicators. These men directed and coordinated production of 17 plants involving over 2,000 employees.

Most product lines acquired had earnings records substantially below TLG's target levels. Thus, the ability to reduce operating costs became equally as important as the record of increasing sales.

The following table sets forth two key expense categories for the four product lines acquired in 1969. The first of these is the "cost to sell." Because of economies of scale, TLG was able to reduce sales commissions, salaries, and expenses as a percentage of sales. As the table below illustrates, these savings were on the order of 1% to 1.5% of sales.

### Reduction in Operating Costs
### (percent of sales)

|  | Cost to Sell* | General and Administrative Costs |
|---|---|---|
| Acquisitions prior to 1969† | 5.3% | 10.3% |
| 1969 Acquisitions |  |  |
|   Sierra Bullets, Inc. | 4.0 | 13.3 |
|   Blazon, Inc. | 3.3 | 5.4 |
|   Mascon Toy Co. | 5.2 | 6.4 |
|   Lyman Gun Sight Corp. | 3.4 | 7.1 |
|     Total‡ | 4.2% | 8.3% |
| Budgeted TLG | 3.1% | 6.1% |

\* Cost to sell was defined as sales commissions, salaries, and expenses as a percentage of sales. Catalogs, advertising, and other promotional costs are not included.
† Actual percentages by acquisition were shown in 1968 annual report.
‡ Weighted average.

Larger savings were typically available in the area of general and administrative costs. Here, through elimination of duplicate management, office consolidation, mechanization, and cost reductions, savings of about 2.2% of sales were achieved.

The impact of these reductions can be illustrated by translating percentages into dollars. If sales and percentage cost levels budgeted for 1970 are achieved, pretax dollar savings compared to percentage costs prior to acquisition could be about $2 million.

### The Issue of Branding

Two issues dealing with the multitude of brand names at TLG had been discussed lately among the marketing group. One had to do with the trade-off between private labeling and selling under a recognized national brand name. Currently, less than 5% of TLG's sales were produced by private labels, yet there was a growing movement among the mass merchandisers to carry a larger number of privately branded products. While the existing opinion had been that the company would never back away from a large account seeking private branding of its products, the company had done very little in supplying private brands.

The second issue dealing with the question of brands concerned the growing number of different brand names as a result of TLG's active acquisition program. Each of the brands called for a certain amount of media advertising to keep its name before the public, and this entailed a significant number of small advertising budgets and accounts. The idea had been put forth by one of the executives at TLG that the company link its products with a corporate trademark or brand in an attempt to realize a synergistic effect among the products. It was believed by some of the TLG marketing executives that this would be a good way to introduce a new product to the trade since it would already have an identity which would in effect be the summation of all the quality brands currently owned by TLG. However, other executives had not been receptive to the idea because they believed that the strength of TLG rested in its large number of brand names that effectively touched those specific market segments solely interested in a particular product.

All of these considerations were running through Mr. Banta's mind when he happened to glance at his desk clock. The orange sunset had faded into the darkness of the Los Angeles evening, and the twinkling lights reflecting from all parts of the city indicated that it was time to leave. Picking up his coat, Mr. Banta wondered about the future of TLG and how it would handle the many issues that had been running through his mind for the last two hours. Tomorrow morning he was to meet with Stephen Hinchliffe to begin drawing up an operational plan for the next five years. It was evident that these considerations would be critical in designing possibly a different strategy for the next five years.

## EXHIBIT 1

### Consolidated Balance Sheets

October 31, 1968 and 1969
(in thousands of dollars)

| Assets | 1969 | 1968 | Liabilities | 1969 | 1968 |
|---|---|---|---|---|---|
| Cash.................. | $ 1,170 | $ 1,915 | Short-term loans........ | $ 9,116 | $ 7,883 |
| Receivables........... | 16,133 | 10,488 | Payables.............. | 7,456 | 3,791 |
| Inventories............ | 12,697 | 7,852 | Accrued liabilities....... | 2,534 | 1,487 |
| Prepaid expenses........ | 583 | 326 | Income taxes.......... | 886 | 1,363 |
| | | | Current long-term debt.. | 1,252 | 775 |
| Total Current Assets...... | $30,583 | $20,581 | Total Current Liabilities... | $21,244 | $14,699 |
| | | | Deferred federal tax..... | $ 1,240 | $ 570 |
| | | | Long-term debt......... | 9,342 | 7,653 |
| Property, plant, and equipment.......... | $15,060 | $ 8,026 | Lease obligation........ | 1,300 | — |
| | | | 7% subordinate notes... | 6,000 | — |
| Other assets........... | 7,324 | 3,304 | Shareholder's equity..... | 13,841 | 8,989 |
| Total Assets... | $52,967 | $31,911 | Total Liabilities. | $52,967 | $31,911 |

Source: 1969 annual report.

## EXHIBIT 2

### Five-Year Operating Summary

| | 1969 | 1968 | 1967 | 1966 | 1965 |
|---|---|---|---|---|---|
| Operating results ($ in thousands) | | | | | |
| Net sales.................... | $39,694 | $30,427 | $22,161 | $19,069 | $10,234 |
| Gross margin................ | 10,528 | 7,572 | 5,403 | 4,051 | 2,068 |
| Operating expenses........... | 6,111 | 4,755 | 3,756 | 3,239 | 1,659 |
| Interest.................... | 1,308 | 717 | 550 | 423 | 128 |
| Net income................. | 1,678 | 1,053 | 571 | 191 | 89 |
| Earnings per share........... | .73 | .54 | .36 | .14 | .10 |
| Financial position ($ in thousands) | | | | | |
| Working capital.............. | $ 9,339 | $ 5,883 | $ 2,777 | $ 2,328 | $ 489 |
| Net property, plant, and equipment................ | 15,060 | 8,026 | 3,635 | 3,326 | 1,479 |
| Shareholders' equity.......... | 13,841 | 8,989 | 1,723 | 1,037 | 521 |
| Other information | | | | | |
| Number of plants............. | 17 | 7 | 4 | 3 | 2 |
| Number of employees......... | 2,600 | 1,700 | 700 | 530 | 120 |
| Space occupied (sq. ft.)........ | 1,370,000 | 750,000 | 491,000 | 281,000 | 50,000 |

**EXHIBIT 3**

**The Leisure Group Table of Organization**

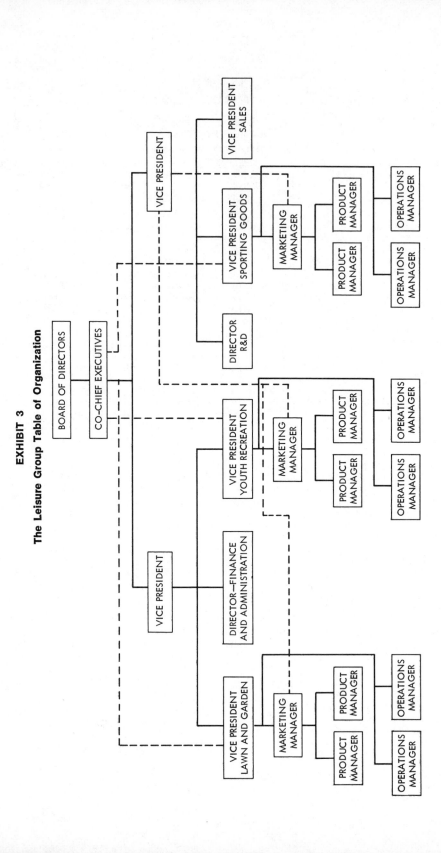

**EXHIBIT 4**

**The Leisure Group Sales Organization**

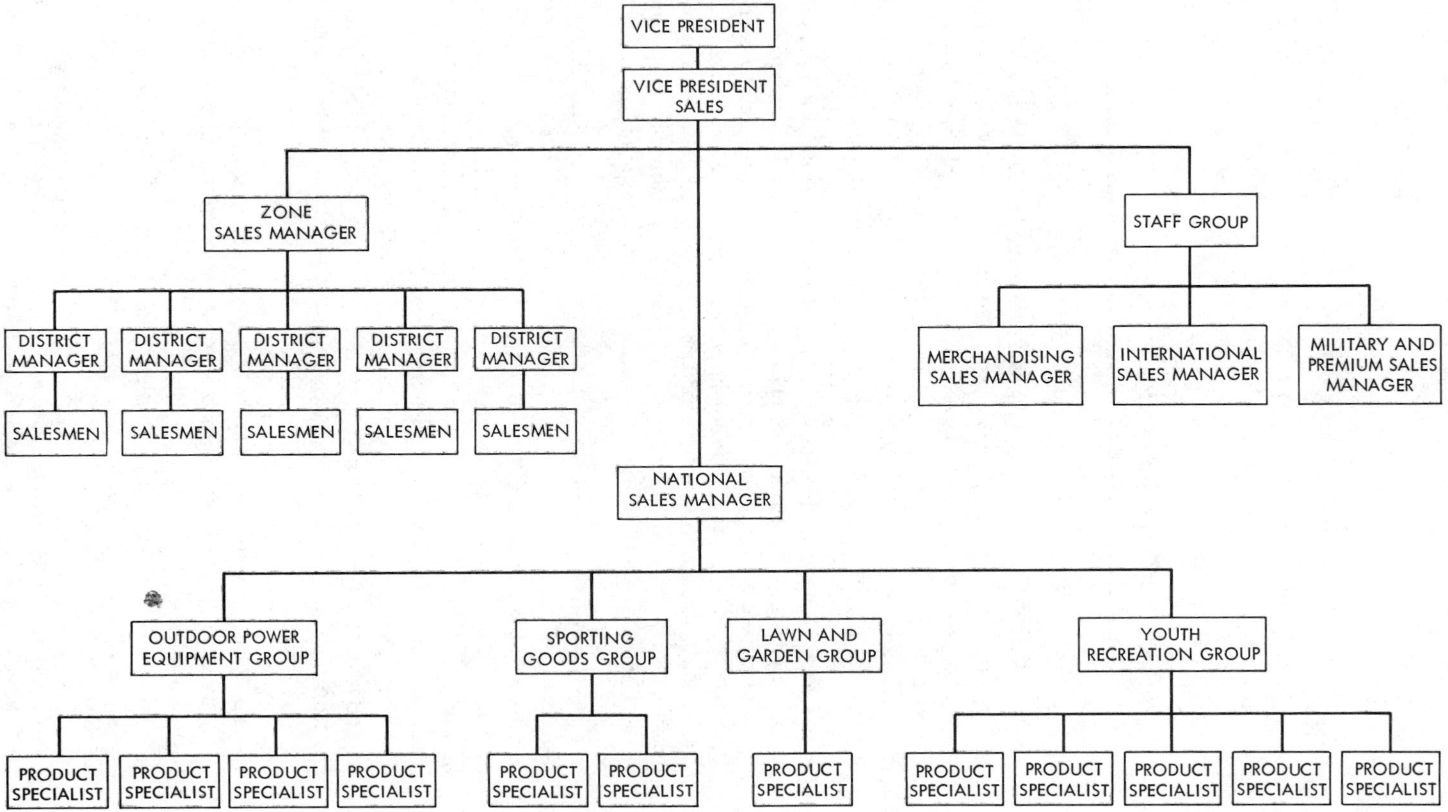

# Spectra-Physics (A)

Spectra-Physics, Inc., was formed in 1961 by Dr. Robert Rempel and four colleagues from Varian Associates. The five founders, who had worked as a team at Varian for two years, envisioned an environment where they could pursue scientific research interests with complete freedom and the ability to control their own destiny. Their philosophy was set forth as the primary objective of Spectra-Physics:

It is essential that the company be founded and operated to respond directly to the weighted ideas of scientific endeavors of the founders or successors. It is of slight value if the company be so constituted, then operated tomorrow in such a way that it becomes void of inspiration, curiosity, and creative ability. The most significant reason the founders are giving up good positions and a measure of security is to create a company that will remain oriented to scientific pursuits and grow and prosper by virtue of their own ability and direction.

Spectra-Physics was born in a one-room office in Palo Alto (soon moved to its current location in Mountain View, California) where the five talented scientists scraped together $150,000 from personal savings to begin their mission to research, develop, design, and manufacture highly technical scientific instruments. Although they had no specific ideas for products, they felt their strong technical backgrounds would yield rapid income results through government contracts. With special expertise in the areas of atomic physics, quantum electronics, and optical electronics, the founders began operating their firm with five primary objectives in mind:

1. To establish a strongly motivating, technically creative environment attractive to the highest quality scientific, engineering, and management talent.
2. To create an enterprise which was financially profitable to the stockholders and employees.

Reprinted from *Stanford Business Cases 1973* with the permission of the publisher, Graduate School of Business, Stanford University. Copyright © 1973 by the Board of Trustees of the Leland Stanford Junior University.

3. To establish sound growth based on internal strength. In accordance with this objective, growth from within was preferred. However, mergers and acquisitions which did not dilute other objectives would be individually considered on their own merits.
4. To establish a strong line of highly technical, unique proprietary products.
5. To provide the capability for custom research and engineering of scientific instrumentation in highly complex fields.

Bob Rempel, having contributed the largest amount of money to founding S-P ($70,000) was named president. He also filled the position of manager of applied research. With a Ph.D. in physics from Stanford, Rempel had compiled an impressive record of discoveries and patents at Varian in the field of atomic physics. It was primarily his enthusiasm and determination which transformed S-P from vision to reality. From its inception the company revolved around Rempel.

Three of the remaining founders headed other technical areas in the new company. William Earl Bell, as manager of experimental physics, brought twenty years of experience to S-P, primarily in atomic physics. Arnold Bloom took the post of manager of theoretical research. With a Ph.D. in physics from the University of California, Bloom was already one of the world's leading experts in atomic physics and optics. Kenneth Ruddock became manager of geophysics and space instrumentation. Ruddock had held a similar post for several years at Varian and had a background in electrical engineering. He received his master's degree from MIT.

The fifth founder was Herbert Dwight, who came to S-P as vice president and business manager. Although his educational background included a master's degree from Stanford in engineering, Dwight brought business experience in the areas of contract administration and sales.

S-P's first business was with NASA to build instruments for spacecraft at the Goddard Space Flight Center near Washington, D.C. The $35,000 contract was obtained by Dwight and Rempel. Due to his strength in electrical engineering Ruddock took charge of this project. Shortly thereafter the company was approached by Perkin-Elmer, an East Coast optical electronics firm with sales of $30 million a year. Impressed with the technical background of S-P personnel, Perkin-Elmer offered to make them a subsidiary for the purpose of building nuclear spectrometers.

Foreseeing a working environment similar to that from which they had just come, Rempel and his colleagues declined the offer. However, the talks led to S-P's first major undertaking, a joint project which was to focus the company's efforts in one direction for the next eight years. The project involved construction of gas lasers. Laser technology, scarcely five years old, presented the founders of S-P with the kind of exciting endeavor they anticipated when they formed the new company. It was in the field of quantum physics—a common thread in the founders' backgrounds. At this time the only lasers in existence were ruby lasers, solid state instruments with limited applications. Gas lasers, although more difficult to build, appeared to have greater potential in scientific research involving coherent light sources.

In 1962, S-P and Perkin-Elmer entered a joint agreement to produce and market the first commercially available helium-neon gas laser. The agreement called for S-P to provide technical and manufacturing capabilities and for Perkin-Elmer to supply precision optics (their major business) and marketing services. The initial agreement was to run for two years or until 75 lasers had been sold, at which time a review would be held to assess the desirability of continuing the venture.

The project was a tremendous success—the first laser was sold for $7,500 before it was even built. Sales were handled entirely by Perkin-Elmer. Due to their novelty and technical potential the units virtually sold themselves. Sales calls to research laboratories inevitably became demonstrations, generally met with wild enthusiasm by the physicists and chemists who had only read about lasers before. Sales were further stimulated by a discovery enabling the use of visible light in the new lasers. (All prior laser wave lengths were located in the infrared portion of the spectrum.)

Seventy-five units were sold in 21 months, thereby hastening a review of the joint agreement. Although Perkin-Elmer was selling the lasers, S-P was providing most of the technical know-how necessary to build them. S-P was also responsible for servicing the units, and the uniqueness and complexity of the product required frequent service calls. As a result, S-P developed a reputation among research laboratories as the dominant company in the joint venture. A lingering reluctance to be attached to a large organization also convinced the founders to terminate the agreement with Perkin-Elmer and build and sell the lasers on their own.

To facilitate the change, S-P created its own sales department. Eugene Watson was hired as manager of marketing. Coming from a similar position with the instrument division of a large electronics manufacturer, Watson was placed in charge of sales, advertising, and promotional activities at S-P. Two salesmen were hired. The eastern half of the United States was assigned to Bob Mortensen, a salesman from Perkin-Elmer who already had experience selling the gas lasers. The western part of the country was assigned to Dick Stark, who came to S-P from Varian Associates.

During 1963 and 1964, S-P produced and marketed a product line of three helium-neon lasers. These lasers differed in power, which made them suitable for different types of research. The 1-milliwatt unit sold for $1,500, the 3-mw for $4,500, and the 10-mw for $9,000. Until 1965 Perkin-Elmer was the only serious competitor in the field of gas lasers. At first, competition was vigorous. S-P had a technically superior product with better servicing, but Perkin-Elmer had the better sales effort. In addition, Perkin-Elmer had a line of laser accessories—instruments designed to modify light beams outside the laser—which complemented their line of gas lasers. By the middle of 1964, S-P was forced to begin building these accessories itself to avoid growing sales losses due to Perkin-Elmer's complementary offerings. S-P created an optics division to engineer and produce laser accessories.

The challenge by Perkin-Elmer was successfully met—by early 1965 Perkin-Elmer began decreasing its efforts to sell gas lasers to research scientists. This was due in part to S-P's complete concentration on this market, while Perkin-Elmer was devoting only a fraction of its resources to this segment. It was also due to Perkin-Elmer's desire to concentrate more heavily on applications of laser technology.

This left S-P the only major producer of gas lasers for research use until mid-1965. Then Optics Technology entered the field with a major innovation—a new method of manufacturing laser tubes. With only a slight decrease in overall quality and virtually no decrease in capability the new company could afford to sell for $400 a helium-neon laser that S-P was selling for $1,200 (which was a significant reduction in price from the original units sold in conjunction with Perkin-Elmer). Shortly thereafter University Laboratories began to market a similar unit, whose new system of mirrors further reduced manufacturing costs; in addition this laser needed no adjustment or alignment in use.

Although S-P was capable of developing the cheaper units, the founders made no move in this direction. Rempel downgraded them as a poor substitute for quality lasers. Marketing manager Gene Watson felt strongly that a market existed for cheap lasers, consisting of a large number of small research labs which could use gas lasers but could not afford those currently on the market. Watson, as well as his two salesmen, believed that saturation was imminent in the market currently served by S-P. Rempel disagreed. Further, he pointed to the founders' original commitment to build only unique, highly technical products.

At first, the other founders were not involved in the conflict. Ken Ruddock was devoting all his time to government contract work. S-P was involved in two long-term contracts in the field of magnetic physics. One was a $250,000 contract with the Air Force Cambridge Research Laboratory to build navigation equipment for spacecraft. The other was a $750,000 contract with NASA to simulate magnetic fields in outer space.

Arnold Bloom had become increasingly dissociated with S-P's laser program as it moved from development stages to production and sales. Bloom had always been a theoretical physicist and wished to remain one, spending much of his time with university contacts working at the frontier of knowledge in atomic physics.

Herb Dwight was inclined to go along with Watson but scarcely had the time to become involved. As business manager, Dwight was responsible for all the nontechnical aspects of S-P's operations. These included finance, accounting, production, and marketing. As the company expanded, his job became tremendously complicated and time-consuming.

The exception was Earl Bell. In 1965 Bell invented the ion laser. This represented a tremendous step forward in laser technology. Bell's invention was the first laser capable of producing light beams in the green and blue portions of the spectrum. Coupled with its capability of operating at very high power levels, Bell foresaw many new applications for the laser. A subsequent seminar involving the nation's leading laser scientists supported his feelings, and Bell took out patent rights on his new discovery. Rempel had decided not to commit the company's resources to engineering and production of the ion laser. Raytheon quickly entered the market with the argon ion laser which sold for $25,000. Although it was a hastily built product, it was the first on the market and sold well.

Rempel was increasingly preoccupied with the development of a new type of camera to be used in the production of integrated circuits. The idea was conceived in 1964 at a time when S-P was looking for applications for their helium-neon lasers. At that time a small Santa Clara based company called Zissen Technical Associates with some experience in the manufacture of integrated circuits incorporating lasers came to S-P looking for a new laser. Integrated circuits require precision measurements (accuracy within millionths of inches) to produce masks which are used in combination to build the circuits. A masking camera incorporating a laser could achieve the necessary level of accuracy. S-P acquired Zissen in 1964 for the purpose of building a laser to fit the camera. Rempel headed this project.

Within the next year the project was elaborated to the point where S-P committed itself to building the entire camera. A whole new technology had to be developed, which absorbed large amounts of research and development funds, and all of Rempel's time and energy. While Rempel was capable of working on more than one thing at a time, he was basically a project engineer—now caught up in the most exciting project of his life.

Still another breakthrough in technology was the invention of the carbon dioxide laser in late 1965. As with the ion laser this new invention appeared to have numerous applications, producing high power infrared light beams which might be used for cutting or welding. Gene Watson was anxious for S-P to enter this market as soon as possible. However, because of the heavy commitment of research and development funds for the masking camera, money was not available to pursue development of the $CO_2$ laser.

Shortly thereafter Watson left S-P to start his own company (Coherent Radiation) for the purpose of producing $CO_2$ lasers and other promising laser products. Bell also left, and at this point Rempel okayed a commitment to develop a $CO_2$ laser. But funds were growing short, markets for S-P lasers were becoming saturated, and profits were falling. While 1966 sales increased 49% over 1965, from $2.7 million to $4.1 million (see Exhibit 1), research and development expenditures increased 91% during the same year—from $700,000 to $1.3 million. Although the company's cash position had been eased somewhat in 1965 by the sale of $500,000 of convertible debentures to a group of 12 San Francisco investors, high research and development expenses coupled with shrinking profit margins forced the company to seek outside financing again in 1966. This time $930,000 worth of debentures were sold through two New York investment houses.

By mid-1966 nearly $1 million had been spent developing the masking camera. For the first time S-P began to doubt the size of the market for the finished product. Early predictions of sales of 10 to 12 cameras now appeared to be overly optimistic as price estimates for each camera climbed continually. With at least another year before completion, estimates of final price now ranged between $150,000 and $250,000 (the laser used in the camera was currently selling for only $5,000). In addition to spiraling development costs, it seemed clear that the camera could not be mass produced. To sell the units at such high prices would require considerable customizing from one unit to the next, cutting into profit margins.

In July of 1967 a series of meetings of Spectra-Physics' board of directors culminated in the following decisions: (1) work on the masking camera would be terminated; (2) engineers hired specifically to work on the masking camera would be released; (3) some cutbacks would be made in manufacturing personnel; (4) Herb Dwight would replace Bob Rempel as president.

These decisions were not made easily by the founders. Since the company's inception in 1961 the founders had always felt they could successfully build and market any product that interested them. Their confidence was repeatedly rewarded in the early days of laser technology. Producing technically superior products which virtually sold themselves, S-P remained the major force in sophisticated research lasers.

The financial situation in 1967 indicated that things had changed. While sales were up 22% from $4.1 million to $5 million, expenses increased 33% from $3.9 million to $5.2 million. Before taxes income went from a 1966 all-time high of $198,000 to a loss of $199,000. Although the masking camera project hastened the necessity of changing the company's course, no one person was blamed; it was a mistake they all shared.

Because he had been running most of the company's operations, Dwight was a logical choice for the presidency. Rempel was invited to stay as vice president and manager of applied research (his former position). Both Dwight and Ruddock were particularly anxious to retain Rempel, due to his tremendous drive and creative ability. Rempel stayed for a short while, but soon left with several members of the optics division to start a new company called Chromatic, a company which produced lasers but one not in competition with S-P's product line.

In thinking about what action to take to bring the company into the black, Dwight knew that he would have to distinguish between the short and long term. In the immediate future new sources of capital would have to be located. In addition, tight budgetary controls would have to be introduced by which each existing product and new product idea would be screened according to its projected cost, profit margin, return on investment, and long-term market potential. The fact that product life cycles for high technology products tended to be three years or less made such financial estimates critically important.

For the long term, Dwight felt that he must change and expand S-P's product line. One of the founders' objectives had been to build a strong line on the base of high technology and to seek government contract work only to the extent that capital was needed to support research and development activities. Dwight was unhappy with the company's efforts to meet this objective. S-P was still involved with two large government contracts. Dwight was considering a policy of not taking on any new government contracts—in effect getting out of contract work completely—and using in some modified form the company's research and development resources to generate mass produced proprietary products.

Dwight was particularly concerned about S-P's failure to expand its product line. Although the company had little competition in its market segments (about 70% of company sales were to laboratory research scientists), technological advances continually reduced the company's prominence. The present line consisted basically of helium-neon lasers and laser tubes of various shapes, sizes, and power and frequency specifications. This market was near saturation, and most sales were for replacement. Production and engineering innovations continually lowered costs which had an adverse effect on S-P. Although the company was committed to a high-quality product, high-price policy, the increasing volume of inexpensive lasers on the market made high-price sales more difficult. For example, S-P had previously sold their 10 milliwatt laser for $9,000 but were now selling a similar 15 milliwatt laser for $4,000. Elsewhere in the industry other companies were capitalizing on recent advances. Optics Technology and University Labs were selling low-cost laser tubes, while Raytheon, Carson, and others were selling ion lasers. Coherent Radiation was selling $CO_2$ lasers and was about to enter the argon ion laser market with a superior product. Each of these markets had a greater growth potential than helium-neon lasers.

Dwight was considering the desirability of adding low-cost tubes similar to those manufactured by a number of small companies which had entered the industry over the past several years. Although profit margins on these items were relatively small on a per unit basis, Dwight reasoned that over time he could obtain sufficient volume to reduce costs to where adequate profits would result. In addition, he was considering the development of a $CO_2$ laser in competition with that produced by Coherent Radiation. The new product would be used by a variety of industries which engaged to some extent in cutting and welding. Another area of interest to Dwight was the argon ion laser. This market was dominated by Raytheon, and there were indications that a new argon ion laser would soon be marketed by Coherent Radiation. Dwight hoped to develop and use a unique technology to develop this product entry.

It was apparent to Dwight and other company officials that laser technology was expanding rapidly to include products with industrial application. In particular, lasers could be used in construction tasks requiring alignment and in surveying activities requiring precise distance measurements. Although S-P had not considered the former, it did have a sophisticated distance measuring instrument called geodolite which had been developed by Rempel and Ruddock in 1963–64. Various versions of this instrument had been sold to scientists for between $50,000 and $80,000 (a $4,000 laser was employed) with sales averaging two to five units a year.

In 1965 BART (the San Francisco Bay Area Rapid Transit) engineers asked S-P to develop a laser which could be used on barges as an alignment device to facilitate digging of the tunnel beneath San Francisco Bay. Although the project represented a one-shot contract similar to those the company wished to de-emphasize, there was the possibility of gaining a foothold in commercial end-user markets by designing the desired laser. The project was, therefore, undertaken, and the result was the successful development of the LT-3 laser.

Dwight planned to market the LT-3 alignment laser as aggressively as possible through the company's existing distribution system. This decision relied heavily on the belief that S-P customers (mostly research scientists) depended on expert sales engineers. Seven high-salaried engineers handled direct sales in the United States. In addition, S-P maintained wholly-owned sales subsidiaries in England, Germany, and France. Independent sales reps carried S-P products in sparsely populated areas of the United States and in 21 foreign countries. Eleven company service engineers operated in California, New Jersey, England, France, and Germany.

A marketing staff of ten technical and administrative personnel was responsible for factory support of the field sales organization. This staff provided services such as technical support, sales order processing, media advertising, data sheets and technical bulletins, trade show exhibits, and periodic visits to customers.

In summary, Dwight believed that his strategy should consist essentially of decreasing research and development expenditures and moving towards the production of proprietary "laser" products for selected commercial end-user markets. To do this would require substantial changes in company operating philosophies and, at some future date, a change in organization structure. At the present time Dwight contemplated making no organizational changes until he better crystallized his plans for the future.

**EXHIBIT 1**

SPECTRA-PHYSICS, INC.
Consolidated Statement of Income (loss)*

|  | 1962 | 1963 | 1964 | 1965 | 1966 |
|---|---|---|---|---|---|
| Net sales.............. | $134,329 | $857,770 | $1,748,379 | $2,749,500 | $4,105,189 |
| Costs and expenses |  |  |  |  |  |
| Cost of sales......... | 104,808 | 612,029 | 1,252,993 | 1,190,814 | 1,510,050 |
| Research and |  |  |  |  |  |
| development....... |  |  |  | 701,681 | 1,337,256 |
| Marketing.......... |  |  |  | 451,312 | 685,829 |
| General and |  |  |  |  |  |
| administrative...... | 38,013 | 159,017 | 401,205 | 219,345 | 333,109 |
| Interest expense...... | 3,462 | 7,108 | 19,441 | 24,094 | 41,128 |
| Totals.......... | $146,283 | $778,154 | $1,673,639 | $2,587,246 | $3,907,372 |
| Income (loss) before |  |  |  |  |  |
| taxes.............. | (11,954) | 79,616 | 74,740 | 162,254 | 197,817 |
| Income tax expense |  |  |  |  |  |
| Current............ |  | 2,750 | 39,501 | 56,313 | 41,277 |
| Deferred........... |  | 27,250 | (19,250) | 6,000 | 13,000 |
|  |  | 30,000 | 20,251 | 62,313 | 54,277 |
| Net income (loss)...... | (11,954) | $49,616 | $54,489 | $99,941 | $143,540 |

* Fiscal year ends September 30.

# The Alhambra State Bank

The Alhambra State Bank, located in a medium-size metropolitan area in the northwestern United States, was founded in 1923. The bank was situated downtown in modernized facilities which had ample parking space nearby. Alhambra had prospered throughout most of its history and over the years had developed a conservative image. The bank concentrated primarily on serving individuals and commercial accounts rather than industrial accounts. This distribution of accounts had occurred, in part, because of the area's history. Originally an agricultural community, the area became somewhat industrialized during and immediately following World War II. There were only a few large industrial firms in the area, however, and these were concerned mainly with the processing of forest products. Furthermore, the headquarters of such activities were located elsewhere, and their financial needs were not serviced locally.

In the mid-1960's the bank came under new management. An evaluation of the bank's profitability at that time revealed that on a relative basis the bank was not performing satisfactorily. A five-year plan-of-action was instituted to improve earnings. The major elements in the plan consisted of modernizing the bank interior, adding more parking space, increasing advertising expenditures, training bank personnel to be better "salesmen," and increasing small loans by adopting less stringent standards.

A statement of corporate purpose was part of this plan and read as follows:

We want our bank to be the quality leader in our area. We will raise banking standards and support and participate in the area's growth. As a result our bank should be exceptionally profitable.

Quality is a result of talent, and we want our bank to attract top-caliber people. We want a working environment where performance is the main cri-

Reprinted from *Stanford Business Cases 1973* with the permission of the publisher, Graduate School of Business, Stanford University. Copyright © 1973 by the Board of Trustees of the Leland Stanford Junior University.

terion for advancement. To be successful, we must build on the talent we now have and attract top-caliber people to all levels of our organization. To all our people we must offer an unusual opportunity for growth in career and growth in income.

We must recognize that we cannot be all things to all people. We must be selective in choosing the customers and customer groups we serve. We cannot serve an uneconomic customer professionally, and our best work will be done with our best customers. Thus, we should not spread ourselves too thinly but rather concentrate our resources—human and capital—on those customers and customer groups that we particularly want to serve. This will take time, but, given time, we can develop customers that truly establish our position of leadership.

In short, we don't want to be the biggest bank in the state, just the best.

During the period 1967–1969 the bank's total deposits grew more rapidly than those of its major competitors. The compounded annual growth rate in total deposits was 20.9% for this period, but the bank's earnings failed to keep pace—primarily because of disappointing growth in demand deposits, which grew only 6.7% annually. A study had shown that overall profits were extremely sensitive to demand deposit growth. Each additional $1 million of demand deposits would yield $38,300 in aftertax profits while the same increase in certificates of deposit would return only $11,100. The difference was due primarily to the fact that a bank had to pay interest on its time deposits but not on its demand deposits. On the other hand, reserve requirements were higher for demand deposits (13%) than for time deposits (6%).

During this same three-year period, savings deposit growth totaled only $2.2 million while the increase in certificates of deposit amounted to $14.2 million. The average return on assets amounted to only .77%. Return on capital was considered "good" (15.5%) but only because of the bank's relatively low capitalization. Returns on loans and investments had, however, been exceptional. The performance of Alhambra and major competitors on these items is shown in Table 1.

### TABLE 1
**Return on Assets, Loans, and Investments
Alhambra Bank and Major Competitors
(1967–1969)**

|  | Return | | | |
|---|---|---|---|---|
|  | Assets* | Capital† | Loans‡ | Investments§ |
| Alhambra................... | 0.77% | 15.5% | 9.1% | 5.5% |
| First National.............. | 1.03 | 19.6 | 8.7 | 4.3 |
| Northwest National......... | 0.98 | 13.6 | 8.5 | 3.8 |
| Pacific State................ | 0.79 | 13.1 | 7.8 | 4.6 |

  \* Profit after tax divided by total assets.
  † Profit after tax divided by end of year capital, excluding loan reserves.
  ‡ Interest income before tax on loans, divided by total loans.
  § Income before tax on investments (securities) divided by total investments.

**TABLE 2**

**Expense Profile**

**(1968–1969 average)**

|  | Alhambra | First National | Northwest National | Pacific State |
|---|---|---|---|---|
| Operating expense.......... | 9.4% | 14.6% | 14.8% | 12.2% |
| Taxes..................... | 2.2 | 7.8 | 1.0 | 5.0 |
| Interest................... | 27.4 | 27.2 | 29.2 | 25.4 |
| Personnel................. | 32.4 | 29.2 | 31.5 | 33.9 |
| Loan losses............... | 4.0 | 3.8 | 1.5 | 3.3 |
| Net occupancy costs........ | 7.0 | 2.7 | 4.7 | 7.3 |
| Other expenses*........... | 17.6 | 14.7 | 17.3 | 12.9 |
| Total.............. | 100.0 | 100.0 | 100.0 | 100.0 |

* Includes depreciation and rent.

High personnel and "other" expenses had overshadowed this performance. Alhambra's head count (employees per $1 million of deposits) was the highest of any of the four leading banks; further, its loan losses as a percent of operating income were the largest. The expense profile of Alhambra and its leading competitors is shown in Table 2.

A factor of concern to the officers of Alhambra was the bank's dependence on time deposits which, if continued, would result in higher interest rates in the future. Data for Alhambra and its competitors are shown in Table 3.

No major bank in the area had shown a significant deposit market share increase in the past several years. Alhambra's share had increased only slightly, and its overall was low when compared to First National and Northwest National. Share data are shown in Table 4.

In its efforts to find ways to develop and maintain a strong customer orientation the bank commissioned a study of the impact of various customer groups on overall bank profitability. Exhibit 1 shows the funds used and supplied by some eleven customer segments as of June 30, 1970. The data were obtained from a sampling of the bank's deposit and loan accounts, and the results were projected to the June 30, 1970, balance sheet. The customer segments were identified by bank officials.

**TABLE 3**

**Demand and Time Deposits as a Percent of Total Deposits**

**(December 1969)**

|  | Demand | Time | Demand Deposit Growth* |
|---|---|---|---|
| Alhambra................... | 29% | 71% | 6.7% |
| First National.............. | 33 | 67 | 10.8 |
| Northwest National......... | 33 | 67 | 12.5 |
| Pacific State............... | 36 | 64 | 20.6 |

* Compound annual growth rate, 1967–1969.

## TABLE 4
### Share of Market for Alhambra and Leading Competitors
### by Total and Demand Deposits
### (December 1967 and June 1970)

| | Share | | | |
|---|---|---|---|---|
| | Total Deposits | | Demand Deposits | |
| | December 1967 | June 1970 | December 1967 | June 1970 |
| Alhambra............... | 8.1% | 8.5% | 8.4% | 8.5% |
| First National........... | 23.6 | 24.7 | 25.6 | 25.9 |
| Northwest National...... | 29.5 | 30.7 | 32.8 | 33.1 |
| Pacific State............. | 7.1 | 7.5 | 8.0 | 9.2 |
| All Other............... | 31.7 | 28.8 | 25.2 | 23.3 |

The analysis of funds used and supplied was relatively straightforward. The total loans outstanding represented simply the amount the bank had lent to the individuals comprising the segment. The total deposits of this group were obtained by tracing the individuals' checking, savings, and other accounts to determine the amount on deposit by type of deposit. The amount the bank was required to hold "on reserve" was then deducted from the total of each type of deposit. In 1970 the bank's net demand reserve requirement was 13%, for savings 3.0%, and for other time deposits 6.0%.

The data contained in the column headed "Net Funds Supplied" represented the difference between the segment's outstanding loans and the amount on deposit, less the amount required for reserves. The "Index" is self-explanatory. Individuals, dealers, and home builders were the largest "cash consumers" in the sense that they required the largest net funds. High-asset individuals, public organizations, and nonprofit groups were the largest cash contributors in that their total deposits (less reserves) far exceeded their outstanding loans.

Next, a profitability analysis was made of each segment. First, the total income for the segment was estimated. The interest received and the service charges paid by the segment members were determined from the bank records pertaining to the individuals involved. The "Credit for Funds" necessitated assigning a monetary value to the segment's "Net Funds Supplied." The same was true—in reverse—in determining the expenses of a segment; i.e., if a segment was a net borrower, then a value had to be assigned to the "deficit."

Thus, it was necessary to assign a transfer price to either the "surplus" or the "deficit" of each segment. The analyst responsible for the profitability study had the option of using a cost- or market-oriented transfer price. He chose the latter since he reasoned that since the bank was trying to attract deposits the market price was more appropriate. As his "rate" he selected the federal funds rate which was the amount charged by one bank lending another bank money on a one-day basis. This was a common practice for banks, and, for the time period involved, the annual rate ranged from 5% to 11%.[1] The analyst used a weighted average which approximated 9% per annum. The profitability analyses by customer segment are shown in Exhibit 2.

Salary and related expenses for each segment were determined on both a direct and indirect basis. First, the analyst allocated all those expenses directly involved with the applicable segment. Thus, certain personnel worked exclusively with selected groups. This was especially true with the petroleum, real estate, and car dealer segments. All remaining expenses were allocated on the basis of number of transactions generated by the segment as a percentage of total transactions. If, for example, a segment was responsible for 10% of all transactions, then it was assigned 10% of all the remaining (unallocated) salaries and expenses.

The analyst also studied a number of factors relating to various customer groups. The purpose of these studies was to gain additional insights into the profitability of each group. The results of these studies are summarized below:

1. *Speed of Customer Service*—A survey taken over a two-week period at busy times of the day revealed that Alhambra's services (judged on the basis of the number of people waiting per teller window) was equal to or slightly better than that of competitors.

2. *Average Size Checking Account*—From a recent FDIC biennial call report it was determined that Alhambra's average size checking account under $1,000 was $255 versus a combined average of $279 for the two larger banks in the area.

3. *Area Economic Forecast*—The population of the area was expected to grow from 280,000 to 370,000 between 1968 and 1975. Total personal income for this period was forecasted to grow from $1.13 billion to $2.50 billion and average personal income from $4,035 to $6,556. In June 1970 the analyst thought these "earlier" forecasts were "on target."

4. *Impact of FHA Loans on Deposits*—From a sample of 50 FHA loans made between January and November 1968, it appeared that FHA loans to noncustomers did not result in additional deposit accounts.

5. *Impact of Installment Loans on Deposits*—From a sample of 95 currently outstanding installment loans made between April 1966 and June 1970, it appeared that such loans to noncustomers did not result in new deposit accounts.

6. *Comparison of Alhambra's Ratios to Those of Two Largest Com-*

---

[1] This was an unusual period in that ordinarily the range would be considerably smaller.

*petitors*—From the 1968 FDIC biennial call report and the ASB summary of deposits report the following was determined:

| | Two Largest Competitors Combined (6/29/68) | Alhambra (6/30/70) | Ratio |
|---|---|---|---|
| Total number of deposit accounts... | 116,307 | 25,205 | 4.61 |
| Total deposits ($ millions)......... | 235.8 | 48.7 | 4.84 |
| Total number of savings accounts, $1,000–$100,000............... | 9,410 | 1,480 | 6.35 |
| Total dollars (in millions) in savings accounts, $1,000–$100,000............... | $   45.0 | $   6.21 | 7.25 |
| Average account size.............. | $ 4,780 | $ 4,190 | — |

If Alhambra could maintain the same ratio of savings deposits between $1,000 and $100,000 to total deposits as the other two banks, then its aftertax profits would increase by $82,500—or 22% of 1969 earnings.

7. *Analysis of High-Asset Individuals*—From an analysis of 217 high-asset individuals with either a checking or savings account, only 25% had both types of accounts. Such individuals were "arbitrarily" defined as ones having $1,000 in checking and/or an average savings account balance of $2,500.

8. *Distribution of Gross Receipts by Type of Activity*—In 1969 (for the entire state) the distribution of gross receipts by industry type was as follows:

| | Industry | Percent of Total Gross Receipts (1969) |
|---|---|---|
| a. | Retail wholesale........................ | 39.9% |
| b. | Construction........................... | 15.2 |
| c. | Finance and real estate................... | 10.8 |
| d. | Transportation, communications and utilities.......................... | 9.8 |
| e. | Manufacturing......................... | 9.4 |
| f. | Service............................... | 3.8 |
| g. | Professional........................... | 3.4 |
| h. | Agriculture and forestry................. | 2.4 |
| i. | Other................................ | 5.3 |
| | Total............................. | 100.0 |

9. *Impact of Automobile Loans*—A sample of automobile loans revealed that out of 49 "customers" some 25 had deposit accounts with the average size account totaling about $300.

The Alhambra State Bank was organized around the "traditional" functional activities (see Exhibit 3.) At one time or another bank officials had discussed a variety of changes. The president felt that the present structure was too functionally oriented and that not enough attention was being paid to different customer groups. As an example of his thinking on this subject he pointed out that organizing around the credit function (e.g., loan officers) led to a neglect of the bank's more profitable groups—i.e., those large depositors with minimal credit needs such as high-asset individuals and public organizations. He felt that by assigning responsibilities for similar accounts to some one person or group within the bank, it would be possible to develop a better understanding of a customer group's unique financial needs.

Other bank officials were not so certain that such an organizational change would be productive, especially if it were not recognized that a whole new way of "running the business" was involved. As one manager said, "It's one thing to talk about organizing around customer groups but quite another to talk about how we proceed to develop target accounts, set up marketing plans, coordinate and control our overall marketing efforts, and reward our lower level managers on the basis of some profitability measure. I see a whole new management philosophy unfolding, and it's hard for me to see at this time what kind of an organizational structure we should have in order to articulate and implement this philosophy."

At a meeting of the executive group (composed of the chairman, the president, the manager of administration, and the manager of operations) the data on overall bank profitability, customer segments, profitability of individual segments, and various related data were reviewed in depth with the analyst. In addition, the subject of organizational change was discussed briefly. At the conclusion of the meeting it was decided that the bank should attempt to state what it hoped to accomplish over the next five years. It was argued by the president that the basic issue was one of setting market share targets. He believed that the bank should seek to increase its market share of demand and time deposits from 8.5% in 1969 to 11.5% by 1975. He admitted that this target might not be realistic but that the group had to "start somewhere." At this point the meeting was adjourned with the request from the chairman that they reassemble a week hence and be prepared to talk specifically about *how* they would attempt to obtain this market share goal, what its attainment might mean from a profit point-of-view, and what the organizational implications would be.

**EXHIBIT 1**

**The Alhambra State Bank, Funds Used and Supplied, June 30, 1970***

**($000)**

| Customer Segment | Total Loans Outstanding | Total Deposits (less reserves) | | | | Net Funds Supplied | Index† |
|---|---|---|---|---|---|---|---|
| | | Demand | Savings | Time | Total | | |
| 1. Individuals.......... | $ 6,445 | $ 2,505 | $1,579 | $ 131 | $ 4,215 | $ (2,230) | − 22.0 |
| 2. High-asset individuals.......... | 855 | 794 | 1,515 | 984 | 3,293 | 2,438 | + 24.4 |
| 3. Retail/wholesale.......... | 1,982 | 1,623 | 79 | 299 | 2,001 | 19 | + 0.2 |
| 4. Dealers‡.......... | 2,923 | 131 | 20 | 30 | 181 | (2,742) | − 27.4 |
| 5. General contractors.......... | 1,789 | 857 | 40 | 96 | 993 | ( 596) | − 5.9 |
| 6. Home builders§.......... | 3,366 | 179 | 27 | 11 | 117 | (3,149) | − 31.5 |
| 7. Public organizations.......... | — | 1,918 | 53 | 14,953 | 16,924 | 16,924 | +169.0 |
| 8. Professional firms.......... | 219 | 606 | 58 | 29 | 693 | 474 | + 4.7 |
| 9. Nonprofit groups.......... | 722 | 1,397 | 421 | 398 | 2,216 | 1,494 | + 14.9 |
| 10. Petroleum companies.......... | 131 | 153 | — | 236 | 389 | 258 | + 2.6 |
| 11. Financial institutions.......... | 638 | 715 | 68 | 91 | 874 | 236 | + 2.4 |
| 12. Other.......... | 2,152 | 1,299 | 391 | 642 | 2,372 | 220 | + 2.2 |
| Total.......... | $21,022 | $12,177 | $4,251 | $17,940 | $34,368 | $13,346 | |

* Based on sample of deposit and loan accounts and expanded to June 30, 1970, balance sheet.
† Funds supplied or used divided by 100,000; minus sign indicates funds used.
‡ Includes all mobile homes and auto dealers and accounts of individuals carrying indirect loans.
§ Includes FHA loans and savings, as well as accounts of individuals carrying FHA loans.

**EXHIBIT 2**

**The Alhambra State Bank, Profitability of Customer Segments, June 30, 1970\***

**($000)**

| Customer Segment | Net Funds Supplied | Total Income | | Interest Paid | Charge for Funds | Salary and Other Expenses | Net Contribution |
|---|---|---|---|---|---|---|---|
| | | Interest and Service Charges | Credit for Funds | | | | |
| 1. Individuals........................ | $(2,230) | $ 789 | — | $ 78 | $201 | $ 948 | $(438) |
| 2. High-asset individuals.......... | 2,438 | 97 | $ 220 | 136 | 11 | 45 | 136 |
| 3. Retail/wholesale companies..... | 19 | 219 | 13 | 25 | | 103 | 93 |
| 4. Dealers†........................ | (2,742) | 281 | — | 2 | 247 | 51 | 13 |
| 5. General contractors............ | ( 596) | 168 | — | 8 | 54 | 64 | 41 |
| 6. Home builders‡................. | (3,149) | 451 | 1 | 2 | 285 | 65 | 100 |
| 7. Public organizations........... | 16,924 | 20 | 1,523 | 989 | — | 30 | 524 |
| 8. Professional firms............. | 474 | 29 | 43 | 5 | — | 39 | 38 |
| 9. Nonprofit groups............... | 1,494 | 97 | 134 | 47 | — | 35 | 149 |
| 10. Petroleum companies............ | 258 | 16 | 23 | 17 | | 63 | (41) |
| 11. Financial institutions......... | 236 | 72 | 35 | 9 | 13 | 35 | 50 |
| 12. Other.......................... | 220 | 233 | 29 | 66 | 9 | 60 | 127 |
| Total........................ | $13,346 | $2,472 | $2,021 | $1,385 | $820 | $1,528 | $ 760 |

\* Based on sample of deposit and loan accounts and projected to June 30, 1970, balance sheet.
† Includes all mobile homes and automobile dealers and accounts of individuals carrying indirect loans.
‡ Includes FHA loans and earnings, as well as accounts of individuals carrying FHA loans.

**EXHIBIT 3**

**The Alhambra State Bank, Organization Chart, June 30, 1970**

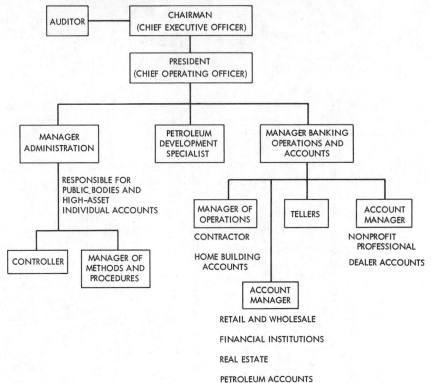

# The Weisman Bottling Company

The Weisman Bottling Company, located in a large mid-western metropolitan area of nearly 2 million people, produced and marketed a line of carbonated beverages consisting mainly of flavored soft drinks, soda water, and tonics. These were sold in a number of different container types and sizes to a wide variety of retail and commercial outlets. In 1974 total company sales were about $3 million.

The company was founded in 1924 by Solomon Weisman and had remained in the family ever since. In 1975 Eli Weisman, the grandson of the founder, succeeded to the presidency upon the death of his father. He had recently completed an evening M.B.A. program at one of the local universities and was anxious to apply what he termed "the newer and more sophisticated management concepts and techniques" to a tradition-oriented firm operating in an increasingly complex and dynamic industry. In particular he wanted to develop a strategic plan for his company. He planned to accomplish this by working with his sales manager, Gerry Stires, and his controller, Irving Tass. Both had served under his father for many years in similar capacities.

The company's marketing area consisted essentially of the metropolitan area which in 1972 numbered 1.8 million. Since 1960 the area had experienced a 20% population increase, and, while the growth rate was slowing, the area was expected to increase to 2.1 million by 1980. As one of the leading areas in the midwest it generated over $6 billion in personal income and had retail sales of $3.8 billion in 1970. Its citizens were, on the average, better educated than for the United States as a whole. Median household income was also higher. Within the area there were 2 major universities, 3 four-year colleges, 7 junior colleges, 80 high schools, and over 300 elementary schools.

The company faced strong competition within its marketing area.

Both the Coca-Cola and Pepsi Cola franchises were large and aggressive units. Mr. Weisman pointed out, however, that while they dominated the cola market—both for the regular and diet products—they by no means dominated the flavor market. Part of the reason for this, he said, was because of their understandable preoccupation with cola which trade sources estimated accounted for some two-thirds of the market expressed in cases. On a dollar basis the cola share was even higher because of the predominance of national brands. The flavor market, on the other hand, tended to be dominated by local bottlers who competed mainly on a price basis. Private labels were considerably more important in flavors than in cola.

Thus, the company faced strong competition which took a variety of forms including local bottlers who also held a national franchise such as 7 Up, Squirt, and a nationally advertised brand of ginger ale. At one time or another the Weisman Company had been offered a franchise for a nationally advertised noncola soft drink. These had been rejected because the company felt acceptance would constrain the way the business was run. Eli Weisman felt that in retrospect such a policy had been a mistake but noted that there were at present no opportunities to pick up a "good" franchise.

Industry competition centered around an everincreasing array of container types and sizes, merchandising "deals" (mostly in "cents-off"), media advertising, and "in-store" activities. Distribution was becoming of major importance because of the growing policy of most outlets to carry only one brand of flavored soft drinks. Often the "one line" was the store's private label. Some large outlets carried two flavor lines—a nationally advertised brand (e.g., those offered by Coke and Pepsi) and a local or private label brand. Eli Weisman stated that while his product was equal in quality to any other brand in the market he was forced to price some 20% lower than the national brands "simply because we don't have the name." In general the company maintained a price parity policy with respect to its local competition.

The company produced a line of ten flavors which was bottled in the same type and size containers used by competitors. Thus, the company packaged its product in glass and disposable bottles and cans. It sold its 12-ounce product in both glass and cans, its 16-ounce in glass, and its 32-ounce in a nonreturnable bottle with a screw cap.

The company had traditionally set aside seven cents per case for advertising, merchandising, and driver-salesmen incentives. Most of this amount was spent on in-store cents-off promotions. Some had gone for incentives to the sales force for opening new accounts and building in-store displays. Rarely did the company spend any monies in media advertising nor did the company allocate funds for the purchase of vending machines or fountain equipment. These two market segments tended to be dominated by the large national brand franchises.

About 90% of the company's sales derived from take-home sales through retailers and on-site cold bottle consumption. Of these sales private labels accounted for 18%. Syrup sales to a number of route vending companies accounted for the remaining 10%. An average of ten truck routes serviced approximately 3,500 accounts of which some 15% accounted for about 50% of total cases sold. The number of routes and accounts varied according to the season of the year. During the summer extra routes were added to service a substantial number of small accounts which were open only during the summer months or who added a line of soft drinks for the "season."

In thinking through the procedures to follow in preparing a strategic plan, Mr. Weisman decided that the first step should consist of obtaining trend data on the company's share of market. Company total case sales had remained relatively static for quite some time, but there had been a change in the mix; e.g., sales of the 12-ounce cases were declining while sales of the 32-ounce cases were increasing. Even so, given the population growth of the area over recent years, it seemed clear that the company had lost share.

In order to determine market share trends, Mr. Weisman had the company's case sales by package size and type tabulated for 1969 and 1974 (the last complete year on which such data were available). He had wanted to go back to 1960, but the type and size packages had shifted to such an extent that he felt they would obscure the trend analysis. Since 1969 the company's product line had remained stable. In his case sale tabulations he excluded soda water and tonics but included syrups (on a case equivalent basis) and his private label "business." Although costs varied slightly by flavor type, he decided not to break them out separately since he reasoned that he could do little to change the sale of any specific one.

The next step was to convert his raw case sales for the two years into case equivalents of 24 units of 8 ounces each which was the way the trade reported its sales data. Following this, he determined what were his dollar marginal contributions per case equivalent.[1] (The results of this analysis are in Exhibit 1.) In 1969 his per case marginal contribution was 45.3, and in 1974 it was 46.9 cents. While this change represented an increase, Mr. Weisman noted that his expenses had increased at a higher rate because of the rapid inflation which had taken place during this period. In any event his profits before taxes over this period had declined despite higher turnover.

Following this analysis, he calculated the area's population growth for the period 1969–1974. In the future, population growth was expected to slow substantially. Some demographic changes had occurred favoring the

---

[1] Marginal contribution was defined as factory price less direct (variable) costs which included plant labor, ingredients, breakage, and container costs.

younger age groups which were the heaviest consumers of soft drinks.
The area's per capita consumption of all soft drinks was estimated by a
reliable trade source as being 275 8-ounce equivalents in 1969 and 331
in 1974. Of these amounts cola and diet drinks (which were dominated by
the cola flavor) were estimated to account for some 68%. Vending sales
were estimated at between 10 and 12% of total sales while fountain sales
were estimated at 16%. Mr. Weisman thought these percentages had
remained relatively constant between 1969 and 1974. In attempting to
get at an estimate of his relevant market, he figured the annual per capita
consumption of his product to be 74 8-ounce units in 1969 and 89 in
1974.[2] He next calculated total industry sales of his company's product
line in 8-ounce equivalent cases of 24 units each and obtained the following:

| Year | Population | Per Capita (flavors) 8-Ounce Units | Total Market Equivalent Case Sales |
|------|-----------|------------------------------------|-------------------------------------|
| 1969............ | 1,680,000 | 74 | 5,180,000 |
| 1974............ | 1,921,000 | 89 | 7,458,000 |

Since company equivalent cases were 1,584,920 in 1969 and 1,636,650
in 1974, market share had dropped from 30.5% to 21.8%. In discussing
these data with his controller and sales manager, the latter pointed out
that the loss should also be interpreted in light of a change in industry
structure. Two small bottling companies selling about 10% of the flavor
market had gone out of business during the past two years thereby reducing the number of competitors to a total of six. Mr. Weisman estimated that Coke and Pepsi together accounted for about 20% of the total
flavor market, that two other competitors each held about 10–12 share
points, and that the largest seller accounted for about a third of the market. In the opinion of the sales manager it was this latter company which
had benefited most from Weisman's loss in share.

In the near term Mr. Weisman was pessimistic about prices and costs.
He felt that competition would continue to force price adjustments to
lag increased costs. In particular he was concerned about the rapid in-

---

[2] These figures were obtained by reducing the total per caps by the amount
represented by cola and diet drinks (68%) and by fountain drinks (16%). The
latter, however, had to be adjusted for the amount of cola and diet product sold by
fountains; thus, the fountain per caps were reduced from 16% to 5.1% (68% ×
16% = 10.88% and 16% − 10.88% = 5.12%). Thus, the "relevant" market was estimated at 26.9% of the total per caps for 1969 and 1974. No adjustment was made
for vend sales since the company sold syrup into that market. Although colas were
an important seller here, it was not known what share they represented. Mr. Weisman knew that by not adjusting for such sales his relevant market figure was somewhat inflated—perhaps by as much as 6 to 7%.

crease which was occurring in connection with deliver costs. His plant was relatively new and could handle up to 25% more sales. He knew, however, that the largest competitor had recently installed a high-speed packaging line which probably reduced marginal per case costs by about two cents.

It seemed clear to Mr. Weisman that he must attempt to strategize in ways which would impact on volume. He expected some "help" from the area's increased population growth, coupled with an increase in per capita consumption of perhaps as much as 3% a year. But he felt that he must seek ways to grow shares. He thought that the private label business—now estimated at 25% of the take-home flavor market—would increase only slightly. He noted that his major competitor was actively seeking such business at prices below those Weisman was quoting.

The three men next turned their attention to the area's store population and the company's accounts. The sales manager had recently put together some information which showed that there were just under 11,000 retail outlets handling soft drinks in the company's marketing area. Of these some 312 were supermarkets, 588 were convenience stores, 712 were small food outlets, and 9,245 were "all other" units. The latter included such outlet types as bars, restaurants, filling stations, discount stores, and liquor stores. Based on an analyses of Weisman accounts it was thought that the company had the following distribution by type of outlet:

| | |
|---|---|
| Supermarkets* | 18% |
| Convenience | 16 |
| All other food | 23 |
| All other | 24 |

\* Includes private label. Six supermarket chains accounted for more than half of all supermarket units in the area and about two-thirds of the dollar sales of such outlets.

The sales manager had located a recent study made by a local newspaper which indicated that supermarkets accounted for about 35% of all bottled soft drinks being sold, that convenience and all other food stores sold 20% of the total, and that all other units sold the remainder.

Given the above data Mr. Weisman instructed his two associates to prepare for a meeting in the near future at which time they would further discuss and, hopefully, come to an agreement on what should be the company's future strategy. Mr. Weisman noted that he hoped each would be as specific as possible in recommending what strategies to adopt and that he expected them to be able to support their recommendation with as much documentation as possible.

## EXHIBIT 1

### Case Sales, Revenues, and Marginal Contributions by Product Item, 1969 and 1974
(includes private label and syrup but not soda and tonic)

| Package | Marginal Contributions (M.C.)* | Sales Price* | Case Sales | Total M.C. | Total Sales | Case Equivalents* |
|---|---|---|---|---|---|---|
| **1969** | | | | | | |
| 12-ounce (returnable) | $.89 | $1.75 | 130,450 | $116,100 | $ 228,287 | 195,675 |
| 12-ounce (can) | .85 | 2.50 | 182,910 | 155,473 | 457,275 | 274,365 |
| 16-ounce (returnable) | .88 | 2.00 | 69,680 | 61,318 | 139,360 | 139,360 |
| 32-ounce (not returnable) | .79 | 2.50 | 487,760 | 385,330 | 1,219,400 | 975,520 |
| Total | | | 870,800 | $718,221 | $2,044,322 | 1,584,920 |

| Package | Marginal Contributions (M.C.)* | Sales Price* | Case Sales | Total M.C. | Total Sales | Case Equivalents* |
|---|---|---|---|---|---|---|
| **1974** | | | | | | |
| 12 ounce (returnable) | $.95 | $2.30 | 110,500 | $104,975 | $ 254,150 | 165,750 |
| 12 ounce (can) | .90 | 3.00 | 206,600 | 185,940 | 619,800 | 309,900 |
| 16-ounce (returnable) | .93 | 2.65 | 48,800 | 45,384 | 129,320 | 97,600 |
| 32-ounce (not returnable) | .83 | 3.05 | 531,700 | 441,311 | 1,621,690 | 1,063,400 |
| Total | | | 897,600 | $777,610 | $2,624,960 | 1,636,650 |

* Per case. All package sizes come in cases of 24 units except the 32-ounce which comes in cases of 12 (case equivalents are 24 units of 8 ounces each). The price per case is that of Weisman to the trade at year's end as is the per case marginal contribution. Marginal contribution is sales price less direct costs such as labor, ingredients, breakage, and container.

Note: Syrup sales converted into 12-ounce units and included in 12-ounce (returnable) data for 1969 and 1974.

# Hayden Manufacturing Company

The Hayden Manufacturing Company of North Carolina was founded in 1936 by Kenneth Hayden to produce a line of women's clothing. From five employees and annual sales of less than $50,000 the company grew to a point where in 1972 it employed 4,800 persons and had annual sales in excess of $60 million. Facilities included a total of nine plants, one of which was perhaps the largest "sewing room" in the world. Until the late 1950's the company experienced continuous growth by concentrating primarily on three merchandising classifications: men's woven underwear, ladies' and children's slips, and children's sportswear. These lines were directed toward the popularly priced volume markets which were controlled to a considerable extent by the large national and regional department store chains.

During this growth period only style changes occurred from year to year. Competitive advantages were gained essentially through manufacturing innovations and by obtaining large orders which led to long production runs. Price, quality, and service dominated the thinking of corporate management. In the mid-1950's foreign imports—primarily from Japan and Taiwan—began entering the U.S. market. Because of the long lead times involved in buying off-shore, imports were concentrated in the staple merchandise categories where price was a significant variable. Hayden—as well as other similar U.S. manufacturers—found it increasingly difficult to meet such competition and turned to the production of more "sophisticated" merchandise lines.

During the late 1950's the company went to more extensive styling of its products; designers were added to upgrade the basic lines. In the early 1960's the company diversified further by buying a small men's shirt

This case originally appeared as "Stone Manufacturing Company." Reprinted from *Stanford Business Cases 1973* with the permission of the publisher, Graduate School of Business, Stanford University. Copyright © 1973 by the Board of Trustees of the Leland Stanford Junior University.

company. Despite these efforts sales remained relatively static and profits continued to decline. Thus, in 1966 the company undertook a major reexamination of itself and a year later changed its organization from a highly centralized type of operation to one consisting of four divisions. Each was established as a profit center with operating control over its own manufacturing and marketing activities. A fifth division which featured higher priced misses' sportswear was formed in 1969. The cost of operating the headquarters unit was allocated to the divisions on the basis of sales. Money borrowed specifically for use by a division was charged "at cost."

From 1968 to 1972 the divisions were given almost complete operating autonomy on the premise that they were separate and distinct business entities. In 1972 the average age of the division managers was 45, and all had had marketing/sales experience in the apparel industry. Each had a merchandising and production staff which reported directly to him. All were paid a salary plus a bonus; the latter was a reflection of the profitability of their division.

By late 1972 management was once again concerned about the effectiveness of its organizational structure. There was a growing feeling that the company was still not functioning properly, especially with respect to its market orientation. Management felt that a reassessment of the company's products and markets was in order.

### The Apparel Industry

The U.S. apparel industry was both highly competitive and highly fragmented. Operating results for the industry tended to be cyclical and strongly influenced by general economic conditions. The industry had suffered from strong import competition over the years, but the bilateral quota agreements of October 1971 provided for a more orderly growth of foreign imports than in the past. The long-term outlook for garment manufacturers was thought to be enhanced by rising personal income, the desire for multiple wardrobes for leisure time activities, the increasing size of the 20–39-year-old group, and the industry's trend toward consolidation and bigger operating units.

The apparel industry comprised over 23,000 firms, of which nearly half employed fewer than 30 workers. It was essentially a labor-intensive industry with payroll costs accounting for about 55% of value added. Despite recent and continuing investments by larger companies in labor-saving machinery (such as laser fabric cutting, ultrasonic sewing, and seam fusing), productivity seemed destined to lag other manufacturing segments.

In recent years garment manufacturers had been forced to introduce an everincreasing and everchanging array of products to meet the demand changes caused by a movement away from traditional dress concepts. The growth rates experienced by the major retail chains selling apparel required increased reliance upon larger resource units. Thus, bigger and better-financed manufacturers who were able to adjust quickly to changes in the marketplace would benefit substantially. At the same time rapid style changes resulted in a reduction in the prices consumers were willing to pay for individual ready-to-wear items. In addition, an increasing proportion of attire was distributed through mass merchandisers and other retailers who relied on lower priced imports for a large part of their stock.

The industry was still heavily dependent upon relatively unskilled labor and was not, for the most part, capital-intensive. Sewing machines remained the principal type of machinery used. Sewing operations took from four to as high as sixteen weeks to learn and, thus, changes in production lines were quite expensive. Workers were paid on a piece-rate basis except when "learning," at which time they were paid an hourly wage. For merchandise of the type produced by Hayden, materials cost about 50% of the selling price, direct labor 15% and overhead 25%. The latter included the unabsorbed labor burden; i.e., the difference between the guaranteed learning wage and the established piece-rate.

Rising incomes in 1971 impacted strongly on domestic garment producers with respect to their labor efficiency—and Hayden was no exception. Since the labor force was essentially comprised of women—many of whom represented the second worker in the family—a rising economy generated a labor shortage which was accompanied by high turnover and absenteeism. In 1971 the company experienced almost 100% labor turnover and rates of 10% or more absenteeism on Mondays and Fridays.

## Company Product Lines

As noted earlier, Hayden's principal business was centered on popularly priced mass market products which were sold to the large general merchandise and discount chains where manufacturers' brands were the exception. The company attempted to price each of its lines so as to attain a 10% gross margin (sales less direct costs less manufacturing overhead). Typically the designers were constrained in their efforts by the retail selling price of the merchandise being produced. These retail price lines were translated into what the store would pay the manufacturer, for example, $24.00 per dozen. These pricing constraints could be handled in a number of different ways, including the amount and type of fabric used, quality of workmanship, and number of manufacturing operations.

As a general rule the company designed and produced its own products; it did little contracting with other manufacturers. The company's reputation reflected strong manufacturing capabilities and the delivery (all F.O.B. factory) of good merchandise values. A brief description of each of the company's divisions follows:

### 1. Children's Playwear/Sportswear.

In 1972 this division accounted for 37.7% of total company sales, employed 41.5% of company assets, and was expected to produce about 18% of the company's profits. It designed, produced, and sold its products primarily to the popularly priced market with about 80% of its sales under its own labels. Its customers were principally general merchandise, variety, and discount stores including regional and local "chains." Over 90% of its sales were generated by the company's wholly commissioned sales force; the remaining 10% of sales were direct sales which involved private label merchandise.

A total of six product lines were manufactured and marketed by the division: (1) toddlers', (2) 3–6X, (3) 7–14, (4) infants', (5) boys' 4–7, and (6) young juniors'. The boys' 4–7 line was added in the 1960's but dropped after two seasons for lack of appropriate merchandising-design personnel. It was reestablished in 1971 with the needed coverage in these areas. Also in the late 1960's a ladies' line was established. It was subsequently converted to a misses' line and moved to another division. At that time it was generating approximately $3 million in sales. In 1970 a young juniors' line was established to replace the transferred line.

The division sold a spring/summer and a fall/winter line for each of its product lines. Typically, between 30 and 40 different fashions were included in *each* line for each selling season—each coming in several different sizes. Even so, the division did not carry a full line of items within each of its different product lines. Toddlers' and infants' wear, for example, specialized in sets (tops and bottoms) and separates (coveralls, shirts, and crawlers). The fall line for both product groups included creepers, play garments, dresses, coats, suits, blouses, skirts, sweaters, swim suits, and jackets.

The division had three designers: one handled the infant and toddler lines, another the 3–6X girls' and 4–7 boys' lines, and the third "all other" lines. In addition to designing company label merchandise, these designers worked with major chains to develop private label lines. Typically, such "business" was the result of "bidding" which involved strong design/price competition for large orders.

Essentially 50% of the division's lines were redesigned each year. The remaining 50% involved relatively staple merchandise which could be carried over to the next year, although color and fabric type changes often made such a possibility impractical. Thus, the division's lines involved considerable risk, and failure to "guess" the market generated high markdowns. These lines were, however, considered to be safe from foreign competition because of their styling. Sales by product line are indicated below.

TABLE 1

Sales by Product Line for Playwear Division

| Product Line | Net Sales by Year (000) | | |
|---|---|---|---|
| | 1969–1970 | 1970–1971 | 1971–1972 |
| Infants'................... | $ 3,178 | $ 3,255 | $ 3,410 |
| Toddlers'.................. | 3,953 | 4,108 | 3,410 |
| 3–6X girls'................ | 7,440 | 7,440 | 7,130 |
| 4–7 boys'................. | — | — | 202 |
| 7–14..................... | 10,230 | 8,448 | 8,680 |
| Juniors'.................. | — | — | 479 |
| Ladies'................... | 1,278 | 2,986 | — |
| Total.................... | $26,079 | $26,237 | $23,311 |

The company was also able to obtain from the U.S. Department of Commerce sales data by item *within* each of the division's major product lines or combination of lines. These data are presented in the following tables. The division did not have records to show their sales of these items.

TABLE 2

Estimated U.S. Manufacturers' Sales by Item within Infants and Toddlers' Category for 1969–1971

| Item* | Yearly Sales (000) | | |
|---|---|---|---|
| | 1969 | 1970 | 1971 |
| Creepers/rompers*............. | $36,700 | $32,100 | $33,000 |
| Play garments*................ | 62,400 | 59,900 | 66,800 |
| Dresses*..................... | 55,700 | 55,100 | 56,100 |
| Coats....................... | 11,400 | 11,100 | 10,900 |
| Suits....................... | 5,700 | 5,600 | 4,900 |
| Ski/snow suits................ | 3,000 | 3,200 | 3,700 |
| Blouses*.................... | 4,300 | 4,100 | 4,400 |
| Skirts*..................... | 2,600 | 2,400 | 1,900 |
| Swim suits.................. | 4,600 | 5,100 | 4,900 |
| Sweaters................... | 9,400 | 7,600 | 8,100 |
| Knit skirts*................. | 24,100 | 24,600 | 25,100 |
| Jackets..................... | n.a. | 4,500 | 3,900 |

n.a. = not available.
* These items are sold by the playwear division.
Source: U.S. Department of Commerce.

The division suffered a severe disruption in sales and profits in 1968–69 when substantial resources were diverted to the creation of a misses' knit sportswear line which would sell at a higher price to a more sophisticated

**TABLE 3**

Estimated U.S. Manufacturers' Sales by Item within Children's
3–6X Category for 1969–1971

| Item* | Yearly Sales (000) | | |
|---|---|---|---|
| | 1969 | 1970 | 1971 |
| Coats..................... | $ 36,000 | $ 34,000 | $ 31,300 |
| Snow/ski suits.............. | n.a. | 8,000 | 8,800 |
| Suits*..................... | 11,400 | 11,200 | 9,800 |
| Jackets.................... | n.a. | 10,500 | 9,800 |
| Dresses.................... | 110,600 | 121,000 | 126,800 |
| Blouses*................... | 8,600 | 8,200 | 8,800 |
| Skirts*.................... | 5,200 | 4,800 | 3,800 |
| Dungarees/jeans*........... | 25,300 | 29,500 | 34,900 |
| Slacks/shorts*.............. | 70,900 | 75,400 | 81,800 |
| Play garments/playsuits*...... | 54,600 | 60,300 | 45,400 |
| Swim suits................. | 9,200 | 10,200 | 9,800 |
| Sweaters................... | 18,800 | 15,200 | 16,200 |
| Knit sports shirts*........... | 41,800 | 37,200 | 50,600 |

n.a. = not available.
* These items are sold by the playwear division.
Source: U.S. Department of Commerce.

market segment. As a result of this attempt to "trade up," profits dropped
from $950,150 to $51,000. In 1970–71 margins and profits improved
primarily because sales of staple merchandise to traditional markets remained steady and division-apportioned overhead was substantially re-

**TABLE 4**

Estimated U.S. Manufacturers' Sales by Item within Girls'
7–14 Category for 1969–1971

| Item* | Sales by Year (000) | | |
|---|---|---|---|
| | 1969 | 1970 | 1971 |
| Coats..................... | $ 45,500 | $ 51,800 | $ 48,700 |
| Ski/snow suits.............. | n.a. | 11,400 | 12,400 |
| Suits...................... | 5,100 | 4,200 | 3,100 |
| Jackets*................... | n.a. | 14,700 | 14,100 |
| Dresses*................... | 173,400 | 160,600 | 153,900 |
| Blouses*................... | 44,700 | 50,200 | 54,300 |
| Skirts*.................... | 27,700 | 32,700 | 30,800 |
| Slacks*.................... | 24,700 | 25,000 | 32,900 |
| Dungarees/jeans*........... | 9,800 | 11,000 | 14,100 |
| Shorts/playsuits*............ | 20,000 | 21,500 | 22,700 |
| Swim suits................. | 13,700 | 12,500 | 9,500 |
| Sweaters................... | 21,600 | 16,000 | 16,400 |
| Knit shirts*................ | 17,900 | 20,900 | 30,100 |

n.a. = not available.
* These items are sold by the playwear division.
Source: U.S. Department of Commerce.

**TABLE 5**

**Estimated U.S. Manufacturers' Sales by Item within Junior
Misses' Category for 1969–1971**

| | Sales by Year (000) | | |
|---|---|---|---|
| Item* | 1969 | 1970 | 1971 |
| Dresses.................. | $2,172,000 | $2,101,000 | $2,311,800 |
| Coats/capes.............. | 575,000 | 543,000 | 541,600 |
| Dress suits.............. | 260,000 | 180,000 | 156,600 |
| Pant suits*.............. | n.a. | 245,000 | 187,600 |
| Blouses*................. | 534,000 | 541,000 | 563,300 |
| Skirts*.................. | 392,000 | 335,000 | 343,100 |
| Jackets.................. | 64,000 | 66,000 | 87,800 |
| Dungarees/jeans*......... | n.a. | 12,000 | 32,400 |
| Jean type slacks......... | n.a. | 72,000 | 105,600 |
| Slacks*.................. | 275,000 | 291,000 | 361,900 |
| Shorts*.................. | 106,000 | 104,000 | 100,000 |
| Playsuits*............... | 18,000 | 24,000 | 24,500 |
| Swim suits*.............. | 119,000 | 123,000 | 117,000 |
| Uniforms................. | 89,000 | 92,000 | 96,000 |
| Sweaters................. | 281,000 | 257,000 | 250,000 |
| Knit sport shirts*....... | 106,000 | 133,000 | 143,800 |

n.a. = not available.
* These items are sold by the playwear division.
Source: U.S. Department of Commerce.

duced as were markdowns. But 1972 saw a return to lower margins, attributed primarily to poor styles in the young juniors' and the boys' 4–7 lines. This caused the division to experience $3.4 million in markdowns. For the future the division planned to place greater emphasis on a new company label for young juniors to be sold in department store budget departments and specialty shops; the "old" company label would be used primarily on styles sold to the discount trade buying in volume.

2. *Lingerie Division.* Since its inception the company had manufactured and marketed children's and ladies' lingerie. Changes in the market, coupled with a fashion revolution, reduced the slip market substantially in recent years. Division sales in slips dropped from a high of about $12.4 million in the early 1960's to currently about $4.65 million. In 1968, partly to offset declining lingerie sales, the division entered the sleepwear market, which was perceived as a large and growing market especially for popularly priced lines like those sold by the company.

Lingerie posed no design problems, but sleepwear did. About two-thirds of the sleepwear items could not be carried over and were, therefore, subject to markdowns. To date, the division's performance in the sleepwear market had been only partially satisfactory due to repeated failure to provide satisfactory delivery. The cause of this difficulty was the need to retrain lingerie workers to produce sleepwear merchandise, coupled with labor shortages, labor turnover, and absenteeism.

This caused both management and the sales force to resort to seeking private label business, which involved longer runs. Scheduled delivery dates could be met because of the long lead times. Thus, volume was built in such national accounts as Sears, Penney's, and Grants. In the last half of 1972 well over 50% of total sleepwear sales were either private label or restricted style house account business. Inevitably, the company's label was subordinated.

In 1971 the division moved aggressively to staff itself with the technical expertise needed to produce flame retardant sleepwear. By early 1972 the division had developed a new line of flame retardant sleepwear which had been well accepted by the trade; indeed, the division could not keep up with the demand throughout 1972. Division sales by product lines are indicated in Table 6 below. Total U.S. sales are given in Tables 7 and 8.

**TABLE 6**

**Sales by Product Line for Lingerie Division for 1969–1971**

|  | Net Sales by Year (000) | | |
|---|---|---|---|
| Product Line | 1969–1970 | 1970–1971 | 1971–1972 |
| Infants'/toddlers' | $   264 | $   194 | $   116 |
| 3–6X | 481 | 473 | 357 |
| Girls' 7–14 | 646 | 1,240 | 2,085 |
| Juniors' 4–14 | 1,418 | 2,117 | 2,978 |
| Ladies' | 2,643 | 3,108 | 4,652 |
| Miscellaneous | 4,603 | 3,420 | 2,322 |
| Total | $10,055 | $10,552 | $12,510 |

**TABLE 7**

**Estimated U.S. Manufacturers' Sales by Item within Children's and Infants' Lingerie and Sleepwear Category for 1969–1971**

|  | Yearly Sales (000) | | |
|---|---|---|---|
| Item* | 1969 | 1970 | 1971 |
| Slips and half slips | $23,000 | $19,400 | $18,700 |
| Panties | 45,200 | 40,700 | 41,600 |
| Undershirts | 7,800 | 6,500 | 7,900 |
| Infants' panties | 17,750 | 20,960 | 17,300 |
| Infants' slips | 14,900 | 17,600 | 15,700 |
| Nightgowns | 19,400 | 19,600 | 22,000 |
| Pajamas | 40,600 | 38,500 | 39,100 |
| Infants' nightgowns | 14,300 | 14,100 | 12,200 |
| Infants' heavy sleepers | 36,200 | 42,400 | 49,000 |
| Infants' pajamas | 11,900 | 12,600 | 11,100 |

* Company lingerie division carries all of these items.
Source: U.S. Department of Commerce.

**TABLE 8**

**Estimated U.S. Manufacturers' Sales by Item within Women's Lingerie and Sleepwear Category for 1969–1971**

|  | Yearly Sales (000) | | |
|---|---|---|---|
| Item* | 1969 | 1970 | 1971 |
| Slips...................... | $191,100 | $171,900 | $136,600 |
| Half slips.................. | 107,600 | 64,400 | 56,300 |
| Panties.................... | 166,800 | 179,900 | 187,500 |
| Vests...................... | 10,600 | 10,000 | 9,100 |
| Nightgowns/sleepcoats........ | 193,700 | 214,000 | 262,000 |
| Baby dolls/short pj's.......... | 43,100 | 32,600 | 43,200 |
| Pajamas................... | 57,800 | 64,200 | 63,800 |
| Robe sets.................. | 35,600 | 48,900 | 60,100 |
| Bed jackets................ | 13,900 | 12,100 | 13,300 |

\* Company's division carries all of these items.
Source: U.S. Department of Commerce.

**3. Halpern Division.** This division was purchased by the company in the 1960's. Over the years the company successfully converted the Halpern image from a popular price volume mass market producer of sometimes questionable quality "fashion" men's dress and sport shirts to a more prestigious brand connoting quality and styling at moderate prices. Sales of this division were aimed at specialty shops and the upstairs departments in department stores. In recent years the division discontinued its ladies' and boys' shirt lines in order to concentrate better on men's shirts. Dress shirts were added, and collars on such shirts were adapted to the new sport shirt look. Knit lines were added to the existing woven lines, and a new line of knit sport shirts was marketed. Even so, about 50% of the line consisted of "basics"—i.e., staple items which could be carried over from selling season to selling season.

The division also eliminated private label accounts and set up a special label for controlled sales to the emerging volume sellers of nonprice protected shirt and pants lines. About 90% of the production of this division, however, carried the Halpern label. The division sold two major seasonal fashion lines and two "transitional" fashion lines. These would be converted to three full-season lines when the knit sport shirts line developed enough volume and when the long and short sleeve sport and dress shirt lines overlapped the spring/summer and fall/winter selling seasons. These would increase the number and proportion of style items in the overall line.

Labor problems—both shortages and turnovers—limited the growth of the division. For the fiscal year 1973–74 sales were projected at $6,789,000 although the Halpern plants had a "rated" capacity to produce between $8.5 and $9.3 million (depending on the product mix), assuming the availability of an adequate and efficient labor force.

The division did not keep records of its sales by item but did know total U.S. sales by item. These are presented in Table 9.

**TABLE 9**

**Estimated U.S. Manufacturers' Sales by Item within Men's and Boys' Shirt Category for 1969–1971**

| | Sales by Year (000) | | |
|---|---|---|---|
| Item* | 1969 | 1970 | 1971 |
| Men's dress/business shirt*.... | $411,000 | $475,900 | $526,600 |
| Men's sport shirts*........... | 324,900 | 316,300 | 324,600 |
| Men's uniform shirts.......... | 42,200 | 37,500 | 33,500 |
| Boys' dress/uniform shirts*.... | 31,200 | 30,700 | 27,600 |
| Boys' sport shirts*............ | 89,200 | 86,800 | 87,800 |
| Men's work shirts............ | 120,600 | 127,200 | 128,100 |
| Boys' work shirts............ | 3,100 | 900 | 900 |

\* These items are sold by the Halpern division although these do not include boys' uniform shirts.
Source: U.S. Department of Commerce.

**4. Sun Island Division.** This division's line contained a higher style component than any of the other company products. As a consequence the line was highly vulnerable to markdowns. Sun Island also operated with the highest margins and highest piece-rates of any of the company divisions. After a profitable and promising start this division suffered two years of heavy losses partly due to its long product line, which had originally included pant suits. It was hoped that the division would achieve a break even position during the 1973–74 fiscal year.

The division concentrated on a line of misses' sportswear (essentially separates, i.e., blouses and pants) which it sold to specialty shops and the upstairs departments of department stores. It was thought that imports would have difficulty penetrating the dynamic four-season brand franchised fashion market for misses' sportswear and that the division had an excellent potential provided it could design the proper lines. Contract label business would be phased out and every effort made to develop the prestige of the Sun Island brand name. Even though sales of $4.8 million were projected for 1973–74 (down from the previous year because of a reduction in contract sales), it was hoped that sales would shortly grow to $7.75 million. No sales records by items were maintained so that it was not known what total U.S. sales were by major sportswear items.

**5. Underwear Division.** This division was a contract manufacturer specializing in men's and boys' woven underwear. It supplied about 15% of the national market of approximately 15.5 million dozen annually. The division had the capacity to produce 2.8 million dozen. At present prices this represented $20 million in sales.

The majority of all men's and boys' woven underwear business was done under private label. The rest was sold by such "marketing" firms as Hanes, Van Heusen, Manhattan, Arrow, and Munsingwear, which sold a family of products (including woven underwear) under their advertised brand. The division manufactured boxer shorts for private label to the large national chains as well as for marketing organizations. Three accounts represented 60% of the division's business.

As noted earlier, the division produced woven underwear ("boxer shorts"). U.S. sales by type of men's underwear item are shown in Table 10.

### TABLE 10
#### Estimated U.S. Manufacturers' Sales by Item in the Men's Underwear Category for 1969–1971

| | Sales by Year (000) | | |
|---|---|---|---|
| *Item\** | *1969* | *1970* | *1971* |
| Boxer shorts\*................. | $ 73,100 | $ 68,800 | $ 70,700 |
| Knit briefs.................. | 125,200 | 122,900 | 134,900 |
| T-shirts.................... | 145,300 | 147,700 | 160,700 |
| A-shirts.................... | 24,500 | 23,000 | 23,700 |
| Drawers.................... | 26,200 | 26,700 | 26,300 |
| Union suits................. | n.a. | 2,700 | 2,900 |

n.a. = not available.
\* Items carried by company's underwear division.
Source: U.S. Department of Commerce.

## Marketing and Sales

The Hayden Company followed a consistent marketing organization structure within each division. Each had a merchandise manager responsible for designing and pricing the products for the target segments. This same individual was responsible for production scheduling and inventories. In addition, merchandising was responsible for the development of samples, sales literature, advertising, and order processing. In the smaller divisions the division manager also served as the merchandise manager. This was the case with the Sun Island, underwear, and Halpern divisions. Because of their size and the type of merchandise handled the latter two divisions employed no designer; the division manager also served in this capacity.

For all the merchandise divisions, with the exception of Sun Island and underwear, there were two major selling seasons—fall/winter and spring/summer. For the former the divisions had to commit themselves to purchasing fabric as early as February—some seven to eight months in advance of the selling season. Production was started in March; at the same time the sales force started its selling from samples. About half of the production for the fall/winter season was completed by June, although production by line item was constantly juggled based on orders received from the field. Substantial reallocations against plan were made at the time when 15%, 40%, and 75% of the orders were received. The same kind of lead times applied to the spring/summer season. One half of the total assets of the Hayden Company were tied up in inventories.

The Sun Island division had four major selling seasons—spring, summer, fall and holiday. To some extent the last overlapped with the spring line. This division produced four distinct lines, thereby accentuating the problems of design, inventory, and production scheduling. Because the underwear division produced essentially a staple product line, production scheduling and inventories produced no special problems. Markdowns were an extremely important determinant of a division's profitability. Typically, the division got rid of its carryover by making a special price offer (e.g., one-third off) to one or more of its large customers.

The Sun Island division sold its line to some 900–1,200 essentially regional (southeast) retail accounts through its own 100% commission sales force. A separate sales force was employed because there were some differences in accounts with the other divisions and because different buyers were usually involved. Further, it was reasoned that the sales forces employed by other divisions, especially playwear and lingerie, were already overloaded. Accounts could only be added with the approval of the divisional manager.

A total of 18 men were employed, of which six handled only the Sun Island lines. Twelve handled Sun Island plus other lines which were noncompetitive to those sold by Hayden. Commissions varied but averaged about 5% on sales. Salesmen were expected to pay their own expenses out of their commissions. Sun Island maintained a New York office, which was manned by one salaried salesman handling national accounts and New York City accounts.

The Halpern division (which sold to between 1500–1800 southeastern accounts) had its own sales force consisting of 23 men; 12 handled the Halpern line exclusively. Commissions approximated 5% of sales. The remainder also handled lines noncompetitive to Hayden. The reasoning behind the separate force for Halpern was essentially the same for the Sun Island. The division manager played a strong role in selecting which new accounts to add. The underwear division had no sales force because of its few accounts; the division manager handled all sales activities. Large contract sales or sales to national chains were treated by Halpern as house accounts on which no commissions were paid. The Halpern and underwear divisions shared a small office in New York City, manned by two salaried salesmen. Halpern paid the underwear division 7% on any sales generated by this office.

The playwear and lingerie divisions shared a national sales force which was also 100% commissioned. Thus, such salesmen sold the lines of both divisions to approximately 28,000 accounts. Salesmen selected their own accounts. Sales to large national accounts and contract label sales were treated as house accounts and typically involved both the merchandise manager and the division manager of these divisions.

The buyers of playwear, lingerie, and sleepwear selected their stocks by shopping for these items in New York or at annual shows or by waiting for the salesmen to appear. Larger stores tended to shop in New York or at the annual shows. There was a trend for the larger stores (especially the chains) to demand samples and then have a committee make the final purchase decision. It was becoming clear that the larger accounts were specializing their buying by items and did not buy the full line(s) from a single manufacturer. Such was not the case with the smaller stores.

The two divisions maintained three regional offices in New York, Chicago, and San Francisco. In New York six salaried employees were paid by the playwear division, and three were paid by the lingerie division. These nine individuals serviced national accounts and sold in New York City for their respective divisions. The expenses of operating the office were split between the two divisions on the basis of their relative sales from this office. The Chicago office had three salaried sales personnel; their costs plus office expenses were prorated in exactly the same manner as in New York. The San Francisco office was paid for by the northern California salesmen out of their commissions. This office was subsidized by the Arizona–southern California salesman who paid one-half of 1% of his sales to compensate for services rendered; the Washington, Alaska, Oregon, and Idaho salesman did the same.

The remainder of the "joint" sales force consisted of salesmen who had been with the company for many years and whose average age was the late 40's. Sales commissions in excess of $1.5 million were paid in 1971–1972. Many of these salesmen maintained offices and showrooms in a major city in their territory at their own expense. These men did not report to a regional sales manager but rather directly to the division manager of the playwear division. In reality they were autonomous agents and were rarely told what to do by anyone within the Hayden organization.

The typical playwear/lingerie salesman drove a van in which various Hayden items were displayed. For medium size and large accounts a "call" could take as long as two days, during which time a number of buyers would shop the offerings. These van sales accounted for 80% of the sales of these divisions since Hayden discouraged "fill in" orders. The job of the company salesman in the case of the smaller accounts was to show the line, quote the price, and write the order. For larger accounts (including regional chains) the salesman could grant exclusives and a discount which came out of his commission. Management considered these decisions to be the salesman's prerogative and made no request to learn more about such activities.

Exhibits 1–5 provide performance data for each division, and Exhibits 6–8 show data for the company as a whole.

**EXHIBIT 1**

**Significant Performance Data,**
**Playwear Division**

| Fiscal Year | Net Sales* $(000) | Profit before Taxes | | Direct Labor Costs $(000) | Division Overhead $(000) | End of Year Inventories† | | Total Assets | |
|---|---|---|---|---|---|---|---|---|---|
| | | $(000) | Percent Sales | | | $(000) | Turns | $(000) | Percent Retained A/T‡ |
| 1969–70............ | 26,079 | 51 | 0.2 | 3,914 | 8,161 | 10,532 | 2.0 | 15,852 | 0.2 |
| 1970–71............ | 26,237 | 1,518 | 5.8 | 3,379 | 6,581 | 8,516 | 2.4 | 12,961 | 5.9 |
| 1971–72............ | 23,311 | 205 | 0.9 | 3,294 | 6,594 | 8,982 | 2.2 | 12,633 | 1.3 |
| 1972–73 (est.)........... | 26,265 | 340 | 1.3 | 4,157 | 7,237 | 8,178 | 3.2 | 12,710 | 1.5 |
| 1973–74 (plan)........... | 28,210 | 1,535 | 5.4 | 5,163 | 3,855 | 7,491 | 3.8 | 12,865 | 5.3 |

* Net of commissions paid to sales force.
† Includes finished goods, goods in process, and raw materials.
‡ After taxes.

**EXHIBIT 2**

**Significant Performance Data,
Lingerie Division**

| Fiscal Year | Net Sales* $(000) | Profit before Taxes | | Direct Labor Costs $(000) | Division Overhead $(000) | End of Year Inventories† | | Total Assets | |
|---|---|---|---|---|---|---|---|---|---|
| | | $(000) | Percent Sales | | | $(000) | Turns | $(000) | Percent Retained A/T‡ |
| 1969–70 | 10,055 | 313 | 3.1 | 1,499 | 3,010 | 3,410 | 2.4 | 5,738 | 2.73 |
| 1970–71 | 10,552 | 550 | 4.3 | 1,697 | 3,345 | 3,548 | 2.4 | 5,512 | 4.08 |
| 1971–72 | 12,510 | 1,097 | 8.8 | 1,849 | 2,931 | 3,982 | 2.4 | 6,248 | 8.78 |
| 1972–73 (est.) | 13,285 | 673 | 5.1 | n.a. | n.a. | n.a. | n.a. | n.a. | n.a. |
| 1973–74 (plan) | 14,725 | 1,023 | 6.9 | 2,460 | n.a. | n.a. | n.a. | n.a. | n.a. |

n.a. = not available.
* Net of commissions paid to sales force.
† Includes finished goods, goods in process, and raw materials.
‡ After taxes.

**EXHIBIT 3**

**Significant Performance Data,**
**Sun Island Division**

| Fiscal Year | Net Sales* $(000) | Profit before Taxes | | Direct Labor Costs $(000) | Division Overhead $(000) | End of Year Inventories† | | Total Assets | |
|---|---|---|---|---|---|---|---|---|---|
| | | $(000) | Percent Sales | | | $(000) | Turns | $(000) | Percent Retained A/T‡ |
| 1969–70 | 3,720 | n.a. | n.a. | n.a. | n.a. | n.a. | n.a. | n.a. | n.a. |
| 1970–71 | 9,150 | 713 | 7.8 | 879 | 2,153 | 2,895 | 3.8 | 3,875 | 9.2 |
| 1971–72 | 8,364 | 1,180 | (14.1) | 916 | 2,327 | 3,272 | 2.6 | 4,236 | (27.8) |
| 1972–73 (est.) | 5,281 | 434 | (8.2) | 663 | 1,798 | 1,922 | 2.7 | 3,333 | (13.6) |
| 1973–74 (plan) | 4,805 | n.a. | n.a. | n.a. | n.a. | n.a. | n.a. | n.a. | n.a. |

n.a. = not available.
* Net of commissions paid to sales force.
† Includes finished goods, goods in process, and raw materials.
‡ After taxes.

## EXHIBIT 4
### Significant Performance Data, Halpern Division

| Fiscal Year | Net Sales* $(000) | Profit before Taxes | | Direct Labor Costs $(000) | Division Overhead $(000) | End of Year Inventories† | | Total Assets | |
|---|---|---|---|---|---|---|---|---|---|
| | | $(000) | Percent Sales | | | $(000) | Turns | $(000) | Percent Retained A/T‡ |
| 1969–70 | 3,365 | 167 | 5.0 | 750 | 818 | 679 | 4.0 | 1,572 | 5.3 |
| 1970–71 | 3,949 | 299 | 7.6 | 801 | 916 | 739 | 4.1 | 1,707 | 8.8 |
| 1971–72 | 4,844 | 395 | 8.2 | 899 | 997 | 1,008 | 3.8 | 2,057 | 9.7 |
| 1972–73 (est.) | 5,679 | 327 | 5.7 | 1,115 | 1,110 | 1,384 | 4.1 | 2,209 | 7.4 |
| 1973–74 (plan) | 6,789 | 543 | 7.9 | 1,304 | n.a. | 1,655 | 4.1 | 2,480 | 10.9 |

n.a. = not available.
* Net of commissions paid to sales force.
† Includes finished goods, goods in process, and raw materials.
‡ After taxes.

## EXHIBIT 5

### Significant Performance Data, Underwear Division

| Fiscal Year | Net Sales* $(000) | Profit before Taxes $(000) | Percent Sales | Direct Labor Costs $(000) | Division Overhead $(000) | End of Year† Inventories $(000) | Turns | Total Assets $(000) | Percent Retained A/T‡ |
|---|---|---|---|---|---|---|---|---|---|
| 1969–70 | 8,421 | (171) | (2.1) | 1,865 | 1,907 | 2,849 | 2.8 | 4,194 | — |
| 1970–71 | 11,157 | 73 | 0.7 | 2,055 | 2,080 | 2,541 | 4.1 | 4,204 | 0.86 |
| 1971–72 | 13,271 | 282 | 2.1 | 2,629 | 2,740 | 2,167 | 5.7 | 4,246 | 3.31 |
| 1972–73 (est.) | 14,948 | 894 | 5.2 | 3,117 | 3,055 | 2,716 | 5.5 | 4,766 | 9.14 |
| 1973–74 (plan) | 17,050 | 930 | 5.4 | 3,553 | n.a. | 3,157 | 5.4 | 5,270 | 8.77 |

n.a. = not available.

* Net of commissions paid to sales force.

† Includes finished goods, goods in process, and raw materials.

‡ After taxes.

## EXHIBIT 6

### Significant Performance Data, Hayden Company, 1969–1971

| Fiscal Year | Net Sales* $(000) | Profit before Taxes | | Direct Labor $(000) | Over-head† $(000) | End of Year Inventories† $(000) | Total Assets† | |
|---|---|---|---|---|---|---|---|---|
| | | $(000) | Percent Sales | | | | $(000) | Percent Retained after Taxes† |
| 1969–70 | 51,640 | 360 | 0.69 | 5,028 | 13,896 | 17,370 | 27,356 | 0.66 |
| 1970–71 | 61,045 | 3,153 | 5.10 | 8,811 | 15,075 | 18,239 | 28,259 | 5.58 |
| 1971–72 | 62,300 | 799 | 1.29 | 9,587 | 15,589 | 19,411 | 29,470 | 1.39 |

* Net of commissions paid to sales force.
† Not including Sun Island division for 1969–70.

**EXHIBIT 7**

**Historical Recap of Markdowns by Divisions**

| Years | Playwear $(000) | Percent Sales | Lingerie $(000) | Percent Sales | Underwear $(000) | Percent Sales | Sun Island $(000) | Percent Sales | Halpern $(000) | Percent Sales | Total $(000) | Percent Sales |
|---|---|---|---|---|---|---|---|---|---|---|---|---|
| 1966–67 | 1,039 | 4.7 | 127 | 1.1 | n.a. | n.a. | — | — | 147 | 4.5 | 1,313 | 3.0 |
| 1967–68 | 1,124 | 4.8 | 112 | 1.1 | n.a. | n.a. | — | — | 183 | 5.4 | 1,418 | 3.2 |
| 1968–69 | 1,071 | 3.8 | 400 | 3.3 | n.a. | n.a. | — | — | 178 | 5.5 | 1,649 | 3.2 |
| 1969–70 | 2,006 | 7.1 | 276 | 2.7 | n.a. | n.a. | — | — | 118 | 3.4 | 2,399 | 5.0 |
| 1970–71 | 1,741 | 6.2 | 299 | 2.8 | 62 | 0.6 | 234 | 2.5 | 121 | 3.0 | 2,612 | 4.5 |
| 1971–72 | 1,612 | 6.9 | 574 | 4.6 | 36 | 0.3 | 1,429 | 17.1 | 102 | 2.1 | 3,753 | 6.5 |
| 1972–73 (budget) | 1,837 | 6.9 | 532 | 4.0 | 14 | 0.1 | 589 | 11.2 | 147 | 2.6 | 3,117 | 4.9 |
| 1973–74 (plan) | 946 | 5.0 | 589 | 4.0 | 14 | 0.1 | 639 | 13.3 | 143 | 2.1 | 2,640 | 3.7 |

n.a. = not available.

**EXHIBIT 8**

**Percent Utilization of Rated Manufacturing
Facilities by Division
(1972)**

| Division | Percent Utilization Rated Capacity* |
|---|---|
| Sun Island | 50 |
| Playwear | 75 |
| Lingerie/sleepwear | 80 |
| Halpern | 75 |
| Men's underwear | 100 |

* Rated capacity assumes the present product line mix but that all workers are on piece-rates and that the maximum number which can be used in the particular plant are present (i.e., no absenteeism).

# General Foods—Birds-Eye Division

The end of the calendar year was always a critical time for Riley Smith, product manager of Birds-Eye frozen regular vegetables, who at that time had to prepare the annual forecast of the demand for each of the 35 different regular vegetables that were his responsibility. This forecast largely determined the extent of the Birds-Eye Division's commitment to buy the acceptable vegetable production of scores of farmers during the coming 12 to 18 months. There was little room for error in the preparation. A forecast that was too high would lead ultimately to large inventories, price reductions to move the excess, and a reduction in profits and return on funds employed. On the other hand, a forecast that was short of demand meant a possible irreversible loss of franchise, or a reduction in profits if the resulting price increases, designed to slow product movement and conserve inventories, were not successful. Another factor was that the realization of the forecast could always be confused by unexpectedly large or small crop yields, which automatically led to unbalanced inventories; although this generally did not happen to the whole product line, but rather to individual vegetables.

The forecast to be made at the end of 1966 presented special problems. For the previous seven years the volume demand for Birds-Eye regular vegetables had been declining between 5% and 10% each year as private and controlled labels increasingly dominated the market. However, there was some evidence that the growth of these brands had stabilized during 1966. A potentially greater influence on the forecast was a test which was being conducted by the Birds-Eye Division to determine possible changes in the pricing and promotion strategy for regular vegetables. Because these tests had been initiated in April of 1966, Riley Smith had only limited evidence on their probable impact available to him by November, 1966. Yet he knew that he had to use this evidence in making at least some tentative judgments on the pricing and promotion strategy that would be used during 1967, before he could meaningfully work on the details of the related volume forecast.

In addition to regular vegetables, the Birds-Eye Division also marketed: (*a*) frozen vegetable combinations, a premium line of vegetables, pre-prepared through the addition of a sauce or another vegetable, such as, peas with pearl onions and French green beans with almonds; (*b*) vacuum sealed or boil-in-bag vegetables, which were frozen in a vacuum sealed pliofilm pouch along with a butter and seasoning sauce; and (*c*) southern vegetables, such as black-eyed peas, which had a regional and/or ethnic appeal. To a considerable, although undefined, extent these specialty lines competed with regular vegetables, so that their prospects also had to be weighed for any adverse impact on the forecast for regular vegetables.

## ELEMENTS OF FORECASTING FOR VEGETABLES

The major factor which Riley Smith had to take into account in making the year-end forecast were: (1) once a commitment for a certain volume had been made there was virtually no way of getting more product if demand was greater than expected other than the fortuitous circumstance of unusually high crop yields; and (2) the forecast period started in May of the coming year and might extend to September of the following year. In effect, he must estimate demand for periods up to 20 months in the future.

The actual forecast period for each vegetable embraced the twelve months between annual National Distribution Dates (this was the date by which the harvest was usually in, frozen, packaged, distributed to regional warehouses and ready to supply going sales or existing stock shortages). This key date varied according to the vegetable—from late May for asparagus to September for corn—and by the length of the pack period, which might last from three weeks to three months. Most of the high volume items had short pack periods, which insured consistently high quality.

Despite the extreme length of the forecast, and the accuracy with which it had to be made, there was no way of delaying the final decision on the forecast much past the end of the year. The item-by-item volume forecasts determined the course of negotiations with growers, and the extent of the contracts of acreage which were made for all vegetables on the same day in March. Each grower contracted to sell all the production of a certain crop from his acreage, and Birds-Eye, or any packer, agreed to buy everything from that acreage as long as it met agreed upon quality specifications. Each party to the contract had a good idea as to the usual yield to be expected. A high percentage of growers always contracted for the same packer. However, in recent years, a number of growers had given up certain risky crops, which meant considerable competition for the remaining growers of that crop.

## BACKGROUND TO THE MARKET

Frozen foods were first sold to retail stores in 1930. Initial acceptance was very slow because of formidable technical problems. The major problems to be overcome were: (*a*) achieving distribution in retail stores, which meant developing small inexpensive freezer units that could be rented to retailers; (*b*) supplying these freezers meant providing insulated facilities for storing and transporting frozen foods at a constant temperature of 0°; (*c*) there was a serious capacity bottleneck because of the lack of efficient portable quick freeze units for handling large harvests.

In addition, a major educational campaign was necessary to teach consumers the difference between quick freezing and the existing "cold storage" method. Consumers needed to be convinced that quick freezing was a vastly superior means of preserving the qualities of the food product, whereas slow freezing was uncertain, uncontrolled and often caused quality deterioration. In many products quick freezing formed small ice crystals, readily absorbed without damage to the product. The existing slow freezing or cold storage method formed large ice crystals which damaged the cells of the tissue structure.

The marketing strategy followed in the mid-1930's emphasized exposure of the product and technological improvements. The war assisted greatly in expanding the distribution of frozen foods. The industry was judged essential to the war effort, for among other advantages, it required less steel than cans. The growing demand from the 24% of all housewives who were war workers and appreciated the convenience of frozen foods was magnified by the needs of the armed services. This set the stage for uninterrupted postwar growth in consumption:

### Per Capita Consumption of Frozen Foods
### (In edible pounds)

| 1940 | 1945 | 1950 | 1955 | 1956 | 1957 |
|------|------|------|------|------|------|
| 0.58 | 1.88 | 3.38 | 6.64 | 7.26 | 7.48 |

The attraction of explosive growth, plus low initial capital requirements, crowded over 1,500 separate producers into the freezing business by the early 1950's. Most of these producers were oriented toward serving a particular region, crop, or group of farmers. The growing need to deal with the expanding regional and national supermarket chains led to considerable consolidation of these individual producers. Because growth prospects continued excellent, each consolidation resulted in an expansion of capacity which cumulated into a temporary over-capacity situation by 1955.

To gain market volume, many of the consolidated processors went directly to the food chains with offers of regionally controlled labels or special private label packs. By selling direct, the processors were able to keep their margins down. This enabled the retailers to price items from 15% to 20% below comparable national brand items without reducing their high margins on frozen foods. The availability of these lower product prices coincided with a period of growing retailer interest in having private brands throughout the store. By 1954, frozen vegetables were the second largest frozen food item (see Exhibit 1), and between 1955 and 1961 became one of the most successful private brand items.

### Frozen Vegetables—Annual Share Trends
### (pound volume basis—percent)

| Fiscal Year | National Brands | Private Label | Others* | Total |
|---|---|---|---|---|
| 1955............. | 59 | 14 | 27 | 100 |
| 1956............. | 57 | 20 | 23 | 100 |
| 1957............. | 47 | 28 | 25 | 100 |
| 1961............. | 31 | 39 | 30 | 100 |
| 1962............. | 30 | 39 | 31 | 100 |
| 1963............. | 29 | 40 | 31 | 100 |
| 1964............. | 28 | 39 | 33 | 100 |
| 1965 (Mar. 1965 to Feb. 1966)........ | 29 | 40 | 31 | 100 |

* Controlled and regional packer brands.
SOURCE: Birds-Eye Market Research Group.

The apparent leveling out of the sharp decline in national brand market share by the early 1960's was a welcome trend to Birds-Eye and other national brand manufacturers. There was no obvious single reason for the stability of the market shares at the 1963 level. One possibility was that private and controlled labels could not effectively penetrate a hard core of buyers who were "more national brand loyal than private label interested." Also the remaining national brands had learned to live with the situation by adjusting their price and trade promotion strategies. Another factor was the recognition by retailers that variety of choice was important to their customers, and that familiar national brand names had a drawing power that should not be ignored. Finally, some national brand manufacturers had succeeded in bringing out new frozen vegetable items such as vegetable combinations and boil-in-bag vegetables that were often not immediately copied by the private labels.

In the 1960's the frozen vegetable market continued to grow, but at a considerably reduced rate. Average annual growth between 1961 and 1966 was 2.75% on a volume basis, with population growth accounting for an increase of 1.5% per year. The growth of frozen vegetables was entirely at the expense of fresh vegetables:

**Total Vegetable Consumption by Process Type**
**(percent)**

| Year | Frozen | Canned | Fresh | Total |
|------|--------|--------|-------|-------|
| 1954............... | 6.2 | 39.2 | 54.6 | 100 |
| 1955............... | 6.6 | 40.5 | 52.9 | 100 |
| 1956............... | 6.8 | 40.3 | 52.9 | 100 |
| 1957............... | 7.0 | 40.3 | 52.7 | 100 |
| 1958............... | 7.6 | 41.0 | 51.4 | 100 |
| 1959............... | 7.7 | 41.1 | 51.2 | 100 |
| 1960............... | 7.7 | 40.7 | 51.6 | 100 |
| 1961............... | 7.9 | 40.8 | 51.3 | 100 |
| 1962............... | 8.6 | 41.7 | 49.7 | 100 |
| 1963............... | 8.3 | 42.4 | 49.3 | 100 |
| 1964............... | 9.0 | 42.7 | 48.3 | 100 |
| 1965............... | 9.1 | 43.0 | 47.9 | 100 |

SOURCE: Vegetable Situation (USDA; TVS-104).

Specialty vegetables were introduced in 1962 and accounted for much of the growth of frozen vegetables.

**Retail—Frozen Vegetable Market Growth**
**(volume in millions of dozens)**

| Fiscal Year | Frozen Vegetables | Specialty Vegetables | Regular Vegetables |
|-------------|-------------------|----------------------|--------------------|
| 1960............ | 123.6 | — | 123.6 |
| 1961............ | 130.0 | — | 130.0 |
| 1962............ | 131.8 | 0.6 | 131.2 |
| 1963............ | 137.9 | 3.0 | 134.9 |
| 1964............ | 144.6 | 4.3 | 140.3 |
| 1965............ | 144.1 | 8.5 | 136.1 |
| 1966(est.)........ | 148.0 | 13.5 | 134.5 |

SOURCE: Birds-Eye Market Research Group.

One reason for the difference in growth of regular versus specialty frozen vegetables was the extent of promotional support each received. Trade sources stated that virtually nothing was spent on media advertising (exclusive of supermarket flyers and other local media) for all regular vegetables in 1966. This was approximately ⅓ of 1% of total industry sales of $325 million. Another reason for the success of specialty vegetables was that they offered a means for overcoming the general feeling of consumers that vegetables were dull, uninteresting, and difficult to make interesting. (See summary of consumer survey, Exhibit 2.)

Those housewives who did not use frozen vegetables were bound by habit, and either a strong preference for the freshness and economy of fresh vegetables or the long shelf life, softer texture, and quick, foolproof preparation of canned vegetables. The fact that frozen vegetables were approximately the same price per edible ounce as canned vegetables while delivering more nutritional value (by not precooking nutritional value out of the solid to the same extent) seemed to have little influence on the preferences for each type. Thus, a study of consumer menus in 1956 (see Exhibit 3) showed that frozen vegetables were more popular among high income families, who apparently were willing to pay for the convenience plus flavor benefits of frozen vegetables and were relatively less concerned over differences in value between canned and frozen.

## BIRDS-EYE REGULAR VEGETABLE MARKETING STRATEGIES (TO DECEMBER 1965)

The most enduring features of the regular vegetable marketing strategies were: high product quality, national distribution, wide product line and high individual product prices. Between 1955 and 1965 a variety of advertising and price dealing plans had been used to take advantage of these basic elements.

(A)   *Product quality* first received significant emphasis by Birds-Eye during the widespread introduction of private label frozen vegetables. To maintain a consistent superiority over private label quality, Birds-Eye kept upgrading its product standards and exerting closer control over the growers of its vegetables. Through such control it was possible to ensure that the best seeds were used, growing conditions were uniform among all growers, and the latest agricultural technology was properly used.

Disposal of that portion of the product that did not quite meet these new high product standards was relieved by the growth of institutional business, as well as the establishment of a number of Birds-Eye house brands. These house brands were generally offered to local food chains on an exclusive basis and served the same function as a private label for that chain. This business was not profitable in itself, but did provide some contribution to fixed plant costs.

(B)   The ability to maintain *national distribution* was a major factor in the relative success of Birds-Eye regular vegetables compared to the other national brand competitors. (See Exhibit 4.)

Most of the difficulties of gaining and/or maintaining distribution were a direct consequence of an almost uniform policy practiced by retailers of displaying only their private or controlled brand and one national brand of any frozen food item. Such a policy was made necessary by the proliferation of frozen food products and brands, plus the high unit handling costs and the lack of freezer display space (see Appendix A).

Birds-Eye had enough frozen food volume to support company salesmen in very large metropolitan areas such as New York. However, about 80% of the area of the country was covered by food brokers who received a fixed commission. Other large competitors used brokers to the same or even greater extent.

The claim of national distribution for Birds-Eye regular vegetables was subject to the qualification that the degree of success within a specific region was highly variable. For example, a high volume item in the Birds-Eye line, such as French green beans, might be stocked by 77% of the stores in one marketing district and 10% in another (see Exhibit 5 for details). As a result of these disparities, 80% of the Birds-Eye regular vegetable sales came from areas that accounted for only 50% of the total sales of frozen vegetables in the country.

Some of the extreme differences between districts could be accounted for by regional preferences, or unusual national or private label competitive strength. In other cases the Birds-Eye brand had been historically weak or strong. During the period of retrenchment in the face of private label advances, these long-term differences were magnified by a policy of concentrating company resources to protect strong products in the strongest districts. One result was that large districts which were already weak, lost so much ground that they could no longer justify the use of company salesmen. Sales experience between 1964 and 1966 showed that the switch to brokers had improved the situation in these weak districts. However, much of the improvement was thought to be the result of the extra effort a broker usually put into a new line in the first year, so there was little expectation that it would continue.

(C)  The depth of the sales coverage helped to support one of the *widest lines* of regular and specialty vegetables (over and above southern vegetables) in the industry. Having a wide line was regarded as a significant advantage, even though it tended to diffuse the time the salesman could devote to regular vegetables. Firstly, it meant that Birds-Eye could maximize its share of freezer cabinet space by getting more items into the freezer. Secondly, freezing and packing facilities were already available for high volume items but only used during short harvest seasons. A new vegetable that could be packed and frozen during a different harvest season became a profit contributor even if sales were low. The distribution penetration of the small volume items depended on regional preferences, degree of sales push, and the private label orientation of the retailer. Generally when the retailer had his own brand of a small volume item, he was not willing to stock a national brand.

(D)  *Pricing* was one of the most contentious issues in the marketing of Birds-Eye regular vegetables. Birds-Eye had always been premium priced, but how much premium should be required was a pervading question. Until 1964 the governing feature had been the necessity of meeting unit profit goals, generally at the expense of volume. By late 1964 this approach was being increasingly questioned, and evidence was being gathered in the hope of demonstrating that excessive retail price spreads were damaging to total profit performance. A complicating feature was the product line price structure which had evolved into a separate price for each item in the line. However, the following is representative of the price structure in a district with low private label prices (District A), and other districts with high private label prices resulting from an umbrella of very high national brand prices (District B).

| | Wholesale Price/Dozen | | | Retail Price/Package | | | Retail Profit Margins | |
|---|---|---|---|---|---|---|---|---|
| | Birds-Eye | Private Label | Spread | Birds-Eye | Private Label | Spread | Birds-Eye | Private Label |
| *District A* | | | | | | | | |
| Peas.............. | $2.08 | $1.65 | $0.43 | 22.5¢ | 18.3¢ | 4.2¢ | 21.5% | 23.5% |
| Corn.............. | 1.95 | 1.35 | 0.50 | 22.5 | 16.5 | 6.0 | 25.6 | 29.3 |
| *District B* | | | | | | | | |
| Peas.............. | $2.08 | $1.65 | $0.43 | 24.5¢ | 21.5¢ | 3.0¢ | 28.5% | 35.9% |
| Corn.............. | 1.95 | 1.35 | 0.50 | 24.5 | 21.5 | 3.0 | 32.2 | 47.4 |

(E)    The role of *advertising* in the regular vegetable promotion mix had varied widely since the upsurge of private brand competition. Up to 1964 most of the effort had been concerned with strengthening the Birds-Eye premium quality image. However, the impact of private labels had caused volume and profit declines in most of the company's staple frozen food lines by the end of 1964. Since there was no prospect of an immediate end to these declines it was decided that the company should: (1) concentrate its resources on new products with prospects for long-term distinction from private label competition, and (2) use defensive strategies to slow and if possible halt sales and profit declines.

These considerations, plus the judgment that advertising effectiveness was reduced by the fact that Birds-Eye and certain varieties of private label regular vegetables were sometimes not perceptibly different in quality, led to the decision to stop all media advertising at the end of calendar 1964. The monies saved were largely invested in the new specialty vegetable lines. It was expected there would be some carry-over benefit to regular vegetables from this move, since the Birds-Eye name itself would be constantly associated with quality vegetables. By the end of calendar 1965 the specialty vegetables were 20% of total Birds-Eye vegetable dollar sales and 13% of the weight volume.

(F)    *Trade dealing* was chosen as the main tool with which to defend current authorizations by stores to stock Birds-Eye regular vegetables. During calendar 1965 and 1966 trade dealing took the place of all media advertising and most of the consumer promotional activity such as coupons, contests and refund offers for regular vegetables. Two different approaches were used during this period: (1) *Buying allowances* were offered to chain headquarters or wholesaler distributors acting for independent stores or buying chains. Depending on the size of the allowance, the retailer might receive a 10 to 30 cent reduction in the per dozen invoice price. The offer applied to all purchases during a given month, but might only be made two or three times a year to a specific chain or wholesaler. This type of promotion was only regarded as effective if the trade became over-loaded with stock and had to cut retail prices to move the excess inventory. Thus, the stated objective was, "creating the impression of value to the consumer." (2) *Direct account performance offers* were intended to serve a different purpose in that they demanded some specific promotional performance by the retailer or wholesaler before any payment was made. One unfortunate feature of this incentive was the legal requirement that payment had to be made to the wholesaler or chain headquarters. Thus a distributor could qualify by placing a small ad in a catalogue and the payment from Birds-Eye would not reach the retailer as intended. Nor was it necessary for the distributor to pass on to the retailer any payment made for an advertisement or promotion of Birds-Eye regular vegetables run locally by the retailer.

(G) *Consumer Dealing.* The cents-off promotion which was independent of retailer cooperation and always benefited the customer was used sparingly, and usually only when there was a particularly heavy inventory to move. One of the reasons for this was that the trade objected to the duplication of inventory extra bookkeeping and freezer space demands and the confusion of regular and special packs. The cost to Birds-Eye of gaining cooperation through extended terms and trade allowances was high. Secondly, there was little of the flexibility usually associated with cents-off promotions because all the packaging and over-wrapping was done once per year. Packaging at some date after freezing cost between 12 and 20 cents per dozen. Finally, experience had shown that cents-off did not help low volume items, apparently because of consumer reluctance to devote valuable freezer space to something that might not be wanted by the family.

Other forms of consumer dealing, such as coupons and contests, were seldom used (see below) because it was felt that they did not address the key problem of protecting distribution.

### Per Dozen Advertising and Deal Expenditures

| Fiscal Year | Trade Deals | Consumer Deals | Advertising | Total |
|---|---|---|---|---|
| 1958 | Nil | .012 | .105 | .117 |
| 1959 | .008 | .015 | .085 | .108 |
| 1960 | .018 | .032 | .099 | .149 |
| 1961 | .025 | .012 | .096 | .133 |
| 1962 | .060 | .004 | .110 | .174 |
| 1963 | .029 | .018 | .084 | .131 |
| 1964 | .119 | .027 | .095 | .241 |
| 1965 | .094 | .079 | .061 | .234 |
| 1966 (est.) | .169 | .021 | .009 | .199 |

However, in early 1965, frustration over the dependence on trade deals led to an attempt to combine trade and consumer deals. The offer consisted of payment to the trade of heavy allowances, amounting in total to $500,000 during the March quarter. These allowances were to be used to cut prices on all Birds-Eye products to a specific level. Seven to sixteen weeks' normal volume (depending on the vegetable) had earlier been packed with an overwrap on the package which left room for the retailer to mark in the reduced price. It was expected that the volume packed would suffice for a two-week feature period.

The majority of the trade took advantage of the promotion to stock up. But the unexpected element was the willingness of most of the trade to treat the specially labelled merchandise as regular—sometimes without bothering to reduce the price at all. In few instances was the allowance reflected in reduced retail prices for more than a week. Many consumers were confused or irritated at the pronouncement of a non-existent saving.

## THE SEARCH FOR A NEW STRATEGY

By the close of fiscal 1966,[1] it was clear that the strategy of high price, heavy dealing and no advertising had not succeeded in halting the deterioration in volume and profits.

### Birds-Eye Regular Vegetables—Volume and Profits

| Fiscal | Regular Vegetable Volume (millions of dozens) | Gross Profits (millions of dollars) | Profits before Taxes (millions of dollars) |
|---|---|---|---|
| 1955 | 16.9 | 8.0 | 3.3 |
| 1961 | 16.8 | 9.2 | 4.0 |
| 1962 | 16.2 | 11.4 | 5.3 |
| 1963 | 15.1 | 9.1 | 4.0 |
| 1964 | 13.8 | 8.9 | 2.9 |
| 1965 | 11.4 | 7.5 | 2.4 |

Nor had two years of promotional emphasis on specialty vegetables contributed profits that could offset the above decline. The unexpectedly long pay-back period was attributed largely to problems in achieving distribution and the strong franchise of the competitors who had entered the market first. The effect on the return on funds employed was even

---

[1] Fiscal year 1966 started April 1, 1965 and ended March 31, 1966.

more drastic since both inventory and allocated plant investment had actually increased.

The skepticism toward the existing strategy gained impetus from disquieting evidence on the inefficiency of trade deals. During calendar 1965 and 1966, over 40% of Birds-Eye regular vegetables were sold to the trade on a buying allowance price and 25% of the total movement was linked to some kind of performance offer. Yet a study of the actual prices paid by the buyer revealed that only 30% to 50% of the buying allowance expenditure had any effect on the retail price.

At this time, evidence on possible alternative strategies were accumulated in a series of *pricing* tests. In addition, a number of potentially useful suggestions about possible shifts in consumer buying behavior were made. Management requested a series of research studies to be completed by early 1967, and it was expected that the results of the studies would be used as the basis for any long-term shifts in strategy.

## NEW IDEAS ABOUT VEGETABLE BUYING BEHAVIOR

The following is a review of some hypotheses which were brought to the attention of Birds-Eye management about possible ways of encouraging more interest and usage of vegetables, frozen vegetables, and Birds-Eye frozen vegetables in particular. Many of these ideas had some basis on fact, gathered through various research studies or analyses of specific problems. The problem for management lay in the contradictory nature of some hypotheses and the lack of evidence on their relative importance.

(A) *Overcoming Birds-Eye Regular Vegetable Problems.* The traditional superiority of Birds-Eye regular vegetables was based largely on the consistency of the quality across the entire product line which led to a strong and durable consumer image of reliability. It was probable that the slowly improving image of private-label vegetables was eroding the Birds-Eye position, although the extent of the erosion was difficult to appraise. Some Birds-Eye executives thought that the extent could be appraised by the degree to which Birds-Eye was only thought of in connection with special occasions, rather than as regular everyday frozen vegetables. Others in the division, who agreed with this approach, also questioned what effect the lack of promotion was having on the perceived quality gap between Birds-Eye and private label frozen vegetables. These questions were not easy to answer because of variability in the consumer's criteria of quality. Past experience showed that richness and consistency of color, price level, and evenness of cut and size were all influential to some degree.

One attractive, although hard to accept, hypothesis argued that the strength of the Birds-Eye line should be capitalized on through an advertising approach that linked regular and specialty vegetables. The big unanswered question, that made the hypotheses hard to accept, concerned the degree to which regular and specialty vegetables competed.

The notion of a central theme was somewhat at variance with another hypothesis about a possible quality continuum. According to one researcher:

The consumer perceives three different points: the high point typified by brands like Birds-Eye (the most "carefully selected" and highest price) and the low point by what she describes as "off" brands (brands other than private label or advertised brands *and* low priced). In the middle, housewives position private label brands. The private label user therefore feels she is being a "good shopper" when she selects private label—rejecting both the low priced brand and the high-priced, self-indulgent brand."

If this is true, it suggests that perhaps one way to get some of the private label business is to push private label's "middle of the road" image off center. In other words, if there were brands added *on top*, in terms of the perceived quality continuum, private label brands could no longer be plunk in the middle. This might cause some consumers to upscale their buying.

(B) *Possible Shifts in the Relationship of Types of Vegetables.* Throughout the industry there was a growing conviction that the heavy users of fresh vegetables were more likely to partially or wholly convert to frozen, than were heavy users of canned. This hypothesis was largely based on observations of a growing dissatisfaction with fresh vegetables— *as they were found in the supermarket.* Examples of consumer's complaints were: the time which elapsed between picking and purchasing actually rendered the vegetables less fresh than frozen; the price was too high and didn't seem to go down during the picking season; the waste added to the final cost; and fresh vegetables were often not uniform in quality. Support for the hypothesis came from company research which showed that canned users would be hard to shift because of: (1) a general lack of interest in the flavors and appearance of food or food preparation and serving; (2) a firm attachment to the traditional flavors and textures of canned vegetables; (3) a lack of confidence in their ability to cook well, and a reliance on canned vegetables as the "safest" to prepare; and (4) a strong budget orientation with "low cost" being a significant factor in the choice of the canned type.

(C) *Identification of Market Segments for Frozen Vegetables.* There was a constant need for information on the size and characteristics of various market groups which might offer opportunities for increased Birds-Eye usage. Among the groups suggested were: (1) present users; (2) multiple vegetable type users; (3) weight watchers who desired a sensible nutritious eating plan; (4) young mothers—particularly because children who become used to the texture and taste of canned vegetables are hard to switch to fresh; (5) working women who desire quick and easy preparation without sacrifice of quality and appearance, and have the additional money to contribute to the family budget; (6) young and old couples—representing the two periods in the life cycle with maximum interest in self-satisfaction and no diversion from family demands. Some evidence on the size of these market targets was available from existing knowledge about family characteristics (see Exhibit 6).

Other questions concerned the potential in each of the above groups if some of the problems of frozen vegetable usage could be overcome in new ways. Two notable problems were the need to watch frozen vegetables closely while they were being cooked, and the inability of a standard 10 ounce package to exactly satisfy most family needs.

The problem of package size was borne out by the growing popularity of the 20 or 32 ounce see-through economy size plastic bags.

### Frozen Vegetables Annual Volume
### Trend by Package Size
### (percent)

|  | 1962 | 1963 | 1965 | 1966 |
|---|---|---|---|---|
| 20–32 ounce size.......... | 11 | 14 | 16 | 20 |
| Other sizes.............. | 89 | 86 | 84 | 80 |

SOURCE: Birds-Eye Market Research Group.

Not only did these bags offer a free flowing product so the housewife could use as much as necessary, but the package apparently also enhanced the appearance of the vegetables. As of late 1966 Birds-Eye had not been able to discover how to take advantage of the demand for the large package. There was a feeling that retailers would not permit two different economy size bags in the freezer at the same time, and it would be very hard to differentiate the bags because of lack of space for advertising.

### RESULTS OF PRICING TESTS

During calendar year 1964 and 1965 three low price tests were in effect in different parts of the country—one by design and two in response to peculiarities of the market. Meanwhile, the rest of the country conformed to the company policy of a single national price to all distributors.

From these price tests came the first evidence of the effect of lower list prices and reduced deal rates on volume and profitability. The evidence, while encouraging, was very tentative since product movement results were not based on store audits and thus were subject to inaccuracies, as well as to inflation, by transshipments to neighboring districts where higher prices prevailed.

*Test 1 (Washington-Oregon).* For reasons relating to freight costs, Birds-Eye peas sold in this area were historically priced 20 cents a dozen (about 10%), below the national price. Deal rates were adjusted downward to partly compensate for the reduced gross profit. The effect of this long run price reduction on sales is shown below for a six months period in 1964.

|  | District Sales as % of National Birds-Eye Sales | | Birds-Eye Share of Market within District | |
|---|---|---|---|---|
|  | All Vegetables | Peas | All Vegetables | Peas |
| Seattle | 5.1% | 6.5% | 10.1% | 10.8% |
| Portland | 3.0 | 5.1 | 5.0 | 9.1 |

*Test 2 (Buffalo-Syracuse).* During the spring, summer and fall quarters of 1965, prices and deal rates on beans and spinach were reduced together to a level where the net price after deals in the area approximated the national net price. Birds-Eye sales of these products decreased 9.5%, over the same period of the year before in the test area, compared to a decline of 20% in the adjacent areas.

*Test 3 (San Francisco-Los Angeles).* By December, 1964, the combination of high Birds-Eye regular vegetable prices and low private label margins and retail prices in the San Francisco district caused: (1) unusually wide price spreads with Birds-Eye prices from 15% to 40% higher than typical private label prices on the same item, (2) an acceleration in the decline of consumer demand for Birds-Eye vegetables, and (3) loss of authorization in the Apex grocery chain, which represented 15.6% of that district's volume. The Apex business was taken over by a competitor, who offered lower retail prices and higher margins.

To protect the San Francisco market from further deterioration an immediate price cut was made. The amount of the cut per item varied, but generally put Birds-Eye close to the new national brand competitive prices (see Exhibit 7). This move, however, caused a negative reaction in the Los Angeles market where price spreads were also large. Existing authorizations in Los Angeles were under attack as national brand competitors tried to lower their prices. The disparity in wholesale price between San Francisco and Los Angeles led to considerable bootlegging (reshipping) and prospects of legal problems. The move to equalize San Francisco and Los Angeles prices in July, 1965 was unavoidable. To protect profit margins the new equalized price structure was somewhat higher than that put into effect in San Francisco in January, 1965 (see Exhibit 7 and below).

| Product | Existing San Francisco Price | Existing Los Angeles Price | New San Francisco— Los Angeles Price |
|---|---|---|---|
| French beans............ | $2.07 | $2.52 | $2.31 |
| Broccoli................ | 2.36 | 2.90 | 2.42 |
| Cut corn............... | 1.78 | 2.01 | 1.92 |
| Peas................... | 1.98 | 2.12 | 1.98 |
| Leaf spinach........... | 1.68 | 1.98 | 1.74 |

A break-even analysis showed that the new prices in the two districts would have to result in a volume performance 7% better than the balance of the country, to maintain the existing contribution less deals margin:

**Break-Even Analysis (June 1965)**
**(rate per dozen)**

| | National Price | San Francisco— Los Angeles Current Price |
|---|---|---|
| Gross sales..................... | $2.52 | $2.30 |
| Net sales....................... | 2.06 | 1.90 |
| Contribution margin............... | 1.09 | 0.97 |
| Promotions..................... | 0.25 | 0.18 |
| Contributions (less promotions)...... | $0.84 | $0.79 |

Interim results showed that the price cut did improve the over-all contribution less deals margin. Whereas national regular vegetable sales (excluding San Francisco and Los Angeles) were down 8.7% between September, 1964 and September, 1965, San Francisco sales were up 7.6% for the same period and Los Angeles was up 0.2%.

## FISCAL 1967 MARKETING STRATEGY

The results of the pricing tests were sufficiently convincing that Birds-Eye management permitted the regular vegetables manager to move gradually toward a structure of lower everyday pricing for regular vegetables. Experience was to be gained by offering several alternative plans in three areas which varied in competitive conditions, price levels and price spreads. (See Exhibit 8 for a description of areas chosen.) The results of these tests would be used to specify the new established prices on regular vegetables. The plan called for one of the new low-price structures to be extended to the whole country by March, 1967, *IF* results were satisfactory.

The alternative plans had the following features in common:

(A)   Reduced price spreads between Birds-Eye and private label on most products—but maintaining some premium for Birds-Eye.

(B)   Elimination of the existing structure of individual item wholesale prices, in favor of grouped wholesale prices. It was felt that having three prices rather than 20 would: make it easier for the sales force to gain acceptance of the new prices; increase consumer acceptance and awareness through product grouping in the retail cabinet by price level; mask wide price spreads where they still existed; and encourage multiple consumer purchases of Birds-Eye products.

(C)   Psychological pricing which basically meant pricing within the same decile as private label. It was well known that it was more attractive for a higher priced product to have a 2 cent difference at 2/39 cents and 2/37 cents than at 2/41 cents and 2/39 cents.

(D)   Wholesale prices set to give the trade a maximum 25% margin. No product was to be priced at a level that didn't yield some contribution at the merchandising margin level unless the inventory position was long.

(E)   Trade deals were to be accommodated to each plan by the requirement that the net price, after the allowance was taken, be the same under both new and old price plans. It was hoped that this would reduce the volume increase needed to break even. The effect of such a requirement was difficult to appraise, but it was clear that fewer goods would move at deal prices, since there was less incentive for the dealer to maintain stocks that would last from one quarterly deal period to the next.

(F)   Price cuts would be directed at high volume items, which were particularly price sensitive.

The request to proceed with these three price tests, and ultimately a lower everyday price structure, was accompanied by a request for newspaper and radio advertising in support of the reductions. The request was based on: (1) the general lack of buyer awareness of specific prices, because of the multitude of prices that have to be considered, and the likelihood that the price decrease would not be perceived by private label buyers; (2) the need to justify the price decrease and assure the buyer that there would be no decrease in Birds-Eye quality; and (3) the need for additional leverage on the trade to ensure that the wholesale price reduction was reflected adequately in lower retail prices. Past experience indicated that obtaining the price reduction would be the most difficult aspect of the plan. Company management agreed on the extent of the latter problem, but felt that the execution of the plan was entirely a sales department responsibility, and that local advertising would have little useful effect.

## DESCRIPTION OF ALTERNATIVE PLANS BY MARKET

*1. Cleveland Market.*   Pricing was aimed at specific group retail prices, 1 cent per selling unit below the decile break, i.e., 2/39 cents,

2/49 cents, 29 cents. The buying allowance was reduced from an average 20 cents per dozen to 10 cents per dozen. The following sample of items shows the extent of the cuts:

|  |  | Current Price (Dozen) | New Price (Dozen) | Retail Price Objective |
|---|---|---|---|---|
| Group 1: | Peas | $2.12 | $1.80 | 2/39¢ |
|  | Cut beans | 2.52 | 1.80 | 2/39¢ |
|  | French beans | 2.52 | 1.80 | 2/39¢ |
|  | Cut corn | 2.01 | 1.80 | 2/39¢ |
|  | Leaf spinach | 1.98 | 1.80 | 2/39¢ |
| Group 2: | Broccoli | 2.90 | 2.30 | 2/49¢ |
|  | Italian beans | 2.67 | 2.30 | 2/49¢ |
|  | Wax beans | 2.45 | 2.30 | 2/49¢ |

2. *Washington Market.* Pricing was aimed at the above retail price objectives, but with 10 cents per dozen higher wholesale price across the board (see Exhibit 8 for the reason for the difference in approach to this market).

3. *Dallas Market.* Differed by applying the lower retail and wholesale prices to only 60% of the line, and sharply reducing deal rates to totally offset the amount of gross profit loss due to the price reductions.

4. *Metropolitan Boston Market.* Only two products, French beans and cut beans, were adjusted to the new Cleveland price structure. According to the manager, ". . . the purpose of this move was to test trade reactions to reductions, which if reflected at retail at a 25% margin, would have Birds-Eye and private label at approximately the same price. In short, we are walking cautiously in this market where high margins are taken on both private label and Birds-Eye rather than gambling on a full line approach which, if the trade reacted unfavorably, could cost us our vegetable franchise via de-authorization. The equally unattractive alternate result could be our pouring money down the drain if the trade did not reflect reductions at all."

### INFLUENCE OF NEW PRICES ON VOLUME— APPRAISAL OF TEST RESULTS

The first real need for an appraisal of the effectiveness of the price tests, developed from the annual demand forecast which was due at the end of 1966. In the past, forecasts had been strongly influenced by a seemingly inevitable 5% to 8% annual decline in sales. If a new national price structure were put into effect in April, 1967, this would no longer be true. But the product manager realized that the extent to which the historical decline in *volume* (not necessarily profits) was reduced or eliminated would depend on: (*a*) the price alternative chosen (whether Cleveland or Washington test levels, or something higher, and whether applicable to the full line or merely selected items as in Dallas); (*b*) the extent of reduction in deal rates; and (*c*) the projection of the volume increase in the test district to the national market.

The projection to national volume required the manager to recognize and balance: (1) the peculiarities of the test areas (see Exhibit 8); (2) the possibility that the sales force in the test district might have executed the new prices more aggressively than normal because of the test situation; (3) the possibility that retail prices might not stay at the lower level; and (4) the likelihood that 20% to 25% of the country would reject the new prices. Areas where low prices would find disfavor with the trade were usually those dominated by strong private label retailers, who used the high Birds-Eye prices as an umbrella over their relatively high private label prices and very high (35% to 40%) gross margins.

By November, the manager had in a sense decided on the "Cleveland" pricing approach since he had already recommended that the prices tested in this market be extended to Los Angeles and San Francisco as part of the national roll-out of new low prices. This would be a very significant extension since the Los Angeles district accounted for 14% of the sales of Birds-Eye regular vegetables and the San Francisco district accounted for another 5%. However, the price reduction recommendation was still in the discussion stage with company management, having been delayed by requests for more substantive estimates of the volume and profit improvement to be expected. The pressure for more accurate forecasting data in a specific market was added to the existing problem of the annual volume forecast.

By early November, 1966, Riley Smith had the following data to consider in the two forecasts he had to make:

(*A*) *Sales Results: Los Angeles and San Francisco.* The financial analyst reported, "There is evidence that we reversed a consistently declining volume trend immediately upon reducing prices. There is also some indication that the non-price reduced items tended to level off at the same time (see Exhibit 9—giving 12 month rolling total volume) in San Francisco, where reduced prices have been in effect for one and one-half years. There may be some evidence of another downward trend . . ." However, Riley Smith did not feel that the evidence was adequate to establish a definite price-volume relationship.

The volume performance of the Los Angeles–San Francisco market (up 2.9% between fiscal 1965 and 1966) compared to a decline of 7.6% in the rest of the country meant that the price cut had surpassed the 7% volume required to break even. However, a recommended price cut, to the "Cleveland" level, would require a further 6% volume increase in the coming year:

| | National Prices ex Los Angeles San Francisco | San Francisco— Los Angeles Price (as of June 1965) | Recommended "Cleveland" Level Prices |
|---|---|---|---|
| Gross sales | $2.52 | $2.30 | $2.15 |
| Net sales | 2.06 | 1.90 | 1.79 |
| Contribution margin | 1.09 | 0.97 | 0.86 |
| Promotions | 0.25 | 0.18 | 0.11 |
| Contributions less promotions | $0.84 | $0.79 | $0.75 |
| Required volume increase to break even at new price level | | +7% | +6% |

(B)   The analyst reported in the same memo, that, "In the *Buffalo-Syracuse* test, little change in the downward trend has been observed. The price reduced products continue to decline at rates equal to those for non-price-reduced products."

(C)   *Store Audit Results: Cleveland-Washington.*   A total of 40 stores had been audited in these two test areas between April and August of 1966. The overall results were very favorable. The Birds-Eye share of total frozen vegetables sales of 20 test items was up 34 percent and 26 percent in Cleveland and Washington, respectively. Most of the improvement was at the expense of private label regular vegetables. However, interpretation of the results was complicated by: (1) a sharp increase in the number of times Birds-Eye prices were featured in store advertising material; (2) Birds-Eye did not have a direct competitor in a specific vegetable item more than 40% of the time; and (3) in the remaining competitive situations Birds-Eye was out of stock or not stocked 35% of the time and prices were not reduced in a further 25% of the possible occasions. At the same time, factory shipments were up 29% in Cleveland and down 0.6% in Washington over the same period in the previous year. Without considering these two markets, the national shipments were down 8.8% from the year before.

(D)   *Boston Market.*   The only useful result was an object lesson in the difficulties of getting trade cooperation in the toughest markets. Even six months after the 72 cent per dozen reduction on the two vegetables went into effect, there was no effect to be seen on retail prices. Nor was there any promotion by the trade. District sales of Birds-Eye cut beans were up 3% in the six months, while sales of French beans were up 6%. These increases, however, only paralleled a 4% increase in district sales of all Birds-Eye regular vegetables.

## LONG RUN MARKETING STRATEGY

There was a keen awareness among Birds-Eye management that pricing could only achieve short run success in reversing the regular vegetable sales and profit declines. It was felt that true long run success would

# EXHIBIT 1

## Annual Sales Trends—Major Frozen Categories—(Retail Prices)

| | Vegetables* | | Fruits | | Fruit Juices | | Seafoods | | Meat | | Poultry | | Prepared Foods | |
|---|---|---|---|---|---|---|---|---|---|---|---|---|---|---|
| | MM$ | % Change | MM$ | % Change | MM$ | % Change | MM$ | % Change | MM$ | % Change | MM$ | % Change | MM$ | % Change |
| 1955 | 217 | | 53 | | 211 | | 106 | | 57 | | 371 | | 151 | |
| 1956 | 235 | +9 | 56 | +7 | 230 | +9 | 111 | +5 | 72 | +26 | 400 | +8 | 261 | +73 |
| 1957 | 257 | +9 | 60 | +7 | 255 | +11 | 114 | +3 | 83 | +15 | 439 | +10 | 339 | +30 |
| 1958 | 254 | −1 | 57 | −4 | 273 | +7 | 120 | +5 | 87 | +5 | 481 | +10 | 431 | +27 |
| 1959 | 280 | +10 | 56 | −3 | 317 | +16 | 126 | +5 | 84 | −4 | 499 | +4 | 475 | +10 |
| 1960 | 300 | +7 | 56 | +1 | 304 | −4 | 118 | −6 | 78 | −7 | 512 | +3 | 537 | +13 |
| 1961 | 311 | +4 | 58 | +3 | 317 | +4 | 119 | +1 | 75 | −3 | 512 | — | 565 | +5 |
| 1962 | 345 | +11 | 63 | +9 | 348 | +10 | 126 | +6 | 78 | +3 | 498 | −3 | 631 | +12 |
| 1963 | 364 | +6 | 68 | +7 | 330 | −5 | 132 | +5 | 78 | +1 | 522 | +5 | 654 | +4 |
| 1964 | 385 | +6 | 60 | −12 | 341 | +3 | 129 | −2 | 75 | −4 | 533 | +2 | 707 | +8 |

* Includes potatoes.
SOURCE: *Frozen Food Review.*

come from a significant differentiation of Birds-Eye products from private label and other competition. Such an achievement would permit improved margins, a return to consumer advertising and hopefully less dependence on commodity marketing techniques.

## EXHIBIT 2

### Consumer Survey—Attitudes toward Vegetables
### (excerpts only)

Vegetables are the dullest—most "difficult" type of food to make more appetizing, according to almost half the women interviewed.

| | % Selecting as Most Dull Food 1,034 = 100% | % Selecting as Most Difficult to Make More Appetizing 1,034 = 100% |
|---|---|---|
| Vegetables | 42 | 53 |
| Meat | 5 | 9 |
| Salad | 7 | 8 |
| Bread/rolls | 21 | 3 |
| Dessert | 7 | 3 |
| None | 16 | 24 |
| All | 1 | — |
| No answer | 1 | — |
| | 100 | 100 |

Source: USDA Survey.

College educated women, more than any other group, are likely to regard vegetables as the type of food hardest to make appetizing.

The most frequently cited reasons for selecting vegetables as a difficult type of food include . . .

Narrow range of vegetable recipes ............................ 39%
  ("Only a few ways to fix . . .")
Personal and/or family disliking of vegetables ................. 21%
Tendency to "stick to only a few kinds of vegetables" .......... 19%

Additional evidence of women's frustration with vegetables is the large majority of women agreeing with these two statements:

"It's hard to think up new ways of serving vegetables." (79% agree)
*and*
"I often wish there were some ways to make vegetables more interesting." (81% agree)

### Difficulty in Getting Children to Eat Vegetables

Almost three-fifths of the mothers in the sample claimed to have difficulty in getting their children to eat vegetables. Of these mothers, about half said they prepare vegetables in special ways, the most popular preparations being:

**EXHIBIT 2 (Continued)**

cream sauce (46% of responses), cheese sauce (16%), butter (12%), casseroles (18%), sauces in general (9%) and several vegetables together (7%).

*Receptiveness to a New Product Designed to Make Vegetables More Appetizing*

Women were asked which type of new product they would prefer, one designed to make vegetables more appetizing, another to make meat more appetizing, and the other to make desserts more appetizing. The resulting vote on this question gave a slight edge to the meat product over the one for vegetables.

| *New Product For* | % |
|---|---|
| Meat | 42 |
| Vegetables | 39 |
| Desserts | 15 |
| None | 3 |
| All | 1 |

Only half of the women who originally said vegetables were "most difficult to make appetizing" indicated a preference for the new vegetable product. Most of the "defectors" decided that a meat product would be more important to them. Basically, the appeal for the meat product was attributable to the perceived importance of meat, relative to other foods, in the overall success of a meal.

The most frequently noted reason for preferring the vegetable product was its possible use as a means of inducing family members (particularly children) to eat more vegetables. The other major reasons centered on the women's own frustrations in their search for new ways of preparing vegetables.

Women who preferred the vegetable product tended to be somewhat better educated and of higher income than the women who preferred the meat product.

**EXHIBIT 3**

**Results of 1956 Menu Study**

**(based on one week's consumption by 4,000 families)**

| Vegetable | Form | Income Class | | |
|---|---|---|---|---|
| | | $7,000+ | $4,000 to $6,999 | Under $4,000 |
| 1. Green beans......... | Fresh | 700 | 791 | 1,327 |
| | Frozen (% of total) | 221 (15%) | 157 (10.2%) | 72 (3.8%) |
| | Canned | 558 | 593 | 520 |
| | | 1,479 | 1,541 | 1,919 |
| 2. Corn......... | Fresh | 231 | 313 | 500 |
| | Frozen (% of total) | 139 (11%) | 126 (9.5%) | 77 (5.9%) |
| | Canned | 806 | 881 | 732 |
| | | 1,176 | 1,320 | 1,309 |
| 3. Peas......... | Fresh | 187 | 268 | 605 |
| | Frozen | 503 (31%) | 365 (21.8%) | 287 (15.9%) |
| | Canned | 932 | 1,044 | 910 |
| | | 1,622 | 1,677 | 1,802 |

Number of families/income class.........

$7,000+.................. 11  million

$4,000 to 6,999.......... 22.6 million

Under $4,000............. 17.6 million

NOTE: All figures are expressed in servings per 1000 people.

**EXHIBIT 4**

**Share of Market Trends—By Brand**

**(percent)**

| | FY 1956 | FY 1957 | FY 1958 | FY 1961 | FY 1962 | FY 1963 | FY 1964 | FY 1965 | FY 1966 | Calendar 1966 | | | |
| --- | --- | --- | --- | --- | --- | --- | --- | --- | --- | --- | --- | --- | --- |
| | | | | | | | | | | Feb.– Mar. | April– May | June– July | Aug.– Sept. |
| Birds-Eye............ | 19.6 | 18.9 | 16.8 | 13.3 | 13.2 | 12.5 | 11.1 | 10.6 | 9.2 | 12.1 | 11.5 | 12.1 | 12.2 (AVG) |
| Four largest competitive brands............ | 39.4 | 38.1 | 32.2 | 17.7 | 16.8 | 16.5 | 16.9 | 18.4 | 18.8 | | | | 12.1 |
| Private, controlled house labels and insignificant regional labels............ | 41 | 43 | 53 | 69 | 70 | 71 | 72 | 71 | 73 | | | | (AVG) 75.7 |

SOURCES: Birds-Eye Market Research Department; consumer panel data until February 1966 when store audit data substituted.

## EXHIBIT 5

### Distribution Analysis
### (based on % of store's stocking)

|  | Chopped Spinach | Green Beans (French) | Green Peas |
|---|---|---|---|
| National (Metropolitan)............ | 41 | 50 | 67 |
| New York District................. | 74 | 65 | 76 |
| Boston District................... | 31 | 30 | 42 |
| Youngstown District............... | 77 | 77 | 81 |
| Philadelphia District.............. | 43 | 65 | 80 |
| Detroit District................... | 74 | 65 | 76 |
| Atlanta District................... | 35 | 48 | 61 |
| Chicago District.................. | 31 | 41 | 82 |
| St. Louis District................. | 31 | 41 | 82 |
| Dallas District.................... | 15 | 26 | 42 |
| Los Angeles District.............. | 31 | 53 | 75 |
| San Francisco District............. | 20 | 26 | 42 |

SOURCE: Birds-Eye Market Research Department.

## EXHIBIT 6

### Regular Vegetables, Family Characteristics, April 1965–March 1966

|  | % of Total U.S. Families | Total Households Buying | | % of Total Pound Volume | |
|---|---|---|---|---|---|
|  |  | Total | Birds-Eye | Total | Birds-Eye |
| *Housewife Employment* |  |  |  |  |  |
| Employed................ | 35 | 35 | 35 | 34 | 33 |
| Unemployed............. | 65 | 65 | 64 | 66 | 67 |
| *Occupation* |  |  |  |  |  |
| Blue Collar.............. | 42 | 35 | 44 | 34 | 35 |
| White Collar............. | 33 | 43 | 28 | 50 | 48 |
| Farmer, Unclassified...... | 25 | 22 | 28 | 16 | 17 |
| *Age of Housewife* |  |  |  |  |  |
| Under 35................ | 29 | 28 | 26 | 30 | 26 |
| 35–54................... | 42 | 42 | 43 | 46 | 46 |
| 55 & over............... | 29 | 30 | 31 | 24 | 28 |
| *Household Size* |  |  |  |  |  |
| 1 or 2................... | 41 | 36 | 40 | 31 | 41 |
| 3....................... | 19 | 17 | 14 | 21 | 19 |
| 4 or more............... | 40 | 47 | 46 | 49 | 40 |
| *Income* |  |  |  |  |  |
| $8,000 or over........... | 23 | 39 | 50 | 44 | 50 |
| $4,000–$7,999........... | 44 | 39 | 32 | 39 | 37 |
| Under $4,000........... | 33 | 22 | 18 | 17 | 13 |
| *City Size* |  |  |  |  |  |
| Urban over 500 M........ | 18 | 20 | 25 | 26 | 27 |
| Urban 50M–500M........ | 15 | 17 | 16 | 16 | 14 |
| Suburban over 500M...... | 15 | 19 | 22 | 22 | 26 |
| Suburban 50M–500M...... | 12 | 15 | 16 | 14 | 18 |
| Under 50M.............. | 40 | 29 | 21 | 22 | 15 |

SOURCE: Birds-Eye Market Research Department.

## EXHIBIT 7

### Price and Deal Schedule—January 1965, San Francisco District

| Item* | 1964 Retail Prices (per 10 Ounce Package) | | Wholesale Prices (Per Dozen) | | | | Promotional Offer‡ | |
| | Birds-Eye | Private Label | Birds-Eye† (Dec. '64) | Birds-Eye (Jan. '65) | National Competitor | Private Label | Birds-Eye Deals and Allowances (Effective Jan. '65) | Net Variance Birds-Eye versus Private Label |
|---|---|---|---|---|---|---|---|---|
| French beans | 29.0¢ | 20–21.5¢ | $2.52 | $2.07 | $2.15 | $1.82 | $.18 | $(.08) |
| Cut corn | 23 | 17–19.5 | 2.01 | 1.78 | 1.79 | 1.48 | .30 | — |
| Peas | 21.5 | 18.5–20 | 2.12 | 1.98 | 1.99 | 1.76 | .23 | .01 |
| Chopped spinach | 23 | 14–15 | 1.98 | 1.59 | 1.56 | 1.24 | .15 | (.20) |
| Wax beans | — | — | 2.45 | 2.45 | 2.40 | 2.01 | — | — |

* This is a partial list only.
† This was the national price.
‡ Offered once per quarter.

## EXHIBIT 8

### Manager's Memo on Areas Selected for Price Tests Nov. 2, 1965

"The markets selected for expansion of low pricing should be representative of probable extremes in trade reaction or in extremes in facility of accomplishing objectives.

1. Washington is judged as a relatively easy market to accomplish the stated objectives because trade margins on Birds-Eye are low, and the current spreads with Private Label high. Therefore, it is judged the trade, in general, will not resent the low price approach.

2. Cleveland, because of high margins on Private Label and Birds-Eye, will be a tougher market to crack, since the accomplishment of our retail price objectives will, in many instances, leave the trade the alternates of having Birds-Eye and Private Label at the same price or reducing the margins on Private Label to maintain a price differential.

3. The metropolitan Boston area, where Regular Vegetables have been declining at a faster pace than national, is also a market where the trade takes high margins, particularly on Private Label. Because of the importance of the market (and the risk involved with reducing the complete line), it is judged that extreme reductions on two products may answer the question of trade reaction as well as pinpointing volume increases we could expect in major areas with pricing close to Private Label.

4. The Dallas District contains market extremes within the district. The Fort Worth trade is accustomed to high margins, and Birds-Eye has competition from two "national" competitors which are priced considerably under Birds-Eye. The solution to this problem is an additional reason for price action. Dallas is a market where the trade works on close margins on Birds-Eye, and it could be expected that reductions in wholesale prices will be reflected to a lower level than the 27% margin objective while reducing spreads with Private Label."

## EXHIBIT 9

### San Francisco–Los Angeles Pricing

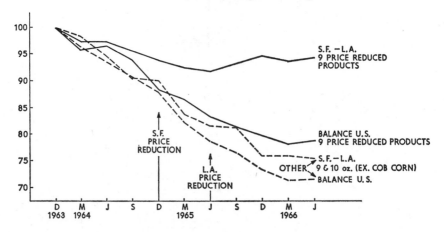

## Appendix A: The Economics of Frozen Foods at the Retail Level

Using the concept of direct product profit or DPP (equal to gross profit less direct product costs of warehousing, delivery to stores, shelving and frozen food space) McKinsey found frozen food departments to be consistently more profitable than other departments. At the same time they found considerable ignorance and confusion regarding the true profitability of frozen foods.

The favorable profit picture was largely due to: (1) a high ratio of sales unit of space, from 1.5 to 3 times that of groceries, coupled with (2) high gross margins to cover higher handling and space costs; while overall handling costs were not as high as was generally believed. As a consequence the leverage on profits from volume changes were found to be very high. That is, when volume was sufficient to cover space costs each additional unit of volume contributed importantly to profits.

Thus, in a typical store it was found:

|  | (Percent) | |
| --- | --- | --- |
|  | Retail Sales | D.P.P. |
| Grocery...................... | 61 | 57 |
| Meat........................ | 22 | 17 |
| Produce..................... | 10 | 12 |
| Total frozen foods............. | 7 | 14 |
|  | 100 | 100 |

SOURCE: Abstracts of a study by McKinsey and Co., published in March 1964.

## Implications for Manufacturers of Specific Items

1. Frozen food profits were found to be heavily concentrated in the fast moving items, i.e., top 10% of items accounted for the following percentages of:

|  | (Percent) | |
| --- | --- | --- |
|  | Dry Groceries | Frozen Foods |
| Sales......................... | 42 | 48 |
| Gross profits.................. | 35 | 48 |
| Direct prod. profits (before space costs)...... | 29 | 48 |

SOURCE: Abstracts of a study by McKinsey and Co., published in March 1964.

2. Despite wide variations in movement of various items (leading to absorption of gross profit by direct product costs that varied from 24%

to 120%) there was no relationship between movement and gross margin for frozen foods:

| Items | Percentage of Total Retail Sales | Average Frozen Food Gross Margin | Average Dry Grocery Gross Margin |
|---|---|---|---|
| Top 20%..................... | 62 | 28.1% | 16.0% |
| Next 20%.................... | 19 | 28.4 | 20.9 |
| Next 20%.................... | 11 | 28.0 | 22.1 |
| Next 20%.................... | 6 | 29.5 | 23.9 |
| Bottom 20%................. | 2 | 27.4 | 31.8 |
|  | 100 | 28.3% | 18.2% |

3.   There was nothing very consistent—or factual—about the basis on which most retailers decided on the number of items to stock. For example, three chains with 50 to 80 stores, stocked 392, 379 and 275 items of comparable product categories.

4.   The complexity of the item selection problem is compounded by: (1) the large numbers of sizes, brands and types available in each frozen food category (according to the Nielsen Researcher, Vol. 3, 1964, there were 639 sizes, brands and types of vegetables available) and (2) new product activity. One distributor estimated he was offered roughly 200 new items each year.

5.   The prevailing price structure of most groceries didn't encourage the use of significant price cuts. Even substantial gains in volume would not offset the revenue loss due to small price cuts. However, the high margins for frozen foods meant a much higher percentage of sales income could be profitably spent on features, displays, etc. In many stores this opportunity was not being put to use to build volume.

6.   Evidence showed that it was often profitable to use promotional efforts to shift volume from dry groceries, meat or produce to frozen foods, despite many opinions to the contrary.

7.   Much of the variation in frozen food sales between stores, other than related to the size of the operation, was accounted for by the level of income in the trading area."

# Meriden Company: Marketing Strategy

Paul Adams, president of the Meriden Company, was interested in creativity as applied to marketing strategy. It had long been his belief that marketing managers were too prone to copy competitive strategies or, when working with an established strategy, loathe to change it. Despite their enthusiastic support of creative approaches most marketing managers, in the opinion of Mr. Adams, were operationally cautious. They talked new approaches but operated traditionally. Mr. Adams was convinced that the record in his company followed that pattern.

Meriden manufactured and marketed a line of measuring instruments for the geophysical trade. Customers included government research laboratories, petroleum companies, universities, and mining companies. Sales had grown slowly but steadily since the firm's founding in 1962. By 1975 sales exceeded $30 million, and Meriden had about a 25% share of its markets. During the past three years, however, the company had lost six points of market share despite the introduction of two major new instruments. Even with apparent product superiority Meriden was not able to offset the reduced price and two-year guarantee policies introduced by the competitors in 1973. Mr. Adams felt that his company could not afford to surrender any of its margins, particularly when the product superiority was so apparent.

Sales were made through a direct sales force of 22 men operating out of five district offices. Small amounts were spent for trade advertising, trade shows, and technical literature; the bulk of the marketing expenses was devoted to the field sales force with costs averaging about $30,000 per man.

In an effort to stir the thinking of his marketing group, Mr. Adams commissioned a friend of his who was a faculty member of a nearby university to prepare a number of strategy examples pulled from business, the military, and other relevant sources. The consultant's report appears below.

1. From these many examples how would you classify the alternative concepts?
2. Which of the various strategy concepts should Mr. Adams consider for application at Meriden?

### U.S. Time Company (Timex)

The post World War II strategy of Timex was to create and maintain a leading market position in one clearly defined user segment—people who wanted stylish watches at very low cost. Such buyers were tired of having a Swiss watch that had to be cleaned and adjusted every three or so years for ±$15.

At the same time Timex identified an underutilized retailing outlet—retail drug stores—resulting in a coordinated product/market niche. This niche was left untouched by other watch companies. The beauty of the strategy lay in its consumable nature. For the low price, people apparently were willing to forego longevity, which ensured substantial replacement sales. This fast replacement tendency was encouraged through an emphasis upon style and design. As new markets emerged, such as electronic timepieces, Timex has been able to garner its share, still in the low-price range, thus increasing its market depth while maintaining its position within its segment.

### Stop-ette Spray Deodorant

Jules Montenier, Inc., in 1948 decided to introduce its innovative squeeze bottle spray deodorant, Stop-ette, to a public that knew nothing of the company or the product. The strategy was to ride in on the reputation of several prestigious women's specialty and department stores, banking on the theory that women would endorse whatever those stores considered good enough to carry. The initial price and markup were higher than competition.

Once established in this limited market, the company placed Stop-ette in beauty shops, further confirming the product's credibility. Having established distribution and a reputation, Stop-ette was moved finally into mass merchandising outlets and national brand advertising was emphasized.

### Sears, Roebuck and Company

During the postwar period, Sears developed a highly successful strategy based on the primary consideration that its customers did not belong to any clearly definable group. Its segmentation approach was *not* to segment the market; the average American, wherever he lived, was a Sears target. The success of the Sears retailing operation derived mainly from its ability to provide easy access to its stores. Sears moved with the suburban trend—away from downtown locations—thus anticipating the onrush of shopping centers. Sales were effectively supplemented by catalog retailing, thus extending the Sears arm into virtually every home in America.

### Marks & Spencer

In Britain during a period characterized by "stagflation," exactly as in the United States in 1975, Marks & Spencer experienced booming sales and profits. The company began as a conventional variety store chain, but its success was obtained through a careful redefinition of its goals and, consequently, its marketing strategy.

First, it decided to concentrate on wearing apparel for the working and lower middle classes at prices they could afford but with upper-class quality—made possible by mass production procedures and recently developed new textile fibers. Second, M&S deliberately restricted its new store openings, electing instead to increase throughout in existing stores. By continually upgrading its merchandising, display, and sales per customer, M&S was able to maintain a per-store sales level of about $4 million a year on only 20,000 square feet of selling space.

### Waltham Watch Company

In 1930 Waltham made a very decent watch for one dollar. To increase sales and develop a quality image, the company in 1938 introduced a $75 watch comparable to the most expensive watch on the market. Although sales of its top line were minimal, management's real objective was to increase buyer confidence in the dollar watch. If Waltham made a fine quality watch, its dollar watch must be good.

On the other hand, in 1946 the Ford Motor Company aggressively pushed its newest model, the Mercury. The same body shell was used as for the prestigious Lincoln. Mercury's sales boomed—at one point it was among the first three in sales of American cars. But the Lincoln lost position rapidly and had to be withdrawn from production. Several years later the Lincoln was redesigned and reintroduced as the Continental.

### Kroehler Manufacturing Company

As the nation's largest furniture manufacturer, Kroehler has chosen to concentrate on a fairly broad user segment—low to upper-middle class families. In line with this overall target the company provides a rugged, moderately priced line with emphasis on conventional styling and combination groups of furniture. Kroehler uses heavy magazine advertising and sells through an extensive dealer network. From its established base the company could well provide interior decorating services on a consulting basis or as part of its more expensive line package. This would serve as a promotional tool, as well as provide greater market depth.

### Levitz

On the assumption that furniture can be an "impulse" item—something never considered by the industry before—Levitz opened huge warehouse/showrooms where furniture in a great array, immediately available, was displayed in "home" settings. Display stressed packages of products, not just single units. Pricing was conventional though the image of large savings was evident in the physical layout and "carry it yourself" alternative.

### Grantree

Grantree rents furniture to young homeowners and apartment dwellers. The company capitalizes on the fact that buying furniture on time costs between $35–$50 a month for the average customer, and the furniture is worn out by the time it's paid off. What Grantree offers is, in effect, perennially new furniture for the same price—$35–$50 per month. The renter has the option of exchanging the furniture at any time for a nominal fee.

Grantree also extends its market by selling this same used furniture at almost its original buying cost, after getting maximum mileage from the leases. If the tenant moves, he turns in his now used furniture and get a replacement at the next location. Grantree's "system" includes bulk buying, a company-owned financial institution, and second-hand outlets.

### Raychem

A Fabian strategy is an indirect approach consisting primarily of evasion. In ancient times Thebes avoided contact with Spartan armies while developing a powerful spearhead composed of picked professionals. This model force, though inferior to the Spartan army in actual number, soundly defeated its enemy.

A modern business example of this type of strategy is Raychem, a West Coast firm. The company developed a process of irradiating a proprietary plastic with "memory"—that is, under a broad range of temperature and pressure extremes the plastic returns to its original shape. It is used in numerous applications such as airtight wrapping, solderless wire connections and the like.

During its first three years Raychem selected out-of-the-way markets and applications with limited potential—deliberately choosing small, secondary segments. When the company had acquired the skills and wherewithall to prove its basic discipline, it then rapidly expanded into its major markets.

## Steuben Glass

This ultraexclusive art glass manufacturer started in the 1930's as a national manufacturer and distributor of ordinary glassware, a unit of Owens-Corning. As such the company was not profitable, and a new president was brought in to turn Steuben around. The line was redesigned by artisans, and the number of retail outlets slashed to ten and then finally to only one in New York City. Advertising was limited to such high-class magazines as *The New Yorker* and *Vogue*. Prices started about $50 and ranged to many thousands of dollars.

From a company with no distinctive difference Steuben had become one of the world's most highly acclaimed producers of one-of-a-kind glass sculptures and objets d'art. The strategy was purely one of prestige appeal. If you could afford Steuben, you could afford to fly from wherever you were to New York to get it.

## Prender N.V.

This Dutch company started 50 years ago and built a strong brand reputation during the post World War II days in the Benelux countries for its line of wire products for consumers—hangers, kitchen gadgets, strainers, baskets, stepladders, etc. By 1973 Prender offered 1,400 different items, tried to enter the large French and German markets, and was losing money, reputation, and market share in Belgium, Holland, and Luxembourg. The base consumers had a high awareness of the name but viewed the firm as "old-fashioned."

The company decided to regroup and reorient itself. First, it reduced its catalog from 1,400 to 400 items in one year. Then, it withdrew from France and Germany (where it was essentially unknown) and concentrated fully on its Benelux markets. Finally, as part of its product positioning strategy Prender elected to concentrate only on those items with comparatively high value added—items which required expensive manufacturing equipment not available to the many small "garage" competitors. Through retrenchment and product-line consolidation the company has achieved once again a dominant position in its core markets.

## Macleans Toothpaste

Faced with a formidable array of well-established toothpaste competitors—all positioned approximately to emphasize decay prevention—Macleans dug into their market research and discovered two things which formed the basis for introduction: (1) the test sample who liked Macleans liked it very much; and (2) there was a significant number, though much less than 50%, of people who were more concerned about sex-appeal than cavity prevention.

Macleans devised a strategy consisting of positioning the product through test marketing, promotional campaigns, and concurrent evaluation to appeal to these people. The toothpaste successfully carved out for itself a hitherto hidden market segment and captured fourth place behind Crest, Gleem, and Colgate.

## IBM—Copiers

Xerox is to the copier industry what IBM is to computers. In an effort to gain a foothold in what is foreseen as a huge growth market, IBM decided to introduce its own copiers. In order to save time, only a single model was launched initially. The machine was slower than Xerox's for copies exceeding ten (though faster under ten) and priced higher than the comparable Xerox models. It used roll paper rather than single sheets and had less flexibility than Xerox.

Since IBM was already well entrenched in the office equipment business with its typewriters (electric and programmed) and a well-respected line of dictating equipment, the copier was positioned as part of a system —"word processing." It was advertised as "the answer to your unduly high duplicating costs," i.e., speed encourages proliferation of copies and therefore costs.

## Pillsbury—Funny Face

Until Funny Face (a drink mix for kids) Pillsbury was mostly involved in flour and baking. The introduction of Funny Face entailed an entirely new approach, both to the market and to top management.

As to the market Pillsbury began with the discovery that its Sweet 10, an artificial sweetener, was being used by some mothers instead of sugar to sweeten Kool-Aid, a competitor's product. Pillsbury's thinking progressed through various stages until it decided to market its own drink mix with the premeasured sweetener already included. The early strategy sessions, however, were nearsightedly focused on the same issue as that of the competition—selling a drink mix to mothers for their children.

Finally, Pillsbury broke through the well-entrenched position of Kool-Aid by deciding to merchandise—not a drink mix—but *fun*. All marketing efforts were then brought into line with this concept; in particular, the strategy would be aimed at selling to kids, not their mothers. Instead of practical pictures of pitchers on the envelope Pillsbury struck on the plan (using their own kids as idea-men) of putting funny-face oranges, apples, etc., on the packages. In line with the basic concept the Pillsbury name was de-emphasized, and Sweet 10 as an ingredient was also played down. Both of these decisions involved risks and moved substantially away from the original plan, which was to build business for the sweetener—in other words, a manufacturing, product-oriented approach. But Funny Face came through and provided a new base for launching other nonflour products.

As a result of its experience with Funny Face, Pillsbury freed its new products people from individual division relationships, forming an entirely new group directly responsible to the president. Thus, their vision is not limited to the particular processes or products of any one division but is free to move in any direction.

### Miller High Life

Originally positioned as the "champagne of bottled beer," Miller attracted primarily light beer drinkers, as well as drinkers of light beer. When it appeared that this market segment was perhaps unnecessarily limited, Miller decided to reposition the product so as to appeal to a wider range of people including the more serious beer drinkers—without losing its existing base of consumers. The company's constraint was "to take the beer out of the champagne bucket but not to put it into the bathtub."

The strategy, developed through exploratory research, was to change the promotionals to reflect quality and leisurely enjoyment; "If you've got the time, we've got the beer." In this way repositioning the product was accomplished without a change in the product, and sales were increased by effective use of promotional techniques.

### Courtship

There is an infinite variety of strategies designed to gain the exclusive favors of a woman—or a man—ranging from blunt solicitation through blind blundering to elaborate, time-phased plans. The degree of success usually is a function of a single-minded, clearly defined goal with all resources brought to bear on the matter at hand. The "marketing mix" is limited only by the imagination of the wooer and can include such diverse things as poetry, Jade East, Cabernet Sauvignon, correspondence, flowers, singing telegrams, yachts, and the ever-popular etchings.

The first phase is usually to secure the attention of the wooee, and surprise is often a successful tactic. Once a base of operations is securely established, the next phase involves extending the influence of the wooer, usually based on careful market research combined with cautious—or bold (depending on the entrepreneurial character of the wooer)—reconnaissance. Careful timing is crucial during this phase, but if successful the next phase, negotiating for a joint venture, may be initiated. (At any time the wooer must be prepared to drop back and resecure weakened defenses should competition come into the field. Thus, the plan must be flexible, continually adapting to changing conditions in the environment.)

It is often effective to utilize a judo technique against a competitor, overpowering him by apparently yielding to his attack. Once the opponent is successfully overcome and the wooee is thoroughly convinced of her/his essential need for the wooer, the final phase may be implemented, securing the franchise.

### Specialty Brands

Specialty Brands had two superior specialty products, "Spice Islands" and "Marie's Dressing." When the chance to buy "Vita Crunch" arose, the company grabbed it. Amidst a swarming mass of cereal producers, all big guns, the company had presumably discovered a small, unattended niche. It saw a specialized market for a granola-type cereal product, too insignificant for the big guys to bother with. The company believed it could take and defend a commanding position with this specialty. And, in fact, Vita Crunch soon became the No. 1 brand of granola.

However, as it turned out, the health food idea was a good one; consequently, a host of very large competitors moved in with advertising budgets that swamped Specialty Brands, i.e., Quaker, General Mills, General Foods. The company had not been able to foresee the tremendous appeal of the product category and was faced with the difficult problem of deciding what strategy to use now.

### Zenith

Zenith's strategy to double market share during the 1960's was to limit its product to a small line of radios and TV sets for household use. Its market segmentation strategy was to capture and expand one specific user group, thus avoiding direct confrontation with the competition who were fragmenting their markets through line proliferation. Specializing in high-quality, relatively high-priced products, the company projected a superior quality image and obtained dealer loyalty through high-margin sales. It spent considerable money on product design and an advertising campaign that stressed the "quality" of Zenith because it was "still made by hand" with vacuum tubes, rather than the "new-fangled" semiconductors.

## Maxwell House Coffee

Maxwell House has made effective use of the concept of brand proliferation, in which several entries compete against each other. Decaffeinated Sanka and Brim—both regular and instant—overlap and extend the company's coverage of this segment. Maxwell House, regular and instant, competes with Yuban, regular and instant, with a slight differentiation in quality, implied by price differences. With Maxim the company had its foot in the freeze-dried segment.

The strategy is to play down the Maxwell House name on all brands except one, thus encouraging consumers to try "different" brands. Maxwell House implements its marketing through emphasis on deals and promotions directed at the retail trade, with proportionately less aimed directly at the consumer. Consumer advertising is, nonetheless, heavy.

## Versatec

Between 1964 and 1970 Varian and Gould, both high technology firms, tried to build significant sales in electrostatic printers. These machines were nonimpact printers that could print electronically about 10,000 characters per second, a speed that was in keeping with the speed of large computers. The firms had limited success though they managed to push the technology to its maximum.

In 1969 Versatec was formed and by 1974 was the leader in a now rapidly growing industry. Instead of concentrating on maximum speed (which is costly), Versatec designed a machine that did 1,000 characters per second (still far ahead of alternative output devices), made all parts modular and interchangeable so that printers and plotters were assembled from the same standard parts, selected specifically the small computer, end user, and OEM research markets, set the price (at one-half) and the competitive level (with a gross margin of 50%), sold through exclusive representatives (rather than company salesmen), and restricted its communication to trade shows, technical literature, and customer-slanted brochures.

## Litton Company

During the early 1960's Litton's microwave tube divisions, along with such competitors as Raytheon, Varian, and G.E., tried with little success to build strong positions in the commercial markets. Litton concentrated on microwave ovens for commercial cooking institutions. It grew modestly until it finally purchased Stauffers in Cleveland, to whom it turned over the task of marketing the new line of ovens. Sales have been successful—divisional sales by 1974 were well over $100 million.

### DuPont-Nylon

Before sales curves for nylon hosiery had flattened appreciably, Du-Pont began to take action to ward off old age in the product life-cycle. Its strategy took the following phased-in steps. First, through advertising it reinforced the social necessity of wearing hose. Next, a full range of colors and textures was introduced for the first time to encourage more varied usage. Third, still within the hosiery market the company added new users by appealing to the teenage group. And, finally, new products were generated—using the same basic material—to open up completely new markets such as rugs, tires, and bearings.

### Small TV

In the mid-1960's, General Electric committed itself to a significant investment in plant and equipment to produce a small portable color television set called Porta Color. The firm decided to follow its successful small set black and white strategy. Early sales were encouraging.

Most competitors were committed already to large picture sets and had two choices with respect to GE—ignore them or introduce small sets of their own.

An effective reaction from some was to subcontract with Far Eastern suppliers for small sets which could be used defensively in selected markets.

### Soft-Drink Manufacturers: Pepsi-Cola and Coca-Cola

The companies are, of course, soft-drink manufacturers. However, they define their business as distribution.

The consumer market has two major parts; on-site sales and take-home sales. Pepsi launched its attack on Coca-Cola by concentrating on only one—the take-home segment. Using a heavy promotional campaign, Pepsi created a new image for itself, aimed at increasing the usage within a selected group of retailers. Furthermore, Pepsi broke away from the standard 6½-ounce bottle and offered its product in a variety of sizes, based on the discovery that hard-core soft drink addicts will buy large sizes as frequently as smaller bottles. Thus, Pepsi increased the usage by increasing the volume consumed of its products.

Coca-Cola responded but, nonetheless, found it difficult to retaliate because its ads were geared to the total market and its bottlers had varying attitudes about changing their traditional approaches.

### GM and Carborundum

In the 1920's, General Motors developed tetraethyl lead to cure knocking in automobile engines. Since this was a chemical product rather than a mechanical one, GM realized the need to find a suitable means of marketing it, other than directly through its own system. One option would have been to buy a fair-sized oil company to distribute tetraethyl lead through its gas stations. But GM's decision was to team up with Standard Oil of New Jersey in a joint venture—Ethyl Corporation. Thus, with minimal capital investment, GM was able to market successfully its product while retaining its own essential unity.

In another situation, Carborundum had developed technical skills with a polymer product which promised high growth. Nevertheless, the company realized its production capabilities and capital resources were insufficient to carry the product through to its full potential. Its strategy was to form a joint venture with several Japanese firms that had the necessary resources. The result was twofold; the market potential for the product was realized, and additional markets were opened up in Japan.

**American Airlines**

Competitive variables within the airline industry are rates, routes, equipment, schedules, service, advertising, and ancillary services. There has been a continuous scramble throughout their history between competing airlines for the safest, fastest, quietest equipment available. As technology evolved, acquiring a competitive fleet was for a time nearly the primary concern for all airlines. American Airlines consistently managed to keep ahead of the advances and was able to pioneer in the other areas of importance to the customer. For example, it was an industry leader in the "fly now—pay later" concept of flying. Also, a primary thrust of its strategy was to focus heavy advertising and promotional campaigns on easing the customer's fear of flying and promoting special services such as VIP lounges, gourmet meals, coach flights, and special coach services.

**Airlines: The Dilemma**

*Fly now—pay later! Fly me I'm Gloria! Catch the Spirit! Friendship Service. Delta is ready when you are! We move our tail for you! Mother Grinning Bird PSA gives you a lift! Japan Air Lines Executive Service. Fly the friendly skies of United.* And now—the booze war. Airlines are apparently reduced to desperate squabbling over customers, with reactionary adjustments to each others' thrusts.

The most recent scrimmage focuses on the question of free drinks. Delta started it all, with its offer of steak and complimentary champagne on coach flights. National and Eastern have been forced to follow suit, fighting all the way, in moves that will ultimately cost them millions. It would seem that the airlines are desperately in need of constructive market strategies that will more clearly differentiate them from one another.

## Texas Instruments

Transistors were once prohibitively expensive to make and thus enjoyed only a very limited market. A development in mass production techniques effectively lowered the unit price, but wider markets were still to be identified. Texas Instruments chose to approach the portable radio market. This entailed finding a way to get through, or around, the vacuum tube producers, who enjoyed a close relationship with radio manufacturers. TI elected to sneak around by the way of the independent radio manufacturers. These, however, lacked the capital, desire, and expertise to produce such small radios, so TI took on the burden of circuit design and otherwise supported the independents, thus building a profitable mass market.

## Pioneer Tape Company

Pioneer originally was in the business of making and marketing tape recordings, featuring the less well-known, new artists, to appeal to the youth market. Its distribution outlets were conventional, its pricing standard, and its promotion achieved through plan exposure on radio stations. Problems arose when Pioneer tried to extend its product offerings into the broader market and entertainment. The company bought a TV station, a radio station, and a small publishing house but did not have the distribution, management, pricing, or communications expertise to market successfully these activities. As a result, the company took enormous losses—close to $10 million on sales of $30 million in 1973. It disposed of its acquisitions and by 1974 was again making profits on its tapes.

## Wineries

Every winery must go through approximately the same process to produce wine. Product positioning ranges from concentration on the affluent sector (the wine connoisseurs) to providing moderate to low-priced average wines for mass consumption.

Oakville, a small winery, concentrates its efforts in producing a few premium wines for limited distribution. Its marketing strategy includes heavy investment in personalized public relations through "private" tastings at the beautiful family estate, combined with old-world hospitality in the form of elegant lawn banquets. The convivial atmosphere leads easily into liberal purchases. The company does not have heavy investment in vineyards; rather its wine is made primarily from grapes purchased from other vintners. Its prices are comparable to others in its class.

Gallo, on the other hand, produces huge quantities of blended wines. The taste and quality are consistent, the prices moderate, great emphasis is placed upon dominating the retail shelves, and there is a steady stream of new products, labels, bottle sizes, point-of-sales promotions, and national advertising.

### Weight-Watchers

Market strategy zeroes in on the extremely widespread concern for weight control. The firm has focused on the nonfad segment of the market, beginning with a carefully controlled program for balanced nutrition and weight control provided for a modest fee. "Product positioning" eliminates extremes—fast weight loss, single focus dieting. Appeal is thus to people who are serious about losing weight. After developing an established base through national "distribution" centers, the company has increased its depth through the introduction of food products and whole meals derived from the elements of its weight-control program.

In a sense the weight-loss programs have provided a secure test base from which to launch clearly related products. Weight-Watchers presumably has a comparatively low advertising budget, since primary (and effective) communications are accomplished by word-of-mouth.

### Foreman-Ali

Ali's successful strategy was based on the element of surprise. Ali secretly conditioned his body to take hard punishment, while openly declaring he would "sting like a bee." In the championship fight instead of an elusive Ali, Foreman found himself pounding away on a strangely positioned opponent who was leaning far back on the ropes. All Foreman got for a target was "nothing." After eight rounds of heavy punching Foreman was exhausted. This was Ali's moment to move in and finish off his astounded foe.

## MILITARY PRINCIPLES

### B. H. Liddell Hart

"Effective results in war have rarely been attained unless the approach had such indirectness as to ensure the opponent's unreadiness to meet it. The indirectness has usually been physical, and always psychological. In strategy, the longest way round is often the shortest way home. . . . While the strength of an opposing force or country lies outwardly in its numbers and resources, these are fundamentally dependent upon stability of control, morale, and supply."[1]

Summarizing the concept of indirect approach, the strategy is to suddenly dislocate the enemy physically by taking the line of least resistance and psychologically by taking the line of least expectation. Further, the aim is to distract the enemy, thus depriving him of his freedom of action. Finally, a concentration of forces may be brought to bear on the now weakened and demoralized enemy forces. "True concentration is the fruit of calculated dispersion."

1.   Adjust your end to your means.
2.   Keep your object always in mind.
3.   Choose the line of least expectation.
4.   Exploit the line of least resistance.
5.   Take a line of operation which offers alternative objectives.
6.   Keep plan and disposition flexible.
7.   Don't hit where your opponent is strong.
8.   Don't renew an attack on the same line after it once has failed.

### Hitler's Success

Early in 1940 Hitler's strategy was specifically to avoid any direct assault on the heavily fortified French Maginot Line. Instead, he chose to bait the Allies into a vulnerable position away from their defenses on the Belgian frontier. When they had been lured deep into Belgium (having been allowed to advance without opposition), the Germans struck a deadly thrust in behind them. The Germans made effective use of their armored divisions, relying on mechanics rather than mass. The success of this approach was largely due to the inability of the French to depart from convention, in that they concentrated almost their entire fighting power in the advance into Belgium and left only a few second-rate divisions to guard their rear. Their thought apparently was that the naturally rough terrain at their back offered enough resistance to the mechanized divisions of the Germans. On the contrary, the Germans had learned that natural obstacles are not nearly so formidable as human resistance in strong defenses.

### Nimitz

During World War II when the Japanese were thoroughly dug in throughout the Pacific, the Navy strategy was to leapfrog from one key island to another, cutting off Japanese supply lines and starving out

---

[1] From B. H. Liddell Hart, *Strategy*, 2d rev. ed. (New York: Frederick A. Praeger, 1967), p. 25.

everything behind. The Navy was therefore able to bypass the big fixed Japanese base at Truk as well as many other well-defended positions.

## General Alexander

Alexander of the Allied forces successfully outmaneuvered the Germans on a line between Tunis and Bizerta by stretching the enemy's front in order to produce a weak joint. His flexible plan called for drawing the enemy's attention to their left flank, then pressing hard on their right, following with his main punch at their left center. When this was effectively checked, Alexander swung to the right, where the Germans believed themselves to be strong enough. This process of distraction allowed Alexander to succeed with a final blow, using his forces to attack simultaneously Tunis and Bizerta, which collapsed German resistance along the northern half of the front. The battle was concluded with a successful attack on the enemy's rear, where the Germans had not been able to recover quickly enough.

## Napoleon

In attacking the enemy, logic may dictate that attacking the enemy's strongest point directly will yield victory. This theory, however, may not take cost into account, nor a recognition that the leverage point could be elsewhere. It was Napoleon's strategy to attack not the strong point, but the vulnerable critical joint of the enemy's alliance. Thus, instead of battering away at Austria directly, his plan was first to knock out the frontier of Piedmont in Northern Italy—Austria's junior partner —from whence he could gain an open road into Austria.

## Schriever's Puzzle

For General Bernard Schriever the objective was to develop an intercontinental ballistic missile system. Schriever had to develop a complex system, which reasonably could be expected to take ten years. Even five years, however, was longer than the experts considered safe, so Schriever devised a method in which all facets of the system would be designed, tested, and built at the same time—the technique of concurrency, very like independently fashioning the pieces of a jigsaw puzzle in the hopes that the pieces would all fit when brought together. Through the use of independent contractors, thousands of scientists and engineers—each assigned to a specific aspect of the project—the latest in computer control systems, and a massive "war room" command post to monitor all phases, the Atlas was successfully launched just four years after the start of the program.

**General Lundendorff**

In spring 1917 German commander Lundendorff, anticipating a renewed offensive by the French and British, conceived a strategy calculated to dislocate the whole Allied offensive plan. From his position along a broad arc he systematically withdrew his forces, destroying everything within the arc, to a trench line straight across its base. From this new and shorter line of great apparent strength he was successful in gaining a year's time for the Germans.

SECTION **III**

## PRODUCT AND PRODUCT LINE

# Hewlett-Packard Corporation

### COMPUTER DIVISION

In the late 1930's the Hewlett-Packard Corporation was founded on $535 by two young engineers, Mr. William Hewlett and Mr. David Packard. The partnership was formed in Palo Alto, California, to manufacture a new type of measuring instrument which had been developed by Mr. Hewlett. The company grew over the ensuing decades to become one of the major commercial successes in American industry. In its early days the company captured a lead in instrumentation which it has successfully preserved despite severe competition. Hewlett-Packard grew entirely through the reinvestment of profits with only occasional short-term borrowing. During the decade of the 1950's the firm diversified into medical instrumentation and during the 1960's further diversified into instrumentation for analytical chemistry and data products, including computers, calculators, and associated peripheral equipment.

By 1973 the company achieved an annual volume of over half a billion dollars and employed some 23,000 people both in the United States and overseas. Hewlett-Packard maintained 185 sales offices, of which 60 were in the United States. The company operated a total of 22 plants; seven of these were located abroad. This case describes the early years of H-P's entry into the minicomputer market. Minicomputers have become extremely important in a large number of H-P's markets, and the corporation currently has a strong computer "flavor." This case, however, deals solely with the early phases of this program during which the fundamental direction and emphasis for this product line were established.

### Company Organizational Structure

Exhibit 1 presents a simplified organizational chart for the corporation as of 1965. The operating divisions were located throughout the United

Reprinted from *Stanford Business Cases 1973* with the permission of the publisher, Graduate School of Business, Stanford University. Copyright © 1973 by the Board of Trustees of the Leland Stanford Junior University.

States, Europe, and Japan. Each operated under the direction of a general manager with profit responsibility, and each encompassed engineering, manufacturing, finance (basically accounting and control), marketing, and various other support functions such as personnel and security. All of the division managers reported directly to Messrs. Hewlett and Packard as did the corporate staff. The latter comprised the "executive council" of the corporation and met monthly; the principal guidance and direction for the organization, however, were determined by the founders.

Most of the operating divisions were engaged in manufacturing various types of testing devices for essentially the same markets. Because of this commonality all sales activities were centralized under either the domestic or international sales manager. The marketing functions within the operating divisions consisted largely of product management and support for the centralized selling efforts.

Product innovation was an extremely important activity in all of the operating divisions, especially since the life cycle of a typical instrument was five years or less. In order to maintain a strong competitive position, major engineering programs to upgrade and introduce new devices were constantly under way in all divisions. Because of the "similarity" between divisions, various benchmarks and guidelines for measuring division performance had evolved over the years. A "good" division was expected to grow at approximately 20% per year, to generate an operating profit of about 30%, to spend some 8% on engineering and development, 5% on administration, 7% on internal marketing, and to have a manufacturing cost of approximately 50% (percentages based on net sales). Some divisions, however, did not meet these guidelines; this was apt to be the case with those divisions entering new markets.

In 1965 the company decided to establish a central research laboratory at corporate headquarters. The rationale was that the development programs at the division level were too product-oriented and that insufficient attention was being given to high-risk technologies which might have long-range fallout for the corporation as a whole. Accordingly, a group of over 100 engineers and scientists was drawn from the operating divisions and established under the direction of the vice president in charge of research and development. The central laboratory was supported by a "tax" of 1.5% on the revenues of the divisions. This amount, plus the average 8.5% being spent within the divisions, brought the total development dollars for the corporation to 10%—a major annual investment in new programs.

### Genesis of the Hewlett-Packard Computer

The rapid pace of digital technology led to the development of the "minicomputer concept" within the electronics industry in the early 1960's. Minicomputers were basically scaled-down versions of larger computers manufactured by such industry giants as IBM, Honeywell, and General Electric. The architecture of the minicomputers resembled that of the large processors, but the memory capability and ability to handle large numbers of peripherals were significantly limited; consequently, they were sold for a fraction of the price of the larger machines. The first company to recognize the possibility of an important market for minicomputers was the Digital Equipment Corporation (DEC) of Maynard, Massachusetts. By 1965 DEC had grown to a volume of several million dollars annually, primarily by selling minicomputers to scientists and engineers seeking lower cost solutions to their data handling problems and to original equipment manufacturers (OEM's) who built the minicomputers into various systems. DEC and other small competitors had not developed applications for minicomputers in the business data processing domain of IBM. In 1965 the total annual market for minicomputers was estimated to be roughly $50 million and growing at a rate of 40–60% per year.

Various engineers within the H-P organization advocated that the company develop a minicomputer. They believed that H-P possessed the necessary technology to accomplish this task; and, more importantly, they expected that the minicomputer would become increasingly necessary for the control of many test and measuring devices which the company manufactured. In fact, scientists within the central research laboratory had experimented with a DEC computer by applying it to a number of instrumentation applications within the company. They believed that significant improvements could be made to the basic architecture of the DEC machine and that H-P could make a unique contribution to the minicomputer field. In 1965 the opportunity to acquire a small company consisting of five computer designers and software experts became available. The acquisition was made, and the acquired individuals were assigned to the central laboratory to initiate a minicomputer program for H-P.

**Palo Alto Division**

As the development work on the minicomputer moved smoothly and rapidly forward, it became necessary to decide where the future home should be for this product. After considerable discussion it was decided to transfer the program at the checkpoint of an operating prototype into the Palo Alto division. It was believed that the systems business in which this division competed was closest to the markets which might be developed for the minicomputer. The division manager, who had no previous computer background, acquainted himself with the essentials of the program through conferences with the central lab staff working on the project. He quickly realized that, while the minicomputer incorporated a number of technical innovations, little thought was being given to marketing the minicomputer or developing software applications. He therefore invested a significant portion of his time in recruiting the nucleus of a computer marketing and software group. One of the key individuals hired was a young Ph.D. in computer applications. He became the product manager of the minicomputer and began to think about marketing implications. A second key individual hired was a man who had been in charge of the software research laboratory of one of the major computer manufacturers. Both men were fascinated with the opportunity to develop a computer program from "scratch," and through their enthusiasm they were able to attract a few additional individuals into the computer department within the Palo Alto division.

In mid-1966, the minicomputer was operating successfully as a prototype within the corporate laboratory. At that time the task force of roughly ten individuals who had developed the product were transferred to the Palo Alto division.

The announcement of the new minicomputer was planned for a large trade show—the Fall Joint Computer Conference of 1966. The product manager and others in the Palo Alto division had hoped to use the trade show to indicate clearly that H-P was making a strong commitment to its new minicomputer products. The senior H-P marketing executive and other corporate officials, however, were concerned about the direction of the computer marketing program and the way the computer would be announced to the trade. They were particularly concerned that the marketing program tentatively proposed might lead H-P into the business data processing field where strong competition from firmly entrenched competitors could be expected. It was finally decided that the new product could be announced only under the following conditions:

1. The word "computer" was not to be used in discussing the new product; "controller" and/or "information processor" would be used as substitutes.
2. The new line would be introduced only if it were available for "off-the-shelf" delivery.

H-P had been careful in the past to prevent premature introduction of products which later could not be readily delivered.

The computer product manager was troubled by these guidelines but was assured that it would be possible to have the product in production in time for announcement at the show. He had planned to announce the computer considerably in advance of the actual demonstration at the show in order to develop prospective customers and to give prospective customers time to write programs in the computer software language, so that the computer would be usefully applied at the time of delivery. He realized that a "staggering" job of training and marketing development lay ahead, and he felt uneasy about the company's ability to accomplish what had to be done.

## Organization of H-P Marketing

As indicated in Exhibit 1, the domestic sales and sales support activities (such as order processing, servicing, and corporate image advertising) reported to the vice president of marketing. The international operations similarly reported to the international vice president. The sales operations had a very strong geographic orientation. In the United States, activities were divided into four sales regions: East, Midwest, West and South. The H-P sales force had evolved from a background of manufacturers' representatives. As the company grew, it had been remarkably successful in carrying the representative system to a size and scope which exceeded those of most other manufacturers in the industry.

In the late 1950's it was reasoned that the company was large enough to establish its own sales arm. Accordingly, the company acquired its sales representatives for whom, by this time, H-P was the dominant product line. The acquisition was carried out smoothly, and very few salesmen left the combined companies. The sales organization, now wholly owned by H-P, continued to operate under the direction of the previous entrepreneurially oriented owners. Commissions continued to be paid, though of course such expenses were consolidated out of the combined operating statements. It was believed that one of the company's greatest strengths was its in-depth knowledge of its customer base which had been successfully preserved by the acquisition of the representatives.

Within a given sales region, operations were organized by districts with the geographical form of structure carried down to the community level. With the exception of the medical and analytical chemistry instruments which in 1965 accounted for but a small percentage of H-P's total business, each salesman sold the company's entire line of products. The medical and analytical lines were handled by separate sales forces, both of which had been obtained as part of the acquisition of medical and analytical businesses during the 1950's and early 1960's. These sales forces had simply been annexed to the existing geographical structure. Thus, the medical sales manager for the Midwest, for example, reported to the Midwest regional manager, rather than to the medical division manager. A similarly oriented structure existed throughout Europe and the balance of the firm's international organization, which in 1965 accounted for approximately 30% of total sales.

As the computer product manager developed his marketing program, he realized it would be necessary to build upon the existing sales organization, although he preferred to establish his own direct selling operation. While he realized that ultimately a major marketing effort would be required, he was able to get approval to hire only one specialist for each of the sales regions. The selection of these sales specialists was delegated to the regional managers. In the Western region, a senior computer systems designer was hired. In the Eastern region, a salesman from a competitive minicomputer firm was employed. In the Midwest a repair technician with no previous computer background was promoted to the new job. In the Southern region, a computer programmer was hired to fill the opening. No one was retained in Europe at this time. The four specialists were sent to the Palo Alto division to be thoroughly trained in the new H-P product. They, in turn, were to transfer this knowledge to all of the salesmen in their home regions.

### Status of Computer Program in Mid-1967

The Palo Alto division introduced their new "information processor" at the Fall Joint Computer Conference in 1966. The marketing group was disappointed that their minicomputer appeared to have little impact on those attending the conference. They felt they had not been successful in positioning their product.

The field specialists were trained and returned to their regions where they quickly began to train large numbers of H-P salesmen. Despite this effort, however, results continued to be disappointing. In particular, the computer was not contributing to either the volume or profits of the division but rather was consuming engineering and marketing resources at an increasing rate. The initial computer was priced at approximately $40,000, and only five orders had been obtained. Several dozen, however, had been sold as capital equipment to other H-P divisions—at manufacturing cost.

By mid-1967 H-P executives were understandably concerned over the lack of progress being made. A major meeting was held in June to discuss the problem. Approximately 75 individuals were invited to attend, including all the top management, the Palo Alto division management, the key individuals in the computer program, the sales specialists, and the area regional managers. Mr. Packard opened the meeting by asking why so few computers had been sold, particularly in view of the fact that DEC had been experiencing substantial increases in sales.

Nearly everyone had ideas on the situation. It was pointed out that diversification into new markets could not proceed with lightning speed, that it would be a mistake for H-P to rush pell-mell into the new field, and that particular caution should be exercised in avoiding confrontation with IBM. Many questions were directed to the four regional sales specialists. There was general agreement among them that certain particular problems prevented ready sale of the H-P computer:

*a.* The software was still quite limited; few application programs existed.

b. Only a few computer peripherals had thus far been interfaced with the processor—a teletypewriter, a card reader, and several H-P instruments would work in conjunction with the computer—but there was a long list of other necessary items which were required.

c. Not enough documentation and sales literature existed.

d. Despite the training which was continually given to members of the H-P sales force, most of the salesmen were clearly "afraid" of the computer. They felt far from being computer experts and were afraid to discuss the computer in front of their customers for fear of being embarrassed technically. The only exception was Mr. Slocum, the Eastern sales specialist who had a previous sales background in minicomputers. He had sold all five of the computers which had been ordered to date and said that if he "did not have to spend so much time trying to teach other salesmen what a computer was all about, I could have sold a hundred."

The computer meeting lasted a full day. At the conclusion of the meeting H-P management remained convinced that a major opportunity existed for the company in the minicomputer market. It was concluded that it should be possible to obtain at least $10 million in orders over the next 12 months. In a meeting the following week with Mr. Packard, division management asked for additional help in undertaking this marketing challenge. It was agreed that Mr. Perkins of the corporate laboratories should become the new marketing manager for the Palo Alto division. Mr. Perkins had no previous computer background.

In his new role of marketing manager for the Palo Alto division Mr. Perkins tried to assess the strengths and weaknesses of the division and his marketing organization. He had inherited a department of over 100 people, most of whom were concerned with the sales-support, proposal-writing, documentation, and training for the conventional product line of the division. The product line consisted of several hundred instruments and accessories which were sold into what was called the "data acquisition" market. Customers used these products to collect and process information from such electronic transducers as strain gauges, thermocouples, tachometers, and load cells. These kinds of data were then converted from analog to digital form for data reduction. A typical application would be the measurement of horsepower and efficiency of a turbine or engine at the manufacturer's research facility. None of the division's products had yet been incorporated into the new computer, although work was under way to produce a computer-based, data acquisition system.

In order to better understand the computer, its problems and potential, Mr. Perkins disappeared for two weeks which were spent entirely with Mr. Slocum, making sales calls and talking with him about the computer, the opportunities and the problems. Following this, Mr. Perkins was confident that the product was saleable but that a number of very basic marketing decisions and programs would have to be initiated. He was pleased with the product manager's grasp of the situation and his enthusiasm for the opportunities. On the other hand, the computer product had accumulated a staff of very junior, but bright, new employees who had no background in the H-P organization or credibility with the field force.

**The First Strategic Plan**

In late summer of 1967 Mr. Perkins developed a marketing plan for the Palo Alto division. He proposed a reorganization of the marketing department into two groups, computers and the old product line. He believed that computers had to be elevated in both stature and visibility. Secondly, he proposed discontinuing a large number of instruments and accessories of the Palo Alto division product line which in total added little to volume but which radically increased the complexity and expense of doing business. A 10% price increase was requested for the balance of the line. Mr. Perkins felt that with these changes it should be possible to hold the overall old product sales volume at least constant—while significantly improving the profit situation. He believed that the old product line managers would be capable of supporting this plan and that it would be most appropriate for his own time to be primarily devoted to the computer situation.

Mr. Perkins had been looking into the various segments of the minicomputer market. In order to display the market situation graphically, he constructed a three-dimensional model. The first axis showed a product characteristic scale; the second, a market sector scale; and the third, or vertical scale, showed total volume available. The total market was estimated to be roughly $120 million in 1967. A major sector was medium-priced computers for sale to OEM customers. A second sector was lower-priced computers for use in scientific and laboratory problem solving. One of the smaller sectors (but important to H-P) was the use of computers for the control of instrumentation. (A copy of this model is shown in Exhibit 2. The numbers in the squares represent the estimated dollar volume available. The model also points out that H-P's marketing and technology strengths were not properly coupled.)

The marketing plan indicated that it would be necessary to replace most of the field specialists with more experienced individuals and to substantially expand their number. Earlier, Mr. Perkins had envisaged the development of a specialized computer sales force, reporting back to the Palo Alto division and oriented toward penetrating the most important market sectors. But while management conceded that more and better specialists would be required, they would not contemplate the establishment of a separate sales force, nor did they want H-P to make any product which every H-P salesman was not free to sell.

The plan contained a concept which was termed "technology cycle." The essence of this concept was that the marketing importance of technical innovation at the time of the introduction of a new computer appealed primarily to OEM customers—such customers developed applications software only once and, therefore, wished to take advantage of the latest technology. The technology inevitably would become obsolete over time; but, if end-user-oriented software applications were developed, the software could counterbalance the decay in raw technology, and the overall competitive position might be maintained. As time passed, the nature of the customer target would have to change.

The plan contended that the best current target was the OEM market and that H-P would have to establish functional and quantity discounts (competitive with minicomputer industry practice) in order to compete successfully in the market. The Hewlett-Packard Corporation had not previously granted such discounts on any products.

Further, the plan maintained that a greatly expanded software effort would be necessary to develop end-user applications. It was proposed that a special group within the marketing department be created to research such applications. Perkins predicted that it would be possible to introduce rather quickly two or three such software/computer products which might contribute an annualized volume of several million dollars.

In addition to more field specialists it was proposed that two "internal salesmen" be added to work with other H-P divisions in developing computer/instrumentation applications for sale to specialized instrumentation customers. In other words, H-P itself should be considered an OEM customer by the Palo Alto division.

In summary a forecast was presented indicating that $12–15 million worth of new business could be obtained in the computer area within a year if the new plan was adopted. The computer operation would become profitable at this volume, but Perkins suggested deferring profitability in favor of accelerating software and other technology investments.

Perkins was encouraged to "sell his program" to the four regional sales managers and to the international sales manager who would have the ultimate decision as to whether or not additional specialists would be hired. In the following weeks Perkins visited all of the sales regions and presented his plan. He volunteered to help the sales regions find a total of 20 additional specialists and over the next few months, in fact, took on the total responsibility of recruiting and training this number.

### Operations in 1967–1968

Throughout the balance of 1967 and through mid-1968, the essential elements of the first strategic plan were implemented. Many additional specialists were hired, and, while they were not designated as salesmen, they did bring in orders. The other H-P divisions were cultivated by "the internal salesmen," and approximately 20% of the order volume began to be internally generated. More important, many major contracts with OEMs were written, based upon the new pricing and discount schedules. Additional engineers and software development specialists were hired. The special group within the marketing department pioneered two major software/computer systems which were introduced in early 1968.

The first, and most important, was a new computer time-sharing system developed around the H-P product. This time-sharing system was the first to use a minicomputer. It was restricted to only 16 terminals and to operating in only one computer language. But it was offered for sale at one tenth the price of the nearest competitive system. The time-sharing system was developed at a minimum of expense and was introduced at the Spring Joint Computer Conference of 1968. A strike of telephone equipment installers rendered all the expensive time-sharing systems inoperative; the H-P system was the only one operating. It received widespread publicity, and several million dollars of orders were written with a variety of customers, mostly in commercial applications. At this show the H-P booth was dominated by a huge sign announcing "H-P Computers."

The second software/computer system developed was for the control of automatic machine tools using minicomputers. A large order was obtained for this system from the leading machine tool manufacturer, although the system was not yet fully developed. The announcement of products in advance of production had gradually become the policy of the computer marketing group. A third new market development was that of computer-aided instruction using the newly developed time-sharing system. Software already written to teach math drill and practice was obtained at a nominal cost and reprogrammed for the H-P system. Four departmental specialists were assigned the task of marketing this product to secondary schools around the United States.

By the end of 1968, $15 million of orders had been booked with the following approximate breakdown:

20% for resale through other H-P divisions.

30% for resale through OEMs.

20% for sale to scientific end users.

30% for "new" market sectors—education, time-sharing, and machine tools.

The financial results through 1968 are shown in Exhibit 3.

By mid-1968 the computer business dominated the Palo Alto division's product line. During the summer of 1968 the computer operation was established as a free-standing division, and Perkins was appointed division manager. Although pleased with some of the progress that had been made, Perkins was concerned over a number of problems including:

1. Increased competition. DEC, the principal competitor, was still growing rapidly, and a host of new competitors had emerged. In the past two years the list of producers had grown from approximately 5 to 50 with a wide variety of products being offered between them.
2. Control of the sales "specialists" through the classical geographical marketing structure.
3. The increasing difficulty of hiring and training new personnel as fast as the opportunities demanded.
4. The salary structure and age of employees in the computer operation. The product manager, for example, was in his mid-30's and was beginning to develop a hierarchy of management of youthful individuals. The average age of the emerging computer operation's management in marketing, engineering, and manufacturing was 15 years younger than the average for the overall H-P corporation.
5. The last and most worrisome problem was that H-P management believed it was possible to achieve a shipment level of at least $70 million annually within another two years. Mr. Perkins was concerned that the present line of minicomputers (which had by now expanded to four models, priced from $10,000 to $60,000) was too narrow to compete in the larger markets required by this kind of growth.

## The Second Strategic Plan

In order to meet the division's growth objectives and to capitalize on opportunities believed available, it was necessary to develop a longer range strategy for the new computer division. After numerous discussions it was concluded that an expanded line of minicomputers would have to be developed.

The key points of the new plan were:

1. A hierarchy of computers should be developed so that a customer might start with a small H-P system and graduate upward to more and more powerful equipment without having to reprogram or change his computer vendor.
2. The problem of rapid technological obsolescence had to be faced. It would be desirable to be able to reimplement computers in new technologies (as large-scale integration and domain memories emerged) without having to revamp the entire product line and change the basic software operating systems. The fundamental importance of software was stressed. It was believed that the new software operating systems should have a life cycle of ten years or

longer. During this period the hardware processors might be re-implemented through several technology cycles.

The new plan which evolved among the marketing, engineering and software groups (now numbering several hundred people) called for the development of the "A" system. The heart of this system was a radical new concept in software which would make possible the development of an interrelated series of computers, modular in size, and re-implementable without software changes. The first product was to be a processor of about the same general size as the present line of H-P computers. However, this processor would primarily be a building block of a much larger processor which would follow the first unit by one year into production. The availability of these two computers would enable the marketing program to span applications of $10,000 per computer unit, upward to a major system of $2.5 million with all of the memories and peripherals included. It was believed that the "A" line would secure the company's position in its current markets and additionally open new possibilities in factory automation, process control, and digital communications. These were markets in which IBM and the others were beginning to compete but in which no vendor had yet achieved dominance.

The "A" concept was discussed in detail, especially its emphasis on new markets. The "A" program was projected to require an investment of approximately $9–10 million through the end of 1971. About $6 million of this would be spent in engineering and software and the balance in incremental marketing. The program would represent the largest technical and marketing commitment ever undertaken by the corporation.

In addition to the "A" program new investments were proposed for the establishment of "data centers" throughout the United States and Europe. The data centers were to be provided with a full line of H-P computer equipment and staffed with a group of application engineers. The purpose was primarily to strengthen the support for customer-oriented marketing within the field. To do this required training a substantial number of additional field specialists in customer software programming. The data centers were called "greenhouses," which would be self-supporting in addition to developing the additional staff necessary to expand the marketing effort.

Mr. Perkins submitted pro forma projections as shown in Exhibit 4. If these projections could be achieved, the "A" project could be funded without violating the traditional guidelines on engineering expense as a percent of sales. H-P management continued to consider this guideline very important. The other guidelines, however, could not be made to apply to the computer division which, although increasingly profitable, had marketing costs triple those of the other H-P divisions and manufacturing costs less than half of the norm.

The projections were ambitious compared to the current size of the computer operations. Top management considered the "expenditures" a good long-term investment but expressed concern about the impact on overall short-term company earnings.

The computer division grew rapidly throughout 1969. Over $27 million of computer products were shipped, and operating profit was over 20% of sales. Data centers and additional application analysts now existed in the field. The specialists had been converted to full-fledged salesmen who carried the full responsibility for the computer line. They were, in turn, backed up by the application analysts within the data centers. One analyst could support two salesmen in the field.

Despite this success a number of problems continued to worry division management. The principal concern was the "A" program. In order to introduce the smaller computer, the larger one had to be thoroughly developed and prototyped in advance. By ensuring practicality of the largest possible system, it would be possible to introduce the submodel with full assurance of upward compatibility. Unfortunately, the larger computer was consuming software and engineering resources at a rate 10–15% higher than that originally contemplated. It was becoming increasingly difficult to continue to hold engineering expense within guidelines and support the necessary development of peripherals, systems, computer-aided instruction, time-sharing, and machine control, all of which required on-going effort. Further, the number of competitors continued to grow, and the first signs that the emerging recession would also affect the minicomputer industry began to appear.

## The Decisions of 1970

During the early months of 1970 the impact of the domestic recession was experienced by H-P. For the first time in 30 years the "mainstream" divisions' domestic order rate declined with a commensurate drop in earnings. (See Exhibit 5 for an eight-year summary of corporate earnings).

In the computer division, unit volume continued to increase, but price pressure was more severe than ever. As the order growth rate began to slow, it became necessary to stretch out the hiring program and support for the "A" system in order to stay within the financial guidelines laid down by corporate management. This, in turn, raised serious questions regarding the 1970 shipment goal of $40 million and the sales goals for 1971 and subsequent years.

By mid-1970 in the face of difficult general business conditions the "A" program, and especially the larger marketing commitment it would require, caused continuing concern. Some suggested that the project be rescheduled so that the development cycle could be spread over a much longer period and spending reduced to a lower rate. Others were convinced that the technology cycle in the computer industry was inexorable: if H-P lost its position, the program would be so seriously jeopardized that continuation would be unwarranted. They also thought that the new small computer was too "mini" to stand alone and that H-P had to develop both machines or neither.

There was no alternative product to the "A" system on the drawing boards. As the mid-year financial review approached, rumors circulated throughout the division that the "A" project would be canceled. As of mid-1970 several million dollars had been invested in the development of the system.

At this point top management met to consider essentially the following alternatives:

a. Continue the "A" program, risk short-term earnings against long-term profit growth.
b. Modify the "A" program to fit better the current economic situation (less R&D, slower market investment).
c. Cancel the entire project and abandon computer activities, except for the original minicomputer line.

**EXHIBIT 1**

**Hewlett-Packard Corporation Organization Chart—1965**

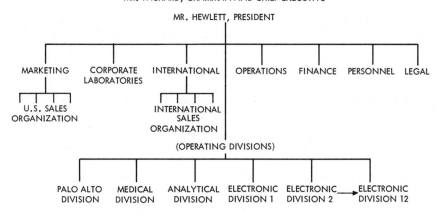

## EXHIBIT 2

**Hewlett-Packard Corporation—Small Computer Market Profile—July 1967**

| | Development/ Manufacturing | Laboratory | Data Handling | Marketing Strength |
|---|---|---|---|---|
| *"Package" Computer/ Software Solutions* | Example: Production Testing $15m | Example: Network Analyzers $5m | Example: Order Processing System $5m | |
| *Instrument Systems* | Example: Engine Testing $25m | Example: Gas Chromatography Systems $10m | Example: Medical Laboratory Data Handling $5m | |
| *Free-Standing Computers* | Example: IC Testing OEM $30m | Example: Scientific Computer $10m | Example: Card to Tape Converters $5m | |

Engineering Strength

*Marketing and Engineering Strength* ←——————————————————

## EXHIBIT 3

**Hewlett-Packard Corporation—Computer Division Operating Results—1965–1968**

| Fiscal Year | Ending Backlog | Net Shipments | Operating Profit |
|---|---|---|---|
| 1965.......... | — | — | ($   200,000) |
| 1966.......... | — | — | (   300,000) |
| 1967.......... | $ 2,000,000 | $1,173,000 | ( 1,000,000) |
| 1968.......... | 15,000,000 | 5,141,000 | (   620,000) |

## EXHIBIT 4

**Hewlett-Packard Corporation—Computer Division Pro Forma Projections**

| Fiscal Year | Shipments | Operating Profit | Comments |
|---|---|---|---|
| 1969.......... | $ 20,000,000 | $ 5,000,000 | Existing products |
| 1970.......... | 40,000,000 | 8,000,000 | "A" 16 announced |
| 1971.......... | 70,000,000 | 14,000,000 | "A" 16 in production |
| 1972.......... | 140,000,000 | 28,000,000 | "A" 32 announced |

**EXHIBIT 5**

**Hewlett-Packard Corporation Eight-Year Earnings Summary**
**(shipments and after-tax profits in millions of dollars)**

|  | 1963 | 1964 | 1965 | 1966 | 1967 | 1968 | 1969 | 1970 |
|---|---|---|---|---|---|---|---|---|
| Shipments........... | $124.2 | $136.3 | $167.6 | $208.3 | $251.2 | $279.6 | $336.2 | $366.4 |
| After-tax profits..... | 7.6 | 9.9 | 13.7 | 17.2 | 20.3 | 21.2 | 26.0 | 23.5 |
| Earnings per share... | $  .30 | $  .39 | $  .55 | $  .70 | $  .82 | $  .84 | $ 1.03 | $  .92 |

# Henkel-Trifft

In late January 1969 Herr Krabbe, product planner at Henkel Cie GmbH, was preparing for the next "weekly conceptual talks" with his colleagues and supervisors. In that meeting, ideas, developments, and problems within the product line would be discussed. One of the products which had been Herr Krabbe's responsibility for the last month was the new liquid spray cleaner "Trifft," launched in August 1968 nationally on the German market. Trifft had not gained as wide consumer acceptance as expected. Facing a disappointing sales performance, product management was wondering how or whether Trifft's market performance could be improved. Herr Krabbe had a report from the advertising agency, Euro Ad, on his desk, suggesting that Trifft should be repositioned closer to other liquid household cleaners to share their success.

In 1876 Fritz Henkel founded a company in Dusseldorf, Germany, for bleaching powder, employing three workers. By 1900 Henkel & Cie employed 80 persons and was the first to apply a brand name to a product normally sold in bulk. Henkel's bleaching powder was produced in uniform quality, packaged in standard sizes, and supported by newspaper advertising. At that time laundry still had to be scrubbed with laundry soap. Henkel's was the world's first self-acting washing preparation, i.e., the laundry had only to be boiled. On June 6, 1907, a Dusseldorf newspaper contained the first advertisement for this product called "Persil," and a year later the company could claim "millions of housewives" used it. The original package has been retained over Persil's 62-year life. This brand was still the biggest selling brand on the market in 1969.

In 1969 Henkel was competing successfully with Procter and Gamble, Colgate, and Unilever—and was the world's fourth largest producer of detergents and cleaning agents. It employed some 32,000 people, one-third of whom worked outside Germany. In Dusseldorf its plants and offices spread over 275 acres. Henkel's sales in 1968 were close to DM 4,000 million, and its line was comprised of 8,000 products ranging from industrial chemicals, adhesives, detergents, to cosmetics, with detergents representing about half the total turnover.[1]

Some Henkel brands had been sold successfully for a long time—for example, Persil. Others were modified or dropped as market conditions changed. Thus, new products were constantly being developed by the firm. Henkel's established policy in "cleaners" was to obtain at least a 13% share for any new product in a particular market one year after its introduction. Otherwise, the product was deemed unsuccessful and phased out. Although the procedure for the development and introduction of a new product could vary substantially from one single product to the next, the company followed the policy of thoroughly testing the product concept and the physical product itself under a variety of conditions including "test" markets. Labels, containers, pricing, and advertising were similarly tested.

All-purpose household cleaners (APHCs) were defined as "cleaning agents for all household washable surfaces." APHCs had somewhat different chemical features which permitted them to perform in a different mix of applications (see Exhibit 1 for current market products). A number of studies performed for Henkel in 1965–67 showed, however, that they were used basically for the "big cleaning jobs." Other applications of APHCs included intermediate cleaning and stain removal, bathroom, kitchen, and door cleaning. Most of this cleaning occurred in the kitchen during and after cooking; therefore, besides cleaners and soap, housewives generally used dishwater. For manual dishwashing (automatic dishwashers at that time in Germany had a negligible share) housewives prepared a solution comprised of a special detergent and warm water. Dishwater was, thus, considered to be the strongest competitor of APHCs as far as intermediate cleaning was concerned.

In 1967, all-purpose household cleaners in Germany could be divided into powders and concentrated liquid cleaners. Both had to be diluted with water before application. Total industry sales for 1962–1967 are given below in Table 1.

Henkel had already innovated twice in this field by introducing Dor, a powdered cleaner, which was the first mild, modern household cleaner for delicate surfaces (launched nationally in 1961) in Germany, and Clin, a concentrated liquid cleaner (national in 1963). The latter was the first concentrated liquid APHC to gain a significant market share. In 1967, APHCs represented about 5% of Henkel's washing and cleaning agent sales in Germany. In spite of this small relative share management

---

[1] Compiled from company sources, *Internal Management*, February 1972, and *Fortune*, August 1972. In 1969 $1 U.S. = DM 4.20.

## TABLE 1
### Market Data for APHCs in Germany

|  | 1962 | 1963 | 1964 | 1965 | 1966 | 1967 |
|---|---|---|---|---|---|---|
| Market size |  |  |  |  |  |  |
| (million DM) | 39 | 62 | 80 | 97 | 100 | 100 |
| Market shares (%) |  |  |  |  |  |  |
| Henkel | 79.5 | 63.5 | 49.5 | 43.0 | 43.9 | 42.0 |
| Colgate (Ajax) | 0 | 0 | 20.4 | 33.6 | 37.8 | 32.5 |
| P&G (Fairy, Mr. |  |  |  |  |  |  |
| Proper) | 20.4 | 31.4 | 19.7 | 14.5 | 11.5 | 20.5 |
| Unilever | 0 | 4.0 | 9.5 | 7.9 | 5.0 | 2.5 |
| Others | 0.1 | 1.1 | 0.9 | 1.0 | 1.8 | 2.5 |
|  | 100.0 | 100.0 | 100.0 | 100.0 | 100.0 | 100.0 |
| Shares by texture (%) |  |  |  |  |  |  |
| Powder | 96.8 | 82.5 | 64.2 | 61.4 | 59.2 | 52.0 |
| Concentrated liquid | 3.2 | 17.5 | 35.8 | 38.6 | 40.8 | 48.0 |
|  | 100.0 | 100.0 | 100.0 | 100.0 | 100.0 | 100.0 |
| Henkel's APHC |  |  |  |  |  |  |
| product line (%) |  |  |  |  |  |  |
| Dor powder | 65.0 | 36.6 | 25.8 | 22.3 | 23.3 | 26.0 |
| Other powders | 11.3 | 10.2 | 8.6 | 11.0 | 10.9 | 10.0 |
| Concentrated liquid | 3.2 | 16.7 | 15.1 | 9.7 | 9.7 | 6.0 |
| Total | 79.5 | 63.5 | 49.5 | 43.0 | 43.9 | 42.0 |

was increasingly concerned about its declining share in the APHC market and about the success of competitive concentrated liquid APHCs.

The U.S. market was used by Henkel as one source of new product ideas. In 1967 liquid cleaners held 70% of the American APHC market. In addition to concentrated liquid and powder cleaners there were (since 1966) so-called spray cleaners (included in the 70% market share for liquid cleaners). They were applied directly to the surface by squirting a pump which served also as a container cap and were promoted as "heavy duty cleaners" for spots and special purposes. The pump was used in Germany only in connection with a liquid window cleaner ("Sidolin").

Spray cleaner prices were well above those of liquid cleaners—on the average they were 30% higher per ounce of liquid. However, they came in larger bottles (22-ounce average versus 15-ounce) which made price comparisons difficult for shoppers. Two brands dominated the spray-cleaner segment (Fantastik and Formula 409).

In autumn 1967 Mr. Bertold, who observed the U.S. market for Henkel in New York City, reported that spray APHCs were estimated to have obtained a 23% market share of the APHC market. This figure was used subsequently by product management in comparing the United States and the German market and its trends.

In the spring of 1967 Henkel received three U.S. spray cleaners, (Fantastik, Formula 409, and Cinch) for laboratory testing. The laboratory director in reporting the results to product management noted that, while he was impressed with the spray principle, these formulas were, in his opinion, chemically too aggressive for the German market. At the same time product management was becoming increasingly concerned with Henkel's position in the growing market for liquid APHCs in Germany. While P&G (Meister Proper) and Colgate (Ajax) were successful in this field, Henkel's effort had not been very successful. The popular Dor powder had been developed in liquid form but had not yet been marketed. "The idea was not to jeopardize sales of Dor powder, when it still has a large market share, and to save the liquid for a later date when powder sales had become too small," said Herr Krabbe.

Product management saw in the spray cleaner an opportunity to market a new liquid cleaner. It was felt that such a cleaner could improve Henkel's position in the liquid APHC segment and also anticipate competitive developments, since it was suspected that U.S. based German competitors were preparing to launch similar products. It was planned to sell the Henkel spray cleaner for large surface cleaning, as well as for spots and intermediate cleaning.

In September 1967 following several meetings, the desired features of the new spray cleaner were agreed upon. At this stage two names were being considered, "Hit" or "Swing." Eventually, neither "Hit" nor "Swing" would be used, since they had already been registered by other companies. The name finally selected was "Trifft," a common expression in German for "hit the spot."

A study was carried out in September 1967 among 750 housewives who tested a strong formula and another 750 who tested the milder formula. This was done even though product management knew that the products being tested were not yet "perfect." The spray pump leaked and the fluid contained in the transparent bottles was sensitive to light, i.e., it changed color when exposed to light over a long period of time. Despite these technical problems, product management felt that work on the project should proceed rapidly. A month after the initiation of the field study it was decided to brief the Euro Ad agency to develop bottle and label ideas. The urgent need for fast development was stressed by a pencil note put on the product conception document by a leading marketing manager, "Es soll in dieser Richtung schnell weitergearbeitet werden" (We should work fast in this direction).

The final product conception document which was completed in November 1967 (detailed in Exhibit 2) summarized the market opportunity; confirmed the positioning of Trifft as a convenient cleaner that could be sprayed undiluted on surfaces; gave details on the formulas, bottle capacity, and pricing policies; and forecast market shares of 8% in 1968, 14% in 1969, and 18% in 1970. Introduction was scheduled for autumn 1968.

The results of the formula test among housewives became available in January 1968. The report stated that:

Trifft has the potential to be well accepted by consumers in comparison to other cleaners, if well introduced with advertising support. During the introduction phase Trifft should be differentiated from window cleaners in order to avoid confusion. The strong version Trifft had better results in most areas and results equal to the mild version in other areas. We therefore recommend production of the stronger type.

The results provide some insights concerning:

Housewives' opinion about household work (only 10% dislike household work);
Surfaces cleaned with Trifft (75% used it on both surfaces and spots);
Little use of Trifft on furniture (60% did not use it on kitchen furniture);
Complaints about spots and stains on lacquers (about 5%) after application (both types); and
Trifft's cleaning power (90% saying either "good" or "very good").

There was no indication of differences by region, social class, or any other criteria. (For more details see Exhibit 3.)

In January 1968 a spray cleaner (Nifti by Cyanamid) was introduced in Denmark, and product management had evidence that Colgate and Unilever were working on similar developments. Herr Krabbe (product management) put it this way: "When we knew that competition intended to do the same as we did, we agreed on not going regional first, as usual, but to go national with Trifft as soon as possible."

A conference with Euro Ad held in January 1968 produced the following agreement regarding the introductory advertising campaign:

1. Use the name "Trifft" in the advertising copy;
2. Show the easy handling ("It's like playing");
3. Emphasize partial cleaning but also show large surface cleaning;
4. Devise a good slogan which contains the new cleaning method;
5. Avoid using the name "Henkel";
6. The target group should be all housewives, with emphasis on the 25–35-year-olds; and
7. Avoid confusion with existing window cleaners by clear advertising and usage instructions.

The next step included setting up operational plans, designing the introductory campaign, and final selection of the label and the bottle.

A marketing research study showed that the most popular label was very similar to that of a competitor's laundry detergent (OMO). "Therefore," said Herr Krabbe, "we chose the second best rated label and changed the color from blue to green, because many housewives said they didn't like the blue with the red; it was too aggressive."

In May 1968 the results of another research study became available. This one tested the concept of spray cleaning through the use of depth-interviews with 40 housewives who discussed their cleaning needs, how they classified cleaners, and how they reacted to the spray concept. During the interview they were shown a spray cleaner and allowed to use it. The results revealed considerable skepticism and insecurity about the new concept, the most important of which was they perceived no real need for a spray cleaner. While it was recognized that these reactions presented obstacles to the success of Trifft, it was felt that they could be overcome by advertising and consumer education (see Exhibit 4).

In April 1968 Colgate introduced on a regional basis its liquid spray cleaner "Schnip." It was milder than Trifft and advertised for intermediate spot cleaning (see Exhibit 5). Unilever/Sunlicht introduced Vigor, a heavy duty spray cleaner for dirt and stains, regionally in the Saarland in May 1968.

The following cost calculations for Trifft and corresponding estimates for Schnip and Vigor were prepared in May 1968.

Trifft was to be introduced with three million bottles at the lower price and then with the regular price. Schnip and Vigor were planned

| | | Trifft (400 g)* | | Schnip (500 g) | | Vigor (450 g) |
|---|---|---|---|---|---|---|
| Introductory period | | | | | | |
| Retail price/unit (DM) | | 1.95 | | 1.95 | | 1.10 |
| Factory list price to the wholesaler | | 1.27 | | 1.30 | | .73 |
| 10% discounts for introduction and quantity discounts | .27 | | .27 | | .15 | |
| Freight | .06 | | .07 | | .07 | |
| Manufacturing costs | .70 | | .75 | | .73 | |
| Total variable costs | | (1.03) | | (1.09) | | (.95) |
| Contribution per unit for marketing budget, overheads and profits | | .24 | | .21 | | (.22) |
| After introduction period | | | | | | |
| Retail price/unit (DM) | | 2.35 | | 2.65 | | 2.25 |
| Factory list price to the wholesaler | | 1.53 | | 1.75 | | 1.50 |
| Quantity discounts | .15 | | .17 | | .15 | |
| Freight† | .06 | | .07 | | .07 | |
| Manufacturing costs‡ | .70 | | .75 | | .73 | |
| Total variable costs | | (.91) | | (.99) | | (.95) |
| Contribution per unit for marketing budget, overheads, and profits | | .62 | | .76 | | .55 |

* g = grams.
† Freight for Trifft was less because of the use of 15-bottle cartons versus 10-bottle carton.
‡ The largest "manufacturing" cost items were the pump (Trifft: .28) and the bottle (.22)—not the liquid itself (.06).

to start with 100,000 bottles each on regional markets, one-third of which were to be sold at the introductory price. The production for Trifft started in June with four million bottles which were to be in retail markets in August, and advertising was planned to start in September.

## Introduction and Initial Results

Trifft was launched nationally in early August 1968 with a special introductory retail price of DM 1.95, compared to a "normal" price of DM 2.35. Within one month about 15 consumers made complaints concerning stripes and stains on lacquers and two about insufficient cleaning power. Tests, however, in the laboratory showed that Trifft did not cause more damage than did other spray cleaners and less than strong cleaners. The damage resulted from the chemical features of old lacquers and could be avoided by careful application (spraying the cleaner on a cleaning towel first and then applying). The complaints were taken seriously enough by product management to change the use instructions on the label.

The point-of-sale promotion budget of DM 1 million was considerably larger than that which was normally used to introduce a new product. The advertising budget (DM 2 million) was spent mainly on television. It was beyond the usual advertising/sales ratio for other APHCs (see Exhibit 6).

Another research study with 80 housewives ranked Trifft-TV spots higher than those of the competition both in recall and empathy. Housewives liked the down-to-earth educational approach towards the new cleaning principle. Based on this study, the following recommendations were made:

Confusion with window cleaners should be avoided at all costs (not even showing windows in TV spots!). Emphasis should be placed on consumer education because there is still a need for information. TV spots should be dominated by a "static line," not by turbulent, fast-moving pictures. Application to delicate surfaces should be stressed, in order to keep well away from Ajax and Mr. Proper. Trifft ranges below them in cleaning power and slightly above Dor. To avoid criticism of high pricing, economy in use should be strongly emphasized.

A further conclusion from this study was that consumer acceptance for Trifft was still low. This conclusion was supported by the slowing sales of Trifft whose market share in December 1968 fell to 5.4%. Actual monthly sales until the end of 1968 are shown on page 204.

In January 1969 Trifft was sold in 10,000 retail stores. Consumer awareness was at 30% with some 10% having tried Trifft and 5% still using it. Another research study again revealed favorable reaction to the TV spots but also reservations towards the product. Some 40% felt that they did not need Trifft, and 22% thought it would be too expensive to use.

**Actual Monthly Sales ex Works**

| Month | Bottles (000) | Market Share in the German APHC Market Percent |
|---|---|---|
| August 1968................... | 500 | — |
| September 1968............... | 1,200 | 10.21 |
| October 1968................. | 990 | 9.91 |
| November 1968............... | 590 | 8.0 |
| December 1968............... | 390 | 5.4 |

The report recommended the following:

Awareness is too high to explain the slowdown of Trifft sales so far. It is rather that existing cleaning habits regarding intermediate cleaning are too fixed, and there is a lack of emotional involvement with Trifft. The task-oriented spots, therefore, have advantages on the one hand but should be much more lively and emotionally engaging to compete innovatively against the "competition" of cleaning habits and dishwater.

Trifft's direct competitors, Schnip and Vigor, also had experienced a disappointing sales performance in their regional test markets; Schnip, which had achieved at one time a 7% market share of the regional APHC market, was faced with declining sales, and Vigor never got beyond 1% in its test market.

By January 1969 more precise information concerning the U.S. market was obtained, which revised previous estimates about the market share of sprays as follows:

**U.S. Market Data on APHCs**

|  | 1966 | 1967 | 1968 | 1969 (est.) |
|---|---|---|---|---|
| Market size (million $)........... | 138 | 152 | 170 | 175 |
| Shares by texture (%) |  |  |  |  |
| Powder....................... | 30.0 | 26.0 | 23.0 | 14.0 |
| Liquid (without spray).......... | 66.2 | 68.4 | 62.0 | 63.0 |
| Spray........................ | 3.0 | 5.6 | 15.0 | 23.0 |
| Total.................... | 100.0 | 100.0 | 100.0 | 100.0 |

**U.S. Market Shares of Spray Cleaners (percent)**

|  | 1966 | 1967 | 1968 | 1969 (est.) |
|---|---|---|---|---|
| Fantastik............................ | 1.2 | 2.7 | 6.2 | 9.2 |
| Formula 409......................... | 1.8 | 2.7 | 5.0 | 6.9 |
| Others (Cinch, Ajax, Power-On, |  |  |  |  |
| Whistle, Clean and Kill)............ | 0.0 | 0.2 | 3.8 | 6.9 |
| Total....................... | 3.0 | 5.6 | 15.0 | 23.0 |

**Advertising/Sales Ratios of U.S. APHCs**

|  | *1967* | *1968* | *1969* |
|---|---|---|---|
| Average advertising to sales ratio of spray APHC.................... | 1.00 | .50 | .14 |
| Average/sales ratio of all APHCs (total average).................. | .20 | .19 | .15 |

The latest critical market review which had been prepared by Euro Ad now lay on Herr Krabbe's desk, and he was reviewing it in preparation for the weekly concept talks. It concluded as follows:

Trifft was introduced in August 1968 in a market dominated by Ajax, Mr. Proper, and Dor. Trifft's disappointing sales performance reflects very fixed consumer cleaning habits towards which the three main products are oriented.

The agency recommendation for immediate action is to change the present Trifft concept (retaining the spray) to get closer to existing household cleaners, i.e., to accept existing consumer habits. Therefore, the formula should be changed for heavy dirt.

## EXHIBIT 1
### Products on the Market in 1967 and 1968

| Company | Product | Form | Cleaning Power* | Color | Perfume | Use | On the Market since | MS† 1967 (percent) | MS† Last Quarter 1968 (percent) |
|---|---|---|---|---|---|---|---|---|---|
| Henkel........ | Dor | Powder | Low | Light green | Lavender | Not for big dirt-"shine" | 1961 | 25.8% | 23% |
|  | Clin | Liquid | Low | — | Pine/ammonia‡ | All purposes | 1963 | 2.5 | — |
|  | WR Kraftreiniger | Liquid viscous | Medium | Milky | Soap/ammonia‡ | All purposes, big dirt | 1967 test marketed | 0.5 | — |
|  | Imi Pulver | Powder | High | — | None | Not for delicate surfaces, esp. for grease | 1929 | 9.9 | Not known |
| Sunlicht........ | Imi Flussig | Liquid viscous | Medium | Milky | Pine/ammonia‡ | All purposes | 1966 | 3.2 | Not known |
|  | Trifft | Liquid spray | Medium | Green | Pine/ammonia‡ | All purposes | 1968 | — | 8.9 |
|  | Andy | Powder | High | — | — | Not for delicate surfaces | 1963 |  |  |
| Unilever........ | Andy Flussig | Liquid | Medium | Green | Pine/ammonia‡ | All purposes | 1965 | — | None |
|  | Vigor | Liquid spray | High | Blue | Pine/ammonia‡ | Not for delicate surfaces | 1968 test marketed |  |  |
| Procter & Gamble........ | Fairy | Powder | High | None | None | Not for delicate surfaces | 1961 | 8.3 | Not known |
| Colgate........ | Mr. Proper | Liquid | Medium | Green | Pine/ammonia‡ | All purposes | 1967 | 12.0 | 18 |
|  | Ajax Floor | Powder | High | None | None | Not for delicate surfaces | — |  |  |
| Palmolive........ | Ajax | Liquid | Medium | Milky | Pine/ammonia‡ | All purposes | 1974 | 28.1 | 28 |
|  | Schnip | Liquid spray | Low | None | Fruit | All purposes | 1968 test marketed | — | 1–7 in test market |
| Others........ | — | — | — | — | — | — | — | 7.2 | Not known |

Notes: Very strong cleaners are aggressive on lacquers. Strength can be felt by the skin during use, especially in case of small scratches.

* This column expresses the alkalinity of the various cleaners corresponding, in general, to the perceived power in cleaning.

† MS = Market shares. These could vary between ±20% geographically. This effect is especially true in test market areas where two products come into the most direct competition.

‡ Ammonia was perceived (due to extensive Ajax advertising) as a very good cleaning ingredient by users.

## EXHIBIT 2

### Summary of the Product Conception Report

Liquid household cleaners have achieved more than 50% share in Germany and more than 75% in the United States.

Henkel has no significant product in the liquid market.

In the United States, spray cleaners have already obtained 25% of the market. We believe that the German market will also be receptive to this new cleaner.

The main ideas of such a spray cleaner from Henkel are:

Easy and convenient application of a liquid household cleaner by means of a spray pump;
Without diluting with water; and
Without rinsing and polishing.

A product test is being carried out to investigate which type will be the most likely to succeed in Germany:

A mild cleaner.
A stronger, better cleaning type.
A universal type between the two, with emphasis on the easy application.

Other data:

Content: 300–400 g, eventually larger refill bottle.
Price (retail): DM 2.10–2.30 for 350 g.
Price level due to calculated necessities and to high-quality positioning.

Calculation:

|  | 1969 | 1970 | 1971 |
|---|---|---|---|
| Market share.............. | 8% | 14% | 18% |
| Market size*.............. | 105 DM | 109 | 112 |
| Revenue Trifft*........... | 12 DM† | 15.3 | 20 |
| Tons sold................ | 2,500 | 3,600 | 4,700 |
| Contributions*........... | 5 DM | 6.3 | 13 |

* In millions of DM.
† 8% market share + inventory.

**EXHIBIT 3**

**Excerpts of a Field Study for Henkel on a Liquid Spray Cleaner**

Samples of Trifft were given free to two groups of 750 housewives. One group received the strong version (SP) and the other the milder one (MP). Interviews took place two weeks later.

| Results | SP (trialists) | MP (trialists) |
|---|---|---|
| Cleaning power "good" or "very good"......... | 90% | |
| Cleaning power "very good".................. | 44% | 36% |
| Good all-around cleaning..................... | 80% | |
| Good stain cleaning.......................... | 52% | 37% |
| "Practical when used"........................ | 75% | 72% |
| Economical.................................. | 71% | 73% |
| "Practical bottle"............................ | 64% | 66% |
| Color and smell............................. | positively judged | |
| Normally used cleaner smells better............. | 3% | 9% |
| Normally used cleaner cleans stains better....... | 0% | 17% |
| Normally used cleaner is less practical as to its bottle................................... | 7% | |
| Spray cleaner is a new thing................... | 50% | |
| Spray is known from window cleaner (Sidolin).... | 25% | |
| I recommend Trifft for spot and large surface cleaning................................. | 62% | 57% |
| I recommend Trifft for larger surfaces.......... | 17% | 29% |
| I recommend Trifft for spot cleaning........... | 19% | 21% |
| Trifft was sprayed directly on the surface to clean.................................... | 75% | |
| Trifft was sprayed on the cleaning rag.......... | 10% | |
| Pump is functioning perfectly.................. | 71% | 66% |
| Product needs improvement.................... | 24% | 31% |
|    Especially the pump...................... | 12% | |
|    Especially the bottle..................... | 6% | |
| I would pay more than DM 2 for the product.... | 60% | 52% |
|    (average price)........................... | DM 2.22 | DM 2.13 |
| Advantages of the spray mechanism: | | |
|    Economical.............................. | 50% | 38% |
|    Good dosing............................. | 15% | 25% |
|    Practical................................ | 17% | 16% |
|    Direct application....................... | 8% | 8% |
|    Clean working........................... | 5% | 4% |
|    Time-saving............................. | 4% | 4% |
| I like household work......................... | 68% | |
| I am indifferent to household work............. | 22% | |

Other cleaners normally used were: Dor (35%) and Ajax All-Purpose Cleaner (17%).

Most housewives think that Trifft is most closely related to Sidolin (25%) than to Dor (9% versus 16%).

## EXHIBIT 4

### Excerpts from a Research Study among 40 Housewives
### Using Depth-Interviewing—May 1968

In a laboratory test with 40 housewives, the results of the depth interviews were:

A. General Findings
   Major classifying dimensions relating to APHCs offered by interviewees were:

   Application area.
   Cleaning power.
   Texture.

   Liquid cleaners are said to be modern, practical. Having a broad range of uses, they are convenient, time-saving, and easy to mix—but expensive. There is a need for precise instructions as to the appropriate mixture for the surface type.

B. Spray Cleaners
   1. Reactions to new concepts
      The new principle raised immediately a negative reaction due to inability to identify the concept. The spray principle is associated with aerosol spray cosmetics (hair spray) and slightly with window cleaning. It is rejected for household cleaning because:

      Difficult to control the amount used,
      Risk of spraying on a wider area than needed, and
      Doesn't seem superior to conventional liquid cleaners.

      Spray APHC's can only be imagined in a form like window cleaners; i.e., in plastic bottle with a squirt top. But skepticism should, on the other hand, not be overestimated. If such a product is introduced, however, a long learning process will be necessary along with a very attractive presentation of the product.

   2. Expectations of a spray APHC
      Basic areas of application were thought to be larger pieces of furniture (like tables and cupboards), but the product is perceived as being uneconomical. Doors, tiles, and windows were mentioned. These attitudes again stress the need for consumer education.

   3. Reactions to a Trifft concept
      a. Spot cleaning endangers the whole product conception. Emphasis on spot cleaning power and use for delicate surfaces are important. The price, substantially higher than for comparable products, represents an economic barrier.
      b. Brand name "Trifft": very original and appealing but lacks product specificity.
      c. Package: positively judged; close to window cleaners and dishwashing liquids. The label does not give precise areas of application. The bottle is easy to handle.
      d. Trifft on today's market: Trifft's image is close to Henkel's

## EXHIBIT 4 (Continued)

Dor and Mr. Proper but can be a good competitor given the following recommended changes:

Dynamic, colorful package (against Mr. Proper!);
Clear product profile, clear instruction of use;
Emphasis on use for large surfaces to avoid "specialization"; and
Stress on easy, time-saving applications.

## EXHIBIT 5
### Profile and Prices of Some APHCs in Germany in 1968

| | | *Price* (*in DM per Kg*) |
|---|---|---|
| Trifft*................ | All purpose cleaner, convenient because of the spray principle, concentration on a new application principle that needs no water, and is good for the hands. | 4.87 (introduction) 5.87 |
| Vigor*................ | Fights against the tough dirt and greyness, destroys the dirt from the inside without water, and restores shine without rinsing. | 2.44 (introduction) 5.00 |
| Schnip*................ | Gives a guaranteed shine and is always there to deal with a "disaster spot." | 3.90 (introduction) 5.30 |
| Mr. Proper............. | Concentrated liquid cleaner that leaves no marks and shades, restores every surface to a "mirror-like" condition, and also emphasizes fast and efficient cleaning. | 3.97 |
| Ajax liquid.............. | Concentrated liquid cleaner (the "White Tornado") with tough cleaning power, especially for cleaning thoroughly and quickly in difficult situations. | 3.26 |
| Dor powder............. | Shine for tiles, doors, and furniture in kitchen and bathroom without attacking the surface in any way, mild for the hands, efficient when used. | 5.70 |
| Imi (powder and liquid).... | Universal for kitchen, bathroom, cellar, stairs and floors, "cuts the grease" in these places, and can also be used for dirty work clothes. | 2.00 (powder) 3.30 (liquid) |

* These cleaners were the only ones to be applied directly on a surface to be cleaned. Other cleaners were concentrated and had to be diluted with water before application with a sponge or a cleaning rag. Therefore, spray APHC's already consisted of a nonconcentrated liquid.

On the other hand, due to the spray principle, only a very small quantity of liquid was sprayed onto a given surface to be cleaned, whereas much more water/cleaner mixture was used with the other types of cleaners.

## EXHIBIT 6

### Advertising Expenditures for All-Purpose Household Cleaners in Germany 1967–1968
#### (in 000 DM)

| Product | 1967 Total (000) DM | 1967 Percent | Monthly Spendings for 1968 | | | | | | | | | | | | 1968 Total (000) DM | 1968 Percent† |
|---|---|---|---|---|---|---|---|---|---|---|---|---|---|---|---|---|
| | | | Jan. | Feb. | Mar. | Apr. | May | June | July | Aug. | Sept. | Oct. | Nov. | Dec. | | |
| Dor.......... | 3,882.7 | 24.3 | 2.0 | 69.9 | 639.2 | 897.4 | 642.2 | 23.0 | 447.4 | 498.0 | 418.7 | 301.1 | 136.1 | | 4075.0 | 22.2 |
| Trifft........ | | | | | | | | | | 42.8 | 651.6 | 633.0 | 547.5 | 511.8 | 3387.5 | 18.4 |
| Imi Flussig.... | 1,601.5 | 10.0 | | | | 313.2 | 292.5 | 144.0 | | | | | | | 261.5 | 1.4 |
| W. R. Krafter.. | 473.7 | 3.0 | 50.4 | 33.9 | 57.1 | 40.4 | 25.4 | 32.3 | 18.1 | 3.9 | | | | | 145.8 | 0.8 |
| Saugermacht..... | | | | | | | | 35.9 | 29.0 | | 24.6 | 35.6 | 16.4 | 16.4 | 235.3 | 1.3 |
| Vigor.......... | | | | | | | | 30.9 | 59.0 | 30.1 | 54.7 | | 25.0 | | 677.1 | 3.7 |
| Fairy........ | 1,172.4 | 7.4 | 50.2 | 50.5 | 54.2 | 169.3 | 166.3 | 150.1 | 38.2 | 16.5 | | 117.2 | 26.1 | 38.5 | 3889.4 | 21.2 |
| Meister RR*..... | 4,568.3 | 28.6 | 389.0 | 319.8 | 320.6 | 466.1 | 432.6 | 588.5 | 320.2 | 275.3 | 194.7 | 187.6 | 233.1 | 191.9 | 4716.5 | 25 |
| Ajax A lizw...... | 4,258.3 | 27.6 | 441.4 | 662.2 | 581.9 | 533.4 | 224.7 | 235.9 | 274.8 | 326.8 | 474.8 | 377.7 | 304.6 | 278.5 | 777.2 | 4.2 |
| Schnip........ | | | | | | | 146.0 | 136.7 | 140.1 | 77.6 | 81.0 | 70.9 | 57.4 | 67.5 | 260.1 | 1.4 |
| Pinarom..... | | | 18.5 | 12.4 | 98.7 | 59.2 | 11.7 | 10.0 | 7.9 | 7.2 | 4.5 | 7.3 | 10.8 | 12.0 | 260.1 | 1.4 |
| Total...... | 15,956.9 | 100% | 951.5 | 1,148.7 | 1,751.7 | 2,479.0 | 1,941.4 | 1,357.3 | 1,534.7 | 1,273.2 | 1,904.6 | 1,755.8 | 1,357.0 | 1,116.4 | 18,376.1 | 100% |
| Quarters........ | I—3,851.9 | | | | | | | I and II—9,629.6 | | | I–III—14,147.1 | | | | | |

* The 1967 media expenditure for Mr. Proper does not include seven million trial bottles distributed free in 1967.
† Exceed 100% due to rounding.

# The Leisure Group (B)

In late June 1969 S. F. Hinchliffe, chairman and co-chief executive officer of The Leisure Group, received an early morning telephone call from a corporate "finder" who reported a company that TLG might be interested in acquiring. The company, Himalayan Industries of Monterey, California, was engaged in the manufacturing and marketing of backpacking equipment for hikers and campers. The finder indicated that there was considerable urgency in deciding whether or not to acquire Himalayan since it was about to terminate a three-year distribution contract with Bear Archery Company of Grayling, Michigan. Since Himalayan was too small an organization to field its own sales force, it might sign another distribution contract which would lock up the company for an additional three years. If TLG was interested, the finder would set up an appointment with TLG's management to talk to the owner of Himalayan, Richard Mack, but he again stressed that if Hinchliffe was interested, he should act quickly. (See TLG (A) for a description of the company's activities.)

As soon as Mr. Hinchliffe had hung up, he had his secretary contact Rick Berthold, a corporate vice president, and Tom Porter, a marketing manager, and ask them to come to his office. When they appeared a few minutes later, Mr. Hinchliffe quickly outlined the sketchy details he had received from the finder and asked if either of them knew anything about backpacking, or the industry. Since neither of them did, Tom Porter was asked to gather as much information as he could about the industry, its growth history, projections, and Himalayan Industries, in order to decide as soon as possible whether to pursue the potential acquisition any further. With that injunction Mr. Hinchliffe turned

This case was prepared by Sterling B. Sessions. Reprinted from *Stanford Business Cases 1970* with the permission of the publisher, Graduate School of Business, Stanford University. Copyright © 1970 by the Board of Trustees of the Leland Stanford Junior University.

back to some work on his desk, and Tom walked out of the office wondering what the backpacking industry was all about. By five o'clock that afternoon he would be TLG's expert on backpacking.

Tom was able to assemble a report on both the industry and Himalayan after a visit to the library and making several telephone calls to friends who were much more familiar with the industry than he. (See Exhibit 1 for a reproduction of the relevant data.)

After reviewing the data on the market which were submitted by Tom, Mr. Hinchliffe decided that there was enough information available to warrant a trip to the company to secure more information about its internal operation. Hinchliffe called the finder the next morning to arrange for a representative of TLG to fly to Monterey for a day to talk to the company's president and founder, Mr. Mack. A summary of Tom's day with Mr. Mack and an evaluation of the report which appeared on Mr. Hinchliffe's desk a few days later are seen in Exhibit 2.

## HISTORY OF HIMALAYAN INDUSTRIES

Himalayan Industries was a relatively young company in the highly competitive world of sporting goods equipment manufacturers. Founded in 1953 by Richard G. Mack, a Yale-trained mammalogist who had participated in numerous scientific expeditions, the company had steadily grown and diversified its product line.

Mr. Mack participated in the first Nepal Expedition co-sponsored by the National Geographic Society, Yale, and the Smithsonian Institute. He also was a member of the U.S. Information Service in Indo-China. He had backpacked, collected mammals, and hiked all over the world. Most of the products that were later to be manufactured by Himalayan Industries were a result of his backpacking experience on these many expeditions.

The first and one of the most successful products developed by Himalayan and the Hike-A-Poose child carrier—30 ounces of aluminum and canvas, worn on the back, and used to transport small children. As the company grew, Mr. Mack also developed backpacks for camping purposes. Through the first difficult six months of the company's history, an eastern manufacturer produced Himalayan's products, but this proved to be a very costly arrangement. Within a year of its founding Himalayan moved west. Mack opened a shop in a 1,400 square foot storage shed in San Jose, California. Together with a friend, he did double duty as manufacturer by night and salesman by day. The company got its first real break when the Hike-A-Poose made news at a 1955 National Sporting Goods Show. The company began jobbing out distribution, and Himalayan products were sold in 44 states and overseas within a year.

In 1957 the company moved from San Jose to an abandoned cannery in Monterey, California. The new location gave Himalayan about 12,000 square feet of space. In these early years of development Mack cited marketing limitations in the distribution of his products as the greatest single factor holding back growth and expansion. The agreement made with Bear in 1966 was thought to be the solution for this problem, although it proved to be not as valuable as anticipated.

The Himalayan Company had been relatively static in its development over the last several years, as could be seen from the background information accumulated. This could be traced primarily to its distribution methods which had been extremely weak. Through an exclusive distribution agreement Himalayan had agreed to sell a certain quantity of its production every year to the Bear Archery Company, which, in turn, gave the products to its sales force to sell. Bear also developed the advertising and promotional activity for the product. The exclusive distributorship arrangement resulted in a period of level sales for Himalayan, largely because the salesmen for Bear were not given a good introduction to the product and never really understood very much about it. Himalayan had little control over the salesmen from the standpoint of motivating them to sell Himalayan equipment because of the terms of the agreement. Consequently, many salesmen had done little, if any, sales work for Himalayan. One of the major reasons for this situation was created by the fact that Bear's salesmen earned handsome commissions on Bear's equipment but very little on the Himalayan equipment. (Bear salesmen were earning $20–$25,000 annually on the sales of archery equipment, while sales work for Himalayan involved developing new channels of distribution with smaller possible rewards for the salesman.) Hence, it really didn't pay for a salesman to make a special call to a store which didn't also carry Bear's archery equipment. Moreover, since Himalayan marked up its products 20–25% and Bear applied another 25–30%, the net effect was that Bear's prices on Himalayan equipment were at least 15% higher than its competitors', and it was extremely difficult to explain the price differential to the retail buyer. This not only caused a loss of customers and consumer franchise but allowed other producers to raise their prices, realizing larger profit margins. For these reasons, Mr. Mack decided against continuing the distribution contract with Bear. At the time of the discontinuance, Bear still held $450,000 worth of Himalayan packs in inventory in its warehouses across the country, and TLG would have to decide what to do with this surplus inventory if it acquired the company.

## FURTHER DISCUSSIONS

Tom Porter explained to Mr. Hinchliffe and Mr. Berthold that financially the company was worth little; although the company had over $500,000 in sales in 1969 and earned a modest profit, it was having problems generating sufficient working capital to continue operations. What TLG would be purchasing would be a marketing opportunity in a new area and a limited distribution system. A comparison between Himalayan's customer list and TLG's showed very little overlap, with much of Himalayan's sales being made through the small specialty shops dealing in camping and hiking equipment. Only 13% of Himalayan's sales were through what could be considered mass merchandising channels, and most of this business was an offshoot of Himalayan's line—a baby back carrier which could be used for biking or shopping mothers and fathers. By 1969 the company only had 550 active customers, and the largest customer only purchased $6,000 worth of Himalayan products. There were 1,000 accounts selling next to nothing. An approximate breakdown of Himalayan sales volume through its various distribution channels is seen in Exhibit 4.

On the plus side, the company appeared to have an acceptable brand, although it had not exploited it, a basically good product, some good people, as Tom's report indicated, and, perhaps most importantly, it appeared to be in a new industry, one that TLG had not yet attempted to enter. Himalayan had captured 8% of the high-priced segment of the backpacking market and 5% of the total market, but it was believed by Hinchliffe and Porter that if this product could be introduced into mass merchandised retail outlets the market share would sharply improve. The products also had patent coverage which was one of TLG's criteria for an acquired brand.

One of the chief problems that several people in the TLG organization anticipated with this product line was that it was technically complex, and they wondered how easily TLG's sales force might be able to handle it. For instance, backpacking equipment came in many variations, depending upon the nature of the hike, the build of the person carrying the pack, and the needs and demands that would be placed on the equipment. It was not the type of product which could be placed into a large mass merchandising outlet and allowed to sell itself. For this reason some changes would have to be made in the marketing of the product were it to be incorporated into TLG's product lines, so that the salesman could sell it along with TLG's other products. Also, in keeping with its product specialists, TLG would probably have to obtain a staff of backpacking experts both to promote the product and to aid in the development of new or improved equipment.

Now that these data had been collected, Mr. Hinchliffe, with the help of Tom Porter, knew he must make a decision. He thought that he should act quickly, since several other companies were also looking at Himalayan. There seemed to be an equal number of pluses and minuses for acquiring Himalayan, but Hinchliffe was not certain as to which course of action to take.

## EXHIBIT 1

### 1970 Himalayan Program

REVIEW OF THE BACKPACK MARKET

A. THE MARKET

The backpack market is approaching $18 million in retail sales annually and appears to be growing at a rate of 15% per year. By comparison, the backpack market is about the size of the hockey market. While most packs are sold to hikers, many backpacks are also sold for such diverse uses as hunting, fishing, mountain climbing, skiing, cycling, camping, and bird watching.

*Future Growth*

We expect the minimum rate of growth for the backpack market to be 15% annually. However, for the reasons listed below, annual growth for the next several years could be as high as 25% per year:

1. *Increased Leisure Time and Affluence*
   Increased leisure time and affluence are channeling more and more Americans into the kinds of activities which utilize backpacks, i.e., hiking, walking, fishing, hunting, skiing, mountain climbing, bird watching, cycling, and camping. This will result in an expansion of the backpack market at a rate greater than the expansion of any one of these outdoor activities.

2. *Increased Participation in Camping*
   The popularity of camping has increased spectacularly in recent years and since backpacks are used most frequently in conjunction with camping, sales of backpacks have soared accordingly. In 1965 only 10% of the population went camping, while in 1969 nearly a third of the population went camping. In the western states nearly 60% of all adult men took at least one camping trip during the year. It is estimated (by the U.S. Forest Service) that, in 1970, 45 million Americans will trek to this country's 35 national parks, each representing a potential user of a backpack.

3. *Need to Get away from People*
   As this country's rapid growth and population are concentrated in large urban areas, more and more people want to get away from noisy neighbors and crowded cities and find that the backpack is the vehicle for doing this. Since many of the more popular campgrounds in this country are becoming as crowded as the cities, there is even more need for backpacking. The U.S. Forest Service says an estimated 2.2 million people will visit U.S. wilderness areas this year, about double the number of five years ago. They further estimate that the number of wilderness users is rising twice as fast as the number of visitors to the nation's campgrounds.

4. *Increase in Trail Systems*
   In addition to the expansion of national trail systems and newly created wilderness areas, many states and counties are creating trail

**EXHIBIT 1 (Continued)**

systems as outlets for recreation. As these trail systems expand, there are more and more opportunities for people to go backpacking.

5. *Increase in Backpacking Clubs*

It has been estimated by experts in the field that the number of backpacking clubs is increasing by over 25% annually. This helps build a nucleus of loyal consumers in the backpacking area.

## B. THE MAJOR COMPETITORS

There appear to be two basic segments of the backpacking market today—the high-priced segment which includes primarily nylon bags and the low-priced segment which includes primarily cotton imported bags. The market is split with 60% of the dollar volume in high-priced bags and 40% in low-priced bags. Of course, in units the distribution would be skewed much more heavily to the low-priced segment of the market. Himalayan competes only in the high-priced segment of the market and has an estimated 12% of that market. However, it should be noted that Himalayan's dollar volume has remained fairly constant during the last three years, and, consequently, their market share has slipped considerably during this period of time. We are targeting a doubling of the market share for Himalayan in 1970. Listed below are Himalayan's major competitors; Table 1 compares them to Himalayan.

### Backpack Market Competition

| Firm (major competitors) | Estimated Market Share (%) | Comments |
|---|---|---|
| Camptrails | 19 | Have both high and low end products. Sold through all types of outlets including mass merchandisers. |
| Himalayan | 5 | |
| Kelty | 6 | The top name in the industry based on the design of their frames. Making an effort to sell more through mass merchandisers. |
| Trager's | 3 | |
| Gerry (Colorado Outdoor Sports) | 3 | |
| Universal | 2 | New company. |
| White Stag | 2 | Very low-priced and poorly-designed product. |
| Denali | 1 | |
| Alp Sport | 1 | Known mostly for their bags. |
| All other | 1 | |
| *Other Market Segments* | | |
| Surplus Army-Navy | 3 | |
| Imports | 32 | |
| Boy Scouts | 23 | |
| Total | 100% | |

**EXHIBIT 1 (Continued)**

C. MARKET SEGMENTS

Today 40–45% of the market is in low-priced bags, most of which are imported from Japan or France. However, one reason why the low-priced imported bags have such a large market share is because the makers of high-priced equipment have not merchandised their products in such a way that mass merchandisers can easily sell them. The consumer is willing to pay more for a backpack as long as he can see the value he is getting for the money. The segments of the high-priced line break out as follows:

| Item | Percent of Market |
|---|---|
| Day bags | 40 |
| Overnighter and weekender bags and frames | 30 |
| Expedition and vacation bags | 20 |
| Accessories | 10 |
| Total | 100 |

D. DISTRIBUTION CHANNELS

Currently most backpack items are sold through the backpack specialty shops and sporting goods stores. However, as seen below, we expect sales of backpacks to increase drastically through the mass merchandiser channel in the next few years.

Backpack Distribution

| Type of Outlet | 1969 | 1970 | 1971 | 1972 |
|---|---|---|---|---|
| Mass merchandiser | 5% | 12% | 20% | 26% |
| Specialty shop | 60 | 52 | 44 | 38 |
| Sporting goods store | 29 | 30 | 31 | 31 |
| Surplus store | 3 | 3 | 2 | 2 |
| Other | 3 | 3 | 3 | 3 |
| Total | 100% | 100% | 100% | 100% |

E. GEOGRAPHIC DISTRIBUTION OF SALES

According to the Omnibus Study the purchases of backpacks are skewed to the western areas. As the table below indicates, nearly 34% of backpack purchases are in the mountain and Pacific regions. Relative to the purchases of the total United States, these two areas have an index of 163 and 145 respectively.

## TABLE 1
### Himalayan Compared with Its Competitors

| | Price Structure | Method of Selling | Average Mark-Up | Private Label | Total Market Strength | Consumer Packaging | General Consumer Regard | Parent Company |
|---|---|---|---|---|---|---|---|---|
| Himalayan.................. | Medium to high | Own sales force | 50% | No | 5% | Boxes | Medium | Himalayan |
| Camptrails................. | Low to medium | Jobbers | 50–55% | Yes (Co-op and North Face) | 19% | None for packs | Low | Camptrails |
| Kelty..................... | Medium to high | Dealer and direct | 37% | No | 6% | Boxes | High (tops) | Kelty |
| Mountain Master (Denali)... | Medium to high | Reps | 40% | No | Less than 1% | None | Low | Mountain Master |
| Trailwise................. | Medium to high | Through Ski Hut Alp Sport | 40% | No | 1% | None | Medium | Donner Mountain Corporation |
| Alp Sport................. | Medium to high | Alp Sport | 40% | No | 1% | None | Medium | Ithaca Gun |
| Gerry..................... | Medium | Reps | 40% | No | 3% | Plastic bags | Medium | Outdoor Sports Industries |
| Holubar................... | Medium | Holubar | 40% | No | Less than 1% | None | Medium | Holubar, Ltd. |
| North Face................ | High for soft packs | Own stores and reps | 40% | No | Less than 1% | None | Medium | North Face |
| Recreational Equipment Cooperative Organizations..... | Low to medium | Mail order and retail | Under 40% because of Co-op policy | Made for them by someone else | Good | None | Medium to high because of bargains | Recreational Equipment |
| Imports................... | Low | Jobbers | 50%+ | Yes | 23% | None | Bargain | |

SOURCE: A trade salesman.

### Percent U.S. Households Purchasing Backpacks by Region

| Region | Percent Households Purchase 1 or More Backpacks | Index |
|---|---|---|
| New England | 12.0 | 109 |
| Middle Atlantic | 10.9 | 98 |
| East North Central | 9.8 | 89 |
| West North Central | 8.7 | 79 |
| South Atlantic | 10.4 | 94 |
| East South Central | 7.3 | 66 |
| West South Central | 7.8 | 71 |
| Mountain | 17.9 | 163 |
| Pacific | 15.9 | 145 |
| Total U.S. | 11.0 | 100 |

SOURCE: Market Facts—Omnibus Study.

The New England area also represents an area of strong development of backpacking equipment.

### EXHIBIT 2
### MEMO

TO: S. F. Hinchliffe, Jr.

CC: J. R. Berthold

FROM: T. S. Porter

SUBJECT: *Himalayan Industries*

DATE: July 10, 1969

This is to outline my initial observations from spending Wednesday, July 2, with the president (Richard Mack) and general manager (Robert Collier) of Himalayan Industries in Monterey, California. Since we have already agreed to pursue Himalayan further as an acquisition candidate, this is less a recommendation for acquisition and more a background document to be used as negotiations continue and should Himalayan become acquired.

I. MANAGEMENT

    A. *President*—Richard Mack is the president of Himalayan Industries. He started the company approximately 20 years ago and has been scraping by at a fairly static sales level of between $150–$250,000 for the last 15 years. Mack's main interest seemed to be product development and marketing, and he is interested in staying active in the business. However, we suspect he may be willing to stay on a part-time basis.

    B. *General Manager*—Robert Collier is responsible for production and finance/accounting. His background is that of accountant, financial consultant, and cost accounting for the aerospace industry. Collier has a strong option position in the company (over 6,000 shares) and is very anxious to stay on in his current capacity. Collier appears to have done an excellent job and would probably be a satisfactory operations manager should The Leisure Group acquire Himalayan. Other key people in the operation are:

C. *Bookkeeper*—who is thought of very highly by the management.

D. *Sewing Department Foreman*—who has had eight years of sewing school education.

E. *Head of Juvenile Sales*—This is the woman who runs the retail factory outlet store at the plant and is also responsible for supervising the reps for juvenile (backpacks for infants) items. This woman would probably not be needed with the TLG sales force.

II. PERSONNEL NEEDS

The company is in the process of interviewing for a marketing manager. However, they will probably discontinue this search if The Leisure Group appears to be attractive to them. Also, the company feels a need to have additional mechanical engineering talent but can probably not justify hiring a full-time man at this time.

III. OPERATIONS

Himalayan's production facilities, while cramped in a garage-like condition, seem to be very efficient and technologically up to date. Key points are as follows:

A. *Raw Materials*—The biggest raw materials are aluminum and textile materials for pack bags. Due to almost no warehouse space, all raw materials are tightly scheduled to coincide with production so there is almost no raw materials inventory. Almost no raw materials are preassembled by outside vendors.

B. *Operations*—The process for making backpacks at Himalayan is almost fully integrated. A heat-treating process is used which eliminates the welding used by most backpack companies. This superior technology enables Himalayan to make a lighter pack on a mass production basis.

C. *Aluminum Department*—Collier indicates that the aluminum department which makes the pack frames may be operating at only 1/10 capacity.

D. *Sewing Department*—The sewing department currently employs 55 people and operates on two shifts. Introduction of a third shift could improve output considerably but not in the dimension needed if The Leisure Group were really to expand Himalayan's business.

IV. MARKETING

The management was reluctant to talk about their marketing system since they were convinced that if we did not buy Himalayan, we would buy one of their competitors, and they were afraid we might use the information against them someday. Nevertheless, we were able to learn the following:

A. *Distribution Channels*—Himalayan has distribution in mass merchandisers (J.C. Penney, Sears, and Montgomery Ward), sporting goods stores, and archery shops. We suspect that distribution is concentrated in archery shops and specialty sporting goods stores due to Bear Archery's distribution of Himalayan's line for the past three years.

B. *Sales Effort*—Sales to mass merchandisers are made directly by Mack and Collier. These customers are called "house accounts." The backpack line is sold through Bear salesmen and sporting goods reps, and the juvenile products are sold through juvenile reps.

C. *Seasonality*—The peak selling season seems to be between April and August. The fiscal year coincides with the calendar year, and the sales through the first five months of fiscal/calendar 1969 seem to be about one-half of their projected 1969 sales.

D. *Volume by Product Category*—Volume seems to be fairly evenly distributed between all items. However, the juvenile packs are probably the volume leaders with about 25–35% of total sales.

E. *Warehousing*—Himalayan products are currently warehoused in Monterey and Grayling, Michigan. A study is underway to determine the feasibility of opening a warehouse in New York.

F. *Marketing Strategy*—Himalayan strategy is to be the number one volume brand of backpacks. To achieve this objective, they believe it is necessary to achieve penetration at all major distribution channels and to appeal to young people who seem to be the major consumer for their products. Since there is little recognized brand identification among backpack companies, they believe it is imperative to establish brand recognition and superiority immediately.

V. FINANCE/ACCOUNTING

Financial data were obtained and may be found in the Himalayan file. It was not our purpose to summarize the data in this report.

INDICATED ACTIONS

Of all the companies in the backpack business, Himalayan Industries appears to have the best name and best production facilities for becoming the leading brand in a mushrooming industry. Consequently, we urge that Himalayan be actively pursued as an acquisition candidate. While Himalayan's 1969 sales are estimated at about $600,000, we believe it is realistic to expect sales to double in each of the next two years under TLG management. These gains would come largely as a result of the ability of the TLG sales force to secure increased distribution among mass merchandisers and large sporting goods stores where Himalayan's position is currently weak.

If TLG were to acquire Himalayan, we believe the following actions would have to take place:

1. *Operations*—Basically the operations seem to be running on a sound basis. However, for sales to double in the next two years, substantial capacity increases will have to be made in the sewing department. Additionally, the finished goods warehouse needs to be reorganized or moved to increase its efficiency. While there are probably other actions which our operations

people will be able to spot, these seem to be the most obvious problem areas in what appears to be a very smooth-running operation.

2. *Marketing*—We believe a marketing budget equal to about 10% of estimated 1970 sales or $120,000 is needed. The main thrust of this marketing program would be to define consumer needs through market research, substantially improve the company's brand identification by improving the brand's logo and its use on all packaging, to presell the consumer through consumer advertising, and to develop a point-of-purchase program which makes selling backpacks easy for the trade and buying easy for the consumer.

We are ready to discuss this subject further at your convenience.

**EXHIBIT 3**

**Himalayan Industries Customer Mix 1969 and 1970**

| | Percent | |
|---|---|---|
| *Customer* | *1969* | *1970* |
| Bear Archery Company | 59 | –0– |
| Sears, Roebuck (mail order only) | 13 | 20 |
| Boy Scouts of America* | 5 | –0– |
| Industrial | 8 | 12 |
| Retail | 5 | 4 |
| Export | 5 | 6 |
| Dealer direct | –0– | 43 |
| Governmental agencies | 5 | 5 |
| Mail order | –0– | 10 |
| | 100 | 100 |
| Gross Sales | $600,000 | $900,000† |

* Account not profitable.

† This gross figure does not include juvenile sales. Recently a marketing plan was implemented incorporating nine representatives throughout the major cities in the United States. Annual sales from this line are expected to be in excess of $500,000.

# Spectra-Physics (B)[1]

In the summer of 1967 Mr. Herb Dwight, president and chief executive officer of Spectra-Physics set forth the policies that henceforth all research and development activities would be guided primarily by inputs from customers and that profitable market opportunities would be pursued by integrating forward into systems and end-user markets. He hoped that if these could be implemented successfully the company would achieve a consistent record of substantial profitability. In order to make these policies operational the following changes in corporate strategy would be made: R&D expenses would be decreased substantially, marketing and sales expenditures would be increased, and acquisitions designed to facilitate forward integration would be bought aggressively. The last would broaden the company's base in the systems and end-user markets, thereby decreasing dependence upon scientific applications of the laser.

While no important organizational changes were made when Dwight took over the company, he did introduce a number of changes into S-P operations. First, he set up a budgeting model by which each existing product and new product idea would be screened according to its projected cost, profit margin, return on investment, and long-term market potential. Product life cycles are short (generally three years or less) for high technology products such as lasers, thereby making such financial estimates critically important.

Over the next three years S-P's difficulties continued. The masking camera was sold to Hewlett-Packard, and a $170,000 write-off was entered as an extraordinary item on the 1967 income statement. The company's carbon dioxide laser was another failure; it was not powerful enough for cutting and welding in industrial use. The company neglected to seek the advice of users who wanted a 1,000-watt model, instead of

Reprinted from *Stanford Business Cases 1973* with the permission of the publisher, Graduate School of Business, Stanford University. Copyright 1973 by the Board of Trustees of the Leland Stanford Junior University.

[1] See Spectra-Physics (A) for company background information and the events leading to the action described in this case.

S-P's 100-watt model. Coherent Radiation had a superior $CO_2$ laser which forced S-P out of the market.

In the ion laser market S-P used its own unique technology to develop its model 140 argon ion laser, but the new product failed to match the required specifications. The unit competed reasonably well against Raytheon's ion laser for two years, but in 1968 Coherent Radiation put their argon laser on the market. Since this product was superior to S-P's, it soon captured the market to such an extent that S-P withdraw its laser from the market.

While S-P was struggling to gain a foothold in the commercial market with its LT-3, a new development dramatically changed the direction of the commercial laser industry. It was discovered that use of an inexpensive laser greatly facilitated the laying of sewer pipes because increased accuracy in long distance alignment permitted the use of longer, cheaper pipe sections.

S-P immediately set out to adapt their alignment laser for use in sewer construction. Once again, the lack of knowledge of what features would be important in such a laser kept them from developing a good product. The lead in the new market was taken by Blount & George (Automated Grade Light) and Laser Alignment. S-P developed and attempted to market its own sewer laser but could not make any sales.

Frustrated by failure to penetrate commercial markets, and facing saturation in current research markets, Dwight began looking for a possible acquisition which would get the company into the construction laser business. After analyzing several possibilities, University Laboratories of Berkeley, California, was chosen as the best candidate.

University Labs (U-L) was founded in 1966 by Dick Jaenicke, a product sales manager from Optics Technology, and Tom Perkins, an investor from Hewlett-Packard, to manufacture a new kind of laser tube called a coherent lightbulb—the first tube which required no alignment of any kind. U-L developed a helium laser for use in universities, but, when U-L failed to penetrate this market, Jaenicke searched for field applications for his product, uncovering the construction industry as a potentially profitable market. With an aggressive marketing effort U-L was able to sell its lasers to contractors for alignment purposes. Company sales grew from $230,000 in 1967 to $730,000 in 1968 to $1,240,000 in 1969.

When Dwight and Stark approached U-L in 1969, the two companies appeared to complement each other perfectly. U-L was in the process of building a sewer alignment laser (called Dialgrade)—the very product S-P was looking for. With considerable experience in engineering and marketing of construction laser equipment, U-L had the strength S-P lacked in this market segment. U-L, on the other hand, was handicapped by lack of manufacturing expertise, which could be overcome by merger with S-P. In addition to the Dialgrade laser, U-L's low-cost laser tubes complemented S-P's line of high-quality, high-priced research-oriented lasers. This segment, ignored by S-P in its early years of operation, was becoming increasingly lucrative as applications for low-cost lasers expanded. Finally, in addition to the complementarity of product lines, U-L's distribution network for its construction laser line consisted of a complete network of independent sales distributors. This set-up, entirely lacking in S-P's operations, was well suited to selling lasers to contractors. (See Exhibit 1 for S-P's product mix as of 1969.)

U-L matched S-P's ambitions so well that the acquisition was executed by vote of the respective boards of directors, despite some misgivings on the part of S-P management. Dissenters felt that the price paid by S-P was too high. The terms of the acquisition called for an exchange of 227,000 shares of S-P stock (valued at $22 per share at the time of acquisition in February 1970) for all 170,000 outstanding shares of U-L stock. The terms were based on pro forma sales predictions for fiscal 1970 of $2.8 million for U-L (with an estimated $240,000 in earnings before taxes) and $6.6 million for S-P (with estimated pretax earnings of $500,000).

Several key personnel came to S-P as a result of the acquisition. Dick Jaenicke, former U-L president, became executive vice president. Harv Berger (an electrical engineer with an M.B.A.) became head of construction laser equipment. Berger had been responsible for establishing U-L's construction engineering distributor network. In addition to these key line personnel, Tom Perkins, general manager of Hewlett-Packard's computer division and chairman of U-L's board of directors, came to S-P as a director.

Dwight felt that the company had now become difficult to manage— too unwieldly. The product line was now extremely complex, with different sales organizations and different marketing strategies existing side by side. Managers from both S-P and U-L were not being used efficiently in their own roles. In mid-1970 the decision was made to reorganize the company into four major profit centers, each with its own engineering and marketing departments (see Exhibit 2):

a.  Laser products division (LPD) consisting of research lasers and laser tubes;

b.  Engineering laser systems division (ELS) whose products were construction-oriented;

c.  Optical products division encompassing laser accessories and coating operations for laser mirrors; and

d.  European operations.

Dick Stark, then S-P's marketing manager, was put in charge of LPD. Jaenicke took over ELS while Bob Mortensen remained head of the optics division. Jon Tompkins, formerly a product marketing manager, went to Europe as the new head of overseas operations.

The objects of the new organization were to:

a.  Facilitate delegation of individual profit management responsibilities.

    *b.*  Add a new dimension to product planning by insuring a more tightly coupled interaction between marketing and development efforts within well-defined product areas.

    *c.*  Insure rapid product reaction to new technical and marketing developments in the field of electro-optics.

    *d.*  Stimulate utilization of more innovative approaches to the development of new products.

Three additional changes were made. Technically trained marketing men were placed in key positions to achieve better coordination between marketing and engineering. A formal financial planning procedure with an 18-month planning horizon was initiated. Finally, a profit incentive program was instituted for all top management personnel, tying salaries to profits; a manager could receive up to an additional 80% of his base salary if his division exceeded its yearly target by more than a specified amount.

By early 1971, ELS was aggressively selling an improved Dialgrade sewer laser. While the unit was not the best in the industry (AGL and LA dominated the market with 40% and 33% market shares respectively), S-P was able to sell 315 units in 1971 for a 22% market share. With a further improved product scheduled for introduction in mid-1972, prospects looked good for S-P in the sewer laser market.

At the same time, Dwight was able to devote more time to seeking new product ideas through acquisition. Late in 1971 S-P negotiated the acquisition of the Autolab division of the Vidar Corporation. Autolab, a two-year-old wing of Vidar, produced digital automation equipment for chromatographs (instruments used by chemists to determine exact composition of substances). When Vidar was purchased by Continental Telephone, the diversification venture no longer interested them, and Autolab went looking for a new home. Autolab sought a small growth company willing to diversify. S-P matched these desires and was greatly impressed with Autolab's product offerings[2] and its short record of financial success. In 1970, its first year of operation, Autolab had sales of $320,000 and a pretax loss of $135,000. In 1971 on sales of $1,265,000, Autolab showed pretax earnings of $225,000. Furthermore, Autolab offered an opportunity to decrease the company's dependence on scientific laser products and markets.

Autolab's initial success was due to its superior product offering in a large but highly specialized market, a solid sales force with a competitive incentive system of compensation, and management with worldwide experience in marketing high technology equipment (35% of Autolab's 1971 sales were in Europe with another 10% in other foreign countries).

The acquisition, consummated on December 31, 1971, called for a

---

[2] The $60 million-a-year chromatograph market, dominated by Varian, Perkin-Elmer, and Hewlett-Packard, was badly in need of sophisticated digital input/output devices which had not been provided by the industry leaders.

cash payment of $560,000 from S-P to Autolab for tangible assets and $1.1 million for intangible assets. No S-P stock was included in the terms of the acquisition. Autolab became S-P's third major product division, joining ELS and LPD.

In 1971 S-P showed its first profits since 1966 with a pretax income of $1.1 million on sales of $8.7 million. (See Exhibit 3.) The following year was even more successful for S-P: Sales increased 62% over 1971 and income more than doubled.

In early fiscal 1972 (S-P's fiscal year begins October 1) S-P's top management reflected upon their record over the last four years and their predictions for 1972. Sales had grown at a compound rate of 28%. That figure was 41% for 1971–1972. After four years of successive losses earnings showed a pretax margin of 13% for 1971 and a 19% margin for 1972. President Herb Dwight set an earnings per share goal at a compound annual growth rate of 25%. This figure was considerably below S-P's performance in 1971–1972, but these years were considered turn-around years following poor performances in the late 1960's. In setting such a corporate objective, Herb Dwight studied the growth and earnings records of a number of successful companies (see Exhibit 4).

After the long-range objective of 25% growth in EPS was established, the next step was to assess the likelihood of achieving that goal under S-P's current operating characteristics. Although S-P was producing an extensive line of products in its three divisions, 47% of the company's sales were attributable to only three products. Two of these products appeared to be within two years of reaching maturity and faced increasing competition. The third product, recently introduced, showed a healthy growth rate with an optimistic horizon. However, it was positioned in a market segment where competitors possessed substantially greater resources than S-P.

The laser systems markets had a projected long-term annual growth rate of no higher than 20%, while laser device markets (laser components) had a projected annual sales growth of about 10%. (See Exhibit 5.) These figures had serious implications for S-P; since current operations were divided between systems and components markets (in nearly equal proportions), unless a dramatic change occurred in market shares, a compound annual growth rate in sales of 15% was the best estimate of long-term performance.

A 15% internal growth rate in sales would not be enough to produce a compound annual growth rate of 25% in EPS. Dwight concluded that a formal growth plan should be made, which would help S-P close the gap between the best estimate of potential from existing markets and the growth objective. In addition, Dwight felt that the likelihood of achieving long-range objectives would be enhanced by increasing the planning horizon—that simply going through the exercise of constructing a long-range plan would increase the probability of meeting its goals. It was decided that internal growth should be supplemented by growth through acquisition. Two such types were possible—corporate acquisitions and product acquisitions. Terms could include cash purchase, exchange of stock, or some combination of the two.

S-P felt it had the ability to manage acquisitions effectively. Their experience ranged all the way back to 1964 with the acquisition of Zissen Technical Associates. Although this proved costly in the end (the masking camera was abandoned in 1967), it set the stage for two subsequent acquisitions (University Laboratories in 1970 and Autolab in 1971–72) which contributed greatly to the company's successful turnaround in 1971–1972.

In late 1971 the optics division of S-P was absorbed by the laser products division. The optics division produced and marketed laser accessories (devices designed to modify light beams outside the laser) and thin film coated substances (used as mirrors inside the laser). Since all its products were used in conjunction with gas lasers, the reorganization appeared desirable in order to better coordinate development, engineering, and marketing.

One effect of the reorganization was to leave Bob Mortensen,[3] manager of the optics division, without a job. Dwight saw the opportunity to pursue his long-range planning goals. He created the staff function of corporate development and installed Mortensen as manager. Mortensen's job was to assist Dwight in preparing a five-year plan for the company's growth.

All of the company's divisions were in the process of preparing their detailed plans for fiscal 1973. As part of the new planning project, each division was required to include a section on long-range planning (with a five-year time horizon). These forecasts were to include a statement of general industry trends, detailed sales and profit forecasts by product line, three-year marketing strategies for each existing product (with detailed information on competition, S-P's strengths and weaknesses vis-à-vis competition, and pricing strategies), and new product opportunities. The divisional forecasts were then combined to project an internal growth forecast for the company as a whole over the five-year planning period. This was then used to determine what acquisition strategy was necessary to supplement internal growth and meet the desired goal of 25% compound annual growth in EPS.

The first draft of the five-year plan was completed in April, 1972. Following a series of meetings with divisional leaders and presentations to the board of directors, criticisms, contingencies, and revisions were

---

[3] Mortensen had been with S-P since 1963 and had served in a number of positions with the company. With a B.S. in physics and an M.B.A., Mortensen had come to S-P from Perkin-Elmer; he was hired as one of two national sales managers, and assumed responsibility for coordinating sales representatives and factory sales east of the Rocky Mountains. In 1965, when Gene Watson left to form Coherent Radiation, Mortensen became marketing manager for S-P. When Dwight took over as president in 1967, Mortensen became manager of the optics division, where he remained until its absorption by the laser products division.

incorporated into the plan. The final draft was submitted to the board for approval in July 1972.

The board considered the plan specific enough to be operational but flexible enough to accommodate revisions. Dwight's personal reactions were also favorable, although he felt the section on acquisition strategy was too general. He thought that management had learned a tremendous amount about divisional strengths and weaknesses, future opportunities, and interdivisional communication and coordination. The plan itself, however, would need constant updating to remain operational. A summary outline of the highlights of this plan appears as the Appendix. The details are not presented—especially those related to internal development—for reasons of confidentiality.

### EXHIBIT 1
#### S-P Product Mix—1969

| Product | Principal Uses | Principal Market | Percent of Sales (1968 figures) |
|---|---|---|---|
| Gas lasers | Research in chemistry, metrology, holography, optical testing, alignment, data processing | Research laboratories | 68 |
| Laser accessories | Optical and mechanical activities employing lasers | Research laboratories | 9 |
| Ranging and construction instruments | Construction alignment, precise distance measurement | Construction industry | 6 |
| Precision optical components | Laser components | Laser manufacturers | 6 |
| Nonrecurring revenues | — | — | 11 |

### EXHIBIT 2
#### Spectra-Physics, Inc., Organization Chart—September 1970

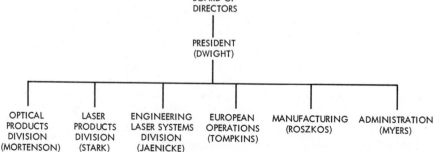

## EXHIBIT 3

### SPECTRA-PHYSICS, INC.
#### Consolidated Statement of Income (Loss)

| | 1966 | 1967 | 1968 | 1969 | 1970 | 1971 | 1972 |
|---|---|---|---|---|---|---|---|
| Net sales | $4,105,189 | $4,998,844 | $6,036,434 | $6,961,304 | $7,468,701 | $8,708,603 | $13,916,039 |
| Costs and expenses | | | | | | | |
| Costs of sales | 1,510,050 | 2,290,216 | 3,290,841 | 3,775,582 | 4,087,479 | 4,071,183 | 6,143,905 |
| Research and development | 1,337,256 | 1,408,655 | 1,033,690 | 1,039,403 | 869,811 | 771,925 | 1,094,305 |
| Marketing | 685,829 | 1,043,233 | 1,216,987 | 1,505,797 | 1,742,032 | 2,058,091 | 2,788,768 |
| General and administrative | 333,109 | 326,109 | 402,531 | 562,571 | 705,843 | 647,662 | 859,741 |
| Interest expense | 41,128 | 129,210 | 229,703 | 141,639 | 108,560 | 66,559 | 70,538 |
| | $3,907,372 | $5,197,423 | $6,173,752 | $7,024,992 | $7,513,725 | $7,615,420 | $10,957,257 |
| Income (loss) before taxes | $ 197,817 | $ (198,579) | $ (137,318) | $ (63,688) | $ (45,024) | $1,093,183 | $ 2,958,782 |
| Provision (credit) for taxes on income | 54,277 | (79,313) | 15,565 | 28,516 | 10,235 | 542,128 | 1,412,865 |
| Extraordinary income | — | (167,949)* | — | 39,000† | (51,062) | 127,592§ | — |
| | | | | | (74,667)‡ | | |
| Net income (loss) | $ 143,540 | $ (287,215) | $ (152,883) | $ (53,204) | $ (180,988) | $ 678,647 | $ 1,545,917 |
| Weighted average number of capital shares outstanding | | 527,583 | 581,340 | 727,325 | 934,912 | 950,873 | 1,545,917 |
| Net income (loss) per share | | $ (.54) | $ (.26) | $ (.07) | $ (.19) | $ .58 | $ 1.51 |

* Write-off for photo masking camera.
† Elimination of deferred taxes on foreign operations due to change in method of reporting.
‡ Write-off of license agreement—$(129,667).
  Settlement of patent claims dispute—$55,000.
§ Income tax benefits from application of operating loss carry forward.

**EXHIBIT 4**

**Compound Growth Rates of Selected Companies**

| Company | Period | Sales ($000,000) | | | EPS | | |
|---|---|---|---|---|---|---|---|
| | | From | To | Compound Rate % | From ¢ | To ¢ | Compound Rate % |
| Hewlett-Packard.... | 1962–56 | 11.0 | 20.0 | 15 | 23 | 59 | 25 |
| Hewlett-Packard.... | 1961–65 | 92.0 | 164.0 | 15 | 26 | 56 | 21 |
| D.E.C.............. | 1965–69 | 15.0 | 91.0 | 56 | 10 | 104 | 78 |
| D.E.C.............. | 1966–70 | 23.0 | 135.0 | 56 | 24 | 151 | 58 |
| IBM.............. | 1961–65 | 2,200.0 | 3,600.0 | 13 | 239 | 440 | 16 |
| Industrial Nucleonics........ | 1966–70 | 12.0 | 27.0 | 25 | 28 | 74 | 26 |
| Cubic............. | 1967–71 | 19.0 | 45.0 | 24 | 63 | 96 | 15 |
| Dymo............. | 1961–65 | 6.0 | 38.0 | 58 | 41 | 109 | 26 |
| Wang............. | 1967–71 | 9.0 | 37.0 | 44 | 26 | 93 | 37 |

**EXHIBIT 5**

**Projected Growth of the Laser Industry (from SRI Report 12/70)**

| | Sales ($000,000) | | | |
|---|---|---|---|---|
| | 1970 | 1975 | 1980 | Rate % |
| Systems markets* | | | | |
| Research.................. | 16.2 | 25.3 | 39.0 | 9.5 |
| Information processing†...... | 7.5 | 34.5 | 115.0 | 26.0 |
| Engineering construction..... | 6.2 | 12.4 | 25.0 | 15.0 |
| Total................ | 29.9 | 72.2 | 179.0 | 19.6 |
| Laser device market........... | 15.0 | 24.0 | 58.0 | 9.9 |

\* Markets in which Spectra-Physics is involved.
† Excludes RCA's SelectaVision.

## APPENDIX: A SYNOPSIS OF SPECTRA-PHYSICS' FIVE-YEAR PLAN FOR CORPORATE GROWTH

*General Business:*

1. Achieve substantial compound growth in EPS based on *sale of high technology products*.
2. Preserve worldwide *product leadership in laser* sources, especially gas lasers, and laser accessory products.
3. Build on established sales, engineering, and manufacturing bases by *expanding current businesses* to gain more dominant market shares.
4. Enter sizable *new applications markets* with proprietary products sold to the end users and preferably (but not necessarily) with the laser as a component of the end product.
5. Depend on growth from both internal development and acquisition of products and businesses.

*Financial Objectives:*

1. Grow 25% per year in earnings per share.
2. Grow 42% per year in sales.
3. Supplement internal growth with product acquisitions for cash.

*Market Strategy:*

1. Emphasize end-user applications markets.
2. Stress proprietary products.
3. Emphasize high technology products.
4. Build on established bases.

**TABLE 1**

**Projected Spectra-Physics Internal Growth**

|  | 1972 | 1973 | 1974 | 1975 | 1976 | 1977 |
|---|---|---|---|---|---|---|
| Forecast |  |  |  |  |  |  |
| Total sales ($000,000)........... | 13.6 | 17.2 | 22.4 | 27.7 | 31.8 | 36.3 |
| Profit after taxes ($000,000)....... | 1.4 | 1.7 | 2.0 | 2.3 | 2.7 | 3.1 |
| Profit after taxes (% margin)...... | 10 | 10 | 9 | 8.5 | 8.5 | 8.5 |
| Shares (000,000)................ | 1.06 | 1.10 | 1.14 | 1.19 | 1.24 | 1.29 |
| Earnings per share (dollars)........ | 1.28 | 1.57 | 1.77 | 1.96 | 2.18 | 2.38 |
| Growth over previous year (%).... |  | 22 | 13 | 11 | 11 | 9 |
| Corporate objectives |  |  |  |  |  |  |
| Earnings per share − 25% |  |  |  |  |  |  |
| growth (dollars)............... | 1.25 | 1.60 | 2.00 | 2.50 | 3.13 | 3.93 |

*Products and Markets:*

1. Utilize *laser technology* wherever possible.
2. Maintain *market leadership* in laser sources and accessories.
3. Add products compatible with ELS sales and marketing capability.
4. Expand Autolab technology into new market areas.
5. Add related laboratory products to LPD product line.

*Implementation:*

1. Keep corporate staff small and highly focused.
2. Involve total top management group in growth plan.

It is clear from Table 1 that additional earnings must be generated if S-P is to meet its objective of 25% compound earnings per share growth. An acquisition program is needed to supplement internal growth.

Two types of acquisitions may be pursued—product acquisitions for cash and corporate acquisitions for stock. Table 2 shows the proposed combination of internal growth and acquisitions necessary to achieve the the 25% EPS growth objective. The figures are derived sequentially in the following way. Projected internal growth figures were taken from

Table 1. From projected cash flows and estimated borrowing power over the planning horizon, potential product acquisitions for cash were derived. Finally, corporate acquisitions for stock were determined as that increment necessary to reach the desired long-range objective of 25% growth per year in EPS.

*Growth Strategies:*

1. Assumes adequate and suitable opportunities for investment through internal development or acquisition exist in fields related to the company's current activities. The strength of the company's three divisional sales/marketing organizations *makes it desirable to invest in products which can be sold by these organizations.*

### TABLE 2
#### Summary: Sales and Earnings Per Share Buildup

|  | 1972 | 1973 | 1974 | 1975 | 1976 | 1977 | Compound Rate % |
|---|---|---|---|---|---|---|---|
| **Sales ($000,000)** | | | | | | | |
| Internal.................... | 13.6 | 17.2 | 22.4 | 27.7 | 31.8 | 36.3 | 22 |
| Product acquisitions for cash.... | | 1.1 | 3.0 | 5.0 | 7.7 | 11.1 | |
| Total.................. | 13.6 | 18.3 | 25.4 | 32.7 | 39.5 | 47.4 | 30 |
| Corporate acquisitions for stock. | | 3.0 | 7.7 | 12.7 | 18.9 | 23.6 | |
| Total.................. | 13.6 | 21.3 | 33.1 | 45.4 | 58.4 | 71.0 | 42 |
| **EPS ($)** | | | | | | | |
| Internal.................... | 1.25 | 1.57 | 1.77 | 1.96 | 2.18 | 2.38 | 14 |
| Internal plus product acquisitions for cash......... | 1.25 | 1.60 | 1.93 | 2.27 | 2.65 | 3.05 | 20 |
| Internal plus product and corporate acquisitions........ | 1.25 | 1.60 | 2.05 | 2.55 | 3.10 | 3.70 | 25 |

2. Primary emphasis on exploiting opportunities to sell new products with existing staff or to existing customers.
3. Secondary emphasis on products which are sold to similar or related customer cross-sections and can be adequately served with existing sales/marketing staffs.
4. Avoid making investments in new products sold to new customers which are justified solely on the basis of technological continuity.
5. Best opportunities for entry into new markets are start-up ventures, corporate acquisition, or new divisions created around products from advanced development.

*Desirable Characteristics of Potential Acquisition Candidates—Corporate:*

1. Control a large share of principal market (be at least as large as next largest competition).

2. Serve end-user markets.
3. Product line: readily expandable, compatible with S-P's image of excellence.
4. Products: high technology content at early stage of growth cycle.
5. Business philosophy compatible.
6. Professional management.
7. Business not highly capital-intensive.
8. Grow at the compound rate of 25% per year.
9. Earn 8.5% after tax profits after break-even operations for the first six months.

*Product:*

1. Marketed by existing staff.
2. Sold to existing customers.
3. Similar manufacturing operations.
4. Grow at the compound rate of 25% per year.
5. Earn 8.5% after break-even operation for the first six months.
6. Be acquired for cash equivalent to realizable sales during the first year of acquisition.

*Organization and Staffing—Corporate Development—*
*Participation of Management:*

1. A successful acquisition program requires the personal involvement of the president. He carries a selling prestige into all phases of the negotiations, especially in making the important, initial contact to a major potential acquisition. The involvement of the president gives him first-hand knowledge he needs to persuade the board of directors to accept a deal.
2. Almost as important the top management personnel who will eventually integrate the acquired company into Spectra-Physics must involve themselves in the evaluation and negotiation phase of the acquisition process.
3. Since our program concentrates on a build-up of our business from established bases, it is particularly important that divisional management be involved in the acquisition program. Of course, this imples that division managers will have added pressures to delegate day-to-day activities to others within their acquisition program. Perhaps future management incentive programs will have to be geared to help accomplish this goal.

*Staffing:*

1. Assuming routine line management participation in the acquisition program, there is no need to build a large corporate support staff. Inputs into the program can be developed by employing consulting firms, research organizations, and other independent study groups

to provide specialized information as it is required. These independent organizations provide us with the advantage of an outside perspective, broader geographic coverage, and more diverse exposure.

2. Because of the inevitable selective process involved, it will be necessary to explore numerous companies and markets. Therefore, we anticipate adding one highly qualified market analyst to the staff during FY-1973. It should be possible to attract an extremely competent individual into this position because of the career opportunity to gain general management exposure and train for a broader responsibility in the future line position.

*Approach to Gathering Leads:*

1. We have concluded that it is necessary to make either acquisitions or start-up ventures over the next four years. Since the acquisition of companies is a very competitive business, it is reasonable to assume that we might eventually acquire 1% of the qualified leads that we are able to generate. A qualified lead is a company candidate that before initial contact meets our acquisition criteria based on Dun & Bradstreet information and a review of the sales literature of the company. A 1% capture rate requires 100 qualified leads per deal and two deals per year. Further, it requires an average of one new qualified lead per working day. If the conversion rate is 5% from qualified leads, we would require one qualified lead per week in order to reach our objectives. In short, a tremendous inflow of acquisition prospects is required.

2. How can we obtain this flow of possible merger candidates? Certainly we must utilize every resource available to us. Sources of inputs are: Spectra-Physics's sales engineers; all levels of management personnel; editorial and advertising information in all of the periodicals that serve the different business areas in which we have an interest; contacts by members of the board of directors; contacts from commercial and investment bankers.

3. As a prerequisite it is important that we inform these potential sources of our objectives so that they may feed us as many new leads as possible.

# California Canners and Growers, Inc.

Robert Gibson, the newly elected President of California Canners and Growers, Inc. (CCG), was happy as he was driving home this Friday night. It had been a difficult week, but he had managed to sort out all problems, and for the first time in months, his briefcase was empty. It would be nice to spend the weekend with Helen and the children. As soon as he walked in the front door, his wife told him that Dick Moulton[1] had called a few minutes earlier and wanted Bob to call him back as soon as possible. Bob Gibson's face fell as he said, "I think I know what that'll be about."

Dick Moulton's voice sounded tired. "Bob, I had a call from Harry Thomas of Great Western Stores in L.A. a couple of hours ago. He wants our answer on the supply contract for all their private label canned fruit and vegetable requirements by 9:00 A.M. Tuesday morning. This is two weeks earlier than we had expected to have to make this decision, but apparently the dry weather and the supply position have them worried. As you know, this contract involves about 10% of our production, and it will mean that we won't be able to consider marketing a larger proportion of our production under our own brand label."

Bob Gibson sighed. "Dick, let me spend some time over the weekend going over some of the figures we have started to prepare. Then let's meet at 9:00 A.M. sharp on Monday and decide whether we should sign the contract or not. Thanks for the call."

"It's no pleasure, but that's the way it goes in this game. See you on Monday morning then." Dick Moulton hung up.

"So much for my weekend," thought Bob Gibson as he sat down at the table for dinner.

## HISTORY OF THE CCG

By the mid-1950's, it was becoming increasingly apparent to a great many California growers that the production of fruits and vegetables was

---

Reprinted from *Stanford Business Cases 1969* with the permission of the publisher, Graduate School of Business, Stanford University. Copyright © 1969 by the Board of Trustees of the Leland Stanford Junior University.

[1] Richard H. Moulton, Executive Vice President and Marketing Director of CCG.

on the increase and that this trend would continue and perhaps accelerate. After intensive study, a tight-knit group of these growers became convinced that in the food industry the "big would get bigger" and the "small would get smaller." They foresaw, as did a number of independent canning companies, that the chances were great that before too long the big buyers—the so-called majors—would have market control and, with it, increasing control of crops and of canned goods prices.

With growing production and a cost-price squeeze, this group of California growers concluded that, for their own protection, it was vital that *they* move toward establishing greater control over the processing and marketing of their own products.

Further research confirmed the group's opinion that they should move immediately toward the formation of a new California fruit and vegetable co-operative. They were encouraged and backed in this by the state's leading grower associations: the California Canning Peach Association, the California Tomato Growers Association, the California Canning Pear Association, the California Freestone Peach Association, and the California Asparagus Growers Association.

Most of these associations were responsible, among other things, for representing their grower members in bargaining on prices with the canners who bought their crops. They believed that the formation of a strong grower "marketing" co-operative would represent a healthy step forward for California agriculture.

Early in 1957, an aggressive membership drive was launched with prospective members asked to commit all or part of their crops and to make a contribution to capital. The original sign-up for this co-operative organization consisted of 473 growers of various California fruits and vegetables. This group put up just under $1,000,000 in capital with two banks providing considerable additional funds.

In the early talks about the formation of a co-operative with a variety of crops, the growers recognized that this kind of diversification offered them a sort of "insurance" they would never have with a single crop. For example: if it were an off-year for tomatoes but peaches were good, the tomato grower, as a co-op member, would realize some of the profits from peaches even though he didn't grow them. The next year might be the reverse and in the following year another crop might carry the load. Thus, diversification became one of the most attractive elements which the formation of a co-op offered California growers, many of whom were "single crop" operators.

At that time, the growers were faced with a critical decision: whether to build new, modern plants or whether to buy existing canning operations with marketing patterns already esablished. They made the decision to buy existing companies, and, with that, CCG became immediately embroiled in the total marketing spectrum.

Just as the growers who formed Cal Canners had seen the dangers which lay ahead, so did a number of solid but somewhat worried processors of the divergent crops which the growers raised. In the middle and late fifties, canners and marketers of California agricultural products were growing fewer but larger. The independent canners, like the growers, faced the somewhat inevitable cost-price squeeze and more intense competition.

So there was, indeed, a mutuality of interests between the growers and certain processors in the state. It seemed only logical that, with similar motivations, California Canners and Growers, Inc. would do well to buy certain processing and distributing companies as a part of a strong agricultural co-operative. In 1958, the purchase of the first two processing companies was made and they became part of the now correctly named California Canners and Growers, Inc. Three additional processing and marketing organizations were purchased in the succeeding four years and a smaller grower co-op became part of the CCG family in 1966. (See Exhibit 1 for details of product categories and acquisitions made by CCG.) CCG operated the five canning companies as subsidiaries until 1964. By that time it had become obvious that this structure was not in the best interest of the company, and the first steps toward centralization of management and operations were taken. A headquarters office was opened in San Francisco, but a number of managers and executives were unable to adjust to this new way of life, and left CCG to pursue other activities.

By the end of 1964, CCG had become a major factor in California's canning industry with sales of over $90,000,000. With this dollar volume, Cal Canners ranked well up with other large, dominant canned goods companies in the United States.

In terms of case sales of California fruits and vegetables, the figures were as follows:

Pack of total industry in California in 1964*.................... 133,200,000
Pack of California Canners and Growers in 1964*............... 19,700,000

   * Excluding tomato juice.

Thus, CCG's pack represented approximately 15% of the total California fruit and vegetable pack in 1964.

The equity of members in CCG had grown from $1.0 million in 1958 to $15 million in 1964–65. At the time of formation in 1958, it had been hoped that the return to growers would be at least 15% above the market value of their crops. This objective had been accomplished, despite two bad years in 1962 and 1963. (See Exhibit 2.)

By the end of the fiscal year 1966–67 the company had been in existence for ten years, and the record looked very impressive. On May 31, 1967, CCG:

Had 1,100 member-growers and a waiting list of growers who wanted to join the group.
Had record sales of $111,000,000 and assets of over $66 million.

Owned and operated nine processing plants, was a partner in two can manufacturing plants, operated a fleet of trucks and maintained distribution warehouses across the U.S.

Had, on the average, over the ten-year span of its existence, returned 15.5% above the market value of their crops to its growers.

Was the largest grower-owned, canner-marketing co-operative in the United States.

Had completely revamped its organization, emerging as a marketing company to be reckoned with in the canned goods industry; a company with operating and marketing expertise.

The company took another step forward in early 1967 when it hired Mr. Robert L. Gibson to be the new President of CCG. Mr. Gibson had many years of top management experience and for the past five years had been president of Libby, McNeill and Libby, headquartered in Chicago. Gibson and Richard Moulton, Executive Vice President for Marketing, had joined together to head a formidable management team. (See Exhibit 3 for background of Gibson and Moulton.) The appointment of Bob Gibson as President of CCG was a bold move, for it served notice on the competition that Cal Canners was fast emerging as an aggressive, ambitious, growth-minded company, now that it had closed out its first decade with a record of success.

Mr. Henry Schacht, CCG's Vice President, Corporate Relations, summed up the company's current attitude about its future direction in an article written for the *Farmer Cooperative Service Journal* published by the U.S. Department of Agriculture:

Of our general philosophies and operating policies, the key one is our determination to be market-oriented. We attempt to govern our *pack* according to marketing plans. All of our *plans* and *programs* must reflect the needs and demands of the marketplace.

In marketing we have been developing greater brand sales, particularly through wider distribution of our low-calorie canned fruits. At present some two-thirds of our sales fall into what we call trade sales that include our private label, institutional, industrial, and export sales—and the other one-third, approximately, is brand.

We feel that stronger brands will give us a better balance in our marketing program. But the private label business will, of course, continue to be of great importance.

We expect the future will bring further refinements in distribution methods. In pursuit of lower costs and improved customer service, we have established a number of regional distribution centers in the East and Midwest.

We are also anxious to strengthen new product development. Hand-in-hand with new product research and development goes market research. Launching a full scale campaign for a new product would be foolhardy without preliminarty testing of consumer response.

Whatever we do must be done in the best interests of our 1,100 grower-members. In the first 10 years of our growth we feel that we have performed well in their behalf. We look ahead to the next 10 years as a period of opportunity. We feel that our co-operative must be able to compete with the best in the industry, and we do not intend to settle for anything less.

A great deal had been accomplished during Gibson's and Moulton's first year as the top management team of CCG. One of the first things which Bob Gibson and Dick Moulton began looking at in 1967 was the possibility of CCG expansion. Both men knew that to offer a full line to their important private label buyers in the East and Midwest areas, they would have to add peas, corn, and green beans to their product line. This meant expansion into the Midwest, where these products were grown.

Wisconsin seemed to be the best area to investigate and by mid-1967, a feasibility study was set in motion. In February of 1968, the findings of the study were exposed to the grower-owners of CCG, and a recommendation was made by management and accepted by the Board of Directors. It was decided that California Canners and Growers would begin processing corn and peas in the state of Wisconsin for the 1969 packing season and green beans in 1970. Sales and earnings for the first six years of this new venture were projected as follows:

|  | Sales (000's Omitted) | Increase (Decrease) in Earnings of Present CCG Growers |
|---|---|---|
| 1968–69 | $2,518 | $ (414) |
| 1969–70 | 5,893 | (391) |
| 1970–71 | 7,075 | 259 |
| 1971–72 | 7,781 | 567 |
| 1972–73 | 8,560 | 793 |
| 1973–74 |  | 1,056 |
|  |  | $1,870 |

This represented a return on investment on a discounted cash flow basis of 25.8%—the highest return of the alternatives considered during the course of this study.

Other highlights of the fiscal year ending May 31, 1968, included the following:

Highest profit year in Cal Canners' history—approximately $7 million.

Greatest grower equity in CCG history—$28 million.

Second largest sales volume in CCG history—$109 million.

Bob Gibson accomplished a number of other things during his first year in office. He greatly improved the morale of the company by selecting his management team and then giving them clear-cut lines of authority and the whole-hearted backing of management. He decided that his key people were substantially underpaid and he quickly corrected this. Bob Gibson's management philosophy was very simple:

The greatest resource of any company is its people . . . preferably fewer people working harder and being given greater responsibility and higher pay. We must have highly motivated management and have a deep concern for those who are subordinate to them. CCG must create a working environment wherein people can freely express themselves and work up to their full capabilities.

Bob Gibson made this philosophy work in terms of highly motivated management and in terms of dollars and cents. In his first full year of operation, he had cut expenses by $1,200,000, almost 10% of the co-op's total cost of doing business.

The granting of greater responsibility and authority to key people accomplished one other vital thing for CCG. The company suddenly emerged as a leader rather than a follower in such important matters as pricing, which represented a complete switch from the co-op's position of a year or two before. As Gibson put it succinctly:

Our people on the marketing and negotiating ends of the business can hold their heads high and they do! Let me tell you this: Everybody these days is wondering what Cal Can is going to do, not the other way around. These days, I get the feeling that Del Monte and CCG are *the* important leaders in the area of California fruits and vegetables.

Shortly after the Directors of California Canners and Growers had approved the co-op's expansion into the Midwest, Bob Gibson and Dick Moulton began to examine and to talk about other routes which might offer new growth and profit opportunities. There were a number of ways to go but one in particular interested them.

At lunch one day in January 1968 at the World Trade Club, Bob Gibson said to his marketing associate: "Dick, we've just completed our first year or so together, which was the best profit period in CCG's history. But, as we said in April, '67, we've got a great opportunity to make Cal Canners an increasingly important marketer of canned fruits and vegetables. Soon, we'll have the complete line that it takes to really compete with the likes of Del Monte and Libby. I think we should start talking seriously very soon about the economics of shifting our marketing away from private labels and into our own promoted brand products. We know that there are greater profits to be made if we succeed in this, but the risk of bigger losses is equally great. We know, for instance, that on a rule of thumb basis, branded merchandise will give us 10 to 15% more profit than we can provide our growers through private label sales. Let's say, for instance, that we up our volume to $115,000,000 in 1969 and switch from 60/40 in our mix to 50/50. The difference in operating profits would be in the area of a million dollars."

"What we are discussing right now," Moulton said, "is whether this might be the time to aggressively develop our 'brand franchise' business, what with a broader line and more production. But, as you say, Bob, there are pros and cons, and we'd better take a hard look at the whole picture before we start changing our marketing strategy and our 60/40 mix of private label and brand."

Bob Gibson concluded, "Let's get all the facts out on the table as soon as we can. It could be, Dick, that before too long you and I will be making a basic marketing decision that will set the course of Cal Canners for some years to come."

## THE MARKETING OPERATION

Sales were made under either private or brand label to a variety of buyers, chain and wholesale organizations for retail sales, as well as institutional, industrial, and export sales. A typical year's output by CCG would be sold as follows:

40% of the pack was sold under the private labels of most of the country's leading chain and wholesale organizations. It was highly desirable and profitable business. This part of the pack was in the standard shelf sizes with which all grocery shoppers are familiar.

25% of the pack was sold under CCG's own brands, which were promoted and advertised by CCG and which competed with such other brand franchises as Del Monte, Libby, Hunt, and Stokely. (For a list of CCG brands, see Exhibit 4.)

15% of the pack was sold, under private label, to the large institutional wholesalers in the country. These were the large size containers (gallons and up) which were purchased by restaurants, hotels, hospitals, government commissaries, etc.

The remaining 20% of the pack was sold either to industrial buyers or for export. About a quarter of this amount was sold under private label while the remaining three-quarters was sold under CCG's own brands.

CCG sales were made through large broker organizations, which were supervised by company district managers. For brand sales the brokers employed retail men who worked both at chain and wholesale headquarters, as well as at the brochures and P.O.S. material. At the retail level they worked with stores to improve shelf position, get more shelf space for brands, and secure end-aisle displays. At chain and wholesale headquarters, the broker salesmen covered deals and sought chain ads and specials.

For private label sales a straight sales story was told by the brokers, with no merchandising or sales help. It simply covered the price of the goods and the labels under which the merchandise would be packed—straight selling without any attempt at merchandising.

For many years, there had been a strong private label (P/L) position with wholesalers and chains on canned goods. Movement figures on P/L's in the nine San Francisco Bay Area counties, for example, showed that they had about a 25% market share of six leading fruits and vegetables—peaches, apricots, pears, peas, corn, and beans. As far as brand products were concerned, Del Monte would probably average out around 35–40% of this, with the balance spread among such brands as Libby, Hunt, and Stokely.

Private labels in such other major categories as coffee, mayonnaise, and bleach, for example, were somewhat less than canned goods. Again using Bay Area figures, P/L coffees and mayonnaise ran in the area of 10–15% and liquid bleach around 20%.

The situation is simply that P/L is a sizable factor today, has been a substantial factor in the past, and will doubtless continue to be in the future. But it is unlikely that it will grow or regress; it is highly probable, instead, that P/L will continue to be a large factor but not the dominant one.

Promotion of a brand nationally takes a lot of money and is a risky venture. The risk is greatly increased when an attempt is made to introduce a new brand against established competition. For example,

*Del Monte* spends around $9 million a year in advertising alone, plus an additional $2 or $3 million on promotions, point-of-sale, and contests. Of that $11 to $12 million, about $8 million are spent on canned fruits, vegetables, and juices.

*Libby* spends about $5 million annually in advertising and promoting its canned fruits, vegetables, and juices.

*Hunt* spends $3 to $4 million a year promoting its tomato sauces, catsup, and peaches.

*Dole* spends approximately $3 million annually on pineapple of various types and pineapple and mixed juices.

A dollar does not go very far in national advertising. A line such as Diet Delight spent about $1,250,000 for all media advertising. This bought six 4-color pages in six major women's magazines. On television, this amount bought three early evening one-minute spots per week for 26 weeks in the 50 major markets of the country.

The product mix of the so-called brand franchisers was much more heavily weighted toward advertised brands than it was toward private labels. Certainly that was the case with the brand operators such as Del Monte, Libby, Hunt, and Green Giant. Del Monte, for example, sold very little private label merchandise. What little it did place on the market would be surplus "inventory" that they simply wanted to dispose of. Hunt Foods sold no private label and Libby sold only surplus commodities under private label.

This situation might alter at short notice, however. The decline in export markets would place increasing pressure on private label business in the future. There was the danger that, due to the potential loss of export tonnage, companies would "dump" merchandise on the domestic market, resulting in a weakening of prices. There was a possibility, therefore, that CCG's strong position in the private label field might in the future be strongly challenged by companies such as Del Monte and Libby.

## BRAND VERSUS PRIVATE LABEL SALES

Since January 1968, Dick Moulton had studied the question of whether CCG should increase its effort in the brand sales field or remain at the 60/40 split between private label and brand sales which the company currently enjoyed. As a first step, Moulton had looked at the four advertised brands currently marketed by CCG.

*Diet Delight.* This was CCG's line of low calorie fruits, low sodium vegetables, plus a number of low calorie specialties. It was sold nationally, and despite a few geographic areas of weakness, it was the leading national brand in canned diet foods and specialties, and its weaker markets were being gradually strengthened.

The diet fruits market had grown steadily during the last five years. For example, in 1963, 8% of households in the U.S. used some diet fruits and in 1968, the usage figure was 18%. In New York, considered a mature market for diet fruits, 18 to 19% of all canned fruits purchased were in the diet category. Diet fruits cost about 10% more than normal canned fruits.

Diet Delight was by far the dominant brand in its category, holding about 65% share of market in such a major area as New York. The brand had withstood competitive activity very well in the past.

In 1966 and 1967, three major brands came into the New York market with diet fruits: Dole in 1966 with fruit cocktail—heavily promoted and advertised; Del Monte also in 1966 and Libby a year later. Dole did well in the beginning; Del Monte, with heavy advertising and promotion, gained a 25% share in fruit cocktail and a 33⅓% share in diet peaches. However, total sales in this *category* increased about 30%. After a year, Del Monte's share settled down to about 10%. While Diet Delight was down slightly in 1966, the brand's share and sales had returned to normal at the end of 1967.

This was an encouraging trend but the questions management had to ask itself were: How close is Diet Delight to a peak in sales? Can Diet Delight continue to withstand competitive inroads, particularly if a major brand decides to *stay* with promotion and advertising, instead of backing off after a year, as Del Monte did? Can Diet Delight hold its profitable 10% price differential in a growing category which might attract more P/L or brands? Should management of Cal Canners hold firm in its determination to maintain its leadership in the low calorie category through sustained and perhaps increased advertising spending? Or could the company afford to slack off somewhat in hopes that competitive advertising spending would lift sales sharply in the whole category? Or should CCG turn a larger share of its advertising attention to another group of products, in an effort to expand its over-all brand franchise?

**Red Pack.**  This was a line of tomatoes and tomato products, including whole peeled tomatoes, quartered tomatoes, juice, puree, paste, catsup, and tomato sauces. It was a line of premium-priced products; it had a long advertising history and had been profitable for many years.

Red Pack was a regional brand, with most of its sales being made in New York, New Jersey, and Pennsylvania. Gradually, sales had begun to expand geographically, and as they did so, Red Pack's advertising budget grew—to $600,000 in the year ending May 31, 1968.

In 1967–68, three new markets were opened for Red Pack tomatoes— Boston, Cleveland/Akron, and Minneapolis/St. Paul, all supported by advertising and promotion. Sales in established markets had been held at high levels; sales and distribution in the new markets had been quite good, somewhat beyond projections. To the marketing team at CCG, it seemed that Red Pack, principally because of the quality of the products, could be a real breadwinner. Although sales had expanded at the rate of 15% per year since 1965, there were some problems ahead. One of these came from low-priced imports from Italy and Portugal, which were expected to make inroads into Red Pack's sales. Fifty percent of Red Pack sales were institutional, and thus were especially vulnerable to price competition. About 90% of the retail sales of Red Pack were made in the New York area, and if this expected low priced competition materialized, $600,000 for advertising would be difficult to justify. Perhaps substantial additional geographic expansion of the market area and of advertising expenditure should be made, especially since the new sales areas opened up in 1967–68 were doing well.

**Heart's Delight.**  This was a full line of California fruits and vegetables, including fruit nectars. The nectar had been advertised for a number of years, and it seemed that the name "Heart's Delight" had become synonymous with a line of fruit nectars. In the year ending in May, 1968, about $300,000 had been spent to advertise Heart's Delight Apricot Nectar on television in 34 markets, accounting for approximately one-half of the television homes in the U.S., and for promotion at the retail level.

The effort was a joint advertising and promotional plan and the combination did the job. Promotional allowances plus hard work on the part of the brokers resulted in excellent displays and substantial price features for Heart's Delight nectars. The advertising, eight 30-second spots a week in the Midwest, East, Florida, and Texas for sixteen weeks, increased consumer awareness of the product and created the required consumer demand for the line of nectars.

The Heart's Delight line of fruits and vegetables had never been advertised or promoted to any degree. It would be difficult to make a brand line out of it; since Heart's Delight was known as a line of apricot, peach, and pear nectar. However, Heart's Delight and Diet Delight did have a kinship of names, and possibly Diet Delight could pull its companion brand along with it.

Thus the questions to be answered about the Heart's Delight line were difficult ones. Should the brand be confined to nectar only and a new brand name established for fruits and vegetables? Was the association between Diet Delight and Heart's Delight something which should be cultivated, or would it just cause confusion in the consumer's mind? What total sum of advertising dollars would be needed to establish the line as a true national brand, if in fact this is what CCG should do?

*Aunt Penny's.* This was a line of sauces—White, Cheese, and Hollandaise—which enjoyed distribution and sales in the Western states only. While the three sauces had to be considered strictly as specialties, they enjoyed solid distribution, had a good reputation for quality, and had a good, solid brand name.

Sales were steady at about 100,000 cases annually, and the brand, without advertising, showed a good profit. Over the years, only limited advertising dollars had been expended on Aunt Penny's sauces with no measurable increase in sales. In spite of little advertising or promotion in recent years, the product continued to enjoy 100% distribution in the marketplace with two and three shelf facings. The major question with this brand was, if sales held steady with little or no advertising, would not some expenditure on advertising increase sales considerably? The other question was the expansion of the line into areas where CCG already had marketing experience and distribution outlets.

As a second step, Dick Moulton had arranged a meeting at Pebble Beach Lodge in early May of 1968, for the 14 top executives of CCG to discuss many of the marketing problems which faced the company.

Inevitably, the discussion returned to the problem of whether to change the current mix of 60% private and 40% branded products or not. By and large the major advantages and disadvantages of such a move were agreed upon. The major advantages were: (1) There was a much greater gross profit to be made from branded products than from private labels. A figure of 10–15% was thought to be possible, depending upon the nature of the products for which brands were to be established. (2) Greater marketing control could be exercised through having a well-known brand product line. The major disadvantages were the costs of advertising and promotion which would be required to establish the brand in the marketplace. There was sufficient indication that these costs would be very large, because competing brands were well entrenched.

As far as its own present branded products were concerned the company felt it had done reasonably well, at least as far as the Diet Delight and Red Pack lines were concerned. Advertising and promotional costs had been held to a reasonable level, and the lines were profitable. On the other hand, and this was true especially of Diet Delight, the product lines had yet to face sustained competition. Other companies had made several attempts at gaining market share, but had backed off after a year at the longest, for reasons which were not really known to CCG; but the high costs of advertising and promoting three products would no doubt be one of the major ones.

The second major disadvantage was that many of CCG's loyal private label customers would suffer. These buyers had long been a mainstay to CCG. If they thought that CCG was moving toward further brand development, they would begin to look elsewhere for their supplies of California fruits and vegetables. It was also a case of no second chance, because once a private label customer had tied up with another supplier there was no chance of CCG obtaining his business again in the event that the venture into branded products proved to be unsuccessful. There was a limit on how much CCG could physically produce during a season, and if the change to additional branded products was to be made, CCG would have to forego a number of private label supply contracts long before it knew whether its advertised brands were a success or not.

On this issue the group at the Pebble Beach meeting had certain questions that needed answering. There were those who asked why there was any need to change a successful operation for one where the monetary risks were very great indeed. This group argued that even if CCG succeeded in successfully establishing its own line of brand products, this would only invite retaliation from those competitors whose market share was being hurt by inroads from CCG brands. Another group argued that "standing still means retrogression." "Furthermore," members of this group asked, "what guarantee do we have that Del Monte and others will not move in on our private label business, especially in view of the export situation? We could then end up with no additional brand volume and our private label business under considerable pressure."

There were some other subsidiary matters discussed at the Pebble Beach meeting. The first of these was the question of a common brand name for all CCG branded products. Those who favored this proposal argued that such a move to a single brand name would indicate a common look to all "branded" packaging, as was the case with Del Monte. A common name or mark would make possible more efficient use of advertising dollars, greater impact at the retail level, and an easier sales operation for the brokers and their retail man. If such a brand name for all CCG products was decided upon, should the Diet Delight brand be included in this brand family or should it continue to be promoted separately, since it was the leader in its specialized category?

Finally, the company had to consider just where to expand its line of branded products, if this was the course of action decided upon. Should it concentrate on dietary products, and if so, on presently developed products only or should it consider adding new products? Alternatively, should it concentrate on non-dietary products, and if so, on presently marketed products or on new products? If the latter, then specifically what products should be added?

These were just some of the many matters discussed at CCG's first "forward planning" seminar. Returning from Pebble Beach after three days of business and golf, Dick Moulton said to Bob Gibson as they headed home,

You know, Bob, that was a very good meeting and I'm certain that a lot of good will come out of it. We covered many things and we talked about profit opportunities that may be just around the corner or well down the road. But CCG's marketing future looks mighty bright to me.

"I couldn't agree with you more," Gibson added. "But you know as well as I that profit growth doesn't come easy. Alternatives are clearly in front of us; all we've got to do now is to make the right decisions."

After the Pebble Beach meeting, Dick Moulton hoped that during the next few weeks he would have an opportunity to come to a decision on the brand products vs. private label contracts question before the contract with Great Western Stores in Los Angeles came up for signature. However, the phone call from Harry Thomas changed all that. A decision had to be made now.

\*    \*    \*    \*    \*

As Dick Moulton walked into Bob Gibson's office at 9:00 A.M. on Monday, he said, "Bob, I think I have decided what we ought to do about this contract with Great Western Stores. I wonder if you will agree with me?"

### EXHIBIT 1

#### California Canners and Growers

*The Product Categories:* 11 major crops.

Cling peaches, tomatoes and tomato products, apricots, pears, freestone peaches, grapes, figs, cherries, fruit salad, asparagus, and spinach.

*The Acquisitions:*

Filice & Perrelli Canning Company in 1958

Specialized in top quality canned fruits and vegetables since 1914, grew to be one of the largest canning companies in California. At time of purchase by CCG had 3 modern plants, and sales of $20,212,000, 30% in advertised F & P brands, 70% in private label.

Richmond-Chase Company in 1958

One of the largest independently owned canneries in the state, which sold $31,937,000 of fruit, vegetables, and nectars in 1958. Had two large plants and two important advertised lines, Heart's Delight whole fruit nectars and other fruit and vegetable products, and Diet Delight, the leader in low-calorie, low-sodium foods. Sixty percent of the pack was sold under private label, 40% as advertised brands.

## EXHIBIT 1 (Continued)

Thornton Canning Company in 1959

Although this company packed some private label fruits and vegetables, the company sales of $9,451,000 were largely in fruit concentrates and in dehydrated fruits and vegetables in crystal form, both used for remanufacture. Virtually all production in its one large plant in the Sacramento Valley was classified as "Industrial."

San Jose Canning Company in 1960

At the time of acquisition, this 40-year-old company had an outstanding reputation as a packer of high quality, premium priced tomatoes and tomato products. Most of the highly efficient plant's production was sold under the well-established, advertised brand, "Red Pack," in Eastern markets. Sales in 1960 totaled $4,704,000.

Schuckl and Co., Inc., in 1963

Considered one of the finest fruit packers in the country, Schuckl processed and sold 4,000,000 cases in 1963, much of it overseas. Total sales in 1963 were $15,544,000. It had two plants, with headquarters in Sunnyvale where it packed and marketed Aunt Penny's White Sauce, Cheese and Hollandaise sauces. These specialities were advertised and distributed in the Western states only. Ninety percent of sales were in private labels.

In 1966 CCG acquired Wyandotte Olive Growers, an excellent, small cooperative with quality products and a valuable brand franchise in the field.

### EXHIBIT 2

#### California Canners and Growers

|  | 1959 | 1960 | 1961 | 1962 | 1963 |
|---|---|---|---|---|---|
| Sales ($ millions) | 53.9 | 68.2 | 77.0 | 79.2 | 88.8 |
| Members' equity ($ millions) | 2.3 | 4.1 | 6.1 | 9.2 | 11.3 |
| Return to growers | 22.2% | 15.4% | 19.8% | 5.1% | 0.5% |

|  | 1964 | 1965 | 1966 | 1967 | 1968 |
|---|---|---|---|---|---|
| Sales ($ millions) | 92.0 | 97.4 | 104.1 | 111.4 | 109.0 |
| Members equity ($ millions) | 14.0 | 16.8 | 20.9 | 24.3 | 28.0 |
| Return to growers | 26.6% | 17.4% | 21.6% | 17.0% | N.A. |

### EXHIBIT 3

#### California Canners and Growers

*Robert L. Gibson, Jr.*

*Education.* B.S. in Food Technology from the University of California at

**EXHIBIT 3 (Continued)**

Berkeley in 1940. Following service as an officer in the Counterintelligence Corps during World War II, Gibson earned a master's degree in industrial management, as a Sloan Fellow, from the Massachusetts Institute of Technology in 1946.

*Business Career.* Out of graduate school into Libby, McNeill & Libby, rose rapidly in the company's most important and profitable geographic region, the West, becoming VP and General Manager of the Western Division in 1958. On the basis of an outstanding record in sales and profits, elected to the Presidency of Libby in 1962, headquartered in Chicago. After 5 years, resigned to accept the post of President and Chief Executive Officer of California Canners and Growers, Inc., in March of 1967.

*Richard H. Moulton*

*Education.* Graduated from George Washington University in Washington, D.C., where he took his L.L.B. degree in 1929 and was admitted to the bar.

*Business Career.* Joined General Foods Corporation following graduation and, during a highly successful 22 years with General Foods, held a number of key executive posts; he was, among other things, General Foods' first Director of Marketing Research. In 1951, Dick Moulton formed an advertising agency and marketing consultant firm in New England. Later he joined the New York business consulting firm of Lillard Syndications, where he worked closely with a number of the country's leading chains.

First served CCG in a marketing consultant capacity and, in early 1967, was named Executive VP and Director of Marketing.

**EXHIBIT 4**

**California Canners and Growers**

The following is a list of products marketed under various CCG brands:

*Diet Delight,* a line of low calorie fruits and fruit cocktail, vegetables, and speciality items which had long been a brand of Richmond-Chase. This line had wide distribution and was heavily advertised. It had made good sales gains in earlier years but by 1965 its sales curve had flattened.

*Heart's Delight,* a line of whole fruit nectars as well as various fruits and vegetables, had also been a Richmond-Chase advertised brand. It had rather wide distribution but, like Diet Delight, its sales had plateaued.

*F & P Brand* was Filice & Perrelli's line of California fruits and vegetables. Throughout the years it had received advertising support but it had never achieved a position of brand dominance. It was becoming, in fact, a semi-price brand with an increasingly limited distribution. Advertising of this brand was discontinued in 1966.

*Red Pack Tomatoes and Tomato Products,* packed by San Jose Canning Company, was a top-selling brand, mainly distributed in such Eastern states as

**EXHIBIT 4 (Continued)**

New York, Connecticut, New Jersey and Pennsylvania. It was a strongly advertised brand in its marketing area. The line included whole peeled tomatoes, juice, puree, paste, catsup, and tomato sauces. Red Pack was a top quality line, sold at a premium price, and was recognized as a brand leader.

*Aunt Penny's Sauces*, pioneered by Schuckl and Co., consisted of a line of White, Hollandaise, and Cheese sauces which were distributed in the West only. They had been advertised to some extent over the years, and they enjoyed good distribution in their limited marketing area.

# Maxwell House Coffee

The product manager for ground Maxwell House Coffee was at work in his office preparing his budget for the next fiscal year. Unexpectedly, he was interrupted by a long distance telephone call from Stockton, California. One of the company's salesmen called to report that the J. A. Folger Company had just introduced a new keyless one-pound can for its brand of ground coffee in Stockton supermarkets, apparently on a test market basis. He was forwarding samples of the can to headquarters in White Plains, New York by air mail.

The product manager reported the news to his immediate superior, the Advertising and Merchandising Manager, who in turn notified the General Manager of the Maxwell House Division of General Foods Corporation. All three executives would be intimately involved in considering the development because of the large potential impact of a packaging change on the profits of the Maxwell House Division.

## POTENTIAL IMPLICATIONS OF A CHANGE

Maxwell House was the leading brand of ground coffee (drip, regular and fine grind) in the United States, selling about 300,000,000 pounds annually. The brand accounted for about 21% of all ground coffee sold and was followed by Folger's with about 15%. Because of the large volume, a cost reduction of as much as 1 cent per can could save Maxwell House about $3,000,000 a year. If a packaging change should cause the brand to either lose or gain a 1% share of market, factory sales would be affected by about $9,000,000, assuming a selling price of 63 cents per pound, and gross margin would be affected by about $1,000,000.[1]

Approximately 60% of the 300,000,000 pounds of ground Maxwell

---

Reprinted from *Stanford Business Cases 1964* with the permission of the publisher, Graduate School of Business, Stanford University. Copyright © 1964 by the Board of Trustees of the Leland Stanford Junior University.

[1] Gross margin figure disguised.

House Coffee sold annually were packed in one-pound cans; 40% in two-pound cans.

The Maxwell House Division also roasted and marketed ground coffee under the Yuban brand and a decaffeinated ground coffee under the Sanka label. Yuban had about 1.9% and Sanka had 1.5% of the ground coffee market. (See Exhibit 1.) The Maxwell House Division had maintained a position of leadership in the coffee industry for many years. Sales of its three brands in both ground and soluble form had grown to account for 35% of all coffee sold in the United States in 1962.

While Maxwell House led other brands of ground coffee on a nationwide basis, its market position was much stronger in the East than the West. The opposite was true for Folger's. For example, 50% of the sales of Maxwell House were made in the eastern and mideastern sales districts which accounted for only 5% of Folger's sales. In 1962, Folger's was not sold in markets which accounted for about 40% of the sales of ground Maxwell House coffee. They included Boston, New York, Philadelphia, Syracuse, Washington, D.C., Youngstown, Charlotte and Atlanta. The west central and western regions contributed only 15% of the total sales of Maxwell House ground coffee compared to 71% for Folger's. (See Exhibit 2.) In Northern California, Folger's sold about four times as much ground coffee as did Maxwell House.

Maxwell House enjoyed 36.2% of the vacuum packed ground coffee market in its mideastern sales region where Folger's share was 6.1%. In its west central region, Maxwell House had a share of 8.5% compared to 29.1% for Folger's. (See Exhibit 3.)

Matters of packaging and labeling were of concern to the product manager because of his responsibility for the domestic marketing of ground Maxwell House Coffee. Aided by a group of assistants, he established annual sales objectives, worked with the advertising agency to develop and implement advertising and promotional programs, evaluated possible changes in the product, determined what price changes should be recommended, and maintained programs of market testing and consumer research.

## GROUND COFFEE PACKAGING

The packaging of ground coffee in the United States had undergone no major change since the late 1920's when a can developed for shortening products was adopted for coffee. At that time the large can suppliers tooled to produce a key opening can 5⅛ inches in diameter and 3⅝ inches in height. Such a can had been used since then by most brands except during World War II when glass jars were substituted to save metal. After the war, electrolytic tinning replaced the old hot-dip process and a lighter weight "tin plate" (Steel plate coated with tin) was used to reduce costs and improve appearance and resistance to rust. The can companies' tooling did not change, however. Use of a key opening can of the same dimensions continued.

The Folger test in Stockton which prompted the phone call to the Product Manager late in October, 1962, was not the first indication of that company's interest in a keyless can. In August, 1962, Folger's had introduced a three-pound keyless can in Stockton. The move was of no unusual concern to Maxwell House executives who viewed it as a test of the three-pound size which they earlier had decided not to market. They saw no manufacturing economies in it and they believed the number of families who could use three pounds of coffee in two weeks was very limited. Coffee tended to become stale about two weeks after the can was first opened.

After receiving the new keyless, one-pound can from Stockton, the Product Manager sent the following memorandum to the Advertising and Merchandising Manager on October 26, 1962:

Forwarded with this memorandum is the new Folger can. Its principal features are a smaller diameter, a taller shape, and its opening device (regular can opener vs. key strip). The can was picked up in Stockton, California, by our sales force. There is a research questionnaire enclosed in the cap and our intelligence indicates that Folger is testing it only in the Stockton area. The sales force also reports that Folger will be introducing a similar two-pound can in Stockton in the near future.

The new can is made by the American Can Company and it costs (including plastic lid) considerably more than the Maxwell House can (about 15¢ per unit of 12 pounds). To mass produce this can, it would be necessary to invest in molds for the plastic lid and in line conversion parts (estimated total cost for Maxwell House, about $600,000).

We have findings from consumer research on can shapes similar to this one. An American Can Company test conducted by Forbes Research in July, 1962, indicated that consumers preferred a smaller diameter, taller can to the standard shape. Their preference was not great enough, however, to influence them to purchase a brand not normally used just because of the can. Although the can used in this research had a conventional key strip opening device, we still believe the research conclusion is valid as far as preference for the shape is concerned.

With regard to the opening device, we feel this may offer an important consumer appeal. Maxwell House had investigated cans that could be opened with a regular home can opener before, but it was decided not to pursue this further.

Now that the Folger Company has indicated interest in this type of can, we will have to stay on top of the development. Accordingly, we plan to conduct consumer interviews in Stockton to learn of consumer reaction to the Folger can. A research proposal for this study will be available early next week, and either a member of the product group or a representative from the Market Research Department will go to Stockton next week to observe Folger's sales activity.

We have alerted the sales force to be looking for this can in all areas and will keep you advised of any new developments.

The Product Manager approved proposals for consumer interviews and store audits of retail sales of ground coffee in Stockton.

## STOCKTON CONSUMER INTERVIEWS

The Marketing Research Department of the Maxwell House Division planned a survey of women purchasers of Folger's coffee in the new no-key can and by October 29, 1962, it had employed Survey Research Services, Inc., of San Francisco, California, to do the interviewing.

During the weekends starting November 8 and 15, interviewers were stationed in Stockton supermarkets. They introduced themselves to women who had purchased Folger's in the new can. In order to guard against bias, a series of three questions were asked about each of five different product categories, one of which was ground coffee. The questions were aimed at ascertaining the respondent's usual brand; the brand she bought the last time she purchased the given type of product, not counting purchases made on the day of the interview; and the brand purchased on the day of the interview. If Folger's was not the respondent's usual brand of coffee, she was asked why she happened to buy Folger's on the day of the interview. The interviewer also obtained the respondent's name, address and telephone number and noted the name and location of the store in which the interview was conducted. (See Exhibit 4 for questionnaire.)

Ten days to two weeks later, telephone interviews were conducted with 125 women who had been interviewed in the supermarkets.[2] Respondents first were asked open questions about what they thought of the Folger's coffee they bought in the new type of can and how they felt about the container itself. Several more specific questions then were asked. (See Exhibit 5 for questionnaire.)

Eighty-six per cent of the respondents reinterviewed considered the new Folger's container better than the usual kind of coffee can. The corresponding figure for women whose usual brand was not Folger's was 80%. (See Exhibit 6.) The main reasons given were ease of opening, slimmer shape which made for ease of handling, reusability of the can as a cannister, and the plastic lid for resealing which was thought to keep the coffee "better and fresher."

Ninety-three per cent of the spontaneous comments on the new can were favorable. When asked to rate the new container and its contents on each of several points, 86% said it was easier to open and 80% said it was easier to reclose than the key can. Coffee purchased in the new can was

---

[2] Eighty-eight women interviewed in supermarkets were not represented in the telephone survey results. Forty-five refused reinterview, 27 could not be reached and 16 interviews were completed after the established deadline.

seen as superior in flavor, aroma and freshness to that bought in the conventional can.

Sixty-one per cent of the women reinterviewed had purchased ground coffee in the two weeks between the in-store interview and the telephone follow-up. In so doing, 56% of the women reinterviewed had selected Folger's. The corresponding figures for women who usually bought a brand other than Folger's were 53% and 47%. Thirty per cent of the non-regular users of Folger's and 53% of the regular users had purchased Folger's in the new can more than once. (See Exhibit 7.)

Ninety-six per cent of the regular users and 70% of the non-regular users of Folger's stated that their next purchase of ground coffee would be Folger's in the new can. When asked why, 59% referred to the coffee and 48% referred to the container in some way. (See Exhibit 8.)

When women who regularly used a brand other than Folger's were asked in the in-store interview why they had selected Folger's, 57% (17 of 30 women) said they did so because it was on sale and 33% replied by referring to the container. (See Exhibit 9.)

The Marketing Research Department reported as follows on the results of the Stockton interviews:

The available data are extremely favorable to the new Folger's can type. Attempts to generalize from the data, however, must be read within the limitations of one fairly small sample in one city with three quarters of the respondents buyers of a single brand—Folger's.

It is suggested, therefore that further research be carried out to check the favorable reaction indicated here among a larger, more diversified sample. Resultant data might then be collated with comparable data for the several new can prototypes now under development by the Division.

## RETAIL SALES AUDIT

Arrangements were made to have the Burgoyne Index, Inc., of Cincinnati, Ohio, audit retail sales of Folger's, Maxwell House and other selected brands of ground coffee in 21 Stockton stores during the weeks beginning November 5, 12, and 19.

Results of the audits showed that Folger's in one-pound and three-pound no-key cans accounted for 10.1% of the total pounds of ground coffee sold in the first week, 14.7% in the second week, and 10.6% in the third week. (See Exhibit 10.) The larger share in the second week was due to an increase in sales of the three-pound size which did not continue into the third week. The Burgoyne staff reported that special merchandising promotions in Stockton stores during the three-week period were limited to a floor display of Folger's one-pound size in the new can and to "the usual shelf strips." Retail prices were not affected by the change in cans.

During the three-week period of the store audits, the three-pound size accounted for 8.1% of the ground coffee sold in Stockton. The corresponding figure for the Maxwell House San Francisco sales district was

0.6%. Folger's share of ground coffee sales (all sizes and both the key and the keyless containers) during each of the three weeks was 23.9%, 28.5%, and 24.7%. Maxwell House's shares of ground coffee sales in Stockton for the same three weeks were 18.7%, 15.3%, and 18.5%. Folger's accounted for 28.5% of the sales of ground coffee in the San Francisco sales district during the three-week period compared with 7.8% for Maxwell House. (See Exhibit 11.)

The costs to Maxwell House of the research conducted in Stockton and described on the preceding pages were about $2,800 for the retail sales audits and about $2,200 for the consumer interviews.

## CUSTOMER ACCEPTANCE

During November and December, 1962, members of the Maxwell House management engaged in many discussions as they considered what to do about the no-key can.

In studying the question of consumer acceptance, they reviewed available studies made by other organizations of consumer likes and dislikes in packaging. The results contained evidence of dissatisfaction with cans that required a key to open and one survey made in 1960 found that 5% of the women regarded coffee packages as "poor." (See Exhibit 12.)

The finding that Stockton women who tried the keyless can preferred it highlighted questions as to what the effects would be if Folger's converted to that can and Maxwell House did not. Would Folger's thereby gain an advantage in the 20 Maxwell House sales districts in which Maxwell House and Folger's competed? Would Folger's be able to use the new can as a merchandising lever to successfully introduce its brand into the eastern sales districts in which Folger's was not now represented and to increase its share in the eastern and mideastern regions which accounted for half of Maxwell House's sales? Folger's might elect to use any increase in gross margin resulting from lower can costs for additional promotion in an effort to increase market position. Maxwell House executives believed they would have to match such an increase in order to hold position for Maxwell House ground coffee.

In considering what the effects would be if Maxwell House converted to the keyless can, Maxwell House executives noted that the three-week audit of retail sales in Stockton provided no evidence that Folger's sales and share of market had increased. They were unwilling to take action which might lead to a decrease in market share. They feared that a decline in share, once started, could not be contained. Because of the large volume involved, a drop in share for the Maxwell House brand could have a significant adverse effect on General Foods corporate sales figures at a time when great emphasis was being placed on growth and a decline in share was regarded as a red flag signaling possible deterioration of a brand's consumer franchise.

## ADEQUACY OF NO-KEY CAN

The Production Services Manager and the Packaging Development Manager reported that they had investigated possible use of a no-key can in 1956 and again in 1959. On those occasions, decisions were made against the no-key can because of technical problems affecting the strength of the metal, the high cost of polyethylene lids and the feeling of the marketing group that its appearance was not of high quality. At the same time, however, it was found that the no-key can was easier to make than the key can. If the cost of the polyethylene lid were excluded, it also was less expensive to manufacture.

The Folger's no-key can was $4\frac{1}{16}$ inches in diameter (called a 401 can) as compared to the standard key can of $5\frac{2}{16}$ inches in diameter (called the 502 can). The cylindrical portion of the Folger's no-key can was made from 60-pound tin plate which was less expensive than the 90-pound tin plate used in the conventional key can. After studying no-key can packaging alternatives in 1962, Maxwell House's researchers concluded that a can made from 90-pound tin plate for the sides and 75-pound tin plate for the ends would be necessary to satisfactorily withstand the pressures which characteristically built up inside a coffee can a few days after it was packed. The Maxwell House production manager believed that a can made with 60-pound tin plate would be vulnerable to bulging and structural failure.

## COST CONSIDERATIONS

Maxwell House production personnel investigated what the costs of a keyless can would be both if Maxwell House should manufacture it and if the can were purchased from suppliers. While the make or buy study was under way, several large United States oil companies switched from steel tin plate cans $4\frac{1}{16}$ inches in diameter (401 cans) to plastic coated paper containers for packaging oil. Their move left some of the machines of the American Can Company and the Continental Can Company available for other uses. While the can companies no doubt would prefer to continue producing coffee cans from their key can machines, the General Foods Purchasing Manager reasoned that they nevertheless recognized that the coffee industry was interested in a packaging change and now might be willing to quote an attractive price on the 401 can.

The following cost figures were compiled from prices quoted by can companies and from the manufacturing cost study made by Maxwell House purchasing, accounting and engineering personnel:

| | Cost per Thousand Cans with Lithographed Labels | | | |
|---|---|---|---|---|
| | One-Pound Size | | Two-Pound Size | |
| | If Make | If Buy | If Make | If Buy |
| No-key can.................... | $46.00 | $55.00 | $67.00 | $ 78.00 |
| Polyethylene lid................ | 6.50 | 8.00 | 7.75 | 9.50 |
| Total.................. | $52.50 | $63.00 | $74.75 | $ 87.50 |
| Key can currently in use.......... | $60.00 | $75.00 | $87.00 | $120.00 |

In the past, Maxwell House had purchased its cans. The $46.00 and the $67.00 figures in the above table included both variable and fixed costs for the Hoboken, N.J. plant production of about 75,000,000 one-pound cans and about 25,000,000 two-pound cans a year. Plant and equipment needed if the Hoboken plant were to make the no-key can would cost an estimated $2,800,000. The comparable figure for the key can was $4,000,000. It was the company's practice to write off machinery over a 15-year period and buildings over a 40-year period. Cans for the other Maxwell House plants in Jacksonville, Florida; Houston, Texas; and San Leandro, California, would continue to be purchased because of their lower volume requirements.

The cost estimates for the 401 can assumed the use of 90-pound tin plate for the sides and 75-pound plate for the ends. Producers of polyethylene lids had quoted $12 per thousand for initial orders filled while they would be expanding their capacity. The Purchasing Manager estimated $8.00 as the future price after mass production techniques had been perfected and capacity had been expanded.

The "buy" figures in the above table did not include the costs of converting the 10 Maxwell House production lines for handling the keyless can. These costs were estimated at $600,000 for capital equipment and $800,000 for labor and expense for a total of about $1,400,000. The costs pertained almost entirely to the one-pound size because the two-pound keyless can had the same dimensions as the two-pound key can.

Another factor which the Maxwell House management attempted to weigh was the probable drop in plant efficiency which would result during plant conversion and continue for some time thereafter. Use of the same methods of packing for many years had resulted in high levels of productivity. Maxwell House executives did not wish to unnecessarily take on new problems which would add to costs. They noted that can company representatives had expressed the opinion that Folger's no-key can was merely an experiment that would not develop into anything beyond a test.

## WAIT FOR A NEW QUICK STRIP CAN?

A further important consideration was that Maxwell House was working with the American Can Company in the development of another major innovation in can design which would use neither a key nor a plastic lid. Its metal cover would be sealed on the side just below the top with a flexible aluminum coated plastic strip one-half inch wide. The can would be reclosed with its own cover which would have deeper side wells than the lid of the key can, providing a tighter fit which would help keep contents fresher.

Maxwell House executives were convinced that the can being developed, which they called "quick strip," would be superior to both the traditional key can and the new keyless can, combining their advantages. Its cost was expected to be comparable to that of the key can. The American Can Company had applied for several patents covering the tear-strip opening principle. While there was no exclusivity arrangement, Maxwell House executives were confident that they would obtain first rights to receive the can for their needs until such time as American Can had developed sufficient capacity to supply the total industry. Since the cost and time necessary for developing such capacity were expected to be great, Maxwell House executives felt that from a practical standpoint they would enjoy lead time ranging from three or four months in all areas and up to 12 months in many areas of the United States before the quick strip can would be available to competition.

In January 1963, the American Can Company representatives estimated that with a reasonable amount of luck, the developmental work on the quick strip would proceed so that 100,000 units could be supplied for test marketing by May or June; and that one production line capable of producing 1,000,000 cans a week could be in operation by September or October, 1963. Full scale production which would permit Maxwell House to use the can for its total output of ground coffee was expected to be possible three or four months after the first production line was put in operation or by January, 1964, in accordance with the above schedule.

Maxwell House executives were inclined to be less optimistic. They thought that there was only about a 50% chance that 100,000 cans would be available by October, 1963, and they believed it would be unrealistic to assume that tests on the first 100,000 units would find the can technically perfect. They recognized the possibility that technical problems might arise which would delay introduction of the quick strip can indefinitely. Once test results permitted a decision to go ahead, about six months would be required before the can company could achieve a production rate which would satisfy the total container needs of ground Maxwell House Coffee.[3]

In reviewing the situation, the Maxwell House executives wondered

---

[3] In response to questioning a year later, the Advertising and Merchandising Manager said that in January, 1963, Maxwell House executives probably would have given the following estimates of probabilities as to when the American Can Company's first production line would be turning out 1,000,000 cans a week: by December, 1963, 50%; by March, 1964, 75%; by June, 1964, 85%; and never, 10%. They expected that full production for Maxwell House's total needs could be attained about four months after the first production line had started operations.

whether it would be better to wait and make one large move from the 502 to the quick strip can or convert in the near future to the keyless can which they regarded as an interim step in coffee packaging. Costs of converting production lines from the keyless to the quick strip can would be minor because the cans were of the same size.

## A NEW STOCKTON SURVEY

On December 12, 1962, a Maxwell House production manager received by telephone findings of research done for the Continental Can Company on the acceptance of Folger's keyless can in Stockton. While details about the study were lacking, the notes made during the phone conversation contained the information that 186 telephone calls had been completed to Stockton homes. One hundred of the 186 respondents said they were aware of Folger's keyless can and 55 had bought it. Of the 55, 69% said they usually bought Folger's; 31% said they normally bought other brands although only 25% reported doing so the last time they bought coffee prior to the telephone interview. Of the 55 people who had tried Folger's in the keyless can, 51% had repurchased it at least once; 16% had repurchased it three times; and 16% had repurchased it more than three times. Forty-nine percent of the 55 people who had tried the keyless can either had not repurchased it or said they did not intend to do so.

Of the regular Folger's users who had purchased Folger's in the keyless can, 17% mentioned the container when asked for reasons. Among respondents who said they usually bought brands other than Folger's, 64% said they purchased Folger's in the keyless can because they "were curious." Explanations of their purchases by respondents who did not buy Folger's in the keyless can when they had the opportunity to do so did not reveal much in the way of negative feelings about the can itself. (See Exhibit 13.)

## FOLGER ADDS THREE MARKETS

Folger had introduced its one-pound no-key can in Sacramento, California; St. Louis, Missouri; and Muncie, Indiana, by mid-January, 1963. While Folger's plans for the future were not known to Maxwell House, rumors were abundant and had been reported by all levels of Maxwell House Division management and by General Foods corporate executives as well.

Contributing to the tension of the situation was the fact that the rumors often were conflicting. One day, for example, a Maxwell House manager heard that Folger's was dropping all distribution of the no-key can. The next day, he received word from a source regarded "equally as reliable" that Folger's would have the no-key can in national distribution within a few weeks. A variety of rumors circulated in the trade and were being relayed to headquarters by the company's sales force. The situation led one executive to remark that the rumor factory was working overtime and that the Maxwell House ground coffee group was receiving much phony intelligence.

## PRESSURE FOR DECISION

The consensus in late January was that no outside party really knew how far Folger had committed itself to national distribution of the keyless can. At the same time, however, there were strong pressures on Maxwell House executives to decide what to do. One Maxwell House manager commented that the speed at which decisions had to be made did not allow anyone to have a comfortable grasp of the situation and it did not permit normal test market procedures.

Although store audits had not been continued in Stockton, the Maxwell House sales force reported in January their observations that the sales of Folger's ground coffee had remained about the same there as they had been before the introduction of the no-key can. Folger's recently had switched from 60-pound to 90-pound tin plate for the sides of the can.

Consideration was being given to converting only the San Leandro plant in order to gain both manufacturing and marketing experience with the keyless can. A majority of the families which purchased coffee in the one-pound size did so at least once every two weeks. In view of this fact, the market research manager estimated that observation of a minimum of two months of sales results from retail store audits in selected markets would be required to ascertain whether the change to the keyless can would not adversely affect Maxwell House's share of market.

By converting the San Leandro plant, Maxwell House might be able to supply the keyless can to sales districts in which Folger had introduced the new can. Following a policy of matching Folger's packaging on a market to market basis, however, could create inventory and transportation problems. While the San Leandro plant could conveniently supply western sales districts, it would have difficulty in supplying a market like St. Louis which normally was served by the Houston plant.

Investigation revealed that suppliers with injection molding equipment capable of producing plastic tops for the no-key can badly lacked capacity sufficient to fill Maxwell House's needs should the brand convert to the keyless can. No single supplier could produce as much as 2,000,000 lids a year. Time would be required to increase lid capacity and to acquire and install can closing machines and new parts needed for packing lines.

None of the four plants in which Maxwell House Coffee was roasted and packed had unused capacity. The San Leandro plant accounted for about 15% of the company's production for domestic sales and the Hoboken plant about 40%. The remaining 45% was split about evenly between Jacksonville and Houston.[4] Conversion could be accomplished one production line at a time. It would have to be carried out on a rotational basis in order to keep retail stores supplied with Maxwell House Coffee. The Hoboken plant had four lines, the other plants two each.

It was estimated that once a decision was made to convert to the keyless can nationally, four months would be required for conversion before the keyless can output could start. Volume could be expected to build up smoothly from that time until six months later when the full output of Maxwell House ground coffee would be in keyless cans. In other words, the equivalent of five full months of output in the keyless can could be achieved during the first year after a decision had been made to convert.

In late January, the General Manager was attempting to determine what course of action the Maxwell House Division should follow in regard to the keyless can.

**EXHIBIT 1**

**Estimated Percentage Share of Ground Coffee Sales for Maxwell House, Folger's, Sanka and Yuban Brands, in the United States, 1953–1962**

|  | 1953 | 1954 | 1955 | 1956 | 1957 |
|---|---|---|---|---|---|
| Maxwell House | 15.6 | 16.5 | 16.3 | 17.3 | 16.7 |
| Folger's | — | — | — | — | — |
| Sanka | 1.1 | 1.0 | 0.8 | 0.9 | 1.0 |
| Yuban | — | — | — | 0.5 | 0.7 |

|  | 1958 | 1959 | 1960 | 1961 | 1962 |
|---|---|---|---|---|---|
| Maxwell House | 17.3 | 19.1 | 20.8 | 21.6 | 21.4 |
| Folger's | — | — | 14.6 | 14.8 | 14.7 |
| Sanka | 1.1 | 1.1 | 1.2 | 1.3 | 1.5 |
| Yuban | 0.8 | 0.8 | 1.0 | 1.8 | 1.9 |

SOURCE: Maxwell House Division, Market Research Department.

---

[4] Figures disguised.

**EXHIBIT 2**

**Estimated Percentage Distribution of Sales of Vacuum Packed
Ground Coffee and Sales of Selected Brands
by Maxwell House Sales Regions, 1962**

| Region (and Sales Districts in Each) | All Brands | Maxwell House | Yuban | Folger's | Chase & Sanborn | Hills |
|---|---|---|---|---|---|---|
| Eastern.................... <br>(Boston, New York, Philadelphia, Syracuse) | 18.7 | 29.0 | 24.1 | 0 | 26.7 | 0.7 |
| Mideastern................. <br>(Washington, Youngstown, Cincinnati, Louisville) | 13.2 | 22.4 | 8.6 | 5.0 | 22.4 | 5.0 |
| Southern.................... <br>(Charlotte, Atlanta, Jacksonville, Memphis, New Orleans) | 13.0 | 19.9 | 5.3 | 9.3 | 13.9 | 0.5 |
| Central.................... <br>(Detroit, Indianapolis, Chicago, Milwaukee, St. Louis) | 18.4 | 13.9 | 5.0 | 14.2 | 21.2 | 48.3 |
| West Central............... <br>(Minneapolis, Omaha, Kansas City, Dallas, Houston) | 16.4 | 6.2 | 1.0 | 34.6 | 4.1 | 10.3 |
| Western.................... <br>(Portland, San Francisco, Los Angeles, Denver, Phoenix) | 20.3 | 8.6 | 56.0 | 36.9 | 11.7 | 35.2 |
| | 100.0 | 100.0 | 100.0 | 100.0 | 100.0 | 100.0 |

SOURCE: Maxwell House Division, Market Research Department.

**EXHIBIT 3**

**Estimated Percentage of Vacuum Packed Ground Coffee Sales
for Selected Brands by Maxwell House Sales Regions, Late in 1962**

| Region (and Sales Districts in Each) | Maxwell House | Yuban | Folger's | Chase & Sanborn | Hills |
|---|---|---|---|---|---|
| Eastern............................ 32.1 | | 1.8 | — | 6.4 | 0.4 |
| (Boston, New York, Philadelphia, Syracuse) | | | | | |
| Mideastern........................ 36.2 | | 1.2 | 6.1 | 10.1 | 4.4 |
| (Washington, Youngstown, Cincinnati, Louisville) | | | | | |
| Southern.......................... 32.8 | | 0.7 | 9.5 | 7.0 | 0.5 |
| (Charlotte, Atlanta, Jacksonville, Memphis, New Orleans) | | | | | |
| Central............................ 14.9 | | 0.5 | 12.1 | 7.1 | 27.1 |
| (Detroit, Indianapolis, Chicago, Milwaukee, St. Louis) | | | | | |
| West Central....................... 8.5 | | 0.1 | 29.1 | 1.7 | 7.4 |
| (Minneapolis, Omaha, Kansas City, Dallas, Houston) | | | | | |
| Western........................... 8.5 | | 5.3 | 26.3 | 4.4 | 17.4 |
| (Portland, San Francisco, Los Angeles, Denver, Phoenix) | | | | | |

SOURCE: Maxwell House Division, Market Research Department.

## EXHIBIT 4

### Questionnaire for the Stockton In-Store Consumer Interviews

We are doing a study of the different products people buy. (IF NECESSARY, EXPLAIN THAT YOU ARE WITH SURVEY RESEARCH SERVICES, AN INDEPENDENT MARKET RESEARCH COMPANY AND THAT YOU ARE NOT SELLING ANYTHING) (INTERVIEW ONLY PEOPLE WHO ARE BUYING THE NEW FOLGER CAN WHICH CAN BE OPENED WITH A CAN OPENER)

Ques. 1a:  What brand do you usually buy of each of the following products . . . detergent? toothpaste? regular ground coffee? paper toweling? margarine? WRITE IN BRAND BELOW.

Ques. 1b:  (ASK FOR EACH PRODUCT)   The last time you bought_____, not counting today, what brand did you buy?

Ques. 1c:  (ASK FOR EACH PRODUCT)   If you bought any _____ today, would you tell me which brand you bought?

|  | *Ques. 1a* | *Ques. 1b* | *Ques. 1c* |
|---|---|---|---|
|  | Usual brand | Last brand | Brand today |
| Detergent | _____ | _____ | _____ |
| Toothpaste | _____ | _____ | _____ |
| Ground coffee (regular coffee) | _____ | _____ | _____ |
| Paper toweling | _____ | _____ | _____ |
| Margarine | _____ | _____ | _____ |

*IF FOLGER'S NOT USUAL BRAND (QUES. 1a) ASK:*

Ques. 2:  Why did you happen to buy Folger's coffee today?

BE SURE TO OBTAIN THE FOLLOWING INFORMATION:

Name _____        Telephone no. _____

Address _____        Interviewer's initials_____

Store name_____

Location _____

## EXHIBIT 5

### Questionnaire for Telephone Interviews of Consumers in Stockton

Hello, my name is _____ from Survey Research Services. We're conducting a survey in this area . . . about two weeks ago you bought some Folger's coffee in a new type of can . . .

1a.    What did you think of the Folger's coffee you bought in the new type of can? (PROBE: Why is that?)

1b.    How about the new container itself, how did you feel about that?

2a.    Would you say that the new type of coffee can was, generally speaking, better or worse or about the same as the usual kind of coffee can?

        SAME............ 1
        BETTER.......... 2
        WORSE........... 3

2b.    Why is that?

3.    Now, for each of the following, would you tell me whether the Folger's coffee in the new type of can was as good as what you used to get in the usual kind of can, or better or worse.

| | As good | Better | Worse |
|---|---|---|---|
| The freshness of the coffee | 1 | 2 | 3 |
| The aroma of the coffee | 4 | 5 | 6 |
| The flavor of the coffee | 1 | 2 | 3 |
| Ease of opening the can | 4 | 5 | 6 |
| Ease of reclosing the can | 7 | 8 | 9 |

4a.    Have you bought any ground coffee since the time you were interviewed in the store about two weeks ago?

        YES........ 1
        NO......... X

        (IF YES):    What brand?_____

4b.    The next time you buy ground coffee do you think it will be Folger's in the new can or some other kind?

        FOLGER'S IN THE NEW CAN.... 1
        SOME OTHER KIND............. 2

4c.    Why is that?

5.    Have you bought this Folger's brand of coffee in this new can before, or is this the first time?

        HAVE BOUGHT BEFORE........ 1
        FIRST TIME.................... 2

**EXHIBIT 5 (Continued)**

*CLASSIFICATION*

A.  Which of the following groups comes    A.  UNDER 25.................. 1
    closest to your own age? (READ        B.  25—34...................... 2
    LETTER AND GROUP)                     C.  35—44...................... 3
                                          D.  45 AND OVER.............. 4
                                              REFUSED.................. 0

B.  Would you tell me the last grade      8th GRADE OR LESS................. 1
    you completed in school?              1–3 YEARS HIGH SCHOOL.......... 2
                                          4 YEARS HIGH SCHOOL........... 3
                                          ANY COLLEGE..................... 4
                                          REFUSED......................... 0

C.  What is the occupation of the head of the household?
    _____

D.  Which of the following comes closest  A.  UNDER $3,000.............. 1
    to your family's total annual income? B.  $3,000—$4,999............... 2
    (READ LETTER AND GROUP)               C.  $5,000—$7,499.............. 3
                                          D.  $7,500—$9,999.............. 4
                                          E.  $10,000 and over............. 5
                                              REFUSED.................. 0

NAME_____     PHONE NO._____
ADDRESS_____
CITY_____   STATE_____
INTERVIEWER'S NAME_____        DATE_____


**EXHIBIT 6**

**Percentages of Respondents Who Considered Folger's No-Key Can
Better Than, Same As, or Worse Than Conventional Key Can**

|  | *All Respondents* | *Respondents by Usual Brand of Ground Coffee* | |
|---|---|---|---|
|  |  | *Folger's* | *Other* |
| (Number of Respondents) | (125) | (95) | (30)* |
|  | 100% | 100% | 100% |
| *Consider New Container* |  |  |  |
| *Better* than the usual coffee can............... | 86 | 88 | 80 |
| About the *same* as the usual coffee can........... | 12 | 10 | 17 |
| *Worse* than the usual coffee can............... | 2 | 2 | 3 |

* Percentages should be interpreted with caution because of the small base.

Question asked: Would you say that the new type of coffee can was, generally speaking,
        better or worse or about the same as the usual kind of coffee can?
Respondents were women who had purchased Folger's ground coffee in the no-key can in
Stockton, California, during the weekends of November 8 and 15, 1962.

**EXHIBIT 7**

**Ground Coffee Purchasing by Respondents since and before First Interview**

| | All Respondents | Respondents by Usual Brand of Ground Coffee | |
| --- | --- | --- | --- |
| | | Folger's | Other |
| (Number of Respondents) | (125) | (95) | (30) |
| | 100% | 100% | 100% |
| Purchases of Coffee since Initial Interview | | | |
| Have Bought Ground Coffee in Past Two Weeks (since Initial Interview) | 61% | 63% | 53% |
| Folger's...................... | 56 | 59 | 47 |
| Hills Brothers.................. | 2 | 1 | 3 |
| Maxwell House............... | 1 | 1 | — |
| Chase & Sanborn.............. | 1 | 1 | — |
| Edwards...................... | 1 | — | 3 |
| Sanka........................ | 1 | — | 3 |
| Don't remember............... | 1 | 1 | — |
| Have Not Bought Ground Coffee Since Initial Interview............. | 39 | 37 | 47 |
| Purchases of Folger's in New Can before Initial Interview | | | |
| Had Bought Folger's in New Can Before Day of In-Store Interview.... | 47% | 53% | 30% |
| Purchase on Day of In-Store Interview Was the First........... | 53 | 47 | 70 |

Questions:  Have you bought any ground coffee since the time you were interviewed in the store about two weeks ago? What brand?
Have you bought this Folger's brand of coffee in this new can before, or is this the first time?

Respondents were women who had purchased Folger's ground coffee in the no-key can in Stockton, California, during the weekends of November 8 and 15, 1962.

## EXHIBIT 8

**Percentages of Respondents Who Said Their Next Ground Coffee Purchase Would Be Folger's in the New Can and Reasons Why**

| | *All* *Respondents* | *Respondents by Usual Brand of Ground Coffee* | |
| --- | --- | --- | --- |
| | | *Folger's* | *Other* |
| (Number of Respondents)..... | (125) 100% | (95) 100% | (30) 100% |
| Next Purchase of Ground Coffee Will Be: | | | |
| Folger's in new can............ | 90 | 96 | 70 |
| Some other kind............... | 2 | 1 | 7 |
| Will buy what is on sale........ | 6 | 2 | 20 |
| Don't know................... | 2 | 1 | 3 |

| | *Totals* |
| --- | --- |
| (Number of Respondents Who Said Next Ground Coffee Purchase Would Be Folger's in New Can)........................ | (112) 100% |
| Percent Referring to Coffee in Explaining Why........... | 59 |
| Always buy Folger's; like it better; never use any other brand................................. | 48 |
| Like the coffee.................................... | 11 |
| Percent Referring to Container in Explaining Why........ | 48 |
| Like the new can (unspecified).................... | 30 |
| Like the top...................................... | 2 |
| Can is easier to open............................ | 1 |
| Can keeps coffee fresher......................... | 1 |
| Can is reusable.................................. | 16 |
| Can is handy; easier to handle.................... | 2 |
| Easy to store; doesn't take up so much room........ | 2 |
| No answer....................................... | 6 |

Question asked: The next time you buy ground coffee do you think it will be Folger's in the new can or some other kind? Why is that?

Respondents were women who had purchased Folger's ground coffee in the no-key can in Stockton, California, during the weekends of November 8 and 15, 1962.

## EXHIBIT 9

**Percentages of Respondents Who Usually Bought Ground Coffee Other Than Folger's by Reasons Given for Buying Folger's in the No-Key Can**

|  | *Totals* |
|---|---|
| (Number of Respondents) | (30) |
|  | 100% |
| *Bought Folger's because It Was on Sale* | 57 |
| *Referred to Container in Explaining Why* | 33 |
| Can use container for other purposes: cookie jar, puddings, fruitcakes, freezer container | 13 |
| Wanted to try new can; liked it | 10 |
| New can looked easy to open | 7 |
| Liked the new lid | 7 |
| Can looked easier to handle | 3 |
| Can looked easy to empty into canister | 3 |
| Don't know; no answer | 10 |

Question asked: Why did you happen to buy Folger's coffee today? (Day of in-store interview)
Respondents were women who had purchased Folger's ground coffee in the no-key can in Stockton, California, during the weekends of November 8 and 15, 1962, but who said they usually bought another brand.

## EXHIBIT 10

**Percentage Shares of Total Pounds of Ground Coffee Sold in 21 Stockton, California Stores during Weeks of November 5, 12 and 19, 1962**

| Brand and Type of Container | Size of Can (lbs.) | Nov. 5–Nov. 11 | Nov. 12–Nov. 18 | Nov. 19–Nov. 26 | Number of Stores Stocking |
|---|---|---|---|---|---|
| Folgers: New (no-key)............ | 1 | 7.0 | 6.9 | 8.6 | 21 |
| New (no-key)............ | 3 | 3.1 | 7.8 | 2.0 | 5 |
| Total New Can........ | | 10.1 | 14.7 | 10.6 | 21 |
| Old (key)............... | ½ | 0.7 | 1.6 | 0.7 | 18 |
| Old (key).............._... | 1 | 0.1 | — | 0.2 | 4 |
| Old (key)............... | 2 | 12.9 | 12.1 | 12.6 | 21 |
| Old (key)............... | 4 | 0.1 | 0.1 | 0.6 | 3 |
| Total Old Cans........ | | 13.8 | 13.8 | 14.1 | 21 |
| Total Folger's........... | | 23.9 | 28.5 | 24.7 | 21 |
| Maxwell House: Old.............. | 1 | 6.5 | 3.4 | 4.5 | 21 |
| Old (5 cents off)........... | 1 | 0.1 | 0.2 | — | 6 |
| Old.............. | 2 | 12.1 | 11.7 | 13.7 | 21 |
| Old (12 cents off)........... | 2 | — | — | 0.3 | 3 |
| Total Maxwell House...... | | 18.7 | 15.3 | 18.5 | 21 |
| Yuban: Old.................... | 1 | 2.2 | 2.3 | 3.1 | 21 |
| Old.................... | 2 | 1.0 | 1.6 | 1.1 | 9 |
| Total Yuban........... | | 3.2 | 3.9 | 4.2 | 21 |
| Sanka: Old.................... | 1 | 3.4 | 1.5 | 1.3 | 21 |
| Old (6 cents off)............ | 1 | — | — | — | 1 |
| Total Sanka............ | | 3.4 | 1.5 | 1.3 | 21 |
| Total General Foods...... | | 25.3 | 20.7 | 24.0 | 21 |
| MJB........................... | all | 14.7 | 14.0 | 21.4 | 21 |
| Hills......................... | all | 17.9 | 23.9 | 15.1 | 21 |
| Butternut...................... | all | 3.9 | 1.8 | 2.2 | 9 |
| Chase and Sanborn................ | all | 4.9 | 4.2 | 4.7 | 7 |
| All Others...................... | all | 9.4 | 6.9 | 7.9 | 19 |
| Total All Brands.............. | | 100.0 | 100.0 | 100.0 | — |

SOURCE: Store audits made for Maxwell House Division.

## EXHIBIT 11

### Ground Coffee Sold in Stockton and San Francisco by Brand and Size of Container During Weeks of November 5, 12 and 19, 1962
### (in per cent of total pounds)

| | | Stockton, Calif.† | | |
| | San Francisco* | Week of | Week of | Week of |
| Size of Can; Brand | (3-week period) | Nov. 5 | Nov. 12 | Nov. 19 |
|---|---|---|---|---|
| 1 Lb. and Under | | | | |
| All Brands | 42.6 | 40.5 | 37.0 | 36.1 |
| Folger's | 13.2 | 7.0 | 8.5 | 9.5 |
| Maxwell House | 2.7 | 6.6 | 3.6 | 4.5 |
| 2 Lbs. | | | | |
| All Brands | 56.8 | 56.3 | 54.9 | 61.3 |
| Folger's | 14.9 | 12.9 | 12.1 | 12.6 |
| Maxwell House | 5.1 | 12.1 | 11.7 | 14.0 |
| 3 Lbs. | | | | |
| All Brands | 0.6 | 3.2 | 8.1 | 2.6 |
| Folger's | 0.4 | 3.2 | 7.9 | 2.6 |
| Maxwell House | — | — | — | — |
| All Sizes Combined | | | | |
| Folger's | 28.5 | 23.9 | 28.5 | 24.7 |
| Maxwell House | 7.8 | 18.7 | 15.3 | 18.5 |

\* Maxwell House's San Francisco sales district.
† In sample of 21 Stockton stores.
SOURCE: Store audits conducted for Maxwell House Division.

## EXHIBIT 12

### (Excerpts from a Maxwell House Division Interdepartmental Memorandum)
CONSUMER DISSATISFACTION WITH PACKAGING

In line with emphasis on maintaining and improving a brand's competitive position with consumer-accepted packaging innovations, it is advantageous to identify available documented consumer dissatisfactions with current packages. This is the purpose of this memorandum.

Unfortunately, documented information, i.e., research findings on this subject are sparse and much of the material is biased by the vested interests of the disseminators.

Packaging per se may in many instances be only a contributing factor in a brand purchase decision. Yet it may be the pivot point in this decision if product and merchandising (both advertising and promotion) do not strongly differentiate between brands. In examining past trade articles, it is apparent that innovations in coffee packaging have been lagging behind many other product categories. One available study on the subject indicated that packaging ranked fifth in what the consumer thought influenced her purchase decision, outranked by the shopper's own experience, recommendation of friends, price and advertising.

Two studies, a 1960 study by *Sales Management* utilizing a National Family Opinion panel of 1,000 respondents and a 1962 study conducted for the Chicago Printed String Company by Market Facts, Inc., will be used to demonstrate consumer packaging dissatisfactions and preferences.

First, consumers are vocal about packaging because at every turn they are confronted with a package of some type. Ninety-four percent of male heads-of-households, when asked if their wives ever asked them to assist in opening a package, answered "yes." Certainly this is manifest proof that there are areas for improvement. The most frequent type of container the husband is asked to open is the "jar" (76%), followed by the bottles (40%), containers with keys (27%), and plastic containers (8%). Yet 68% of the women open most of the packages in the family.

At the time of the 1960 survey, the women interviewed felt these packages were "poor:"

**EXHIBIT 12 (Continued)**

| Item | % of Women |
|------|------------|
| Frozen foods | 15 |
| Paper flour sacks | 8 |
| Rice | 6 |
| Cereals | 6 |
| Bread | 6 |
| Coffee | 5 |
| Packaged lunch meats | 4 |
| Crackers | 3 |
| Cheese | 2 |

What package gave the housewife the most trouble?

| Item | % of Women |
|------|------------|
| Cartons which are stapled | 52 |
| Cartons which are glued shut | 43 |
| Plastic bags or coverings | 41 |
| Cardboard box | 37 |
| Cartons which need to be closed again | 35 |
| Packages with metal binding (required key to open) | 35 |
| Pry-open lids | 32 |
| Screw top jars | 27 |
| Tied packages (string or wire) | 22 |
| Vacuum sealed containers | 14 |
| Cartons which are taped shut | 14 |
| Paper wrapped packages | 8 |
| Containers with opening tear tapes | 7 |
| Other | 4 |

To judge the magnitude of the package opening problem, the findings showed that 70% of the women found most packages fairly easy to open and 14% found most packages fairly difficult to open. Only 3% mentioned coffee as a product with which they had specific difficulty. Three percent said coffee was a "really good package."

Consumers when asked their likes and dislikes about different closures and containers, responded as indicated below:

| Container or Closure | Like | Dislike | Don't Care |
|----------------------|------|---------|------------|
| Package with spout | 87 | 4 | 7 |
| Inner wrap of foil | 85 | 3 | 10 |
| Packages that reveal product | 85 | 1 | 12 |
| Containers usable for other purposes | 85 | 1 | 16 |
| Pull tab openings | 76 | 8 | 13 |
| Aluminum screw tops | 71 | 7 | 19 |
| ¼ Twist off lid | 69 | 11 | 17 |
| Other metal screw tops | 63 | 10 | 22 |
| Tuck in top on cardboard package | 68 | 17 | 14 |
| Square glass bottle or jar | 63 | 12 | 22 |
| Inner wrap of paper | 61 | 19 | 16 |
| Large economy size container | 59 | 18 | 20 |
| Plastic screw tops | 53 | 18 | 25 |
| Plastic flip caps | 52 | 10 | 33 |
| Plastic squeeze containers | 52 | 22 | 22 |
| Individual serving container | 49 | 12 | 37 |
| Stretched tops on bags | 38 | 42 | 15 |
| *CANS THAT OPEN WITH A KEY* | *35* | *48* | *15* |
| Metal lids on cardboard containers | 27 | 35 | 36 |
| Tear open cylindrical containers | 26 | 33 | 36 |

**EXHIBIT 12 (Continued)**

Available data clearly point out that consumer oriented packaging improvements which have added to ease of opening and resealing have been well accepted in recent years and that they still represent a major target area for future functional packaging improvements. The value of the material available is that it has largely excluded product and design elements while concentrating on a very manifest level of dissatisfaction.

There are two other areas of concern in the adaptation of functional packaging improvements to varying food categories, i.e., how these relate to frequency of usage, expectations for product freshness, in-home storage and previous dissatisfaction within the product category, just to mention a few. This does not try to include the functional attributes of size and shape.

One note of caution is pointed out in these studies. "The best liked features are relatively recent innovations. The least liked are those that have been around the longest."

(In 1951, for example, 54% liked cans that opened with a key. Today (1962) 35% like them and 48% do not.)

## EXHIBIT 13

### Notes on December 1962 Telephone Report of Findings of Continental Can Company Study of Acceptance of Folger's Keyless Can in Stockton

186 telephone calls were made to people in Stockton, California. 100 people were aware of the new containers. Of those who were aware of the new can, 55 had tried it and 45 had not. Of the 55 people who had tried the new container:

69% were Folger's users
<u>31%</u> were users of brands other than Folger's
100%

The reasons for purchasing the new container among:
Respondents who usually bought Folger's:

52% always used it
20 were curious
10 thought the container was attractive and cute
7 thought they could use the container for other things
<u>11</u> had various other reasons
100%

Respondents who usually bought brands other than Folger's:

64% were curious
<u>36</u> other
100%

Of the 45 people who did not purchase the new container originally:

2% thought the flavor would not be as good
36 (reason not available)
33 always bought another brand
7 did not because another brand was on sale
10 bought Folger's in the 2-lb. size (key can)
<u>12</u> other
100%

Of those who had tried the new container:

49% normally purchased the 1-lb. size
44 normally purchased the 2-lb. size
5 normally purchased the 3-lb. size
<u>2</u> varied the size of container normally purchased
100%

Of the 55 respondents who had tried Folger's in the no-key can:

51% had repurchased it at least once
44 had not repurchased it
<u>5</u> did not intend to repurchase
100%

20% had repurchased it twice
16 had repurchased it three times
16 had repurchased it more than three times

What brand did you buy the last time?

75% bought Folger's
<u>25</u> bought brands other than Folger's
100%

Ninety-five per cent normally purchased their coffee in a can.

# SECTION **IV**

## PRICE

# Grey Electronics, Inc.

Grey Electronics, Inc., a multi-divisional producer of electronics equipment headquartered in Iowa, was founded in 1936 by John Forman, a graduate engineer with an interest in electronics. During its early years the company survived by assembling various types of radio equipment for Midwestern manufacturers. Operations expanded substantially during World War II as the company obtained large amounts of subcontracting work, mainly of an assembly nature. During and immediately following the war, Forman changed the character of his firm in an attempt to develop a proprietary product. His first effort was an improved version of a high frequency radio receiver which one of his associates had designed. The "new" product was immediately successful and the profits generated enabled Forman to invest heavily in research and development. During the late 1940's and early 1950's the company successfully introduced a series of new products and by 1960 sales had grown to almost $40 million a year. By 1965 the company consisted of three major producing divisions (consumer products, radio equipment and solid state) as well as several staff departments (see Exhibit 1).

The solid state division's products were high quality, technically sophisticated electronic subassembles and integrated circuits designed for limited, specialized uses, with about 75 percent of division sales going to the U.S. government. The products were constantly changing and the division regularly worked near the "state of the art" in either its product development work or its production methods.

The division was organized with four major departments—all of which reported to a division manager. In 1964 a solid state oscillator department

Reprinted from *Stanford Business Cases 1967* with the permission of the publisher, Graduate School of Business, Stanford University. Copyright © 1967 by the Board of Trustees of the Leland Stanford Junior University.
[1] An oscillator is a source of power used in technically advanced laboratory and field test sets. A test set might contain a series of oscillators, each capable of producing a signal over a given frequency range, making the set useful for checking the accuracy and receiving power of a piece of electronic equipment.

was added to the division.[1] (See Exhibit 2.) This department was responsible for its own research and development, engineering, manufacturing, and marketing activities. Grey's market share for this product was estimated to be about 35 percent versus 40 percent for the industry's largest producer, Standard Parts.

Because such a large portion of its sales were to the government, the manager of the oscillator department, Ned Seymoure, was constantly troubled by the problem of bid pricing. Competition was severe and he was often forced to bid on a variable cost basis—or even below—to secure some business. In 1965, Seymoure asked Tom Moore, Director of Corporate Operations Research, to investigate the feasibility of preparing a model which would help in determining the price to bid on contracts.

In his preliminary work, Moore found that the oscillator subassembly group's cost on a job was often a function of the price bid. Thus, if a low bid was submitted and accepted the manufacturing group worked hard to keep its costs down. Conversely if a "profitable" bid had been accepted, the manufacturing group did not strive as hard to hold down its costs. He also determined that substantial variations existed between contracts and bids in the gathering and utilizing of marketing information concerning the customer's needs and competitor's strengths, weaknesses, and probably bids.

At the end of three months, Moore and other members of the Operations Research Group had completed the job of constructing and programming the model. The actual construction consisted of two steps:

1. **Determining the Objectives of the Model.** After careful deliberation it was decided that, since the manager of the oscillator department was the person who would ultimately accept or reject the model, it would be useless to try to sell him a model which did not meet his objectives. "Therefore," stated Moore, "I asked Seymoure what his own goals were relative to the operations of the division. It would have been possible for us to construct a model which best served the interests of the corporation, the product managers working for Seymoure, and/or of Seymoure himself. We knew, in advance, that the objectives of these three parties were not necessarily compatible. For example, the corporation tends to set year to year objectives on return on investment while product managers often become excessively concerned about winning or losing a particular contract. Seymoure, on the other hand, tends to look at the long run—the next five years. He worries about getting enough volume to hold his research group together, to hold his manufacturing schedule fairly constant throughout the year, and about getting a big share of the market. We finally decided we'd try to construct a model which would be predicated on the long run, but which would show what would happen in the short run also."

2. **Determining the Bidding Process.** The Bidding Procedure in the oscillator department involved the representatives of several functional areas. Chronologically, the steps appeared as follows:

1. A request to submit a bid was received by the department's Marketing Manager.
2. He referred the bid request to a Product Marketing Specialist whose specialty was within the product line concerned.
3. The Product Marketing Specialist requested a cost estimate from the Accounting Department.
4. A cost estimator from the Accounting Department obtained from the Product Line Manager estimates of the cost of manufacturing the product; i.e., the cost data, both historical and estimated, that he could use to produce a bid. This bid was always based on full-cost-recovery pricing.
5. This analysis was returned to the Product Marketing Specialist who prepared an analysis of the market to supplement the financial analysis.
6. These analyses were presented to the Product Line Manager. The Product Marketing Specialist and the Product Line Manager jointly prepared a bid which was submitted to the Marketing Manager for approval.
7. If the Product Line Manager and the Product Marketing Specialist could not agree on a bid, the Marketing Manager would resolve their differences.
8. If the contract to be bid was large or particularly significant for other reasons, the Division Manager approved the final bid. He also resolved any remaining disagreements or even changed the suggested bid to one which he felt was more appropriate.

## FULL-COST-RECOVERY PRICING

A full-cost-recovery price, as prepared by the cost estimator, was designed to recover *all* variable costs plus all allocated costs of a contract. The procedure for preparing such a bid was:

1. Direct labor for the contract was estimated. Direct labor included a 25 percent charge for employee fringe benefits.
2. An overhead charge was allocated based on 70 percent of direct labor. Overhead included depreciation on the division's equipment, the costs of the machine shop and service departments of the division (e.g., divisional R & D, etc.), and all fixed charges not included in the General and Administrative allocation.
3. Material costs were estimated.
4. (1), (2), and (3) were totaled to get manufacturing cost.
5. General and Administrative burden was computed as a percentage of manufacturing cost. G & A included: an allocation for the expenses of the corporate staff; corporate building; corporate service; the division manager's salary and his staff salaries; and costs of moving and

rearranging equipment. G & A normally ranged from 35 to 65 percent of manufacturing cost.

6. An allocation for profit was computed as a percent of the total of (4) and (5). The percentage used depended on the type of contract being negotiated and also varied according to the Federal Government's pricing guidelines.

## Description of the Model

The basic model represented an attempt to simulate the process by which an experienced manager prepared a bid. The probability of getting the contract if a given price was bid was of critical importance. By multiplying this probability with the expected payoff, the model showed the probable value of submitting a particular bid. Mr. Moore explained: "We repeat their process for many different bids until we find the optimal price, that is, the bid which was the highest expected value of those bids we are willing to submit. Naturally, we don't blindly accept what the model puts out. We know we can't describe all bidding situations in this one model and even if we could, the cost would be exorbitant. We submit the model's output to the department manager for further action. If his intuition agrees with the model, we'll have done a pretty good job. If not, either some factor has been left out of the model or the manager is biased by some personal consideration. Once we determine what the problem is, the model's suggested bids can be accepted or rejected."

## Inputs to the Model

In its completed form, the model made use of four inputs. The first input was an estimate of the most critical competitor's probable bids. Factors considered in preparing this estimate included the opposing firm's financial condition, the capacity at which the firm was estimated to be operating, its bidding history, and the bidding history of the person preparing that firm's bid, the firm's estimated cost structure, its capacity to develop or produce the product involved, the firm's policies relating to long-run versus short-run gains, any unique rivalry existing between Grey and that firm, the firm's position in (or out of) the market involved, the price structure of the market (e.g., firm or deteriorating), and any other information relevant to the opposing firm's probable bid.

One or several people might prepare this assessment. Usually those persons most familiar with the market would be the manager of the manufacturing group for that product and his counterpart in the marketing department. Their estimates were quantified in the model using a probability distribution. A normal-type distribution was assumed with the competitor's most likely bid equalling the mode.

(As an example, if a competitor's most probable bid was expected to be $50,000 and there was felt to be 1 chance out of 40 that he would bid below $35,000, a normal-type distribution was created with $50,000 equalling the mode while $35,000 and $65,000 equalled the plus and minus two standard deviation points.)

The second input involved an estimate of the amount of bias which the customer held for or against Grey or its products. To prepare this estimate it was necessary to determine the basis on which the contract would be let. A customer might be concerned about a number of factors including price, the ability of the supplier to meet delivery schedules, unusual technical characteristics of a product, the back-up service which a firm offered—or any of a number of other factors peculiar to a customer and a contract.

This estimate was quantified in terms of the probability of Grey being awarded the contract if its bid was a certain percent above or below the competitor's bid. Such an estimate might appear as follows, for example:

| *Percent Grey's Bid Above (+) or Below (−) Competitor's Bid* | *Probability Grey Will Get Contract* |
|---|---|
| +20% | .025 |
| + 5% | .5 |
| − 10% | .975 |

Once again, a normal-type distribution was assumed with the mean equalling the point at which there was a 50–50 chance Grey would get the bid. This estimate was prepared by the product sales manager and the manufacturing group manager.

The third input consisted of the production costs of the contract. An estimate of the labor and material costs was prepared by the manager of the manufacturing group. He considered historical performance, learning curve effects, start-up costs, equipment required and all other factors which influenced his production costs. Overhead rates were allocated by the Division Controller.

The fourth input was the long-run effects of the contract. Effects of the contract on catalogue prices and prices which would have to be submitted on succeeding bids such as follow-on contracts, reduced overhead allowances on renegotiable contracts, gains and losses in market position and prestige, and any other factors not included in the costs of production were computed to determine the rewards and penalties of losing the contract. These payoffs or losses were present-valued at an annual rate of 10 percent to determine the "extra" benefits and costs of the contract. The manufacturing group manager and the marketing manager prepared this estimate.

### Output of the Model

The model's output was a payoff table showing the expected value of a given bid. This table might appear as follows, for example:

| Bid | Probability of Winning | Profits (Losses) | Probable Profits (Losses) |
|---|---|---|---|
| $70,000................. | .05 | $40,000 | $ 2,000 |
| 60,000................. | .3 | 30,000 | 9,000 |
| 50,000................. | .55 | 20,000 | 11,000 |
| 40,000................. | .70 | 10,000 | 7,000 |
| 30,000................. | 1.0 | –0– | –0– |

### Other Factors

Several additional factors were built into the model. The model could produce two suggested bids, one based on full-cost and the other on variable cost. The model could also be used to compare the effect of several different estimates of cost and market inputs.

### The SSI Job

An opportunity for the oscillator department to reach its goal of becoming the leader in the solid state oscillator field arose in April, 1966 when Systems Suppliers Incorporated (SSI) solicited bids for a large number of oscillators to be used in laboratory test sets designed for the military. SSI received the contract from Redstone Arsenal at a time when SSI was reportedly in financial trouble due to low sales volume.

The contract was for 57 sets. Each set contained two separate oscillator units each of which required one oscillator subassembly for each of eight frequency bands, A, B, C, D, E, F, G, and H. Bids were therefore being solicited on 912 subassemblies in total or 114 in each frequency band. In addition, bids were requested for a possible follow-on order should Systems Suppliers wish to raise the total procurement to either 1,200 or 1,600 units.

SSI did not restrict itself to one supplier for the entire contract. Bids were requested on several options so that SSI could split the contract if it wished. The options were:

| Option Number | Frequency Bands to Be Covered |
|---|---|
| 1................... | A, B, C, D, E, F, G, & H |
| 2................... | A, B, C, D, E, F, & G |
| 3................... | H |
| 4................... | A, B, & C |
| 5................... | D, E, F, & G |

Grey asked for and received permission to bid on one other option:

| Option Number | Frequency Bands to Be Covered |
|---|---|
| 6................... | A, B, C, D, & E |

Grey requested this option because it closely matched Grey's present capabilities and its market expansion plans. Option number 6, therefore, was the option the company was most interested in winning.

Grey believed it held a technical advantage in three frequency bands (A, B, and C) amounting to a virtual monopoly. Standard Parts, Grey's only significant competitor, was known to have started working on these oscillator subassemblies, but had not yet displayed any capacity to produce or deliver in quantity any oscillators in these frequency ranges. In the past year, Grey had successfully marketed an oscillator at H band, one which was expected to be extremely competitive in terms of the SSI contract. Grey did not have, or plan to develop, an oscillator at G band, but at F band, an oscillator was in the final stages of development. At E band, the company was preparing a pilot production run, while both Grey and Standard Parts had successfully marketed D band subassemblies.

Grey believed it held a technical advantage on all oscillators from A through E band, and in H band, because its products were magnetically shielded. Magnetic shielding was important to SSI as Redstone's specifications required close physical storage of the oscillators, a layout which might cause equipment failure if their magnetic fields interacted. It was known that Standard Parts proposed to overcome this weakness by lining the storage containers with magnetic shielding material. It was not known with certainty if this technique would work.

## The Customer

Determining the basis on which SSI would award the contract was relatively easy. SSI had the reputation of making decisions which maximized short-term profits. In other words, they were thought to be willing to take a high risk of a long-term loss in return for a high assurance of a short-term gain. Price, therefore, was thought to be the key to obtaining the contract.

This situation operated to Grey's disadvantage because, in issuing the contract, Redstone Arsenal had specified Standard Parts oscillators rather than "Standard Parts or equivalent." This oversight on Redstone's part had probably occurred because Redstone copied SSI's specifications when the contract was written. Grey was not successful in attempting to get Redstone to change this specification. Although Grey might legally have forced Redstone to change the specifications, this would have created ill-will which the company was reluctant to incur.

Redstone's oversight worked to both SSI and Standard Part's advantage. SSI told Grey it would be willing to purchase Standard's oscillators in all frequency bands despite the risk of technical difficulties and failure to meet delivery schedules, knowing they could escape any repercussions by maintaining they had exactly followed the contract's specifications.

On the other hand, Grey was reasonably sure that SSI did not really wish to do this. Grey felt that SSI probably wanted to split the order, with Standard Parts getting options 3 and 5, and Grey getting option 4. It was also felt that Standard Parts would be determined to get as much of the contract as possible since their market share had dropped substantially over the past two years. This contract was quite large and the firm which got the contract would probably gain or hold a leadership position in the market for some time to come. The combination of these circumstances meant that the SSI job was a prize well worth seeking but one that would be difficult to attain.

### Estimates of Competitive Bids

Assuming the contract would be let on price alone, Grey prepared estimates of Standard Part's probable bids.[2]

| Option | Frequency Band | Bid Range Estimate A | Estimate B |
|---|---|---|---|
| 1................ | A | $1,990–1,390 | $1,530–1,630 |
| | B | 1,170–1,420 | 1,020–1,120 |
| | C | 765– 865 | 765– 720 |
| | D | 690– 740 | 665– 765 |
| | E | 665– 740 | 640– 690 |
| | F | 665– 740 | 640– 690 |
| | G | 690– 765 | 690– 740 |
| | H | 2,500–2,750 | 2,100–2,500 |
| 2......Same as 1 above except eliminate H Band | | | |
| 3................ | H | $2,500–2,750 | $2,100–2,500 |
| 4................ | A | $2,040–3,040 | $1,840–1,940 |
| | B | 1,220–1,720 | 1,220–1,320 |
| | C | 820– 920 | 870– 970 |
| 5................ | D | $ 720– 770 | $ 720– 770 |
| | E | 690– 765 | 665– 720 |
| | F | 690– 740 | 665– 720 |
| | G | 720– 820 | 720– 770 |
| 6................ | A | $1,990–2,390 | $1,530–1,630 |
| | B | 1,170–1,420 | 1,020–1,120 |
| | C | 765– 865 | 765– 715 |
| | D | 690– 740 | 665– 765 |
| | E | 665– 740 | 640– 690 |
| 7 Standard Parts Reaction to Option 6......... | F | $ 690– 665 | $ 714– 765 |
| | G | 700– 800 | 790– 840 |
| | H | 2,325–2,550 | 2,375–2,495 |

Estimates A and B were made by knowledgeable people who were intimately familiar with the market, historical bids made by Standard Parts, their general financial position, and other intangibles which might

[2] While Grey was preparing bids on all seven options, only option number 3 will be costed in this case; the cost per oscillator is given in Exhibit 3.

influence Standard's bid. They were made independently, and there was no attempt to "correct" the estimates once each estimator knew what the other had estimated. They were therefore a reliable indicator of Grey's knowledge of Standard Part's intentions.

## Historical Costs

The company possessed a substantial amount of cost data on oscillator subassemblies in bands A, B, C, and D; several successful bids had been made for contracts involving these subassemblies, and the company was confident that this information could provide the basis for a successful bid on this occasion. The company had only been marketing band H subassemblies, on the other hand, for some four months. The technical breakthrough which had enabled Grey to manufacture band H oscillator subassemblies at relatively short notice had led to wide customer acceptance of the product. Nevertheless, Grey was a little uncertain of the value of the five months' cost data on band H components, in view of the relative experience of its competitors. In spite of this, Grey was very anxious that the company's bid on Option 3 should be competitive, in view of the boost to development that would be provided by winning the band H contract. The first five months' labor and material costs (Exhibit 3), are those actually incurred during the first production runs of band H components. The last seven months' costs (of the full year's contract) were estimated by the Product Line Manager.[3]

Although lacking marketing experience in bands E, F, and G, the company prepared bids using the following criteria:

1. Costs for the band E oscillator should equal band D. Equivalent effort should be the same.
2. Costs for band F should be the same as those for band D except that the costs for labor category 2 should be doubled. Equivalent effort should be the same.
3. Costs for the G band oscillator should be the same as for D band for labor category 1, the same as the F band for labor category 2, 1.25 times the cost of D band for labor category 3, and the same as D band for material cost. Equivalent effort should be the same as the D band.

All labor costs included an overhead charge of 70 percent.

## Additional Labor Costs

If Grey obtained the order, it was felt that additional people would be required. Estimates of these needs were as follows:

---

[3] The company felt it had a good chance of being awarded the contract for option 4. At all events, Grey anticipated spreading the production of the subassemblies over a year's operations.

| Labor | Salary (Not Including 25% Fringe Benefits) | Order Size* |
|-------|------|------|
| Jr. Tech. | $115/wk | Three or more bands |
| Assembler A | $2.75/hr | Three or more bands |
| Assembler A | $2.75/hr | Six or more bands |
| Assembler B | $2.41/hr | Three or more bands |
| Experimental Assembler | $2.75/hr | Any order |
| Assembler B | $2.41/hr | Four or more bands |
| Technician | $136/wk | Six or more bands |
| Prod. Eng. B | $180/wk | Four or more bands |
| Clerk (half time) | $88/wk | Four or more bands |

* The necessity for these labor force additions varied with the number of types for which an order was received. If Grey received an order for any three oscillators, for example, it would have to hire four people: a senior technician; an Assembler A; an Assembler B; and an Experimental Assembler. If it obtained an order for all eight oscillators, it would have to hire all of the people listed.

## Equipment Required

In addition to labor force additions, an order from SSI would force Grey to purchase equipment. The following table summarizes these requirements:

| Equipment | Approximate Cost* | Order |
|-----------|------|------|
| Assembly Station | $ 5,000 | Three or more bands |
| Assembly Station | 5,000 | Four or more bands |
| Processor | 1,200/pair | Any order |
| Console | 10,000 | Any order |
| Console | 10,000 | Four or more bands |
| Microscope | 600 | Each added assembler |
| Spotwelder | 1,000 | Any order |
| Spotwelder | 1,000 | Three or more bands |
| Two Spotwelders | 1,000 ea. | Six or more bands |
| Test Bench | 500 | Each added assembler |
| Furnace | 7,500 | Seven or more bands |

* Installation costs included.

## Other Costs

Several miscellaneous costs had to be considered. Training costs historically equalled about six weeks' salary per person. There were also warranty provisions; about 5 percent of the oscillators in each of the top five bands would have to be replaced, while in the lower three bands, about 15 percent would have to be replaced. Royalties were also a factor; a royalty consisting of one-half of 1 percent of the selling price would have to be paid on the top six oscillators. Finally, there was the problem of deciding which, if any, of the bids would bear the departmental overhead of $480,000 a year. The management assumed that the contract, if awarded, would run for one year, and that the overhead rate on all of the oscillator business was effectively the same. This did not mean, however, that a marginal cost bid could not be made.

In addition to these costs, increases would be necessary in some liquid assets. In general, a contract would increase cash requirements by about two or three weeks' total cost, receivables by between three and four weeks total cost, and inventories by about seven to eight weeks' total cost.

### Intangibles

No matter what the factory costs, Grey did not want to lose all of the SSI business. Recent technical developments in test sets indicated the feasibility of substituting integrated equipment for low frequency oscillators. If Standard Parts got a contract for high frequency units, they could develop a shielded oscillator subassembly and compete more favorably with Grey elsewhere. Grey, therefore, did not want Standard Parts to get the order for high frequency oscillator subassemblies.

### Output

The final output of the program, based on the information given in the case for band H subassemblies, is presented in Exhibit 5.

**EXHIBIT 1**

**Organizational Chart of the Grey Electronics Company in 1965**

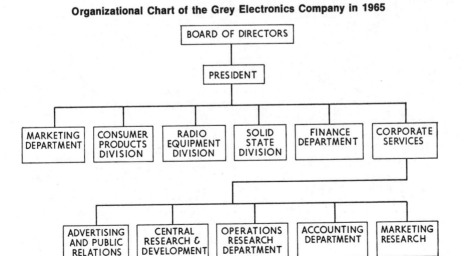

## EXHIBIT 2

### Organization Chart of the Solid State Division of the Grey Electronics Company in 1965

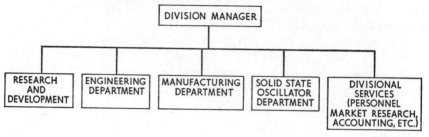

## EXHIBIT 3

### Grey Cost Data for Frequency Band H

| Month | No. of Weeks | Labor Category | | | Total Labor | Material | Equivalent Effort* |
|---|---|---|---|---|---|---|---|
| | | 1 | 2 | 3 | | | |
| 1..... | 4 | $ 4,290 | $ 5,110 | $ 2,450 | $ 11,850 | $ 4,700 | 11.70 |
| 2..... | 4 | 3,330 | 4,330 | 3,860 | 11,520 | 2,420 | 8.65 |
| 3..... | 4 | 2,865 | 3,870 | 2,370 | 9,105 | 3,440 | 8.50 |
| 4..... | 5 | 3,905 | 2,480 | 2,125 | 8,510 | 2,820 | 1.15 |
| 5..... | 5 | 3,120 | 3,860 | 4,050 | 11,030 | 1,775 | 12.25 |
| 6..... | 4 | 3,770 | 2,825 | 3,115 | 9,710 | 1,570 | 13.35 |
| 7..... | 4 | 3,535 | 3,165 | 2,655 | 9,355 | 1,570 | 12.65 |
| 8..... | 4 | 2,170 | 3,350 | 2,830 | 8,350 | 1,175 | 8.25 |
| 9..... | 5 | 2,285 | 2,110 | 3,160 | 7,555 | 590 | 8.15 |
| 10..... | 4 | 3,410 | 2,735 | 2,660 | 8,805 | 785 | 9.35 |
| 11..... | 4 | 3,265 | 3,150 | 2,210 | 8,625 | 980 | '9.55 |
| 12..... | 5 | 2,985 | 2,845 | 3,615 | 9,445 | 590 | 10.45 |
| | | $38,930 | $39,830 | $35,100 | $113,860 | $22,415 | 114.00 |

* "Equivalent effort" referred to the number of oscillator subassemblies produced during the period. With respect to the above, for example, output at the end of the first month might consist of the following:

| No. of Oscillators | Percent Completed | Equivalent Effort |
|---|---|---|
| 1...................... | 100 | 1 |
| 20...................... | 50 | 10 |
| 2...................... | 25 | 0.5 |
| 1...................... | 20 | 0.2 |
| Equivalent effort at end of 1st month | | 11.70 |

**EXHIBIT 4**

**Evaluation of Cost of H Band Oscillator**
**Subassembly: Options 1 & 3**

| | | |
|---|---|---|
| Direct labor............................ | $113,860 | |
| Material............................... | 22,415 | |
| Additional labor........................ | 11,690 | |
| Training costs.......................... | 660 | |
| Additional equipment.................... | 1,590 | |
| Manufacturing cost..................... | $150,215 | $150,215 |
| Warranty provisions.................... | $ 22,530 | |
| Royalties.............................. | — | |
| Other costs............................ | 485 | |
| Miscellaneous costs..................... | $ 23,015 | 23,015 |
| Allocation of department overhead.......... | $ 42,860 | 42,860 |
| Cash.................................. | 10,660 | |
| Receivables cost........................ | 15,275 | |
| Inventory cost.......................... | 30,545 | |
| Total increase in liquid assets.............. | $ 56,480 | 56,480 |
| Total cost: | | $272,570 |
| Units produced: | | 114 |
| Full cost per unit: | | $   2,391 |
| Marginal cost per unit: | | $   2,015 |

NOTE: Costs are calculated on the basis of information given on pages 345–346 and in Exhibit 3 of this case. General & Administrative overhead of $42,860 (29% of manufacturing cost) was a result of (1) allocating the total factory overhead "reasonably" between not only the expected SSI contracts, but also over the other work on which the department was engaged; (2) an assessment of the major long term benefits to which success with the Option 3 bid was expected to lead.

**EXHIBIT 5**

**Grey Electronics, Inc.**

```
GREY ELECT FULL COST

        Q =        0.95

        A =     2100.00

        M =     2500.00

        B =     2750.00

        ALPHA =        0.0  Percent (competitive advantage)

        FIRST TRIAL PRICE =      2000.00

        TRIAL PRICE INTERVAL =       10.00

        NUMBER OF TRIAL PRICES =       80.00

        PRODUCT COST =     2391.00

        NUMBER OF UNITS =      114.00

        EXTRA PROFIT =       0.0

        EXTRA PENALTY =       0.0

        PSTAR INTERPOLATION PERMISSIBLE ERROR =        0.10 Cents
```

## EXHIBIT 5 (Continued)

GREY ELECT FULL COST

| BID PRICE | PROBABILITY OF WINNING | EXPECTED PROFIT |
|-----------|------------------------|-----------------|
| 2CCC.CO | 0.991 | -44182.81 |
| 2010.CO | 0.990 | -42997.70 |
| 2C20.OO | C.989 | -41808.76 |
| 2C3C.CC | 0.987 | -40615.91 |
| 2C40.00 | 0.985 | -39419.04 |
| 205C.CC | C.983 | -38218.12 |
| 2C6C.00 | 0.981 | -37013.14 |
| 2C7O.00 | C.978 | -35804.15 |
| 2080.0U | 0.976 | -34591.25 |
| 2C90.00 | C.973 | -33374.60 |
| 210U.00 | 0.969 | -32154.44 |
| 211C.00 | 0.966 | -30931.10 |
| 2120.0C | 0.962 | -29704.97 |
| 2130.00 | C.957 | -28476.56 |
| 2140.C0 | C.952 | -27246.46 |
| 2150.0C | 0.947 | -26015.39 |
| 2160.C0 | 0.941 | -24784.16 |
| 2170.0C | 0.935 | -23553.72 |
| 218C.00 | C.928 | -22325.13 |
| 2190.0C | 0.921 | -21099.59 |
| 22C0.0C | C.913 | -19878.41 |
| 2210.00 | 0.904 | -18663.04 |
| 2220.00 | 0.895 | -17455.07 |
| 223C.C0 | 0.886 | -16256.20 |
| 2240.00 | C.875 | -15068.27 |
| 225C.CC | 0.864 | -13893.22 |
| 2260.00 | C.853 | -12733.11 |
| 2270.C0 | 0.840 | -11590.11 |
| 2280.0C | 0.827 | -10466.46 |
| 229C.0C | C.813 | -9364.50 |
| 23CC.CC | 0.799 | -8286.62 |
| 2310.00 | 0.784 | -7235.26 |
| 2320.0C | C.768 | -6212.89 |
| 2330.00 | C.751 | -5221.99 |
| 2340.00 | C.734 | -4265.04 |
| 2350.0C | C.716 | -3344.48 |
| 2360.C0 | C.697 | -2462.69 |
| 2370.00 | 0.678 | -1621.99 |
| 238C.0C | 0.658 | -824.60 |
| 2390.0C | 0.637 | -72.62 |

**EXHIBIT 5 (Continued)**

GREY ELECT FULL COST

| BID PRICE | PROBABILITY OF WINNING | EXPECTED PROFIT |
|---|---|---|
| 2400.0C | C.616 | 631.98 |
| 2410.CC | 0.594 | 1287.42 |
| 2420.00 | 0.572 | 1892.06 |
| 2430.0C | 0.550 | 2444.51 |
| 2440.00 | 0.527 | 2943.54 |
| 245C.0C | C.504 | 3388.19 |
| 2460.00 | C.480 | 3777.74 |
| 2470.CC | C.457 | 4111.70 |
| 2480.00 | 0.433 | 4389.86 |
| 2490.0C | 0.409 | 4612.25 |
| 2500.C0 | C.385 | 4779.23 |
| 2510.CC | 0.361 | 4891.56 |
| 2520.CC | C.337 | 4951.25 |
| 2530.C0 | 0.313 | 4961.09 |
| 254C.CC | C.290 | 4924.44 |
| 2550.CC | 0.267 | 4845.16 |
| 2560.C0 | 0.245 | 4727.52 |
| 2570.CC | 0.224 | 4576.08 |
| 2580.CC | 0.204 | 4395.64 |
| 2590.CC | 0.185 | 4191.08 |
| 2600.00 | 0.167 | 3967.30 |
| 261C.0C | 0.149 | 3729.09 |
| 2620.00 | 0.133 | 3481.05 |
| 263C.00 | C.118 | 3227.52 |
| 2640.00 | 0.105 | 2972.51 |
| 265C.CC | C.092 | 2719.61 |
| 2660.00 | C.081 | 2472.02 |
| 267C.0C | 0.070 | 2232.47 |
| 268C.0C | 0.061 | 2003.22 |
| 269C.00 | C.C52 | 1786.08 |
| 27CC.CC | 0.045 | 1582.41 |
| 2710.00 | C.C38 | 1393.14 |
| 2720.C0 | 0.032 | 1218.82 |
| 2730.00 | 0.027 | 1059.66 |
| 2740.00 | 0.023 | 915.55 |
| 2750.CC | C.C19 | 786.13 |
| 276C.CC | 0.016 | 670.82 |
| 2770.00 | 0.013 | 568.89 |
| 278C.CC | 0.011 | 479.47 |
| 2790.00 | C.C09 | 401.62 |

MAXIMUM PROFIT =    4963.18    PRICE =    2527.10

## EXHIBIT 5 (Continued)

GREY ELECT. MARGINAL

$Q =$           0.95

$A =$      2100.00

$M =$      2500.00

$B =$      2750.00

ALPHA =          0.0  Percent (competitive advantage)

FIRST TRIAL PRICE =      2000.00

TRIAL PRICE INTERVAL =          10.00

NUMBER OF TRIAL PRICES =          80.00

PRODUCT COST =      2015.00

NUMBER OF UNITS =          114.00

EXTRA PROFIT =          0.0

EXTRA PENALTY =          0.0

PSTAR INTERPOLATION PERMISSIBLE ERROR =          0.10 Cents

## EXHIBIT 5 (Continued)

GREY ELECT. MARGINAL

| BID PRICE | PROBABILITY OF WINNING | EXPECTED PROFIT |
|---|---|---|
| 2CCC.00 | 0.991 | -1694.99 |
| 2010.CC | 0.990 | -564.27 |
| 2020.00 | C.989 | 563.46 |
| 2C3C.CC | 0.987 | 1687.64 |
| 2C4C.00 | 0.985 | 2807.62 |
| 2C5C.CC | C.983 | 3922.68 |
| 2C60.00 | C.981 | 5032.00 |
| 2070.00 | C.S78 | 6134.66 |
| 2080.00 | C.976 | 7229.68 |
| 2C9C.00 | C.973 | 8315.93 |
| 2100.00 | C.969 | 9392.19 |
| 2110.00 | 0.966 | 10457.13 |
| 2120.CC | 0.962 | 11509.30 |
| 2130.00 | C.957 | 12547.14 |
| 214C.CC | 0.952 | 13568.95 |
| 2150.0C | 0.947 | 14572.93 |
| 2160.8C | 0.941 | 15557.16 |
| 217C.00 | 0.935 | 16519.58 |
| 2180.00 | C.928 | 17458.04 |
| 2190.00 | 0.921 | 18370.29 |
| 22C0.0C | C.913 | 19253.95 |
| 2210.0C | C.904 | 20106.59 |
| 2220.0C | 0.895 | 20925.67 |
| 2230.00 | 0.886 | 21708.59 |
| 2240.00 | C.875 | 22452.72 |
| 2250.0C | C.864 | 23155.37 |
| 2260.00 | C.853 | 23813.83 |
| 227C.0C | C.840 | 24425.44 |
| 228C.00 | 0.827 | 24987.50 |
| 229C.00 | C.813 | 25497.41 |
| 2300.0C | 0.799 | 25952.61 |
| 2310.00 | C.784 | 26350.65 |
| 2320.00 | 0.768 | 26689.19 |
| 233C.0C | 0.751 | 26966.04 |
| 234C.CC | 0.734 | 27179.20 |
| 2350.0C | C.716 | 27326.81 |
| 23CC.CC | 0.697 | 27407.32 |
| 2370.0C | C.678 | 27419.31 |
| 238C.CC | C.658 | 27361.74 |
| 2390.0C | 0.637 | 27233.72 |

## EXHIBIT 5 (Concluded)

### GREY ELECT. MARGINAL

| BID PRICE | PROBABILITY OF WINNING | EXPECTED PROFIT |
|---|---|---|
| 2400.00 | 0.616 | 27034.78 |
| 2410.00 | 0.594 | 26764.75 |
| 2420.00 | 0.572 | 26423.66 |
| 2430.00 | 0.550 | 26012.09 |
| 2440.00 | 0.527 | 25530.72 |
| 2450.00 | 0.504 | 24980.73 |
| 2460.00 | 0.480 | 24363.70 |
| 2470.00 | 0.457 | 23681.29 |
| 2480.00 | 0.433 | 22935.79 |
| 2490.00 | 0.409 | 22129.52 |
| 2500.00 | 0.385 | 21265.38 |
| 2510.00 | 0.361 | 20347.27 |
| 2520.00 | 0.337 | 19382.81 |
| 2530.00 | 0.313 | 18381.02 |
| 2540.00 | 0.290 | 17351.23 |
| 2550.00 | 0.267 | 16302.91 |
| 2560.00 | 0.245 | 15245.55 |
| 2570.00 | 0.224 | 14188.41 |
| 2580.00 | 0.204 | 13140.41 |
| 2590.00 | 0.185 | 12109.92 |
| 2600.00 | 0.167 | 11104.65 |
| 2610.00 | 0.149 | 10131.54 |
| 2620.00 | 0.133 | 9196.65 |
| 2630.00 | 0.118 | 8305.12 |
| 2640.00 | 0.105 | 7461.11 |
| 2650.00 | 0.092 | 6667.77 |
| 2660.00 | 0.081 | 5927.34 |
| 2670.00 | 0.070 | 5241.11 |
| 2680.00 | 0.061 | 4609.49 |
| 2690.00 | 0.052 | 4032.13 |
| 2700.00 | 0.045 | 3507.93 |
| 2710.00 | 0.038 | 3035.21 |
| 2720.00 | 0.032 | 2611.76 |
| 2730.00 | 0.027 | 2234.97 |
| 2740.00 | 0.023 | 1901.93 |
| 2750.00 | 0.019 | 1609.48 |
| 2760.00 | 0.016 | 1354.37 |
| 2770.00 | 0.013 | 1133.28 |
| 2780.00 | 0.011 | 942.92 |
| 2790.00 | 0.009 | 780.09 |

MAXIMUM PROFIT =    27422.98    PRICE =    2366.70

NOTES *to Output, Exhibit 5*

1. "Q" relates to the degree of certainty which Grey had for the estimates of its competitors' most probable bids; figure A refers to the minus 2 standard deviation point; figure B to the plus 2 SD point, and M to the mode. See pages 284–287, this case.

2. "Alpha" is an input measure of any (non-price) competitive advantage which Grey was thought to have over the competitor. Alpha = 0.5, for example, would mean that Grey could bid 5 percent more than the competitor and still win the contract. If the contract was being let on price alone, then there could be no competitive advantage, and Alpha would equal zero. See page 287.

3. Extra Profit, Extra Penalty: These dollar inputs quantify the extra (particularly longer term) benefits (or penalties) which the company might expect as a result of winning (or losing) the contract. For example, success in this contract might lead to a reduction of costs in the production of another assembly. See page 287.

4. P* is the allowed error in the estimate of the price (to produce the expected maximum profit).

## APPENDIX A

### Government Contracts

Among the problems faced by firms supplying sophisticated parts and equipment to the government or its suppliers is the contracts which the government negotiates.

As a first-order generalization, government contracts are very precise in terms of specifications, both technical and other. The custom of phoning or writing a customer to submit an order, common in some business and industries, is not common when doing business with the government. Technical specifications in government contracts are very specific and inclusive in describing the desired product. Other specific provisions of these contracts might include delivery dates, profits which the supplying firm is allowed to make, sharing of research and development costs, and privileges which the government reserves for itself with respect to the product, its development, and the knowledge which a firm gains from developing that product.

With respect to systems, the government reserves the right to accept or authorize the manufacture of a system until the pilot models have been demonstrated to be fully workable and the supplying firms have proved their capacity to supply the system and its components. Thus, if five firms are supplying components to a systems manufacturer and one of the components fails, neither the systems manufacturer nor the components manufacturers will receive authorization to commence production until the problem is solved. This can create many scheduling problems as a firm might receive a contract for a component but not get authorization for production until some time later, with that time depending on another supplier.

Contracts which the government might negotiate with respect to profits can also create problems. In general, there are three types of contracts: a "fixed-price" contract; a "cost-plus-fixed-fee" contract (CPFF); and a "target-incentive" contract.

A fixed-price contract means that a company agrees to supply a given quantity of a given product for a fixed amount of money. If the company loses money on the contract, it suffers the entire loss. If the company makes money on the contract, it enjoys the entire gain.

A cost-plus-fixed-fee contract might cover a research and development project with the government agreeing to pay for the cost of the project plus some amount or percent of profit. Such contracts are renegotiable as differences of opinion may arise concerning exactly what the costs are or were. Disagreements can arise over whether machinery investments should be allocated fully to a given contract or should be partially supported by other aspects of a firm's operations. Overhead and administrative expenses are also common areas of disagreement, not only because of the difficulties involved in allocating these costs, but also because of the difficulties created by the fluctuating volume of business which a company might do. For example, an overhead allocation rate based on the level of business a firm is doing now might be unacceptable to the government six months from now if the firm's business increased significantly in the interim. The opposite would be true if the firm's business declined.

A target-incentive contract involves several negotiated figures—a target price, a target cost, a ceiling price, and a profit formula. Target cost represents the expected cost of the job. Target price is the price the government expects to pay and represents target cost plus an allowance for profit. Ceiling price is the highest amount which the government will pay for the job. The profit formula represents the division which will be made of the costs or profits if they differ from the targets. If target cost is less than actual cost, the government shares part of the cost and the company takes the rest. If actual cost is less than target cost, the government shares part of the savings and the company gets the remainder.

The government handles problems over CPFF and target-incentive contracts by reserving the right to audit a company's books whenever it chooses. For example, if a company is working on a CPFF contract and the company receives another large contract from the government or a significant amount of business from elsewhere, the government might audit the company's books to renegotiate the overhead and administrative allowances on the CPFF contract. As a consequence, when a company is bidding on contracts, it must consider the effect of those contracts on any government business it currently has if that government business is renegotiable or requires cost breakdowns.

The government also audits a firm's books before it negotiates a fixed-price contract if there is insufficient competition for the contract.

Another aspect of government contracts deals with the ownership of products developed through government sponsored research. If the government has financed the development of a product, it can require the firm which performed the work to supply blueprints to competing firms to allow the government to develop alternative sources of supply. It should be noted, however, that supplying blueprints does not imply that production know-how must also be supplied. In practice, the difficulties involved in manufacturing many technical items reduces substantially the usefulness of blueprints.

## APPENDIX B

### Some Competitive Characteristics of the SSO Market

SSO's are utilized as subassemblies of systems designed mainly for military use. It has been estimated that as much as 90 percent of the SSO's produced are ultimately delivered to the government. In this field, Grey is an "independent" producer. That is, Grey is not a systems designer but, instead, supplies SSO's to other firms which are systems designers and which often have their own SSO departments. Independent producers sometimes find that a systems designer will ask for bids from the independents, then offer the contract to their own division if it can produce the SSO's at a lower cost.

About 25 percent of Grey's SSO sales are the result of contracts for which bids are required. However, these bid contracts serve as the price leaders in the field. As the price structure of this and other electronics markets is historically deteriorating, it is necessary for a manager to consider not only the effect of a bid price on a given contract, but also the effect of that bid on his "catalogue" prices and the profits resulting from these sales.

Producers compete in several ways in this market but not all firms elect to follow the same paths. As the products are often "state-of-the-art" in terms of their advanced technical design, the capacity to develop and produce high-quality, technically advanced and often highly-specialized equipment is one area of competition.

In general too, allegedly competitive items produced by different manufacturers are not directly interchangeable. For example, if a system is designed to use Company A's SSO's, it might be very difficult or expensive to alter that system in order to use Company B's SSO's. This situation places a premium on being either the first producer of an item or getting a firm to design their system specifically to use your products.

Firms may compete by having an intelligence system which informs them of the probable need for a given new product or an adaptation of an existing product in order that they can develop the item. They may also compete through the use of highly-skilled, technical field men whose job it is to sell the systems designer on the merits of their company's products and to suggest to the systems designer ways in which new uses or adaptations can be made of existing products. It is sometimes said that the field men must "live in the customer's pocket."

The importance of price in this market is very great. Systems designers must submit bids to the government which force the designer to seek the lowest-cost suppliers he can. In addition, contracts with suppliers are usually negotiated by the business managers of a system design firm rather than by the technical men. Thus, even though the technical designers may be convinced of the merits of Company A's products, it may be very difficult to convince the business managers of this fact. This problem is compounded by the fact that technical specifications of competing products are often the same while their performance characteristics may not be.

Several other factors also compound the price problem. The effect of volume on the costs of production is substantial. Learning curves play an important role in this industry so that the variable costs of producing SSO's is significantly reduced with increased volume. In addition, the high costs of research and development represent a substantial fixed investment in a given product which often requires a large volume of production to recover. As government contracts are often followed by additional "follow-on" contracts for the same products, the necessity for volume production places another premium on securing the initial contract. Finally, as initial contracts sometimes include an allowance for R & D, yet another premium is placed on securing the first contract.

The characteristics described so far also apply to the systems manufacturers so that price pressures are extremely strong throughout the industry. Systems designers and components manufacturers will sometimes deliberately take a loss on an initial contract in order to gain a competitive advantage. When a systems designer has done this, he will exert pressure on the components manufacturers for lower prices in order to recover part of the expected loss. Similarly, a components manufacturer may do the same thing to its suppliers or to its own manufacturing groups in order to reduce costs.

One of the more interesting ways in which suppliers may be pressured is by means of a practice referred to as a "Chinese Auction." A systems manufacturer might solicit bids from components manufacturers with the understanding that the contract will be awarded to the low bidder. After bids have been submitted, the customer might call components manufacturer company X and hint that he would prefer X's products but that company Y submitted a lower bid. If X responds by submitting a lower bid, the process is then repeated with Y. Since X and Y do not know what the competing firm has bid or whether or not the customer is in fact telling the truth, the amount of uncertainty faced by a supplier is very great. X and Y cannot reveal their respective bids for competitive reasons nor will they do so for fear the Justice Department might regard this as collusion. They cannot mutually agree to stop bidding since that would definitely be collusion. The only alternative is to unilaterally elect to stop bidding, inform the customer of this decision, and run the risk of losing the contract. Needless to say, the customer may not believe a company when it has made this decision and may find itself placed in an untenable position as a consequence. The Chinese Auction is a practice followed by only part of the industry, so a supplier must know who might engage in this practice and be prepared to act accordingly.

Another practice consists of varying the technical specifications of a contract. A customer might specify loose or misleading technical specifications in a contract to be bid on. After the contract has been awarded, the customer will tighten and reinterpret the specifications, so that he gets an expensive part or component for the price of a cheap one.

It would be misleading to say that these practices prevail in the electronics industry. However, they are practiced enough, particularly on large contracts, that they must be taken into account by suppliers through strategic bidding. Some of the ways in which a supplier might combat these practices would include submitting an initially higher bid than the contract is expected to go for in order to be able to reduce the bid later. Alternatively, a supplier might demand technical concessions in exchange for a lower bid or even demand that his technical specifications be written into the customer's contract.

Another way in which a supplier might combat the Chinese Auction problem or escape price pressures consists of reject-bidding. If a components manufacturer is producing an SSO which must produce a certain amount of power, he may find that he is getting a significant number of rejects which do not meet the power requirements for the item he is selling. If he can find a customer for these rejects, he has the opportunity to make very large profits since, in effect, the cost of these items is virtually minimal to him.

Reject bidding, however, is also quite hazardous. It is based on the assumption that rejects will be available to be sold. If a production improvement eliminates the rejects or the market for higher-power products runs out, the supplier may find himself trapped with an unrealistic price. Alternatively, if the lower-power products are not acceptable, renegotiating the contract would be both difficult and embarrassing, if not impossible. The problem of renegotiation is further hampered by the responsibility a manufacturer assumes when he accepts a contract. If a system fails, even though it is the fault of the designer, the manufacturers whose components are involved suffer a very real loss of reputation and feel called upon to do what they can to correct the problem. If this involves supplying primary rather than reject products, they may be forced into this position to avoid the stigma attached to the failure of the system.

# Cryovac Division, W. R. Grace & Company

Cryovac introduced a new process for packaging and preserving such foods as fresh meats, poultry, cheese, and fish in 1947. Although there were some 20 other firms manufacturing fresh food packaging materials, none had the patented features of the Cryovac process, which management considered to be the only truly satisfactory method of packer packaging for self-service retail sale. From its inception, therefore, Cryovac sold its process at a considerably higher price, generally 50–100 percent higher, than other packaging materials. The firm's sales climbed rapidly from $1.5 million in 1947 to about $40 million. Sales in recent years had not been up to expectations. Cryovac executives believed that this failure to achieve the planned sales volume was the result of prices higher than competitive prices and that this was especially true during a period when economic and competitive factors were unfavorable.

Cryovac is the name of a vacuum-sealing process designed to protect products from damage and deterioration during handling, storing, and shipping. The process involves four steps:

1. The item to be packaged is placed in a loose-fitting bag made from special plastic.
2. Air is withdrawn from the bag by a vacuum pump.
3. The neck of the bag is twisted tightly and sealed with a metal clip.
4. The package is then dipped in hot water at about 200° F., which causes the plastic to shrink and to cling tightly to the contours of the product like a second skin.

Cryovac bags are made from an airtight film that is a modified type of Saran, a plastic resin produced by Dow Chemical Corporation. When a food is sealed in a Cryovac bag and the air withdrawn, the food is protected against spoilage and shrinkage (loss of weight from loss of moisture), and the flavor does not deteriorate. The food can be seen clearly through the plastic. When so packaged, the meat loses its red color because of the absence of oxygen. The red or natural color returns when the package is opened and the contents are exposed to fresh air. The loss of color was but one of the reasons why Cryovac had not been able to sell its process to retailers who sold precut meat on a self-service basis. Many foods wrapped by Cryovac can be kept under refrigeration for many weeks without spoiling, whereas with other wrappers spoiling sets in within a week.

Cryovac's strongest selling points to food packers were that the Cryovac package would (1) stop shrinkage of the product completely, (2) control the color of the product, and (3) prevent spoilage and thus permit retail shelf life of from three to seven weeks versus a shelf life of only a few days to a week with other types of packages. Competitors in food-packaging materials had processes for packaging foods in plastic bags, but none had the airtight vacuum or the durability features of Cryovac.

Cryovac licensed their entire process to packers. This included sale of three items: the bags, the clips, and the equipment. Manual, semiautomatic or automatic equipment was available, depending on the needs and desires of the packer. The equipment included (1) a vacuumizing unit that drew out the air in the bags, (2) a clipping machine that fastened clips on the bags, and (3) a bath unit that shrank the bag tightly around the product. One person could operate one complete unit. Working with small-unit products, one man in an eight-hour day could package 1,000–1,200 units; with the automatic or semiautomatic equipment, he could do 2,000–3,000 units. On products packaged in larger units, one man could handle 800–1,000 units in a day with the manual equipment and 1,500–1,750 units with the automatic equipment.

Manual equipment generally costs $500–$700 for each set, and the automatic equipment $5,000–$7,000 a set. The equipment wore out very slowly, so that replacement sales were negligible. Small packers might buy one set; large national packers might buy 75 to 100 sets. The bags were sold at prices that varied with the quantity bought, the size of the bag, the type, and the printing desired. About 60 percent of all bags sold were printed. The price schedule for a typical bag size is shown on page 306.

It was possible for a packer to purchase bags on a split-shipment basis. He could place an order for a number of bags and have portions of the order shipped at different times within a six-month period; however, a minimum of 20,000 bags had to be shipped at any one time. The clips were sold in three sizes in cases of 10,000; medium clips sold at about $25 per case.

A small meat packer who did about 25 percent of his dollar volume in

| Nonprinted Bags | | Printed Bags* | |
|---|---|---|---|
| Quantity Purchased | Price per Thousand | Quantity Purchased | Price per Thousand |
| 1,000 | $40.00 | 2,500† | $83.00 |
| 5,000 | 38.00 | 5,000 | 63.00 |
| 10,000 | 36.00 | 10,000 | 53.00 |
| 20,000 | 34.00 | 20,000 | 48.00 |
| 50,000 | 32.00 | 50,000 | 45.00 |
| 100,000 | 30.00 | 100,000 | 44.00 |
| 250,000 | 29.00 | 250,000 | 43.50 |
| 500,000 | 28.50 | 500,000 | 43.00 |

\* The prices shown are for three-color printing.
† Minimum order.

package meats would use the following Cryovac equipment: one semiautomatic vacuum and fastening machine set, one manual vacuum and fastening machine set, and one automatic shrink tunnel. This equipment would cost about $6,000 and would enable him to package up to 2,000 units a day. This packer would use $10,000 to $15,000 worth of bags and clips in a year.

Initially, the packers of poultry, especially turkeys, were the biggest customers for the Cryovac process. It was estimated that some 86,000 farms produced 82 million turkeys but that about 2,000 of these accounted for 56 million. Many of the larger farms were owned by large meat packers, grocery manufacturers, and animal feed processors. Others were owned cooperatively. Cryovac management estimated that its process was used by a substantial majority of the large turkey managers but that its penetration was low among the smaller packers who typically sold their output locally. Early in its career Cryovac began an all-out campaign to convince meat and poultry packers of the desirability of prepackaged goods for consumers, a somewhat new concept at the time. To accomplish this task, Cryovac made extensive appeal to retailers, in the hope that retailers would encourage food packers to prepackage more products. Direct mail pieces, articles in trade publications, demonstrations at trade shows and conventions, and calls by Cryovac salesmen were used. Cryovac salesmen also called on food packers with a presentation that included (1) a list of items to prepackage, (2) a description of how to prepackage them, (3) a statement of how to prepare the food for prepackaging, and (4) a blueprint of how to install a production line using the Cryovac process.

Cheese packers, especially those in Wisconsin, were next in using the Cryovac process because they could age the cheese in the package. While not as concentrated an industry as poultry, the natural cheese industry was nevertheless dominated by a relatively few large brands including large co-ops who sold regionally. This does not mean that the large brand sellers produced all their own natural cheeses, since their practice was to buy from a large number of small producers and package their cheese for sale under their brand. Fish and meat packers were also beginning to be important sales sources, but turkey packers were still the largest customers.

The firm split into three regional divisions, each having its own plant and personnel. The western division included the territory west of Michigan to the Texan line, with headquarters in Cedar Rapids, Iowa; the eastern division was centered in Greenville, South Carolina; and the third division was in Canada. The general administrative office, where all research, promotion, and general policies were developed, was located in Cambridge, Massachusetts. In addition, a Chicago office was maintained to handle a group of large national accounts, which included Armour, Swift, Kraft, Wilson, A & P, and National Food Stores. These large accounts generally produced sales of between $100,000 and $1 million each per year. One salesman was required to handle two to four accounts. National accounts represented approximately 25 percent of Cryovac's volume.

Originally Cryovac had five salesmen, who called on some 25 to 30 distributors who sold the product to packers. The distributors were selected on the basis of experience in the food industry, ability to merchandise, and willingness to crusade for a new process that was costlier than competitive processes. The distributors realized an average 18 percent discount from list price. After several years the company reappraised this policy in the light of the growing frozen food market and the general consumer acceptance of prepackaged fresh foods. The executives believed that an all-out sales campaign was needed, if Cryovac were to receive its share of the packaging market, and that distributors could not do as effective a job as could Cryovac's own sales force. Prospects had to be sold aggressively because of the high cost of the Cryovac process, and accounts had to be serviced. Cryovac salesmen were more skilled in handling the service problems than were distributor salesmen. In addition, the Cryovac management believed that Cryovac salesmen were actually doing most of the selling for distributors. Therefore, all distributors were dropped, and 60 salesmen were added to Cryovac's existing force which had grown to 20.

Only two years later the management decided on another major expansion of the sales force and about 80 salesmen were added, bringing the total to more than 160. Each salesman had an assigned territory and was expected to call on each account at least once every 30 days. A sizable and growing volume of business had been developed with smoked meats which constituted in part a line of so-called luncheon meats. Typically, these meats were sold in small size packages through refrigerated self-service display boxes in food stores which were usually serviced weekly by local packers or wholesalers.

The company then campaigned to get the packers and wholesalers of red meats to use the Cryovac process. The advantages of aging such meats in the Cryovac package rather than unwrapped was emphasized. The Cryovac salesmen could cite the following problems in aging by this method: (1) weight loss due to shrinkage; (2) color loss from bacteria activity; and (3) the trimming required to take off the edges that had spoiled. Shrinkage ran to as much as 8 percent of the weight of some meats but averaged about 4 percent. Generally, only the finest meats were aged—those sold to high-class restaurants and similar customers. Aging was believed to make the meat more tender and to improve its flavor. Despite aggressive selling Cryovac salesmen found considerable resistance to dropping the traditional method of aging red meat. This market segment, however, represented a large potential. The primary market here was considered to be the restaurant wholesaler who sold aged beef—often on a portion control basis. Such business units were local and often family-owned. While the exact number of such units was not known, it was estimated that there were several thousand.

Cryovac faced competition from a few large firms and some twenty smaller firms. The larger ones were Visking, Tee-Pak, Milprint, Dobeckmun, Continental Can, and Goodyear. These firms had many other packaging lines that did not compete with Cryovac's line, but it was estimated that they had combined sales of $40 to $50 million that might be replaced by Cryovac.

All competitive firms sold packaging materials, but few sold a packaging process, and none had all the features of Cryovac's vacuum-sealing method. Cryovac, therefore, offered the best method for preventing shrinkage and assuring longer shelf life. It was generally accepted in the field that the Cryovac bag was of a quality superior to that of competitors. How much the added quality was worth was not clear. A typical comparison was a bag used for smoked luncheon meats. Cryovac's bag sold for $44 per thousand and would preserve a butt for three weeks or more, compared to $30 per thousand for a competitor's bag that would be adequate protection for only 10 to 14 days.

Although the company sold flat film, pouches, and equipment, bags were the key item in the line. They represented the major part of the sales volume and produced the greatest margin. Therefore, it was the price competition in bags that was crucial; equipment sales and prices were relatively unimportant. Cryovac bags were priced from 50 to 80 percent above competing bags.

During a recession there was a rather pronounced effort by most food packagers to reduce expenses because of a profit squeeze. Many firms reported to Cryovac that they were well satisfied with the line but that the advantages gained from Cryovac over other packaging lines in terms of what was needed did not justify the additional costs of the Cryovac line.

Cryovac's competitors generally used the argument that meat packers should package to sell, not to keep, and that the most effective way to maximize profits was to package as cheaply as possible while maintaining minimum package requirements. Cryovac salesmen also ran into other objections as follows:

1. The labor costs of operating the Cryovac process were generally 10–15 percent higher than others because somewhat more skilled workers were needed. The manual and semiautomatic machines, especially, required a great deal of dexterity on the part of the operator.
2. The initial cost of the packaging line averaged 50 percent more than competitive lines.
3. Cryovac offered no cash discount or free weight, as was the general practice in the field. All Cryovac prices were F.O.B. factory, and terms were net 30 days.
4. Cryovac-wrapped fresh red meats changed color because of the absence of air. When the package was opened, however, the original color returned.

In considering the problem, the Cryovac general manager listed the things that Cryovac salesmen had to offer:

1. A process that would stop shrinkage of the product completely, which would mean that a packer would incur virtually no weight loss during aging or handling.
2. A process that would retard color fade in smoked meat, making it more inviting to purchase, with resultant higher turnover.
3. A process that permitted the package to have a retail shelf life of three to seven weeks, depending on the product, which meant fewer returns and less dissatisfaction from consumers and retailers.
4. A bag that was stronger and clearer than any other plastic bag on the market.
5. The only process that permitted aging of product, when desirable, right in the package.

As an example of the savings possible through prevention of shrinkage loss, one Cryovac customer, a hotel and restaurant meat purveyor, reported the following savings from using the Cryovac process: A choice boneless sirloin strip steak might weigh 17 pounds and, at $1.50 per pound, be worth $25.50. The cost to package it with Cryovac, including the bag, clip, and labor, was 26.5 cents. Shrinkage during aging of such steaks usually ran 4 percent or more. Such shrinkage in this case cost the purveyor over $1.00 in loss of weight, an amount far more than the cost of packaging. Meats aged outside of Cryovac developed mold, which had to be trimmed off, causing further loss of weight.

Figures from the various industries showed that average shrinkages were as follows: cheese, 3 percent; smoked meats, 4 percent; red meats, 6 percent; and poultry, 3 percent.

Meat wholesalers also gained a saving in the use of Cryovac in that the longer shelf life it gave meat permitted them to build up inventory during slack periods. This resulted in labor savings and also permitted the wholesalers to buy larger quantities when they had opportunities to get lower prices.

Cryovac's management was disturbed by the apparent resistance in the market to its prices. This was particularly noticeable among smoked meat packers, whose preservation requirements were not as critical as in some other lines. Cryovac's margins were such that it could cut prices to some degree, but it could not meet the prices of lower-quality bags. If it cut prices, however, it would lose margin on all sales. There was a possibility that an intensified sales and promotion program could offset a price cut.

What pricing action, if any, should the Cryovac management take?

# Container Corporation of America

Increased competition and its resultant pressures on salesmen and profits led the Container Corporation of America, the largest manufacturer of corrugated and solid fiber shipping containers in the United States, to reappraise its market objectives. Part of the pressure on profits, in the opinion of management, was the result of salesmen's taking any orders they could get without regard to plant operating efficiency or profit. It was proposed that this tendency be controlled by changing the pricing procedure to make all types of orders approximately equal in profitability, even though this might result in lost sales. Since prices were established from cost estimates for each job, a program was outlined to revise the estimating system so that it would more accurately reflect the marketing objectives of the company.

The Container Corporation was a completely integrated company, with sales exceeding $250 million. Its own forests and wastepaper processing plants supplied its fifteen paper mills with raw materials. The paper mills supplied paperboard to the company's twenty-five shipping container factories and twenty folding carton and fiber can factories. Each of the forty-five container and carton plants operated independently and was responsible for meeting competition in its area and for making a profit. Paperboard was sold by the mills to the plants at market prices.

The shipping container market extended to all manufacturers who needed to package their products. Potential order sizes ranged from orders of one hundred or less units from a small manufacturer of specialized products to orders for five or more carloads at a time from large canners and brewers. Variations in types of materials ordered ranged from display materials, which required complicated manufacturing procedures, to plain regular "slotted containers," the industry term for ordinary boxes, which were run routinely at the rate of 10,000 per hour.

Container's shipping container factories were primarily designed for large-volume operation. For example, the Chicago plant had two corrugators for producing corrugated paperboard with a capacity in excess of 2.5 million square feet of corrugated board per day, which represented thirteen to fifteen carloads of finished boxes per day. The company did not manufacture any stock items or maintain an inventory of finished material. Everything was made to order.

The manufacture of an ordinary box, one for canned foods or beer, normally involved three operations. First, the order went to the corrugator, where the corrugated sheets were made, cut to size, and scored[1] to make the flaps of the box. The sheets then went to a printer-slotter machine, where they were printed, scored to form the sides, and slotted to separate the flaps of the boxes. In the final operation, the ends of the sheets were folded and joined either by taping, stitching (stapling), or gluing to form the finished box. The finished boxes were tied in bundles or palletized and moved almost immediately into trucks or freight cars for shipment. Orders were timed to be finished at the scheduled time for shipment, since the volume of materials produced each day made storage impractical.

To get maximum production out of a box plant such as Container's Chicago plant, it was necessary to have a major proportion of large orders. This reduced the down time of machines for changing "setups" for each new order. But the large-volume business was generally low-profit business because of competition. Therefore, to maximize profits, it was necessary to have a mixture of large-volume orders and small or more specialized but more profitable orders.

Management believed that the cost-estimating methods led to prices that did not indicate the real profitability of an order. The estimating methods were thought to overstate profits on small-volume business and understate profits on large-volume business. This had led to a situation in which the plants were getting too many small orders to operate efficiently, because these orders looked more profitable than they were. Furthermore, some large-volume business was being lost because it did not look profitable when actually it was. A study of sales records revealed less than 10 per cent of the company's customers accounted for 90 per cent of the volume.

Further thought on this problem led management to the conclusion that a box factory was not primarily selling paper, but was selling the skills and process of converting paper into boxes. It was on these conversion costs that profits should be based. Under the existing system, sales and administrative expenses and profits were estimated as percentages of full cost, including materials. Also, under the existing estimating system,

---

[1] "Score" is the industry term for creases put in the corrugated board so that it will fold at the proper points.

costs of certain groups of similar operations were averaged. It was thought that a new method should be found that would be based on the specific cost of each operation. This would make it possible to determine much more accurately the profitability of an individual order.

Exhibit 1 shows the prices arrived at from costs estimated by the existing average cost method and by the proposed specific cost system, with overhead and profits based on conversion costs. Four examples are shown. The first illustrates the case of an ordinary box, for which material costs were large in proportion to factory conversion costs, and the fourth example illustrates the case of a more complicated item, for which factory costs greatly exceeded material costs. The second and third examples are in between. Factory conversion costs consisted of two parts, the setup cost, or cost of preparing the machines for a particular operation, and the base cost, which was the cost of the machine time and labor used to run 1,000 units. All material and factory costs were for 1,000 units.

The profit percentage, 10.9 per cent of total conversion cost, including materials for the average cost method and 24 per cent of total conversion costs for the specific cost method, was calculated to bring a return of 20 per cent on invested capital after taxes. Factory costs that were included in factory conversion costs were allocated to units on the basis of an assumed minimum volume. The sales and administration cost percentage and the profit percentage were also based on this assumed minimum volume. In the case of the Chicago plant the assumed minimum volume was 63 million square feet of corrugated board per month.

Base and setup costs were not ordinarily quoted to customers. Prices were quoted for a specific quantity or quantities and were always quoted on a per thousand basis. These prices were arrived at by dividing the setup cost by the quantity in thousands and adding the base cost. For example, given a setup cost of $10 and a base cost of $100, the price quoted for 1,000 units would be $110 per thousand; for 500 units, $120 per thousand; and for 5,000 units, $102 per thousand.

Exhibit 2 shows the prices that would be quoted for orders of different quantities when the prices were determined by both the old and the new methods. Prices are shown for the same four hypothetical products shown in Examples 1, 2, 3, and 4 of Exhibit 1. The specific cost method resulted in generally higher prices, especially for small quantities. Where factory conversion costs were less than material costs, as in Examples 1 and 2, however, the specific cost method of computing prices resulted in lower prices than the average cost method. For products in which the conversion costs exceeded material costs, prices were consistently higher under the specific cost method than under the average cost method. Since most of the company's business, particularly the large-volume business, resulted from items similar to Examples 1 and 2, the specific cost system would improve Container's competitive position.

The responsibility for establishing the actual prices quoted to cus-

# EXHIBIT 1

## Two Methods of Cost Estimating for Four Hypothetical Jobs

|  | Example | | | | | | | |
|---|---|---|---|---|---|---|---|---|
|  | 1 | | 2 | | 3 | | 4 | |
|  | Setup | Base | Setup | Base | Setup | Base | Setup | Base |

*Average Cost Method with Profit Calculated on Full Cost*

|  | Setup | Base | Setup | Base | Setup | Base | Setup | Base |
|---|---|---|---|---|---|---|---|---|
| Material | | $ 70 | | $ 60 | | $ 40 | | $ 30 |
| Factory conversion costs | $10 | 20 | $10 | 30 | $10 | 50 | $10 | 60 |
| Total factory conversion costs, including materials | $10 | $ 90 | $10 | $ 90 | $10 | $ 90 | $10 | $ 90 |
| Sales and administration costs, 10 per cent of total factory conversion costs | 1 | 9 | 1 | 9 | 1 | 9 | 1 | 9 |
| Total conversion-cost, including materials | $11 | $ 99 | $11 | $ 99 | $11 | $ 99 | $11 | $ 99 |
| Profit, 10.9 per cent of full cost | 1.20 | 10.80 | 1.20 | 10.80 | 1.20 | 10.80 | 1.20 | 10.80 |
| Price | $12.20 | $109.80 | $12.20 | $109.80 | $12.20 | $109.80 | $12.20 | $109.80 |

*Specific Cost Method with Profit Calculated on Total Conversion Costs*

|  | Setup | Base | Setup | Base | Setup | Base | Setup | Base |
|---|---|---|---|---|---|---|---|---|
| Factory conversion costs | $10 | $ 20 | $10 | $ 30 | $10 | $ 50 | $10 | $ 60 |
| Sales and administration costs, 25 per cent of factory conversion costs | 2.50 | 5 | 2.50 | 7.50 | 2.50 | 12.50 | 2.50 | 14 |
| Total conversion costs | $12.50 | $ 25 | $12.50 | $ 37.50 | $12.50 | $ 62.50 | $12.50 | $ 74 |
| Profit, 24 per cent of total conversion costs | 3 | 6 | 3 | 9 | 3 | 15 | 3 | 18 |
| Materials | | 70 | | 60 | | 40 | | 30 |
| Price | $15.50 | $101.00 | $15.50 | $106.50 | $15.50 | $117.50 | $15.50 | $122.00 |

**EXHIBIT 2**

**Prices Calculated from Exhibit 1**

| Quantity | Example | Price per Thousand | |
|---|---|---|---|
| | | *Average Cost* | *Specific Cost* |
| 100.................. | 1 | $231.80 | $256.00 |
| | 2 | " | 261.50 |
| | 3 | " | 272.50 |
| | 4 | " | 277.50 |
| 500.................. | 1 | 134.20 | 132.00 |
| | 2 | " | 137.50 |
| | 3 | " | 148.50 |
| | 4 | " | 153.00 |
| 1,000.................. | 1 | 122.00 | 116.50 |
| | 2 | " | 122.00 |
| | 3 | " | 133.00 |
| | 4 | " | 137.50 |
| 10,000.................. | 1 | 111.02 | 102.55 |
| | 2 | " | 108.05 |
| | 3 | " | 119.05 |
| | 4 | " | 123.05 |

tomers rested with the sales managers at a step beyond the cost-estimating process described above. The estimated price was the price needed to give the standard profit. The price actually quoted to a customer might vary up or down from the level, depending on information sales manager had on market conditions and competition for the specific account involved. There were no "standard prices" in the industry. It was not unusual for two companies buying boxes identical in size and material from the same box manufacturer to pay different prices. Some box companies tried using a "price list" that would permit the customer to calculate what the price would be on a given box by using the number of square feet of corrugated board in the box, multiplying this by a price per square foot, and then adding special charges for printing or other special features. In all cases, these "price lists" had been short-lived.

Examples of two typical pricing situations are shown in Exhibit 3. In both situations the estimating department figured estimated prices based on the minimum return desired by management. The sales manager established the market prices, i.e., competitive prices, on the basis of his knowledge of the market and information from salesmen as to competitors and the prices they usually quoted these accounts. In the first situation the market price was lower than the estimated prices. It offered no profit under the average cost method of estimating costs, but it showed a profit of 12.4 per cent on conversion costs if the specific cost estimating method was used. In the second situation, which represents a small order that required more conversion, the market price was above the average

## EXHIBIT 3

### Two Typical Pricing Situations

| | Average Cost Method | Specific Cost Method |
|---|---|---|
| *Price per Thousand for 20,000 Ordinary Boxes Similar to Example 1, Exhibit 1* | | |
| Estimated price.......................... | $110.41 | $101.78 |
| Full cost............................. | 99.55 | 95.63 |
| Market price.......................... | 99.55 | 99.55 |
| Profit................................ | ... | 3.92 |
| Per cent profit | | |
| On total conversion cost.............. | N.A. | 12.4% |
| On full cost......................... | 0 | 3.9% |
| *Price per Thousand for 500 Complicated Boxes Similar to Example 4, Exhibit 1* | | |
| Estimated price.......................... | $134.20 | $153.00 |
| Full cost............................. | 121.00 | 129.00 |
| Market price.......................... | 146.20 | 146.20 |
| Profit................................ | 25.20 | 17.20 |
| Per cent profit | | |
| On total conversion cost.............. | N.A. | 17.4% |
| On full cost......................... | 20.8% | 13.3% |

cost price and below the specific cost price, but showed a profit in both cases. The average cost method showed more profit on market price than did the specific cost method.

With this information at hand, the sales manager could decide how badly he wanted these particular orders. Container's policy was to develop long-standing accounts that were profitable. Once a profitable price level was established in these accounts, it was generally maintained to the best of the company's ability. Constant attention was necessary, however, because of possible price cutting by competitors.

Constant attrition of accounts because of product changes, moves, and losses to competitors required the regular addition of new accounts if the company was to maintain its position. Container's main emphasis in acquiring a new account was on quality and design rather than on price. Price competition was avoided whenever possible, but it was sometimes necessary, particularly in large accounts using relatively standard types of boxes. Generally, when a company designed a new package for an account, it got the first order before the other box companies quoted on the item. Competitors could be expected to bid on later orders.

Salesmen were given some latitude for bargaining with an account. If the price the sales manager quoted was high, the salesmen could, if the customer was willing to bargain, meet the competitive price to get the order. Experienced salesmen were even given the authority to go below competitors' prices for some accounts.

Management did not expect that a change to the specific cost method of estimating prices would result in radical price changes and immediate improvement in profits. The estimating system approximated prices, actual prices were established by the sales manager in light of market conditions. Since the latter would not change, no great changes could be made in Container's prices. Management believed, however, that the new pricing system would cause sales managers to re-evaluate the importance of various accounts and hence to make some price adjustments.

1. Would the new pricing system lead to higher profits for Container Corporation?
2. What other actions, if any, could have been taken in lieu of or in addition to the new pricing system to accomplish the same objectives?

# CHANNELS OF DISTRIBUTION

# North Star Shipping Company (A)

In January 1974 Mr. Peter Kruger, marketing manager of the North Star Shipping Company's North Continent subsidiary (which serviced the Benelux countries, Italy, Austria, Switzerland, and West Germany) was studying the latest company report on shipments from Germany to North America. Sales and revenue tonnage were again below budget—sales more so than volume (tonnage). Because of the importance of the German market both short and long term Mr. Kruger knew that he had to take remedial action immediately.

In 1973 German exports provided about 25% of the subsidiary's total revenues but less than 5% of those of the parent company. In tons the ratios were approximately the same although per ton revenues and contributions were somewhat lower than for other countries. North Star's share of the total German North Atlantic tonnage was lower—much lower—than for other countries where a share of 30% was typical. The market share for Germany had never exceeded much more than 11% and in recent years had been declining. The budget for Germany, set on a port basis and shown in both tons and dollar revenues, had almost never been attained. The German personnel involved generally explained this "failure" by the longer transit time of North Star's service versus that of leading competitors and by the frequent changes made by the parent company in the type and amount of ship space allotted to them.

North Star Shipping was formed in the early 1960's by a merger of several companies to serve the highly competitive North Atlantic trade route via containerization. It was one of the first shipping companies to apply the "through" transportation concept; i.e., providing house-to-house service through the use of containers versus the more traditional port-to-port approach. North Star provided a variety of special equipment for both sea and land transportation, insured the use of the least expensive and fastest land routings, and even provided for fast customs clearance. Its sophisticated communication system which included computers and private telex wires made it possible to adopt a high-quality integrated sales-service approach to the problems posed by shippers, forwarders, and consignees. These services coupled with convenient and dependable sailing schedules had made North Star a successful company.

Subsidiary organizations in Canada, the United States, England, France, Scandinavia, and Holland were responsible for marketing the company's services. The central organization was located in New York City and served to control the operation of the vessels, coordinate marketing efforts between subsidiaries, allocate ships and space between ports, undertake general promotional activities, supply marketing information, and prepare budgets. Understandably, the company's North American operation was the largest of any of the country organizations, numbering in excess of 400 individuals.

## THE GERMAN MARKET FOR WESTBOUND NORTH ATLANTIC LINER TRADE

In 1973 West Germany was the biggest European exporter to the United States and the second largest importer from there. German exports to the United States included machinery and transport equipment (60%) and manufactured goods (15%). For Canada, Germany was second after Great Britain, and exports to Canada typically represented only 10% of total U.S. exports. In 1973 the United States had imported goods worth approximately $6 billion from West Germany, representing nearly 5 million tons, of which about 40% moved over the North Atlantic.[1] About half of the North Atlantic cargo tonnage was transported by liners; i.e., regularly scheduled ships which were, in 80% of the cases, container ships. Exports from Germany fluctuated year to year and were difficult to forecast because they depended on the general economic conditions and particularly on the current exchange rate for the dollar.

Basically, yearly exports from one country were assumed to be connected with its GNP. Any forecast for the lines was made difficult by a lack of current market data; e.g., official statistics in Germany were restricted to classifications by value, and so were OECD statistics for different commodity groups. The most suitable data were those of the U.S. Department of Commerce (DOC) which classified imports by country, commodity, tons of commodity, percent share of North Atlantic liners, and percent share by shipping company. These data were, however, available with a time lag of at least eight months and were, therefore, of only limited relevance to the lines for planning purposes.

Many North Atlantic shippers used liners because they needed a regular service. They often used more than one line in order to balance risks.

---

[1] Compiled from OECD and U.S. Department of Commerce statistics.

Typically, less than 50 shippers provided more than half the volume for a particular line. The interest of a shipper in the North Atlantic shipment itself depended largely on the contract by which he sold his goods. If he sold ex works, either the consignee asked for a particular line, or the cargo was simply handed over to a forwarder. In ex work sales the shipper was only slightly interested in the whole transport. This was different when goods were sold on a c.i.f. basis—then the shipper paid greater attention to the transport problem.[2] About 25% of the shipments were done on a c.i.f. basis. Consequently, in many cases not the shippers but the forwarders dealt with the lines and, thus, constituted a large customer group. Approximately ten forwarders dominated the German market. Overall it was estimated that forwarders handled over half of all shipments on a tonnage basis.

It was difficult to separate customer groups by services used, because car shippers, for instance, would also ship automobile spare parts in containers. Statistical groupings were often done by commodities. These groupings, however, gave no indication concerning geographical factors, and little of the profitability per ton cargo for the line, because rates could vary within a commodity group and the cost per ton or per TEU[3] was not always the same.

According to Mr. Kruger a shipper chose a line based on the following:

1. Availability of service.

   House-to-house transit time.

   Availability, regularity, and reliability of shipments.

   Availability of special equipment—special containers or trailers.

   Reliability of the line.

   Availability of special services.

2. Sometimes a shipper had problems in availability on non-North Atlantic shipping routes. Therefore, he had to close a "package deal" with a line serving both the North Atlantic and other routes. Such a situation worked to the disadvantage of North Star which served only the North Atlantic trade.

3. Price, although conference liners had to maintain price parity. Price sensitivity was greatest with forwarders and could vary with clients.

4. Use of German ports, since German railways offered special rates to these ports.

In most companies, a traffic manager was in charge of shipments. This made personal contact very important and, at the same time, limited a more general approach to transport problems. For instance, it was difficult

---

[2] c.i.f = cost, insurance, and freight included port of destination.

[3] TEU = 20-foot equivalent unit, i.e., unit equivalent to a 20-foot container.

to convince a traffic manager of the long-term positive effects on investments and costs that could be obtained using a different mode of transportation, such as roll-on, roll-off which was especially important for shipping vehicles of almost any size or type. North Star had more RORO capacity than did any of its competition. Sometimes emotional arguments favored a German line.

It was expected that in the future transportation would be viewed on a more integrated systems basis—incorporating it into plant location and investment decisions. Moreover, other companies were expected to follow the example of Volkswagen, who operated its own integrated transport system by owning its own trucks and ships.

## THE TRANSPORTATION INDUSTRY IN GERMANY FOR THE NORTH ATLANTIC LINER TRADE

The "container revolution" had already taken place in Germany. Container shipping required a more careful planning of investments and operations, and, therefore, the industry was forced to apply more and more sophisticated technology and management techniques. The old port-to-port approach had given way to an integrated approach. Many difficulties still had to be overcome including the need to close information gaps and update an outmoded and overly complex tariff. Companies had difficulty in determining the profitability by individual units. In general, high-value cargo paid better than did low-value cargo, although there were exceptions to this rule. Conference tariffs in Germany were the lowest in Europe due to the competitive situation. Some shippers from abroad even shipped goods to Germany for transshipment elsewhere in order to obtain tariff advantages (e.g., automobile spare parts from Sweden).

The largest lines were organized in a "conference" which was mainly a tariff agreement. The other lines, the outsiders, were not coordinated as to their prices. Their total capacity was estimated to be about 40% of that of the conference lines, but according to the latest statistics (see Exhibit 1) conference liners transported in the third quarter of 1973 only about 50% of the German North Atlantic tonnage. The remaining 50% was done by outsiders. The success of the various lines (see Exhibit 2) was based mainly on three factors:

1. Quality of service offered.
2. Representation in Germany.
3. Personal contacts.

Hapag Lloyd, one of the members of the conference, was the most successful line in Germany. It had a 50–60% market share of the total conference German tonnage. It offered transportation to all parts of the world and was known for reliable and reasonably fast schedules as well as for special services which facilitated customs clearance. Their own

**EXHIBIT 1**

**Germany—United States North Atlantic Traffic**
**(1971–1973 in thousands of tons)**

| | 1971 | 1972 | 1973 by Quarters | | | Average for All 1973 (Quarters I + II + III) (0.75) |
| | | | I | II | III | |
|---|---|---|---|---|---|---|
| Total Germany—U.S............ | 4,179 | 4,051 | 895 | 1,161 | 1,233 | 4,385 |
| Total North Atlantic............ | 1,487 | 1,595 | 425 | 538 | 615 | 2,104 |
| Total liner North Atlantic....... | 1,108 | 990 | 267 | 267 | 230 | 1,018 |
| Total conference liners......... | 790* | 700* | 151 | 130 | 127 | 544 |
| Total North Star.............. | 95 | 89 | 26 | 22 | 21 | 88 |

* Estimated.
SOURCE: U.S. Department of Commerce statistics.

suborganization, DCD (Deutscher Containter Dienst) was able to provide containers and special equipment on short notice. Hapag Lloyd used mainly German ports (Hamburg, the largest German port, and Bremen). Approximately half the ocean cargo leaving Germany used these two ports. Hapag had substantially more offices and salesmen than did North Star. Sealand, the next biggest line, had fast ships and could promise an unbeatable transit time to New York, where two-thirds of the freight to the United States came in. It served most routes and had substantially more reefer (refrigerated) boxes than any competitor. Sealand had approximately 25% of the pool share in Germany.

**EXHIBIT 2**

**Competitive Profile on Major Shippers**
**Servicing West Germany—1974**

| | North Star | Hapag Lloyd | Sealand |
|---|---|---|---|
| Estimated market share of conference liner traffic in tons.............. | 8% | 50–60% | Over 25% |
| Services.................. | Container, RORO | Container, break-bulk | Container |
| Frequency................ | Weekly | Weekly | Weekly |
| Ship speed (knots)......... | 22 | 19 | 33 |
| Transit days.............. | 12 | 10 | 6–7 |
| Direct ports in North Continent................. | Antwerp, Rotterdam (Rot.) and Bremerhaven (Bhv.) | Rot., Bhv. Hamburg | Rot., Bhv. |
| Direct ports in North America.................. | Halifax, N.Y., Baltimore, Portsmouth, Montreal, Quebec | N.Y., Philadelphia, Baltimore, Norfolk | N.Y. |

SOURCES: Company sources; U.S. Department of Commerce statistics; trade journals.

Traditionally, forwarders had a strong grip on the market. The ten largest forwarders who dominated the market had their own lorry fleets and booked whole trains for inland moves. They often chartered planes and ship space. Besides their commissions they earned money by packing goods (an operation typically costing 2–5% of cargo value and sometimes up to 12%). There were indications that in the future forwarders would be "nonvessel operating carriers"; i.e., they would subcontract the sea transportation part of the shipping.

The growth in the total liner North Atlantic trade had slowed during recent years, although the fuel crisis of 1973 somewhat boosted the business for liners since they were the only ones to have made long-term contracts for fuel supply and, thus, were assured of a ready supply. Annual growth in tons transported by liners was estimated to be around 3–4%, and there was no indication that the market would become less competitive. One threat for the future was the U.S.-based lines which transported a good deal of cargo back and forth for U.S. forces in Europe. Since these forces were decreasing yearly, the U.S.-based lines had begun to seek nonmilitary cargo aggressively.

## NORTH STAR POSITION IN THE GERMAN MARKET

North Star's activities consisted of marketing containers and RORO (roll-on, roll-off) space. Air charter and other air transport services had a low priority given the manpower constraints in the German sales organization. The declining trend in North Star German sales in 1971–72 was reversed in 1973 (see Exhibits 3 and 4), but sales and market share were still low compared to other areas. The revenue per ton averaged $75 compared to other areas where North Star averaged approximately $85. The contribution from Germany was 20–25% of sales versus 30% from other areas. The reasons for this were manifold according to Mr. Kruger and included low tariffs and the fact that two competitors dominated the market, thereby picking up the better paying cargo.

The partial "success" of North Star in Germany was explained largely on the basis of personal contacts, a reliable organization, a relatively good service to Canada, and especially by the availability of special equipment. Competitors had problems with large equipment, whereas North Star could use RORO. In 1973, 75% of North Star's German clients were regular users of their service, and some 35 (if forwarders were included) provided 70% of the total volume.

Selling in Germany was handled by the Werther Agency which was paid a commission of 2½% of sales. This agency, headquartered in Frankfurt, was formed in 1953 to represent a number of shipping lines. In addition to representing North Star, it served 14 other lines all of which were conventional, noncontainerized lines; most did not service the North Atlantic route. The agency was headed by Mr. Werther who concerned

**EXHIBIT 3**

**Exports by West Germany to U.S. via North Atlantic Route**
(selected commodity groups 1971–1973 in tons)

| Commodity | 1971 | | | 1972 | | | 1973 (extrapolated from 1st 9 months) | | |
|---|---|---|---|---|---|---|---|---|---|
| | Total Liner Carryings | North Star Carryings | North Star Market Share | Total Liner Carryings | North Star Carryings | North Star Market Share | Total Liner Carryings | North Star Carryings | North Star Market Share |
| Cars and trucks | 245,546 | 31,903 | 13% | 202,848 | 42,448 | 20.9% | 135,000 | 40,000 | 29.5% |
| Beer | 53,747 | 6,437 | 12 | 52,957 | 2,217 | 4.2 | 64,000 | 900 | 1.4 |
| Organic chemicals | 40,028 | 3,909 | 9.8 | 37,271 | 4,262 | 11.4 | 43,000 | 2,900 | 6.6 |
| Inorganic chemicals | 16,234 | 4,148 | 25.6 | 35,690 | 6,999 | 19.6 | 34,000 | 5,600 | 16.4 |
| Plastics | 19,980 | 2,647 | 13.2 | 17,490 | 1,441 | 8.2 | 33,000 | 2,500 | 7.7 |
| Yarn, thread | 44,402 | 4,904 | 11 | 27,086 | 1,746 | 6.4 | 25,000 | 2,400 | 9.5 |
| Iron, steel bars | 34,601 | 27 | .1 | 25,338 | 72 | .3 | 35,000 | 140 | .4 |
| Steel sheets | 158,688 | 125 | .1 | 111,671 | 584 | .5 | 140,000 | 1,400 | 1.0 |
| Copper | 19,189 | 272 | 1.4 | 20,042 | 68 | .3 | 23,000 | 500 | 2.1 |
| Power generating machinery | 28,883 | 1,094 | 3.8 | 26,488 | 1,808 | 6.8 | 29,000 | 1,500 | 5.2 |
| Machinery | 39,339 | 6,202 | 15.8 | 41,507 | 3,145 | 7.6 | 41,000 | 3,500 | 8.6 |
| *Subtotal for the cited commodities* | 725,000 | 66,756 | 9.2 | 628,956 | 70,823 | 11.3 | 638,000 | 67,500 | 10.6 |
| Total for *all* commodities | 1,108,000 | 95,000 | | 991,000 | 89,000 | | 1,020,000 | 88,000 | |

**EXHIBIT 4**

**Revenue Data on a Sample of Selected Commodity Groups Moving out of Bremerhaven between December 1973 and February 1974 on North Star Ships**

| Denomination | Port of Destination | Equipment* | Rate† ($) | Average‡ Tons per TEU | Average $ Revenue per Ton | Average $ Revenue per TEU |
|---|---|---|---|---|---|---|
| Cars and trucks............ | | — | — | — | 151 | 180 |
| Alcoholic beverages........ | NYC | 1–20 ft. | 85 | 9 | 88 | 794 |
| | HFX | 1–20 ft. | 85 | 9 | 88 | 794 |
| Organic chemicals.......... | NYC | 30–20 ft., 10–40 ft. | 53–63 | 13 | 58 | 750 |
| | HFX | 3–20 ft., 1–40 ft. | 63 | 11 | 64 | 731 |
| Inorganic chemicals........ | NYC | 11–20 ft. | 34–45 | 16 | 40 | 654 |
| | HFX | 12–20 ft. | 45–48 | 17 | 46 | 773 |
| Plastics................... | NYC | 5–20 ft., 2–40 ft. | 51–62 | 14 | 49 | 700 |
| | HFX | 3–20 ft., 1–40 ft. | 51–59 | 14 | 49 | 672 |
| Yarn, thread .............. | NYC | 1–20 ft. | M40 | — | — | 123 |
| Copper.................... | HFX | 4–20 ft., 1–40 ft. | M19–28 | 6 | 80 | 496 |
| | NYC | 19 flat-bed | 55 | 18 | 56 | 500 |
| | | 50 trailers 40 ft. | 55–59 | 7 | 58 | 190 |
| Machinery................. | NYC | 1–40 ft. | M67 | 1 | 128 | 128 |
| | HFX | 1–20 ft., 4–40 ft. | 40–51 | 8 | 52 | 444 |
| | BAL | 9–40 ft. trailers | — | 5 | 256 | 1,195 |
| | PTM | 1–40 ft., 1–40 ft. trailers | M39–43 | 6 | 110 | 607 |

* If not otherwise specified, containers (20′ and 40′).
† Per ton, unless an M appears, in which case the rate is per cubic metre.
‡ Rounded.
Source: Compiled from company statistics.

himself mainly with handling relationships with the various lines his agency represented. His son handled the day-to-day operations which were carried out by some 40 persons of whom 15 were on-the-road salesmen operating mainly out of agency offices located in Frankfurt, Dusseldorf, Berlin, Munich, and Hamburg.

At headquarters three persons worked full time to coordinate the agency's North Star marketing effort. Salesmen, of course, sold the services of all lines represented by the agency. They called mainly on traffic managers and occasionally on the large freight forwarders and did as much of their work as possible by phone. The Werther Agency accounted for approximately 80% of North Star's German traffic. The remainder was taken by port agents who handled shipments which were brought to the port location by the shipper. North Star's business here was but a small percentage of their total sales.

### Coping with the Constraints

North Star had developed a budgeting planning system in which profitability per port was carefully watched. Agent commissions were expressed in fixed percentages, but cost performance was reflected in the "revenue guidelines." These guidelines served as a basis for salesmen to determine whether a cargo would be profitable—or profitable enough to accept. The implicit assignment given to the German sales organization was to improve market share and, in the process, to cut costs and increase revenues. This could be done by obtaining better paying cargo and achieving the optimal container balance per area so as to lower "positioning" costs as much as possible (at the end of 1973 they ranged between $24 and $140 per container). A typical revenue for a 20–foot container was $800.

The quarterly German budget was set in tons and dollar revenue by port and type of equipment. This budget had been developed using estimates from computer forecasts prepared by North Star's central office (essentially an extrapolation of historical data) modified by the German "situation." Forecasts received from each subsidiary were reviewed at central office and revised only after discussions with the applicable marketing managers. They were then used to prepare a final budget which was presented to the shareholders for approval. The budget for the following year was processed during the period August/October of the previous year. Additionally, a rolling forecast was made each quarter showing tons and revenues by ports broken down by equipment. The budget had never been split up by area within Germany, and targets were always in gross terms; i.e., they were not broken down by commodity.

The actual volumes and revenues were compared monthly with the budget, in the "trade report." The RORO traffic was further analyzed monthly in the RORO report. Contribution was watched monthly in the "contribution report" which analyzed volumes, revenues, revenue per TEU, and contributions per TEU. Another monthly report received from each subsidiary dealt (both quantitatively and qualitatively) with past marketing and operational activities.

### The Action Plan for 1974

In order to change the approach of more or less soliciting day-to-day cargo as had been done in the past, Mr. Kruger had worked out a new approach which was aimed at increasing revenues and market share in the German market. This was termed the 1974 action plan. This latest planning effort was in line with corporate efforts to take a longer term view of German problems. The latest step in this effort was the preparation of a five-year tonnage and revenue forecast by port in Germany which was tied to an expected annual growth of some 3 to 4%. The goal for Germany was set at a growth in market share during this time period of five share points.

The 1974 budget had already been set by the normal procedure. Tonnage figures were set about 5% higher than the previous year, but revenue was expected to grow between 10 and 15%. For the first time the budget presented data of a detailed type for Germany, and Werther was asked to split them up by sales area. The new marketing effort provided that the sales force would be helped out by Mr. Kruger and two salesmen from Holland. A list of potential customers was compiled for Germany by area which listed several companies local salesmen had not heard of. This list had been compiled from Germany on port data and was thought to be reasonably good in identifying large high-value shippers.

A so-called task force was constituted; i.e., Mr. Kruger and/or the salesmen from Holland would spend time with local sales people, discussing their future call efforts and visiting difficult and new accounts in their area. This way North Star's services would be sold more aggressively than before to a prospective client since Werther salesmen were responsible for selling the services of all the lines they represented. If a better performance in Germany could be obtained, then Werther received increased commissions. In addition, Mr. Kruger hoped that in the future it could improve his bargaining position versus the other subsidiaries in obtaining more space allocation for his operation overall. This, in turn, would have a positive effect on market share in the future.

Mr. Kruger was considering whether the described new efforts could achieve the goals set and to what extent he could undertake further action. He was particularly concerned about the reaction of large forwarders to his plan, since North Star was literally in competition with its own customers. While he recognized that other shipping companies competed against the forwarders, he wasn't sure but what they could do so better, because of their size, and dominate market share. To what extent forwarders would switch their business from North Star to competitive lines was difficult to estimate. Just what could be done to minimize this possibility was not clear.

# Oak Creek Furniture Company

Each December was budget time at the Oak Creek Furniture Company and Sales Manager, Jack Renfro, like other division heads, turned his full attention to this task. Renfro considered for some time, but with little satisfaction, the approaches he might take in preparing what he hoped would be an ideal sales budget. Last year's budget, in his opinion, was unsatisfactory because it had lacked the flexibility necessary to combat an unfavorable sales trend which caused Oak Creek's net profit to drop to its lowest level since 1960. When it became obvious in the previous May that Oak Creek sales would fall short of the forecasted $3,300,-000 by $300,000, Renfro could take little action because the money set aside for advertising and sales promotion was already either spent or committed and there was no other ready source of funds. Unfortunately a big portion of the sales budget was committed to such fixed expenses as salaries, showroom rental, freight, catalog printing costs, and so forth. The largest of costs was the amount earmarked each year for agents' commissions—5.9 percent of sales and approximately 50 percent of the entire sales budget.

As Renfro faced the problem, he knew that to meet the company's objective of a 20 percent sales increase next year, he would have to base his budget on a $3,600,000 volume. This meant that assuming the same percentage of expenses as in the current year, about $215,000 of an expected $540,000 sales budget had to be earmarked for agents' commissions. The remainder, which represented only a slight increase over the funds available in the current year, had to support the projected increase in sales. (The distribution of the sales division's expenses for the past three years are presented in Exhibit 1.)

Renfro thought that one answer to the budget problem might be to have the agents agree to take a smaller commission on sales up to 80 per-

Reprinted from *Stanford Business Cases 1970* with the permission of the publisher, Graduate School of Business, Stanford University. Copyright © 1970 by the Board of Trustees of the Leland Stanford Junior University.

cent of their budgeted volume. Then, if it became obvious that the forecast would not be reached, Renfro would have some reserve funds for stepped-up advertising and promotion. If forecasted sales were achieved without added stimulus, the reserve would then be distributed to the agents to bring their commissions up to 7 percent.

Over the long run, Renfro felt that it could not be possible for sales commissions to remain as large a percentage of total sales and the sales budget. In fact, commissions to some agents were already becoming so large that Renfro questioned the reasonableness of the company's existing distribution system. Obviously, when Oak Creek Furniture Company was in its infancy and its product line unknown, the agents were the key to its success. In the meantime, however, the Oak Creek name had become well enough known that Renfro believed continued sales gains were no longer entirely related to the agents' efforts.

The recurring temptation was to replace sales agents with company salesmen on a salary plus commission basis. Sales in some areas, however, had not yet reached a volume sufficient to sustain the salary and travel expenses of a company man. To make the change in areas with higher volume would be to lose the best of the sales agents and would certainly be demoralizing to sales agents in those areas where they are retained. Assuming a change to direct salesmen Renfro also anticipated disproportionate initial costs and the possibility of a serious public relations problem with Oak Creek Furniture's customers who, in many cases, had a strong personal loyalty to the sales agent with whom they had been working for so many years.

## THE COMPANY AND THE INDUSTRY

The Oak Creek Furniture Company was founded in 1952 in Oak Creek, Wisconsin, by Aaron Forester. Until that time, Forester had been the chief furniture designer for the Logan Furniture Company of North Carolina. He broke from this firm over a disagreement with the president concerning the style trend that the Logan Company should follow. Forester advocated a shift to the clean straight lines characterizing the modern furniture that had become so popular since World War II, but the president of the Logan Company insisted on staying with traditional carved and curved surfaces.

Early in 1952, Forester found financial backing to start his own company, and the end of the year witnessed the first piece of furniture emerge from the Oak Creek plant. Forester had earlier designed a full line of home furniture of contemporary style. The line included seating units for both living and dining rooms, dining room tables and cabinets, and bedroom furniture. Forester chose to manufacture a high quality line which maximized the use of carefully selected hard woods. Consequently, the price of Oak Creek furniture was in the more expensive range for manufactured furniture. Only antiques and other unique pieces sold for more.

A number of people apparently agreed with Forester's designing, because Oak Creek furniture was well received from the start and sales grew rapidly. The price of the furniture dictated that it reach the consumer through fine furniture stores and interior decorators. Several of the country's better department stores eventually accepted the line, but since the individual pieces were manufactured to order, Oak Creek furniture was not the rapid turnover type of merchandise desired by the average department store.

The company competed in an industry that had been long established as an important segment of the U.S. economy. Of the twenty major industrial groups used in the Census of Manufacturers, the furniture industry ranked 16th in the number of employees and 17th in value added by manufacture. Manufacturers' shipments of wood (and upholstered) furniture were estimated to be over $2.5 billion.

The furniture industry was highly competitive, nonintegrated and characterized by a number of relatively small, closely held companies. No one, or even few companies, dominated the industry. There were about 700 metal furniture plants, 1,700 upholstered furniture plants, and 2,500 wood furniture plants. Few employed as many as 500 workers. In fact, 50% of the establishments employed less than 21 and the industry average was about 50. Only 1,200 plants in the industry topped $400,000 a year in sales and these plants accounted for better than 80 percent of industry sales.

Two-thirds of all furniture plants were located in the Middle Atlantic Southeast and Great Lakes States. North Carolina, with 12 percent of the plants, led all the states. The trend in industry location, however, was to the Middle West following the population shift. An excellent supply of hardwood in Michigan and other midwestern states further encouraged this move.

Most furniture companies produced a wide range of style patterns and suites in particular lines. Consumer tastes varied widely and retailers felt the need to keep a broad selection on the floor in order to meet these diverse needs. Moreover, retailers preferred new styles to feature in their sales talks and in their advertising programs. Consequently, most furniture manufacturers used designers, some with original and creative talent and others who adapted from successful items. This preoccupation with design was matched by the larger furniture department stores, most of which employed full time decorators.

Distribution in the furniture industry centered around a number of furniture markets located throughout the United States. At these markets, manufacturers periodically displayed their products to the trade. Retailers representing 29,000 furniture outlets from all parts of the country visited the markets to select stock to see what was being offered for the coming year. Manufacturers maintaining booths went all out to induce visiting retailers to make purchase commitments. Needless to say, salesmen had to follow-up such voluntary commitments, but the difficult part of selling the line—actually showing the pieces—had already been accomplished. Most retail buyers would not consider taking on a line unless they had seen it at one of the markets. These markets, which were closed to the public, lasted from one to two weeks and were held twice a year. In order of importance, the furniture markets were located in Chicago, Highpoint, N.C., Los Angeles, New York, San Francisco, Grand Rapids, Dallas, Jamestown (N.Y.), and Boston.

Chicago set the pace of industry activity. The other cities waited until Chicago established its semiannual market dates—usually in January and June—and then scheduled their dates accordingly. Between 500 and 1,000 manufacturers participated in the Chicago market.

Widespread distribution of its products was the typical pattern for the furniture manufacturer. Because each manufacturer concentrated on particular groups of furniture he needed a wide market to secure volume. The demand for furniture, moreover, was sensitive to business conditions and a regional economic down-turn could easily destroy a market. No manufacturer, nonetheless, had ever achieved intensive national distribution. The largest firms were able to place their products in about one-third of the furniture outlets.

Manufacturers typically used sales representatives who carried the products of noncompeting manufacturers and who were paid a commission of 5 to 10 percent of the sales that they made. Few manufacturers had been able to establish sales forces to handle their products exclusively.

Attempts by manufacturers to create brand preference were relatively unheard of until 1949. Since then, the number of firms spending over $25,000 a year for advertising had increased substantially. With many firms in the industry grossing less than $500,000, however, few had much of a chance to launch costly advertising programs.

Retailers, in many cases, tended to discourage the development of manufacturers' brands. Some even went so far as to conceal the identity of a manufacturer on floor samples. Retailers taking this position did so for several reasons. They believed that no manufacturer advertised enough to make his brand mean more to a community than the name of a reputable local store. Furthermore, retailers were concerned that advertised names would be disparaged by unscrupulous salesmen in other stores. The average consumer's inability to ascertain the quality of furniture by visual inspection made him particularly vulnerable to such tactics. Finally, the retailers did not want to promote manufacturers' brands because they feared they would become the "showrooms" for many of the small decorators and dealers not maintaining such a facility. Decorators could easily place an order for a customer once they knew who manufactured the pieces the customer wanted.

To stock a furniture store, retailers found it necessary to buy from several different manufacturers in order to obtain the styles, types and quality grades required. While a typical store might buy from six to eight different manufacturers, they did try to limit the number as much as possible in order to minimize inward freight costs.

Most of the dealings between furniture stores and manufacturers were carried on by sales representatives and store buyers. The number of buyers in a store depended largely on the store size. A large store would probably have a buyer in each department, i.e., lamps, upholstered furniture, modern furniture, etc. A buyer had complete responsibility for the purchase and sale of the items in his department. He supervised the sales force and was responsible for its training and performance.

Buyers selected new lines of merchandise and dropped other lines generally with the approval of the store merchandise manager. When a buyer selected a new line, he asked the following questions:

Is it an accepted name and style?
Will the quality of the line fit in with the other items in the store?
Will it add prestige to the store and the department?
Does the price fit into the pattern in the store?
Does the price represent the true value of the item?
Is there an adequate markup?
Is similar merchandise sold in the area?
Is the price protected?
Is there adequate selectivity in the fabrics, finishes, frames, etc.?
Can I get rapid delivery?
Is the line advertised?

Of equal importance were another set of questions regarding the agent selling the furniture:

Do I already know the agent? (Possibly he is already selling me a line.)
Does he have a good personal reputation?
Is he experienced in selling this type of merchandise?
Will he visit me often enough to give me the selling support required?
Will he immediately take care of my complaints about damaged pieces and delivery errors?
Will he spend time with the floor salesmen to support the training that I give them?

## OAK CREEK DISTRIBUTION POLICY

Oak Creek, in 1965, employed nine selling agents and one company salesman. Eight of the agents were independent and carried other, non-competing lines. The ninth sold Oak Creek furniture exclusively. The company salesman, holding the title of Eastern Sales Manager, was located in New York City. There he sold to furniture stores and contract dealers,[1] and also directed the operation of Oak Creek's New York showroom. The showroom was one of five that Oak Creek maintained in major U.S. cities. (These showrooms were used to exhibit the Oak Creek line to visiting retailers. The remainder of the year, the showrooms were open usually one day a week for conducting business with local decorators, architects, non-stocking dealers, and in some cases, retailers.)

Future plans called for the ten Oak Creek territories to be organized under three field sales managers. In 1965 the eastern sales manager who sold in territory #2 supervised the agents in territories 1, 3 and 4. Jack Renfro supervised the remaining agents. Renfro's responsibilities as sales manager included selecting and supervising agents, managing the company's advertising and promotional activities, preparing the sales budget, and providing company representation at the various furniture markets.

## SALES AGENTS

Renfro believed that he had assembled a highly competent group of agents. Most had joined Oak Creek during the company's first two or three years and worked hard to establish the line. Renfro exercised great care whenever it was necessary to select a new agent. He did not use personality or sales ability tests, but thoroughly screened each applicant by interview and carefully investigated their backgrounds. Renfro relied much upon recommendations from other manufacturers who had used or were using the agent. He looked particularly at the following elements when considering prospective agents:

1. Sales experience with furniture.
2. Amount of uncommitted sales time which could be given to the Oak Creek line.
3. Types of other merchandise sold by the agent.
4. Types of outlets covered by the agent.
5. Appearance and carriage of the applicant. Does he have the "Oak Creek look?"[2]

Probably the most important determinant for selecting a new sales agent was the candidate's present territory. The most effective agents sold Oak Creek furniture through channels which they had already set up; thus it was important that these channels did not overlap those of other sales agents.

Oak Creek agents generally represented several manufacturers of

---

[1] Contract dealers were individuals who sold only to commercial accounts.

[2] Renfro explained that the agent's appearance was extremely important since the company tried to maintain the quality image in its salesmen that it maintained in its furniture.

furniture or home furnishings. A typical mix might include the Oak Creek line and lines of traditional furniture, lamps, garden furniture and accessories. In larger stores, the agent often sold each line to a different buyer, although this was not considered the optimum use of the agent's time.

Because Oak Creek furniture was not intensively distributed there were only a few franchise dealers in a given area. The agents called about every two weeks on stores which sold large volumes of Oak Creek furniture, but only two or three times a year on remote stores that did not show particularly active sales.

On a typical visit to a furniture store, the agent first made an appointment to see the buyer. During the interview, the agent presented new pieces and fabrics which had been added to the Oak Creek line. He talked over the items which were moving most easily in the area and told of new promotions sponsored by the company. The buyer then ordered the items that he believed he would need in the interval between the agent's visits. Sometimes the agent had to suggest tactfully to the buyer that the order was either too large or too small. Most buyers respected the agent's opinion on such suggestions.

After visiting the buyer, the agent usually inspected the floor samples. He looked for soiled or damaged pieces which would reflect poorly on the quality of the line. (The majority of the stores selling Oak Creek furniture were on a basic stock plan which meant they displayed representative items of the line. The amount of basic stock was generally decided upon by the agent and the buyer in terms of the store's size and volume.) If the agent found that any of the basic stock had been sold from the floor, he noted this along with data on soiled pieces. While on the floor, the agent talked with the furniture salesmen explaining many of the same details about the line that he had with the buyer earlier. One of the agent's prime objectives was to develop the floor salesmen's enthusiasm for the Oak Creek line.

After inspecting floor samples and talking to the floor salesmen, the agent returned to the buyer and wrote up the order. He suggested that soiled pieces be marked down and sold, and he made arrangements to have damaged pieces repaired at one of the company's warehouses.

## AGENT SUPERVISION

Renfro exercised little direct selling supervision over the eight independent agents. He did not attempt to tell the agents to whom they could sell, except that it was understood that the agents would not sell to discount houses or other cut-rate merchandisers. The agents recommended the discount to be allowed to various retail dealers. The established discount schedule was:

50 percent of retail—to furniture and department stores stocking and displaying Oak Creek furniture.

40 percent of retail—to furniture and department stores not stocking and displaying Oak Creek furniture, and to interior decorators having a legitimate office and showroom.

33 percent of retail—to interior decorators not having an office or showroom.

Agents were watched carefully to see that they were selling up to their area's potential. If they were considerably low, Renfro could threaten to withdraw the agency. Renfro determined area potential, which he called a "style quota," through a city-by-city analysis of the national market. An index published by *Sales Management* gave the relative buyer power of each metropolitan area. This index was based upon population, retail sales and family income. The index gave Renfro a tool with which to compare the efforts of each agent against the others and against the country as a whole. Sales data were collected weekly and graphs were drawn monthly for each agent comparing territorial sales and total sales for the country.

In the fall of 1965, Renfro sent a questionnaire to each agent requesting information about the other lines carried and the percent of the agents' income each represented. Some agents responded with complete details while others provided only fragmentary information. Because of the great quantity of data, Renfro grouped the style quotas and corresponding sales figures by state rather than by city. A sampling of the reports is included in the Appendix.

**SELLING AIDS**

Renfro attempted to provide his agents as much help in making a sale as possible. He regularly placed Oak Creek ads in *Holiday, Town & Country*, and *Bride*. (Exhibit 2 outlines the 1965 advertising schedule.) Renfro also supplied the agents with various descriptive materials about new items or lines of furniture, gave the agents samples of new fabrics, and offered special merchandise for sales and promotions. Agents received monthly a letter from Renfro informing them of how they were doing with respect to the total sales picture and how the merchandise was moving in the various territories. Moreover, each sales agent was given a "Manual of Standard Procedures" which contained descriptive material about all the Oak Creek products and prices as well as reprints of current magazine ads and samples of the advertising mats which were available to the retailers.

**THE 1966 BUDGET**

If he could find a way to cut back the dollars going out as agents' commissions, Renfro planned to redistribute the budget to place emphasis on the following:

1. A total reduction in the overall sales budget to assist in delaying possible price increases owing to: (*a*) Increased costs of design and product research; (*b*) Increased costs of labor and materials.
2. Funds to support hiring two more field sales managers.
3. A larger investment in advertising space and production, dealer aids and printing (catalogs, consumer brochures, etc.).

### EXHIBIT 1

#### Sales Division Expenses
#### (1963–1965)

|  | *1965** | *1964* | *1963* |
|---|---|---|---|
| TOTAL SALES | 3,300,000 | 2,858,710 | 2,308,500 |
| Commissions | 185,900† | 200,400 | 161,500 |
| Salaries | 45,400 | 29,800 | 29,500 |
| (Agency fee) | 2,900‡ | 7,600 | 4,200 |
| Travel | 6,400 | 4,500 | 13,800§ |
| Entertainment | 2,200 | 1,200 | 9,340§ |
| Sales promotion | 6,850 | 5,900 | 9,250§ |
| Advertising space | 38,400 | 19,650 | 27,900 |
| Advertising production | 7,740 | 2,460 | 3,500 |
| Photography | 5,800 | 4,900 | 3,000 |
| Dealer aids | 7,600 | 5,750 | 4,560 |
| Printing | 24,300 | 10,800 | 14,850 |
| Sample expense | 13,600 | 6,150 | 9,500 |
| Freight | 3,500 | 4,090 | . . . |
| Postage | 6,800 | 6,100 | . . . |
| Repairs & maintenance | 1,450 | 715 | 1,060 |
| Showroom rent | 28,500‖ | 8,700 | 1,020 |
| Miscellaneous | 3,870 | 3,700 | 3,600 |
|  | 391,210 | 322,415 | 296,580 |

* 1965 figures are as budgeted.

† During 1964, a 22 percent commission was paid to the separately owned New York showroom. The drop in commission in 1965 reflects the beginning of a company owned showroom there, but overall expenses were increased to cover the cost of the company's showroom in salaries, showroom rent, etc.

‡ Agency fee was substantially reduced when the company hired its own full time Advertising Public Relations Manager.

§ In 1963 and before the travel and entertainment expenses of all executives in the company as well as all company gifts and gratuities normally charged to sales promotion were charged against the sales budget.

‖ 1965 was the first full calendar year reflecting cost of rent of showrooms in New York and San Francisco.

**EXHIBIT 2**

**Advertising Schedule, 1965**

| Book | Space | Color | Months |  |  |  |  |  |  |  |  |  |  |  | Total |
|---|---|---|---|---|---|---|---|---|---|---|---|---|---|---|---|
| | | | 1 | 2 | 3 | 4 | 5 | 6 | 7 | 8 | 9 | 10 | 11 | 12 | |
| Holiday | 1/4 | 2 | | | | | | 1 | | 1 | 1 | 1 | 1 | | 5 |
| Town & Country | 1/4 | 2 | 1 | 1 | 1 | 1 | 1 | | | | 1 | 1 | 1 | | 10 |
| Bride | 1/4 | 2 | | 1 | | 1 | 1 | | | | | 1 | | | 3 |
| | | | 1 | 2 | 1 | 3 | 2 | 1 | | 1 | 2 | 3 | 2 | | 18 |
| Furniture Forum | | B/W | | | | | 1 | | | 1 | 1 | | 1 | | 4 |
| Int. Dec. Hand-book | | 2 | | | | | | | | | | 1 | | | 2 |
| Interiors | 1 | B/W | 1 | 1 | 1 | | 1 | | | | 1 | 1 | | | 6 |
| Interior Design | 1 | B/W | 1 | 1 | | 1 | | | | | 1 | | | | 4 |
| | | | 2 | 2 | 1 | 1 | 2 | | | 1 | 3 | 3 | 2 | | 16 |
| | | | 3 | 4 | 2 | 4 | 4 | 1 | | 1 | 5 | 6 | 4 | | 34 |

Oak Creek Furniture

| AGENT: | Dick Newton | TERRITORY: | 1 |
| HOME: | Massachusetts | JOINED OAK CREEK: | 1956 |
| OTHER LINES: | | | |

| NATURE OF LINE | APPROX. % OF INCOME |
|---|---|
| Rattan furniture | NA |
| Fabrics | NA |
| Accessories | NA |

| YEARLY SALES VOLUME: | 1965 | 1964 | 1963 |
|---|---|---|---|
| | (11 mo. total) | | |
| | $228,300 | $228,400 | $158,000 |

QUOTA PERFORMANCE:  STYLE QUOTA ACTUAL SALES
(1st 6 mos.)

| | STYLE QUOTA | ACTUAL SALES | |
|---|---|---|---|
| Connecticut........................... | $ 25,193 | $ 12,965 | |
| Maine................................ | 3,619 | 548 | |
| Massachusetts.......................... | 44,957 | 49,379 | |
| New Hampshire........................ | 2,227 | 100 | |
| NY (excluding NY City)................. | 49,343 | 48,673 | |
| Rhode Island.......................... | 6,263 | 6,962 | |
| Vermont.............................. | 5,217 | 1,450 | % of U.S. |

| TERRITORY COMPARISON (1965 Data) | % of Co. Sales | % of U.S. Population | % of U.S. Metropolitan Population |
|---|---|---|---|
| | 8.0 | 10.3 | 12.3 |

| AGENT: | Allan Connell | TERRITORY: | 2 |
| HOME: | New York | JOINED OAK CREEK: | 1957 |
| OTHER LINES: | None— | | |

Employed by company as Eastern sales manager and also responsible for the New York City territory and showroom. Paid a $16,000 salary in 1965.

| YEARLY SALES VOLUME: | 1965 | 1964 | 1963 |
|---|---|---|---|
| | (11 mo. total) | | |
| | $242,600[1] | $271,200 | $169,500 |

QUOTA PERFORMANCE:  STYLE QUOTA ACTUAL SALES
(1st 6 mos.)

| | STYLE QUOTA | ACTUAL SALES |
|---|---|---|
| New York City....................... | $214,972 | $126,067 |

| TERRITORY COMPARISON: | % of Co. Sales | % of U.S. Population | % of U.S. Cosmopolitan Population |
|---|---|---|---|
| | 9.5 | 4.9 | 18.2 |

[1] Include sales through N.Y. showroom which became company owned and operated in 1965. Showroom sales for first 11 months of 1965 were $151,800. Connell's sales outside the showroom for the same period were $90,800.

AGENT:   Paul Kearns
HOME:    New Jersey
OTHER LINES:  Would not list

TERRITORY:   1
JOINED OAK CREEK:   1952

| YEARLY SALES VOLUME: | 1965 | 1964 | 1963 |
|---|---|---|---|
| | (11 mo. total) | | |
| | $285,100 | $323,900 | $258,700 |

QUOTA PERFORMANCE:
(1st 6 mos.)

| STYLE | QUOTA | ACTUAL SALES |
|---|---|---|
| Delaware | $ 3,201 | $ 11,236 |
| District of Columbia | 33,900 | 25,155 |
| Maryland | 21,991 | 27,643 |
| New Jersey | 62,912 | 32,872 |
| Pennsylvania | 84,208 | 52,071 |

| % of Co. Sales | % of U.S. Population | % of U.S. Cosmopolitan Population |
|---|---|---|
| 11.3 | 12.6 | 18.1 |

AGENT:   Carl Gilman
HOME:    Florida
OTHER LINES:

TERRITORY:   4
JOINED OAK CREEK:   1955

| NATURE OF LINE | APPROX. % OF INCOME |
|---|---|
| Traditional | NA |
| Woven Woods | NA |
| Lamps | NA |
| Accessories | NA |

| YEARLY SALES VOLUME: | 1965 | 1964 | 1963 |
|---|---|---|---|
| | (11 mo. total) | | |
| | $116,000 | $110,000 | $116,600 |

QUOTA PERFORMANCE:
(1st 6 mos.)

| STYLE | QUOTA | ACTUAL SALES |
|---|---|---|
| Alabama | $ 8,073 | $ 2,424 |
| Florida | 30,064 | 21,246 |
| Georgia | 13,222 | 8,207 |
| Mississippi | 3,480 | 1,182 |
| N. Carolina | 12,109 | 4,431 |
| S. Carolina | 5,567 | 475 |
| Tennessee | 11,692 | 6,560 |
| Virginia | 12,031 | 2,540 |
| W. Virginia | 7,658 | 2,303 |

| TERRITORY COMPARISON: | % of Co. Sales | % of U.S. Population | % of U.S. Cosmopolitan Population |
|---|---|---|---|
| | 3.9 | 17.2 | 6.1 |

AGENT:    Dean Metcalf                                TERRITORY:                9
HOME:     Southern California                          JOINED OAK CREEK:    1958
OTHER LINES:

| NATURE OF LINE | APPROX. % OF INCOME |
|---|---|
| Garden Furniture | 15% |
| Custom Designs | 5% |
| Accessories | 5% |

YEARLY SALES VOLUME:

| 1965 | 1964 | 1963 |
|---|---|---|
| (11 mo. total) | | |
| $371,100 | $294,700 | $245,600 |

QUOTA PERFORMANCE:          STYLE QUOTA  ACTUAL SALES
(1st 6 mos. 1959)

| | STYLE QUOTA | ACTUAL SALES |
|---|---|---|
| Southern California...................... | $120,084 | $173,017 |

TERRITORY COMPARISON:

| % of Co. Sales | % of U.S. Population | % of U.S. Cosmopolitan Population |
|---|---|---|
| 10.3 | 4.1 | 3.7 |

AGENT:    Harry Preston                               TERRITORY:               10
HOME:     California                                   JOINED OAK CREEK:    1954
OTHER LINES:    Exclusive Oak Creek
Preston received a 5% commission on all sales. Oak Creek
provided Preston a completely financed showroom in lieu of
the normal 7% commission.

YEARLY SALES VOLUME:

| 1965 | 1964 | 1963 |
|---|---|---|
| (11 mo. total) | | |
| $360,600 | $375,500 | $350,400 |

QUOTA PERFORMANCE:          STYLE QUOTA  ACTUAL SALES
(1st 6 mo.)

| | STYLE QUOTA | ACTUAL SALES |
|---|---|---|
| California (Northern).................... | $ 60,399 | $ 80,601 |
| Oregon.............................. | 12,388 | 25,968 |
| Washington.......................... | 21,574 | 65,968 |
| Nevada.............................. | 1,854 | 299 |
| Idaho............................... | 2,784 | 2,285 |
| Montana............................. | 3,201 | 2,834 |
| Alaska.............................. | ... | 5,220 |

TERRITORY COMPARISON:

| % of Co. Sales | % of U.S. Population | % of U.S. Cosmopolitan Population |
|---|---|---|
| 13.1 | 7.8 | 13.5 |

# Skyline Petroleum Company

"Congratulations, Joe," said Phil Keller, a regional credit manager for the Skyline Petroleum Company, "your new assignment to the Watertown Sales District is a good promotion." Joe Smith was the district sales manager of Skyline's small River Bend Sales District, and had recently received word of his transfer to Watertown. "Just think," Phil continued, "old Dick Owen has finally reached retirement age. Forty-two years is a lot of service."

The Skyline Petroleum Company, a large and well-established oil distributor, operated in Texas, Oklahoma and Louisiana. The company's marketing division was divided into Wholesale and Retail Departments. Both the River Bend and Watertown Districts were part of the Wholesale Marketing Department.

Wholesale distribution involved all customers not buying through service stations of the Retail Marketing Department. Customers included farmers, contractors, truckers, and manufacturing and commercial establishments. The three-state marketing area was divided into regions which in turn were organized into sales districts. As shown in Figure 1, a sales district was a purely line organization; staff support was centralized at the regional headquarters.

District organizations varied depending on the business density and volume of the area served. Typically, however, districts consisted of some ten bulk plants or depots, a majority of which were operated on a commission basis. Facilities included storage tanks for gasoline and diesel products and a warehouse for lubricating oils, greases, and other packaged materials. Tank trucks distributed Skyline products from the local bulk plant to the customer, although certain customers with large requirements and adequate storage were served direct from the refinery or major distribution terminal. The company owned bulk plant facilities and leased them to Commission Agents.

Reprinted from *Stanford Business Cases 1959* with the permission of the publisher, Graduate School of Business, Stanford University. Copyright © 1959 by the Board of Trustees of the Leland Stanford Junior University.

A sales manager headed each district, but staffing below that level again depended on the size and nature of the area. Assistant sales managers were assigned to larger districts. An average-sized district employed two to three Wholesale Salesmen, a Fuel and Lubricant Engineer, and the necessary operating personnel to receive, store, and deliver the products. All operating personnel engaged in some way in direct contact with customers. Office personnel sold to walk-in customers, while truck

**FIGURE 1**

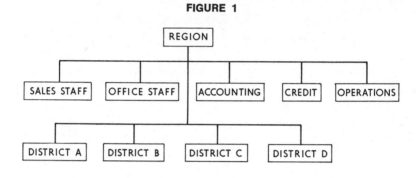

drivers delivered and sold products from tank trucks. Job titles and brief job descriptions of all district positions follow:

*District Sales Manager*—manages the activities of the sales district and administers established policies and procedures relating to sales, delivery, accounting, credit, operations and personnel to secure a representative portion of the available business at maximum realization and minimum operating cost.

*Assistant District Sales Manager*—assists the district sales manager in managing the activities of the sales district and administering established policies and procedures relating to sales, delivery, accounting, credit, plant-operations and personnel to secure a representative proportion of the available business and maximum realization at minimum operating cost.

*Fuel & Lubricant*—provides technical and specialized solicitation and service to accounts which require full engineering help, technical service and experienced assistance beyond the ability of general sales organization through one or a combination of the following activities: (1) solicitation of all product requirements and servicing of accounts which requires constant fuel and lubricant engineering effort beyond the ability of other sales positions; (2) furnishing regularly assigned support to other sales positions on accounts requiring a high degree of fuel and lubricant engineering effort; or (3) providing on-call technical specialized service to accounts requiring fuel and lubricant engineering effort at intermittant or infrequent intervals.

*Wholesale Salesman*—responsible for sale of the full line of products and related services to an assigned group of accounts (both Skyline and competitive) within a designated area. Keeps constantly alert to the entrance of new accounts into the field, and programs solicitation efforts to best serve such accounts. As appropriate, and when so directed, performs designated administrative and clerical functions closely related to sales and operations.

*Office Salesman*—directs and performs plant sales and clerical work for the district sales manager. In the absence of the district sales manager, acts as a company representative at the station and coordinates station activities. Responsible for meeting standards in the preparation of reports, records and correspondence; for accurate advice to customers on products, prices and sales policies; for securing maximum orders from each customer contacting the plant; and for direction of warehouse and delivery functions as required to coordinate station activities.

*Assistant Office Salesman*—as a primary function, i.e., at least 25% of the time, performs one or a combination of the following duties: (1) taking orders and soliciting business at the counter and on the phone, advising customers on product characteristics, applications, prices and sales, operating or credit policies; (2) performs negotiation-type credit control duties such as soliciting payments on accounts from customers on the phone or in person; (3) dispatches delivery trucks. Responsible for giving accurate information to customers and for completing assigned clerical and operating duties accurately and expeditiously.

*Head Route Salesman*—operates a small sales office and bulk plant at a location remote from the district sales office to provide service and facilities for the receipt, storage, sale and delivery of bulk and packaged petroleum products in the area. Performs all functions involved in the receipt, storage and delivery of packaged and bulk petroleum products. Responsible for plant and operations, safety practices, solicits business of regular and new accounts, collects and arranges for banking of funds, performs accounting functions, prepares sales, stock, credit, personnel and accounting forms, and reports, and necessary correspondence.

*Route Salesman*—delivers company products by tank, combination or package truck to accounts within an assigned area or an assigned route. Loads or assists in loading trucks, drives truck, delivers product from truck, collects for product at the time of delivery or in accordance with established line of credit. Accounts for all products and funds handled. Reports any pertinent competitive activities observed. Services the truck.

## THE JOB OF THE DISTRICT SALES MANAGER

One of Skyline's top wholesale marketing executives explained that the job of the district sales manager consisted of three basic functions—

He has to make day-to-day operating decisions to keep the business running smoothly.

He has to plan ahead, setting worthy objectives for each component of the organization; and follows through to assure that progress actually made is in keeping with goals established.

And finally, he has to train, counsel and motivate the people comprising the organization.

Administering these functions required a number of skills on the part of the district sales manager. He maintained a good deal of the physical plant; he sought out and reported price actions by competitors; he assigned sales territories; was the company representative in the community; recommended manpower changes; and so forth. The regional office reserved final approval on price changes, hiring, wage and salary matters, etc., but the district sales manager initiated such recommendations.

Forms for recording district activity were important to the manager in the effective discharge of his basic responsibilities. Several served as the basis for recommendations to regions. For example, Exhibit 1 is the form used for determining the delivery work load for the route salesmen. The district sales manager used this information periodically to reapportion the work load within the district or to recommend additional personnel to the region.

Sales personnel were expected to record available business information on the customer data sheet, D102 (Exhibit 2). This form provided up-to-date data on the pertinent circumstances surrounding each account, including responsibility for solicitation. Form D105 (Exhibit 3), the account change card, kept the manager informed on sales gains and losses. District managers varied in their insistence on current maintenance of these forms. Some felt that this attention to detail was burdensome and not overly productive, while others insisted that the reported information was their only way of keeping aware of district activity.

The Commission Agents submitted monthly operating and financial statements which the sales managers were to evaluate and use in consultation with the agents. Agents had no formal business training and relied greatly on the supervision of the district sales manager.

The Regional Office provided the district with information compiled by three staff services. Form R30, for instance, reported cumulative monthly sales results by product for the district and its components. Form R31 showed the number of accounts to which credit has been extended. Form R35 provided expenses per gallon delivered.

## THE WATERTOWN DISTRICT

Following several trips to the Watertown district, Joe wondered just what his course of action would be on assuming his new duties. Dick Owen had been at Watertown for 29 years and appeared to be an established part of the community. Joe noted during visits at several service clubs that Dick knew nearly all the town's business people. In fact, at one time or other Dick had served as president of several of the organizations.

Also going through Joe's mind was the material he had encountered at a recent administrative functions course for district sales managers held at Skyline's home office in Dallas. Joe had not been back at River Bend long enough to really apply the material but he recalled how they had covered the basic management responsibilities of planning, organizing, directing, coordinating and controlling.

The Watertown District spread over a large area, with a concentration of business activity and population as shown on the map in Exhibit 4. Petroleum and related needs were diversified to the extent that the portion south of the Blue River was highly industrialized while to the north the mainstay was agriculture. District population figures recorded at 321,000 in 1964 had reached 400,000 in 1968 and were projected to 675,-000 in 1980. This growth was based primarily on expected manpower requirements for new business establishments moving into the area. The following figures show new plant construction since 1964:

**Number of New Plants and Expansions (and of Capitalization—Millions)**

| 1964 | | 1965 | | 1966 | | 1967 | | 1968 | |
|------|------|------|------|------|------|------|------|------|------|
| 55 | ($10.5) | 82 | ($12.0) | 99 | ($15.0) | 153 | ($24.6) | 176 | ($35.1) |

Fabricated metal products manufacturers ranked first in number of firms followed by electrical machinery, chemicals, and food and kindred products. Active promotion of five major industrial parks promised a continuation of this trend.

Navigable waters along the Blue River, adequate rail and trucking facilities, and moderate year-round weather were considered basic attractions to new plant growth.

With the increase in population and industrialization, the area within the district devoted to agriculture had been declining over the past five years. However, mechanical efficiencies in farming and an improved price structure in 1968 helped achieve a record value for agricultural production of $16,500,000. Flowers, vegetables and livestock accounted for the major share of the total.

*Watertown,* the heart of the area's heavy industrial growth, was the home of the district office and the main salaried sales office. Encouraged by liberal zoning laws, "smoke-stack" type operations had increased 40% over the last five years. A new industrial park consisting of 300 acres was soon to open near the city.

There were four rather sizable airports in the Sales District—located at Watertown, Alpine, Poplar Bluff and Garden City. The Watertown Airport, five miles outside the city limits, was the largest, providing facilities for commercial and private aircraft. The District had been successful in establishing dealerships at each of these airports. Bulk storage facilities at the Watertown Airport were under supervision of the District Sales Manager and required the services of four warehousemen.

A smaller salaried sales office was located 20 miles from Watertown, in the city of *Poplar Bluff.* This was primarily a residential center, but a recently developed light industrial tract brought 20 new manufacturing firms to the city within the past two years. Commercial establishments, warehousing facilities, and some farming rounded out the activities of the area. Several large accounts were important in maintaining the gallonage position at this station. The light industrial plants, in general, were not large users of petroleum products.

The city of *Alpine,* served by a Commission Agent, was involved in an overnight transition from an agricultural-commercial economy to one centered around light industry. Electronics and precision-type manufacturing firms were predominant in the area. Industrial sites covering 250 acres were at the time being sold along the Blue River with reports that actual sales and inquiries had already exceeded expectations. Keeping pace with industrial growth, the city's population now at 50,000, had doubled in the past five years. Joe was visiting the Watertown office when it was learned that Mac McMurtry, a commissioned distributor for Skyline's largest Alpine competitor, was going to retire in several months. McMurtry had always been a leader in Alpine (mayor, city council, etc.) and was held in high esteem by many accounts in the area. A salaried plant was scheduled to replace the old operation.

*Garden City* and *Mansfield* were both unincorporated farming centers served by Commission Agents. The total number of agricultural accounts had been declining over the last three years due to the failure of the marginal operators to keep up with new farm innovations. However, those still in business were producing larger quantities through use of more and more mechanized equipment. The Garden City area showed the most promise in terms of agricultural growth, while the future of Mansfield was uncertain. Recent plans for improving Highway 7 and the low cost of land had attracted the interest of several real estate promoters to the Mansfield area. One manufacturing firm had already constructed plant facilities near Mansfield, and from all reports its management was quite happy with the results.

An organization chart for the Watertown sales district would have been as shown in Figure 2.

Exhibit 5 shows the district's 1968 market position in terms of number of accounts and percent of gallonage for both motor gasoline and diesel sales. These figures were developed from existing customer data sheets, Form D102, which admittedly had received very little attention from the district sales manager. Comparable figures for prior years had never been developed. Some picture of district growth, however, can be gained from

**FIGURE 2**

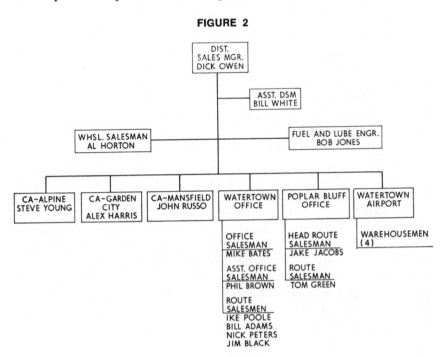

a composite of the R31 Credit statements. Quarterly and yearly averages of accounts to which credit had been extended are shown in Exhibit 6 for the last four years.

Sales results for the district and its components are shown in Exhibit 7 for the period covering 1966–1968. Dick set the district goals for 1968 at a general increase over the 1967 results. Several large losses, as noted in the exhibit, resulted from situations over which the district had no control. Expenses, as listed in Exhibit 8, showed some improvement for the year. The large decrease per gallon at the Poplar Bluff Plant related to the elimination of a Route Salesman following a regular workload study.

Credit collections for the district ran below the Company objectives of 75% current. Figures ($ & Accounts Current) for September, 1967, and September, 1968 are indicative of the yearly results.

| | Sept. '67* | | Sept. '68* | |
|---|---|---|---|---|
| | $ | Accts. | $ | Accts. |
| District.................... | 71 | 62 | 66 | 63 |
| Watertown................. | 77 | 68 | 71 | 70 |
| Poplar Bluff................ | 78 | 63 | 68 | 60 |
| Alpine...................... | 75 | 54 | 63 | 60 |
| Mansfield................... | 52 | 48 | 53 | 50 |
| Garden City................ | 54 | 61 | 71 | 59 |

\* SOURCE: CD-35.

Commission Agent operations are outlined in Exhibit 9 which shows the number of employees, major expense items, gross commissions, total expenses, net commissions, commission rates, and equipment. Several monthly statements (Exhibit 10) are included for the operation at Mansfield. Realizing that such earnings would not support the distributorship, John Russo was paid, as a common carrier, for picking up and transporting the product needs for both his own and the Garden City operation. As a part of the trucking business Russo often hauled farm products for other members of the community. Such trips might cover a distance of 200 miles, with fertilizers often making up the load for the return haul. Russo's 22 year old son tended the CA operations during these absences.

Dick Owen, the retiring District Sales Manager, had, during his tenure, advanced with the organizational changes of the company. His duties over the past 29 years had changed from Agency Manager to Resident Manager and finally District Sales Manager. He was alert, enthusiastic and a good personal salesman. As a result of his long association in Watertown he knew most of the accounts in the immediate area and often supplemented the solicitation efforts of other district employees. To make sure operations continued smoothly, Dick was quite active in checking on clerical details, handling many himself. He insisted on opening all the company mail as a precaution against missing any important correspondence.

The following people were relied upon to carry out district operations:

## White Collar Personnel

*Bill White—Assistant District Sales Manager.* Age 36, had been with the company 11 years and in his present position 3 years. Held a B.S. degree in engineering and started with Skyline as a route salesman. His ability was obvious as he moved rapidly through the positions of head route salesman, Fuel and Lubricant Engineer, and regional specialist. As Asst. D.S.M., he handled a number of accounts, which greatly relieved the load on the wholesale salesman. He also took the responsibility for planning the activities of the Fuel & Lubricant engineer. Joe had formed the impression that Bill was not being used to his full capabilities and was not functioning within the proposed scope of the A.D.S.M. position.

*Bob Jones—Fuel & Lubricant.*  Age 62, had been with the company 35 years and in his present position 16 years. A graduate engineer, he had held a previous position as a home office specialist. He was very conscientious but needed to be told exactly what to do, where to be at a given time, etc. The A.D.S.M. had set up certain days when the Engineer was to be at stations in the district. He reported to the District Office twice a week for instructions.

*Al Horton—Wholesale Salesman.*  Age 60, with the company 35 years and in his present position 12 years. A high school graduate, previously a bottled gas salesman, he was considered to be a good salesman; was energetic and enthusiastic. While not particularly effective in organizing his own time, once told to do something he required little follow-up. He reported each day to the District Office, left (about 9:30 A.M.) to make his calls, returned in the afternoon to set up appointments on the telephone and then out again about 3:00 P.M. Al seemed to be left pretty much on his own in terms of planning his sales approach and setting up his calls for the day. Very little of his time was actually spent in the area north of the Blue River. Occasionally, when a problem was heard of through one of the Commission Agents, Dick would instruct him to take a run out and see what was taking place. According to both Dick and Al, the nature of these accounts did not warrant a more intensive solicitation effort.

## Operating Personnel: Watertown Sales Office

*Mike Bates—Office Salesman.*  Age 32, with the company 10 years and in present assignment for the last 4 years. Had completed two years of college and seemed to possess the necessary qualifications for the job although it was noted that he was not particularly exacting in his work. There was evidence that he needed training in the clerical aspects of his job but this seemed to stem from the fact that he had not been delegated the full responsibility called for in this position. Normally Mike should have been the spokesman for the rest of the operating personnel, but very seldom was he included in problem solving or planning conferences held by Dick Owen.

*Phil Brown—Asst. Office Salesman.*  59 years old, had been with the company 35 years and in his present assignment for the past six months. Previous positions included time as a field salesman and head field salesman. There were indications that he didn't work well under pressure and lacked knowledge of many company policies.

*Ike Poole—Route Salesman.*  57 years old and had been with the company for 30 years in his present position. Performed his work well.

*Bill Adams—Route Salesman.*  59 years old and had been with the company for 40 years as a field salesman. Performed work well and required a minimum of supervision.

*Nick Peters—Route Salesman.* Age 45, with the company as a field salesman for 20 years. An energetic and enthusiastic worker with real concern for company welfare. Well acquainted with company policy and required little supervision.

*Jim Black—Route Salesman.* Age 38, had been a field salesman for 11 years. Had potential for position of head field salesman or head office salesman. Followed directions well.

It was noted that the work done by the above men consisted principally of delivering to accounts, taking orders, truck maintenance, etc. However, in terms of solicitation of new and existing small accounts, all needed development of sales desire and techniques. Few tangible results were being recognized from their efforts to gain new accounts or increase sales from present customers.

### Personnel: Poplar Bluff Sales Office

*Jake Jacobs—Head Route Salesman.* Age 58, had been with the company 38 years. Very energetic and conscientious. Required a minimum of supervision but did require occasional counseling from the district management. Noted as a good salesman.

*Tom Green—Route Salesman.* 58 years old and with the company 35 of these. Had no formal sales training but was very alert to duties involving filling orders, maintenance, etc.

### Commission Agents

*Steve Young—Alpine.* 50 years old with eight years as agent. Was at one time a bottled gas salesman for the company. Steve was sized up as a rather retiring individual and, while effective in selling agricultural accounts, was not particularly suited to the growing industrial trend of his area. It was felt that he was making little effort to keep the district office posted on potential business that entered the area.

*John Russo—Mansfield.* Age 59, had been agent for 15 years. Previously worked 15 years for the company. In addition to the low area potential his operation was somewhat sloppily run. John did not seem to be particularly concerned with company welfare. Much of the area was of the same nationality and was extremely clannish. Consequently, there was danger that business could well follow the distributor rather than the company, should he become alienated. The present CA agreement was soon due to expire and regional reports that always preceded renewal of such contracts showed considerable weakness, particularly in the areas of plant maintenance and credit collections.

*Alex Harris—Garden City.* 58 years old, with 16 years as agent. Was head field salesman at the same station before it was converted to an agency. Similar to John Russo, he had greatly tied up the area business in an extremely clannish community. Although he needed considerable supervision the operation had always been independently profitable. Alex had always been very cooperative and receptive to suggestions.

*   *   *   *   *

As implied earlier, supervision of district functions was closely held by Dick Owens. Having grown with most of the local accounts, he seemed to feel that he owed personal attention to them. During one of the visits Dick said to Joe, "I know everything that happens in this district. If I walk into the front office of any of our accounts here in Watertown they know who I am. Knowing as much as I do about the accounts saves a lot of time in working with my sales personnel. Unless a special problem arises, it's very seldom that we have to sit down and plan an approach to a particular customer."

"One thing I've really limited," continued Dick, "is the use of sales meetings for district personnel. If you ask me, they are a pure waste of time; most people form a negative attitude when they are asked to attend these meetings. I see all of my white collar people every day, and believe me, the grapevine takes care of passing on information of interest to the operating personnel."

Apparently Dick was satisfied with the job being done by his sales force, as he spent relatively little time with them observing sales techniques. "If I play nursemaid to these people," he said, "they would never learn to go out on their own. Hell, I'll know anyway when one of them goofs-up."

District sales coverage logically broke down into geographical areas with the Wholesale Salesman and Fuel and Lubricant Engineer providing white-collar support to the entire district. Alpine, Poplar Bluff, Garden City and Mansfield, with their relatively limited number of accounts, posed no real problem of area breakdown. Within the Watertown area, the responsibility of the four route salesmen was originally organized by geographical boundaries. However, local revisions over a period of time had finally resulted in each route salesman serving a certain list of accounts. This occurred as account status changed and Dick found it necessary to add or subtract gallonage as a means of maintaining an equal workload for each salesman. Finally, Jim Black was pulled off regular business and given the responsibility to service contractor accounts only. The net result of the shifting had been a composite of accounts for each salesman which no longer followed the original geographical breakdown. A two-year record by route salesmen of miles run, gallons delivered, number of deliveries, and average gallons delivered is offered in Exhibit 11.

**EXHIBIT 1**

**Tank Truck Performance Analysis**

| 1 | 2 | 3 | 4 | 5 | 6 |
|---|---|---|---|---|---|
| Truck No. | Capa-city | Gals. Delv'd | # of Loads | # of Del'ys | Miles Run |
|  |  |  |  |  |  |
|  |  |  |  |  |  |
|  |  |  |  |  |  |
|  |  |  |  |  |  |
|  |  |  |  |  |  |

| 7 | 8 | 9 | 10 | 11 | 12 |
|---|---|---|---|---|---|
| Loads @ 25/min | Del'ys @ 20/min | Drive @ 20 mph | Total #7, #8 & #9 | Office Plant Solic. Etc. | Total Hours Required |
|  |  |  |  |  |  |
|  |  |  |  |  |  |
|  |  |  |  |  |  |
|  |  |  |  |  |  |
|  |  |  |  |  |  |

The following indicates the source of data entered in Columns 1–2–3–4–5–6 and the basis as well as method of computation of figures entered in Columns 4–7–8–9–10–11:

Column 1 —*Truck Number*
     From Statement of Miles Run by Motor Equipment, D-123.
Column 2 —*Capacity*
     If the exact truck capacity in gallons is not known, average ca-
     pacities can be used, i.e., 750 for T1, 950 for T2, 1,250 for T3
     and 1,650 for T4.
Column 3 —*Gallons Delivered*
     From Statement of Miles Run—D-123.
Column 4 —*Number of Loads*
     Divide gallons delivered (Col. 3) by truck capacity (Col. 2).
Column 5 —*Number of Deliveries*
     From Statement of Miles Run—D-123.
Column 6 —*Miles Run*
     From Statement of Miles Run—D-123.
Column 7 —*Loading*

Multiply Col. 4 by .42 (the fractional hour equivalent of 25 minutes per load). For package trucks, full loads, multiply Col. 4 by 1 hour.

Column 8 —*Delivering*

Divide Col. 5 by 3 (hourly equivalent of 20 minutes per delivery —a liberal average for all types of deliveries).

Column 9 —*Driving*

Divide Col. 6 by 20 (average truck speed under normal operating conditions).

Column 10—*Total of Loading, Delivery and Driving Time.*

Column 11—*Office, Plant, Solicitation, Collection and Miscellaneous*

Multiply Col. 10 by .28 which is the standard percentage of tank truck workload time allowed for these functions. (The office and plant standard allowance to handle daily turn-ins, checking orders, servicing and garaging equipment, etc., is 40 minutes a day. Allowance for solicitation, collection and miscellaneous is 60 minutes per day. This total, plus 20 minutes for personal time, reduces the average available time for delivery operations to 360 minutes. 100 minutes is 28% of 360 minutes.)

## EXHIBIT 2

### Customer Data Sheet—D102

| ASSIGNED TO: | CALLS ASSIGNED | NAME | | | | | |
|---|---|---|---|---|---|---|---|
| | | LOCATION | | | | | |
| SUPPORTED BY: | | HEADQUARTERS | | | | | |
| | | TYPE OF BUSINESS | | | | | |
| | | EQUIP. OPERATED: PASS. CARS ___ | TRUCKS ___ | | TRACTORS ___ | NO. CREDIT CARDS ___ | |
| | | OTHER EQUIP.: | | | | | |

| KEY PERSONNEL—SPECIAL DATA—CONTRACT INFO. — ETC. | ANNUAL AVAILABLE BUSINESS | | | | | |
|---|---|---|---|---|---|---|
| | PRODUCT | STGE. TANKS | TOTAL | SKYLINE | COMPETITIVE | CO. |
| | GASOLINE (Gals.) | | | | | |
| | DIESEL (Gals.) | | | | | |
| | FURNACE (Gals.) | | | | | |
| | STOVE/KERO. (Gals.) | | | | | |
| | AUTO OILS (Gals.) | | | | | |
| | AUTO LUBS./GRS. (Lbs.) | | | | | |
| | INDUSTRIAL OILS (Gals.) | | | | | |
| | INDUSTRIAL GRS. (Lbs.) | | | | | |
| | THNRS./SOLVS. (Gals.) | | | | | |
| | WAXES (Lbs.) | | | | | |
| | OTHER SPECIAL PRODUCTS (Gals.) | | | | | |
| | | | | | | |
| | | | | | | |
| | TOTAL LIGHT PRODUCTS | | | | | |

| CALLS MADE | YEAR | JAN. | FEB. | MAR. | APR. | MAY | JUNE | JULY | AUG. | SEPT. | OCT. | NOV. | DEC. |
|---|---|---|---|---|---|---|---|---|---|---|---|---|---|
| | | | | | | | | | | | | | |
| | | | | | | | | | | | | | |

**EXHIBIT 3**

**Skyline Petroleum Company
Account Change Card—D105**

| Account Change | | | | | |
|---|---|---|---|---|---|

District_____  Office_____  Date_____

Name of Account_____

Type of Business_____

| Product | Annual Require-ments | Volume Gained Lost | Distribution of Requirements after Change | | Compet. Gained from or Lost to |
|---|---|---|---|---|---|
| | | | Skyline | Compet. | |
| Gasoline–gals Motor Aviation | | | | | |
| Diesel fuel–gals | | | | | |
| Furnace oil–gals | | | | | |
| Stove oil–gals | | | | | |
| Kerosene–gals | | | | | |
| Fuel oil–gals | | | | | |
| Auto oils–gals | | | | | |
| Auto grease–lbs | | | | | |
| Ind. oils–gals | | | | | |
| Ind. greases–lbs | | | | | |
| Thinners and Solvents–gals | | | | | |
| Liquified pet. gases–gals | | | | | |
| Other gal or lbs | | | | | |

Reason for Gain or Loss_____

_____

_____

Office Manager_____
Sales Rep _____ District Manager_____
(over)          D-105

Contracts in Effect (if Gained, What Type Signed: If Lost, What Paper in Effect):_____

_____

_____

If Account Lost, What Action Taken to Regain:_____

_____

_____

_____

_____

_____

Should Appreciation Letter Be Sent to Account

Yes ☐   No ☐

Changes in Key Personnel, Subsidiaries, Etc.:_____

_____

_____

_____

_____

_____

_____

**EXHIBIT 4**

**Geography of Watertown Sales District**

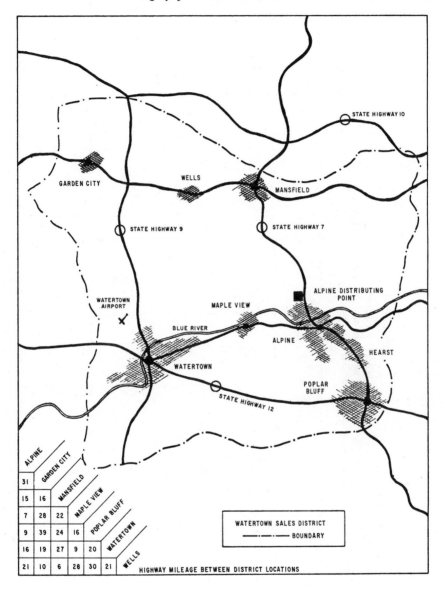

EXHIBIT 5
## Market Position* 1968
### (by number of accounts and per cent of gallonage)

*Watertown District*—(5,000 gal. per year and over)

| Company | Motor Gasoline | | | | Diesel Fuels | | | |
| --- | --- | --- | --- | --- | --- | --- | --- | --- |
| | *C.A & I* | | *Other* | | *C.A & I* | | *Other* | |
| | # Accts. | % of Gallonage | # Accts. | % of Gallonage | # Accts. | % of Gallonage | # Accts. | % of Gallonage |
| Skyline | 244 | 38.3 | 8 | 34.1 | 69 | 30.6 | 2 | 12.3 |
| Company A | 61 | 14.7 | 2 | 11.7 | 18 | 15.3 | 1 | 5.5 |
| Company B | 95 | 25.7 | — | — | 20 | 19.8 | — | — |
| Company C | 86 | 11.3 | 6 | 19.0 | 16 | 5.6 | — | — |
| Company D | 6 | 1.1 | 11 | 25.5 | 5 | 20.1 | 1 | 54.3 |
| Company E | 10 | 2.4 | 2 | 2.3 | 1 | .5 | 1 | 27.9 |
| Other | 55 | 6.5 | 2 | 7.4 | 11 | 8.1 | | |
| Accounts Available | 557 | | 31 | | 140 | | 5 | |
| Total Gallonage | 8,918,800 | | 1,118,400 | | 2,776,700 | | 107,200 | |

*Watertown Office—(5,000 gal. per year and over)*

|  |  |  |  |  |  |  |  |  |
|---|---|---|---|---|---|---|---|---|
| Skyline | 81 | 46.1 | 3 | 24.3 | 27 | 25.7 | — | — |
| Company A | 14 | 15.8 | 1 | 16.0 | 1 | 7.9 | — | — |
| Company B | 56 | 25.3 | — | — | 7 | 20.9 | — | — |
| Company E | 5 | 2.5 | — | — | 1 | 1. | 1 | 34.1 |
| Company C | 19 | 6.4 | 3 | 26.4 | 3 | 4.1 | — | — |
| Company D | 1 | .9 | 6 | 22.6 | 3 | 36.4 | 1 | 65.9 |
| Other | 16 | 3.0 | 1 | 10.7 | 2 | 4.0 | — | — |
| Accounts Available | 192 | | 14 | | 44 | | 2 | |
| Total Gallonage | 5,009,000 | | 409,000 | | 1,515,000 | | 88,000 | |

* Source D-102. Excludes some company's activities where minor sales involved.

## EXHIBIT 5 (Continued)

*Poplar Bluff Office—(5,000 gal. per year and over)*

| | Motor Gasoline | | | | Diesel Fuels | | | |
| | CA & I | | Other | | CA & I | | Other | |
| Company | # Accts. | % of Gallonage | # Accts. | % of Gallonage | # Accts. | % of Gallonage | # Accts. | % of Gallonage |
|---|---|---|---|---|---|---|---|---|
| Skyline | 27 | 25.6 | 1 | 70.8 | 3 | 17.0 | 1 | 100 |
| Company A | 13 | 14.1 | 1 | 26.4 | 5 | 49.3 | — | — |
| Company B | 3 | 8.2 | — | — | — | — | — | — |
| Company F | 4 | 5.4 | — | — | 1 | 19.7 | — | — |
| Company G | 3 | 10.8 | — | — | 1 | 9.8 | — | — |
| Company C | 23 | 28.5 | — | — | 3 | 4.2 | — | — |
| Other | 2 | 7.4 | 1 | 2.8 | — | — | — | — |
| Accounts Available | 75 | | 3 | | 13 | | 1 | |
| Total Gallonage | 1,980,000 | | 212,000 | | 507,000 | | 12,000 | |

Alpine—(1,200 gal. per year and over)

| | | | | | | | | |
|---|---|---|---|---|---|---|---|---|
| Skyline | 34 | 23.0 | 2 | 24.0 | 6 | 48.5 | 1 | 100 |
| Company A | 16 | 13.9 | — | — | 3 | 5.3 | | |
| Company B | 35 | 38.9 | — | — | 13 | 41.3 | | |
| Company C | 31 | 12.9 | 2 | 20.4 | 2 | 3.2 | | |
| Company D | 5 | 2.3 | 5 | 48.5 | 2 | 1.7 | | |
| Other | 18 | 9.0 | 2 | 92.9 | — | — | — | — |
| Accounts Available | 139 | | 11 | | 26 | | 1 | |
| Total Gallonage | 2,391,000 | | 416,000 | | 562,000 | | 13,000 | |

**EXHIBIT 5 (Concluded)**

*Mansfield—(1,200 gal. per year and over)*

| Company | Gasoline | | | | Diesel Fuels | | | |
|---|---|---|---|---|---|---|---|---|
| | CA & I | | Other | | CA & I | | Other | |
| | # Accts. | % of Gallonage | # Accts. | % of Gallonage | # Accts. | % of Gallonage | # Accts. | % of Gallonage |
| Skyline | 49 | 52.8 | — | — | 10 | 62.1 | — | — |
| Company A | 5 | 7.5 | — | — | 5 | 12.2 | — | — |
| Company F | 6 | 10.1 | — | — | 3 | 6.2 | — | — |
| Company C | 10 | 29.6 | 1 | 100 | 7 | 19.5 | — | — |
| Accounts Available | 70 | | 1 | | 25 | | | |
| Total Gallonage | 199,000 | | 4,000 | | 98,000 | | — | |

*Garden City*—(1,200 gal. per year and over)

| | | | | | | | | |
|---|---|---|---|---|---|---|---|---|
| Skyline | 53 | 76.6 | 2 | 100 | 23 | 43.3 | 1 | 100 |
| Company A | 13 | 8.1 | | | 4 | 12.8 | | |
| Company F | 11 | 8.3 | | | 4 | 6.9 | | |
| Company C | 3 | 7.0 | | | 1 | 37.0 | | |
| Accounts Available | 81 | | 2 | | 32 | | 1 | |
| Total Gallonage | 239,800 | | 17,400 | | 94,700 | | 1,200 | |

**EXHIBIT 6**

**Number of Accounts to Which Credit Has Been Extended**

|  | 1968 | 1967 | 1966 | 1965 |
|---|---|---|---|---|
| **District** | | | | |
| 1st Qtr.................... | 701 | 648 | 730 | 677 |
| 2nd Qtr.................... | 706 | 651 | 705 | 685 |
| 3rd Qtr.................... | 721 | 659 | 680 | 685 |
| 4th Qtr.................... | 713 | 676 | 689 | 650 |
| Year Avg................. | 710 | 659 | 701 | 674 |
| **Watertown** | | | | |
| 1st Qtr.................... | 223 | 177 | 188 | 167 |
| 2nd Qtr.................... | 224 | 172 | 184 | 183 |
| 3rd Qtr.................... | 238 | 173 | 174 | 177 |
| 4th Qtr.................... | 234 | 220 | 184 | 163 |
| Year..................... | 230 | 186 | 182 | 172 |
| **Poplar Bluff** | | | | |
| 1st Qtr.................... | 91 | 78 | 88 | 85 |
| 2nd Qtr.................... | 88 | 83 | 81 | 86 |
| 3rd Qtr.................... | 96 | 93 | 89 | 85 |
| 4th Qtr.................... | 93 | 81 | 87 | 79 |
| Year..................... | 92 | 84 | 86 | 84 |
| **Alpine** | | | | |
| 1st Qtr.................... | 123 | 119 | 148 | 121 |
| 2nd Qtr.................... | 131 | 118 | 142 | 129 |
| 3rd Qtr.................... | 132 | 130 | 135 | 129 |
| 4th Qtr.................... | 133 | 121 | 123 | 129 |
| Year..................... | 130 | 122 | 137 | 127 |
| **Mansfield** | | | | |
| 1st Qtr.................... | 93 | 84 | 112 | 104 |
| 2nd Qtr.................... | 96 | 95 | 109 | 104 |
| 3rd Qtr.................... | 94 | 96 | 111 | 104 |
| 4th Qtr.................... | 86 | 89 | 108 | 102 |
| Year..................... | 92 | 91 | 110 | 103 |
| **Garden City** | | | | |
| 1st Qtr.................... | 171 | 190 | 194 | 200 |
| 2nd Qtr.................... | 167 | 182 | 189 | 183 |
| 3rd Qtr.................... | 161 | 167 | 171 | 190 |
| 4th Qtr.................... | 167 | 165 | 187 | 178 |
| Year..................... | 166 | 176 | 185 | 188 |

SOURCE: R 31 (compiled through averaging to obtain data by quarters).

**EXHIBIT 7**

**Sales Results by Product, 1966–1969**
**(gallons)**

|  | 1968 | 1967 | 1966 |
|---|---|---|---|
| **DISTRICT** | | | |
| Motor gasoline | | | |
| Agriculture................. | 413,211 | 410,733 | 423,592 |
| Const. & contr............. | 675,031 | 518,116 | 634,570 |
| Comm. & ind.............. | 2,316,641 | 2,187,287 | 1,973,751 |
| Jobbers.................. | 30,264 | 137,998 | 25,861 |
| Government............... | 429,345 | 146,052 | 179,462 |
| Total................... | 3,864,492 | 3,400,186 | 3,237,236 |
| Auto diesel.................. | 126,705 | 114,517 | 114,100 |
| Truck diesel................. | 695,846* | 1,083,705 | 877,275 |
| Aviation gasoline............. | 18,699,930 | 18,961,370 | 16,483,800 |
| Auto oils.................... | 113,000 | 118,899 | 112,000 |
| Thinners & solvents........... | 2,350,074 | 2,334,249 | 2,561,540 |
| Refined wax................. | 476,344 | 660,778 | 191,297 |
| Total light products........... | 26,326,391 | 26,673,704 | 23,577,248 |
| **WATERTOWN PLANT** | | | |
| Motor gasoline | | | |
| Agriculture................. | 141,119 | 137,365 | 144,307 |
| Const. & contr............. | 304,499 | 287,146 | 292,250 |
| Comm. & ind.............. | 1,876,132 | 1,832,996 | 1,559,580 |
| Jobbers.................. | 11,014† | 125,015† | 12,500 |
| Government............... | 209,300 | 100,105 | 50,674 |
| Total................... | 2,542,064 | 2,482,627 | 2,059,311 |
| Auto diesel.................. | 76,443 | 78,388 | 82,647 |
| Truck diesel................. | 346,360 | 454,469 | 406,284 |
| Auto oils.................... | 52,543 | 54,997 | 50,674 |
| Thinners & solvents........... | 2,046,644 | 2,149,941 | 2,180,938 |
| Refined wax................. | 367,334 | 264,037 | 287,653 |
| Total light products........... | 5,431,388 | 5,484,459 | 5,067,497 |
| **POPLAR BLUFF PLANT** | | | |
| Motor gasoline | | | |
| Agriculture................. | 8,934 | 12,699 | 8,710 |
| Const. & contr............. | 136,126 | 94,674 | 96,852 |
| Comm. & ind.............. | 173,003 | 168,020 | 164,412 |
| Government............... | 115,884 | 34,169 | 36,358 |
| Total................... | 433,947 | 309,562 | 306,332 |
| Truck diesel................. | 77,975‡ | 182,892 | 92,783 |
| Aviation gasoline............. | 137,859 | 117,468 | 100,848 |
| Auto oils.................... | 9,245 | 10,327 | 9,503 |
| Thinners.................... | 48,493 | 62,564 | 81,098 |
| Total light products........... | 707,519 | 682,813 | 590,564 |
| **ALPINE** | | | |
| Motor Gasoline | | | |
| Agriculture................. | 29,842 | 25,315 | 22,358 |
| Constr. & contr............. | 232,033 | 121,384 | 218,095 |
| Comm. & ind.............. | 202,618 | 258,345 | 282,590 |
| Jobbers.................. | 19,250 | 0 | 0 |
| Total................... | 483,743 | 405,044 | 523,043 |

## EXHIBIT 7 (Continued)

|  | 1968 | 1967 | 1966 |
|---|---|---|---|
| Auto diesel................... | 5,740 | 7,644 | 7,534 |
| Truck diesel.................. | 191,378 | 351,600 | 269,199 |
| Aviation gasoline............. | 136,937 | 127,613 | 105,006 |
| Auto oils..................... | 20,856 | 22,447 | 18,142 |
| Thinners & solvents........... | 253,776 | 145,277 | 230,305 |
| Refined wax.................. | 10,010 | 49,737 | 20,013 |
| Total light products........... | 1,102,440 | 1,109,362 | 1,173,242 |

### MANSFIELD

| Motor gasoline | | | |
|---|---|---|---|
| Agriculture................. | 82,455 | 77,448 | 87,824 |
| Constr. & contr............. | 311 | 5,432 | 15,131 |
| Comm. & ind............... | 28,507 | 29,228 | 32,977 |
| Total................... | 111,273 | 112,108 | 135,932 |
| Auto diesel................... | 14,961 | 16,450 | 10,741 |
| Truck diesel.................. | 40,879 | 49,092 | 81,668 |
| Auto oils..................... | 3,122 | 3,220 | 4,720 |
| Bottled gas.................. | 58,968 | 61,969 | 64,831 |
| Total light products........... | 229,203 | 242,839 | 297,892 |

### GARDEN CITY

| Motor Gasoline | | | |
|---|---|---|---|
| Agriculture................. | 150,861 | 142,304 | 148,142 |
| Constr. & contr............. | 1,062 | 0 | 0 |
| Comm. & ind............... | 33,650 | 37,673 | 44,042 |
| Government................ | 13,800 | 2,400 | 2,111 |
| Total................... | 199,373 | 182,377 | 194,295 |
| Auto diesel................... | 21,766 | 3,871 | 3,377 |
| Truck diesel.................. | 39,245 | 45,644 | 51,080 |
| Aviation gasoline............. | 28,640 | 25,844 | 25,413 |
| Auto oils..................... | 4,043 | 4,274 | 4,067 |
| Refined wax.................. | 99,000 | 61,600 | 64,000 |
| Total light products.......... | 392,067 | 323,710 | 342,232 |

### WATERTOWN AIRPORT

| Aviation gasoline............. | 18,396,500 | 18,690,445 | 16,252,433 |
|---|---|---|---|

* Lost (completed) highway contract—nonrecurring business.
† Gained and lost jobber—not under District or Region control.
‡ Loss of large account—moved to other District.
SOURCE: R 30 (Based on 10-month period).

**EXHIBIT 3**

**Expenses Per Gallon Delivered***
**(1967–1968)**

|  |  | 1967 (cents) | 1968 (cents) |
|---|---|---|---|
| Total Sales District. . . . . . . . . . . . . . . . . . . . | 1st Qtr. | 3.34 | 3.06 |
|  | 2nd Qtr. | 3.00 | 2.93 |
|  | 3rd Qtr. | 3.20 | 2.75 |
|  | 4th Qtr. | 3.30 | 2.94 |
|  | YEAR | 3.21 | 2.92 |
| Supervision/Solicitation. . . . . . . . . . . . . . . . | 1st Qtr. | 0.64 | 0.69 |
|  | 2nd Qtr. | 0.57 | 0.58 |
|  | 3rd Qtr. | 0.49 | 0.48 |
|  | 4th Qtr. | 0.56 | 0.57 |
|  | YEAR | 0.56 | 0.57 |
| Plant Cost—Watertown. . . . . . . . . . . . . . . . . | 1st Qtr. | 1.05 | 0.71 |
| Sales Office. . . . . . . . . . . . . . . . . . . . . . . . . | 2nd Qtr. | 0.50 | 0.75 |
|  | 3rd Qtr. | 0.82 | 0.86 |
|  | 4th Qtr. | 0.80 | 0.83 |
|  | YEAR | 0.79 | 0.79 |
| Marketing Delivery Cost—. . . . . . . . . . . . . . | 1st Qtr. | 2.07 | 1.90 |
| Watertown Sales Office. . . . . . . . . . . . . . . | 2nd Qtr. | 1.78 | 1.72 |
|  | 3rd Qtr. | 2.04 | 1.47 |
|  | 4th Qtr. | 1.95 | 1.70 |
|  | YEAR | 1.96 | 1.70 |
| Total Cost—Watertown. . . . . . . . . . . . . . . . | 1st Qtr. | 3.12 | 2.61 |
| Sales Office. . . . . . . . . . . . . . . . . . . . . . . . . | 2nd Qtr. | 2.28 | 2.47 |
|  | 3rd Qtr. | 2.86 | 2.33 |
|  | 4th Qtr. | 2.75 | 2.53 |
|  | YEAR | 2.75 | 2.49 |
| Plant Cost—Poplar Bluff. . . . . . . . . . . . . . . | 1st Qtr. | 0.78 | 0.51 |
| Sales Office. . . . . . . . . . . . . . . . . . . . . . . . . | 2nd Qtr. | 0.76 | 0.27 |
|  | 3rd Qtr. | 0.72 | 0.42 |
|  | 4th Qtr. | 0.77 | 0.40 |
|  | YEAR | 0.76 | 0.40 |
| Marketing Delivery Costs—. . . . . . . . . . . . . | 1st Qtr. | 2.12 | 2.24 |
| Poplar Bluff Sales Office. . . . . . . . . . . . . . | 2nd Qtr. | 2.15 | 2.04 |
|  | 3rd Qtr. | 2.27 | 1.75 |
|  | 4th Qtr. | 2.17 | 2.01 |
|  | YEAR | 2.18 | 2.00 |
| Total Cost—Poplar Bluff. . . . . . . . . . . . . . . | 1st Qtr. | 2.90 | 2.75 |
| Sales Office. . . . . . . . . . . . . . . . . . . . . . . . . | 2nd Qtr. | 2.91 | 2.31 |
|  | 3rd Qtr. | 2.99 | 2.17 |
|  | 4th Qtr. | 2.94 | 2.41 |
|  | YEAR | 2.94 | 2.40 |
| Total Cost—Commission Agents. . . . . . . . . | 1st Qtr. | 1.99 | 1.89 |
|  | 2nd Qtr. | 2.35 | 2.02 |
|  | 3rd Qtr. | 2.35 | 1.89 |
|  | 4th Qtr. | 2.36 | 1.91 |
|  | YEAR | 2.26 | 1.93 |

* Excludes airport gallonage.
SOURCE: R 35.

## EXHIBIT 9
### Commission Agent Operations

|  | 1966 | 1967 | 1968 |
|---|---|---|---|
| | *ALPINE* | | |
| Gross Commissions.... | $24,240 | $23,395 | $25,193 |
| Expenses | | | |
| Salaries............. | $7,621 | $7,986 | $8,274 |
| Gas & oil........... | 1,225 | 1,091 | 1,294 |
| Tires & batteries..... | 195 | 178 | 329 |
| Repairs............. | 923 | 711 | 383 |
| Rental............. | — | — | — |
| Dep............... | 2,136 | 637 | 323 |
| Lic. & tax.......... | 191 | 145 | 195 |
| Ins................ | 723 | 769 | 774 |
| Bus. lic............. | 56 | 130 | 126 |
| Work. comp........ | 103 | 190 | 138 |
| U. C. tax.......... | — | — | — |
| F.O.A.B........... | 201 | 147 | 173 |
| Utilities........... | 137 | 111 | 137 |
| Postage............ | 268 | 301 | 307 |
| Tel. & tel.......... | 572 | 390 | 409 |
| Tool & sup......... | 243 | 164 | 228 |
| Dues & dons........ | 212 | 231 | 194 |
| Adv............... | 196 | — | — |
| Dep. P & T........ | — | — | — |
| Stor. ded........... | — | — | — |
| W/D allow......... | 739 | 13 | — |
| Spec. allow......... | — | — | — |
| Enter.............. | 381 | 548 | 680 |
| Other............. | 64 | 161 | 110 |
| Total Expenses....... | $16,186 | $13,903 | $14,074 |
| Net Commissions..... | 8,054 | 9,492 | 11,119 |

| | Commission Rates | Equipment | Full-Time Employees |
|---|---|---|---|
| Airport & Airline................ | 1.10¢ | 1962 Dodge—710 Gal. | 1 @ $500 per month |
| All Other Resale................. | 1.10¢ | 1961 Ford—12 BBL | |
| Government.................... | .80¢ | 1966 Dodge—Pickup | |
| Other Consumer—gasoline and kerosene.................... | 1.70¢ | | |
| Diesel/Furnace & Auto........... | 1.35¢ + .2¢ = 1.55¢ Gas Oil | | |
| Stove Oil...................... | 1.45¢ + .2¢ = 1.65¢ | | |

**EXHIBIT 9 (Continued)**

**Commission Agent Operations**

|  | 1966 | 1967 | 1968 |
|---|---|---|---|
| | *GARDEN CITY* | | |
| Gross Commissions.... | $15,457 | $14,464 | $18,222 |
| Expenses | | | |
| Salaries............. $3,900 | | $3,900 | $5,608 |
| Gas & oil.......... 650 | | 574 | 721 |
| Tires & batteries..... 394 | | 465 | 356 |
| Repairs............ 1,009 | | 720 | 550 |
| Rental............. — | | — | — |
| Dep............... 1,320 | | 1,320 | 1,416 |
| Lic. & tax.......... 217 | | 175 | 342 |
| Ins................ 712 | | 1,011 | 759 |
| Bus. lic............ — | | — | — |
| Work. comp........ — | | — | — |
| U. C. tax.......... — | | — | — |
| F.O.A.B........... — | | — | — |
| Utilities........... 144 | | 144 | 145 |
| Postage........... 122 | | 121 | 144 |
| Tel. & tel......... 562 | | 561 | 516 |
| Tool & sup........ — | | — | — |
| Dues & dons....... 300 | | 275 | 300 |
| Adv.............. — | | — | — |
| Dep. P & T....... — | | — | 12 |
| Stor. ded.......... 87 | | 115 | 54 |
| W/D allow......... — | | — | — |
| Spec. allow........ — | | — | 47 |
| Enter............. — | | — | — |
| Other............ — | | — | — |
| Total Expenses....... | $ 9,417 | $ 9,381 | $10,970 |
| Net Commissions..... | 6,040 | 5,083 | 7,252 |

| | Commission Rates | Equipment | Full-Time Employees |
|---|---|---|---|
| Airport and airline*.............. | 1.60¢ | 1967 Chev—970 Gal. | 1 @ $457 per month |
| Gov't—All bulk products......... | 1.60¢ | 1956 Chev—930 Gal. | |
| All other resale*................. | 1.60¢ | 1959 Ford—Pickup | |
| Other consumer—gasoline and kerosene*..................... | 2.10¢ | | |
| Diesel/furnace & auto*........... | 1.95¢ | | |
| Stove oil*....................... | 2.05¢ | | |

## EXHIBIT 9 (Concluded)
### Commission Agent Operations

|  | 1966 | 1967 | 1968 |
|---|---|---|---|
| | *MANSFIELD* | | |
| Gross commissions........ | $7,971 | $6,812 | $6,986 |
| Expenses | | | |
| Salaries................ | $1,597 | $1,812 | $1,956 |
| Gas & oil.............. | 690 | 724 | 678 |
| Tires & batteries....... | 506 | 161 | 408 |
| Repairs................ | 1,830 | 280 | 270 |
| Rental................. | — | — | — |
| Dep................... | 564 | 564 | 654 |
| Lic. & tax.............. | 132 | 150 | 138 |
| Ins.................... | 337 | 458 | 162 |
| Bus. lic................ | 10 | — | — |
| Work. comp........... | — | — | — |
| U. C. tax.............. | — | — | — |
| F.O.A.B.............. | — | — | — |
| Utilities.............. | 54 | 54 | 52 |
| Postage............... | 50 | 38 | 43 |
| Tel. & tel............. | 118 | 108 | 131 |
| Tool & sup............ | 73 | 53 | 29 |
| Dues & dons........... | 47 | 42 | 36 |
| Adv................... | 27 | — | — |
| Dep. P & T............ | — | — | — |
| Stor. ded.............. | 22 | 12 | 19 |
| W/D allow............ | — | — | — |
| Spec. allow............ | — | — | — |
| Enter................. | 343 | 327 | 387 |
| Other................. | 114 | 178 | 9 |
| Total Expenses.......... | $6,514 | $4,961 | $4,972 |
| Net Commissions........ | 1,457 | 1,851 | 2,014 |

|  | Commission Rates† | Equipment | Full-Time Employees |
|---|---|---|---|
| All other resale.................. | 1.40¢ | 1959 Chev—760 Gal. | 1 @ $163 per month |
| Consumer—all gasoline and | | | |
| kerosene...................... | 2.10¢ | 1958 Ford—Stake | |
| Diesel/furnace & auto............. | 1.95¢ | 1962 De Soto—Sedan | |
| Stove oil........................ | 2.05¢ | # Pd. to Pete Russo, | |
| | | John's son | |

\* Plus .50¢ TSC (Temporary Supplemental Commission)
† Workload shows that TSC's not warranted.

**EXHIBIT 10**

**Monthly Statements for Mansfield**

### JUNE—68

| | | | |
|---|---|---|---|
| Gross Commissions...................... | | | 607.35 |
| Expenses.............................. | | | |
| Wages............................. | | 163.13 | |
| General | | | |
| Gas and oil........................ | 57.03 | | |
| Tire and battery.................... | 53.48 | | |
| Repairs........................... | 11.53 | | |
| Depreciation....................... | 57.00 | | |
| Licenses..   ................ | 2.40 | | |
| Insurance  ...................... | 15.64 | | |
| Utilities.......................... | 13.85 | | |
| Miscellaneous..................... | 7.89 | | |
| Club dues......................... | 2.50 | | |
| Advertising and entertainment.......... | 22.20 | | |
| Total Expenses................. | | 243.52 | 406.65 |
| Total Net Commissions.................. | | | 200.70 |

### JULY—68

| | | | |
|---|---|---|---|
| Gross Commissions...................... | | | 591.49 |
| Expenses | | | |
| Wages............................. | | 163.13 | |
| General | | | |
| Gas and oil........................ | 45.47 | | |
| Tire and battery.................... | 156.06 | | |
| Repairs........................... | 7.94 | | |
| Depreciation....................... | 57.00 | | |
| Licenses.......................... | 2.36 | | |
| Insurance......................... | 15.64 | | |
| Utilities.......................... | 24.98 | | |
| Club dues......................... | 2.50 | | |
| Advertising and entertainment......... | 19.90 | | |
| Total Expenses................. | | 331.85 | 494.98 |
| Total Net Commissions.................. | | | 96.51 |

**EXHIBIT 10 (Continued)**

AUGUST—68

| | | |
|---|---|---|
| Gross Commissions...................... | | 608.06 |
| Expenses | | |
| Wages.............................. | 163.13 | |
| General | | |
| Gas and oil......................... 75.71 | | |
| Repairs............................ 52.95 | | |
| Depreciation....................... 57.00 | | |
| Licenses........................... 2.61 | | |
| Insurance.......................... 15.64 | | |
| Utilities........................... 18.82 | | |
| Club dues......................... 2.50 | | |
| Advertising and entertainment......... 32.70 | | |
| Total Expenses.................. | 257.93 | 421.06 |
| Total Net Commissions................... | | 187.00 |

SEPTEMBER—68

| | | |
|---|---|---|
| Gross Commissions..................... | | 533.65 |
| Expenses | | |
| Wages.............................. | 163.13 | |
| General | | |
| Gas and oil......................... 61.76 | | |
| Repairs............................ 34.06 | | |
| Depreciation....................... 57.00 | | |
| Licenses........................... 2.22 | | |
| Insurance.......................... 15.64 | | |
| Utilities........................... 25.27 | | |
| Club dues......................... 2.50 | | |
| Advertising and entertainment.......... 20.95 | | |
| Total Expenses.................. | 219.40 | 382.53 |
| Total Net Commissions................... | | 151.12 |

**EXHIBIT 11**

**Route Salesman Performance**
**(1967–1968)**

| Route Salesman | Miles Run | | Light Products Delivered (Gal.) | | Number of Deliveries | | Average Gal./Del. | |
|---|---|---|---|---|---|---|---|---|
| | 1967 | 1968 | 1967 | 1968 | 1967 | 1968 | 1967 | 1968 |
| *Jim Black—T2—Capacity 850* | | | | | | | | |
| 1st Qtr. | 3,146 | 2,547 | 78,697 | 99,554 | 217 | 318 | 312 | 313 |
| 2nd Qtr. | 3,473 | 5,044 | 89,256 | 124,525 | 258 | 440 | 344 | 287 |
| 3rd Qtr. | 2,899 | 3,404 | 58,282 | 119,132 | 167 | 330 | 304 | 358 |
| 4th Qtr. | 3,133 | 3,191 | 62,878 | 118,005 | 209 | 410 | 292 | 282 |
| Year. | 12,651 | 14,186 | 289,113 | 461,216 | 851 | 1,498 | 313 | 310 |
| *Bill Adams—T2—Capacity 977* | | | | | | | | |
| 1st Qtr. | 2,719 | 1,963 | 114,693 | 141,621 | 406 | 431 | 281 | 328 |
| 2nd Qtr. | 2,664 | 2,113 | 127,813 | 157,392 | 457 | 484 | 280 | 325 |
| 3rd Qtr. | 2,687 | 2,182 | 127,633 | 176,900 | 451 | 629 | 283 | 283 |
| 4th Qtr. | 2,369 | 2,023 | 120,889 | 177,000 | 452 | 590 | 252 | 300 |
| Year. | 10,439 | 8,281 | 491,028 | 652,913 | 1,766 | 2,134 | 274 | 313 |
| *Ike Poole—T2—Capacity 814* | | | | | | | | |
| 1st Qtr. | 3,225 | 3,293 | 168,433 | 128,564 | 487 | 435 | 342 | 296 |
| 2nd Qtr. | 2,813 | 3,585 | 162,500 | 157,624 | 503 | 509 | 329 | 310 |
| 3rd Qtr. | 3,317 | 3,490 | 156,824 | 178,958 | 487 | 522 | 322 | 348 |
| 4th Qtr. | 3,050 | 3,030 | 133,122 | 134,368 | 383 | 442 | 366 | 299 |
| Year. | 12,405 | 13,398 | 620,879 | 599,514 | 1,860 | 1,908 | 340 | 313 |
| *Nick Peters—T3—Capacity 1130* | | | | | | | | |
| 1st Qtr. | 2,360 | 3,457 | 157,020 | 126,627 | 449 | 408 | 351 | 288 |
| 2nd Qtr. | 1,970 | 3,938 | 166,070 | 158,651 | 435 | 430 | 375 | 369 |
| 3rd Qtr. | 2,178 | 3,688 | 162,693 | 170,154 | 452 | 520 | 339 | 329 |
| 4th Qtr. | 3,033 | 4,462 | 152,109 | 157,885 | 474 | 468 | 299 | 358 |
| Year. | 9,541 | 15,545 | 637,892 | 613,317 | 1,810 | 1,826 | 341 | 336 |
| Composite. | 45,036 | 51,410 | 2,038,912 | 2,326,960 | 6,287 | 7,366 | 317 | 318 |

SOURCE: D-123.

# Four Generations

Four Generations, a firm dedicated to producing quality wooden toys and games that would last "four generations," took form in a forest ranger's cabin at Big Sur, California, in 1966. The founding partners, Dick Benton and Harry Batlan, designed and produced their earliest products on a part-time basis. In 1968 the firm was relocated in Sebastopol, among the rolling hills and vineyards of the wine country north of San Francisco. Throughout 1968 and 1969 a number of innovative designs were added to the product line. In addition, stemming from the unorthodox outlook of its owners, an unusual system of employer-employee relations evolved. Sales had doubled each year since 1968, and over time the product mix had shifted away from toys and into adult games; yet Four Generations had never earned a profit. Sales for 1972 were projected to exceed $300,000. While management expected to break even at this level, further moves to achieve a more economical production volume and broaden the product mix were being contemplated.

## EVOLUTION OF THE COMPANY

The majority owner and president of the firm, Dick Benton, graduated from the University of Colorado in civil engineering. His work experience included a stint with Caterpillar Tractor's export sales division, several years as a field engineer for Morrison-Knudsen Construction, and three years as a special agent for the FBI. A position in engineering marketing attracted him to Inland Steel where he worked for ten years. His final assignment for that firm brought him to California. "After we moved to California," recalls Benton, "I became interested in efforts to design a construction system that would systemize building. My interest in this problem culminated in a patented design of a flexible steel system—

This case was prepared by Associate Professor Richard T. Johnson and Karen H. Campbell. Reprinted from *Stanford Business Cases 1972* with the permission of the publisher, Graduate School of Business, Stanford University. Copyright © 1972 by the Board of Trustees of the Leland Stanford Junior University.

much like an erector set—that was appropriate for schools and other similar institutional construction. While still working at Inland Steel, I founded Design Systems. Stanford University was one of our first contracts; we built the Student Credit Union."

At Inland Steel, Benton relaxed some of the strict regulations. He gave employees responsibility for their jobs and did not require them to punch in and out on the time clock. As a result morale improved. Employees took shorter coffee breaks, absenteeism decreased, and productivity went up.

During this same period I met a forest ranger one weekend at Big Sur. He had four children and I had four children, and we became friends. He was educated as an artist, and for one reason or another we both shared an interest in being in business for ourselves. Somehow, our discussion turned to children's toys, and Harry had dreams of interesting toy trucks that he thought he could make and sell. So we decided to make children's playthings—toys that would last, that were well put together and geometrically "right," designed so a child could play with them by himself and learn about himself and his environment.

Between us we had $6,000 in savings; we bought some used equipment and materials and began making toys in Harry's cabin at Big Sur and selling them at the shop of Nepenthe Restaurant on Highway 1. It was such a shoestring operation that we both kept our regular jobs and did our manufacturing on weekends.

It didn't take long to see that $6,000 wasn't enough to start a company— we needed volume, and volume required dollars to finance inventory and equipment; but getting those dollars meant that neither of us could quit our jobs. However, about this time Design Systems began to bear fruit and did sufficiently well that by the end of the year I was able to sell my share for $25,000. Thus, by the end of 1967, I really had enough money to make a full-time commitment. Harry had been transferred to Fort Ross so we started looking for a location that was near San Francisco and a major freeway and yet enough in the country to be "real California" . . . like it was when Steinbeck wrote about it. After a while we gave up on rentals . . . industrial sites are so ugly and commonplace. So we ended up buying a sort of small farm with a barn-like shed. In retrospect, it is probably unwise for a starting company to buy anything . . . you don't know what you'll need or how fast you'll grow. But having our own place probably helped us in some ways because it enabled us to do our thing in our own way . . . to come up with a lot of ideas we couldn't have used if we had taken a rented space.

You know there are a lot of things that just happen to you in business . . . it's not always sifting among alternatives and picking the best move. It's the problem of crisis response . . . of selecting among too few alternatives . . . of being constrained by time and space, and money running out. And once you've built an organization of people, your maneuvering room gets even more limited.

About this time Harry dropped out. He's really a philosophical guy. As matters of money and management began to inject themselves into the venture, he had to excuse himself. Basically, he was unwilling to quit his job with the Forest Service and make the concessions that being in business requires. But with Harry gone, it sure got lonely in that shed . . . me, a few machines . . . and a stack of lumber. Then one day Michael Gonzalez walked down the driveway and asked if he could help. I said I'd split my salary with him if he'd join me. He did. He's had a tremendous influence on all our products and policies ever since.

Throughout 1968 Michael and I developed a whole batch of toys (Exhibit 1). We lived there, sacking out in sleeping bags, cooking on the pot-bellied stove, working all day in the factory and talking at night about the future. One of the first things Michael asked when he started was about working hours. All I could say was "Let's get the job done." That basic approach to things became our operating philosophy. Why should there be double standards between employer and employee? So, as we began to grow and hire other people, they just moved in with us. At one time we had as many as six people living there. Mike and I had worked in factories ourselves; he had felt the boredom of working on one machine all day. We knew that accident rates and low efficiencies were all related to whether a person felt involved with the company he was working for and whether or not he had a way of expressing himself.

We didn't make any money in 1968; in 1969 our sales were $20,000, and we still lost several thousand dollars. At times I just didn't see how we could make it. I tried everything I could think of to make the company work . . . to make people more productive . . . to make it happy, safe, pleasant, and also successful. We paid people when we could . . . and, if we couldn't pay them, they moved in and we paid for their food. It's corny, but I think we evolved a kind of "do unto others" philosophy. That's how our various payments systems evolved. At first we paid people by the hour. But on some routine jobs people preferred to have a *quota* so they could work like hell and go home. We'd all vote to set the quota based on our production requirements. Then if a guy came in at 7:00 A.M., and left at 12:30, it was better for him and fine for us. Of course, most people can't work like that every day . . . and, besides, it gets boring. So that's where our system of job rotation came from—letting employees pick the machine they wanted to work on each day—depending upon how they felt—and rotating into different jobs throughout the day to keep them alive and creative. We developed other payment systems, too . . . a *piece rate* (like one cent per cut on the table saw), and a *contract* system so that employees could bid on one whole job and perform that job over a week or two in any manner they wanted. These four payment systems enabled our employees not only to choose what they wanted to do each day but how they wanted to be paid for it. It also contributed to a lot of innovation in the production process. At first employees feared we'd take advantage of them if they found a way to improve productivity. Our solution was to vote the inventor a higher rate of pay depending upon his contributions.

Our payment system gives us a lot of flexibility. For example, in those first years we'd have no orders and then suddenly an order for 100 units . . . due *yesterday!* We were always building up our work force and then collapsing it back like an accordian; you couldn't afford to hang on to ten or twelve employees, but you hated to lose depth by cutting back to only one or two.

So we started looking for odd jobs to keep the factory busy. We got into the business of making trophy plaques and other special order items in wood; we'd underbid and bank on our ingenuity to improve efficiency. Our contract payment system enabled us to be a broker for our employees' labor. They bid on the job to us; we bid on it to the customer.

Presently, most of the people have elected the hourly rate. They say it was too nerve-wracking to have their earnings tied to production . . . they wanted to know what next week's pay would be regardless of how they felt or how fast they worked. Some thought the quota system was too demanding and too competitive. The speedy employees would start at 7:00 A.M., go straight through with no breaks, and leave at noon. Others, who maybe lacked the ability to work like that, had a slight uneasiness about it. Still, we are way ahead of competition in terms of productivity. Our cost savings are not very apparent because we're always running out of work or having to design a new jig or interrupt the production process for a crisis order. But there's one unionized woodshop nearby, and I'm told their contract specifies an operator limit of 800 cuts on the rip saw per day. We get 2,000 cuts per day on ours without straining. Actually unions periodically come and talk about organizing the factory. The workers listen but reject unionization because they feel they have better conditions, wages, and benefits now than they would with the union.

The key to our production process is Michael. He and our mechanic, Jeff, have made most of the big production innovations. Michael keeps us all together. . . . He's part school teacher, part fire fighter, part therapist. He's only got an elementary school education, but he's a genius. We've never had a conflict. I've never given him a command . . . we just understand each other.

## GROWTH AND THE PRODUCT LINE

Throughout 1968 and 1969 the Four Generations product line grew rapidly. A large proportion of the product designs were contributed by Dick Benton and plant foreman Michael Gonzalez. In addition, the firm's unusual organization and style of management enabled and encouraged employees to participate in the design process. The factory was open after hours and on weekends for employee use; scrap lumber was made available free of charge. A number of important ideas and projects have resulted from work force involvement with the factory. Employees have created new products and innovative production methods and have built facilities such as a sauna and shower. At the end of 1969 there were 32 items in the product line, ranging from wheeled toys to blocks, easels, toy boats, and geometric puzzles. Every item was made of wood and offered in seven different finishes. Samples of the product line are shown in Exhibit 1.

We did nearly all our $20,000 in sales in 1969 in the last four months. Michael and I were really deluged. It was just about impossible to handle production and selling too. That's why when Bill Moore approached me and expressed an interest in selling for us, I almost hugged him. I had to play a little coy since he was interested in participating in the ownership as well as helping us sell. But I felt like giving him half the firm in return for a little assistance. Bill joined us early in 1970.

As soon as Bill arrived, he started to push the toys. We made him a wooden display box in the plant, loaded up with toys, and he headed off to the toy shows in Chicago and New York. Lots of stores—big stores like Macy's and Bloomingdale's and Marshall Field's—made good opening orders. But it never developed into big volume business. We had also gone after kindergartens and nursery schools, but that's a very limited market too. The problem is that parents buy toys as a result of a verbal exchange with the child. The child decides what he wants as a result of what his peers have or what he sees on Captain Kangaroo. So the parent as an act of self-protection buys the item— even if he knows he'll be lucky to get it home before it breaks. Of course, this is not true for the infant market. In that segment what the parent buys is sort of a function of "keeping up with the Joneses." For a while, Creative Play-things was "in" . . . and that helped our business. But the problem remained that our product line looked like a kindergarten. We opened up a store in Ghirardelli Square during Christmas in 1969, and people came in not to buy things but to *leave their children.* They thought our store was a day care facility provided by the Ghirardelli merchants!

Michael, in addition to developing toys, had come up with some in-genious adult games. As always, we were looking for something to offset the seasonality of production during the post-Christmas slump, so Bill took four of our best games to Skor-Mor—one of the largest adult game manufacturers. They were enthusiastic but they wanted an exclusive. As the negotiations proceeded, they kept lowering the price. We were faced with a tough choice and finally decided to build up a network of jobbers and go it on our own. By the close of 1970 our sales had reached $97,000 . . . and 80 percent of it was in games. We discovered we had stumbled into a new field; adult games put us in a brand new ball game.

As 1970 unfolded, we planned to have two separate lines—toys and adult games. But by the end of that year, I decided . . . or maybe the group de-cided . . . not to make toys any more. It was an agonizing decision. But we had lost $20,000 in 1970, and you come to a point where if you want to survive you've got to do something. By all rights the company should have been dead a long time ago. Until you reach a certain volume, there is no economical way to buy raw materials, you can't buy efficient equipment or manage time and production effectively. It's all piecemeal, and it's hell on our labor force. You get a guy for a rush job, then you find out he's skilled so you try to keep him, and when production slackens overhead goes up; or you let him go and then encounter training and recruiting delays during the next crisis.

I wanted a line that would really grow to a company. I could have made it as a mom and pop operation with one or two items, but I didn't want to do it that way. I don't want a mommy-daddy shop. I want a business and an or-ganization with secretaries, a marketing manager, a treasurer . . . with literature and catalogs.

All during 1969 we were getting orders for one tractor, one set of blocks, two rattles; in the factory it was sort of "you do this, I'll do that." What you need is a line where people say "I'll take 100 of these." Then you can buy the automated equipment. We were finally able to purchase an automatic sander this year. I designed it from scratch, and it cost $25,000. But at peak capacity of 5,000 units per day it replaces ten people.

I think the climate we've created here is important. We're probably the most innovative company in adult games in the United States. Michael has invented most of the games that we have developed internally. More recently we have been approached by game designers from the outside who have heard of our reputation. We invite them out here, and invariably they like the place. They tour the plant and sense the atmosphere and feel comfortable. What a designer wants is a place that will give his idea love and care. If they go to Parker Brothers or Skor-Mor, they get to sit and tremble in a waiting room until some executive summons them to present their prototype. Here they feel safe.

## MARKETING

Marketing manager Bill Moore joined Four Generations in early 1970. As one of three major stockholders in the firm he has watched the sales grow from $20,000 in 1969 to $97,000 in 1970, to $170,000 in 1971, and to an estimated $300,000 in 1972.

"I got involved right after the 1969 season," says Moore. "At that time Dick had been selling strictly to preschool education programs."

The real problem was to transform those toys to a volume product once the preschool market was too limited . . . we needed retail sales. I decided to do a market survey. We were making toys of birch . . . but for the retail market this type of toy didn't really have a lot of appeal. We realized we couldn't make it out of plastic and compete with Mattel. It was clear that our target was the educated parent. So we decided to try to make a toy that would be useful to the child but appeal to the adult. We started making toys out of black walnut and other more decorative woods. We geared our selling to better stores and tried to have our products displayed so they would catch the adult's eye and appeal to the parent who wanted to give his child a fine, lasting thing of beauty. We went to the toy shows and had reasonable success—we got a few in Marshall Field's catalog, several of the big national chains picked them up, and we sold a number to specialty shops.

Throughout this period we hadn't done much with the games Michael had invented. I decided to see if I could peddle a few. One of the first of the big game outfits I showed it to—Skor-Mor—offered to buy 10,000 each of three of our games. They wanted an exclusive and their margins were tight. They would be putting their name on it—not ours. So after a lot of sweating we decided to turn them down and try it on our own. That was a big decision— to turn down an order for 30,000 games. Instead, we went out to build a network of 18 manufacturers representatives. Fortunately, our product was good, and by the fall of 1970 we were deluged with orders of games. As the games began to take off, several things became clear. First, they were twice as profitable as toys. Secondly, they were far easier for us to produce. Toys were slow to build and handle, and they took up so much more space. In a small factory like this big toys with lots of parts and assembly operations really tie everything up. We can manufacture a lot more games under the same roof.

In 1971 we decided to come out with some new games. Once again virtually all of them were invented by Michael Gonzalez . . . games like Odd Ball, Revolutions, and Sculpture Puzzle. (See Exhibit 3.) They were good sellers, but with hindsight I think we're encountering many of the same problems with them that we had with toys. They require multiple operations and lots of handwork. Next year we'll be coming out with games with some wood and some plastic parts.

We made tremendous inroads in 1971 with our adult games—we sold them to Sears, Bloomingdale's, Lord & Taylor, Joseph Magnin, Gimbal's, and elsewhere. We did this despite the important disadvantage of being a small firm with a limited line. Skor-Mor or Parker Brothers can walk into a store and offer them a whole game *system*. If the buyer accepts the package, he usually doesn't have much left for extra items like ours.

At the end of the year we took a look and saw that games were just about as seasonal as toys. Our games are good, but they're sold primarily at Christmas time—bought more as gifts than by the end user himself. We also found a market among big firms that would special order our games for Christmas giveaways. This was good business, but it didn't help the seasonal problem.

For a company to grow in a seasonal business you need a lot of cash in a big chunk, and you don't get it back until much later. You need the cash to build up inventories for the Christmas season. But ours isn't exactly the kind of inventory you can borrow a lot of money on. . . . A banker looks at us and says, "Why do I want to own 10,000 Magic Marbles?" It's not the same as 10,000 gallons of gasoline or similar commodities that are easy to liquidate.

We tried to keep our good games but wanted to add something else to level production. One partial solution was to add a line of classic games in 1971. Presently, we are making poker chips, cribbage boards, and a domino set in a wooden box. These products account for nearly half our sales, and we plan to introduce chess sets in 1973. We're also making cutting boards and spice racks. We sell our spice racks as an exclusive to Spice Islands. At one point we got into the trophy thing, but it didn't fit our factory. Trophies come in jillions of sizes and shapes, they are ordered in small quantities and with lots of specials . . . and invariably there is an impossible deadline. We found that they had an insidious way of altering our whole production process. We've discontinued them.

Over time I guess we have evolved a product philosophy. We are offered lots of things, and we try to select those things which fit our style. Basically, we market products that hit the top of the middle price range; we design our products to be attractive and nicely done . . . but at a good volume range. We'd make a $30 chess set but not a $100 one; on the other hand, we wouldn't make a $10 chess set either.

One real nightmare for us has been costing. Take the Euclidian Puzzle— it's a $20.00 thing, except that our costing wasn't too good, and it sold like hot cakes for $5.00 retail. Our rule of thumb around here—if we can figure out what an item costs—is to sell it at two times its variable cost. I think these costing problems are some of the reason why we still lost $40,000 in 1971 despite the fact that our sales doubled to $170,000. Another problem is that you need a large revenue to cover overhead—you need people like Dick and me and Mike and Jeff to run the operation, but it takes a lot of sales to cover it.

Our sales projections as a whole have been quite accurate. The aggregate demand projections are right, but projections for individual products are all wrong. Here we are at the end of 1972, and we have stocked out on several items—but we have 5,000 of one game I have no idea what to do with.

Reflecting on the overall operation, marketing manager Bill Moore made the following comments:

Dick and I handle the external affairs of this company. On the manufacturing side things are done in a way so that our employees can make a statement. It makes sense to try to run a factory where employees get a feeling of being more than just a number. If someone asks me what I do, I tell them I work for a company which manufactures games and puzzles. I really don't get into the way we operate. Our employees are free, creative-type people who are in an environment that achieves higher rates of production than in a typical factory. They are more willing to change jobs as our production needs change and to get behind things. Everything gets done just like in any factory, but we don't make one guy work one machine for a year. But management's job is to make a product—not to create a happening.

## RECENT PRODUCT IDEAS

One interesting development in 1972 appeared to result from Four Generations' expanding reputation as an innovator in adult games. Game designers began to approach the firm with various ideas. One well-known designer presented five new games, two of which were added to the product line. Both of these games offered the potential of high-volume sales but were prohibitively expensive if totally made of wood. As a result, wood and plastic combinations were developed—a first for Four Generations. Even more recently the firm had been approached by an inventor in Oregon whose mysterious "perpetually spinning top" (see Exhibit 4) captured the imagination of management. This item, made with no wooden parts, was to be manufactured entirely outside Four Generations' premises. Four Generations had contributed the product's name and packaging and had entered into a licensing agreement to distribute the product for the inventor. Originally, the product's name was to have been "Black Magic." But just before the promotional material was sent to press, a member of the Four Generations work force entered the office, picked up the new product, and dubbed it "Top Secret."

## COMPETITION

The adult puzzle game market was highly fragmented and comprised of many small firms—most of them privately held. Skor-Mor, one of the larger firms in this segment, had sales in excess of $2 million in 1972. The total market was estimated to be about $50 million. No published market projections were available; however, major competitors expected continued rapid expansion.

Skor-Mor contracted out production of its product line. The company's 1972 catalog was a 5 × 8 inch brochure featuring descriptions and color photographs of about 35 puzzle games, 15 desk-top accessories, 11 boxed games, and numerous novelty items. The catalog was used in department store advertising. Skor-Mor would supply its brochures (with the store's name on the cover) for inclusion with the store's other mailings—if the store would place a minimum order. Thus Skor-Mor created a competitive advantage in getting shelf and display space.

## FINANCE

"I've never been sure exactly how much money I've put into the company," said President Benton. "It's probably around $60,000. I sold my house, my car, my stocks, my boat—everything I owned plus all the earnings from Design Systems."

But even that wasn't enough. In 1969 we went for three or four months with no income. We had to raise money so I went to friends and raised $1,000 here, another $5,000 there . . . it's all on a little list somewhere. Someday they'll be stockholders.

When Bill Moore came on board, he invested in the firm. All in all by early 1970 we had raised an additional $70,000. Our biggest problem is that 80 percent of our sales occur in the last four months of the year. It's hard to borrow on our inventory . . . and besides, I've never enjoyed doing business with banks. They want a lot of financial information. Financial statements are just not informative.

Under our circumstances we've got to enter the market gradually. You need time and money to build up big inventories, and we certainly lack the latter. I think we're also afraid to have high hopes. Top Secret could be a big seller this season, but you can't really intelligently plan for a bonanza. And for too many years we've had too much capacity, too many items, so it wouldn't bother me to have $100,000 in unfilled orders.

Maybe some of our financial problems will be ironed out now that John Kellog has come on board as our treasurer and production control man. John became an investor in 1971 and also wanted to be involved in management. With his investment and outside help we raised another $70,000. Altogether now, we probably have around $200,000 in the firm. John also helped us borrow $75,000 so we could build up a little pre-Christmas inventory. The trouble still remains, however: our games sell about 8,000 units per year and we need a volume of 30,000 to 40,000 per year to really take advantage of volume. With automatic production equipment we could make 8,000 units in six to eight days—but what's the sense of buying automatic equipment for those kind of runs—and besides, you don't dare even run off 8,000 because you're never sure you'll sell them. And on top of that you can't afford to put all the capital into one big pile of boxes . . . so instead you make 2,000 units which is uneconomical; you can't spread the set-up cost with small batches, and you have to use unsophisticated equipment which takes twice as long to do the job.

Perhaps we will find the volume somewhere. We expect 50 percent of our sales this year to come from first-time products—like Top Secret, Impasse, and Tau. But because they are new, all the set-ups will be firsts—and that means money. It's a real problem for us . . . generating the cash to build inventories. Maybe Top Secret will do it. But most of the other nonseasonal stuff just hasn't made it. Take the chopping boards—a great idea, but they require a whole different distribution network. They're gifts—not games. They just haven't worked for us.

## PRODUCTION

In 1971 John Kellog, with a master's degree in history and experience as office manager of a small midwestern printing firm, joined the management team of Four Generations. As part of a package he took a stock option, lent the firm $50,000, and assumed the responsibilities of production control and bookkeeping:

It's hell just keeping the plant going. If I had known more about manufacturing, I certainly would have thought twice. There's always a crisis. In September as we were building up for the Christmas rush, we had no increase in productivity but a 40% increase in labor. What had happened is that we added people to work on the last of the trophy contracts, and there was quite a bit of down time.

We take a month-by-month look at our percent labor costs. Some months it's good and some months it's terrible. It's very hard for us to get cost figures in the plant. We've been very reluctant to ask people to make out detailed time cards. But last month I finally asked one of the secretaries to do it. She asks people how many units they produced and keeps her eye on her watch. We can't tell yet how the employees are taking it; those who resent it she just leaves alone. If we can get some cost figures, I think we can drop some products. Sculpture Puzzle is a likely candidate.

October has been a great month . . . almost too good to be true. A partial reason is that we're making cribbage boards and poker chip holders, and both items lend themselves to smooth production. One requires the saw and gang drill, the other uses the drill press and the router. Between the two we make good use of the whole shop. I still think it will take sales in excess of $500,000 to get the volumes we need. It's tough competition in the mass production business, and over time we are going to need steadier production and mass production equipment to keep up.

The big dividend of this labor force is its flexibility. These people can really adjust to changes in mid-stream. Last year we had a fire which destroyed the old plant. Our employees helped us find a new location, pitched in, and moved the machines to the new site. We were back in production in four days. We have virtually no absenteeism. There is more turnover than we'd like, but most of it is management-caused. People want to stay, but we can't keep production steady. Over time, I think we're getting more employee specialization by department. We're also getting into plastics—but all that work is done by outside contractors.

## THE FUTURE

Despite prospects of further change management was looking forward to significant sales growth in 1973. The introduction of traditional games such as cribbage offers a hedge against seasonality and these products are seen as within Four Generations' established market segment. The new additions among the innovative games (Tau, Impasse, Top Secret) were all projected to have considerable growth potential.

"Planning is almost impossible in this business," said president Benton. "I guess I don't live too much in the future because I like the 'now' too much. It's too unpredictable a business to think much about projections . . . and I know from history that we can overcome any obstacle. It just depends upon our ability to expend energy and effort. Maybe someday I'll be interested in becoming a publicly held firm. But maybe that will have to wait until I get bored with what I'm doing now."

Bill Moore felt that the company faced a number of critical marketing decisions in the years ahead. He was not at all certain that the company had settled upon the right product line. There were some people like Michael Gonzalez who felt strongly that the company should try to market toys again. They argue that making toys was more fun and rewarding than making games and that the company had learned how to design and to produce them better over the past couple of years.

Wooden toys of the type previously produced by Four Generations were thought to be similar—from a marketing point-of-view—to the educational toy segment of the toy industry. This segment was thought to account for some 10 percent of the toy industry's 1.3 billion annual sales volume. Overall annual growth in recent years was between 8 percent and 12 percent, and most industry analysts were optimistic about the future.

The educational toy segment of the market had fewer seasonal sales than did the rest of the industry which sold some 75 percent of its output during the Christmas season. Further, it was thought that people tended to shop for specific types of educational toys, whereas the greater share of most other toys was bought on impulse.

About 40 companies made educational toys, but only a few concentrated on wooden toys. Playskool was a well-known brand in the field which had enjoyed considerable success over the years by concentrating on this segment of the industry. Its line consisted mainly of wooden items such as pull toys, push toys, blocks, coordination toys, construction toys, puzzle plaques, and pounding toys. This company priced its line somewhat higher than did the remainder of the industry.

If the company decided to reenter the preschool educational toy market, it would have to give serious thought to how to establish a favorable image. A variety of magazines were available which specialized in editorial content for parents. In addition, package inserts featuring the entire line could be used. Direct mail to school officials and teachers, plus booths at school conventions, were other possibilities. A reasonable promotion program using such media could, in Bill Moore's opinion, be mounted for $50,000. "Of course," he noted, "we would start much smaller probably by attending some school conventions and placing one or two ads in a prominent home magazine. We could get by with about $25,000 the first year."

Many toy wholesalers used a catalog which they offered literally without charge to retailers for mailing to their customers. These catalogs were paid for by the toy manufacturers on a co-op basis. Large department stores followed much the same practice. Average costs were about 5 percent to retailers and 2½ percent to the wholesalers; i.e., the toy manufacturers gave a co-op advertising allocation of 5 percent of sales to a particular store. Mr. Moore thought that such catalogs were of particular value to a company such as Four Generations.

The distribution posed yet another problem. Large stores had to be sold direct. They often made their decisions on the basis of displays at the larger toy shows. Because the company's line of preschool educational toys would be less seasonal and involve more rationality in selection than most other toys, Mr. Moore reasoned that the larger accounts would have to be handled by a high-quality sales force. He estimated the number of such accounts at between 300–400 in addition to the several hundred large wholesalers which would also have to be serviced on a regular basis. He pointed out, however, that the company did not have to go national at the outset. California alone represented a market of some 19 million people and could be covered by himself and one other salesman. In addition, the two men could display the company's line at the major shows and contact personally 50–60 of the larger retailers located throughout the nation.

Of the $150 million (at retail) spent on adult games in 1972 about $50 million was spent on adult puzzle games, sold by the company. While less seasonal than toys, a substantial percentage of their sales did occur at Christmas.

Distribution channels were approximately the same as for toys, although according to some industry observers advertising was considerably more important as was in-store display. The remainder of the company's present line consisted of more-or-less standard games (see Exhibit 3). These faced substantial competition from both domestic and foreign companies. In general they would use the same channels as the puzzle games and the preschool educational wooden toys, although it was possible that for some distribution gift shops would be important.

In thinking about the company's future, Mr. Moore concluded that the most critical decision lay in a specification of the product line which had to be selected on the basis of the company's resources, the needs of certain market segments and where price competition would not be too great. Following this, a marketing plan could be determined.

**EXHIBIT 1**
**Four Generations Sample Toys in Product Line, 1968–1970**

**EXHIBIT 2**

**Four Generations Organization Chart**

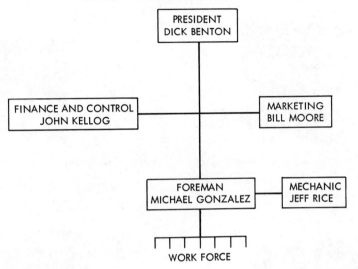

## EXHIBIT 3
### Four Generations Current Products

**MAGIC MARBLE**          **CAT. NO. 203**

Drop the marble into the internal maze and then attempt to remove the marble by shaking, tipping or rotating the walnut block. You'll need your sense of touch and hearing with some logic to be successful.          4" x 4" x 1¾"

**PLUNGING PEG**          **CAT. NO. 204**

Eight pegs that fit into four holes of different lengths. There are over 2500 ways to replace them, but only two combinations will result in the tops all being level. Six other games are shown on the box.          4" x 4" x 1¾"

**NEW TIC TAC TOE**          **CAT. NO. 205**

A beautiful black walnut playing base with an internal storage for the eight black and white playing marbles and instructions on how to play a new way.          4" x 4" x 1¾"

**SHREWD MOVE**          **CAT. NO. 207**

A mathematical game for two people that is easy enough for the young, but complex enough for anybody. A solid black walnut base with fifteen solid steel balls.          4" x 4" x 1¾"

**AFRICAN STONE GAME**          **CAT. NO. 208**

Natural oil finish on black walnut with authentic ocean bottom smooth stones for playing pieces. A classic game from Africa for all ages. 24" x 5" x 1"

## EXHIBIT 3 (Continued)

**ODD BALL**                **CAT. NO. 209**

A dexterity, minipulation game. There are nine marbles trapped within a black walnut block. The object of the game is to move the marbles around so that all of one color are in one chamber and all of another color are in the second chamber.          4'' x 4'' x 1¾''

**REVOLUTIONS**            **CAT. NO. 210**

A black walnut block with a large hole in the center and two internal grooves. The object is to place the two marbles in separate grooves and move the block in such a manner that the marbles rotate around the inside of the block in the grooves in opposite directions.    4' x' 4i x l1¾

**SCULPTURE PUZZLE**        **CAT. NO. 212**

This is a sculpture for the place where you live and a puzzle to challange your patience. All you have to do is drop the small sphere on the large sphere until, in one drop, the small sphere will jump into the small hole . . . and then without moving the block of wood in any manner, retreive the small sphere . 4'' x 4'' x 1¾

**GRAVITY TRAP**           **CAT. NO. 214**

A handsome black walnut block and three steel balls combine to challenge anyone's mental and physical ability. The three balls can be trapped within the block if you put them in just right and if you don't, gravity will get them                 4'' x 4'' x 1¾''

**LEVEL LEARNER**                                        **CAT. NO. 211**

The pegs are all different lengths, and the holes in the playing block are all different depths. The large pegs are easy to hold and a child will learn about depth and measuring while playing with this instructional toy.    12'' x 3'' x 1¾''

## EXHIBIT 3 (Continued)

**POKER CHIP RACK, SMALL**
**8" X 4" X 2"    120 CHIPS**
**CAT. NO. 217**

Solid American Walnut in a unique design packed with either 240, or 120 quality poker chips. Stores easily and looks handsome on the shelf.

**POKER CHIP RACK, LARGE**
**16" X 4" X 2"    240 CHIPS**
**CAT. NO. 218**

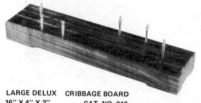

**LARGE DELUX   CRIBBAGE BOARD**
**16" X 4" X 2"    CAT. NO. 216**

A beautiful, sculptured, solid American Walnut traditional cribbage board. Six aluminum and brass pegs included.

**DELUXE CRIBBAGE BOARD   16" x 4" x ¾"**
**CAT. NO. 216A**

Sculptured with the same lines as the Large Deluxe board in select dark hardwoods. Six handsome playing pegs included.

**WALNUT DOMINO BOX   9" X 6" X 2½"**
**RED    CAT. NO. 219**
**IVORY   CAT. NO. 220**

A hand crafted, carefully fitted solid Walnut box with traditional beauty. Lined with a soft velvet like material and containing a full double six set of superb professional dominoes in either red or ivory.

**LARGE DOMINOES WITH GIFT BOX**
**8 x 5 x 1    RED    CAT. NO. 221**
**IVORY   CAT. NO. 222**

Large size, extra thick, marblelike Dominoes. A double six set in either red or ivory. Packed in an attractive white and silver gift box.

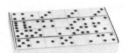

**REGULAR DOMINOES WITH GIFT BOX**
**IVORY    7 X 4 X 1    CAT. NO. 223**

Regular size, thick, marble-like smooth Dominoes, a double six set packed in an attractive white and black gift box in ivory only.

**EXHIBIT 3 (Concluded)**

ADULT GAME SET NO. 2    12″ X 4″ X 2″
CAT. NO. 215

A gift set which includes Sculpture Puzzle, Odd Balling, and Shrewd Move, in an attractive silver and black gift box. Includes instructions.

TAU    12″ X 5″ X 1″
CAT. NO. 213

A new and original game created by Philip Shoptaugh which is simple to play, yet broad enough to inspire deep thought and, interesting tactics. The game is for two players who alternate turns in an attempt to place three playing sticks of the same color in a row. The game utilizes the six basic colors on the standard color wheel and players who do not already know the color wheel will learn much about the relationship of colors while enjoying a fascinating game. The base is solid walnut with 14 hardwood playing sticks all finished in natural oil and hand rubbed for a deep finish.

IMPASSE    10 X 8 X 1
CAT. NO. 224

An original game created by Philip Shoptaugh for those people who like games of skill and action. This new game is played by two people and can be learned in a few minutes. Players attempt to be the first to move their marbles across a movable board. Your opponent can trap your marble and cause you many extra moves. Strategy and skill are required to win consistently. The playing base is solid walnut with a hand rubbed, penetrating oil finish.

GOMOKU (JAPANESE FIVE)  14″ x 8″ x 1½″
CAT. NO. 225

A traditional Japanese Folk game over 4,000 years old. Designed in select hardwoods with 78 playing pieces. A game of skill and logic for two people which can be studied for years, but can be played with ease in a few moments. The object of the game is to be the first player to place 5 pegs in a row.

ADULT GAME SET NO. 1    12″ X 4″ X 2″
CAT. NO. 206

A gift set which includes Magic Marble, Plunging Peg and the New Tic Tac Toe in an attractive silver and black box. Includes instructions.

**EXHIBIT 4**

**Four Generations**

### INTRODUCING "TOP SECRET"

We know it's late but this promises to be one of the top sellers of the year. Our market testing in the California area shows excellent public acceptance. Its quality is typical of our products. If you display this item near your register it will attract a great deal of attention and increase your sales. Order a dozen or more now!    Product is in stock. Immediate delivery is assured.

### WHAT IS IT?

A deep, rich, black base with a concave top surface on which a small Saturn shape spins like a top - well almost like a top - the Saturn spinner is started like a top - with your hand - but then the fun and mystery starts.  Watch for a moment and suddenly you will realize that the top is moving faster and faster, until it reaches almost 2500 revolutions per minute - and it moves - it moves all over the top of the base in some strange irregular pattern - and it goes and goes - start it in the morning - it will still be running at night and the next morning and the next.  Well for a long, long time. Maybe a month, maybe a year.  As long as you own it you can make it work - for ever and that's fascinating, but that's all we can tell you because it's a "TOP SECRET".

### ORDERING DETAILS

Top Secrets are packed in cases containing 12 pieces and weighing approximately 6 pounds.

**No Broken Cases**

Cost Per Case  . . . . . .    $60.00
Suggested List Price .  .  .  .    $  9.95

Price F.O.B. Sebastopol, California

## FOUR GENERATIONS

6005 Gravenstein Hwy. South
Sebastopol, Ca.  95472

**EXHIBIT 5**

**Four Generations Price List, February 1, 1972**

| No. | Product | No. per Case | Wt. per Case (pounds) | Case Price | Cost Each | Suggested List |
|-----|---------|-------------|----------------------|-----------|-----------|----------------|
| 203 | Magic Marble......................... | 6 | 4 | $12.00 | $ 2.00 | $ 3.95 |
| 204 | Plunging Peg.......................... | 6 | 4 | 12.00 | 2.00 | 3.95 |
| 205 | New Tic Tac Toe..................... | 6 | 4 | 12.00 | 2.00 | 3.95 |
| 206 | Adult Game Set #1.................... | 4 | 9 | 24.00 | 6.00 | 11.95 |
| 207 | Shrewd Move.......................... | 6 | 5 | 15.00 | 2.50 | 4.95 |
| 208 | African Stone Game................... | 6 | 15 | 24.00 | 4.00 | 7.95 |
| 209 | Odd Ball.............................. | 6 | 4 | 15.00 | 2.50 | 4.95 |
| 210 | Revolutions.......................... | 6 | 4 | 12.00 | 2.00 | 3.95 |
| 211 | Level Learner........................ | 6 | 9 | 15.00 | 2.50 | 4.95 |
| 212 | Sculpture Puzzle...................... | 6 | 5 | 15.00 | 2.50 | 4.95 |
| 213 | Tau—Available 6/1/72................. | 6 | 7 | 24.00 | 4.00 | 7.95 |
| 214 | Gravity Trap.......................... | 6 | 4 | 12.00 | 2.00 | 3.95 |
| 215 | Adult Game Set #2.................... | 4 | 10 | 30.00 | 7.50 | 14.95 |
| 216 | Large Walnut Cribbage Board........... | 6 | 16 | 24.00 | 4.00 | 7.95 |
| 217 | Poker Chip Rack/120 Chips............. | 3 | 5 | 9.00 | 3.00 | 5.95 |
| 218 | Poker Chip Rack/240 Chips............. | 3 | 8 | 16.50 | 5.50 | 10.95 |
| 219 | Walnut Domino Box/Red dbl. 6......... | 1 | 4 | 10.00 | 10.00 | 19.95 |
| 220 | Walnut Domino Box/Ivory dbl. 6........ | 1 | 4 | 10.00 | 10.00 | 19.95 |
| 221 | Large Double Six Dominoes—Red........ | 3 | 6 | 13.50 | 4.50 | 8.95 |
| 222 | Large Double Six Dominoes—Ivory....... | 3 | 6 | 13.50 | 4.50 | 8.95 |
| 223 | Regular Double Six Dominoes—Ivory..... | 6 | 8 | 15.00 | 2.50 | 4.95 |
| 224 | Impasse—Available 6/1/72............. | 3 | 12 | 19.50 | 6.50 | 12.95 |

*Minimum Order:* Case lots only.
*Freight:* FOB Factory—Sebastopol, California.
*Terms:* 1% 10th Prox. EOM.
*Advertising Allowance:* 10% cumulative from January 1 through December 31 annually, paid upon receipt of tear sheet.

Duns Number 02–917–3424.

**EXHIBIT 6**

**Four Generations**

## GAMES PEOPLE PLAY KEEP
## MANUFACTURERS OPTIMISTIC

Throughout the year—every year, even during a recession—the kids have to play. More and more adults have found that they do, too, and the toy and game market has grown steadfastly through soft and hard economies.

Only twice in the last decade did annual sales drop off from the year before—in 1962 and 1967, by 3 percent and 4 percent respectively. Strong recoveries of 11 percent and 12 percent were made in the years immediately following the declines.

In 1970's recession, sales increased more than 5 percent, and reached $1.35 billion. They should gain another 6 percent this year, says Penton Publishing Company's research division.

Casually optimistic—Toymakers are almost casually optimistic about their future. They see no end to the 8 to 12 percent annual growth rates they've been experiencing. (The figures provided by Penton do not include dolls or children's vehicles. Total toy industry statistics, which include these fast-growing products, show last year's sales at $2.26 billion, nearly 11 percent ahead of 1969.)

Several factors point to continued growth of the market, not the least of which is rising disposable income, which more than doubled in the 1960's and should grow another 35 percent between 1970 and 1975.

More subtly a national attitude that favors playthings makes the purchase of these products almost inevitable.

Consumer demands—In fact, Fred Ertl, president, Toy Manufacturers of America, Inc. (New York), and president, Ertl Co. (Dyersville, Iowa), a subsidiary of Victor Comptometer Corp., maintains that toys and games comprise a new category of consumer products that defy current classification.

"They are not the necessities without which life could not exist," he says. "Nor are they luxuries which consumers are willing to curtail in emergencies. They are quite simply the goods and services people have decided they will not do without."

He cites last year's 10.7 percent sales gain at a time when consumer spending was sharply curtailed. That figure, he says, is "the industry's normal rate of gain—and it is a greater increase than can be accounted for by population growth."

For that reason he "feels safe in predicting that 1971 will see another industry gain between 8 and 12 percent."

Major manufacturers agree with his forecast wholeheartedly. "Our increases will be the same as they have been—around 10 percent a year," says Don Knutzen, vice president, marketing, Parker Brothers, Inc., Salem, Mass.

Monopoly proliferates—Games, he says, have a way of spurting on age. His firm's *Monopoly*, for instance, which is now 36 years old, has

**EXHIBIT 6 (Continued)**

Trends and Forecasts

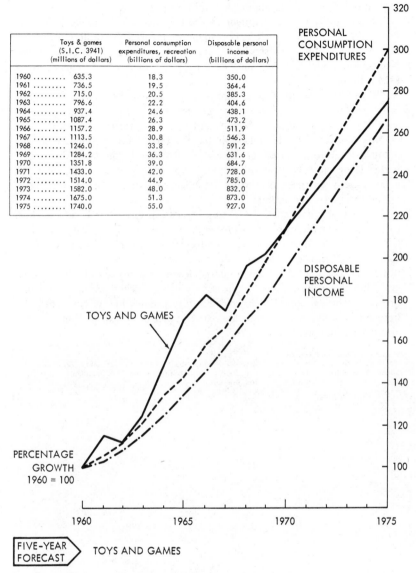

| | Toys & games (S.I.C. 3941) (millions of dollars) | Personal consumption expenditures, recreation (billions of dollars) | Disposable personal income (billions of dollars) |
|---|---|---|---|
| 1960 ........ | 635.3 | 18.3 | 350.0 |
| 1961 ........ | 736.5 | 19.5 | 364.4 |
| 1962 ........ | 715.0 | 20.5 | 385.3 |
| 1963 ........ | 796.6 | 22.2 | 404.6 |
| 1964 ........ | 937.4 | 24.6 | 438.1 |
| 1965 ........ | 1087.4 | 26.3 | 473.2 |
| 1966 ........ | 1157.2 | 28.9 | 511.9 |
| 1967 ........ | 1113.5 | 30.8 | 546.3 |
| 1968 ........ | 1246.0 | 33.8 | 591.2 |
| 1969 ........ | 1284.2 | 36.3 | 631.6 |
| 1970 ........ | 1351.8 | 39.0 | 684.7 |
| 1971 ........ | 1433.0 | 42.0 | 728.0 |
| 1972 ........ | 1514.0 | 44.9 | 785.0 |
| 1973 ........ | 1582.0 | 48.0 | 832.0 |
| 1974 ........ | 1675.0 | 51.3 | 873.0 |
| 1975 ........ | 1740.0 | 55.0 | 927.0 |

PERSONAL CONSUMPTION EXPENDITURES

DISPOSABLE PERSONAL INCOME

TOYS AND GAMES

PERCENTAGE GROWTH 1960 = 100

FIVE-YEAR FORECAST  TOYS AND GAMES

SOURCE: Data prepared by Penton Publishing Company's Research Division.

been selling better in each recent year than it did the year before. Total sales to date are somewhere around 70 million sets, and the game is played in 16 languages, he says.

Growth of leisure time, the move to the suburbs, and the shooting up of discount stores are all cited as having favorable effects on sales.

The leisure time effect is probably best exemplified in the growth of

**EXHIBIT 6 (Concluded)**

the hobby industry, where sales grew more than $100 million between 1968 and 1970, reaching about $850 million last year.

The mainstay of that segment of the toy industry is model kits. Last year, plastic models of all types accounted for $230 million of sales, reports the Hobby Industry Association of America, Inc., New York. Nonplastic model sales of racing cars, railroads, planes, and boats reached $324 million.

"These kits are aimed at all age levels," the association says, "and the sales trend is more stable than the general toy industry because models appeal to all ages and to both sexes and have an educational appeal."

Not obsolete—Model kits will hardly fade from popularity as do many toys. Manufacturers of games and toys have combated this problem in large measure by diversifying, however. Many maintain a careful balance between those toys with stable year-to-year demand, and those which can be related to fads.

Product obsolescence is becoming less of a problem, as is season. The toy industry, which used to experience extremely heavy seasonal (pre-Christmas) sales, has found the trend evening out in recent years. One spokesman estimates that pre-Christmas business used to account for nearly 75 percent of all sales but is down now to about 60 percent.

"The nice thing about it," he says, "is that other seasons have not grown at the expense of Christmas business. Sales in the three months before Christmas have steadily increased, but the overall market all year around has increased even more."

SOURCE: *Industry Week*, April 26, 1971.

Researcher's Note: Of the approximately $1.5 billion spent on toys and games in 1972, around $150 million was spent on adult games. Approximately one-third of this amount—or $50 million—was spent on adult puzzle games of the sort sold by Four Generations.

# Marex Communications—Telshop

### INTRODUCTION

At the beginning of October 1969 Mr. George Shine, managing director of Marex Communications, Inc., was preparing for a board meeting later that month. He had just received a marketing consultant's report, from which he had concluded that a grocery "telephone shop" should be considered by Marex as a spearhead for its computerized Telshop system.

Telshop, Marex's latest development, was a new automated order-entry system, which was designed to create a new dynamic "shopping center" for consumer purchasing by telephone and computer. The system would therefore benefit suppliers to whom Marex intended to sell the system by enabling them to capitalize on a new market of "telephone shoppers," as well as providing them with an accurate and economical system of receiving and processing orders and of inventory control. In time, as more sophisticated communication devices were added, the method was designed to lead to a totally revolutionary marketing system.

Unfortunately, Mr. Shine had been unsuccessful in his attempts to sell Telshop to sufficient subscribers. They showed interest but felt that the market risks of this radical new service were too great to justify the investment involved. Others wanted exclusive rights to a much larger sales territory than Marex was prepared to assign them. Mr. Shine, therefore, intended to recommend to the board that Marex itself run a demonstration of Telshop in one test area, to serve as a "shop-window" to help sell the new system. He hoped that the success of this operating model would convince potential subscribers of a good return on their investment.

Marex was a successful participant in the growing market generated by the use of computer and telecommunications for data processing. Specifically, Marex specialized in creating systems that would provide data processing services to as yet noncomputerized businesses. These clients would use the Marex IBM 360/65 computer and personnel under service contracts with Marex.

The Telshop system was one application of the Marex method. It seemed particularly promising as retailing experts in numerous publications were forecasting that direct consumer shopping by telephone, eventually with the assistance of TV screens, would be a future buoyant sector of the direct-selling industry. Mail order was already an advanced branch of that industry.

Door-to-door selling was perhaps the oldest method of direct selling. With the development of communications and transport, other methods emerged. They included mail order and shopping by telephone. The former was comprised of many small and a few medium-sized firms which specialized in novelty items such as gifts, books and records; and larger firms which sold virtually everything. The "big five" (Sears, Ward, Spiegel, Aldens, and Penney) sent out 60 million catalogs annually, selling merchandise worth approximately $2.2 billion. Specialized mail-order houses for novelties and the like were dominated by the "big six" (Breck's, Foster & Gallagher, Hanover House, Miles Kimball, Spencer Gifts, and Sunset House), who in 1967 had a total of 15.5 million customers and sales of about $100 million.

Both groups in the mail-order business reported an annual growth of about 10%. However, growth within mail-order houses selling every kind of merchandise was generated basically by the opening of new catalog-order centers and retail outlets. Direct mail sales of the "big five" represented only 20% of total catalog sales.

Telephone shopping was already widespread in many consumer and industrial markets. One basis for this was the personal acquaintance between buyer and seller (regular customers of local garages, spare-part stores, grocery shops, or drug stores). Another use was to meet the fast pick-up and delivery needs, for example, in the fast food and laundry businesses. A few department stores in major cities also used a telephone sales system. It was generally used for special offers advertised in newspapers and was restricted to customers holding the store's credit card. The customer ordered the goods by telephone, his credit was verified, and upon delivery he signed a credit slip to be included in his monthly bill. An alternative payment method in some stores was C.O.D. (cash on delivery). In this area, computers were sometimes used for sales statistics, accounting, and screening of target groups.

The new market place for consumer transactions planned by Telshop was to consist of suppliers grouped by region into entities capable of receiving and sending out orders for consumer goods. It was hoped that a maximum of five suppliers per region would be able to meet demands for all types of merchandise eventually offered by Telshop. These suppliers would probably be responsible for the buying of the merchandise, ware-housing, and delivery of orders to consumers.

The Telshop computer system would be used for automatically processing those orders in a number of steps leading to a final order entry and processing. The steps would involve the following computer system: 1) basic order processing and delivery instructions; 2) credit evaluation; 3) billing; 4) inventory maintenance (updating of inventory stock position); 5) accounts receivable handling; 6) sales analysis; 7) inventory control; 8) production planning; and 9) management systems.

The consumer would be able to phone in her order for merchandise which she would see advertised in newspapers, shopping newsletters, and catalogs. She would also hear about Telshop from TV and radio commercials. The option to receive mailed orders had been left open. In the initial stages, access by consumers, either by mail or telephone, would not be completely automated. Initially Telshop sales personnel would enter all orders upon receipt into the automated basic processing system.

Some of the advantages of the method to the consumers were seen as follows:

1.  It was time-saving.
2.  One could shop at one's time convenience.
3.  The consumer does not have to carry home the merchandise herself.
4.  There is a clear choice of item.
5.  The consumer is not "harassed" at the point of sale.
6.  The consumer might benefit from lower prices by taking advantage of special sales offers.

The advantages to the suppliers were seen as follows:

1.  The availability of a new untapped market.
2.  The facility to sell goods via Telshop to consumers without having the expense of physical display at point of purchase.
3.  Because of the limited number of suppliers per region the supplier would have a competition-free market within the Telshop system.
4.  A supplier could use a number of credit card systems and obtain cash periodically directly from them with no further administrative procedures.

It was anticipated that suppliers would not work under their own names but, instead, that deliveries would be made under the Telshop name.

The decision to operate a demonstration model for Telshop involved running a warehouse of merchandise, a fleet of delivery trucks, and having sufficient personnel to fill and deliver orders. The Telshop computer system would serve as the communication and data processing part of the facility.

One of the areas the marketing consultant had been asked to report on was the line of merchandise most likely to be ordered by telephone. (Excerpts of the report are in Exhibit 1.) From these findings Mr. Shine concluded that target consumers would use telephone shopping most regularly and with maximum convenience for groceries and that grocery merchandise was, therefore, the best fit to be used in the demonstration model.

He was also encouraged by the fact that according to a Bell Telephone Company report (on a study carried out by National Family Opinion, Inc.) 36% of all shoppers were "locked in" (i.e., they could not get out of the house to buy goods when required) and that 10% of the housewives in the United States would like to use telephone shopping on a regular basis for continuously needed items like groceries.

Industry sources disclosed that in an average supermarket a family's weekly shopping bill was about $30–$40.[1] A medium-sized supermarket served approximately 1,200 families regularly and had annual sales of about $2 million. Its cost structure was as follows:

### Supermarket Cost Structure

| | | | |
|---|---|---|---|
| Sales................. | | $2,000,000 | 100% |
| Cost of goods sold....... | $1,570,000 | | 78.5% |
| Gross margin........... | | $ 430,000 | 21.5% |
| Warehouse and delivery expenses............. | $ 46,000 | | |
| Operating expenses and interest.............. | $ 320,000 | | |
| Advertising and promotion............ | $ 30,000 | | |
| | | $ 396,000 | |
| Net profit............ | $ 34,000 | | |

Mr. Shine assumed his demonstration model would have an annual turnover similar to that of a medium-size supermarket; i.e., approximately $2 million in annual sales. He further assumed a similar order size and geographical service area. He drew up his calculations as follows:

### Cost Estimate for a Telshop Distribution Facility

| | | | |
|---|---|---|---|
| Sales................. | | $2,000,000 | 100% |
| Cost of goods sold....... | $1,570,000 | | 78.5% |
| Credit card billing costs................ | $ 60,000 | | 3% |
| Gross margin........... | | $ 370,000 | 18.5% |
| Delivery costs (12 trucks; $10,000 per truck with driver............... | $ 120,000 | | |
| Operating expenses and interest.............. | $ 150,000 | | |
| Contribution before order processing and advertising costs....... | | $ 100,000 | |

---

[1] For a breakdown of spendings, see Exhibit 2.

Mr. Shine realized that out of the final contribution he would have to spend some money for advertising and promotion (see Exhibit 3). With respect to computer order processing he figured the required sales volume would be generated by approximately 60,000 orders. Because Telshop offered substantial convenience to the consumer, he was considering charging customers a one-dollar fee per delivery to compensate for the processing costs. The costs to process 60,000 orders would be as follows:

### Costs to Process 60,000 Orders*
### (estimates)

| | |
|---|---|
| CPU rental............................... | $24,000 |
| Peripheral equipment rental.................. | 5,000 |
| WATS lines for communications............. | 6,000 |
| Personnel................................ | 16,000 |
| Rent.................................... | 4,500 |
| Total processing costs for 60,000 orders....... | $56,500 |

* These costs were fixed for each block of 60,000 orders, i.e., 70,000 orders would cost twice as much.

At the board meeting Mr. Shine said:

We can't sell our service. Nobody wants to be the first Telshop subscriber, and the few seriously considering Telshop requested unreasonably large exclusive territories.

OK, then let's do the whole thing ourselves! We can hire consultants to solve the technical problems; we have cost figures on supermarkets, and we have data on shoppers. I am convinced that this system is more profitable than a conventional supermarket. Let's set up our own telephone shop! The idea seems even better if we take a look at convenience stores, offering the same kind of advantages as Telshop—quick shopping and convenience. Do you realize what this means? It means a lot of profit for us and, at the same time, proof of our success to all the suppliers we talked to during the last few months who are afraid to subscribe.

I already have some contacts with investors who are interested in helping substantially with financing this demonstration move. Now it's our turn to make up our minds where to start, how to attract the consumer, and which market to aim at. In many markets Telshop is a radically new service, and its implementation has to be planned very carefully. In order to acquire some know-how, I wouldn't object to putting up a joint venture with an experienced supermarket or any other type of experienced merchandiser. We must move carefully and quickly because we now know that we aren't the first to think about such an operation.[2]

But I'm sure that when we've proved we can operate successfully sub-

[2] Mr. Shine was referring to the California company "TeleMart" which had just started up a system similar to Telshop in San Diego. This name had been used by Marex before but had not been protected; and Marex was forced by a court order to use the name "Telshop" instead. An article describing the founding of TeleMart is presented in Exhibit 4. In Montreal a company named "Homemart" was just starting a similar operation.

scribers will rush to get in on the Telshop system. We'd better fix up now all the necessary subscription conditions. On the other hand, we must also look toward Europe, where the changeover from the around-the-corner grocery store to the modern supermarket has not yet fully taken place. Here we might well be able to attract customers away from the grocery store straight to our system, avoiding the transitory stages of grocery store/supermarket/Telshop.

**EXHIBIT 1**

**Consultant's Report on Telshop and Telephone Shopping—
Summary and Conclusions**

There are difficulties in using a telephone-shopping system as a sales medium because of the risk, perceived by the customer who does not have the conventional means of reducing his risk.

On the other hand, the system offers convenience which the shopper did not have before. The problem, in brief, is to match the particular array of products which project the least risk with the most convenience-seeking segment in the market. This coupling will produce the initial core of customers for the system.

Experience and word-of-mouth advertising will gradually promote the system to additional lines of merchandise and additional segments of customers in the market.

All this will be conditioned by superior service in terms of delivery pick-ups, well-trained telephone sales personnel, and satisfaction-enhancing on the part of the system.

The suburban housewife who is under 40 with children living at home is suggested as the target customer, and several lines of products are suggested thereby.

On the supply side of the system it is viewed that the system can either buy or resell the merchandise or be used by independent suppliers as an additional medium for sales. A primary consideration here is to have enough control of the suppliers or the goods so that all the servicing conditions mentioned before will be met.

Certain promotional and operational implications are also pointed out for further elaboration.

INTRODUCTION

The purpose of this report is to assess, on the basis of studies that were done in the past, the ideal posture or positioning of a telephone-shopping service. Regarding the crucial question of prospective merchandise, studies and investigations available were initially applied to a limited number of product lines. However, as will be shown, the emerging concept can be applied to a large variety of products and services.

In the projected business the consumer will be able to shop at home by using his telephone. He will talk to a salesclerk backed up by a number of suppliers who will have merchandise ready for delivery at his order. At the same time the system should serve the supplier with extra sales which otherwise would not have occurred via his marketing channels.

Positioning of the service will yield operational guides for the marketing of the system. This should be done by determining first the amount of information the system planners have to work with and which pieces of information carry most weight. This could be referred to as a "strategy of positioning."

I. STRATEGY OF POSITIONING

As a first step, a "target customer" of the system should be defined. By orienting the system towards this customer and tailoring it to his needs, the system's prospects for success will be increased. There are three alternative target customers to consider:

1. The shopper.
2. The supplier.
3. Simultaneously both.

Let us first consider the implication of starting with the supplier as our target customer. We might then save ourselves the search for information about the individual shopper as a target customer. Our role here would be to define and explain how the supplier would be entering another medium of marketing transactions. This would be especially appropriate to the vast number of smaller specialty goods suppliers and stores who depend on orders and sidewalk shoppers.

The problem with this approach is the dependence of the system on the marketing and delivery methods and success of the supplier. The system could not and should not be a slave to the fluctuations of telephone orders to a particular supplier. By having a supplier as the target customer, we have no control over sales, and, further, it would be too risky to have the suppliers turn away from the system in the event that it did not live up to their expectations.

Therefore, in order to retain maximum control and to reduce uncertainty to the minimum, we must have as target customers the ultimate users of the system. Once we have enough information about the ultimate users and can tailor the system, the products and the promotional tools to him, we then can turn to the supplier; and with our planning and information we have a much better position to negotiate and control the system. At that stage, we shall be able to assess whether a prospective supplier has a relevant line of products, whether he is able to supply prompt delivery and accept rejected merchandise, and whether his operating methods are adequate.

II. THE TARGET CUSTOMER

There are two major considerations which determine who is the prospective customer, how frequent will his telephone shopping be, and to what extent (in terms of product and cost) he will shop by telephone:

1. Perceived risk.
2. Convenience.

PERCEIVED RISK

The consumer might risk facing detrimental consequences because of making a decision to buy. These consist of:

1. Economic cost.
2. Time loss.

3. "Ego loss" and frustration.
4. Not achieving buying goals.

As far as we are concerned, these risks will either bar him from telephone shopping, or, if he tries it once and either one or some of these consequences occur, he will not use the system any more and, by word of mouth, may even hurt our efforts.

In order to make the transaction, the shopper must reduce his uncertainty regarding possible detrimental consequences. The consumer will reduce his uncertainty by collecting more information or imitating someone credible to him. The common uncertainty-reduction tools which are not available to the telephone shopper are:

1. Personal inspection of the merchandise.
2. Comparisons.
3. Reference to sales personnel.

The uncertainty-reduction tools which are available are:

1. Reliance on past experience with product brand or store;
2. Reliance on advertising;
3. Reliance on someone else's experience.

In short, we can say that the less the number of decisions the shopper has to make, the less risk he will perceive. Studies and experience show that confidence was expressed in ordering particular kinds of merchandise by phone or mail in two cases:

1. When there was an ability to identify the items by brand, size, color, and other properties;
2. When standard reorder items were involved.

CONVENIENCE

Telephone shopping offers solutions to the following problems which the shopper may face:

1. Having to carry the merchandise;
2. Crowds, boredom, and fatigue;
3. Poor or confusing arrays of merchandise and difficulty in finding the wanted items;
4. Traveling;
5. Spending time and money on traveling;
6. Inconveniences of making shopping trip arrangements and then getting to the store.

This suggests that we should define our target customer as one who has to overcome these problems. We have to consider the following attributes:

1. Women with greater-than-average need for convenience in shopping;
2. Women with restricted mobility because of children at home;
3. Women residing in suburbs;
4. Women who are in possession of means to shop (income, possession of credit cards etc.,);

5. Customers temporarily tied down at home or unable to get into town for special promotions;
6. Customers who may rely on newspaper and catalog advertising (as TV advertising has proved to be deficient in generating telephone orders);
7. Customers with intelligence and education who are aware of specific brands offered in a market which contains a number of different products;
8. Customers who are educated enough to compile a shopping list and assess shopping needs;
9. Customers who are enterprising enough to be willing to explore this new way of shopping;
10. Customers who are affiliated with formal and informal organizations;
11. Customers who are actively interested in leisure activities.

III. Prospective Products

A category of products with proven success in telephone shopping and mail ordering was packaged grocery products ordered on a weekly basis, to be complemented by the daily fresh foodstuffs bought in the local grocery.

Studies done on telephone shopping in department stores and mail-order houses have revealed a number of products appropriate to the target customer. As this new way of shopping spreads and is reinforced, other products and lines could be incorporated. The initial products are:

1. Bed linens.
2. Women's stockings.
3. Women's underwear and housedresses.
5. Toys and games.
6. Blankets.
7. Table linens.
8. Children's clothing.
9. Gifts (holidays and family events).
10. Branded small appliances.

It could not be stressed too strongly that telephone shopping involves a high degree of perceived risk which could be overcome in a learning process based upon shopping experience with those products mentioned and involving a minimum number of decisions. The consumer will learn to telephone-shop and eventually will shop for other products by telephone as well.

IV. Operational Implications

1. Advertising
   a. Informative;
   b. Facilitate ordering by brand, size, color or code;
   c. Easy identification of items should be emphasized.
2. Service
   a. Well-informed telephone salesclerks;
   b. Well-trained salesclerks for suggestion and solicitation selling;
   c. Customer confidence and satisfaction should be increased by the manner in which telephone contacts are handled;
   d. Delivery and prompt pick-up service are a major property of the system;

    *e.* Catalogs should be designed to be personal and of top quality;
    *f.* Service should be available after hours when stores usually close;
    *g.* Accurate filling of orders;
    *h.* An up-to-date inventory status information facility.

## V. PROMOTION

1. Two promotional tools have to be used simultaneously at first until a certain momentum picks up. Specifically, we should reach the suburban housewife, who has most of our target customer's attributes, by way of mail and meetings. The affiliation with formal and informal organizations should help stimulate word-of-mouth advertising. By reaching wives of professional associations' members, we should increase the probability of reaching the opinion leaders among the women of suburban communities. Simultaneously, newspaper and other mass media advertising should be aimed at increasing the confidence in the system as a credible, well-known organization. This tool could be dropped once repeat purchases and word-of-mouth advertising are dominant.

2. Catalogs should be updated periodically with a sufficient visual distinction between the issues.

3. The use of the system could be promoted as a sign of sophistication and a status symbol. For example, delivery should be very distinctive in terms of delivery packages (boxes, bags, etc.) and satisfaction should be enhanced with each delivery, possibly through special courtesies.

4. Distinctive stationery and insignia should be used.

5. The system should have its own free membership card in addition to any credit cards accepted by the system.

6. Salesclerks should be very well-trained in order to maintain contacts in a personal and friendly atmosphere all the time.

## VI. COMPETITION

By catering to this particular segment of customer and taking into account the target customer's prepurchase deliberations, gaining his purchase activities and postpurchase satisfaction in the operation, a competitive advantage over conventional suppliers should be achieved. This has to be coupled with a prompt delivery and pick-up service and rapid order processing. It is imperative to use sophisticated communications equipment in order to maintain the competitive edge.

## VII. EXPERIENCE OF TELEPHONE SHOPPING

Studies report that telephone sales represent a substantial portion of the catalog operation of the two leading mail-order firms. They operate separate organizations for telephone shopping and work directly with the warehouses. Telephone sales of mail-order firms have grown faster than any other phase of their operation.

The drawback a mail-order house has in this respect is its commitments to its own brand names. The new telephone-shopping system will work with nationally or locally accepted brand names.

In the supermarket-product category, as mentioned, telephone shopping has been tried by one firm, and its success was with that segment of the market which we have defined as our target customer. On the other hand, discount stores in the suburbs have not offered telephone-ordering facilities. This leaves our target customer only with the option of telephone ordering from department stores, which do not operate as recommended here. This leaves the target customer, whom we have defined, with real incentives to use our telephone-shopping system.

## VIII. SUPPLIERS

It should not be a problem to convince a prospective supplier to use the system once a prospective customer who otherwise would not have bought from him is presented to him.

The operators of the system could either buy and resell the name brand or provide a tool to the various levels of suppliers to bypass, with additional sales, their wholesalers, distributors, or other middlemen.

A possible problem with the second alternative may be the fact that a policy decision has to be made by the supplier which may alienate his middleman.

One solution to this problem is having the alienated middleman also participate in the system on a regional basis, compensating him for the additional sales made by the supplier. Again, the conditions of adequate service and personnel should be met, and this poses a problem of control over the delivery channels that should be maintained closely.

## IX. CONCLUSION

The final recommendation of this report is that the proposed telephone shopping should be implemented with the defined target customer in mind and the types of products provided which have a proven appeal to telephone and mail-order purchasers. The unique advantage of the proposed system is that it provides the customer with a wider range of brand name products, more easily identified by code or designation, than a conventional department store normally provides or any of the mail-order establishments have provided to date. Further advantage lies not only in unique ease of ordering but also in special buying incentives, such as clearly defined special sales prices and telephone and personal sales talks from individuals associated with the new system.

The logical approach to suppliers should take into account especially the need for the new system to reduce the complexity of purchasing and packaging the foods purveyed therein. This should be accomplished by seeking a limited number of experienced regional suppliers capable of supplying that merchandise to be sold through our new system. These "participating suppliers" should provide goods at a wholesale price and take the responsibility of packaging for delivery. These participating suppliers should have the capability of arranging through, say, no more than five such suppliers in a given sales region the acquisition and preparation for delivery of all goods ordered in a designated region.

It remains to be decided precisely the manner of delivery, whether by the participating supplier, a third party or the new system itself.

Finally, the new system should have adequate automated inventory, ordering, billing, credit-checking and communications controls.

## EXHIBIT 2

### Typical Supermarket with an Annual Sales Volume of $2 Million
### Product Groups, Margin and Sales—1968

|  | Net Profit* | GM Percent | Percent to Sales |
|---|---|---|---|
| Total store............................... | 1.8% | 21.5 | 100 |
| Meat....................................... |  | 21.3 | 22.6 |
| Produce (fresh vegetables, processed meat)................................... |  | 30.1 | 7.0 |
| Dairy...................................... |  | 14.2 | 10.0 |
| Bakery..................................... |  | 26.2 | 2.0 |
| Frozen food............................... |  | 25.2 | 5.2 |
| Dry grocery (canned and bottled goods, detergents, cigarettes, etc.)............... |  | 20.8 | 47.7 |
| Total nonfood............................. |  | 27.9 | 5.5 |
| Health and beauty aids.................... |  | 29.2 | 3.1 |
| Housewares............................... |  | 24.5 | 1.2 |
| Miscellaneous............................. |  | 29.1 | 1.2 |

Notes: Total store margin 1.1% higher than in 1958, but meat and produce margins remained steady while health and beauty showed decline.

Margins on specific items range from 7.67% (cigarettes) to as high as 39% (instant milk).

* Before taxes.

SOURCE: *Progressive Grocer*, 1969 and 1972.

## EXHIBIT 3

### Selecting Advertising Costs

Four-page newspaper supplements

| | |
|---|---|
| Color............................................. | $10,000 |
| B & W............................................. | 8,000 |
| One 60-second regional TV spot (average)................ | 2,000 |
| One radio announcement (average)...................... | 500 |
| One-page newspaper advertisement (average).............. | 2,000 |
| Cost for 100,000 40-page catalogues (approximate).......... | 30,000 |

## EXHIBIT 4

### Dialing for the Groceries*

In almost anybody's dream of the future the harried housewife never undergoes the agony of dragging the kids through a supermarket. She shops by telephone and television, chatting briskly with a computer that totals her bill with flawless efficiency, and she is forever free from what A. G. Bailey calls a "nerve-wearing time-wasting, fender-bending ordeal."

If 45-year-old "Bill" Bailey succeeds in his grandiose scheme, the San Diego housewife's dream future arrives late this summer. TeleMart Enterprises, Inc., hopes to make grocery shopping by phone and computer a reality for some 3,000 women a day.

A former Beverly Hills advertising executive, now TeleMart's chairman of the board, Bailey is busy setting up the company's first $1.1 million operation, with a distribution center that has a capacity equal to ten major super-

* Reproduced from *Business Week*, March 28, 1970.

markets. And Bailey hopes that by opening day 40,000 women will have paid their $2 permanent membership fee.

TeleMart shopping goes like this: A housewife makes up her grocery list from a shopper's guide that lists 3,000 food and nonfood items, each with a code number. Between 7 A.M. and 11 P.M. she phones one of 90 TeleMart operators who hooks the call into an audio-response computer (dubbed "Clara"). The computer verifies the order, item by item, and quotes various quantity prices—for a single item, several items, or a case. The cost of the order is given, and a delivery time is scheduled—at least four hours later and within a two-hour target period.

When the housewife hangs up, the computer prints out an order sheet to be filled by warehouse clerks. Clara also figures out which of TeleMart's 75 leased trucks should carry the order, over which route within the 415-square mile area the truck should go, and which orders should be loaded first to be delivered last. When the housewife gets her groceries, she pays $1 delivery charge (no tipping allowed) and pays for the order by check or is billed monthly.

"TeleMart housewives," states Bailey with finality, "will more than make up the delivery charge by taking advantage of price breaks on quantity orders. Because we do the carrying, she can afford the case of soda or the 25-pound package of detergent."

More than a year of research and development of the system has prepared him for almost every argument why the operation will not work. Replying to conventional grocers who say that shoppers like to pick such items as meat and produce personally, he points out that a woman can return any unsatisfactory merchandise at the time it is delivered.

Donald S. Perkins, president of Chicago-based Jewel Companies, doubts that the 3,000 items TeleMart will list in its quarterly shopping guides are enough for profitable operation. He notes, too, that supermarkets operate with small staffs—primarily cashiers and clerks who restock the shelves. TeleMart will take more people, more salaries, more equipment, he says.

Bailey counters with the claim that the items on his limited shopping list account for 80% of all grocery dollars spent in San Diego and that the list will be expanded as time goes on. Costs of personnel and equipment will be more than offset by savings on the physical plan. "The biggest cost facing a supermarket is land and building. . . . Our one distribution facility is located on industrial land. We don't need a dozen branches to serve a population center."

"TeleMart," says a skeptical spokesman for Safeway Stores, Inc., "appears a valid concept for a limited market. We'll keep an eye on it, but we have serious reservations about the feasibility of home delivery for a mass market." The president on one southern California grocery chain is more direct: "The system is too error-prone. How are thousands of housewives going to get the code on the No. 10 can of corn correct?"

One of those most interested in TeleMart is Rolf Millqvist, a balding Swede who founded a similar operation 16 years ago in Stockholm. Hemkoep (Home Shop) has virtually everything TeleMart will have, except the computer. It grew from $50,000 in sales its first year to about $6 million in the mid-1960's. But volume has held steady since, and with prices rising about 4%

annually, Hemkoep business actually has declined. One reason is that competitive supermarkets—and cars to get to them—have increased in recent years. To improve his cash flow, Millqvist now opens his warehouse to shopping-cart customers from 4:30 P.M. to 8 P.M.

"TeleMart," says Millqvist, "is part of the wave of the future," but he is not sure how far off that future is. He built his store with the idea that emancipated women of today had more important things to do than shop. "I'm afraid the development of the women's role in society has not come as fast as I had hoped," he says. As for computers, "They are too expensive," he says.

Hemkoep makes no charge for the 35,000 catalogs it sends out every two weeks, and delivery is free on orders of $15 or more.

Everyone connected with TeleMart is aware of skepticism at home and abroad. But the youthful Bailey glibly talks of spending $20,000 or $30,000 a month for TV spots that will send housewives running to their phones to place "impulse buys."

"Though we rate TeleMart as an extremely speculative investment, I've never seen a more thorough documentation behind a beginning operation," says W. C. Richardson, executive vice president of Birr, Wilson Co., Inc., the San Francisco investment banking firm that was going to handle TeleMart's private placement to raise $1 million. Two weeks ago Bailey decided instead to try to sell 250,000 shares of stock at $10 each to Californians—"so that we will have money for expansion." Present operating capital comes from officers of the company and from Food Baron, a San Diego fast-food franchiser.

Another supporter is Rohr Corporation, the largest of the aerospace subcontractors which developed TeleMart's computer system.

Bailey is scheduled to speak to women's groups over the next few months, introducing TeleMart and asking housewives to try it for a month without paying the membership fee. "Our main challenge," he says, "is a marketing one. Our Wheaties are no different than anyone else's. What we've got to sell is service." To be successful, he estimates, he must capture 4% of the San Diego County grocery market. John Mabee, president of San Diego's Big Bear Supermarkets who has been watching Bailey in action, shakes his head, "If anyone can sell the housewife on TeleMart, Bill Bailey can."

# SECTION **VI**

## PERSONAL SELLING
## AND ADVERTISING

# Western Industrial Supply Company

Mr. James Mitchell, vice president and general manager of the Western Industrial Supply Company, faced several provocative situations involving selection of sales personnel for his organization. In each case Mr. Mitchell had his own opinions, and he wanted input from others before making his final decision.

Western Industrial Supply Company, located in Los Angeles, distributed janitorial supplies—waxes, cleaners, equipment, and the like— to industrial and institutional users in California from San Diego to Fresno and east as far as Needles. Salesmen called on custodians who, if sold on the product or products, requisitioned the purchase through the firm's purchasing department. On these direct contact sales where bids were not required, the recommendation of the custodian was usually accepted by the purchasing department without question.

Western Industrial was one of the larger companies of its type west of the Mississippi. Within the Los Angeles area Western Industrial competed with 40 other companies, most of which were small operations employing one or two salesmen. Competition was fierce, with price being a major factor. For instance, almost all 40 firms distributed Crown Zellerbach paper, and obviously the firm with the lowest price was bound to take the business.

Despite pressures for price reductions Mr. Mitchell sought to minimize whenever possible the importance of this competitive factor. Over the last several years he had succeeded in raising the level upon which his company sold. Products that could be demonstrated and glamorized were stressed instead of items with primarily price appeal. The company submitted bids on large orders but was rarely successful. Mr. Mitchell's goal was a reasonable profit on every piece of merchandise sold.

Reprinted from *Stanford Business Cases 1963* with the permission of the publisher, Graduate School of Business, Stanford University. Copyright © 1963 by the Board of Trustees of the Leland Stanford Junior University.

Consequently, the Western Industrial salesmen were taught to merchandise items by demonstration which required them to have a reasonable technical knowledge of the product and to adopt higher level sales approaches than those used by competitors. For example, the term "janitor" had long since been replaced by "custodian" in the salesman's vocabulary and all company literature. Also, custodial schools were set up in which Western Industrial personnel went into a plant and worked with the custodial crew for two-hour sessions on how to make their job easier. Uses of the products were explained and demonstrated, such technical knowledge (but not enough to be boring) was passed on, and an attempt was made to build up the esprit de corps of this group who were charged with "the maintenance of millions of dollars of plant and equipment." Western Industrial salesmen extended invitations to the firm's management to keep them apprised of the program.

A successful Western Industrial salesman, then, had to get his "hands dirty," he had to be energetic, and had to be able to take a product and glamorize it to a point where he could sell it for as much as 50% more than a competitor could get for the same or a similar product.

However, the burden of achieving a reasonable profit was not entirely left to the salesman. For example, a few years earlier Western Industrial sold only 100 gallons of toilet bowl cleaner a month. Competition was taking most of the business on the basis of price. Sizing up the situation, Mr. Mitchell selected an attractive new package and a good name for the product. A sudsing agent and distinctive fragrance were added to a previously uninteresting product. Sales contests were then initiated, and within two years sales had jumped to about 1,300 gallons a month, and the product was at twice its original price.

Mr. Mitchell employed 12 salesmen, each working an assigned territory. Accounts within a territory, however, were protected only to the extent that they are active. Those not being sold or called upon were "open" to other salesmen. Mr. Mitchell explained that in his business personalities played an important part in selling and that many times a change in salesmen could immediately bring a new account.

Salesmen received a commission on top of a monthly guarantee. The guarantee was based on the person's experience, the territory, and related factors. The lowest guarantee offered was $600 a month plus a nominal car expense. A good salesman in the janitorial supply field could expect to earn between $900 and $1,000 a month (guarantee and commission) within his first year. At the end of two years he should make $1,300 a month, and after five years the potential would be in the area of $18,000 annually.

Since taking over the company, Mr. Mitchell had completely turned over his sales force. While he was currently satisfied with his personnel, situations did occur which required replacement of salesmen. One such situation had come about when a salesman handling one of the company's best territories resigned to take a similar job in New York state. Since Mr. Mitchell had no one available to cover this territory, he immediately ran ads in the newspaper and started circulating word that he was looking for a man to take over his territory. Between 40 and 50 people responded to the blind ad, and out of the applications a few were chosen for further consideration. Within three days the list was reduced to two men who appeared to be of the type needed to sell jaintorial products. The two men were contacted for interviews.

The first man interviewed was Samuel Smith. Following are the impressions of Mr. Mitchell based on a series of interviews:

Mr. Smith appeared to me to have all the necessary prerequisites for the job. He was well dressed, extremely neat appearing, had a confident manner and did an excellent job of selling himself. I spent several hours talking to him during the initial interview. He had the right answers for everything we discussed; the man was sharp. As is my general practice, I told him what we had to offer, the starting pay, the potential, and a little about the company. Then I asked him to go home, think it over, talk to his wife, then if he was still interested, to come in the next morning at 10:00, and I would give him a second interview.

The next morning Smith arrived at a quarter of ten and waited until I was able to see him. To me this indicated his reliability and promptness. We had another interview, and I was pretty well satisfied that this was the right man. My administrative assistant interviewed Smith and reported that he was every bit as impressed as I was. There was no question that this was the man for the job.

Again we asked him to go home and think about it for 24 hours. Rather than have him come back for an interview, I asked my administrative assistant to spend a little more time with Smith. It is my opinion that two heads are always better than one, so I had my assistant pick up Smith at his home and take him to lunch to see what his impressions then might be. Mr. Smith lived in a nice neighborhood in an attractive, but not ostentatious, house. My assistant reported that Smith handled himself well at the lunch table and discussed things intelligently. To check Smith's references and background, I sent for a Retail Credit Company Report preliminary to making a final decision.

In the meantime, I interviewed the second applicant selected from the original list, Albert Tonelli. His experience in sales was on a much lower level than Smith's. He worked for a macaroni company—not one of the larger ones, but one which was fairly well-known in southern California. Aggressiveness wasn't needed in this type of selling, since Tonelli's job more or less required creating goodwill with the grocers, i.e., dusting their shelves, arranging their packages, and the like.

Tonelli had been with this company for quite some time. I was impressed with him during the interview. He spoke frankly. His making a modest salary in his present job didn't seem to worry him. He was married, had no children, lived in his own home, and worked Saturdays in a grocery store to earn a little extra money to support his family. They seemed to live quite adequately on his salary. Tonelli spoke well, was neatly dressed, and looked younger than his 29 years. I sent him home after the initial interview and, as with Smith, asked him to think it over and come back the next day.

During 24 hours between the first and second interview Tonelli was offered another job. He immediately informed me and explained that he had been looking over several opportunities to better himself, explaining that the macaroni company had been very good to him, but there his earnings potential was limited. The other job offer was with his wife's uncle, a position as a shoe salesman at approximately 50% increase in income. Certainly, this was more than I was prepared to offer him at the time. I told him that I appreciated his frankness and said I could give him a week in which to make up his mind whether to take the other job. I did impress upon him that once he made up his mind I would accept it as his final decision. Also, I informed him that others had applied for the job, and therefore I could not promise him a job with our company.

At the end of a week he returned and said he had decided definitely against taking the job with his wife's uncle. He was afraid that getting into a family situation would be no real improvement and that the overall potential was not much greater than that of his present position. Subsequently, my administrative assistant interviewed Tonelli, and he was impressed with him but neither of us was quite as sold on him as we had been on Smith.

In the meantime, we had received the Retail Credit Company Reports on both men. (See Exhibits 1 and 2). Of the two, Mr. Smith had more personality, more confidence, was neater appearing, and presented a much more impressive figure. Had I not seen the background report, I would have picked Smith without question.

A second situation requiring the selection of a salesman arose in the company's Bakersfield area. Two salesmen operated out of a branch in Bakersfield. Mr. Mitchell sought to replace one man in an attempt to increase sales in a somewhat dormant area. The Bakersfield branch had, until several years ago, been an independent operation. When Mr. Mitchell assumed responsibility for the branch, he retained the old manager because of the man's long experience in the area. In addition to being a steady man and a good administrator, the branch manager was noted for his conservatism. Mr. Mitchell regulated his responsibility without a change in title, which had been fully accepted. In the search for a new salesman Mr. Mitchell finally found an experienced man, aged 55, who was available for the position. While Mr. Mitchell did not feel that the man was of exceptional caliber, he was satisfied with his knowledge of the merchandise. The man would at least be a definite improvement over the salesman to be replaced.

About the time that Mr. Mitchell was set to hire this man, he was informed of another possible applicant. As he put it, "This applicant happened to be a woman, and I say this advisedly." She was about 42 years of age and the owner of a pet store in Bakersfield. A mutual friend advised Mr. Mitchell that June Brady was a terrific merchandiser but was feeling tied down by the pet shop. A preliminary investigation showed that Miss Brady was so busy in her pet shop on weekends that she had to hand out numbered tickets to her customers. Mr. Mitchell also found Miss Brady's selling methods interesting. She boasted of the quality of the dog food that she sold, and if a customer asked her if she were sure that it was good quality she would say, "Oh, it's the best," and eat some.

Deciding that he had nothing to lose, Mr. Mitchell arranged an interview with June Brady. The following is Mr. Mitchell's impression of the interview:

Miss Brady was hardly what you would call genteel. I am not exaggerating when I say that several times she sent me sprawling across the room with slaps on the back. She was loaded with personality. She was sold on herself and her ability, and she didn't mind letting me know that she was going to set the world on fire. I've always liked to gamble to a certain extent in business. I knew the operation in Bakersfield wasn't getting anywhere at present, and I felt the innovation of a woman might be something that would, if nothing else, make known the fact that Mitchell was in southern California. However, I didn't make up my mind before going to Bakersfield to discuss this with our branch manager. To say that he told me I was crazy is a mild understatement. He said that it absolutely couldn't work. I was then faced with the decision to either take the gamble or go ahead with a man who had some experience in the business.

The final situation involved a recent call that Mr. Mitchell received from the sales manager of Western Industrial's largest competitor. The sales manager, Paul Jacobs, asked Mr. Mitchell to lunch, whereupon he stated that he wanted to go to work for Western Industrial. Jacobs was a controversial figure and had previously attracted Mr. Mitchell's attention. The background and impact of the statement by Jacobs can best be expressed by Mr. Mitchell, who relates the situation as follows:

You have to go back several years really to appreciate this situation. At that time, I spent seven months negotiating to purchase our largest competitor, the company for which Jacobs works. In the local area this company does twice the volume that Western Industrial does, even though on the whole we are larger. Theirs is an interesting organization, staffed by politicians, men who are too old to run the business, and Paul Jacobs.

The type of man Jacobs is can best be explained by the contacts my men have had with him in the field. Often I would ask, "Did you get any business from the XYZ company?" They would reply, "No, I didn't get any this year because Paul Jacobs really sold them a bill of goods. He really loaded them." As you probably suspect, the following year they'd call on the same account and come back with the same answer. One of my salesmen now carries a picture of Jacobs in his wallet, and when someone mentions the name of his company my salesman says, "Oh, you mean my competitor!" and produces the picture.

At the time we were negotiating to purchase the company, I asked one of the owners of the company, "What's the story on Paul Jacobs? Why is he with your organization?" In asking this, I was trying to determine whether I would retain Jacobs if the negotiations were successful. The owner replied, "Write down these figures: 15, 15, and 70." So I did and said, "Okay, I've written them down; now what do they mean?" He said, "Well, 15% of the accounts that he calls on will give you a phone call and tell you they never want to see the (censored) again, and they never want to do business with your company again, either. The other 15% will not call you, but you just won't get any more business from them. The 70% will love him, they will give him ALL their business, and he will do a tremendous job with them."

Soon thereafter these negotiations broke down, but my interest in Jacobs continued. On one occasion I asked a former employee of mine, who worked for this competitor as a purchasing agent, the following question: "Well, Jim, how do you get along with this fellow Jacobs?" He answered that he couldn't stand him but that "Jacobs does a tremendous job with the salesmen. In fact, the salesmen love him. He talks to them every night on the phone, plays cards with them, and fights for everything that the salesmen feel is right; they really think he's a terrific guy. No one else in the organization, however, can stand him."

A little searching revealed that Jacobs had been my competitor's sales manager for 17 years. During this time he had increased their sales staff from 13 to 22 men. He never had a man quit his organization. He had discharged two or three men during the 17 years but never did a man leave because of him or the company. It's hard for me to understand all this knowing the particular individual, but that's how it was.

When he called me on the phone and asked me to have lunch with him, I suspected the reason and agreed to the meeting mainly out of curiosity. I spent some time mulling over how to tell him I wouldn't use him under any circumstances. However, when he talked of his record, development of salesmen, increasing sales, etc., my planned words never came out, and I was convinced I should give the matter more consideration.

One thing for sure, Jacobs is really a salesman. He was available to us due to a serious illness of his this last summer. His doctor told him that if he expected to live past 50—he's now 47—he would have to change completely his mode of living. Jacobs went to his bosses and broke the news that he was going to leave the company. They accepted the resignation but retained Jacobs as a consultant at a greatly reduced salary. Two months later the doctors reevaluated his case and decided there was no longer any reason that Jacobs could not continue his normal working habits and mode of living. Meanwhile, our competitor brought two men in to replace Jacobs—one for in-town and one for out-of-town—and both worked well in the organization. Jacobs, of course, wanted to return to full-time work, but the only place for him was his company's San Francisco office. For personal reasons he refused this offer, and this is when he approached me.

My problem is, first: Should I hire him? Second, if I do hire him, in what position? And third: What would be the reaction of my organization?

Jacobs has stated that he is not interested in working as a salesman. However, presently I don't really need a sales manager. With only 12 salesmen in the field my administrative assistant and I can handle this function adequately.

Eventually, I intend to add a sales manager so that I can spend more time merchandising new products, etc., although, as I implied, this is several years off. If I bring Jacobs into the organization, I would also bring in a great deal of business and a number of my competitor's better salesmen. I guess I have to weigh this against the repercussions in my own organization.

## EXHIBIT 1
### Retail Credit Company Salesman Selection Report

Name: Smith, Samuel
Address: Redonda, California
Age or Date of Birth: 7/28/40

| | |
|---|---|
| 1. Number of years known: | 3,1,2,2,2 Years |
| | File: 6 years |
| 2. Racial descent: | Hebrew |
| 3. Net worth: | $25,000 (est.) |
| 4. Annual income: | $10,000 (est.) |
| 5. General impression of sales ability | See remarks |
| 6. Any unfavorable health information developed? | None learned |
| 7. Any criticism of drink habits? | No |
| 8. Is reputation good? | See remarks |
| 9. Recommended? | No: finance, ability employment |

*Scope of Investigation:* Other locations:

The following information was obtained through interviews held with three sources at a former place of employment and two sources at his present place of residence as well as file information from our own files. We also checked all available civil and federal records in Los Angeles County.

*Exact dates of Employment or Unemployment:*

| | | |
|---|---|---|
| 2/10/1971 to 8/?/1972 | Vari-Typer Corporation | Los Angeles, California |
| 2/23/1967 to 2/2/1971 | Hoover Vacuum Cleaner Company | Los Angeles, California |
| 7/9/1965 to 11/28/1966 | Metropolitan Life Insurance Company | Los Angeles, California |

*Summary of Employment:* Your inquiry indicates the Subject, Samuel Smith, as having been very recently employed by Allied Distributors, 555 Washington Street, Los Angeles. We called at listed address and learn that this firm left this address over a year ago and moved to San Francisco. We learn, through a former employment source, that the Subject has been employed by a local blueprint service company (name unknown) since he left Allied Distributors. Telephone book lists another firm by the name of Allied Distributors at 148 Spear Street, Los Angeles. We contacted this firm and learn they are not connected in any way with the Subject's former employer.

The Subject was employed by the Vari-Typer Corporation as a salesman of office machines. The Subject was terminated and is not eligible for rehire. The Subject was not a successful salesman and was described as a "poor mouth." The Subject was constantly telling his troubles to anyone who would listen and disrupted the routine of the office. This former employer has had numerous inquiries from bill collectors concerning the whereabouts of the Subject. The Subject had often stated he had financial troubles and how difficult it is to raise four children (financially).

He was employed by the Hoover Vacuum Cleaner Company as a sales supervisor during dates indicated. He resigned of his own accord for a better future elsewhere and is considered eligible for rehire. File information indicates he had an excellent job/sales rating and no criticisms indicated. He was employed by Metropolitan Life Insurance Company as a Debit Agent. He had a fair job/sales rating and resigned voluntarily for personal reasons. His sales production was described as insufficient.

*Education:* He is believed to have had some college training and appears to possess above average intelligence.

*Sales Experience:* The Subject has been selling for approximately 7½ years. His selling background has included selling office machines, vacuum cleaners, and insurance. Subject's most recent employer, where he sold office machines, indicated the Subject "does not have it as a salesman."

*Sales Aptitude:* We learn of no criticisms of his honesty, dependability, or ability to get along with others. He is described as a "complainer" and is a disrupting influence in the office. He displays an average amount of ambition and initiative, and we learn of no peculiarities.

*Finances:* His financial worth is estimated to consist of equity in a home and auto, cash, savings and personal effects, and household furnishings. A former employment source indicates the Subject has had some financial difficulties indicated when the firm was contacted by numerous bill collectors desiring to know the Subject's whereabouts. A check of court records in Marin County revealed no suits, judgments, bankruptcies or heavy indebtedness. Residence sources had no knowledge of any financial difficulties.

*Health Habits:* He presents a normal, unimpaired appearance and has no known appreciable drink habits. He is not known to use narcotics, and we learn of no serious illnesses.

*Personal Reputation:* He is married, residing with wife, Joan, and four children, ages 11, 10, 8, 3. Subject and his family are well regarded in the community, and we learn of no criticisms of habits, morals, financial standing, or mode of living. Subject is not known to have any special interests or hobbies, and we learn of no club activities. Home is located in a middle-class residential district where home surroundings are favorable.

*Police Records:* Are not available. A check of all locally available civil and federal records are negative.

## EXHIBIT 2

### Retail Credit Company Salesman Selection Report

Name: Tonelli, Albert
Address: Pasadena, California, 703 1st Ave.
Age or Date of Birth: 11/19/44

| | |
|---|---|
| 1. Numbers of years known: | 7,7,6,6,3,3, Years |
| 2. Racial descent: | Italian |
| 3. Net worth: | $16,000 (est.) |
| 4. Annual income: | $ 9,500 (est.) |
| 5. General impression of sales ability: | Average to above |
| 6. Any unfavorable health information developed? | No |
| 7. Any criticism of drink habits? | No |
| 8. Is reputation good? | Yes |
| 9. Recommended? | Yes |

*Scope of Investigation:* Other locations:

Information contained in this report was obtained through interviews with two present employment superiors, two former employment superiors, and two present residence sources. In addition, all locally available court records were checked and sources at a former residence address contacted.

*Exact Date of Employment or Unemployment:*

| | | | |
|---|---|---|---|
| 4/16/1970 | to | present | Firenze Macaroni Company |
| 1967 | to | 12/1969 (approx.) | Los Angeles, California |
| | | | Luigi Brothers Grocery |
| | | | Los Angeles, California |

*Summary of Employment:* The Subject is employed as a macaroni and paste products salesman for the Firenze Macaroni Company. He has been so employed for the period shown above. He is regarded by superiors here as a steady, consistent, and reliable worker and is well regarded here. He works regularly and steadily, and his work record is good. He is not known to be seeking other employment as known to informants here.

Prior to above, he was known to have been employed by the Little City Market, 570 Gray Street, Los Angeles, for approximately four to five months. This address was contacted, and it was noted that this market is no longer in business and location of former owners is unknown to sources in the vicinity of this address.

Prior to above, Subject was employed for approximately the period shown as a grocery clerk for the Luigi Brothers Grocery, Los Angeles. Exact dates of employment are not known to owners of this business; however, sources recalled the Subject as employed for approximately period shown above. Subject was a steady, competent, and capable worker here, and he was very well liked personally by owners of this establishment who were interviewed.

Subject was considered to have resigned from this employment of his own accord in order to accept a better position, and he is eligible for rehire here.

*Education:* His exact educational background was not known to the informants here. However, he was considered to be of average intelligence and I.Q., and he was considered to be at least a high school graduate.

*Sales Experience:* He has had all his known sales experience in the food sales line. He has had most experience in retail grocery sales. However, for the past three years he has been selling paste products to various hotels, restaurants, and retail stores with his present employer. He is considered to be capable and reliable in this work and is considered to be experienced in this line.

*Sales Aptitude:* He is aggressive, enthusiastic, and resourceful in his work, and he works regularly and steadily with no excessive time lost due to minor or recurring illnesses. He is cooperative and personable and gets along well with associates and superiors at past and present employments. He presents a favorable appearance and dresses neatly and in good taste. He is considered to enjoy sales work.

*Finances:* He is financially stable and reliable. He is considered to be living moderately and within his income. He is not known to have any excessive debts or expenditures.

*Health Habits:* He is in good health and presents a favorable physical appearance. He is not known to be impaired, and he has no known excessive use of intoxicants or narcotics. He is not known to engage in any hazardous or dangerous sports or pastimes, and no major past or present illness or injury is known.

*Personal Reputation:* He is married and living congenially with his wife, Maria, and two small children: a son, estimated age 6, and daughter, estimated age 5 years. Family are living at present residence address at 703 1st Avenue, Pasadena, California, in their own home where they have been since 5/1967, and personal reputation and standing in the residence area is excellent. Home surroundings and environment are excellent and no criticism of habits, morals, or associates noted.

*Court Records:* All local civil, criminal, and divorce court records have been screened, and no record of any actions by or against the Subject are noted. We learn of no suits, judgments, or bankruptcies through local handling and informant contacts. Local police records are not available.

# Imperial Belting Company

For over fifty years Imperial Belting Company had been the sales leader of stitched canvas belting, which was used primarily with conveyors and elevators. Each of the nine men on the sales force was a highly trained industrial salesman with considerable knowledge of engineering problems, who earned between $12,000 and $15,000 annually. The general sales manager was concerned with salesman turnover; at least one salesman had left the company each year for the past several years. The sales that were lost while these men were being replaced plus the cost of training a new man, which was estimated at $15,000, made this turnover expensive.

The belting industry consisted of two major segments, manufacturers of rubber belts and manufacturers of canvas belts. There were approximately fifty companies making belts, of which some forty manufactured the rubber type and ten the canvas and cotton woven type. Imperial accounted for about 40 per cent of the total quality canvas belting business, or more than the next three largest canvas belting manufacturers combined. Canvas belts were considered to have a major advantage over the rubber variety—they resisted oils and acids and cost less to maintain. Imperial produced quality belts that sold for 5–15 per cent more than most competitive belts. The company executives believed that their belts lasted two to five times longer than most ordinary rubber or canvas belts.

Each Imperial salesman was expected to make about one hundred calls a month, of which 20 per cent should produce sales; the typical order was for about $1,200. The sales manager expected that about 40 per cent of all calls would be made on new prospects and the remaining 60 per cent on established accounts. All established accounts were to be called on at least once a year. Larger-volume accounts were expected to receive from four to eight calls a year, depending on their size.

A new salesman normally needed nearly a year to acquire the technical information needed to be fully versed on the entire line. An ability to read blueprints was essential. Each salesman was on his own, once he was out in the field, except for monthly visits by the general sales manager. A two-day sales meeting was held once a year. All other contact with the home office was by mail or telephone. The nine sales territories are shown in Exhibit 1. Each salesman had to adapt his sales personality to a number

### EXHIBIT 1

#### Geographic Territory Assignments

Salesman 1: Connecticut, Massachusetts, Vermont, New Hampshire, Maine, 50 per cent of New York, and 50 per cent of New Jersey.

Salesman 2: Maryland, Delaware, Virginia, 50 per cent of West Virginia, 50 per cent of North Carolina, 50 per cent of Pennsylvania, and 50 per cent of New Jersey.

Salesman 3: Canada (basically Montreal and Toronto), 50 per cent of New York, 50 per cent of Pennsylvania, and 25 per cent of Ohio.

Salesman 4: Kentucky, 50 per cent of West Virginia, 75 per cent of Ohio, and 75 per cent of Indiana.

Salesman 5: Alabama, Georgia, S. Carolina, Tennessee, and 50 per cent of North Carolina.

Salesman 6: Michigan exclusively.

Salesman 7: Wisconsin, Minnesota, 50 per cent of Iowa, and 50 per cent of Illinois.

Salesman 8: 50 per cent of Illinois, 25 per cent of Indiana, and 50 per cent of Iowa.

Salesman 9: Arkansas, Colorado, Kansas, Mississippi, Nebraska, and Oklahoma.

of varied situations. On one occasion he might deal with the plant superintendent or with the maintenance foreman, who often had worked his way up from the ranks; at other times his contact would be with the chief engineer, who perhaps had one or more college degrees. The job description for an Imperial sales engineer is shown in Exhibit 2.

All salesmen received the same base salary—$8,000 a year—and expenses which averaged about $6,000. In addition, each salesman received a bonus of 10 per cent on all sales that exceeded the quota established for his territory.

The general sales manager recruited new salesmen primarily through newspaper advertising, employment agencies, and referral of noncompetitive salesmen by Imperial's customers. Management believed that the sales force was not large enough to justify a sales training man; therefore, all training was done by the general sales manager. Since he had many other responsibilities, he was willing to pay a premium to obtain the services of an experienced industrial salesman.

Imperial executives had developed the following list of characteristics, which they believed a salesman would need to have in order to be successful with their firm:

1. Be married.
2. Have two or more children.
3. Be 28–35 years old.
4. Have had some engineering courses.

5.  Be a college graduate.
6.  Not be an only child in his family.
7.  Enjoy traveling and being on his own.
8.  Have a wife who would be a social asset.

A candidate for a selling position usually went through the following procedure:

1.  Filled out an application blank.
2.  Had preliminary interview with general sales manager (generally 15–20 minutes).

### EXHIBIT 2
#### Job Description of an Imperial Sales Engineer

A job description is a written record of the duties, responsibilities, skills, and requirements of a particular job. It is concerned with the job itself and not with the individual. The individual is selected and trained to perform the duties it outlines.

An Imperial representative is the sales manager of his territory and must perform the following essential functions for best performance. (1) sales, (2) service, (3) territory management, (4) sales promotion, (5) executive duties, and (6) goodwill.

1.  Sales:
    Make regular, productive calls.
    Sell the line, demonstrate.
    Handle questions and objections.
    Estimate customer's potential needs.
    Emphasize quality.
    Explain company policies on price, delivery, credit.
    Explain benefits of product to customer.
    Get the order.
2.  Service:
    Report product adaptability, complaints.
    Handle adjustments, returns, and allowances.
    Show customer how to get the most from the product.
    Advise and assist customer on his belt problems.
3.  Territory Management:
    Arrange route for best coverage.
    Balance effort with customer against potential.
    Maintain sales portfolio, samples, kits.
4.  Sales Promotion:
    Develop new prospects and new accounts.
    Call on conveyor manufacturers' headquarters.
    Present suggestions, layouts, and proposals.
5.  Executive:
    Each night make a daily work plan for the next day.
    Prepare and submit daily reports to home office.
    Organize field activity for minimum travel and maximum calls.
    Prepare and submit special reports on trends and competition.
    Collect and submit data requested by home office.
    Investigate lost sales and the reasons for loss.
    Prepare reports on developments, trends, new objections met, and new ideas on meeting objections.
    Attend sales meetings.
    Build a prospect list.
6.  Goodwill:
    Counsel customers on their problems.
    Maintain loyalty and respect for firm represented.

3. Awaited word relative to (1) checking on references given on application blank and (2) evaluation of interview.

4. If step 3 was favorable, he was asked to return with his wife for a final interview.

The general sales manager believed that the yearly turnover of at least one salesman was primarily the result of faulty selection, since he was not able to determine whether or not a candidate possessed the psychological attitudes that would fit him for the job. He could only guess at answers to such questions as: How well can he take being on his own? How well can he take company direction? Does he resist help? Should he be in selling at all?

To help him select salesmen, the sales manager decided to use the services of a psychological testing company, which would test prospective salesmen for $50 per candidate. The testing company suggested that each candidate be given a battery of six tests:

1. Mental ability (Otis Employment Test).
2. Personality portrait (Washburne S-A Inventory).
3. Social intelligence (George Washington University Series).
4. Personality adjustment (Bernreuter Personality Inventory).
5. Interests other than selling (Strong Vocational Interest Test for Men).
6. Sales aptitude (sales sense).

To verify the validity of these tests, the battery was given to each salesman in the company. From analysis of each salesman's test and the correlation of test scores, criteria were established to evaluate the test scores of potential salesmen as shown in Exhibit 3. Upon seeing the results of these tests the sales manager was convinced that they could be a useful tool to help separate the undesirable from the potentially good salesmen. Shortly after completion of this validity work, he was faced with the problem of hiring a salesman. After several months of recruiting, a number of candidates were obtained. Of the group, two men, Mr. Harold R. Overstreet and Mr. George Paddock, appeared to be the best prospects. The selection problem was a difficult one for the general sales manager because both candidates appeared to have equal abilities:

1. Both were married and had children.
2. Both had wives who would be social assets to their work.
3. Both had their own homes.
4. Both had about equal previous industrial selling experience.
5. Both were college graduates with over a year of study in engineering.
6. Both had been in the service as officers.
7. Both were in their early thirties.

Paddock and Overstreet took the aptitude tests, after which the testing firm submitted the reports shown as Exhibits 4 and 5. Each report consisted of a "graphic analysis" and a commentary by an analyst.

**EXHIBIT 3**

**Graphic Test Analysis**

|  | Score to Be Not Less than | Score to Be Not More than |
|---|---|---|
| 1. Mental ability |  |  |
| Speed in arriving at conclusions on new problems | 35 | 90 |
| Accuracy in finding the right answers under time pressure | 35 | 100 |
| Capacity—mental adaptability and trainability | 35 | 100 |
| 2. Personality portrait |  |  |
| Stability—ability to take adversities or turndowns | 65 | 90 |
| Self-sufficiency—capacity to stand on one's own two feet | 30 | 75 |
| Objective-mindedness—treating situations unaffected by own feelings | 75 | 95 |
| Dominance—ability to control interviews and situations | 60 | 90 |
| Self-confidence—confidence in one's own ability to achieve | 65 | 90 |
| Social mixing qualities—need for group sociability | 70 | 90 |
| Aggressiveness and driving power | 50 | 90 |
| 3. Social intelligence |  |  |
| Tact and diplomacy—knowledge of diplomatic things to say and do | 50 | 100 |
| Sizing up—sizing up people in face-to-face social situations | 75 | 100 |
| Judging behavior—judging human behavior correctly | 75 | 90 |
| Sense of humor—ability to take kidding at one's own expense | 75 | 95 |
| 4. Personal adjustment |  |  |
| Sincerity in taking these tests | 30 | 100 |
| Happiness—tendency toward personal and domestic happiness | 90 | 100 |
| How others take to him—feeling of being accepted | 50 | 95 |
| How he takes to others—sympathetic interest in others | 15 | 75 |
| Purposiveness—goals and objectives in business | 75 | 95 |
| First things first—in business situations | 90 | 100 |
| Self-control—capacity for control in business situations | 80 | 100 |
| 5. Sales aptitude |  |  |
| Interest in selling as expressed by sales managers | A | ... |
| Interest in selling tangibles | A | ... |
| Interest in selling intangibles | A | ... |
| Sales sense | 85 | 100 |
| 6. Interests other than selling |  |  |
| Engineer | C | ... |
| Chemist | A | ... |
| Production | B | ... |
| Personnel | B | ... |
| Accountant | No rating | ... |
| Office worker | No rating | ... |
| Purchasing agent | No rating | ... |
| Advertising | No rating | ... |

## EXHIBIT 4

### Graphic Test Analysis
### George R. Paddock

|  | Danger | Desirable | Caution |
|---|---|---|---|
| **1. Mental ability** | | | |
| Speed in arriving at conclusions on new problems......... | | 40 | |
| Accuracy in finding the right answers under time pressure......................................... | | 35 | |
| Capacity—mental adaptability and trainability............. | | 35 | |
| **2. Personality portrait** | | | |
| Stability—ability to take adversities or turndowns......... | | 84 | |
| Self-sufficiency—capacity to stand on one's own two feet................................................. | | 35 | |
| Objective-mindedness—treating situations unaffected by own feelings...................................... | | 93 | |
| Dominance—ability to control interviews and situations.... | | 58 | |
| Self-confidence—confidence in one's own ability to achieve........................................... | | 65 | |
| Social mixing qualities—need for group sociability......... | | 88 | |
| Aggressiveness and driving power...................... | | 34 | |
| **3. Social intelligence** | | | |
| Tact and diplomacy—knowledge of diplomatic things to say and do......................................... | | 34 | |
| Sizing up—sizing up people in face-to-face social situations....................................... | | 99 | |
| Judging behavior—judging human behavior correctly...... | | 29 | |
| Sense of humor—ability to take kidding at one's own expense.......................................... | | | 99 |
| **4. Personal adjustment** | | | |
| Sincerity in taking these tests........................ | | 30 | |
| Happiness—tendency toward personal and domestic happiness........................................ | | 99 | |
| How others take to him—feeling of being accepted....... | | | 20 |
| How he takes to others—sympathetic interest in others..... | | 35 | |
| Purposiveness—goals and objectives in business........... | | 75 | |
| First things first—in business situations.................. | | 99 | |
| Self-control—capacity for control in business situations..... | | 74 | |
| **5. Sales aptitude** | | | |
| Interest in selling as expressed by sales managers.......... | | A | |
| Interest in selling tangibles........................... | | A | |
| Interest in selling intangibles.......................... | | B | |
| Sales sense........................................... | | | 15 |
| **6. Interests other than selling** | | | |
| Engineer............................................. | | | |
| Chemist.............................................. | | | |
| Production........................................... | | B-plus | |
| Personnel............................................ | | | |
| Accountant........................................... | | A | |
| Office worker......................................... | | A | |
| Purchasing agent...................................... | | A | |
| Advertising........................................... | | | |
| **7. Other factors** | | | |
| Analytical tendency................................... | | | X |

## EXHIBIT 5

### Graphic Test Analysis
### Harold R. Overstreet

| | *Danger* | *Desirable* | *Caution* |
|---|---|---|---|
| 1. Mental ability | | | |
| Speed in arriving at conclusions on new problems......... | | 55 | |
| Accuracy in finding the right answers under time pressure..................................... | | 80 | |
| Capacity—mental adaptability and trainability........... | | 45 | |
| 2. Personality portrait | | | |
| Stability—ability to take adversities or turndowns........ | | 65 | |
| Self-sufficiency—capacity to stand on one's own two feet................................................. | | | 21 |
| Objective-mindedness—treating situations unaffected by own feelings....................................... | | 86 | |
| Dominance—ability to control interviews and situations.... | | 78 | |
| Self-confidence—confidence in one's own ability to achieve......................................... | | 75 | |
| Social mixing qualities—need for group sociability......... | | 75 | |
| Aggressiveness and driving power..................... | | 84 | |
| 3. Social intelligence | | | |
| Tact and diplomacy—knowledge of diplomatic things to say and do...................................... | | 99 | |
| Sizing up—sizing up people in face-to-face social situations....................................... | | 89 | |
| Judging behavior—judging human behavior correctly...... | | 54 | |
| Sense of humor—ability to take kidding at one's own expense......................................... | | 94 | |
| 4. Personal adjustment | | | |
| Sincerity in taking these tests....................... | | 35 | |
| Happiness—tendency toward personal and domestic happiness........................................ | | 99 | |
| How others take to him—feeling of being accepted....... | | 94 | |
| How he takes to others—sympathetic interest in others..... | | 15 | |
| Purposiveness—goals and objectives in business........... | | 95 | |
| First things first—in business situations................. | | 99 | |
| Self-control—capacity for control in business situations..... | | 99 | |
| 5. Sales aptitude | | | |
| Interest in selling as expressed by sales managers......... | | A | |
| Interest in selling tangibles.......................... | | A | |
| Interest in selling intangibles......................... | | A | |
| Sales sense....................................... | | 90 | |
| 6. Interests other than selling | | | |
| Engineer......................................... | | | |
| Chemist.......................................... | | | |
| Production........................................ | | | |
| Personnel......................................... | | A | |
| Accountant....................................... | | | |
| Office worker..................................... | | | |
| Purchasing agent.................................. | | | |
| Advertising....................................... | | B-plus | |
| 7. Other factors | | | |

## DETAILED ANALYSIS: PADDOCK

*Objective of This Report.* To evaluate Paddock for the position of industrial salesman.

1. *Mental Ability.* The ratings are in line for the job. Paddock has the capacity for absorbing the essentials of new duties and responsibilities.

2. *Personality Portrait.* Paddock has a strong personality portrait. He reveals capacities for taking it when it comes to the impact of disappointments, defeats, and obstacles and resistances. He has aggressiveness, inner energy, dominance, and driving power, as well as confidence in himself and his abilities and high objective-mindedness.

The following factors should be explored: Paddock was analytical in his approach to the test. Many technical men tend to be analytical, are accustomed to weighing carefully the pros and cons of situations before reaching decisions or making commitments. We have placed this tendency in the caution zone on the color chart because it is important to determine whether or not Paddock may still be in the state of "analysis" relative to the job opportunity being offered him with Imperial Belting. In other words, does Paddock have any uncertainties or doubts or mental reservations concerning the job or his ability to handle the job or the future. If so, these should be completely resolved before he is put on the payroll.

3. *Social Intelligence.* Paddock has capacities for tact and for sizing up people in face-to-face social situations. He earned a fairly good rating for judging behavior.

Paddock earned a top rating for sense of humor. We have placed this in the caution zone on the color chart because it is important for him to recognize the fact that many of the people with whom he will be working out in the field cannot begin to match his own high sense of humor. He must be alerted against impressing such individuals as taking too lightly or airily situations that they would rather have him consider seriously.

4. *Personal Adjustment.* Paddock seems to feel that others may not take to him too readily. Why? Is there any aspect of his appearance, speech, personal mannerisms, or background about which he is sensitive and which he believes others do not like in him?

Ratings for the other adjustment factors are in line for the job.

5. *Sales Aptitude.* Paddock has live interest in selling, but his rating for sales sense is that of the individualist, and usually the individualist sells the hard way and only the rugged survives.

Paddock is not bringing what might be termed an inherent or intrinsic sales sense to the new job with Imperial Belting. Thus he is a risk for employment unless he has had very thorough and specific experience in exactly the same field of work in which he will be operating if employed as an Imperial Belting industrial salesman. If he has this experience, then he is a fair or calculated risk for employment by Imperial Belting; perhaps he will carry over in the new job some specific sales experiences he has had in the same or related field.

It is important in working with Paddock to make certain that at all times he follow through on specific Imperial Belting methods and techniques of selling rather than depend on his own individualist's approach to sales situations.

6. *Interests Other Than Sales.* Paddock's other interests are in line for industrial selling, particularly his interests in manufacturing processes and in purchasing.

*Conclusion and Recommendation.* Paddock is recommended for employment as an industrial salesman with Imperial Belting Company.

## DETAILED ANALYSIS: OVERSTREET

*Objective of This Report.* To evaluate Overstreet's potentials for a sales position with the Imperial Belting Company. In this capacity he would be covering New England and New York City, being away from home for several days to a week at a time but never for week ends.

1. *Mental Ability.* Overstreet's performance on the mental ability test is quite good. It indicates that he should be able to absorb training, new information, and new ideas without any particular difficulty.

2. *Personality Portrait.* Overstreet appears to be a generally sociable individual who is quite amiable and amenable to guidance. He should be a good company man in terms of being willing to follow through on established policies and procedures without making sudden and unexpected changes on his own.

From that standpoint, he should be a good company man. He shows good over-all self-confidence, can take most emotional pressures without becoming easily discouraged, and is sufficiently objective-minded to be able to keep most personal worries or troubles apart from his work. He shows good dominance, drive, and aggressiveness.

The marginal rating for self-sufficiency has positive as well as negative implications. From the positive standpoint, it reflects the type of individual who fits well into a large, smoothly running organization, where he is expected to operate as a member of a closely knit and well co-ordinated team.

By the same token, such a man typically needs to feel that he has the support of his organization and of his manager behind him if he is to function at his best. It is also important, from the standpoint of the traveling aspects of his job, that he have the full support of his family and those who are nearest and dearest to him, since otherwise it may be difficult for him to "take" traveling which keeps him away from home for days and nights at a time. Not only his attitude but the attitude of his wife and family should be checked carefully to be sure that all are in full accord with the desirability of his entering into a position of this type.

It should also be noted that Overstreet apparently has high hopes and great expectations for the future. He seems to expect big things to happen and great events to occur. The question is: Are his "great expectations" realistic and in accordance with the plans and expectations that management has for him? If not, they could lead to ultimate disappointment and a letdown in his efforts.

3. *Social Intelligence.* Overstreet has a fine understanding of what it takes to get along well with other people. He can be so highly tactful and diplomatic as to be almost suave, and he has fine capacity for sizing up other people face to face. He has a good understanding of human nature generally and a fine sense of humor.

4. *Personal Adjustment.* The indications are that Overstreet has made a good adjustment to his home, personal, and business environments.

5. *Sales Aptitude.* Overstreet has a strong interest in the selling field, or the type commonly associated with men who regard that general field of work as a career. Furthermore, he has an excellent understanding of and insight into the "sales-wise" approach to situations.

6. *Interests Other than Sales.* Overstreet also has a strong interest in working with and handling personnel and a secondary interest along advertising, merchandising and sales promotional lines.

*Conclusion and Recommendation.* On the basis of the over-all test pattern, Overstreet is recommended for employment as a salesman with the Imperial Belting Company.

Which candidate, if any, should Imperial hire?

Evaluate the use of this psychological testing program in recruiting salesmen.

# Brewer Company

The Brewer Company, located in a large city in the Southwest, had a 450,000 annual barrel capacity brewery and sold its line of malt beverages in parts of the states of Arizona, New Mexico, and Texas.[1] A family-owned business, the company had enjoyed almost continuous success since its founding in the 1880's. Although the company was currently enjoying an accelerating demand for its line of products, the company's vice president and general manager, Mr. James Brewer, was concerned about what strategies to employ over the next several years.

## THE MALT BEVERAGE INDUSTRY AND CONSUMER

Since the repeal of prohibition the growth of the malt beverage industry had been subject to ups and downs but in recent years had experienced a steady growth. The outlook for the next decade was considered excellent. Malt beverages were served in about two-thirds of the homes in America. While beer drinkers were not restricted to any one particular social or economic group, the bulk—as would be expected—came from the broad middle class (about 75 percent). Surveys indicated that slightly over 64 percent of all men and approximately 40 percent of all women were beer consumers. However, the quantity consumed by each drinker varied sharply. Over two-thirds (68.7 percent) of all beer sold was consumed by only 14.3 percent of the total population. This 14.3 percent comprised the "prime beer market."

The 21–39-year-old age bracket was the top malt beverage consuming group, in terms of both consumer quantity and consumption frequency. Because a major portion of this group consisted of "World War II babies," this segment was experiencing a rapid growth in relation to

Reprinted from *Stanford Business Cases 1970* with the permission of the publisher, Graduate School of Business, Stanford University. Copyright © 1970 by the Board of Trustees of the Leland Stanford Junior University.

[1] Capacity was computed at ten times the greatest monthly output in any yearly period. One barrel equals 31 gallons or 14 cases, each of 24, 12-ounce containers.

the rest of the population. The young market was important since it offered brewers customers with maximum longevity. The older age groups consumed less beer per drinker but, due to increased longevity, were increasing in number.

Approximately 87 percent of the total U.S. beer consumption occurred in urban places and only 13 percent in rural areas. Men accounted for over 80 percent of all beer consumed, even though they represented only some 60 percent of all beer drinkers. Thus, the 21–39-year-old male heavy beer drinker (one of the 14.3 percent who drank over two-thirds of the beer sold) was worth several light drinkers.

Surveys reported that people drank beer at social gatherings because it was refreshing and relaxing and permitted them to break down social barriers. Beer was also a beverage which could be enjoyed "alone." It could be consumed while reading, watching TV, or working. Most people associated beer drinking with events surrounding the evening meal and after-dinner relaxation. This did not mean, however, that most beer was consumed at the evening meal. As a matter of fact less than 30 percent was consumed at a meal.

In considering when beer was consumed during the week, nearly 75 percent was consumed from Monday through Friday and slightly more than 25 percent on Saturday and Sunday. Because there had been a pronounced trend toward more beer drinking in the home, there had been a substantial swing toward packaged beer. More than 80% of all beer consumed was packaged, and 75% of this was bought in container sizes of 12 ounces and under. Food stores—for the nation as a whole—accounted for over 50 percent of all off-premise beer sales. In such outlets nearly three out of five shoppers were women. Package liquor stores accounted for between 25 and 30 percent of total beer sales, and two out of three customers were men. Taverns and bars represented about 15 percent of all off-premise sales, and three out of four customers were men. The past decade had witnessed a substantial trend toward heavier beer purchasing in supermarkets and a decline in purchases made in smaller grocery outlets.

## THE SOUTHWEST BEER CONSUMER

The beer drinker in the Southwest was thought to be the same as the beer drinker nationally. He was visualized as being typically a blue collar worker, male, 21–39 years of age, with an income between $7,000 and $10,000 annually. He was apt to visit on-premise outlets on his way home from work, and he or his wife bought additional beer for home consumption. The Southwest had historically been a heavy on-premise beer area; however, in recent years, approximately 50 percent of the beer sold in the Southwest area served by the Brewer Company was consumed on-premise and 50 percent off-premise.

## COMPANY'S PRODUCT LINE

The company's product line consisted of the Brewer and Fargo brands. The latter was a creation of the Brewer Company and was a price beer which did not receive any media advertising support. Special in-store displays, however, were made available to distributors.[2]

The Brewer brand was by far the company's biggest selling brand. It was heavily advertised, and the company's sales force spent a vast majority of its time promoting this brand. Slightly over 85 percent of the company's volume was sold under the Brewer label. The company estimated that the Brewer brand contributed $9.89 per barrel to the gross margin account versus $4.62 for Fargo. If more of the brewery capacity could be employed, the contributions would increase substantially. Thus, at full (or near full) capacity the Brewer brand contribution would increase to $15.25 and Fargo to $6.15.

### Past and Present Brewer Market Shares

It was clear that Brewer was enjoying a favorable and accelerating demand for its product. To a considerable extent this could be traced to changes in the beer industry—primarily those within that part of the state of Texas which sold the company's brands. The four leading companies accounted for about 75 percent of total beer sales in that part of the Southwest served by Brewer. Over the past several years, however, all but Brewer lost market share as follows:

| | Market Share (estimated) (four-year period) | | |
| Brand | Previous | Current | Gain or Loss |
|---|---|---|---|
| Brand A. | 24.6 | 22.9 | − 1.7 |
| Brewer. | 19.7 | 23.8 | + 4.8 |
| Brand B. | 16.3 | 11.2 | − 5.1 |
| Brand C. | 10.1 | 8.5 | − 1.6 |

The general manager pointed out that a loss in market share did not necessarily imply a loss in the number of barrels sold since the total number of barrels sold in the area increased by about 100,000 during this period. Thus, despite a loss in brand share of 1.7 percentage points, Brand A actually increased its sales during the period. Brand B, of course, lost heavily. He went on to say that a gain in market share during a period when total industry sales were increasing rapidly increased the

---

[2] Although the aging process was essentially the same for both the Brewer and Fargo brands, the latter had less alcoholic content and sold at retail for about 25 percent less.

number of barrels sold substantially, as witness the rise in the Brewer brand sales from 162,473 barrels to 220,793. Brewer sales increase, therefore, had to be in part a function of such losses. During this same period one national brand (Brand D) picked up in excess of 12,000 barrels, and another (Brand E) did almost as well with 10,000 barrels.

During this period Brewer did a number of things which strengthened its position. These included an improvement in its quality control, a change in labels, the addition of new distributors, and the use of a consistent advertising campaign.

A recent market survey among malt beer drinkers in the company's marketing area indicated the following:

1. That Brewer had made its primary gains at the expense of Brand B. Earlier, this brand (a local one) had been purchased by a large national brewery which immediately reduced the brand's advertising. This "saving" was diverted to their national brand.
2. Brewer had greater loyalty among its customers than did the other brands.
3. Brand A was the brand people said they would buy if Brewer was not available.
4. In response to a question dealing with what was liked about the brand used most often, people replied:

**Brand Used Most Often***

| Reason | Brand A (percent) | Brewer (percent) | Brand B (percent) |
|---|---|---|---|
| Long habit | 17 | 34 | 32 |
| Mild, light | 65 | 30 | 27 |
| Local product | 5 | 28 | — |
| Better flavor | 12 | 11 | 24 |
| Tangy taste | — | 9 | 4 |
| Stronger taste | — | 8 | — |
| Smooth and mellow | 5 | 7 | 5 |
| Consistent quality | — | 5 | 2 |
| The hops and malt | 1 | 3 | — |
| Refreshing | 2 | 3 | 2 |
| More body | 2 | 1 | — |
| Good blend | 2 | — | 4 |

*Many respondents gave several reasons. Percentages based on number of men saying Brand A (or Brewer or Brand B) was the beer they used most often.

5. That, in part, the Brewer success had been based on positioning itself opposite from Brand A—letting Brand A have the mild, light story and instead going after and keeping the real beer drinker, the person who wanted taste, tang, hops, malt, quality, and aging.
6. Individual brand images were reported as follows (among all beer drinkers in the study):

| | Brand A (percent) | Brewer (percent) | Brand B (percent) | Brand C (percent) |
|---|---|---|---|---|
| Mild......................... | 61 | 25 | 20 | 20 |
| Aged......................... | 12 | 23 | 18 | 25 |
| Harsh......................... | — | 7 | 2 | 4 |
| Watery......................... | 15 | 1 | 1 | 4 |
| Dependable.................... | 16 | 17 | 15 | 10 |
| Well-brewed................... | 20 | 30 | 20 | 12 |
| Green......................... | 2 | 4 | 2 | 5 |
| Refreshing.................... | 28 | 24 | 14 | 14 |
| Light......................... | 30 | 14 | 11 | 8 |
| Slow-brewed................... | 10 | 16 | 14 | 11 |
| Heavy......................... | — | 6 | 2 | 4 |
| Good flavor................... | 27 | 31 | 26 | 14 |
| Strong. .................... | 1 | 9 | 2 | 5 |
| Stimulating................... | 11 | 10 | 5 | 5 |
| Bitter......................... | 2 | 10 | 5 | 6 |
| It's the hops................. | 7 | 2 | 4 | 7 |
| Quality....................... | 12 | 9 | 6 | 5 |
| Old-fashioned................. | 3 | 4 | 2 | 6 |
| Prestige...................... | 5 | 7 | 5 | 5 |
| Premium....................... | 6 | 7 | 5 | 5 |
| Popular....................... | 20 | 25 | 9 | 9 |

## Brewer's Future Market Coverage and Sales

The company's marketing area was expected to experience good population growth and an annual growth in barrels of 56,000 for the next five to seven years. The most likely explanations for such an increase were shifting age groups and rising incomes. Higher per capita beer consumption was also forecasted for the future, but the company followed a conservative policy of assuming in its forecast that per capita consumption would remain at 15.1 gallons on an annual basis.

Despite the fact that the trend favored the sale of packaged beer versus draft beer and that the former was more profitable, the company's draft sales (in barrels) were up in all but seven distributor areas. The city in which the company's headquarters and brewery were located had shown the largest drop—800 barrels—over the past four years, although package beer had increased during this same period by 10,800 barrels.

Mr. Brewer was concerned about a number of matters pertaining to market coverage. He felt that there was a definite limit to the amount of brand share the company should seek in its present marketing area. "After all," he said, "we've got all our eggs in one basket if we concentrate on only our present market. The higher our brand share the more vulnerable we are. Our growth has to be in Texas. That's where the people are. More specifically we should be looking at the Dallas, Fort Worth, and Houston markets. But the competition is fierce there, and it would take a lot of money even to try to enter these markets. Besides, we have to demonstrate that we know how to enter, successfully, new markets."

In referring to the company's problems in entering new markets, Mr. Brewer was specifically concerned with the company's failure to gain a foothold for its brand in two "new" nearby small Texas areas. In the closest one the advertising budget had been doubled over the past year to $50,000. A full-time salesman was hired to devote all of his time to helping the distributor procure distribution. Although Brewer had managed to get good distribution, brand share was less than 2 percent. Management was concerned that sales per outlet were so low that consumers might be buying overage beer. The distributor did sell several thousand barrels of the company's price brands yearly. In the second area the company had experienced similar difficulties.

Mr. Brewer was also considering what to do with the company's price beer which was distributed in many parts of the market. Although price beers were probably less than 5 percent of the market, the president wondered if he should make an aggressive introduction of Fargo throughout the marketing area within the next year or so. He thought this move might be successful if Fargo were positioned against Brand A. It would be promoted as a mild beer through point-of-purchase advertising and its "light" label. All Brewer distributors would be asked to carry Fargo—assuming that a "go" decision was made.

Recently the company had hired a price beer manager with the express purpose of increasing sales. Gaining entry to a market was difficult because most distributors, especially the better ones, already carried a full line of beer. But the company had the advantage of being known as fair and a quality producer. Recently the price beer manager had succeeded in getting a distributor in Dallas to take on Fargo. Mr. Brewer was seriously considering hiring a salesman to work solely in Dallas to help sell Fargo. In addition, the price beer manager had interested six distributors in Texas and southern California. It was still too early to tell what barrelage these and other prospective distributors might move, but it was thought that 10,000–15,000 barrels per year would be a conservative estimate.

### Channels of Distribution and Sales Force

The company distributed its product to a variety of retailers (of which supermarkets were the most important for the sale of packaged beer) through 27 distributors, of which two were company-owned. In general the management was well satisfied with the performance of the distributors, although some 12 were estimated to have a share of less than 10 percent in their areas.

The company's retail prices for the Brewer brand were competitive with other regional beers but below such national brands as Budweiser and Miller. The typical retail price for six-pack cans is given below:

| | |
|---|---|
| Brewer........................ | $1.17 |
| Fargo......................... | 0.89 |
| Budweiser..................... | 1.39 |
| Miller's...................... | 1.39 |

The following were typical retailer and distributor margins:

| | Retail | Distributor |
|---|---|---|
| Brewer...................... | 23% | $0.60* |
| Fargo....................... | 22 | 0.42 |

\* Per case of 24 units (12-ounce can equivalents).

The company's contact with its distributors was through its 14-man sales force which reported to an assistant sales manager. The sales manager was responsible for advertising, selling, and channel relations. The manager of the company-owned home market distributor reported to the sales manager. Salesmen were paid a salary and expenses and could earn annual bonuses of up to about 15% of their annual salary. The sales force was comprised mostly of high school graduates with an average age in the late 30's. The men resided in their individual territories but made frequent trips to the brewery to discuss local problems. Over the past several years the company had done little sales training although several sales meetings were held annually where salesmen exchanged ideas on ways of meeting difficult problems. Turnover of salesmen was low—less than one a year. Most had been with the company for over ten years.

Salesmen were primarily controlled by call reports which were analyzed daily by the assistant sales manager and summarized for the sales manager. Typically follow-up action was taken only when a salesman's report showed a drop-off in calls. Additionally the two managers were supposed to spend enough time in the field to travel with each salesman several times a year. In recent years this objective had not been realized because the assistant sales manager had been bogged down with paper work as well as in poor health. As a result the sales manager had been forced to spend most of his time in the office.

A salesman had the responsibility of checking all A and B accounts (high-volume stores) in his territory. The classification of stores into A, B, C, and D categories had been accomplished by the marketing research director with the help of individual distributors. In calling on the A and B package accounts, the salesman was expected to: check all point-of-purchase displays; install special "new" point-of-purchase displays; check the stock in the back room to determine its adequacy and freshness; rotate and stock collers; check the number of facings and, if possible, increase them; make certain that the account carried the complete Brewer package line; handle any questions or complaints; and check all cold beer stocks and rotate present stocks.

In calling on an A or B draft account, the salesman was supposed to: check all point-of-purchase displays; install new POS (point of sale) displays during new promotions; check to make certain the draft equipment was functioning correctly; provide the owner/manager with ideas for promoting the sale of Brewer draft beer; buy non-Brewer drinkers who were present a glass of Brewer beer; check the package stock for rotation.

One company problem was that many distributors, especially the old timers, frequently went around the sales manager to the president. Another problem was that many, if not most, distributors expected the company salesman assigned to their territories to set up displays. Theoretically, the salesmen were responsible only for checking the distributor's driver sales force and for helping the distributor with his problems. In practice the salesmen often did the distributor's work.

Each distributor was assigned a Brewer "barrel quota" not broken out by individual package types or sizes. The quota took into account the local economy, previous market share, share trends, competitive pressures, and advertising expenditures and was adjusted quarterly. Before setting quotas the marketing research manager discussed them with the salesman involved.

Distributors were not expected to advertise locally or to make any contribution to the Brewer Company for regional advertising or POS (point of sale). They were encouraged, however, to participate in community projects and service groups.

### Advertising

The Brewer Company had long supported a heavy expenditure in advertising. The current budget (including media, point-of-purchase, and production) was $502,000. Almost all of this total was spent on the Brewer label. The company's agency had not done any extensive testing of the advertising copy used. Over the past several years the company had used two advertising themes as follows:

Enjoy The Perfect Beer
> Since the 1890's we have been developing and refining a perfect blend of Brewer's artistry and modern science.

A Refreshing Interlude
> No other brewery in the Southwest can match Brewer's years of brewing *experience* at blending nature's best ingredients into a refreshing beer.

A study of the effectiveness of Brewer advertising versus other leading brands among male beer drinkers had been made two years earlier. The results are shown in Exhibit 1.

### Conclusion

Mr. Brewer hoped to develop a plan of action which he could present to his father and the company's board of directors at their next meeting.

While he could expect some help from the sales manager, the advertising manager, and the marketing research director, he knew that the major burden of preparing the plan would fall on himself. He fully expected that his plan would call for some "investment spending." While he anticipated some questioning of this, he felt that the company's strong profit and financial position would enable him to obtain the extra funds provided he had a well-integrated plan which demonstrated that the investment would "pay off" in the long run. The company had never had a written plan of any consequence although it did operate with fairly detailed budgets. Mr. Brewer thought he should present a one-year plan in some detail and a less detailed three-year plan. The latter, he thought, was important because some of the expenditures would not pay off until later.

**EXHIBIT 1**

**Summary of Advertising Effectiveness Study**

|  | Total (Percent) | Brand A (Percent) | Brewer (Percent) | All Other (Percent) |
|---|---|---|---|---|
| Recall slogan "It's light" | 68 | 62 | 75 | 70 |
| "Pure Ingredients" | 22 | 21 | 15 | 27 |
| Quality | 20 | 22 | 20 | 17 |
| Saw advertising—TV, billboard | 11 | 18 | 7 | 9 |
| Good flavor, good taste | 10 | 11 | 10 | 9 |
| Made in Arizona | 10 | 13 | 8 | 10 |
| Mild, light, smooth | 6 | 10 | 3 | 4 |
| Cool, refreshing | 6 | 4 | 3 | 10 |
| Horse show | 5 | 9 | 5 | 3 |
| Open for tours | 5 | 4 | 5 | 4 |
| All other positive | 4 | 4 | 5 | 3 |
| All other negative | 2 | 2 | 6 | — |
| Confused with other brands' advertising | — | — | — | — |
| Don't know | 7 | 6 | 11 | 3 |

Brand A's advertising is pretty much the same as it has been for the past five years, and it seems to have held up well partly because the overall diffusion of most beer advertising in this area in the past has made Brand A's consistency particularly effective. It has become an oasis of familiarity in an everchanging slogan scene.

Yet for all that it is not, as we have seen, selling beer the way it should. Has it lost its usefulness? Our own feeling would be otherwise. Rather what has happened is that Brand A has not yet learned how to back up the "it's light" story with the kind of strong reason why story.

The light story belongs to Brand A. But it needs a new framework, additional underscoring, solid support to push ahead in the new situation.

## EXHIBIT 1 (Continued)

### Recall of Brand B Advertising

| | Total (Percent) | Brand B Drinkers (Percent) |
|---|---|---|
| Sponsor wrestling | 15 | 23 |
| Singing, yodeling | 8 | 5 |
| Saw ad on billboards, TV | 6 | 24 |
| Old recipe beer | 5 | 9 |
| German type of beer | 5 | 2 |
| Let's have a Brand B | 4 | 7 |
| Sociable, fun, get-together | 4 | 11 |
| Remember German scenes | 3 | 5 |
| Remember little men | 2 | 3 |
| Slow-brewed | 2 | 10 |
| Best quality | 2 | 5 |
| Best flavor, taste | 2 | 2 |
| Light, mild | 2 | 2 |
| All other positive | 3 | 11 |
| Confuse with other brands' advertising | 3 | 2 |
| Don't know | 49 | 31 |

### BRAND B ADVERTISING

Brand B has done little or no advertising for the past several years; thus the recall is rather surprising. The fascinating story here is that three years after Brand B stopped almost all its advertising about half of the beer drinkers' market is unaware of the change; and less than two out of three of the brand's own drinkers note the change. Yet the question, which in all fairness must be asked, is whether this is a tribute to Brand B's former advertising or the lack of individuality and uniqueness of most of the other beer advertising.

For Brand C the "aged" claim is the best feature of the advertising. Without this the advertising would be in trouble. The other factor which may be helping is the "made in the Southwest, local beer" tag line.

Over the past several years Brewer has increased the recall of their advertising from 24% to 40%.

### Recall of Brewer Advertising, 1955–1962

| | 1962 (percent) | 1957 (percent) | 1956 (percent) | 1955 (percent) |
|---|---|---|---|---|
| Recall Brewer advertising | 40 | 41 | 30 | 24 |
| Don't recall | 60 | 59 | 70 | 76 |

But this is considered to be only part of the story, since what was working was not the central advertising theme but the back-up signature of "The Southwest's Oldest and Most Experienced Brewery" and the local appeal.

Experience and local overtones in the image are good, but the basic quality

**EXHIBIT 1 (Continued)**

Brand C Advertising
Recall of Brand C Advertising

|  | Total (Percent) | Brand C Drinkers (Percent) |
|---|---|---|
| The Beer of the Old Southwest................... | 24 | 36 |
| Label with Spurs (Red, Silver, Gold)............ | 15 | 20 |
| Aged...................................... | 13 | 25 |
| Local beer—made in the Southwest............. | 11 | 15 |
| Partying, fun............................... | 4 | 5 |
| Dance time................................ | 4 | 10 |
| Sports..................................... | 4 | — |
| American beer.............................. | 4 | 5 |
| Dislike advertising.......................... | 3 | — |
| People's beer; workingman's beer................ | 2 | 5 |
| Outdoor sports.............................. | 2 | — |
| Old reliable beer............................ | 1 | 10 |
| Less expensive, better buy..................... | 1 | 5 |
| All other positive............................ | 3 | 10 |
| Don't know................................ | 40 | 15 |

Brewer Advertising Recall

|  | Total (Percent) | Brewer Drinkers (Percent) | All Others (Percent) |
|---|---|---|---|
| Remember "Made for Over 60 years by Experienced Craftsmen"...................... | 15 | 21 | 13 |
| Remember "Made locally"...................... | 12 | 21 | 12 |
| Saw advertising on billboards, TV............... | 10 | 12 | 10 |
| Quality, best beer............................ | 7 | 7 | 7 |
| Show outdoor scenes......................... | 5 | 9 | 4 |
| Waterfalls.................................. | 4 | 7 | 2 |
| Sponsor sports.............................. | 4 | 6 | 2 |
| "Perfected"................................. | 3 | 3 | 4 |
| Refreshing, cool............................. | 2 | 2 | 2 |
| Made from old formula........................ | 1 | 2 | — |
| Good flavor................................. | 1 | — | 2 |
| Man pouring beer from glass................... | 1 | 2 | — |
| Light, mild................................. | 1 | 1 | 1 |
| Visit the brewery, tours....................... | 3 | 4 | 3 |
| Confuse with other brands' advertising............ | 3 | 1 | 4 |
| All other positive............................ | 1 | 2 | — |
| All other negative............................ | 1 | — | 2 |
| Don't know................................ | 60 | 39 | 67 |

**EXHIBIT 1 (Continued)**

beer story is not coming through any more than it comes through in the advertising recall.

When we recap the overall beer advertising recall picture, the need for a basic reevaluation of the company's advertising approach is apparent. The evidence speaks for itself,

Comparative Recall of Individual Brand's Advertising
Efforts among All Beer Drinkers

| Brand | Recall Advertising (percent) | Don't Recall (percent) |
|---|---|---|
| Brand A | 93 | 7 |
| Brand C | 60 | 40 |
| Brand B | 51 | 49 |
| Brewer's | 40 | 60 |

In addition, beer drinkers appear to be rather consciously aware of the weakness of Brewer's current theme. This is indicated in the next table which shows their responses to the question: "If you had to choose a brand of beer on the basis of advertising, which one brand would you choose?"

*Observation.* It is a mistake, of course, to try to make advertising experts of consumers. What they do, how they react is the important factor—not what they say.

One step further, before we try to look for further clues on the kind of advertising message which might work best for Brewer. In the following table we have shown, slogan by slogan, how each of the brand's individual slogans are related back to the individual brands by the beer drinkers. In this instance, the drinker was reminded of the slogan and then asked to tell us what brand came to mind for each one.

Yet of all the brands of beer on the shelves, Brewer beer, in actual life, does satisfy the physical beer needs of its users more than any other brand.

The real story for Brewer's advertising lies in the responses of the different brand users to the single question: "When does your brand of beer taste best to you?"

Brand Choice on Basis of Advertising

| Brand | Total (percent) | Brewer Drinkers (percent) |
|---|---|---|
| Brand A | 39 | 32 |
| Brand C | 10 | 9 |
| Brand B | 8 | 12 |
| Brewer's | 7 | 13 |

## EXHIBIT 1 (Continued)

*Observation.* Here we see the real dividing line between a mild, light beer and a real beer. The mild beer is the social beer, the occasional outdoor beer, the summer beer, even the TV-watching beer.

But the real beer—the one with hops and malt, brewed, and aged—with real ingredients—this is the beer for the moments when the beer need is greatest—when thirsty, tired, after work—hot—just plain thirsty for a glass of beer.

This is the Brewer story, which is not now being sold or told. This is the story which, if properly executed, can help Brewer keep its current customers,

### Aided Recall of Brand Slogans

| | *Percent* | | *Percent* | | *Percent* |
|---|---|---|---|---|---|
| *Largest Selling Beer* | | *Aged* | | *Does the Most Advertising* | |
| Brand A | 37 | Brand C | 55 | Brand A | 42 |
| Brewer | 14 | Brewer | 9 | Brand C | 28 |
| Brand B | 14 | Brand A | 4 | Brewer | 6 |
| All others | 20 | Don't know | 32 | All others | 10 |
| Don't know | 19 | | | | |
| *Slow-Brewed* | | *People Like It* | | *Best Tap Beer* | |
| Brand B | 15 | Brand C | 48 | Brewer | 22 |
| Brewer | 11 | Brewer | 8 | Brand A | 18 |
| All others | 20 | All others | 11 | Brand B | 10 |
| Don't know | 43 | Don't know | 31 | All others | 5 |
| | | | | Don't know | 35 |
| | | | | *The Best Packaged Beer* | |
| *Oldest Beer Company* | | *Pure Pleasure* | | | |
| Brewer | 40 | Brand A | 19 | Brand A | 19 |
| Brand A | 13 | Brand C | 12 | Brewer | 12 |
| All others | 7 | Brewer | 7 | Brand B | 9 |
| Dont know | 40 | All others | 10 | Brand C | 8 |
| | | Don't know | 30 | All others | 7 |
| | | | | Don't know | 28 |
| *The Lady's Beer* | | *The Sportsman's Beer* | | | |
| Brand A | 35 | Brand A | 12 | | |
| Brand C | 2 | Brewer | 15 | | |
| Brand B | 2 | Brand B | 10 | | |
| All others | 2 | Brand C | 8 | | |
| Don't know | 50 | All others | 10 | | |
| | | Don't know | 23 | | |

build more loyal users, increase consumption, and extend its present share of customers.

We will recognize that it is an easier story to unlock than it is to tell—but it is the story which does need telling. Only then will Brewer advertising pull its weight and really contribute to the outstanding job being done by Brewer on other scores.

## EXHIBIT 1 (Continued)

### Brand Associations

A measure of brand image is its association with various types of people or occupations. The beer drinkers were read a list of occupations and types of people and asked to associate a beer brand with each. They were also handed a card listing the brand names that they could refer to at any time.

### When Brand Tastes Best

|  | Total (Percent) | Brewer (Percent) | Brand A (Percent) | Brand B (Percent) |
|---|---|---|---|---|
| When I'm hot | 24 | 33 | 24 | 12 |
| When I'm thirsty for a glass of beer | 22 | 35 | 15 | 22 |
| After work | 35 | 46 | 35 | 22 |
| When I'm tired | 14 | 17 | 13 | 17 |
| In the summer | 11 | 8 | 14 | 11 |
| With meals | 4 | 4 | 4 | 5 |
| Social occasions | 9 | 2 | 13 | 7 |
| Any time | 3 | — | 5 | 4 |
| In the evening, after dinner (watching TV) | 22 | 15 | 23 | 25 |
| Outdoors | 9 | 2 | 14 | 11 |
| When I'm relaxing | 9 | 7 | 11 | 10 |
| All others | 9 | 9 | 6 | 8 |

The groups have been separated into these associated more with Brewer and those associated more with Brand A.

As might have been expected, Brand A is strongly associated with women and white collar workers. It is also connected with drinkers who are not very knowledgeable about beer (young people) and those who don't drink much beer (athletes and retired people).

Brewer is a rough, masculine beer—for the heavy beer drinker and the man who is sports-minded.

### Brand Identification

In an attempt to determine the importance of various beer characteristics and to evaluate brand image with these characteristics, respondents were presented with sets of paired values on a five-point rating scale. The "pairs" consisted of matched antonyms. Negative words were avoided and words connoting similar ideas were rotated, thus minimizing bias.

The respondent was asked in the beginning to designate for each "pairing" where he would rate "what he looks for" in a beer. For example, the respondent was asked to indicate whether he looked for a very light beer, a somewhat light beer, neither a light nor a dark beer, a somewhat dark beer, or a very dark beer. The same procedure was used for five other "pairs" of values. The frequencies for the various traits were averaged to derive comparable means for the different brands and subgroups. The means for "look for" ratings will be referred to, in this report, as the "ideal" beer.

The purpose of this design is to provide a workable benchmark for future reference so that trends can be observed and evaluated. Therefore, statistical

## EXHIBIT 1 (Continued)

variance and standard deviation have been determined for every mean average shown. The size of our sample was such that a difference of .02 percent or more in a total column shall be considered significant. Lowering the sample size increases the variability; therefore, when evaluating the means in the heavy user, moderate-light user, or other subgroups, they must be at least .04 percent from one another to be statistically significant.

The data are first presented in tabular form and then reproduced graphically for easier readability and more comprehensive comparison.

### Brands Associated with Different Occupations and Types of People

| | Brewer (Percent) | Brand A (Percent) | Brand B (Percent) | Brand C (Percent) | Don't Know (Percent) |
|---|---|---|---|---|---|
| *Associate More with Brewer's* | | | | | |
| Men.......................... | 27 | 16 | 9 | 6 | 26 |
| Fishermen..................... | 21 | 16 | 3 | 8 | 28 |
| Mechanics..................... | 21 | 12 | 7 | 8 | 36 |
| Truck drivers.................. | 18 | 11 | 10 | 11 | 30 |
| Hunters....................... | 18 | 11 | 8 | 11 | 30 |
| Boaters....................... | 15 | 12 | 7 | 7 | 38 |
| *Associate More with Brand A* | | | | | |
| Women....................... | 7 | 46 | 4 | 2 | 25 |
| College students............... | 11 | 36 | 5 | 5 | 30 |
| Young people.................. | 10 | 35 | 3 | 5 | 30 |
| Retired people................. | 7 | 28 | 4 | 1 | 39 |
| Waiters....................... | 8 | 27 | 4 | 3 | 38 |
| Athletes....................... | 9 | 20 | 8 | 3 | 49 |
| Salesmen...................... | 11 | 15 | 7 | 4 | 40 |
| Doctors....................... | 6 | 14 | 8 | 1 | 40 |
| Farmers....................... | 12 | 13 | 7 | 7 | 44 |
| Military officers............... | 9 | 11 | 9 | 4 | 44 |

**EXHIBIT 1 (Continued)**

**Mean Averages of Ratings Given "Ideal" Beer
Compared with Ratings Given Various Brands**

|  | Ideal Beer (Percent) | Brand A (Percent) | Brewer (Percent) | Brand B (Percent) | Brand C (Percent) |
|---|---|---|---|---|---|
| *Light/Dark* | | | | | |
| Total beer drinkers............ 2.0 | | 1.7 | 2.2 | 2.3 | 2.6 |
| Heavy beer drinkers........... 1.9 | | 1.6 | 2.2 | 2.3 | 2.4 |
| Moderate-light beer drinkers.... 2.0 | | 1.7 | 2.2 | 2.3 | 2.7 |
| *Smooth/Tangy* | | | | | |
| Total beer drinkers............ 2.7 | | 2.4 | 3.4 | 3.2 | 3.4 |
| Heavy beer drinkers........... 2.8 | | 2.4 | 3.5 | 3.2 | 3.2 |
| Moderate-light beer drinkers.... 2.5 | | 2.3 | 3.3 | 3.3 | 3.5 |
| *Bland/Sharp* | | | | | |
| Total beer drinkers............ 2.9 | | 2.5 | 3.4 | 3.2 | 3.4 |
| Heavy beer drinkers........... 3.0 | | 2.5 | 3.4 | 3.1 | 3.4 |
| Moderate-light beer drinkers.... 2.7 | | 2.5 | 3.4 | 3.3 | 3.4 |
| *Light Body/Full Body* | | | | | |
| Total beer drinkers............ 2.9 | | 2.5 | 3.4 | 3.4 | 3.4 |
| Heavy beer drinkers........... 3.1 | | 2.4 | 3.5 | 3.3 | 3.2 |
| Moderate-light beer drinkers.... 2.7 | | 2.6 | 3.3 | 3.4 | 3.7 |
| *Mild Flavor/Strong Flavor* | | | | | |
| Total beer drinkers............ 2.3 | | 2.0 | 3.0 | 2.9 | 3.4 |
| Heavy beer drinkers........... 2.4 | | 1.9 | 3.0 | 2.7 | 3.3 |
| Moderate-light beer drinkers.... 2.2 | | 2.1 | 3.1 | 3.1 | 3.6 |
| *Sweet/Hoppy* | | | | | |
| Total beer drinkers............ 3.6 | | 3.2 | 3.8 | 3.7 | 3.7 |
| Heavy beer drinkers........... 3.7 | | 3.1 | 3.8 | 3.7 | 3.7 |
| Moderate-light beer drinkers.... 3.4 | | 3.2 | 3.7 | 3.7 | 3.7 |

**EXHIBIT 1 (Continued)**

"Ideal" Beer Ratings of Various Groups

| | Drink Brewer (Percent) | Drink Brand A (Percent) | Drink Brand B (Percent) | Drink Brand C (Percent) | Drink Other Brands (Percent) | Heavy Beer Drinkers (Percent) | Moderate-Light Beer Drinkers (Percent) | Males (Percent) | Females (Percent) |
|---|---|---|---|---|---|---|---|---|---|
| Light/dark.......... | 2.1 | 1.8 | 1.9 | 2.0 | 2.0 | 1.9 | 2.0 | 2.0 | 1.8 |
| Smooth/tangy........ | 2.9 | 2.4 | 3.1 | 2.0 | 2.5 | 2.8 | 2.5 | 2.7 | 2.4 |
| Bland/sharp......... | 3.1 | 2.7 | 3.0 | 2.8 | 2.7 | 3.0 | 2.7 | 2.9 | 2.6 |
| Light body/full body... | 3.3 | 2.8 | 2.9 | 2.7 | 2.7 | 3.1 | 2.7 | 3.0 | 2.8 |
| Mild/strong......... | 2.6 | 2.0 | 2.3 | 2.5 | 2.2 | 2.4 | 2.2 | 2.4 | 2.0 |
| Sweet/hoppy........ | 3.7 | 3.4 | 3.4 | 3.6 | 2.4 | 3.7 | 3.4 | 3.7 | 3.2 |

**EXHIBIT 1 (Continued)**

GRAPH NO. 1
All Beer Drinkers Rate "Ideal" Beer, Brewer, and Brand A

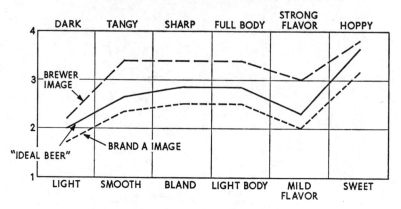

GRAPH NO. 2
Heavy Beer Drinkers Rate "Ideal" Beer, Brewer, and Brand A

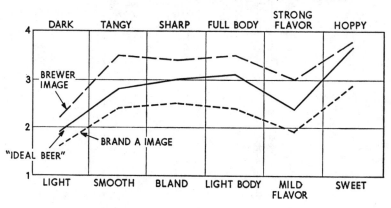

GRAPH NO. 3
Moderate and Light Beer Drinkers Rate "Ideal" Beer, Brewer, and Brand A

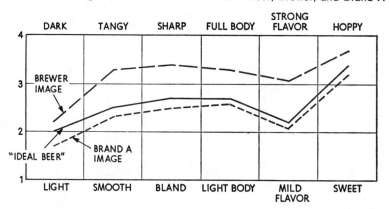

**EXHIBIT 1 (Continued)**

GRAPH NO. 4
All Beer Drinkers Rate Brewer, Brand C, and Brand B

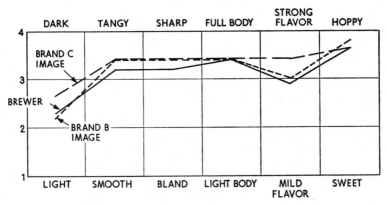

GRAPH NO. 5
Brewer Drinkers, Brand A Drinkers, and Heavy Beer Drinkers Rate "Ideal" Beer

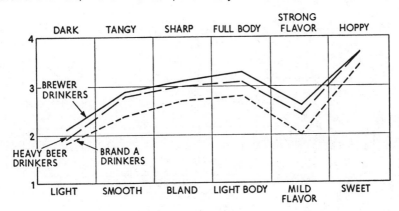

GRAPH NO. 6
Brewer Drinkers, Brand A Drinkers, and Moderate/Light Drinkers Rate "Ideal" Beer

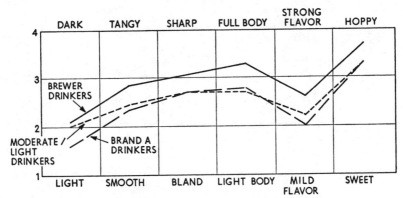

**EXHIBIT 1 (Continued)**

GRAPH NO. 7
Brewer Drinkers, Males, and Females Rate "Ideal" Beer

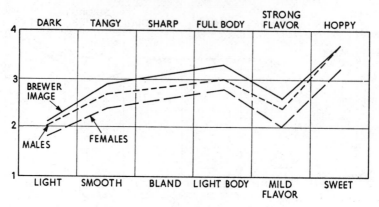

GRAPH NO. 8
Brand A Drinkers, Males, and Females Rate "Ideal" Beer

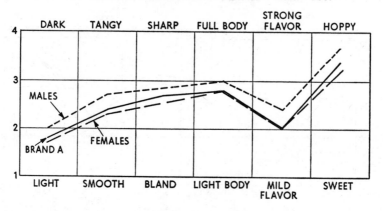

GRAPH NO. 9
Brewer Image Compared with Brand B Drinker and Brand C Drinker "Ideal" Beer

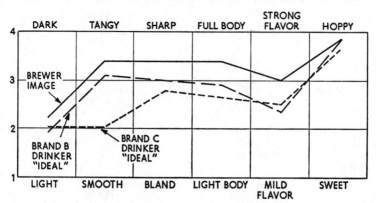

**EXHIBIT 1 (Concluded)**

GRAPH NO. 10
Brewer Image Compared with Heavy Drinkers and Moderate/Light
Drinkers "Ideal" Beer

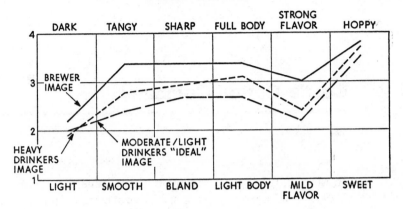

GRAPH NO. 11
Brewer Image Compared with Brewer Drinkers and Brand A Drinkers "Ideal" Beer

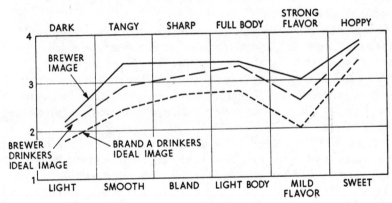

# Castle Coffee Company

In May of 1972 Mr. Adrian Van Tassle, advertising manager for the Castle Coffee Company, tugged at his red mustache and contemplated the latest market share report. This was not one of his happier moments as he exclaimed, "I've got to do something to turn this market around before it's too late for Castle—and me. But I can't afford another mistake like last year. . . ."

Indeed, Mr. William Castle (the president and a major stockholder of the Castle Company) had exhibited a similar reaction when told that Castle Coffee's share of the market was dropping back toward 5.4%—where it had been one year previously. He had remarked rather pointedly to Mr. Van Tassle that if market share and profitability were not improved during the next fiscal year "some rather drastic actions" might need to be taken.

Adrian Van Tassle had been hired by Mr. James Anthoney, vice president of marketing for Castle, in the summer of 1970. Prior to that time he had worked for companies in the Netherlands and Singapore and had gained a reputation as a highly effective advertising executive. Now in the spring of 1972 he was engaged in trying to reverse a long-term downward trend in the market position of Castle Coffee.

## Castle's Market Position

Castle Coffee was an old, established company in the coffee business, with headquarters in Squirrel Hill, Pennsylvania. Its market area included the east coast and southern regions of the United States and a fairly large portion of the midwest. The company had at one time enjoyed as much

Reprinted from *Stanford Business Cases 1973* with the permission of the publisher, Graduate School of Business, Stanford University. Copyright © 1973 by the Board of Trustees of the Leland Stanford Junior University.

This case was developed by Professors William F. Massy, David B. Montgomery, and Charles B. Weinberg of the Graduate School of Business, Stanford University.

as 15% of the market in these areas. These were often referred to as the "good old days," when the brand was strong and growing and the company was able to sponsor such popular radio programs as "The Castle Comedy Hour" and "Castle Capers."

The company's troubles began in the 1950's, when television replaced radio as the primary broadcast medium. Castle experienced increasing competitive difficulty as TV production and time costs increased. Further problems presented themselves as several other old-line companies were absorbed by major marketers. For example, Folger's Coffee was bought by Procter and Gamble and ButterNut by Coca Cola. These giants joined General Foods Corporation (Maxwell House Coffee) among the ranks of Castle's most formidable competitors. Finally, the advent of freeze-dry and the increasing popularity of instant coffee put additional pressure on Castle, which had no entry in these product classes.

The downward trend in share was most pronounced during the 1960's: the company had held 12% of the market at the beginning of the decade but only about 5½% at the end. Share had held fairly stable for the past few years. This was attributed to a "hard-core" group of buyers plus an active (and expensive) program of consumer promotions and price-off deals to the trade. Mr. Anthoney, the vice president of marketing, believed that the erosion of share had been halted just in time. A little more slippage, he said, and Castle would begin to lose its distribution. This would have been the beginning of the end for this venerable company.

**Operation Breakout**

When William Castle was elevated to the presidency in 1968, his main objective was to halt the decline in market position and, if possible, to effect a turnaround. His success in achieving the first objective has already been noted. However, both he and Anthoney agreed that the same strategy, i.e., intensive consumer and trade promotion, would not succeed in winning back any appreciable proportion of the lost market share.

Both men believed that it would be necessary to increase consumer awareness of the Castle brand and develop more favorable attitudes about it if market position were to be improved. This could only be done through advertising. Since the company produced a quality product (it was noticeably richer and more aromatic than many competing coffees), it appeared that a strategy of increasing advertising weight might stand some chance of success. A search for an advertising manager was initiated, which culminated in the hiring of Adrian Van Tassle.

After a period of familiarizing himself with the Castle Company and the American coffee market and advertising scene, Van Tassle began developing a plan to revitalize Castle's advertising program. First, he "released" the company's current advertising agency and requested proposals from a number of others interested in obtaining the account. While it was generally understood that the amount of advertising would increase somewhat, the heaviest emphasis was on the kind of appeal and copy execution to be used. Both the company and the various agencies agreed that nearly all the advertising weight should go into spot television. Network sponsorship was difficult because of the regional character of Castle's markets, and no other medium could match TV's impact for a product like coffee. (There is a great deal of newspaper advertising for coffee, but this is usually placed by retailers under an advertising allowance arrangement with the manufacturer. Castle included such expenditures in its promotional budget rather than as an advertising expense.)

The agency which won the competition did so with an advertising program built around the theme, "Only a Castle is fit for a king or a queen." The new agency recommended that a 30% increase in the quarterly advertising budget be approved, in order to give the new program a fair trial. After considerable negotiation with Messrs. Castle and Anthoney and further discussion with the agency, Van Tassle decided to compromise on a 20% increase. The new campaign was to start in the autumn of 1971, which was the second quarter of the company's 1972 fiscal year (the fiscal year started July 1, 1971, and would end June 30, 1972). It was dubbed "operation breakout."

### Performance During Fiscal 1972

Castle had been advertising at an average rate of $1.0 million per quarter for the last several years. Given current levels of promotional expenditures, this was regarded as sufficient to maintain market share at about its current level of 5.4%. Castle's annual expenditure of $4 million represented somewhat more than 5.4% of industry advertising, though exact figures about competitors' expenditures on ground coffee were difficult to obtain. This relation was regarded as normal, since private brands accounted for a significant fraction of the market and these received little or no advertising. Neither Mr. Van Tassle nor Mr. Anthoney anticipated that competitive expenditures would change much during the next few years regardless of any increase in Castle's advertising.

Advertising of ground coffee followed a regular seasonal pattern, which approximated the seasonal variation of industry sales. The relevant figures are presented in Table 1. Total ground coffee sales in Castle's market area averaged 22 million cases per quarter and were expected to remain at that level for several years. Each case contained 12 pounds of coffee in one-, two-, or three-pound containers. Consumption in winter was about 15% above the yearly average, while in summer the volume was down by 15%.

Advertising expenditures by both Castle and the industry in general followed the same basic pattern, except that the seasonal variation was between 80% and 120%—somewhat greater than the variation in sales. The "maintenance" expenditures on advertising, shown in Table 1, were what the company believed it had to spend to maintain its "normal" 5.4% of the market in each quarter. Van Tassle had wondered whether this was the right seasonal advertising pattern for Castle, given its small percentage of the market, but decided to stay with it during fiscal 1972. Therefore, the 20% planned increase in quarterly advertising rates was simply added to the "sustaining" amount for each quarter, beginning in the second quarter of the year. The planned expenditures for fiscal 1972 are also shown in Table 1.

In speaking with Mr. Castle and Jim Anthoney about the proposed changes in the advertising program, Mr. Van Tassle had indicated that he expected to increase market share to 6% or perhaps a little more. This sounded pretty good to Mr. Castle, especially after he had consulted with the company's controller. Exhibit 1 presents the controller's memorandum on the advertising budget increase.

### TABLE 1
#### Industry Sales and Castle's Advertising Budget

| Quarter | Industry Sales | | Maintenance Advertising | | Planned Advertising for FY 1972 | |
|---|---|---|---|---|---|---|
| | Cases* | Index | Dollars* | Index | Dollars* | % Increase |
| 1. Summer......... | 18.7 | 0.85 | .8 | 0.80 | .8 | 0% |
| 2. Autumn......... | 22.0 | 1.00 | 1.0 | 1.00 | 1.2 | 20% |
| 3. Winter......... | 25.3 | 1.15 | 1.2 | 1.20 | 1.44 | 20% |
| 4. Spring.......... | 22.0 | 1.00 | 1.0 | 1.00 | 1.2 | 20% |
| Average....... | 22.0 | 1.00 | 1.0 | 1.00 | 1.16 | 16% |

\* In millions.

Mr. Van Tassle had, of course, indicated that the hoped-for 6% share was not a "sure thing" and, in any case, that it might take more than one quarter before the full effects of the new advertising program would be felt.

The new advertising campaign broke as scheduled on October 1, 1971, the first day of the second quarter of the fiscal year. Adrian Van Tassle was somewhat disappointed in the commercials prepared by the agency and a little apprehensive about the early reports from the field. The bimonthly store audit report of market share for September–October showed only a fractional increase in share over the 5.4% of the previous period. Nevertheless, Van Tassle thought that, given a little time, things would work out and that the campaign would eventually reach its objective.

The November–December market share report was received in mid-January. It showed Castle's share of the market to be 5.6%. On January 21, 1972, Mr. Van Tassle received a carbon copy of the memorandum in Exhibit 2.

**EXHIBIT 1**

August 1, 1971

Confidential

Memo to:    W. Castle, President
From:        The Controller (I.F.)
Subject:     Proposed 20% Increase in Advertising

I think that Adrian's proposal to increase advertising by 20% (from a quarterly rate of $1.0 million to one of $1.2 million) is a good idea. He predicts that a market share of 6.0 percent will be achieved, compared to our current 5.4 percent. I can't comment about the feasibility of this assumption. That's Adrian's business and I presume he knows what he's doing. I can tell you, however, that such a result would be highly profitable.

As you know, the wholesale price of coffee has been running about $8.60 per 12-pound case. Deducting our average retail advertising and promotional allowance of $0.80 per case, and our variable costs of production and distribution of $5.55 per case, leaves an average gross contribution to fixed costs and profit of $2.25 per case. Figuring a total market of about 22 million cases per quarter and a share change of from 0.054 to 0.060 (a 0.006 increase), we would have the following increase in gross contribution:

$$\text{Change in gross contribution} = \$2.25 \times 22 \text{ million} \times .006$$
$$= \$0.30 \text{ million}$$

Subtracting the change in advertising expense due to the new program and then dividing by this same quantity gives what can be called the advertising payout rate:

$$\text{Advertising payout rate} = \frac{\text{Change in gross contribution} - \text{change in advertising expense}}{\text{Change in advertising expense}}$$

$$= \frac{\$0.10 \text{ million}}{\$0.20 \text{ million}} = .50$$

That is, we can expect to make $.50 in net contribution for each extra dollar spent on advertising. You can see that as long as this quantity is greater than zero (at which point the extra gross contribution just pays for the extra advertising), increasing our advertising is a good deal.

I think Adrian has a good thing going here, and my recommendation is to go ahead. Incidentally, the extra funds we should generate in net contribution (after advertising expense is deducted) should help to relieve the cash flow bind which I mentioned last week. Perhaps we will be able to maintain the quarterly dividend after all.

I. F.

On Monday, January 24, Jim Anthoney telephoned Van Tassle to say that Mr. Castle wanted an immediate review of the new advertising program. Later that week, after several rounds of discussion in which

**EXHIBIT 2**

January 20, 1972

Memo to:    W. Castle, President
From:       The Controller (I.F.)
Subject:    Failure of Advertising Program

I am most alarmed at our failure to achieve the market share target projected by Mr. A. Van Tassle. The 0.2 point increase in market share achieved in November–December is not sufficient to return the cost of increased advertising. Ignoring the month of October, which obviously represents a start-up period, a 0.2 point increase in share generates only $100,000 in extra gross contribution on a quarterly basis. This must be compared to the $200,000 we have expended in extra advertising. The advertising payout rate is thus only—0.50: much less than the break-even point.

I know Mr. Van Tassle expects shares to increase again next quarter, but he has not been able to say by how much. The new program projects an advertising expenditure increase of a quarter of a million dollars over last year's winter quarter level. I don't see how we can continue to make these expenditures without a better prospect of return on our investment.

cc:   Mr. J. Anthoney
      Mr. Van Tassle

Private postscript to Mr. Castle: In view of our autumn 1971 performance we must discuss the question of the quarterly dividend at an early date.

I. F.

Mr. Van Tassle was unable to convince Castle and Anthoney that the program would be successful, it was decided to return to fiscal 1971 advertising levels. The TV spot contracts were renegotiated, and by the middle of February advertising had been cut back substantially toward the $1.2 million per quarter rate that had previously been normal for the winter season. The agency complained that the efficiency of their media "buy" suffered significantly during February and March, due to the abrupt reduction in advertising expenditure. However, they were unable to say by how much. The spring 1972 rate was set at the normal level of $1.0 million. Market share for January–February turned out to be slightly under 5.7%, while that for March–April was about 5.5%.

## Planning for Fiscal 1973

So, in mid-May of 1972 Adrian Van Tassle was faced with the problem of what to recommend as the advertising budget for the four quarters of fiscal 1973. He was already very late in dealing with this assignment, since media buys would have to be upped soon if any substantial increase in weight were to be effected during the summer quarter of 1972. Alternately, fast action would be needed to reduce advertising expenditures below their tentatively budgeted "normal" level of $0.8 million.

During the past month Van Tassle had spent considerable time reviewing the difficulties of fiscal 1972. He had remained convinced that a 20% increase in advertising should produce somewhat around a 6% market share level. He based this partly on "hunch" and partly on a number of studies that had been performed by academic and business market researchers with whom he was acquainted.

One such study which he believed was particularly applicable to Castle's situation indicated that the "advertising elasticity of demand" was equal to about ½. He recalled that the definition of this quantity when applied to market share is:

$$\text{Advertising elasticity of demand} = \frac{\text{Percent change in market share}}{\text{Percent change in advertising}}.$$

The researcher assured him that it was valid to think of "percent changes" as being deviations from "normal levels" (also called maintenance levels) of advertising and share. However, he was worried that any given value of advertising elasticity would be valid only for moderate deviations about the norm. That is, the value of ½ he had noted earlier would not necessarily apply to (say) plus or minus 50% changes in advertising.

Van Tassle noted that his estimate of share change (6.0 − 5.4 = 0.6 percentage points) represented about an 11% increase over the normal share level of 5.4 points. Since this was to be achieved with a 20% increase in advertising, it represented an advertising elasticity of 11%/20% = 0.55. While this was higher than the 0.5 found in the study, he had believed that his advertising appeals and copy would be a bit better than average. He recognized that his ads may not actually have been as great as expected but noted that, "even an elasticity of 0.5 would produce 5.94% of the market—within striking distance of 6%." Of course, the study itself might be applicable to Castle's market situation to a greater or lesser degree.

One lesson which he had learned from his unfortunate experience the last year was the danger inherent in presenting too optimistic a picture to top management. On the other hand, a "conservative" estimate might not have been sufficient to obtain approval for the program in the first place. Besides, he really did believe that the effect of advertising on share was greater than implied by performance in the autumn of 1971. This judgment should be a part of management's information set when they evaluated his proposal. Alternatively, if they had good reason for doubting his judgment, he wanted to know about it—after all, William Castle and Jim Anthoney had been in the coffee business a lot longer than he had and were pretty savvy guys.

Perhaps the problem lay in his assessment of the speed with which the new program would take hold. He had felt it "would take a little time" but had not tried to pin it down further. ("That's pretty hard, after all.") Nothing very precise about this had been communicated to management. Could he blame the controller for adopting the time horizon he did?

As a final complicating factor, Van Tassle had just received a report from the agency about the "quality" of the advertising copy and appeals used the previous autumn and winter. Contrary to expectations these ads rated only about 0.90 on a scale which rated an "average ad" at 1.0. These tests were based on the so-called theater technique, in which various spots were inserted into a filmed "entertainment" program and their effects on choices in a lottery designed to simulate purchasing behavior were determined (see Exhibit 3 on theater tests). Fortunately, the ads currently being shown rated about 1.0 on the same scale. A new series of ads scheduled for showing during the autumn, winter, and spring of 1973 appeared to be much better. Theater testing could not be undertaken until production was completed during the summer, but "experts" in the agency were convinced that they would rate at least as high as 1.15. Mr. Van Tassle was impressed with these ads himself but recalled that such predictions tended to be far from perfect. In the meantime a budget request for all four quarters of fiscal 1973 had to be submitted to management within the next week.

## EXHIBIT 3

### Theater Tests*

In theater testing an audience is recruited either by mail or by phone to attend a showing of test television programs. When the members of the audience arrive, they are given a set of questionnaires, through which an emcee guides them as the session progresses. Usually, data on the audience's opinions and preferences regarding the various brands in the product categories being tested are gathered before the show begins. The show consists of a standard television program episode (or two or more such episodes) in which several television commercials have been inserted. At the close of the showing, audience members are again asked to fill out questionnaires, reporting on the commercials they remember, and are again asked to give their opinions and preferences concerning the various brands of the advertised products. In many cases, the members of the audience (or some proportion of them) also record their interest in the show as it progresses by turning a dial as their interest level rises and falls, which permits the analyst to trace "interest curves" for the program. One service, Audience Studies, Inc., of Los Angeles, also

---

* From Kenneth A. Longman, *Advertising*. (New York: Harcourt, Brace Jovanovich, Inc., 1971), pp. 326–7. Reprinted with their permission.

measures basal skin resistance continuously for some members of the audience, for recent studies have suggested that there is a connection between this measure and the audience's degree of involvement with the material on the screen.

The theater test is one of the most versatile of the available test methods. It can be used to test television commercials in many different stages of development, and it has sometimes been used to test radio commercials and print ads (presented in the form of slides). To offset the high cost of this method, several advertisements for noncompeting products are normally tested in a single session, thus splitting expenses among several advertisers. The method yields fair measures of attention-getting power, credibility, and motivating power. However, it is not very valuable in diagnosing specific problems in the commercials. To some extent, interest curves and measures of skin resistance can help to pinpoint weak spots, but the best way to obtain information that will point the way to improvement is to hold group interview session immediately after the showing, using a few people selected from the audience.

1. State precisely what you think the objectives of Castle's 1972 advertising plan should have been. Were these the objectives of Van Tassle? William Castle? I.F. (the controller)?

2. Evaluate the results obtained from the 1972 advertising campaign prior to and after the cut in advertising funds. What do you think the results would have been if the 20% increase had been continued for the entire year?

3. What should Van Tassle propose as an advertising budget for 1973; how should he justify this budget to top management?

4. How should Van Tassle deal with the issues of seasonality and copy quality?

# Varian Associates, Incorporated

Early in April, 1966, the marketing research director of the Tube Division of Varian Associates, Inc., was faced with the problem of responding to a request made by the manager of the Operations Research Unit to specify exactly what types of decisions could and would be made using data obtained from the media survey now in the field. The media study had been initiated in the fall of 1965 by the advertising manager of the tube division to obtain needed information on the readership of selected magazines and journals. At one time or another a variety of interested parties, including the division's advertising agency, the Corporate Public Relations officer, the Corporate Director of Research, and the division's marketing manager had participated in formulating the study of design.

Varian Associates, with headquarters in Palo Alto, California, is one of the largest electronics companies in the world. Founded as an outgrowth of the pioneering work done before and during World War II on the klystron tube the company grew in some twenty years from 6 people and $22,000 in sales to 6,400 employees and annual sales of $100 million in 1965. The company is organized into three major groups as follows:

## 1.  Microwave Tube Group

This group is comprised of the Palo Alto tube division; the Eimac Division of San Carlos, California; the Bomac Division of Beverly, Massachusetts, S-F-D Laboratories, Inc., of Union, New Jersey; Varian Associates of Canada, Ltd., Georgetown, Ontario; and Semicon Associates, Inc., Lexington, Kentucky. Major products of the group consist of

Reprinted from *Stanford Business Cases 1970* with the permission of the publisher Graduate School of Business, Stanford University. Copyright © 1970 by the Board of Trustees of the Leland Stanford Junior University.

klystron tubes, traveling wave tubes, magnetron tubes, gas switching tubes, microwave components, solid state devices, crossed-field devices, backward wave oscillators, and klystron amplifiers. The basic applications for these products include early warning radar, radar astronomy, satellite communications, missile guidance, air traffic control, weather radar, UHF television, microwave relay systems, beacons, microwave test equipment, navigation aids, and navigation.

### 2.  Instrument Group

This group is comprised of the Analytical Instrument Division of Palo Alto, the Recorder Division also in Palo Alto, and the Quantum Electronics Division of Beverly, Massachusetts and Palo Alto. The major products of the group include spectrometers, laboratory electromagnetics and superconducting magnets, recorders, frequency standards, and magnetometers. The basic applications for these products include quantitative and qualitative nondestructive analysis of chemical compounds, isotope identification, laboratory research, studies of the behavior of matter under the influence of precise magnetic fields, navigation, timekeeping, communications, geophysical exploration, magnetic search, deep space probes, and oceanographic research.

### 3.  Equipment Group

This group produced such products as ultra-high vacuum pumps and systems, vacuum instrumentation, and linear accelerators. The basic applications of these products include appendage pumping, vacuum tube processing, mass spectometers, physics experiments, evaporation and deposition, environmental testing, study of services, metallurgical studies, physical and biological studies, clinical radiation therapy, food irradiation, high energy physics studies, and radiation chemistry studies.

*    *    *    *    *

The Tube Group was the largest in sales of the three groups. It sold its products to both military and industrial companies typically on a contract-bid basis. In 1965 the group employed a total of 40 salesmen and servicemen. In addition, a substantial number of men at the various headquarters offices assisted the field men when the occasion arose. The Tube Group spent several hundred thousands each year in advertising and promotion including media advertising, trade shows, workshops, publicity, direct mail, and catalogs.

The advertising manager of the Tube Group summed up his request for a media study by saying, "I want to know what magazines and journals are the most efficient to use to cover audiences that I specify as needing to receive certain messages." He also indicated that in preparation for a media study of some sort he was revising his master mailing list by omitting individuals who were not influential in the purchase of products produced by the tube group. This master list had been compiled over the years through sales reports, inquiries, trade shows, direct mail, and workshops. In order to bring it up to date all tube sales and service people were asked to indicate the names, titles, and addresses of all those people whom they thought were influential in deciding what supplier to use. The specific request read, "We would like to ask that you prepare a list of the ten most influential people in each of your major accounts; these should be people that you feel we should be reaching with our advertising."

After receiving the names from the field force and further culling, the master list contained approximately 3,500 names of which 600 were indicated as being "prime influentials." It was decided to conduct the survey among all 3,500, but to identify the 600 separately so as to be able to follow up either by phone or mail on them where necessary.

The group's advertising agency was asked what information should be obtained in the media study. The agency's response is shown in Exhibit 1. After evaluating the agency's reply as well as requests from other individuals, a final questionnaire was prepared (see Exhibit 2). Follow-ups were planned on the entire sample to obtain a high rate of returns. The questionnaire was mailed together with a stamped first-class return envelope in February and March, 1966.

At one of the several conferences held to implement the survey the responsibility for analyzing the returns was given to the Operations Research Unit. Since the same survey approach would likely be used by other Varian groups, the OR Unit was anxious to develop a standardized set of procedures for computerizing and analyzing the data. To do this they had to know *exactly* what decisions the advertising manager planned to make using the survey data, what additional information he wished to correlate with the survey data, and what "operational" measures he wanted to use. As an example of the latter the word "coverage" represented a problem. The term could be used in a variety of ways including the number of people reached by the average issue of a given magazine or journal, or it could mean the cumulative audience reached by a given number of issues of a magazine or journal.

The OR Unit requested that the Tube Group marketing research manager get together with the division's advertising manager to respond to numerous suggestions pertaining to the development of a simple media model which could, it was thought, be made operational through the use of the survey data. The proposed model is described in Exhibit 3.

*How should the Marketing Research Manager and Advertising Manager of the Tube Group respond to the request from the OR Unit?*

**EXHIBIT 1**

Hoefer, Dieterich & Brown, Inc. Advertising and Public Relations
414 Jackson Square, San Francisco, California 94111—Yukon 1–1811

November 5, 1965

Mr. Dick Barck
Marketing Department
Varian Associates
611 Hansen Way
Palo Alto, California

Dear Dick:

I enclose an outline of the kinds of information that we would find useful when the media preference survey is completed for the Tube Group.

Taking the groupings in order, we're interested in a breakdown of the company's primary areas of interest because different kinds of products should, obviously, be advertised to different kinds of systems manufacturers. You may be able to provide this information within Varian on most of the companies.

We want some sort of a breakdown on job function, because the new Business Publication Association (BPA) figures on circulation by member publication will be broken down in this manner. The functions that I have suggested are those used by Microwaves magazine in their own circulation analysis.

We would like to break the surveys into groupings by (1) specifying function and (2) approving function. In addition, if possible, we would like to have a "rating" as to degree of actual influence in the actual purchase.

As to the publications themselves, I have listed the magazines now under consideration for Tube Group promotion, plus two amateur-oriented publications being used by Eimac. The list should probably be checked with Bob Landon to make sure that we are covering his market adequately. I have consciously excluded questions dealing with the "most useful" editorial or "do you read the advertisements," because I frankly don't know what to do with this type of information after I have it. We don't care, in my opinion, whether he reads the magazine because it contains information pertinent to his job, or because it contributes interdisciplinary information in which he is interested, or because it provides general news about his industry. We do care whether or not he reads it regularly, and whether or not he considers it "must" reading. As to the advertising readership, it's our job to make the ads sufficiently interesting so that he *will* read them.

After the results are in, we will provide cost information which can be related to publication preferences and market coverage. It should be fairly simple to

**EXHIBIT 1 (Continued)**

determine a "cost efficiency" rating by comparing the weighted percentage of regular readers to the absolute cost of a single advertising page.

Please call me if you have any questions.

Very truly yours,

HOEFER, DIETERICH & BROWN, INC.

/s/ Hal

Hal H. Marquis

sh

Enclosure
cc:  Mr. Paul Warner
     Mr. Bill Engel
     Mr. Jim Kirby

(1)  Company's primary areas of interest:

    Communications systems manufacturers
    Telemetering & data systems manufacturers
    Electronic countermeasures systems manufacturers
    Navigation & guidance systems manufacturers
    Air traffic control & landing systems manufacturers
    Weapon control systems manufacturers
    Miscellaneous radar systems manufacturers
    Research & development laboratories
    U.S. Government & military
    Microwave test equipment manufacturers
    Miscellaneous microwave components manufacturers
    General: materials, plasma, nuclear, magnetics, etc.

(2)  Job function of individual answering questionnaire:

    Application engineering
    Development engineering
    Design engineering
    Research
    Engineering management
    Purchasing
    Administrative management
    Production management

(3)  Individual's influence in buying decision:

    a.  Specify components: (rate 1 to 10)
    b.  Review purchase decision: (rate 1 to 10)

(4)  Readership of the following publications (rated "read occasionally," "read regularly," and "consider *must* reading"):

**EXHIBIT 1 (Concluded)**

PRODUCT:    Electronic Design, Electronics, EDN (Electrical Design News), E.E.E., Electro-Technology, Electronic Industries, Signal, Space Aeronautics, Solid State Design, IEEE Proceedings, IEEE Spectrum

PURCHASING:    Electronic Procurement, Electronic Specifying and Procurement

MILITARY:    Air Force & Space Digest, Armed Forces Management, Army, Ordnance, Data, Journal of the Armed Forces, Naval Institute Proceedings

AMATEUR:    CQ and QST

HORIZONTAL:    Aviation Week, Astronautics & Aeronautics, Electronic News, Industrial Research, International Science & Technology, Missiles & Rockets, Research/Development, Scientific American

(5)  Agency will provide information on circulation, cost-per-thousand-readers, and cost-per-page. Final figures should relate cost-per-page to weighted percentage of regular readers in Varian study.

**EXHIBIT 2**

Varian Associates Executive Offices

Palo Alto, California

Robert T. Davis
Vice President, Marketing
Dear Sir:

Would you please help us in solving one of our marketing problems?

We're trying to improve our communications programs. During the next eighteen months, we will, with your permission, be calling on you for your personal advice on the subject of magazine ads.

This survey is the first of the series and asks for your reading preference; the second will follow in about six months and will deal with the effectiveness of our ads; the third questionnaire, later in the year, will give you the opportunity to help us actually write our ads.

We hope you will take a few minutes to answer this questionnaire. Your response will be very meaningful and greatly appreciated.

Very truly yours,

Robert T. Davis

RTD/bb

Inside are photographs of 28 magazines serving our industry. In the spaces provided, please check how often you read each of these magazines. If you do not read a magazine, simply leave the spaces blank. (Note: This part of the questionnaire is not contained in the case.)

**EXHIBIT 2 (Continued)**

Questionnaire*

*Which of the 28 mentioned magazines do you find most helpful in your work?*
*(Please list in order of importance)*

1. _____     4. _____
2. _____     5. _____
3. _____     6. _____

*In addition, we ask you to indicate your job function and the primary area(s)*
*of your work.*

My work is primarily concerned with the following:

(Check one only)

MANAGEMENT                ENGINEERING
   ☐ Administrative           ☐ Design/Application
   ☐ Engineering Program      ☐ Manufacturing/Production

RESEARCH & DEVELOPMENT     ☐ OTHER _____
   ☐ Basic (No specific end product)   (Specify)
   ☐ Applied (Product development)

The primary technical area(s) of my work is (are) concerned with:

☐ RADAR                      ☐ TEST MEASUREMENT
☐ NAVIGATION, GUIDANCE       ☐ INDUSTRIAL HEATING
   & CONTROL                    PROCESS & CONTROL
☐ ECM/PEN AIDS               ☐ SCIENTIFIC & MEDICAL
☐ TELEMETRY                  ☐ OTHER _____
   COMMUNICATIONS                        (Specify)
      ☐ Broadcast
      ☐ Military
      ☐ Other _____
            (Specify)

*Thank you for taking the time to answer these questions. Your assistance in this*
*phase of our over-all marketing program is sincerely appreciated. All that re-*
*mains is to fold the questionnaire and return it to me in the enclosed self-*
*addressed envelope.*

**EXHIBIT 3**

Excerpts from the Proposal by the OR Unit to Set up a Media Model

The proposed model (called MISER) has as its objective among selected audience groups the generation of a weighted readership scale *and* a readership distribution. The former provides a score based on reach and frequency of exposure within specified time periods while the latter consists of two distributions, the first of which yields the percentage of readers exposed once, twice, etc. The second distribution is cumulative. By comparing the weighted scores

---

* These questions were asked in addition to those pertaining to the readership (if any) of the 28 magazines.

**EXHIBIT 3 (Continued)**

and the readership distribution of two or more alternative media schedules the user can decide which schedule best suits his objectives.

The media vehicle data which is being obtained by individuals from the survey will be collapsed into the following question—"what is the probability of prospect X being exposed to the *average* issue of each of a variety of print media vehicles?" No attempt will be made to measure the extent or degree of exposure. Thus, exposure is defined operationally as whether a respondent reports reading "something" within a particular vehicle.

The probability statement is used because of the problem of time. Assume a quarterly journal. If one knew that a prospect is exposed on the average to three out of four issues then the probability of exposure to the *average* issue would be .75; if the exposure is two out of four it would be .50; and so on. Obviously, if the prospect is exposed to all four issues then it would be certain (1.0) that he read the average issue.

The problem of how to treat additional exposures (either within a specific vehicle through time or between media vehicles) is not easily solved. The problem is complex because of the need to ascertain at the margin the effect of each additional exposure given certain time intervals between exposures. Naturally the effect of repetition has to be evaluated differently for different products. In the case at hand it is proposed that the first exposure be rated at .9, the second at 1.0, the third at .9,—all within a two months' interval on the assumption that your advertising will be centered on products which are relatively new and complex; therefore, the "reader" will need exposure to two ads in order to obtain "full" information. A special feature of the model calls for providing you with the opportunity of inserting the "current" media schedule to inoculate individual prospects following which the schedule to be tested can be better evaluated through the weighting of additional exposures.

We estimate the total cost of building MISER at about $4,000 and that each schedule can be "tested" at a cost not to exceed $40.

# Hatfield versus Duncan[1]

In early 1966, Oregon's Republican governor, Mark O. Hatfield, appeared to be the winner in the race for the seat in the U.S. Senate that had been vacated by Democrat Maurine Neuberger. Hatfield's Democratic opponent, Representative Robert B. Duncan, was largely unknown to voters outside his own Congressional District in southwest Oregon. Moreover, Hatfield had a record as one of the strongest vote-getters in Oregon's political history. Then one issue—Viet Nam with all its personal and political ramifications—began to change the character of the race.

In late July Hatfield's key staff planners and his advertising agency met to consolidate and to alter the direction of the campaign for the final election in November. At this time it was clear that Hatfield, and not Duncan, was the candidate in trouble.

Hatfield's trouble began in April and May. Although he had previously made statements opposing the administration's policy in Viet Nam, his comments began to attract national attention during a speaking tour in Arizona and Texas early in the year. At that point, Hatfield's position did not seem out of line, because his most likely opponent, Representative Edith Green, was even more of a "dove." The May Democratic primary, however, made Hatfield's position on Viet Nam look unsound politically. Representative Duncan, not Green, ran against Howard Morgan, another "dove" on Viet Nam, who was strongly supported in his campaign by Senator Wayne Morse, one of the most vitriolic critics of the administration with respect to Viet Nam. Duncan won with a vote of

Reprinted from *Stanford Business Cases 1970* with the permission of the publisher, Graduate School of Business, Stanford University. Copyright © 1970 by the Board of Trustees of the Leland Stanford Junior University.

[1] This case was prepared by Assistant Professor Michael L. Ray of Stanford and Professor John D. Phillips, a Vice President of Lewis and Clark College, Portland, Oregon. Although the entire case is based on actual events, confidential figures and dates have been changed. The case is merely a description of events and is not meant to be critical of administrative action or political tactics.

130,478, while Hatfield totaled only 131,025, running against several relatively unknown candidates in the Republican primary. Duncan gave unmistakable evidence of the kind of campaign he would run against Hatfield. His successful primary effort was laced with statements on Viet Nam like:

If we don't stop the Communists on the Mekong, we'll have to fight them on the banks of the Columbia River.

Communism can't be contained by debate and argument.

There is no road to peaceful settlement which we have not explored. It cannot help our cause to negotiate with each other while Hanoi refuses to negotiate.

Hatfield himself gave Duncan's "hawkish" emphasis further fuel and meaning in the first week of July at the National Governors' Conference in Los Angeles. There Hatfield's views again stirred local and national comment when he refused to sign a resolution supporting the administration's position on Viet Nam—the "military defense of South Viet Nam against aggression." In casting the only negative vote (49 to 1), Hatfield said he did not support escalation of the war.

It was evident that Duncan had an issue that could coalesce any negative feeling that might have existed against Hatfield in Oregon before the Viet Nam problem. The attitude of many Oregonians after the Governors' Conference was:

We're not sure we want two people representing us back there in the Senate who stand alone.

The statement linked Hatfield's lone dissent with Senator Wayne Morse's stand on Viet Nam. Many Democrats saw Hatfield as another Morse—somebody who would regard himself as "his own man" rather than as a man who would be "loyal" to the administration or the party or Oregon. At the same time, many Republicans recalled that Morse was once a Republican and bolted to the Democrats on the basis of a "position" which they naturally regarded as highly unsatisfactory.

All of these events strongly affected the senatorial contest. In July, a survey conducted by pollster John Kraft for the Oregon AFL-CIO showed the following:

|  | *Percent* |
| --- | --- |
| Duncan | 46 |
| Hatfield | 40 |
| Uncommitted | 14 |

The Hatfield planners now had an uphill battle on their hands.

## THE OREGON POLITICAL ENVIRONMENT

Oregon is a relatively small state in population (about 2 million in 1966), but its political importance is relatively great. Oregon's primaries were quite crucial, for example, in the fortunes of several presidential candidates (e.g., Governor Rockefeller's victory in Oregon in 1964 gave a substantial boost to his campaign), and its senators often had great visibility.

The state could be characterized as Democratic and reasonably "liberal" on most issues. Lumber is the major industry with food and paper products following. The defense industry was showing some growth in Oregon in 1965 and 1966.

Oregonians personally could be classed as rugged outdoor types. Hunting and fishing are very popular. One of the few "liberal" issues that failed to gain substantial support in Oregon was gun control. This failure obviously reflected Oregon's outdoor and "individualistic" style of living.

The Kraft poll taken in July also asked Oregon voters what issues they thought were the most important, and more of them mentioned taxes than anything else. Next came inflation, then "big government," while the fourth ranked area of concern was Viet Nam with about 25 percent.

Oregon was essentially a one-party state until 1954, when Democrat Richard Neuberger was elected to the Senate, and Edith Green launched her career as congressman from the Third District by defeating Republican Tom McCall. In fact, the 1954 elections merely recorded the turning point in a long-term trend of voter registrations toward the Democratic Party. This trend continued during the next ten years, as follows:

| Year | Democrats | % | Republicans | % | Others | % | Total |
|------|-----------|-----|-------------|-----|--------|-----|---------|
| 1954 | 402,283 | 49.1 | 404,694 | 49.4 | 12,562 | 1.5 | 819,539 |
| 1956 | 451,179 | 51.4 | 413,659 | 47.1 | 13,114 | 1.5 | 877,952 |
| 1958 | 447,195 | 52.3 | 395,090 | 46.2 | 12,759 | 1.5 | 855,044 |
| 1960 | 480,588 | 53.4 | 405,195 | 45.0 | 14,833 | 1.6 | 900,616 |
| 1962 | 473,561 | 53.6 | 395,351 | 44.7 | 14,778 | 1.7 | 883,690 |
| 1964 | 511,973 | 54.9 | 402,336 | 43.2 | 18,152 | 1.9 | 932,461 |

These statistics show that registered Republicans were actually *fewer* in 1964 than in 1954, while the Democrats had registered an increase of 109,690, or 27 percent. In view of this continuing trend, it is somewhat surprising that Oregon politics had remained intensely competitive throughout the five elections.

Three major factors may be cited to help in explaining the continued competitiveness of Oregon politics:

1. The new Democratic registrations were composed largely of recent immigrants from Southern and Midwestern states. Their party preferences arose from the force of habit rather than ideological conviction, and, in the context of Oregon politics, they formed a rather "conservative" bloc of voters.

2. Both party organizations were traditionally very weak in Oregon,

dating from the historical commitment to "popular democracy" of the Progressive Era, and reflecting the continuing popular commitment to (a) an open primary system of candidate selection and (b) a system of state administration which is virtually devoid of patronage. (For example, despite fairly uniform support for Sig Unander among GOP leaders in 1958, Mark Hatfield defeated him in the gubernatorial primary. But when he became governor, Hatfield had only two positions on his own office staff to dispense to his loyal supporters.)

3. It may be fairly stated that the Republicans had been remarkably fortunate in developing attractive statewide candidates who contrasted favorably with their Democratic counterparts.

Yet despite all of these factors which tended to neutralize the impact of the Democratic registration advantage, it still exercised a critical influence upon Oregon politics. *The Democratic cross-over vote is the pivotal factor in almost every major race;* the Republican candidate strives to maximize it, and the Democratic candidate struggles to minimize it.

Although final figures would not be available from the Elections Division until October 25, it appeared that total voter registrations for the 1966 General Election would approach 960,000—including 528,000 Democrats, 413,000 Republicans, and 19,000 "others." Past experience with similar off-year elections suggested that Republican turnout in this General Election would be about 75 percent to 78 percent. This would give the Democrats a numerical advantage of 396,000 to 322,000, or about 74,000 actual votes. Assuming that the small "other" vote was equally divided, this meant that *in order to win, a statewide Republican candidate had to net at least 37,000 Democratic votes* over and above those required to offset Republican cross-over votes. Or to state the same point another way, even if he could draw 100 percent of the Republican vote, he would also need to attract one out of every ten voting Democrats in order to win.

Any strategy for victory in Oregon also had to consider the geographic composition of voters. Oregon has 36 counties which were organized into four congressional districts in 1966. The biggest plum in any election was the Portland area composed of Multnomah, Clackamas, and Washington counties. This area alone constituted 41 percent of the population and 45 percent of the registered voters. The concentration of Oregon's population was such that if just seven more counties (Lane, Marion, Jackson, Douglas, Linn, Coos, and Klamath) were added to the Portland counties, over 76 percent of Oregon's registered voters could be accounted for. The bulk of the populous counties were in the western part of the state, moving down the Willamette Valley from Portland.

Although Mark Hatfield had always done well throughout the state, Portland was considered to be a relatively strong area for Duncan because of its strong Democratic composition. Duncan's congressional district was the Fourth which was not in the heavily populated Portland area but was composed of seven counties in the southwestern portion of the state.

## MARK O. HATFIELD

Despite the extreme problems of the 1966 campaign, the Hatfield planners still had an impressive candidate to work with. In his previous political outing for governor in 1962, Hatfield rolled up a plurality of 80,000 votes over Robert Thornton by securing an estimated *net* cross-over of 21 percent of the voting Democrats. Hatfield's personal attractive-ness, his well-advertised church activities, his moderate political posture, and his ten-year exposure as an elected state official gave him a large stock of basic political assets.

Hatfield, born in Dallas, Oregon on July 12, 1922, was often called the "boy wonder" or the "golden boy" because he was the youngest Oregon governor (36) in 1959 and was reelected in 1962.

A former associate professor of political science and dean of students (Willamette U., 1950–1956), Hatfield was a state representative from 1950 to 1954, a state senator from 1954 to 1956 and Oregon's secretary of state from 1957 to 1959.

A lifelong Republican, Hatfield started his political career at 10, carry-ing literature for Herbert Hoover. By 1960, it was Hatfield who placed Richard M. Nixon in nomination for President at the GOP National Con-vention and, at the Republican National Convention in 1964 he was Temporary Chairman and Keynoter. In his keynote address, he urged the party to rid itself of extremists, specifically mentioning the Ku Klux Klan, the John Birch Society, and the Communist Party. Later, in a char-acteristic move for a strong party man, he campaigned actively in Oregon for Barry Goldwater, despite their obvious differences of opinion. This move and others like it led some to charge that Hatfield was a political opportunist who was "wishy-washy" in his views.

A "liberal" of the same ilk as New York's Governor Rockefeller Hat-field prefers calling himself a "moderate" or an exponent of "western Progressivism." Nevertheless, his public record reveals that as a legislator, he took an active role in Oregon's civil rights legislation, one of the most enlightened in the nation, supported strong legislation for the protection of migrant labor, and co-authored the legislation creating Oregon's presidential primary system.

As governor, he supported programs in welfare, education, recreation, and economic development. When he faced an economic crisis (as a re-sult of the legislature refusing to raise the state income tax), he slashed the budget, but refused to institute a sales tax believing such a tax to be "regressive."

Hatfield worked hard to bring industry to Oregon. He advocated "orderly development and growth" and particularly emphasized five areas of growth—wood products, tourism, agriculture, services (auxiliary to transportation and distribution of goods), and industry related to the sciences. Despite his efforts, however, the lumber industry was still of dangerous predominance in the Oregon economy.

Hatfield felt strongly that it was the "challenge of the states to revitalize and retain a powerful position in our federal system," and that reorganization, reform, and consolidation within the states are essential. He contended that there was too much local and too much federal government.

On water-power resources, Hatfield was a "middle-of-the-roader," favoring public or private ownership depending on the circumstances. He did find a need for the states to get together on such matters as the protection of water rights.

Hatfield favored foreign aid for economic development but was against aid to the communist bloc.

The issue about which Hatfield had been most outspoken, of course, was Viet Nam. He continually attempted to make his view clear. He disagreed with Morse's stance in that he did not consider the U.S. position "illegal" nor did he want the withdrawal of troops. But he said that the President's policy was "contradictory" and "unclear," that the administration was not being "candid and truthful" and that he would not give Johnson a "blank check" on the issues of peace or escalation.

Hatfield wanted Johnson to give "guidelines, goals and objectives with regard to the war." Furthermore, he contended that the U.S. should not "go it alone." Alone, he said, the U.S. is "moment by moment in a position of confrontation with Red China." Hatfield believed that the Vietnamese "common man" wanted, above all, to be left alone and to have enough to eat. Judging that a "free" election in the U.S. sense was out of the question, he anticipated that a consensus was the best to be expected at the present in Viet Nam.

Hatfield advocated: "frank and open discussion" on "overall objectives and goals," allied support as well as a halt in their trade with China and North Viet Nam; a look into "every alternative to bloody conflict"; persistence in getting U.N. action; and a reopening of the Geneva Conference.

As a result of his views, Hatfield was dubbed a "duck"—halfway between a "dove" and a "hawk."

Personally, Hatfield is handsome, conservative in dress, and a "cool, competent speaker." This coolness had been turned against him as evidence of his difficulty in dealing with the Oregon legislature. Some critics said he was not competent in the political infighting that would be necessary in the senate. Deeply religious, he neither drinks nor smokes. He is married and has four children. The oldest was seven at the time of the election in 1966.

## ROBERT B. DUNCAN

In contrast to Hatfield, Duncan had never been a candidate for state-wide office, although he obtained a certain amount of general exposure as Speaker of the Oregon House of Representatives. His vote-pulling power among Republicans was unknown, and among Democrats it was subject to considerable doubt. In the balloting for Delegates-at-Large to the 1964 Democratic Convention, Duncan finished seventh with 115,000 votes, while Wayne Morse rolled up almost 196,000 votes to finish first. In the primary election of 1966, Duncan raised his total to 131,000 votes and won the senatorial nomination, but his two competitors still drew a total of almost 98,000.

Duncan was born in Normal, Illinois on December 4, 1920 and had practiced law in Oregon since 1948. Before being elected to the House of Representatives he served three terms in the Oregon legislature (1956–1962) and was the only two-term speaker of the Oregon House. He was a delegate to the Democratic National Convention in 1956, 1960, and 1964.

In 1962, President Kennedy appointed Duncan to the advisory committee on intergovernmental relations.

In 1963, as a freshman congressman, he was chosen one of the "ten most promising new faces in the Congress" by the Washington Press Corps. In the same year, Duncan was congressional advisor to the U.S. delegation to the World Food Conference in Rome.

Duncan was a member of the House Appropriations Committee and since May, 1966 had been serving on the United States–Canadian Parliamentary Council.

On the major issue of Viet Nam, Duncan's support of the Administration's policy was part of his belief that "we are now in a critical stage for the free world. This is a period of overall strife. Although some people describe Viet Nam as an isolated incident, it is not. It is just part of the whole."

Otherwise, internationally, he supported the Peace Corps, Food for Peace, and aid to "underdeveloped" countries. He was critical of the slowness of coming to grips with the world's food and population problems as well as the balance of payments and international liquidity.

In trying to underline his bent toward thrift and as a part of his habitual pointing to his Scots ancestry, Duncan boasted that by his one vote on the House Appropriations Committee, he had often saved more money than the general fund budget of Oregon. Also, although some key projects were sometimes not approved, the appropriations committee had allocated more to Oregon than would have been expected on the basis of population alone.

Duncan favored health-improvement measures, aid to education, air and water anti-pollution measures, full-employment programs, and fiscal stability. He also was for suspending investment tax credit to ease inflation.

A former merchant seaman and U.S. Navy fighter pilot, Duncan is a colorful figure, who enjoys chewing "snoose" (a moist snuff), writes reminders to himself on his hand and arm, and delights in wearing Duncan tartan ties. The father of seven children, Duncan worked in the gold fields of Alaska while attending college and has played semi-professional baseball.

## THE JULY DECISIONS

On Tuesday, July 26, the Hatfield planning group received the results of a state-wide political study that confirmed the grave nature of their position. The study was based on 1,067 personal interviews with a random sample of registered voters, 55 percent Democratic, 45 percent Republican (excluding "other"). Field work for the study was conducted during the last week in June and the first ten days in July. Inasmuch as the Hanoi-Haiphong bombing commenced midway in the survey period, it was possible to do a "before-after" analysis. It was not possible, however, to gauge the precise effect of Hatfield's lone stand on Viet Nam at the Governors' Conference.

Some of the survey results appear in Exhibit 2. In general, they supported and clarified the views that the planners already had about the election. Preferences were closer than the 46–40 split indicated by the Kraft survey, but Hatfield was slightly behind, especially in certain areas, with certain questioning techniques, and among certain groups. The survey gave additional information on what seemed to cause the preferences, and although the Viet Nam issue was important, other issues and candidate characteristics seemed to be important in planning the campaign.

The most important strategy decisions facing the Hatfield group had to do with what their advertising and campaign workers and candidate should say, how it should be said, and when it would be said. Beyond these decisions were certain questions of implementation, many of which had already been answered and others which would have to be answered later. For instance, some of the media time and space had been scheduled and the rest would be purchased when sufficient funds had been raised.

A variety of approaches to content were supported within the group. For instance:

*How much emphasis on Viet Nam?*

The opinion varied from those who thought that Viet Nam should be mentioned prominently to those who felt that every piece of campaign material (including the candidate's statements) should exclude all mention of Viet Nam.

An example of the former position was a letter that Hatfield received early in the campaign saying: "Your position expressing concern reflects the innermost feelings of many Oregonians . . . it supports our men in an awful struggle, while questioning this policy that involves them there. . . ." The writer went on to suggest that the issue of Viet Nam could become the center of many crucial statements⸴ of concern that Hatfield might make.

Others within the Hatfield group suggested various other emphases. They asserted that Hatfield would be seen as inconsistent and wishy-washy if he completely dropped the issue (the *Oregon Journal* called Hatfield "The Dove that Ducks" because he refused to debate with Duncan on Viet Nam) but would stand to lose much if he continued to be vocal about it. Something clearly had to be done because Hatfield was losing the support of contributors and political names within the party in addition to the support of many voters. (Background on the Hatfield Viet Nam position is in Exhibit 3.)

*What other issues should be emphasized?*

A general dissatisfaction existed in the U.S. and in Oregon. The extent to which Hatfield could take advantage of this dissatisfaction was in some sense negatively related to his identification with the causes of the dissatisfaction. For instance, with respect to Oregon's economic health, it was apparent that the lumber industry was feeling the pinch of LBJ's "tight-money" policies. Consumers were bothered by inflation. But Hatfield would have to be careful in dealing with these issues, because he bore much of the responsibility for Oregon's economic health since 1959.

*What stress should be placed on "gut" versus "intellectual" or future issues?*

Hatfield had many concerns that were general and did not strike directly at present-day problems. For instance, he was concerned about world peace and the quality of international relations beyond Viet Nam and beyond Oregonians' present money problems. Some planners felt that he would be best advised to emphasize these statesmanlike stands rather than get involved in everyday problems of Oregon. Others said that, although Hatfield achieved senatorial proportions by emphasizing statesmanship, too much concern with future global and intellectual matters would label him as an "egghead" who cared less about Oregon than about the world and his own career. These advisors suggested that Hatfield should concentrate entirely on "gut" issues that were of immediate relevance to Oregonians.

*Should Duncan be answered or even attacked?*

Duncan's campaign appeared to be shaping up as a negative one in which he would continually attack Hatfield as indecisive, confused on Viet Nam, even "soft on Communism." The question here was how much Hatfield should respond. Should he meet Duncan's constant challenge to debate? Should he answer carefully all of Duncan's charges? And to what extent should advertising, speeches, campaign workers, public relations releases, etc., actually attack Duncan and his position? Some felt that Duncan should be connected directly to the negative aspects of the Administration's policies and attacked in Hatfield communications. These people wanted to brand Duncan as a "rubber stamp" and to circulate political cartoons showing him, for instance, sitting on LBJ's knee. Others felt that Duncan and his position should be almost totally ignored. They felt that strong attacking tactics might be ethically unsound and practically inept because they might give Duncan added exposure.

*Should the Hatfield campaign concentrate on his past record or on what he planned to do as senator?*

Hatfield could make many claims about his administration in education, labor and industry, budget, conservation, agriculture, highway development, and social advancement (see Exhibit 4 for details). On the other hand, this approach presented some dangers because his administration had not been completely successful, because this emphasis might remind voters of negative attitudes which they might have had about Hatfield, and because the job of governor might not be regarded as the best preparation for a senatorial post. Further, Hatfield had to indicate, to some extent, his goals in the Senate.

*What effort should be expended in dealing with Hatfield's personal image?*

Hatfield had a tendency to come over as a "cold fish," as too polished, too intellectual, humorless, and as not ruggedly masculine enough in the context of the "Oregon personality." This was in direct contrast to Duncan's folksy "masculine" approach that was effective on a person-to-person basis. Some of Hatfield's planners felt that his personal appearance and style might reinforce the contention that he was a political opportunist and that he might be a decent administrator but would not fare well in the personal infighting that was necessary in the Senate. These planners felt that Hatfield's personal appearances should be kept to a minimum, that he should be counseled closely as to what to wear, etc., that the bulk of the campaign should be concentrated on mass media advertising, and that maximum advertising attention should be paid to the issues and the candidate's performance rather than to Hatfield himself. The argument here was that voters liked to read an acceptable image into the candidate. Some evidence indicated that personal appearances by the candidate (or any candidate) are less effective and, in fact, might have a zero or negative effect when compared with the effect of the mass media. This might be especially true of Hatfield because he was always asked questions about Viet Nam when he made personal appearances, and his answers tended to remind people of this negative aspect. On the other hand, some argued that Hatfield, while receptive to suggestions from his advisors, could hardly be forced to hold back from personal appearances, despite the demands of his position as governor. And it was hard to imagine Hatfield dramatically changing his personal appearance, even if the ethical aspects of such artificial direction of the candidate's image were dismissed.

The problem of "how to say it" was really two interrelated problems: the question of ad format and the question of advertising media.

The Hatfield planners had a broad array of media open to them, but their problem was that Hatfield's position and his weak early showing limited the extent to which they could use those media. For instance, it was felt that Hatfield would need at least 3,000 campaign workers during the campaign. These would range from precinct workers to office help to well-known people who would be used to make speeches and to lead discussion groups for Hatfield. But, instead of 3,000, the Hatfield staff felt that they were lucky if they had 1,000 committed to the campaign in July. Some evidence suggested that Hatfield's position on Viet Nam, especially his dissenting vote at the Governors' Conference, was something with which campaign workers did not want to be associated. In some quarters, an aura of treason was actually connected with Hatfield, and his planners guessed that many people who normally would have worked for Hatfield were committing themselves to other campaigns (e.g., the Republican gubernatorial campaign) in order to have an excuse for not working for Hatfield. This kind of dropping-out was obviously greater among the more conservative workers, but the situation made the content and form of Hatfield's campaign very important. It would have to meet objections and attract workers who now seemed to be avoiding Hatfield.

The campaign would also have to stimulate contributions in order to utilize the media effectively. It was estimated that the campaign had about $50,000 *pledged* in July and that six times more than this would be necessary to carry out a complete campaign. The candidate, public relations, and the media would have to be used creatively.

Political campaigns used two types of "media"—collateral material and general advertising media. The typical campaign in Oregon used about 50,000 each of a variety of collateral pieces including bumper stickers, campaign buttons, handbills, direct-mail pieces, and door hangers. These ranged in cost from one to 5 cents apiece. Some of the items, such as major brochures and direct-mail pieces, might receive longer press runs (perhaps 150–200,000) and cost 4 or 5 cents apiece. There were also items that could be sold such as hats (25 cents), aprons ($1), and campaign seals ($1 for a sheet of 100 envelope seals). Collateral material would be used in mailings, precinct work and in connection with special events such as key organization meetings, state and county fairs, campaign headquarters openings, and candidate appearances.

All mass media were available in Oregon (see Exhibit 4 for media data). There were about 70 daily and local newspapers headed by *The Oregonian* and the *Oregon Journal*. These two papers were most important in Portland but had coverage and influence throughout the state. The nine key papers and their rates are below. Sunday rates and circulation were approximately 15 percent higher. A Sunday supplement could be run in newspapers throughout the state with a circulation of 600,000 for a cost of $26,000.

| Newspaper | Location | Circulation* (000) | Basic B&W 1 Page Rate* |
|---|---|---|---|
| Oregonian................... | Portland-NW | 240 | $2,000 |
| Oregon Journal................ | Portland-NW | 150 | 1,500 |
| Eugene Register Guard......... | Central-West | 50 | 580 |
| Salem Statesman (Morn.)........ | | | |
| Capital Journal (Even.).......... | Salem-NW | 53 (N&E) | 731 (M&E) |
| Medford Mail Tribune.......... | Southwest | 20 | 423 |
| Coos Bay World.............. | South Coast | 15 | 352 |
| Bend Bulletin................. | Central | 9 | 235 |
| Pendleton East Oregonian........ | East | 10 | 330 |

* There are slight extra charges for color (about 12 percent for 1-color extra). These are approximate rates and circulations.

Portland had four major television stations which reached a large proportion of the state's electorate. One television idea being considered by Hatfield planners was morning and afternoon "coffee with Mark" half-hours that could be combined with neighborhood women's coffees. These would cost about $250 apiece for time and $1,500 for production if, in fact, money could be found. If Hatfield was able to raise sufficient funds, it might also be possible to run an "eleventh-hour" telethon or a two-hour prime time program. This would cost about $30–50,000.

The Portland television stations, rates, and reach are below. There were also stations in Coos Bay, Eugene, Medford, Pendleton, and Salem.

| | Spot Rates* | | |
|---|---|---|---|
| | 60-sec. Daytime | 20-sec. Prime Evenings | Average Homes Reached in Prime ¼ Hour* |
| KATU–TV (ABC)......... | 150 | 320 | 75,000 |
| KGW–TV (NBC)......... | 110 | 350 | 90,000 |
| KOIN–TV (CBS).......... | 125 | 325 | 80,000 |
| KPTV.................. | 80 | 250 | 60,000 |

* Data are approximate and for case purposes only.

Radio spots and programs could be purchased on all kinds of radio stations (rock, classical, news, talk, etc.) for about $10–20 a minute spot. Fifteen-minute radio shows would cost about $100 for time only. Finally, billboard and transit advertising had already been committed throughout the state. The Hatfield campaign had maximum coverage and was spending approximately $40–50,000 on this phase of the effort.

The campaign was already underway to a limited extent in some media. Exhibit 5 gives some idea of some of the media appeals and formats being used. The present billboards showed a picture of Hatfield in front of the U.S. flag with one-word messages like "Courage," "Integrity," etc.

The key question now was how much effort would be put against the more geographically specific media like precinct workers and direct mail as opposed to the mass media like television, radio, and newspapers. And, within the media, the question was how and how much should Hatfield himself be used in illustrations and in actual appearances. The planning group wanted also to pull the campaign together with a slogan that would typify their general approach, but they were not certain if this was possible—given the existing multiplicity of goals and approaches.

On top of all these problems was the issue of timing. Of first consideration, of course, was the expected timing of the Duncan campaign. Hatfield's team knew that Duncan planned to make a big push toward the end of the campaign. He had scheduled a large TV telethon. He expected to receive supportive visits toward the end of the campaign from Vice-President Humphrey, Senator Robert Kennedy, and even President Johnson. Duncan himself would not be able to campaign aggressively until after mid-September when Congress was scheduled to adjourn. He was getting support from the labor unions, several of which were organizing a get-out-the-vote campaign for election day. Duncan's campaign timing also had to be considered from a qualitative standpoint. He might well change campaign emphasis midstream with less emphasis on Viet Nam and more on Oregon's problems—the work that he had done and the work that Hatfield had not been able to do. Some of his campaign material is shown in Exhibit 5.

In addition to Duncan's campaign, the Hatfield planners had to consider the possibility of several events occurring. It was unclear what effect victories in Viet Nam for the U.S. and South Viet Nam might have on Oregonian attitudes toward the war. Political analysts expected President Johnson to make some sort of dramatic move in relation to the war before election time. A new "peace offensive" was rumored. There was also the problem of student disturbances and peace demonstrations. To what extent would they occur? To what extent would Hatfield become identified with these disruptions that were increasingly disturbing to the majority of Oregon voters?

Aside from the war issue, the planners had to consider what changes in the economy were likely to occur and of what significance they would be to Oregon voters. Inflation was a continuing problem and Oregon housewives were organizing "Food Price Wars" with boycotts and picketing. The "tight-money" policy was beginning to affect new housing starts, and the Oregon lumber industry was beginning to feel the pinch. Two thousand workers in the lumber industry had been laid off. Further layoffs were being predicted.

Hatfield had to have a campaign that was flexible enough to meet these changing conditions while strong enough to appeal to important segments

**EXHIBIT 1**

**Statement of Registration by Congressional Districts, General Election 1966**
**(prepared by secretary of state, elections division, November 1, 1966)**

| County* | Precincts | Population† | Democratic | Republican | Other | Total |
|---|---|---|---|---|---|---|
| **FIRST DISTRICT** | | | | | | |
| Benton | 50 | 45,800 | 8,279 | 11,046 | 700 | 20,025 |
| Clackamas | 97 | 134,000 | 37,633 | 31,243 | 1,007 | 69,883 |
| Clatsop | 46 | 27,700 | 7,880 | 6,178 | 223 | 14,281 |
| Columbia | 40 | 24,300 | 7,775 | 3,911 | 176 | 11,862 |
| Lincoln | 44 | 23,200 | 6,988 | 4,896 | 396 | 12,280 |
| Multnomah† | 164 | 92,000 | 21,064 | 24,863 | 1,125 | 47,052 |
| Polk | 51 | 34,200 | 6,723 | 7,530 | 399 | 14,652 |
| Tillamook | 35 | 16,100 | 5,030 | 3,652 | 112 | 8,794 |
| Washington | 180 | 122,000 | 29,154 | 31,673 | 1,292 | 62,119 |
| Yamhill | 42 | 39,900 | 8,638 | 8,856 | 393 | 17,887 |
| TOTALS | 749 | 559,200 | 139,164 | 133,848 | 5,823 | 278,835 |
| **SECOND DISTRICT** | | | | | | |
| Baker | 27 | 15,600 | 4,760 | 2,989 | 128 | 7,877 |
| Crook | 16 | 8,900 | 2,409 | 1,451 | 68 | 3,928 |
| Deschutes | 29 | 27,000 | 6,878 | 5,185 | 142 | 12,205 |
| Gilliam | 6 | 3,200 | 759 | 610 | 15 | 1,384 |
| Grant | 15 | 7,600 | 1,588 | 1,691 | 38 | 3,317 |
| Harney | 18 | 7,100 | 1,894 | 1,326 | 79 | 3,299 |
| Hood River | 22 | 14,200 | 3,309 | 2,618 | 230 | 6,157 |
| Jefferson | 14 | 10,000 | 2,082 | 1,565 | 45 | 3,692 |
| Klamath | 92 | 48,100 | 10,814 | 7,619 | 531 | 18,964 |
| Lake | 19 | 6,200 | 1,455 | 1,412 | 30 | 2,897 |
| Linn | 105 | 65,000 | 15,585 | 11,718 | 497 | 27,800 |
| Malheur | 33 | 25,400 | 4,295 | 4,583 | 210 | 9,088 |
| Marion | 116 | 145,000 | 29,013 | 32,188 | 1,079 | 62,280 |

| County | | | | | |
|---|---|---|---|---|---|
| Morrow | 9 | 4,750 | 1,062 | 991 | 36 | 2,089 |
| Sherman | 5 | 3,250 | 676 | 578 | 36 | 1,290 |
| Umatilla | 56 | 43,100 | 10,141 | 8,524 | 437 | 19,102 |
| Union | 30 | 17,800 | 5,072 | 3,497 | 126 | 8,695 |
| Wallowa | 14 | 6,050 | 1,899 | 1,191 | 22 | 3,112 |
| Wasco | 39 | 23,300 | 5,485 | 4,142 | 145 | 9,772 |
| Wheeler | 6 | 1,800 | 515 | 514 | 3 | 1,032 |
| TOTALS | 671 | 483,350 | 109,691 | 94,392 | 3,897 | 207,980 |

### THIRD DISTRICT

| | | | | | | |
|---|---|---|---|---|---|---|
| Multnomah | 854 | 463,000 | 149,017 | 93,354 | 4,254 | 246,625 |

### FOURTH DISTRICT

| | | | | | | |
|---|---|---|---|---|---|---|
| Coos | 82 | 52,400 | 16,445 | 8,014 | 441 | 24,900 |
| Curry | 21 | 13,000 | 3,304 | 2,504 | 122 | 5,930 |
| Douglas | 105 | 76,000 | 18,442 | 12,856 | 645 | 31,943 |
| Jackson | 125 | 92,100 | 22,041 | 19,976 | 1,571 | 43,588 |
| Josephine | 56 | 35,100 | 8,662 | 8,062 | 260 | 16,984 |
| Lane | 236 | 198,000 | 51,983 | 39,878 | 2,013 | 93,874 |
| TOTALS | 625 | 466,600 | 120,877 | 91,290 | 5,052 | 217,219 |
| COMBINED TOTALS | 2,899 | 1,972,150 | 518,749 | 412,884 | 19,026 | 950,659 |

* The counties listed herein are those which were in the new congressional districts as provided in Chapter 1, Oregon Laws 1965, Special Session.
† The 1965 estimates furnished by the Oregon Bureau of Census.
‡ That portion of Multnomah west of the Willamette River and west of the Stadium Freeway.

of the state. Much depended on a strong early campaign as well as the crucial strong finish. Several important pressure groups and state political figures had not indicated where their support lay, but it was clear that Hatfield was at a disadvantage among the more conservative. Newspaper endorsements were likely to appear in early October and, although Duncan appeared to have the "inside track" in this area, the Hatfield media and press campaign clearly would have to work hard to court these endorsements. An early Hatfield campaign, if successful, would have an important effect on obtaining money for the total effort. There was a strong bandwagon effect in campaign contributions and Hatfield had to show early strength in order to reach the campaign goal of over $300,000 and 3,000 workers. The problem was somewhat circular in that he did not now have adequate monies or workers to conduct a large total campaign at the early stage. Since Hatfield had not shown strength in public preference in either the primary or post-primary periods, the campaign now had to be dramatic enough to turn the tide of opinion optimistically in his direction.

*What campaign strategy would you recommend for Hatfield? Specifically, what should be his target segments? His message? His message format? The timing of his campaign? The media?*

### EXHIBIT 2

#### July Hatfield Survey

*Question:* "As you know, we're going to have another election this fall where Oregon will elect a new U.S. Senator. Do you happen to know the name of the (Democratic) (Republican) candidate for U.S. Senator?"

| (Read across) Group: | (R) Hatfield Correct | (D) Duncan Correct |
|---|---|---|
| Total Sample | 59% | 45% |
| Democrats | 55 | 45 |
| Republicans | 75 | 54 |
| Not registered or other | 36 | 27 |

*Question:* "The two candidates for U.S. Senator from Oregon are Mark Hatfield, Republican, and Robert Duncan, Democrat. If the election were being held today, would you probably vote for Duncan or Hatfield?" (Note: A split-sample approach was used, where the above question was asked of one cross-section, while a comparable cross-section was asked to mark a secret ballot.)

**EXHIBIT 2 (Continued)**

| Group: | Hatfield | Duncan | Undecided | Total |
|---|---|---|---|---|
| Total Sample | 45.8% | 46.6 | 7.6 | 100.0% |
| By Questioning Technique: | | | | |
| Oral | 46% | 43 | 11 | 100% |
| Secret | 45% | 51 | 4 | 100% |
| By Political Party: | | | | |
| Democrats | 21% | 73 | 6 | 100% |
| Republicans | 77% | 16 | 7 | 100% |
| Not registered or other | 44% | 43 | 13 | 100% |
| By Hanoi Bombing: | | | | |
| Before | 46% | 47 | 7 | 100% |
| After | 45% | 47 | 8 | 100% |
| By Congressional District: | | | | |
| No. 1 | 51% | 41 | 8 | 100% |
| No. 2 | 47% | 44 | 9 | 100% |
| No. 3 | 43% | 49 | 8 | 100% |
| No. 4 | 40% | 54 | 6 | 100% |
| Total Sample | 45.8% | 46.6 | 7.6 | 100.0% |
| By Education: | | | | |
| College—complete | 67% | 27 | 6 | 100% |
| College—partial | 53% | 41 | 6 | 100% |
| High school | 41% | 50 | 9 | 100% |
| Grade or no schooling | 34% | 61 | 5 | 100% |
| By Occupation: | | | | |
| Professional—managerial | 63% | 33 | 4 | 100% |
| White collar workers | 51% | 41 | 8 | 100% |
| Blue collar workers | 36% | 55 | 9 | 100% |
| Agricultural | 47% | 47 | 6 | 100% |
| By Union Membership: | | | | |
| Union | 36% | 54 | 10 | 100% |
| Non-union | 52% | 42 | 6 | 100% |
| By Sex: | | | | |
| Male | 45% | 49 | 6 | 100% |
| Female | 47% | 44 | 9 | 100% |
| By Age: | | | | |
| 21–39 years | 47% | 44 | 9 | 100% |
| 40–59 | 44% | 49 | 7 | 100% |
| 60 or over | 47% | 46 | 7 | 100% |
| By Income Level: | | | | |
| Upper | 57% | 40 | 3 | 100% |
| Middle | 44% | 47 | 9 | 100% |
| Lower | 38% | 53 | 9 | 100% |

*Question:* "On this card are a list of words. Will you please read over the words quickly and tell me, offhand, which words you think describe (Mr. Hatfield) (Mr. Duncan)? Choose as many as you like."

**EXHIBIT 2 (Continued)**

| Words: | Hatfield | Duncan |
|---|---|---|
| Intelligent | 55% | 43% |
| Politician | 48 | 31 |
| Religious | 38 | 4 |
| Honest | 34 | 31 |
| Friendly | 32 | 26 |
| Polished | 31 | 7 |
| Works for people | 31 | 33 |
| Leader | 31 | 19 |
| Sincere | 31 | 31 |
| Dignified | 30 | 7 |
| Statesman | 27 | 16 |
| Glory-seeker | 23 | 4 |
| Courageous | 19 | 13 |
| Fence-straddler | 14 | 2 |
| Decisive | 13 | 15 |
| Yes-man | 7 | 6 |
| Stuck-up | 6 | 1 |
| Cocky | 6 | 2 |
| Fresh | 6 | 5 |
| Regular guy | 5 | 9 |
| Stuffy | 4 | 1 |
| Irresponsible | 2 | 1 |
| Rugged | 2 | 5 |
| Stale | 1 | 1 |
| Undecided—No Opinion | 4 | 25 |

*Questions:* "Now, will you please look at this list. Which two of these specific problems do you feel your U.S. Senator should work the hardest on?"

"Which do you feel is the next most important problem?"

"Now, which two on the list do you think are the least important problems?"

| Problems: | Most | Next | Least |
|---|---|---|---|
| Solve the Viet Nam crisis | 25% | 10% | 5% |
| Attract new industry to Oregon | 24 | 8 | 5 |
| Cut down on federal spending | 19 | 9 | 5 |
| Lower property taxes in Oregon | 19 | 8 | 7 |
| Keep Oregon water from going to other states | 16 | 7 | 8 |
| Stop the increase in cost of living | 14 | 8 | 4 |
| Keep Russians out of Oregon fishing waters | 11 | 8 | 7 |
| Protect Oregon interests in federal timber | 11 | 6 | 3 |
| Better representation for Oregon in U.S. Senate | 11 | 6 | 4 |
| Reduce air and water pollution | 11 | 6 | 7 |
| Reduce federal interference in state affairs | 9 | 5 | 15 |
| Increase social security benefits | 7 | 4 | 12 |
| Obtain federal aid for education | 6 | 5 | 10 |
| War on poverty | 5 | 4 | 19 |
| Keep Red China out of the U.N. | 4 | 2 | 17 |
| Do something about Castro and the spread of communism | 4 | 3 | 18 |
| Expand recreational areas in Oregon | 1 | 3 | 26 |
| Undecided or other | 2 | 3 | 13 |

**EXHIBIT 2 (Continued)**

*Question:* "From what you know or have heard, how do you feel about Robert Duncan's stand on Viet Nam . . . ?"

| Group: | Strongly Approve | Approve | Dis-approve | Strongly Disapprove | Undecided |
|---|---|---|---|---|---|
| Total Sample.................. | 10% | 30 | 13 | 5 | 42 |
| Democrats.................. | 15% | 34 | 9 | 3 | 39 |
| Republicans................ | 7% | 25 | 20 | 7 | 41 |
| Not registered or other....... | 7% | 27 | 10 | 5 | 51 |

*Question:* "Which one of the alternatives best describes how you feel about Mr. Hatfield's stand on Viet Nam?"

| Group: | Strongly Approve | Approve | Dis-approve | Strongly Disapprove | Undecided |
|---|---|---|---|---|---|
| Total Sample................ | 6% | 24 | 33 | 10 | 27 |
| Democrats.................. | 4% | 15 | 43 | 12 | 26 |
| Republicans............... | 10% | 36 | 25 | 7 | 22 |
| Not registered or other...... | 4% | 21 | 24 | 11 | 40 |

*Question:* "How do you feel about Wayne Morse's stand on Viet Nam?"

| Group: | Strongly Approve | Approve | Dis-approve | Strongly Disapprove | Undecided |
|---|---|---|---|---|---|
| Total Sample.................. | 8% | 20 | 28 | 27 | 17 |
| Democrats.................. | 6% | 17 | 33 | 31 | 13 |
| Republicans................ | 9% | 27 | 26 | 25 | 13 |
| Not registered or other....... | 9% | 14 | 22 | 22 | 33 |

*Table 4: Reasons for Favoring MR. HATFIELD for U.S. Senator.*

|  | Hatfield Supporters |
|---|---|
| *Experience, Records, Accomplishments:* Experience gained as governor; loyalty to Oregon; record in office; industrial accomplishments; Duncan lacks experience ........................... | 47% |
| *Party Loyalty:* I'm a Republican; he's a member of my party; back party's candidates ........................................ | 20 |
| *Professional Qualifications:* Leader; professional abilities; statesman; better qualified than opponent; job capabilities ............... | 20 |
| *Viet Nam Views:* Agree with Hatfield on Viet Nam; the Viet Nam mess; opposed to Administration's Viet Nam policies; war in Viet Nam ...................................................... | 18 |

## EXHIBIT 2 (Continued)

*Awareness, Knowledge of Candidates:* Know more about Hatfield; familiar with his stands; know little or nothing about Duncan .. 15

*Personal Qualifications:* Conscientious; hard working; high principles; good family man; dignified; interested in youth .......... 13

*Religious* ....................................................... 8

*Policies, Platform:* Agree with his political stands; conservative; like his policies, political beliefs ............................ 8

*Honest, Sincere* ................................................ 5

*Dislike Duncan:* Dislike, disagree with Duncan ................. 3

*Appearance:* Handsome; erect; trim, appeal to women ........... 3

*Intelligence, Education* ........................................ 3

*Courage of Convictions:* Decisive; strong; says what he thinks .... 2

*Speaking Ability* .............................................. 1

*Supports Working Man; Pro-Labor* ........................... 1

*Undecided—Just Prefer Him* ................................... 5

  Total ...................................................... 172%*

\* Totals more than 100%, due to multiple response.

*Table 5. Reasons for Preferring MR. DUNCAN for U.S. Senator.*

|  | Duncan Supporters |
|---|---|

*Party Loyalty:* Vote party ticket; I'm a Democrat; Duncan's our candidate .................................................. 30%

*Dislike Hatfield:* Would not vote for Hatfield; disagree with Hatfield; Duncan is lesser of two evils ........................... 29

*Viet Nam Views:* Agree with Duncan's Viet Nam views; Duncan backs President on Viet Nam; Duncan supports Viet Nam war effort ........................................................ 17

*Experience, Record, Accomplishments:* Record as Congressman; experience in Oregon Legislature; accomplishments in office; has the experience to do the job ............................... 12

*Professional Qualifications:* A leader; capable of carrying out job; better qualified than Hatfield; legal background ................ 10

*General Policies, Platform:* Supports Dunes Park; his platform appeals to me; agree with his policies, political beliefs ............ 9

*Personal Qualifications:* Down-to-earth; good family man; tough; young and aggressive; "Scotsman" .......................... 7

*Supports Working Man* ....................................... 5

*Decisiveness:* Strong; makes decisions and sticks to them; more decisive than Hatfield .......................................... 3

*Honest, Sincere* ................................................ 2

*Awareness:* Know more about Duncan, Duncan's views .......... 2

*Need a Change:* New political blood; change in political scenery .. 1

*Intelligence, Education* ........................................ 1

*Miscellaneous:* Hard campaigner; religious; dignified; reserved .... 1

*Undecided—Just Prefer Him* ................................... 10

  139%

**EXHIBIT 2 (Continued)**

*Table 6.  Reasons for NOT Preferring MR. HATFIELD.*

|  | Non-Hatfield Voters |
|---|---|
| *Party Conflict:* He's a Republican—I'm a Democrat .............. | 20% |
| *Viet Nam Stand:* Disagree with Viet Nam views; Hatfield opposed to Viet Nam war; not supporting U.S. forces in Viet Nam; un-patriotic ...................................................... | 14 |
| *Indecisive:* Fence-straddler; afraid to take a firm stand; wishy-washy; beats around the bush; says one thing, does another; no mind of his own ........................................... | 12 |
| *Political Ambitions:* Places self above state; only interested in him-self; wants to be President instead of Oregon senator; uses office to further personal ambitions ............................... | 9 |
| *Gubernatorial Administration:* Mediocre record as governor; in-efficient administration of office; poor record of running state ... | 6 |
| *Lack of Accomplishment for State:* Has done little, nothing for state; state has not advanced during his administration; lack of results ...................................................... | 6 |
| *Disagree with Political Policies, Stands:* Daylight savings time; Boardman deal; welfare out of Portland; not conservative-minded | 5 |
| *Personal Characteristics:* Stuck-up; arrogant; never has a hair out of place ...................................................... | 5 |
| *Travels:* Out of state too much; too many trips ................. | 5 |
| *Lack of Support of Working Man:* Has done little, nothing for common man; anti-labor .................................... | 4 |
| *Just Don't Like Him* ......................................... | 4 |
| *Lack of Professional Capabilities* ............................. | 3 |
| *Forces Issues Over Public Vote* ............................... | 2 |
| *Like Duncan Better—No Feelings Toward Hatfield* .............. | 2 |
| *Resented Mrs. Hatfield's Remarks on TV* ...................... | 2 |
| *Raised Taxes* ............................................... | 2 |
| *Miscellaneous:* Copying Morse (1%); economic views (1%); need a change (1%); too religious (1%) .................... | 4 |
| *Undecided—No Particular Reason* ............................ | 4 |
|  | 109% |

*Table 7.  Reasons for NOT Preferring MR. DUNCAN.*

|  | Non-Duncan Supporters |
|---|---|
| *Lack of Knowledge of Duncan:* Not familiar with Duncan, Dun-can's stands; know nothing about him; new name .............. | 30% |
| *Party Conflict:* He's a Democrat—I'm a Republican .............. | 20 |
| *"Rubber Stamp" Obedience:* Blindly backing Administration's | |

**EXHIBIT 2 (Continued)**

| | |
|---|---:|
| policies; LBJ "Yes" man ..................................... | 11 |
| *Disagree with Viet Nam Views:* Too strongly for Viet Nam war; can't go along with his Viet Nam stand; we shouldn't be in Viet Nam ......................................................... | 9 |
| *Prefer Hatfield:* Hatfield's record is better; can't vote for both candidates; Hatfield is my man ............................... | 6 |
| *Lack of Experience:* Insufficient experience for job; Hatfield more experienced ...................................... | 4 |
| *Lack of Professional Qualifications:* Lacks qualifications for U.S. Senator; lacks leadership qualities of Hatfield ................. | 3 |
| *Just Don't Like Duncan* ....................................... | 1 |
| *Too Liberal* .................................................... | 1 |
| *Congress too Heavily Weighted with Democrats* ................ | 1 |
| *Lacks Statesmanship Qualities:* Hatfield more of a statesman; Duncan wouldn't get along with UN officials ...................... | 1 |
| *Indecisive* ..................................................... | 1 |
| *Smooth Talker* ................................................ | 1 |
| *Disagree with Political Stands* ................................. | 1 |
| *He's in Favor of Dunes Park* .................................. | 1 |
| *Morse Favors Duncan* .......................................... | 1 |
| *Undecided—No Particular Reason* ............................. | 10 |
| Total .................................................. | 102% |

*Table 13a.  FAVORABLE Facets of MR. HATFIELD'S Image.*

| | *Total* |
|---|---:|
| *Personal Characteristics:* Clean; forthright; charming; dynamic; friendly; humble; unselfish; considerate; conscientious; patriotic; polished ...................................................... | 47% |
| *Professional Capabilities:* Capable and dedicated; leader; shrewd judge of people, situations; influential ........................ | 38 |
| *Experienced, Successful Governor:* Put Oregon on map; expanded Oregon's industry; outstanding job as Governor; highly experienced executive .......................................... | 23 |
| *Honest, Sincere, Truthful* ..................................... | 16 |
| *Ambitious:* Ambitious to carry out goals of office; drives himself; aggressive in actions, accomplishments; energetic .............. | 14 |
| *Intelligent, Well Educated, Keen Mind* ........................ | 11 |
| *Strong, Decisive:* Has courage of his convictions; not afraid to speak out; confident, independent thinker ........................ | 8 |
| *Pleasing Appearance:* Handsome; well dressed; immaculate; appeals to women; clean-cut ............................................ | 7 |
| *Religious* ...................................................... | 7 |
| *Good Politician; Astute Political Stands* ....................... | 4 |
| *Good Speaker* ................................................. | 3 |
| *Well Known, Prominent Figure* ............................... | 2 |
| *Has Right Idea on Viet Nam* .................................. | 2 |

**EXHIBIT 2 (Continued)**

| | |
|---|---|
| *Dignified, Respected* .......................................... | 2 |
| *Interested in Working Class* .................................... | 1 |
| *Miscellaneous* ................................................ | 2 |
| *No response* .................................................. | * |
| Total ...................................................... | 187%† |

\* Less than 0.5 percent.
† Results total more than 100 percent, due to multiple response.

*Table 13b.* UNFAVORABLE *Facets of MR. HATFIELD'S Image.*

Total

*Overriding Political Ambitions:* Everything subordinated to political ambitions; wants to be President; political opportunist; using office as stepping stone; Senate is next political step; shooting for big game ............................................... 30%

*Vacillating:* Wishy-washy; evasive on issues; afraid to show how he feels; hedges; hasn't courage of his convictions; won't take a firm stand ........................................................ 21

*Self-Centered:* Publicity seeker; stuck-up; arrogant; everything revolves around himself; social climber; big-headed; cocky ...... 15

*Unsuccessful Governor:* Accomplished little as Governor; hasn't carried out promises; been a so-so Governor; others could have done better ................................................. 10

*Immature, Unqualified:* Man with school-boy ideas; not ready for the job; too young for Senate; too sissified to work; not qualified for job at this time ........................................ 10

*Traveler:* Would rather travel than stay home; away from job half the time; trips cost money; who pays for his wife's travel expenses; absenteeism ......................................... 8

*Appearance:* Too well-groomed; don't trust handsome man; fashion plate ...................................................... 6

*Has Wrong Idea on Viet Nam* ................................ 5

*Pawn of Special Interest Groups:* Works for big business; not interested in "little people" ....................................... 4

*Weak Fiscal Policies:* Raised taxes; advocated state tax on federal tax ...................................................... 2

*Miscellaneous:* Stand on daylight time didn't appeal to me; don't like his wife; poor advisors; shady politician; has some far-fetched ideas; just don't like him .................................... 9

*No Response* ................................................... *

Total ................................................... 120%†

\* Less than 0.5 percent.
† Results total more than 100 percent, due to multiple response.

**EXHIBIT 2 (Continued)**

*Table 13c.  FAVORABLE Facets of MR. DUNCAN'S Image.*

|  | *Total* |
|---|---|
| *Personal Characteristics:* Regular guy; down-to-earth; good family man; unselfish; nice fellow; conscientious; clean-cut; patriotic; crew-cut | 32% |
| *Professionally Qualified:* Dedicated; has sound ideas; has Oregonians' interests at heart; good lawyer; good judgment | 30 |
| *Honest, Sincere, Truthful* | 13 |
| *Decisive:* Strong; not easily swayed; willing to commit himself on issues; means what he says | 12 |
| *Experienced, Successful Office-Holder:* Experienced through service in Congress and Legislature; done a lot for the state; always present to vote in Congress; good record | 10 |
| *Ambitious:* Hard worker; energetic; drives himself to get things done | 10 |
| *Intelligent, Well Educated, Keen Mind* | 7 |
| *Loyal Democrat:* Supports the Administration; behind LBJ; hard worker for party's cause | 6 |
| *Supports, Helps Workingman* | 6 |
| *Sound Political Stands:* Good politician; well versed in political areas | 6 |
| *Has the Right Idea on Viet Nam* | 4 |
| *Good Speaker* | 4 |
| *Pleasing Appearance* | 1 |
| *Dignified, Respected* | 1 |
| *Miscellaneous* | 1 |
| *No Response* | * |
| Total | 143%† |

\* Less than 0.5 percent.
† Results total more than 100 percent, due to multiple response.

*Table 13d.  UNFAVORABLE Facets of MR. DUNCAN'S Image.*

|  | *Total* |
|---|---|
| *Rubber Stamp, Follower:* Rubber stamp for the great society; LBJ "Yes" man; Democratic follower; blindly follows party lines | 26% |
| *Self-Centered:* Stuffy; acts like a banty rooster; rash; opinionated; egotistical | 17 |
| *Inexperienced, Unsuccessful:* Hasn't any experience to speak of; all talk, no action; can't think of any accomplishments; do-nothing record; junior politician; can't hold a candle to Hatfield | 14 |
| *Politically Motivated:* Political show-off; politics come first, unscrupulous politician; latches on to the thing of the moment; actions dictated by political expediency | 10 |
| *Immature, Unqualified:* Not serious enough; lesser of two evils; not big enough for the Senate; capabilities not up to the job | 10 |

### EXHIBIT 2 (Concluded)

*Has Wrong Idea on Viet Nam* ..............................    8
*Vacillating:* Goes along with the majority; straddles the fence; in-
decisive ...............................................    5
*Poor Fiscal Policies:* Has fat hand in the taxpayer's pocket; no ex-
perience in public money matters .........................    2
*Poor Appearance* ...........................................    1
*Miscellaneous:* Disagree with his educational views; prejudiced
against him; just don't like him; poor political stands; failed to
help war veterans ......................................    6
*No Response* ...............................................    3

   Total  ...............................................    $\overline{102\%}$*

* Results total more than 100 percent, due to multiple response.


### EXHIBIT 3

*EXCLUSIVE INTERVIEW: Oregon Voter,* April 2, 1966.

#### Hatfield's Vietnam Position

When asked: "What do you consider is Gov. Hatfield's position on Vietnam, most people reply, *Oregon Voter* has found, "I'm not sure, but I think
he's against the war and favors withdrawal of our troops."

After criticizing both Gov. Hatfield and the press (March 5) for their
failure to adequately and clearly set forth Gov. Hatfield's views, *Oregon
Voter* was invited to meet privately with the Governor for a "briefing" of his
position on the Vietnam war.

The Governor began: "I do not agree with Sen. (Wayne) Morse's position
. . . we cannot do less than give full support to our men in Vietnam." Hence,
the Governor's support of the $4.8 billion emergency appropriation bill ap-
proved by congress last month.

#### America Committed To Vietnam

Gov. Hatfield continued: "America cannot pull out of Vietnam. We are
there, and we cannot turn our back even if things were wrong at the onset.
We must stay there until an honorable settlement is reached."

Commenting on Sen. Morse's charges of "illegal" and "unconstitutional"
U.S. involvement, Hatfield rose to his feet stating, "It's too late to even discuss
legalities—we've 215,000 men there. We're committed."

"Furthermore," he declared, "When you start arguing legalities, you automatically advocate withdrawal." Withdrawal now, he implied, would be de-
feat in every sense of the word.

Gov. Hatfield, therefore, does not support Sen. Morse's position, nor does
he advocate withdrawal of American troops from Vietnam.

#### Critical of LBJ Policy

The Governor, however, is highly critical of President Johnson's Vietnam
war policy. He refused to back the administration last summer at the Governors' conference in Minneapolis, and following a White House briefing last

EXHIBIT 3 (Continued)

fall, he publicly criticized the president for what he termed "contradictory" and "unclear policy."

He said he could not support giving the president a "blank check" on the issue of making peace or escalating the war when the president had not spelled out to this country his "guidelines, goals and objectives with regard to the war."

And last month he abstained from voting with other governors on a resolution endorsing the president's policy, a resolution unanimously adopted by the 38 governors who attended another White House briefing. Although he had planned to attend the briefing, Gov. Hatfield was forced to change his plans when he came down with influenza.

He later announced he would not sign the resolution, because he had not attended the briefing, and had no evidence the administration had changed its policies on matters with which he (Hatfield) disagrees.

### Gov. Hatfield's Criticisms

What are Gov. Hatfield's criticisms? Essentially they appear two-fold: (1) failure on the part of the administration to be "candid and truthful" with the American people in spelling out exactly what are its goals and objectives in Vietnam; and (2) the administration's "contradictory foreign policy," particularly with regard to communism.

In the first instance, Gov. Hatfield said we have been bombarded with "illusions, myths and secrecy about our goals and objectives in Vietnam . . . we have been told many things and many so-called facts, most of which have not been borne out or correct.

Outlining specifics, Gov. Hatfield displayed quotes from Sec. of Defense Robert McNamara:

In May, 1963, McNamara said: "The corner has been definitely turned toward victory." In Dec., 1963, he said: "We have every reason to believe that plans will be successful in 1964." In Feb., 1964, McNamara declared: "The U.S. hopes to withdraw most of its troops from South Vietnam before the end of 1965." In Oct., 1965: "The major part of the U.S. military task can be completed by the end of 1965." And in early Dec., 1965, he said: "We have stopped losing the war."

Oregon's Chief Executive again quoted McNamara who said at a press conference on April 24, 1964: "I still believe we can win . . . following the current program, and I don't believe that anyone in the government of South Vietnam or our government believes that the addition of U.S. ground combat troops in South Vietnam, or the introduction of such troops in South Vietnam, would favorably affect the situation there."

### Consequences of Buildup

The Governor then quoted U.S. Ambassador to Vietnam Henry Cabot Lodge, who, before returning to Saigon, told reporters in Washington (June 30, 1964) what he thought the consequences of massive American military involvement in Vietnam would be:

"Well," quoting Lodge, "that means we become a colonial power, and I think it's been pretty well established that colonialism is over. I believe that if you start doing that, you will get all kinds of unfortunate results; you'll stir

## EXHIBIT 3 (Continued)

up anti-foreign feelings; there'll be a tendency to lay back and let the Americans do it, and all that. I can't think that that's a good thing to do."

Of this Oregon's Governor asked, "Does this indicate the administration has clearly spelled out its goals to the American people?"

Answering his own question, he said "No!" Despite what Sec. McNamara and Ambassador Lodge have said, we now have the "American nation fully committed to a land war in Vietnam."

"The president," the Governor continued, "says we are committed to guaranteeing the right of self determination for the Vietnamese people—through free elections."

"Just what would happen," asked Gov. Hatfield, "if a hard-core communist were to win a free election? What will we have accomplished? Will our boys have died in vain—for nothing?"

He said. "No one sees any person in South Vietnam capable of winning a free election." Our first task, suggested Gov. Hatfield, is to help build Vietnamese support for a friendly candidate who could win such an election.

He continued: "The Vietnam struggle started as a civil war. Peiping later took advantage of the situation and moved in supplies and equipment to the Viet Cong and the National Liberation Front."

### Ho-Chi-Minh A Symbol

"What we must realize is that Ho-Chi-Minh is a symbol to the Vietnamese of liberation from the French Colonialists prior to and after World War II, and from the Japanese Imperialists during the War.

"Furthermore," said Gov. Hatfield, "the Vietnamese are concerned with only two things: Being left alone and having a full stomach. They do not understand what freedom is, and no people can be expected to fight for freedom if they don't understand it . . . they could care less about the philosophical debate over democracy vs communism."

Gov. Hatfield suggested this is one of the key reasons we have seen so many changes of government and numerous defections in South Vietnamese military ranks.

"Under these circumstances," he asked, "just what are our guidelines, goals and objectives? How can we expect the American people to know what they are when the administration has yet to be candid with us about the war?"

Moving to the subject of American foreign policy, Gov. Hatfield said he is deeply concerned about the universal threat of communism.

He said he has personally seen communism—Chinese communism. European communism and American communism. "It is a deadly enemy and not purely a philosophical ideal. It is a hard-core committed system, antagonistic to anything free or dear to this country."

If Vietnam is the spot where America is making its stand against Chinese communist expansion in Southeast Asia, Gov. Hatfield asked: "Can the containment of Red China be unilaterally successful—can America do it alone?"

He suggested that if the Vietnam war is a containment of Red China, then it must be a "multi-nation containment."

Singly, he fears, we are "moment by moment in a position of confrontation with Red China."

## EXHIBIT 3 (Continued)

### No Allied Support

"But where are our allies?" he asked. "South Korea and Australia (to a limited degree) are the only countries which are supporting us. The rest of the free world, in the words of Ambassador Lodge, 'stir up anti-foreign feelings . . .' and '. . . lay back and let the Americans do it.'"

Our allies, he said, are indirectly supporting North Vietnam and Red China with goods and materials with which to build factories and feed their people. This helps give Red China and North Vietnam the means to wage war and weakens the American position, he declared.

### Position on Escalation

Gov. Hatfield said he doesn't want to see the U.S. "go it alone," and this is one key reason why he has opposed escalation of the war.

He said, if it is the administration's policy to contain, and possibly confront Red China at Vietnam, "we must have the support of the free world in our pocket." He said the Johnson administration has achieved no such support, to his knowledge, and he doubted if any "one country is willing at this point to confront Peiping—Moscow."

Oregon's Governor continued: "And what is so contradictory about our foreign policy against communist expansion is that 7,000 miles from home we are trying to avert its expansion when in Cuba, 90 miles from our shores, the greatest spawning ground for communist subversion and revolution is building stronger every day."

"What has this administration done," he asked, "to strengthen, support and defend our allies in the western hemisphere against the red plot in our own back yard?"

Referring to the Hungarian revolution in 1956 (Eisenhower era) the Governor asked, "Where was this country's pledge to help?" He said the Hungarians "were people who understood freedom and were willing to fight for it." Instead, he declared, we're fighting off communism in an area where the people don't understand freedom, and "don't appear too determined to fight for it."

### Alternatives Offered

Gov. Hatfield offered what he thought are now the alternatives to escalating the war any further:

"There has to be a frank and open discussion with the American people on the administration's over-all objectives and goals.

"We must develop a Get-America-off-the-Spot program by gaining a multination approach to a military and political solution. We've got to persuade our allies to stop supplying our enemy and unite behind us.

"And we must exhaust every alternative to bloody conflict. Escalation hasn't worked yet."

He said we should not be discouraged by the United Nations Security Council's "apparent lack of interest . . . we must be persistent in making the U.N. more effective; and we must insist on re-convening the Geneva Conference where the opportunity of Red China's participation exists. We have to meet them face-to-face."

**EXHIBIT 3 (Concluded)**

Asked could not the rich natural resources of all Southeast Asia be a deciding factor of whether China will be a "have" or a "have not" country in the future, Gov. Hatfield answered: "Perhaps."

"But," he concluded, "if we are to stop its expansion—as I believe we should —the American people should know that every alternative has been fully explored and that this country has the full support of its allies."

**EXHIBIT 4**

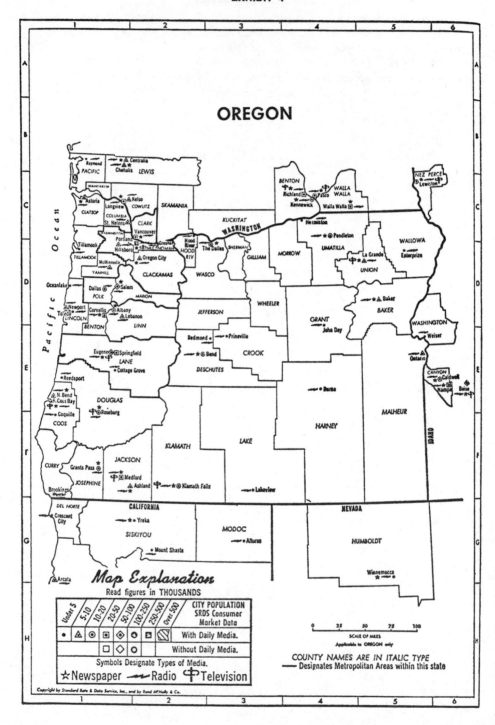

**EXHIBIT 5**

# QUALIFIED
# APPOINTMENTS
### (A Mark of Leadership)

*"... choosing the right individual for the right job at the right time constitutes one of the most important functions of your Governor..."*
*—Inaugural Address*
*January 12, 1959*

Mark Hatfield undertook his job as Governor convinced that teamwork is absolutely essential to effective state government. Throughout his term of office, his impartial appointments have been applauded for their competence.

No Governor in this century has been called upon to fill so many high statewide elective offices including the U. S. Senate (Hall S. Lusk), Secretary of State (Howell Appling, Jr.), Supreme Court (A. "Ted" Goodwin), State Treasurer (Howard Belton), Superintendent of Public Instruction (Leon Minear), Multnomah Circuit Court (James M. Burns).

## Citizens for Mark Hatfield

| | | |
|---|---|---|
| Henry A. Carey, Jr. | Bert S. Gooding | James B. O'Hanlon |
| Edw. L. Casey | John J. Higgins | Frank G. Perri |
| Don Chapman | Robert A. Leipzig | Frank J. Stark |
| Albert D. Corrado | James F. Lonergan | Michael J. Walsh |
| Eugene E. Feltz | Robert W. McMenamin | Charles W. Wentworth |

## MARK ☒ HATFIELD

## FOR UNITED STATES SENATOR

 Hatfield for Senator Committee, Gerald W. Frank, Chairman, 285 Church St., N.E., Salem.

## EXHIBIT 5 (Continued)

### HE KNOWS OREGON...
### OREGON KNOWS HIM
#### AND HE IS RESPECTED BY THE NATION

Hatfield for U. S. Senator Committee, Gerald W. Frank, Chairman, 285 Church N. E., Salem, Oregon. Phone: 585-6275

**MARK ☒ HATFIELD FOR U.S. SENATOR**
**MAKE OREGON'S VOTE COUNT ON CAPITOL HILL**

### *Hatfield leadership launched a Decade of Development*

Hatfield immediately rallied citizens throughout the state and launched a Decade of Development. Oregon again became a state on the move with these significant achievements:

1) **EDUCATION**—The statewide community college system, established and burgeoned during the Hatfield years, now includes 17,909 students in ten institutions; a state scholarship commission was established; services to the mentally retarded have multiplied ten times; the annual school dropout rate has decreased from 11.3% in 1959 to only 2.9% in 1965.

2) **HIGHWAY CONSTRUCTION AND BEAUTIFICATION**—Oregon has led the nation in the percentage of interstate highways completed to acceptable standards during the Hatfield Years—with the dollar value surpassing the corresponding figure for the last 40 years; highway beautification was a reality in Oregon long before it became a national goal—over $3 million has been expended on state-sponsored beautification programs.

### YEARS OF GROWTH FOR OREGON

3) **SOCIAL ADVANCEMENT**—Community mental health clinics have been established throughout the state; welfare administration has been greatly improved and work projects have been initiated for welfare recipients; civil rights programs in Oregon have become a model for the entire nation.

4) **AGRICULTURAL DEVELOPMENT**—The State Department of Agriculture has been reorganized for greater service to farmer producers, allied industries and consumers; a new Agriculture Building has been built on the Capitol Mall; Oregon recognized the importance of the consumer in food marketing by the creation of the Consumer Advisory Committee; a vigorous Agri-Business Council was established to improve market relations.

5) **NATURAL RESOURCES**—Oregon's state park system, largest in the nation, has continued to expand, with 24 new parks. Stronger anti-pollution control and enforcement was initiated. Governor Hatfield won legislative approval for a comprehensive water study to show Oregon needs for decades to come and as chairman of the Western Governors he won their support in establishing a water council for the west. Off-shore oil exploration, already an important contributor to the Oregon economy, holds dramatic promise for the future; oceanography research is tapping the vast potential of our state's lengthy shoreline; and space scientists are using Central Oregon as a key testground.

6) **HOLDING THE TAX LINE**—During the Hatfield Years, Oregon had no income tax rate increase—the result of responsible and efficient administration. In 1958, Oregon was eighth highest in the nation in state and local taxes per $1,000 of personal income. By 1964, Oregon had dropped to 23rd. Only Oregon and Louisiana have been able to avoid major tax increases since 1959. Today, per capita taxes in our state are lowest of all Pacific Coast states.

7) **PAYROLLS AND PROGRESS**—During Oregon's Years of Progress the most dynamic growth period in our state's history, per capita personal income has climbed more than 26%—from below the national average to well above average; more than $3 billion in new construction has been started; 180,000 new jobs (non-agricultural), the equivalent of two cities the size of Salem, have been added; over 313 new plants have been constructed and 327 others have been expanded since 1960 alone.

### *FOR PAYROLLS AND PROGRESS*

### *MARK ☒ HATFIELD*

**EXHIBIT 5 (Continued)**

THE OREGONIAN, THURSDAY, OCTOBER 20, 1966

# Neuberger Supports Duncan Candidacy

WASHINGTON (Special) — What does Sen. Maurine Neuberger think of the two men who are fighting for the privilege of succeeding her in the U.S. Senate?

She knows both of them personally, having served with Gov. Mark Hatfield when she and Hatfield were members of the Oregon Legislature, and having served with Rep. Robert B. Duncan in Congress for the past four years.

Sen. Neuberger favors Duncan. She plans to make a few speeches in his behalf, mainly in Medford Oct. 28 and Eugene Oct. 29, despite her admitted dislike of election campaigning.

Is her preference for Duncan simply because she and he are both Democrats and Hatfield is a Republican and after all, the party expects her to do the proper thing and campaign for Duncan? Or is it to offset the expressed preference of Sen. Wayne Morse for Hatfield?

Not at all, says the senator. Her preference has to do with the different natures of the two senatorial candidates.

**Duncan, Called Fighter**

"Ever since I've known Bob Duncan," she said in an interview, "I've seen a person completely engrossed in the legislative process. He's not an administrator, and he would have been out of his depth as governor for that reason. But he's cut out to be a fighter for legislation. He knows how to maneuver, how to work with his colleagues, how to get legislation passed. He's a fighting cock."

"Hatfield's nature is entirely different," Sen. Neuberger continued.

"Hatfield looks like a governor. He presides well at meetings. He tries to please all groups. I don't know when we've had a governor who has pleased more groups. He has labor support. The utilities are for him. He has support from liberals and conservatives. He plays a very cautious middle-of-the-road role," said the senator.

"I don't think you get real leadership that way," she added. "You've got to get one side to say, 'I won't vote for you.' Then you know you've done something. Instead, he's always juggling things. You never know where he stands. All of these are characteristic of the politician who wants to stay in office. He hasn't been a bad governor and he hasn't been a great governor. He just hasn't shown any leadership."

Also, Sen. Neuberger thinks Duncan would make a better Oregon senator than Hatfield because Duncan would assert more independence, a trait that is difficult to demonstrate in the House where he is now.

"I think Duncan would be a ball of fire," she said. "Why, he'd take on Wayne Morse and the Southern Democrats and all — and I think other senators would like Duncan's outspokenness."

"If Hatfield is elected," she predicted, "he'll just become a regular Republican, operating under Dirksen's direction. I wouldn't expect him to demonstrate the independence of Javits or Case or Margaret Smith or Kuchel, because Hatfield's ambitions are so very great for a place on the national Republican ticket. Defiance of Dirksen would hurt his prospects. The Republicans are much better at whipping party members into line than the Democrats are. With the exception of two or three mavericks, they stay in line."

Finally, Sen. Neuberger observed that Oregon benefits greatly by various federal programs and projects, some of which depend on the effectiveness of members of the Oregon congressional delegation.

"You can't minimize he fact that a Democratic administration is in power," she asserted, "and there is no doubt that Duncan can do more for Oregon."

"I think Duncan would be a ball of fire"

"Duncan's cut out to be a fighter for legislation... he knows how to get legislation passed. He's a fighting cock."

—Senator Neuberger

## KEEP BOB DUNCAN working for Oregon

## EXHIBIT 5 (Concluded)

Bob and Marijane Duncan

*Meet* **BOB DUNCAN**
*Democrat for U.S. SENATOR*

Visiting with
the Green Beret
soldier

The
Duncan
Clan
at home
in Medford

Bob with the youngest,
Jeannie Beth

...experienced, realistic statesman whom AP lists as "one of the HARDEST WORKING Congressmen on Capitol Hill." DUNCAN—the only man to serve two consecutive terms as speaker of Oregon House of Representatives. DUNCAN—the kind of diligent, decisive "shirtsleeve" senator Oregonians can depend upon for intelligent leadership in the U. S. Senate. DUNCAN—father of 7, an Oregon lawyer, WW II Navy pilot and member of the Navy Reserve—a man you can trust to make up his mind, stand and be counted.

Bob commuting
between
Washington, D.C.
and Oregon

Duncan for Senate
Committee, Sid Leiken,
Chm., 2230 W. Harvard,
Roseburg, Oregon.

# SECTION VII

## ORGANIZATION

# Bank of California

On the afternoon of January 26, 1966, Mr. Glenn K. Mowry, the Executive Vice President of the Bank of California, was going over a report referred to him by the bank's Corporate Planning Division. According to Mr. Paul Erickson, Director of Corporate Planning, the report had been written by a recent business school graduate who had been working as a trainee under Mr. Erickson. This report (reproduced in Appendix A) was concerned with the organizational implications of the adoption of a marketing concept in commercial banking. Mr. Mowry had scheduled a meeting for the next morning with Mr. Erickson and Mr. Herbert Foedisch, Senior Vice President and head of the Marketing Division, to discuss the report and to determine what action, if any, should be taken concerning Mr. Cunningham's suggestions. Mr. Mowry wanted to assess the report's value in light of the bank's present strategy and organization.

## BACKGROUND OF THE BANK OF CALIFORNIA

The Bank of California was founded in San Francisco in 1864 by Mr. D. O. Mills and Mr. William C. Ralson. The bank grew steadily and played an important role in the early economic growth of Northern California. The early financing activities of the bank included the granting of loans to mining companies in the Comstock Lode and to the Central Pacific Railroad for its drive eastward to meet the Union Pacific. With the acquisition of the London & San Francisco Bank, Ltd. in 1905, the Bank of California acquired offices in Portland, Tacoma, and Seattle. Five years later, the bank received a unique national charter allowing it to continue its operations in California, Oregon, and Washington. It still has the distinction of being the only bank in the country chartered by the federal government to do business in more than one state.

During the first half of this century the bank continued to place primary emphasis on traditional banking services to commercial customers. In late 1954, however, the Bank of California acquired the Bank of Martinez and entered the retail banking field. This initial move was followed by other acquisitions and by the establishment of regional-type branch banks. The charter of the bank did not permit branching in Oregon or Washington, and, in the 1950's, all new offices were located in Northern California.

In 1962 Charles de Bretteville, who had been a director of the bank and the president of Spreckles Sugar Company, became president of the Bank of California. Under Mr. de Bretteville's direction a number of changes were introduced. A new organization was developed with added emphasis on personnel development, corporate planning, and marketing. (An organization chart is shown in Exhibit 1.) Increased emphasis was placed on developing international business. International offices were opened in nearly all of the bank's port city locations, and in 1964 a branch was established in Manila. Also, in the same year the bank opened an Edge Act subsidiary, which would permit the bank to make foreign investments of a more risky nature. Prior to 1963, the bank had not had offices in Southern California. In 1963, a major office was opened in Los Angeles. In 1964, the bank expanded its operations in Southern California with the acquisition of the 9-branch American National Bank of San Bernardino. During the 1960's the policy of the Bank of California would be characterized as: maintaining the position as a strong wholesale bank while continuing to develop a competitive position in the retail banking industry. Comparative financial data for 1955 and 1965 are shown in Exhibit 2, and a breakdown of loans by types for the 1965 year-end is given in Exhibit 3.

## Marketing Responsibilities in the Bank's Organization

The responsibility for marketing the bank's services was given to several units within its organization.

There were several staff groups which were concerned with business development problems. The Marketing Division, whose organization is shown in Exhibit 4, developed advertising and promotional programs. Their work included both coordination of branch marketing programs and planning of bank-wide promotions. For example, this group had recently arranged for the Bank of California to sponsor the televised broadcasts of San Francisco Giants' games during the coming season. Another promotion program that had been developed by "Marketing" was the Customer-Call Plan. This was a centrally-controlled program by which officers and managers called on present and potential commercial customers to promote the bank's services. In planning these promotions, some marketing research was done by this division.

Mr. Foedisch also headed the bank's National Division, which handled the development of national accounts. As shown in Exhibit 5, the National Division was organized on a geographic basis. The efforts of this group were oriented toward promoting the bank's wholesale services to national companies.

The Corporate Planning Division's work included projects concerned with the bank's marketing policies, especially when the program under study had strategic implications. These studies often involved marketing research activities. The activities and specializations of the seven men in this group are shown in Exhibit 6. Recently the group was trying to determine the primary factors which influence branch growth, and to develop a mathematical model to estimate size of deposits and loans for prospective branch locations. (The actual selection of new branch sites is done by the Branch Expansion Division.) The Corporate Planning Division also worked with the EDP Operations Department in developing new EDP services to attract and hold customers for other bank services. However, as one officer in Corporate Planning said, "Bank of California does not want to become a (computer) service bureau."

The direct business development efforts are the responsibility of the officers and managers of the branches within the bank's system. These men are expected to develop business within their respective areas, using the aid of staff specialists when needed.

# EXHIBIT 1

## The Bank of California, National Association— Organization Nomenclature Chart

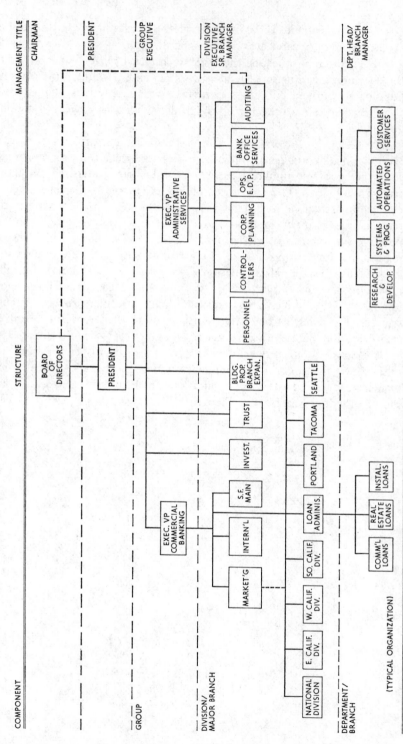

## EXHIBIT 2

### Comparative Balance Sheet

| | December 31 | |
|---|---|---|
| | 1965 | 1955 |
| **Assets** | | |
| Cash and due from banks.......................... | $ 188,091,496 | $104,823,007 |
| U.S. Government securities........................ | 195,435,908 | 149,547,587 |
| State and municipal securities..................... | 132,256,553 | 31,718,650 |
| Other securities................................. | 16,429,988 | 4,630,000 |
| Loans and discounts, less reserve for possible loan losses, 1965–$12,329,917...................... | 763,766,763 | 215,050,267 |
| Customers' liability on acceptances................. | 14,536,464 | 13,452,478 |
| Bank premises and equipment, at cost, less accumulated depreciation and amortization, 1965–$8,081,549..... | 25,693,532 | 4,934,260 |
| Accrued interest................................. | 7,193,262 | 1,240,201 |
| Other assets.................................... | 3,348,547 | 163,401 |
| Total Assets.............................. | $1,346,752,513 | $525,559,851 |
| **Liabilities and Capital Funds** | | |
| Demand deposits................................ | $ 581,798,782 | $310,663,570 |
| Savings and other time deposits.................... | 616,838,280 | 104,646,795 |
| U.S. Government & other public.................. | — | 59,106,626 |
| Total Deposits............................. | 1,198,637,062 | 474,416,991 |
| Funds borrowed................................. | 5,000,000 | — |
| Accrued taxes and other expenses................. | 8,565,975 | 2,883,792 |
| Dividends payable............................... | 836,631 | 344,520 |
| Acceptances outstanding.......................... | 14,761,928 | 13,614,155 |
| Other liabilities................................. | 9,353,755 | 1,296,274 |
| First mortgage notes (4.6% due 1993)............. | 20,000,000 | — |
| Total Liabilities............................ | 1,257,155,351 | 492,555,732 |
| Capital funds | | |
| Capital notes (4.55% due 1989)................. | 20,000,000 | — |
| Shareholders' equity: | | |
| Capital stock, authorized 1,959,180 shares $10 per value—shares outstanding 1,859,180.............. | 18,591,800 | 11,484,000 |
| Surplus......................................... | 38,408,200 | 18,516,000 |
| Undivided profits................................ | 12,597,162 | 3,004,119 |
| Total Shareholders' Equity................... | 69,597,162 | 33,004,119 |
| Total Capital Funds......................... | 89,597,162 | 33,004,119 |
| Total Liabilities and Capital Funds............. | $1,346,752,513 | $525,559,851 |

## EXHIBIT 3

### By Type of Loans

December 31, 1965
(Percent)

| | |
|---|---|
| Real estate loans..................................... | 23.6 |
| Loans to banks and financial institutions................ | 13.0 |
| Loans for purchasing or carrying securities............. | 4.9 |
| Loans to farmers..................................... | 1.1 |
| Commercial and industrial loans....................... | 34.8 |
| Loans to individuals for personal expenditures........... | 21.5 |
| All other loans....................................... | 1.1 |
| | 100.0 |

**EXHIBIT 4**

**Marketing Division**

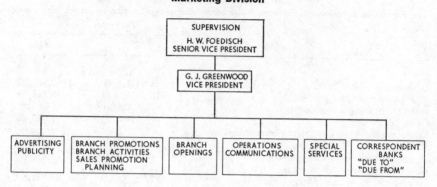

**EXHIBIT 5**

**National Division**

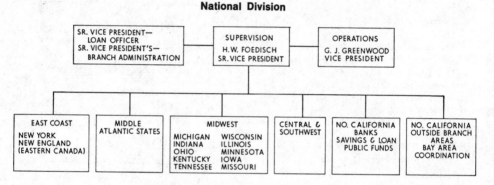

**EXHIBIT 6**

**Organization Planning**
**Manpower Planning**

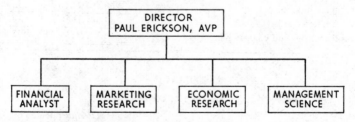

## APPENDIX A: THE MARKETING CONCEPT
## IN COMMERCIAL BANKING

### Introduction

Commercial banking is currently facing strong competitive pressure. It is facing this pressure because it has failed to adapt to the changing needs of its market. The failure to find and implement new and better ways to fill consumers' needs for financial services reflects a shortcoming in the commercial banking industry: the lack of *the marketing concept*. It is the purpose of this report to show the broad implications of the marketing concept for commercial banking. Specifically, we will concentrate on the implications for organizational structure.

The first step will be to identify the major elements of the marketing concept. We will then apply this concept to commercial banking, showing its implications for the proper conduct of this business. Finally, we will describe the organizational structure of a hypothetical bank which has adopted the marketing concept.

## The Marketing Concept

Under the marketing concept, the principal task of management is "not so much to be skillful in making the customer do what suits the interest of the business, as to be skillful in conceiving and then making the business do what suits the interests of the customer."[1] Essentially, the business becomes an organization to fill customer needs, not an organization to produce and sell its products and services to whichever customer it can convince to buy them. A business which adopts this concept—one which becomes oriented towards the customer rather than towards its products, focuses its major efforts on introducing new products and services, and seeks out new classes of customers who heretofore have not used the existing products—will be the business which will compete successfully in today's highly competitive markets.

The marketing concept implies working backward from consumer's needs, not forward from the company's product or service. It implies developing an organization which will thrive on continual change. It stresses the firm's distinctive competence in developing products and services which meet the needs of specific market segments.

## The Marketing Concept as It Relates to Commercial Banking

The commercial banking industry is one which can benefit greatly from adoption of the marketing concept. Commercial banks *sell financial service*. Lending is a means to meet consumers' need for financing. Trust administration is a means for meeting consumers' needs for financial security and investment. Financial counseling is a means for meeting consumers' needs for proper financial planning. Automated services are a means to meet consumers' needs for financial record keeping. In short, it is financial service that a commercial bank offers to the market place.

What is the true criterion for success in this industry? The answer

[1] J. B. McKitterick, "What Is the Marketing Management Concept," *American Marketing Association*, 1957.

lies in the ability of a bank to determine consumers' needs for financial services, to determine how these needs may be segmented, and to determine the ways in which it may organize to most effectively meet these needs. The answer lies in the adoption of the marketing concept. What are the implications of the marketing concept for the commercial bank?

1. The commercial bank should thrive on accepting change, rather than resisting it. It should implement new technological developments and continually strive to develop new and better ways of meeting consumers' needs.

2. The main focus of the creative search for improved performance should be on optimizing the financial service provided to customers, rather than defending against competition.

3. The overall marketing effort should add "consumable value," not merely cost, to the bank's financial services. The commercial bank should use the tools of marketing to improve the "need-satisfying ability" of its products. New products (services) should be developed which will better serve consumer needs. They should be packaged in a way which will further improve their ability to fill consumer demands (repayment flexibility, justifiable deviation from financial restrictions, compensating balance flexibility, etc.), they should be promoted in such a way as to inform a customer of the ways in which they can fill his needs. They should be distributed in a manner (personal call, mail, telephone, or a branch office), and at the time (when he needs it) most optimal to him. If this is done, the marketing effort will add value to the product, further increasing the bank's competitive advantage.

4. The commercial bank should recognize and meet the needs of market segments in order to maximize its ability to solve their unique problems. Commercial banks face many segments. The financial needs of individuals are different from the financial needs of corporations, the needs of domestic corporations are different from the needs of international corporations, the needs of electronic firms are different from the needs of chemical firms, the needs of the wealthy are different from the needs of the poor. A commercial bank should decide which of these segments it wishes to serve, and then develop products which will do this optimally. It must ignore the desire to suppress the differences between these market segments, a desire which is often couched in the philosophy that a dollar is a dollar, no matter who uses it. Instead, recognize that the needs for financial service (which is really its product) will be vastly different for each market segment. It must choose the segments it wishes to deal with, and then tailor its facilities, services, and policies to meet the needs of those segments. If this is done, no competitor who tries to compete by straddling one of these segments will ever be successful. If it is not done, the bank in question will be perpetually vulnerable to any

competitor who sets out specifically to serve the segment it was trying to straddle.

5. The employees of a commercial bank should be "customer's men" rather than "company men." Every employee of a commercial bank who meets the public is a salesman. Tellers, platform officers and callmen are all salesmen. As such they should direct their efforts towards serving the customer, not the company. Their sole concern should be with mobilizing the total resources of the bank towards filling their customer's financial needs. Its efforts should be directed towards discovering customer needs ("Could we set up an automatic savings account for you, sir, in order to save you trips to the bank?"), towards informing management of new ways to solve these needs ("Perhaps we should seriously investigate the establishment of an Edge Act corporation so we can meet the equity needs of our foreign customers?"), and towards tailoring the resources of the bank to meet the particular financial needs of its customers.

6. The commercial bank should focus on its distinctive competence, using its distinctive resources and skills to optimize its ability to serve specific segments of consumer needs. This competence may be in the areas of wholesale banking, or retail banking, or international banking, or trust, and the like. The bank should focus on a limited number of areas, ignoring the temptation to enter into every possible market segment. The bank which focuses on its areas of distinctive competence succeeds because it is more capable of serving the needs of its customers. The bank which does not do so—the bank which straddles all markets—remains vulnerable because it does not optimally serve any specific customer.

In summary, adoption of the marketing concept by commercial banks would require a great change in present attitudes, procedures, and policies. It would require that the bank thrive on the dynamic change which its market has undergone, rather than resist or refuse to recognize it. It would demand that the bank orient itself totally toward consumers' financial needs, rather than simply meeting its competition and selling its traditional products. It would place the marketing function in a position of overriding importance in the bank's power structure. It would mean that the bank would have to segment its markets, spinning off those which it could not serve in an optimal manner, and keeping those which it is uniquely capable of serving.

The author does not mean to imply that nowhere in the field of commercial banking are elements of the marketing concept to be found. Many enlightened bank officials have been able to "sell" certain elements of this concept to their policy makers. The results have been significant. Bank of America's concept of retail banking has resulted in a level of performance that is unmatched across the country and around the world. Morgan Guaranty's market segmentation (wholesale banking only) has been most successful, giving Morgan a distinct advantage over its market-straddling competitors in this area (Chase, City Bank, Manufacturers' Hanover).

### Implications of the Marketing Concept for the Bank's Organizational Structure

An organizational structure may be defined as the vehicle for implementing corporate strategy. It is the set of relationships, the allocation of responsibility and authority, which will carry the stated corporate strategy into effect, thus enabling the corporation to achieve its objectives. From this standpoint, each organizational structure must be unique, for it will reflect the particular objectives and strategic choices of each firm. Thus there is no "right" or "wrong" structure for any firm. On the contrary, the correct structure will be that which will enable the firm to implement its unique strategy and achieve its individual objectives.

Because I do not wish to assume the bank's own area of distinctive competence and its own concept of consumers' needs, I cannot recommend the best organizational structure for the Bank of California. However, we can examine some of the implications of the adoption of this concept for the organizational structure of the bank, whatever choices it makes. And we can show what form organizational structure might take, given a hypothetical set of these choices.

*Selling Financial Service.* The author feels that the first requirement of the adoption of the marketing concept is that individuals throughout all levels of the organization realize that the bank sells financial service, not money, trust, automated services, or the. like. It sells specialized financial services to its customers, providing them with a means to satisfy their financial needs. It is particularly because of "marketing myopia" that some commercial banks have been less progressive than other financial intermediaries. Once bank management accepts the general premise that they are selling financial service to meet specific consumers' needs, they may seriously question certain aspects of the bank's organizational structure.

*Marketing and Top Management.* Another crucial implication of the marketing concept for the organizational structure of this bank is the fact that the marketing function must assume a commanding role in the organizational hierarchy. Top management must have a marketing orientation and must perceive the total market for financial services, so that the bank can foresee and creatively adapt to change. The adoption of the marketing concept means that the marketing function—sales, research, new product analysis, planning, service, and sales training—will assume a role of primary importance in the organizational structure.

*The Marketing Function: Management, Services, Operations.* The adoption of the marketing concept requires that the marketing function be broken down into three basic segments: management, service, and operations. This is done so that marketing management, divorced from the details of operations, and the specifics of service, devotes its time to the broader implications of new product analysis, organizational planning, management training, and marketing policy. Marketing services—such as advertising, promotion, research, forecasting, and public relations—are indirect selling tools and require a special expertise for their proper utilization. Marketing operations—such as field sales, sales training, customer service, product service, and sales administration—are direct selling tools. The separation of the three functions, therefore, insures that each is handled most capably, that each is evaluated in light of its own responsibility, and that each contributes to overall marketing effort.

*Segmentation.* Inherent in the marketing concept is the belief in segmentation. Segmentation is the division of the total market into certain *need* categories, categories which can be identified by some sort of empirical measure. If it adopts the marketing concept, a bank must engage in some sort of market segmentation and structure its organization to reflect the market segments on which it is concentrating. It makes no difference whether it segments by product, by customer type, by geography, or by size of checking account. The important thing is that the method of segmentation give recognition to *differing consumer needs* for financial services.

But ever more important is the fact that the bank cannot properly serve all segments. It cannot force its package of financial services to straddle every part of the market. The bank must choose these segments which it can serve better than anyone else and organize to serve them better.

We emphasize the importance of segmentation in the marketing concept without specifying a procedure by which a bank can determine its "optimal" segments of the market. In general, we urge that bankers examine their total market for financial services, that they try to segment it in the best way possible, and that they then utilize this information to build up a service package which will optimally satisfy those segments which they choose to serve. Finally, they must organize in such a way that this package will be most effectively presented to the segment for which it was produced.

*Market Research.* The adoption of the marketing concept implies that the firm will focus its efforts on a creative search for new and better ways to meet their market's needs for financial services. The tool for this effort is market research. Thus market research must play an important role in the organizational structure of this bank. It must be staffed by a professional who is well versed in the techniques of the field. It must be given proper recognition in all marketing analysis and planning. It must be directed towards continually evaluating the effectiveness of the bank's current package of financial services and towards the complete analysis of creative proposals to improve this package. It must be directed towards determining new and better ways to segment markets, and new and better ways to serve them. Its findings will be the cornerstones for the dynamic development of the marketing concept.

*Sales Training: Creating Customers' Men.*  We have seen the importance of salesmen for the implementation of the marketing concept. We have seen that these men must be customers' men, capable of mobilizing the total resources of the bank towards meeting a customer's financial needs. Thus, the adoption of the marketing concept requires that the commercial bank train and develop its employees so that they may have this capability. Training must assume an important position in the organizational structure. It must be centralized, so that the program will focus on the total resources of the bank, not just on particular functions or products. It must be complete, so that no man will leave the program without the total picture of the bank in his mind. It must be continual, as the bank aggressively adapts to its changing market.

*Planning: Insurance for Success.*  The adoption of the marketing concept implies that the planning function assume a great deal of importance in the organizational structure. Planning insures that the organization is continually equipped to meet the dynamic needs of its market, that the firm goes where it wants to go, and that the total organization and its objectives are the guiding principles, not the fragmented objectives of each department or function. Thus the marketing concept, which implies adaptability to change, market innovation, selective segmentation, and corporate direction dictates that the planning function be placed in a position of great influence and recognition; the very functions which planning fulfills are the means to the successful adoption of this concept. Thus the commercial bank which adopts the marketing concept must place the planning function in a commanding position within the organization.

We have touched on a few of the more important implications of the marketing concept, showing how the commercial bank which adopts it must, in determining its organizational structure, give proper recognition to these facts: that the bank is selling financial service; that marketing is a three-pronged tool consisting of management, service, and operations; that the marketing function must assume a commanding role in the organizational power hierarchy, while operations moves into the background; that segmentation must be practiced; that market research will be the key to success; that salesmen must be trained to sell the total package of the bank's financial services; and that planning should be given all the respect and authority due the importance of its responsibility.

## Organizational Structure: An Example

We will describe briefly the organizational structure of a hypothetical bank. This example incorporates the organizational implications of the marketing concept described above. Our primary assumption is that the bank has decided to concentrate on two primary areas: retail banking and wholesale banking.

The following comments apply to the organization chart shown in Exhibit 7.

*Groups.*  Two major operating groups, Retail and Wholesale, correspond to the two primary market segments on which the bank will concentrate. The major group managers have total responsibility for development of their respective markets, including "sales" of financial assets (gaining new deposits) and "sales" of financing services (gaining new loans).

*Divisions.*  The Retail and Wholesale groups each have three divisions: Sales, Business Development, and Planning.

*Sales* division is segmented geographically for purposes of decentralized control. In the Retail group, district executives supervise branch managers. The Wholesale group also is organized with the goal of specialization, with specific-industry departments and geographical segmentation (U.S., Metropolitan, International).

*Business Development* division includes two departments: Service Managers and Marketing Services. Marketing Services include staff coordination of advertisement, public relations, etc.—sometimes called "indirect selling." Note that so-called "direct selling" is done through the Sales divisions. Service Managers are similar to product managers in manufacturing companies; each Service Manager is responsible for marketing coordination of a specific service, such as installment credit. Service Managers ensure that each "product" or service that the bank sells receives coordinated emphasis in direct and indirect selling operations, e.g., provides service and information on installment credit to all branches.

*Planning* division includes Training, Market Research, New Service Analysis and Organizational Planning departments. Each of these departments works closely with the Corporate Planning staff function. Each is directly responsible to the Retail or Wholesale operating group, so that the special requirements of that segment of the market can be satisfied.

*Corporate Staff Functions.*  Five staff functions assist in corporate-level operations and decision-making but are separate from the line groups that sell the services of the bank. These staff functions are Legal, Bank Investments, Corporate Planning, Control and Operations. The head of Corporate Planning, for example, will have as assistants his counterparts in the Planning Divisions of the Retail and Wholesale groups.

## Conclusion

It has been the hope of the author to present to the reader the organizational implications of the marketing concepts for banking, analyzing them in light of banking's present attitudes and concepts. Specifically, I examined the implications of the marketing concept for the organizational

**EXHIBIT 7**

**Bank Organization Chart with Marketing Concept**

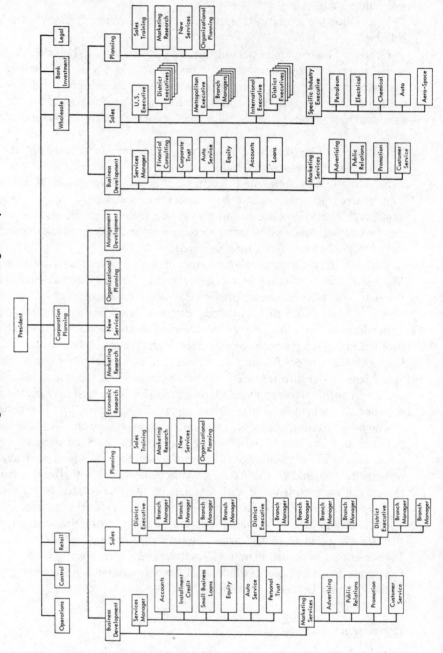

structure of a bank like the Bank of California. I was, of course, unable to present any "organizational truths" or platitudes, for each organizational structure must reflect the unique objectives and strategy of the firm. But I was able to raise the relevant considerations which the bank would have to recognize if it desired to adopt the marketing concept.

I showed how the elements of customer orientation, marketing management, market segmentation, creative innovation, marketing planning, and the like would be reflected in the organizational structure. I also introduced the concept of the Product Manager in an effort to separate the vested influence of products from the primary purpose of customer service. In short, I showed how the bank might organize to reflect the commanding implications of the fully adopted marketing concept.

Above all, the reader must realize that this paper is but a rough beginning to a very complex problem. It handled but a few of the relevant issues, in a manner which barely did them justice. But this does not deny the importance of the marketing concept. Commercial banks have hidden behind their cloaks of conservatism and traditionalism for far too long. Their market has changed. Their customers' demands have changed. Their competitors have changed. For the commercial bank of the future to be successful, it must adopt the marketing concept in its entirety. The nature of its market dictates it, the nature of its product dictates it, the nature of its competition dictates it.

# Barney Corporation

Barney Corporation was founded in 1958 to develop an entirely new field of technology based on the control of the crystalline structure of metals and alloys to a degree not thought possible prior to this development. A whole new product line had been developed from this technology.

Between 1956 and 1967 company sales had grown to about $42 million, and the average growth rate during the past five years had been in excess of 20%. In 1958, Barney stock was offered to the public at a price of $12.50 per share. In 1960, Barney obtained listing on the American Stock Exchange and, in 1967, the stock was trading in the range of $98–$142 after splitting two for one in 1966. The management of Barney felt that this impressive growth rate was due to two factors. Firstly, the vigorous research and development program undertaken by the company, and secondly, a dynamic and aggressive organization which prided itself on modeling its unique technical capabilities to the needs of the market place.

However, conflicts had started to develop within Barney's marketing organization as a result of the rapid expansion experienced by the company. To illustrate some of the problems, the following are excerpts taken from a recent meeting of product managers:

So for the second time in a month I had to ring St. Francis[1] to ask for more time on their order, because you guys in manufacturing don't know the meaning of the word "priority." You also remember the trouble I had persuading R & D to work on this problem in the first place. Now we get a $150,000 order just as a starter, and we can't deliver on time!"

Why do you ask me to spend my time trying to sell tubing when the time given up could be spent on chain, for which I have profit responsibility?

Reprinted from *Stanford Business Cases 19* with the permission of the publisher, Graduate School of Business, Stanford University. Copyright © 1968 by the Board of Trustees of the Leland Stanford Junior University.

[1] St. Francis Roller Bearing Company was a major customer of Barney.

All I do all day long is put out fires. I have no time left to perform my other functions, especially long-range planning.

I wish you guys would wake up and see that we must move away from product management. Market orientation, that's what we need.

Look, we sell metal products; sure it's high-grade stuff, but it's all based on our product technology. A specialized, single-line sales force under these circumstances doesn't make sense to me.

Comments such as these worried the management of Barney, and they wondered what changes, if any, should be made in Barney's marketing organization, to maintain the expected rapid growth rate in the future.

## Company History

In 1955, while working for the Great Western Steel Company's R & D Division 'as metallurgists, Ken Barrington and George Whitney made an important discovery. Using various metals or alloys and subjecting them to a variety of physical and chemical treatments, they were able to produce compounds with extraordinary properties. These included an extreme degree of hardness, lightweight, elasticity and an ability to change the electrical conductivity of the metal.

Toward the end of 1955, Barrington and Whitney resigned from their positions with Great Western Steel, and started their own company, which they called The Barney Corporation. After a great deal of discussing, it was decided that Barney Corporation would manufacture the finished products resulting from the new technological development, rather than license other companies to use the technology, or to manufacture the metal raw materials only. The Company became a supplier to the electronics, aircraft and aerospace industries almost immediately, although some time had to be spent with the engineers of each customer to acquaint them with the attributes and performance of these new materials.

The Company grew rapidly between 1956 and 1960. Barney continued to concentrate on furthering research and development in the whole field of metal technology. Many patents were applied for and new product development was taking place at an extremely rapid rate. Whitney commented that "hardly a day went by without someone calling us up, with the 'greatest' new idea ever! We received a lot of good ideas in this way."

Marketing of the product line also received a good deal of attention. In order to build for long-range growth, management decided upon the following strategies:

1. Manufacturers representatives were to be used initially, in order to gain national distribution and rapid customer acceptance, until a competent internal marketing organization consisting of metallurgical engineers could be developed.

2.  Commercialization of new products would initially be restricted to those with only limited sales potential.

These strategies proved successful and by the early 1960's, Barney had developed to the point where it was able to launch a major expansion program. Existing product lines were greatly expanded, and several new high volume product groups were introduced. The Cincinnati Chain and Cable Company located in Cincinnati, Ohio, was acquired, which opened up markets not served by Barney prior to the acquisition. Barney also purchased the Curtis-Conway Manufacturing Company located in Chicago. Although under the financial direction and control of Barney, this wholly owned subsidiary continued to operate as a separate and autonomous company under the direction of Mr. John Curtis.

At the same time, Barney began the transition to an in-house technically-trained marketing team through the establishment of the product management group and a direct sales force. The marketing group increased from only 10 people in 1960 to 104 in early 1968; in addition, 22 field sales offices were opened. Barney also began a major domestic plant expansion to supplement its leased facilities in an industrial park south of Cleveland. The company purchased 100 acres of land in an industrial park nearby, on which some 420,000 square feet of manufacturing, research and office facilities were constructed. Present facilities had the capacity to handle up to $80 million of business a year. Much of this expansion and construction was financed from the sale of some $7 million of convertible debentures.

Barney also began to expand internationally. In conjunction with Uni-Metals Ltd., Barney set up a subsidiary in England, which had research, manufacturing and marketing facilities, to exploit potential markets in the United Kingdom. Complete control of this British affiliate was acquired in 1966. As overseas marketing efforts were extended to Western Europe, a second manufacturing facility was established in West Germany. Most of the requirements of the European market could be produced by the English and West German facilities.

Although Barney's record had been highly successful to date, management was anxious to maintain the company's impressive growth rate. As such, management's stated financial objectives were to obtain *at least* a 20% increase in sales per year, a 40% annual return on invested capital, and an after-tax profit on sales of 7–9%. Management considered three courses of action prerequisite to fulfilling these objectives: continued technological innovation, adequate patent coverage and vertical integration.

## PRODUCT LINE

### Technology

Nearly all of Barney's products were based on the science of metal crystallography. The company had developed over 100 different metals and alloys, which, when changed by several chemical and physical processes had desired chemical, physical and electrical properties. Barney utilized these properties to develop novel products and applications ranging from ball bearings to top secret materials for defense contracts, and had over 8,000 different types and sizes of products.

## Research and Development

In early 1968, Barney's R & D staff totalled 170, nearly double that of the previous year. Approximately half of the staff were degreed personnel, including 31 with doctorates in metallurgy, engineering and chemistry. Research was carried out in new facilities which included a materials processing area, product development laboratories, and technical service laboratories. England and West Germany had a separate development and technical service group which supplemented the U.S. activity for service to these Western European subsidiaries.

Many of the research projects were initiated by the product management group based on market research or on information from the field sales force. In order to supplement the market research and product development efforts of the product managers, a venture analysis group, which consisted of three men, was set up in early 1967 to explore whole new areas within the technical competence of the company. This group originally reported directly to the President, but was later transferred to the R & D area under Vice President Greenhalgh.

All Barney products were developed through its own research efforts. Over 60% of 1967 company sales were comprised of products introduced in the preceding three years. In addition to patent protection on substantially all of its significant patentable developments, the company had many trade secrets and a large body of confidential technical information and skill. Barney also adopted and used many trademarks. A description of the major product lines follows.

## Electrical Wiring

Prior to the development of special alloys for high-performance electrical wiring by Barney, electrical wiring could be made to withstand only quite narrow extremes of physical conditions. For example, there was high-temperature wire and low-temperature wire, each being suitable for applications only in a fairly narrow temperature range. The alloys developed by Barney allowed one wire to be used under all temperature conditions. Up to 1964, the wire insulating step in the manufacturing process had been subcontracted out, but in 1964, Barney purchased the Wells Insulating Corporation in Toledo, Ohio, and thus acquired its own insulating capability. Many coating materials were used including teflon, rubber, polyethylene, PVC and several other special compounds. This coated wire was sold in many forms including hook-up wire, single and multi-conductor cable, and various configurations of coaxial cables. The line had wide acceptance in the electronics, aircraft, missile, and aerospace industries because of its unique properties. It was also used extensively in uncoated form, in the wiring of special purpose electric motors.

About 50% of the sales of electrical wiring went into government products such as the F-111, the Lockheed C-5A and Poseidon missile.

### Tubing

Another major property, which could be conferred upon alloys by a variety of treatments, was extremely high tensile strength. Coupling this property with the ability to withstand temperature extremes had led to the development of tubing for fuel lines of aircraft and missiles. It had been determined that this particular tubing would not rupture when it was subjected to five times the pressure expected under normal applications. Barney tubing was now specified in government contracts, for a number of aircraft and missiles, as well as for commercial aircraft such as the Boeing and Douglas range of jetliners.

Despite this widespread acceptance in the missile and aircraft industries, tubing sales were only moderate because the number of units (missiles and aircraft) produced and the amount of tubing required per unit were only quite small. Barney was, therefore, actively exploring other outlets for this product line. Barney had recently been successful in switching over the country's major manufacturer of pressure gauges to its own tubing line. Barney was also actively working closely with such other potential major customers, such as boiler manufacturers, and contractors involved in the installation of commercial nuclear reactors. However, since extensive testing of all new products was required by these customers, progress in these applications had been rather slow.

One contractor, Pittsburg-Nuclear Corporation had indicated to the Company recently that it had almost completed testing of Barney tubing, and that the results to date had been extremely promising. The sales engineer handling the account had been given to understand, that Pittsburg-Nuclear could make a complete switch to Barney tubing in about six months time. A major question confronting the Product Manager for this product group was how to capitalize upon this development, once the change became official.

### Ball and Roller Bearings[2]

Barney had made a major breakthrough with this product line recently. For a number of years, Barney had been working in close cooperation with the St. Francis Roller Bearing Company, one of the major

---

[2] The company did not produce finished bearings. It produced only spherical or cylindrical shaped alloy ball and roller bearings, ground and polished to the required tolerances. These "ball bearings" were then sold to bearing manufacturers who made a final polish and then manufactured the bearings.

producers of ball and roller bearings in the U.S.A. In the past, St. Francis had manufactured over 300 different types of bearings, in many different sizes and shapes, depending upon the application, required life, load carrying capacity and many other factors. Many different alloys were used, to produce this large product range. After several years of testing, St. Francis had recently decided to standardize on ball and roller bearings manufactured by Barney. As a result of this change, St. Francis was able to reduce its line of bearings to about 35 basic types, with great savings in manufacturing and inventory costs.

The first commercial order had been received about six months ago, and it would appear that potential business for this application would reach at least $10 million within a very short space of time.

Barney was now actively soliciting business with other bearing manufacturers, and had initiated a study project to determine whether it should begin to manufacture finished bearings. Barney had been approached recently by one of the major motor car manufacturers, regarding the supply of finished bearings manufactured from Barney alloys.

### Chain and Cable

These products were sold to a wide variety of industrial users. The major product advantages over competing lines was a high degree of hardness and high tensile strength. Chain was sold to automobile companies and other engine manufacturers for timing chain, to bicycle and motor bicycle manufacturers as driving chain and to other industrial users for a variety of applications. Another line of chain was manufactured for cutting purposes and found a major outlet in power saw manufacturers either as chain or band saws.

Mechanical cable was also manufactured in a wide variety of alloys depending upon the required application. Some cable went into aircraft, and to automobile manufacturers. Other high tension cable was sold to contractors involved in the construction of bridges and commercial office buildings. One major customer was the Langsford Elevator Corporation, one of the major manufacturers of elevators in the U.S.A. Both the main cable and the safety cable of lifts manufactured by Langsford were made from Barney cable.

### Castings

Barney had developed many alloys for use in a wide variety of castings. In addition to a wide variety of castings manufactured in its own foundries, Barney sold metal to other foundries for casting purposes. This was the only purpose for which Barney sold raw metal or alloy.

Barney owned several foundries in different parts of the U.S.A. located close to major customers. Major use for casting was in a wide variety of precision items. Automobile manufacturers were major customers and others included manufacturers of earthmoving and agricultural equipment. The leading edges of bulldozer blades, power shovels, plows and harrows were major outlets for Barney castings.

Another group of important, potential customers for castings was the nation's railways. Rails are laid in 100-foot lengths but cannot be welded together, since expansion during hot weather would lead to buckling. A gap of about one to one and one-half inches has to be left between these lengths to allow for expansion. This means that the wear at the end of the rail is about three times as great as that on the rest of the rail, leading to costly maintenance problems. Barney had conducted tests for some years with a variety of alloys, whose special attribute was extreme hardness, to combat this problem. It currently had a cast sleeve in the final stages of testing which looked very promising. It appeared that it would need replacement only once during the life of a rail rather than three or four times. If this product proved acceptable to the railways, a market of some $20–25 million annually was projected by the Product Manager responsible for casting products.

### Welding and Soldering Devices

Because of the special nature of Barney alloys, they could not be welded or soldered with ordinary equipment. Barney, therefore, produced a line of welding equipment and soldering guns, as well as special welding and soldering rods for use with its product line. These devices accounted for less than 3% of Barney sales.

### Manufacturing

Manufacturing at Barney took place in two distinct phases:

i. Firstly, a smelting and treatment plant, where metals and alloys were melted, mixed and treated in batch quantities, depending upon the use to which the metal was to be put.

ii. Product lines for wire, bearings, cable, tubing, etc. where the products in question were manufactured from the alloys produced in the smelting and treatment plant.

Conflicts between product groups could, therefore, take place at both of these phases of the manufacturing process. About 80–85% of the time, the conflict occurred in the smelting and treatment plant. Two or more product managers might, for example, ask the plant, at the same time, to produce alloy on an urgent basis for orders which they had obtained and for which manufacture had not been planned.

The remaining 15–20% of conflicts occurred on the product lines, where, for example, two urgent orders for cable might arrive at the same time, and some means of setting priorities had to be arrived at.

## MARKETING

Barney attributed much of its success to its desire and ability to respond quickly and effectively to the needs of the marketplace. If a customer wanted an item at a given time which manufacturing could not fit into the production schedule, then manufacturing would be asked to work overtime to complete the order. Likewise, if a product manager wanted R & D to design a new application for a customer with a significant potential, then R & D would set aside less pressing projects in order to satisfy the customer's requirements.

### Markets and Customers

Barney's sales were concentrated in a relatively small number of accounts and industries. In 1967, the three largest customers accounted for approximately 21% of sales, and the 10 largest customers accounted for 41%. The industry breakdown for 1967 sales was approximately as follows: aircraft (principally military), 29%; missiles and space, 14%; electronics, telecommunications and computers, 26%; automobiles, 18%; other 15%. The profitability of sales to all the industries was roughly comparable.

Sales for United States Government end use (estimated at approximately 48% of sales during fiscal 1967, including approximately 3% direct sales to the United States Government) were dependent upon continuance of appropriations and requirements for national defense and aerospace programs and were subject to renegotiation. Most of Barney's sales for governmental end use were to customers operating under government prime contracts and subcontracts which contained standard provisions for termination or curtailment at the convenience of the government. Sales for commercial use had expanded to approximately 60% in the first six months of fiscal 1968, primarily due to increased commercial aircraft business and to the addition of the ball bearing business, plus much higher sales to the automotive market.

### Competition

Although Barney's products were sold in highly competitive markets, there were few directly comparable products. Barney competed with many companies and divisions of companies both larger and smaller than Barney, but only a few of these companies supplied competitive products that provided similar technical solutions to the functional problems of customers. Barney competed primarily on the basis of its unique technical capabilities and the advantages thereof—high reliability, labor cost savings, less repair work.

## Sales Organization

Barney sales were originally handled primarily through manufacturer's representatives who sold both Barney's entire product line and other related products. These representatives were used to set up a national sales network at a low cost (average 4½% commission). Barney utilized some distributors for casting products and a small direct sales force which handled sales in some eastern states, missionary sales, and contacts with the manufacturer's representatives.

When Barney's rapid expansion made a direct sales force expedient, the manufacturer's representatives were phased out. Barney found it advantageous, however, to retain its distributors for casting sales, even though it built up its own direct sales force. The nature of the casting market lent itself to mass distribution because approximately 80% was sold in small quantities. Furthermore, only the distributors could effectively provide the necessary local service to this diverse market. Because Barney was able to offer its distributors a high markup (45–55%), the distributors pushed Barney casting products, so that Barney became a major line with most of them. And even though castings became more price competitive, the distributor, rather than Barney, absorbed the price erosion; yet the line's volume still commanded a great deal of his time and effort. Moreover, the distributor presently had an added incentive to find new applications for Barney products, in that he was in direct competition with Barney; only if the distributor found a new market or application was he allowed to sell it; otherwise, Barney handled the new accounts directly.

As Barney expanded its direct sales force and district offices were opened throughout the United States, the current sales organization took shape (see Figure 1).

The general sales manager's position was established in December, 1966, to coordinate the activities of the three regional managers who had previously reported directly to Vice President Ron McOnie. Peter Joyner, the current field sales manager, defined his job as mostly administrative at the outset; however, in the long run, he expected to spend about half of his time selling and half on administrative detail.

The regional sales managers were responsible for all accounts within their respective regions. They worked with the salesmen and Branch managers to set priorities and to sell to major or difficult accounts. According to Joyner, "the regional manager should spend at least 80% of his time actually selling."

The Barney sales force in the U.S. consisted of 58 men, of whom 24 were managers of Branch sales offices. The Branch managers had anywhere from one to seven salesmen working out of their individual offices. Much of the sales effort was directed toward project selling. Of the 24

**FIGURE 1**

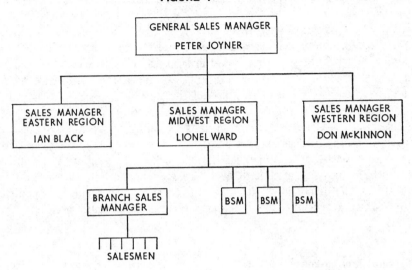

branch sales offices in the United States, most were established in response to the needs of specific projects or accounts. For example, an office was set up in St. Louis, Missouri, to gain and service the St. Francis account.

The Barney sales force ranged in age from 23 to 52 and averaged eight years of sales experience. Sales compensation consisted of a salary (ranging from $12–18,000 per year) plus a bonus based on each salesman's performance. The basis for evaluating performance was the quarterly sales forecast, which was a combination of

1. The forecast made by the salesmen in conjunction with their branch and regional managers, based on key accounts, distributor sales, and new projects
2. The forecast made by the product managers based on their work in the field and new product developments.

Sales performance was reviewed monthly by the sales managers. Of the 58 sophisticated and technically trained salesmen in the U.S., three-quarters had scientific or engineering backgrounds and 12 held MBA degrees. They attempted to create the image of being "consultants" to their accounts based on their high technical competence. Primary emphasis was placed upon working with the engineering and manufacturing departments of customers and potential customers.

Barney had another 31 salesmen working out of its 11 sales offices in Europe and Canada. These offices, staffed with engineering personnel, provided a full range of marketing services and maintained inventories to meet customer requirements. Foreign sales accounted for about 14% of the company total in 1967.

All of the salesmen went through a rigorous three-month training program which emphasized company philosophy, product knowledge, and company capabilities. Nearly two-thirds of the program was devoted to detailed technical information and applications of the company's products and processes. The other third of the time was spent on sales training, including role playing, information on customers and markets, and field experience. Upon completion of the training course, a salesman was assigned to the field either as a multi-line salesman covering a given geographical area, or as a specialized salesman selling a given line of products to specific markets. Although each salesman had originally handled all products, the demands of the marketplace had recently made expedient the use of a specialized sales force, oriented to specific products and markets.

### Product Management

According to one of Barney's six product managers, "The product manager has the best job in the company. The whole structure here is such that things get funnelled to the product manager, and then he crosses whatever lines he needs to get things done. It's where the action is." Each of Barney's major product lines was under the direct control and responsibility of a product manager who coordinated and directed the entire marketing program for his particular product line.

Barney's product managers ranged in age from 29 to 38. All but one had both sales experience and a scientific or engineering background; in addition, all of them held MBA degrees. Their compensation consisted of a salary (ranging from $14–22,000) plus a bonus (based on management's estimates of each man's relative contribution to profitability and sales growth). The organization of the product management group, under the direction of Terry Westwood is shown in Figure 2.

According to Westwood, "the product manager should operate much as a general manager of his own business with P & L responsibility, but without his own sales force or manufacturing facilities." One of the product managers described the role in more detail:

The product manager is responsible for the profitability and growth of his product line, and a major part of that responsibility should be the long-range planning for that line. He is essentially a coordinating function between sales, manufacturing, and R & D. He is responsible for training and equipping the sales force to sell the existing product line, which boils down to training new men, retraining existing people, promotional material, literature, and sales aids. He's also in charge of advertising—where, what media, how much. He is responsible for guiding R & D in the design of new products to meet whatever requirements he finds. The product manager is also directly involved with

**FIGURE 2**

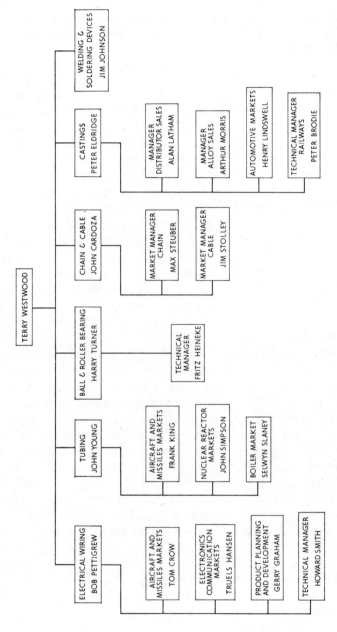

field sales problems. Often he will go to specific areas where there are major problems, or major sales efforts or programs and will assist the local guy in whatever way he can.

The product manager also had pricing responsibility. Since Barney had little direct competition because of the unique properties and applications of its products, customers were often willing to pay a premium for Barney products which offered such advantages as high reliability, or savings in labor and repair costs. Prices were usually based on value to the customer, rather than cost plus a fixed percentage. As such, most of Barney's products were very profitable.

Although the product manager was responsible for the profitability of his product line, he was technically in a staff position with no direct authority. He had to deal directly with the people in manufacturing, R & D, and sales and "sell" them on his projects and ideas. According to another of the product managers, "the basic philosophy at Barney essentially promotes a nonorganizational type of function. In other words, each guy is pretty much on his own to accomplish what has to be done to fulfill his job function without a lot of mickey mouse organization stuff. If I want R & D to work on something, I talk to the guy who knows the most about what I want done, and I get it done."

Occasionally, however, conflicts would arise between product areas, and these conflicts were becoming increasingly difficult to resolve within the growing company framework. The unique characteristics of each product line presented different requirements and marketing problems for each product manager, as the following examples show.

**Welding and Soldering Devices.** This product line, under the direction of Jim Johnson, crossed all other product lines except ball bearings because of its essentially supportive nature. Johnson did not look to the marketplace itself to ascertain the need for his type of product as the other product managers did. He had to deal with the needs of the other product managers and field sales people since his devices provided them with a great deal of leverage to generate sales in other product lines.

Although Johnson theoretically had the same profit and loss responsibility as the other product managers, he did not have the same pricing authority that they did—they could "give away" one of his devices in order to close a sale. Furthermore, his line was characterized by low volume and high unit cost and, thus, he could not be evaluated on the same basis as the other product managers.

**Castings.** This line also differed from the other product lines in several respects. First, most of the casting products were marketed through a series of distributors who took title to the products. Secondly, castings were subject to more direct competition than the other product lines.

Eldridge had three staff marketing assistants to cover the four major markets for his products, and the fourth of Eldridge's assistants was in charge of distributor sales.

*Electrical Wiring.* Bob Pettigrew, who was responsible for the large electrical wiring line, had four men working with him. Howard Smith was primarily involved in the technical aspects of the line including technical problems both in the plant and in the field, writing product specifications, and preparing sales literature. Because of the nature of the product line, electrical wiring experienced far more technical problems than the other lines.

Pettigrew also had one man aiding him with product planning and development. Gerry Graham had recently been transferred to the product management group from his position as Midwestern Regional Sales Manager. Pettigrew himself was very involved with the selling function, and he estimated that 75% of his time was spent dealing directly with the sales force.

Barney's electrical wiring line had significant competition from the many other producers of coated wire products. Since Barney's products were often quite different, the salesmen sometimes had difficulty getting their products specified by the customers, because Barney would then become their sole source of supply.

*Tubing.* John Young was responsible for the tubing product line. Since this product line differed from the others somewhat in that a larger portion of his orders were manufactured on a custom basis, he spent a good deal of his time on new product strategy—determining which had the greatest potential, establishing prices, etc. Recently, two men had been hired to work with him on the nuclear reactor and boiler markets.

John Simpson was in charge of tubing for the nuclear reactor market, and had responsibility for sales development to contractors and industries where the major potential for high pressure tubing was. These included the electric utilities companies, shipyards involved in the nuclear submarine program, and companies working on a variety of other projects, utilizing nuclear reactors, such as desalination. It was anticipated that once all these markets became fully developed, the regular sales force would have to be supplemented with a group of six to seven specialists. The reason for this expansion was the fact that the potential was expected to be very large, and secondly, that the construction work would be carried out by a large number of subcontractors, all of whom would have to be familiarized with the special properties of Barney tubing.

Selwyn Slaney was responsible for the development of sales to the boiler and steam generator markets. Included in his list of potential customers were public and private electric utilities and equipment manufacturers. It was Slaney's job also to identify other possible major markets for high pressure tubing, and to ensure that such products were developed to add to the present line.

There was some duplication in terms of product responsibility between Simpson and Slaney. Often contractors were quoting on both nuclear and conventional power generators so that two sales engineers might be working with the same contractor at the same time. The characteristics of the tubing used in nuclear and conventional power generators were quite different, but Young wondered whether the present system was the best way to utilize very high cost sales resources.

In addition, this line of tubing shared production facilities with tubing required for use in aircraft and missiles. Occasionally a conflict would arise in manufacturing. For example, Simpson recently ordered a considerable quantity of specialized tubing for extensive testing purposes by one of his potential customers, at the same time as Frank King received a large tubing order for an aircraft application. Terry Westwood had to resolve the conflict by authorizing the use of both overtime and subcontracting to complete the two projects in time.

## Product Manager's Meeting

The following dialogue concerning Barney's marketing operations took place at a recent meeting of the product management group.

CARDOZA: One of the basic defects in our present product management setup is that we're too concerned with day-to-day problems, and we're unable to spend as much time as we should looking ahead and planning what direction the product line should be taking. Basically, there's just too much to do, and we've really got to skim the top.

TURNER: Yeah! Day-to-day ticky-tack gobbles up a fierce amount of time. It's easy to put off formal long-range planning and sales forecasting in favor of more pressing immediate needs.

JOHNSON: True. With so many men in the field now, I sometimes never get the phone off my shoulder all day long. But, after all, the open phone-open door policy is our real strength. We've maintained our growth record by being able to react quickly to the customer's needs rather than by sitting down and figuring out by market research what area we really want to shoot at, then designing a product to meet that need, and then going out and promoting it.

YOUNG: But one of the biggest problems ahead is going to be to keep developing new products and new potentials, so that we can sustain that growth rate.

KING: John's right. And the product management concept was set up at Barney to create new products and new markets.

YOUNG: Long-range planning may not be the panacea, but I think you'll agree with me, John, that as the field sales organization grows, product management has got to grow to support the activities of the product in the field.

PETTIGREW: I have to disagree with you, John. This may be a sacrilegious statement in this group, but I think we're going to have to get away from the product management concept toward that of market management, which I've already done to a certain extent in my line. I have two staff marketing assistants in charge of the big potential wiring markets. I've come to the conclusion that if we intend to turn an almost job shop kind of business into a high volume operation, we need market development and emphasis.

SIMPSON: I agree, Bob. After all, I'm basically a market manager myself. I think it's inevitable that we ultimately organize on a market basis, because our products and markets are not clearly and exclusively defined. I say that we should be oriented on a market basis—including the sales force. We've got to fit our company capabilities to the needs of an industry.

JOHNSON: Your product areas may need market specialists, but that doesn't hold for me. We all need more time for planning, etc., but what I need is an applications engineer to do some of my leg-work. I suspect that more technical support might be valid for electrical wiring, too.

SMITH: Well, that's pretty much how Bob and I have things divided now, anyway. I'm taking care of most of the technical problems, but we need a larger technical back-up staff to keep up with them.

TURNER: As I see it, we have a couple of alternatives for evolution. First, if the company organized itself into product divisions—when we're big enough to afford the luxury of it—the product management concept would make some sense, because one guy would have real control and responsibility for manufacturing, marketing, sales, and new product development for his line. Then Terry's definition of a product manager as a mini-general manager with his own business would be realistic. Right now we don't really have that flexibility, because we're single-sourced by manufacturing and R & D, and we always have to work within the framework of the whole company.

An alternative to the division manager would be to have market managers, which probably makes more sense from a growth and marketing standpoint. We already have some market specialists under the product managers, but since they sometimes have to cross product lines, we find ourselves in competition with each other, or the wrong guy gets the credit for making things happen, and so on.

KING: I can vouch for that. The markets I deal with buy tubing, but I'm sure they could use some electrical wire, too. But there's no incentive for me to spend my time trying to sell them wire if it takes time away from the products where I have authority and profit responsibility.

TURNER: Yeah, we keep saying we're marketing oriented, but boy, the whole concept of product management is a very unmarketing oriented way to do things. It's a manufacturing approach. I mean, I will sell bearings to anyone who wants to buy them. But what if my customer needs some castings or cable? I'm not really going to get credit for it on a formal basis unless we install a halfway decent profit-compensation plan which gives credit where it's due.

HANSEN: Isn't that what you guys from Biz School would label the authority/responsibility syndrome? It's inevitable that a conflict will come up now and then, where there's an authority/responsibility gap, but if you can persuade people, it really isn't that much of a problem.

CARDOZA: Right. We're recognized as the guiding group and our requests are respected by the various functions. It may take a certain amount of salesmanship to sell a point, but if the project's any good. . . .

In spite of some problems inherent in the product management system, Terry Westwood felt that it had operated effectively at Barney. He was, however, concerned that additional problems might arise as the company continued its rapid expansion. One of his current concerns was how to allocate R & D time among the various projects recommended by the product managers. The relative importance of each project was not always clear cut, since the product managers frequently did not have enough time to devote to market research.

Current crises generally commanded most of the product manager's time, and the results of the time so expended were often more measurable than that spent on long-range plans or new product development. As a result, Westwood felt that the company might unintentionally exclude itself from new markets or applications. Active evaluation and pursuit of new markets and applications were essential if Barney expected to maintain its ambitious growth rate.

# Fernand Company

The Fernand Company produced a line of machine tools which consisted in the main of drilling machines and lathes. Founded in 1904, the company had consistently maintained its reputation as a quality producer and one which had developed and made operational a substantial number of innovations in both drilling machines and lathes. Most of its $75 million annual sales volume was concentrated in the North American market, although sales to Western Europe were becoming increasingly important. In the late 1960's the company adopted the product manager type of organization, but in 1974 the new marketing director felt that the system was still not functioning properly. In particular he was dissatisfied with the way the product managers handled their planning activities.

The marketing department was divided into four major units: product management, field sales, advertising, and marketing research. Field sales included a technical support group which functioned not only to help the salesmen to "sell" but did service work as well, including the supervision of the installation work (where required) and handling complaints. The advertising group was responsible for producing all catalogs, bulletins, technical data sheets, slides and movies, and the company's house newspaper. In addition, it prepared special mailings, handled publicity releases, and wrote advertising copy.

The product management unit was comprised of eight product managers. Three of these reported to a product group manager who was responsible for drilling presses; the remainder reported to a product group manager in charge of lathes. The main responsibilities of the product managers were as follows:

1. To develop and administer the sales programs for the product items for which they were responsible.

2. To initiate and administer all product design changes once approved by the engineering, manufacturing, and marketing departments.
3. To administer prices under the supervision of the applicable product group manager.
4. To keep all sales and service personnel continuously informed regarding all aspects of his product items including price, delivery, product modifications, and performance.
5. To liason with the advertising unit regarding the development and implementation of printed materials pertaining to the product; further, to plan the extent and type of advertising required to support the product.
6. To prepare all bids and quotations, handle sales correspondence, and handle customer complaints.

The complaint of the new marketing director centered on his belief that the product managers were spending their time mostly servicing the sales force on a day-to-day basis. In his view this was understandable given that the company employed a single sales force to sell its entire line of products. It was only natural that product managers would seek as much time as possible from the sales and service group since they were not billed on a direct basis for the actual time spent.

Product managers did, however, have profit responsibility for their items. Each item sold was billed to them at a price which covered direct and indirect manufacturing costs (including plant overhead, inventory, engineering, and depreciation) and general management overhead. From their dollar sales were substracted their costs (salary, expenses, and secretarial services), any bad debts pertaining to their product, all product specific advertising and marketing research, direct service costs (e.g., repair parts and direct expenses of the services engineers), and an allocated amount designed to cover all sales and service general expenses for their product. Such costs were allocated on a basis of each product's annual dollar sales. Indeed, all allocations were made on this basis.

The new marketing director was disappointed to learn that the individual product managers did little planning beyond one year. They were, in his opinion, too entrepreneurial in their activities and openly competed against one another for the company's scarce resources. This short-term orientation was, he thought, not always conducive to increasing the firm's overall profitability over the longer term.

In order to gain a better understanding of what would be involved in attempting to initiate a new and longer term (three–five years) product planning process, the new manager commissioned a consulting firm to set forth their views on the subject. Their preliminary response in outline form appears as Exhibit 1. It was structured to show what tasks had to be accomplished in order to formulate a longer term plan for a particular product. The outline was used as the basis for a day-long seminar which all product managers attended as did the heads of the various marketing activities and the marketing manager. At the end of this seminar the latter requested an appraisal of the proposed planning system by all those present.

### EXHIBIT 1
#### Suggested Steps in Developing a Marketing Plan

I. Objectives
   A. Longer term—three–five years
      1. What products are involved? What market segments are involved for each?
      2. What is the outlook or forecast for *each* product within each major market segment expressed in terms of units and marginal contribution dollars (sales less direct costs)?
      3. What are the company's market share objectives in terms of the above "breakdowns" by year over the planning horizon?
         *a.* What is the "gap" between the "present" and the "future" share?
         *b.* What is the value of the "increment" expressed in terms of units and marginal contributions? The latter measure should be expressed in both actual and real or constant dollars.
         *c.* Note: In making the above estimates please state your assumptions about the following variables with respect to your marketing area as to:
            (1) Production availability.
            (2) GNP trends and effect on present customer industries regarding their purchases of your item.
            (3) Inflation and its effect on purchases.
            (4) The nature and scope of competition within each major segment.
            (5) Technology changes.
            (6) Price changes.
         *d.* Which of the above items should be monitored on a continuous basis in order to provide you with the data needed to effect a contingency plan?
            (1) What are the sources of such data?
            (2) At what "levels" would the contingency plan take effect?
                What action would you recommend taking at different levels?
            (3) What additional data do you need for contingency planning?
                What are the sources? What is the frequency? What would be the action levels involved? What actions would evolve?
   B. Short term—12–18 months
      1. State what market segments you plan to emphasize by indicating what market share objectives you have for each.

EXHIBIT 1 (Continued)

2. State in generalized form what market share determinants are critical and their relative importance.* Do not attempt at this point to indicate precisely their form by individual market segments.
3. Indicate what you expect major competitors to do during this period for each generalized determinant:
   a. Regardless of what you do.
   b. Based on your action.
4. What sales revenue, profit, and/or cost guidelines constrain your suggested plan? Indicate to what extent you feel these constraints serve to limit your actions in an unreasonable way.
5. Indicate the individuals who have participated in the development of this plan.

II. Action by Individual Segments
   A. For each product market segment indicate what the market share goal is and its value in marginal contribution dollars.
   B. For each share objective indicate the following:
      1. What determinants are involved, listed in order of importance.
      2. How each of these determinants will be accomplished.
      3. Who in the organization is involved in the prosecution of each activity leading to the accomplishment of the determinants.

Note: Knowledge about the segment may be sufficiently primitive that data must be obtained before action can be prescribed. In such cases state what data are to be obtained from what sources in what form and by whom. Also indicate deadlines and when results will be reflected in your plan.

III. General Support Plans for Action across Market Segments
   A. Indicate which determinants have relevance *across* all segments.
   B. Indicate for each such determinant what action you intend taking over what is now being taken and the cost.
   C. For the sales force activity the following questions are suggested.
      1. Upon whom should the sales force call and with what frequency during the coming year?
      2. What information should the sales force have on each potential customer called upon?
      3. What product features should the sales force stress in their presentations to alternative segments by level of respondent?
      4. What questions should the salesmen be prepared to handle in the field? What questions should be referred to the technical service group?
      5. What special training should be given to the salesman to help him sell and provide adequate feedback?
         a. Who should do this training?
         b. When should this training be done? How?

---

* By determinant is meant that action or accomplishment which will affect market share; for example, a change in one or more product features relative to competitive products, improving the service activity, increasing the speed of delivery of the product once ordered, increasing the amount of time spent with an account, and so on.

**EXHIBIT 1 (Continued)**

6. What feedback should be provided by the sales force with respect to your product?
    a. Is the present sales call report adequate? Need for another form?
    b. Who should evaluate the information?
7. What will the use of the sales force as outlined above cost during the coming year? Figure in terms of time spent selling and servicing your product.

D. For advertising and public relations the following questions are suggested:
1. What kinds of people (in what job classifications) should be "contacted" during the coming year?
2. How often should these individuals be contacted?
3. What appeals should be used in these contacts?
4. What media should be used to make each contact? When (month) should each contact be made? What appeal should be used?
5. What trade shows should be entered during the coming year?
    a. Who should be invited?
    b. Who should be responsible?
6. What sales literature needs to be prepared for use during the coming year (e.g., catalog sheets, price lists, brochures, etc.)?
    a. To what group(s) will each be sent?
    b. Who will prepare? In what form? In what quantities?
    c. What will be the total costs involved?

E. What marketing research should be undertaken on a project by project basis during the coming year?
1. What is the purpose or objective of each project? What problem is each designed to "solve"?
2. What information are you attempting to obtain from what sources for each project?
3. Who will undertake each of these studies and what is the expected cost of each?

IV. Control and Reappraisal Contingency Plans
A. What information will you use to control and reappraise the above recommended marketing plan?
B. What precise data do you want, in what form, and from what sources?
C. Who besides yourself is involved in the control and reappraisal process? Exactly what is each person responsible for? At what points in time?
D. What contingency action will you take—or recommend—based on what data? How will you take such action?

V. Budget Format
Product _____ Year _____
    Total U.S. market $_____
    Company market share _____%

Estimated company sales
(transfer net)                        $_____

Less: cost of sales (transfer
price × units sold)              $_____

Gross profit                                                    $_____

*Selling/market expenses:*

Product Manager and staff    $_____

Field sales                              $_____

Service engineering              $_____

Market research                     $_____

Product development            $_____

Advertising

Trade shows $_____

Media              $_____

Direct mail    $_____

Sales literature $_____

Other $_____

Total Advertising              $_____

Total expenses                   $_____

Operating product profit    $_____

SECTION **VIII**

## DEVELOPMENT OF MARKETING PLANS

# General Foods Corporation—Maxim

In 1963 the Maxwell House Division of General Foods was the leading company in both the regular and soluble coffee markets. This dominant position was traceable to the company's historic strength in the regular coffee market, and the early development and introduction of high quality soluble (instant) coffees in the early 1950's. As a result of this flavor improvement in soluble coffee, category sales grew dramatically during the middle and late 1950's and were the leading growth factor in the total coffee market of that period.

Not content with this success, General Foods was aggressively developing another new coffee, produced by a process called freeze drying. This coffee was markedly different (in appearance and flavor) from either regular or "traditional" soluble coffees. The overriding problem during the initial development period was the high per unit production cost. By late 1962 the research group assigned to the problem expressed confidence that a freeze-dried coffee could be produced at a "reasonable" cost. Their recommendation to proceed was followed shortly by the assignment of a new product marketing group to the task of compiling appropriate consumer research and developing the most effective marketing positioning and strategy for the new brand. During 1963 this new product group, headed by Mr. Ken Carter,[1] who served as the product manager, worked towards the goal of preparing a fully defined national marketing plan by February of 1964. This national plan was designed to satisfy three needs:

1. Define the new product's positioning and potential share of market impact, as well as its ability to meet the company's financial guidelines for new entries.
2. Serve as the basis for a decision to either: proceed immediately to the

This case was prepared by George S. Day. Reprinted from *Stanford Business Cases 1968* with the permission of the publisher, Graduate School of Business, Stanford University. Copyright © 1968 by the Board of Trustees of the Leland Stanford Junior University.

[1] A disguised name used here to represent the several product executives who eventually worked on the project.

national introduction stage, test market, or stop the development process.

3. Assuming a favorable decision to proceed with test and/or national market introduction, guide the implementation of these stages. (The marketing plan for a test market or regional introduction would be a scaled down version of the national plan.)

As the deadline for the completion of the marketing plan drew near, the problem of selecting the best "mix" from many alternatives of: *market positioning, pricing strategy, promotion and advertising budgets,* became acute.

In defining the optimum market positioning for the new product, three broad potential market positions became apparent:

1. A totally new kind of coffee
2. The best of the soluble category
3. As good as ground coffee with the convenience of soluble

Another vital consideration in properly positioning the new entry was the selection of a name for the brand. Should it be:

1. Maxwell House Freeze-Dried Coffee?
2. Freeze-Dried Instant Maxwell House?
3. A name with no Maxwell House connotations?

The basic issue involved was the desire to capitalize on the strength of the Maxwell House name and consumer acceptance at minimum cannibalization risk to other Maxwell House brands.

Each of the possible positions would require a different marketing approach. Each would also have its own impact on the final share of market goal identified in the marketing plan. Each would have to be evaluated in estimating the long run financial benefits to be gained by the introduction of the new freeze-dried entry. The determination of the most effective market positioning would also have direct effects on the selection of pricing strategy, promotion and advertising strategies and budgets used to promote the brand.

The critical task of evaluating all viable alternatives involved and developing the best possible combination—to be detailed in the national marketing plan—was the assignment which Mr. Carter and the men of his Product Group faced in the closing months of 1963.

## THE GENERAL FOODS CORPORATION

General Foods grew to its 1964 level of $1,338,000,000 in sales (see Exhibit 1)[2] through a series of mergers and consolidations that had begun in 1926 and that had gradually built up a corporate structure containing over sixty plants divided into six major domestic divisions: Maxwell House, Post, Jell-O, Birds-Eye, Kool-Aid and Institutional Food Service. Each division functioned as a highly autonomous unit. These divisions

___

[2] Unless otherwise noted all exhibits are from company records or reports.

turned out a wide array of food products, including Maxwell House, Yuban and Sanka Coffees; Kool-Aid; Birds-Eye Frozen Foods; Post Cereals; Jell-O Desserts; Gaines Dog Foods; Minute Rice and many more.

*Maxwell House Division.* The organizational structure of the Maxwell House Division reflected its marketing orientation (see Exhibit 2). The Division believed that the size, complexity and competitive nature of the coffee business created the need for the "Business within a business" arrangement of product management. Key to the success of this system was having a small group of managers—such as Ken Carter—literally "run their own business" under general philosophy and strategy guidelines administered by Division's top management. In short, subject to the approval of management, Maxwell House Division Product Managers exercised the functional responsibility and authority of a "General Manager" of a given brand. This "General Manager" responsibility required that the Product Manager initiate the development of an integrated overall plan for marketing his brand, *secure* management's concurrence with this plan and *follow through* to ensure that each element of the plan was successfully and efficiently executed.

To discharge this "General Manager" responsibility to his brand, the Product Manager had to secure management concurrence on these primary objectives: (1) The competitive position the brand expects to occupy in the marketplace, (2) The brand's profit and volume objectives, (3) The advertising, promotion and pricing strategy and execution, (4) All auxiliary plans and operations necessary to realize these profit and sales objectives—including appropriate marketing research plans, product development plans, marketing tests, etc.

*New Projects Evaluation Policy.* An important consideration in the development of the new freeze-dried product's marketing position, objectives and strategies, was the financial requirement specified in General Foods' corporate policy for new entries. General Foods required each division to submit rate-of-return estimates for any project involving incremental outlays of more than $50,000, specifying its expected payback period (from the date the project became operational to the repayment of the original investment) and projecting the anticipated return-on-funds employed (using average flows from the first 3, 5 and 10 years of the project's life). The policy ruled explicitly that any new venture's report must include deductions for anticipated incremental losses to *other* General Foods products occasioned by the new project. Top management generally required a *specified* projected 10 year average profit before taxes on invested funds, but it allowed the payback period to extend the full 10 years to cover losses accumulated during the market development period.

After reviewing the Product Group's profit projections and accompanying budget proposals, top management also bore the responsibility for weighing several factors: (1) duration of the period until break-even, (2) risks, (3) probable competition, (4) quality of forecasts, (5) period of greatest investment.

## THE COFFEE MARKET

Coffee was, without question, the American national drink (see Exhibits 3 and 4). Coffee's position as the largest single beverage category was achieved by a broad demographic appeal and an ability to meet many needs and serve many functions. Thus coffee was seen by many consumers as being appropriate for most social occasions and at almost every time of day (see Exhibits 3 and 4).

A series of inquiries into the general motivational structure that indicated salient consumer needs and desires for the best cup of coffee were of considerable value in the development of freeze-dried coffee. Coffee was perceived as having a wide latitude of functions beyond satisfying thirst or providing warmth and comfort. The functions varied as to time of day, mood of the individual and particular needs at any given time. Some of these functions were: (1) a force to provide energy or stimulation, (2) a tension reliever with an implicit reward and consequently an aid to mental health, (3) a convenience food and a "snack," (4) an appetite-depressant, (5) a medication (with apparent emetic qualities) and (6) a "friend" in and of itself. Also coffee served as a visible symbol of adulthood.

Drinking coffee was universally associated with the sociability of a friendly gathering. Other perceptions of the coffee drinking situation were (1) an opportunity to relax, (2) a thought lubricator to help achieve concentrated thought, and (3) an excuse for sociability. The coffee break had an almost unique status as a reward for work well done, or as a legitimate escape from routinized drudgery.

Although consumers perceived coffee in a variety of ways, most agreed on what constituted the important attributes in a cup of coffee. These attributes, ranked according to the number of times they were mentioned, are shown below for two different ways of viewing the attributes:

|  | Attributes Desired in Everyday Cup of Coffee (Percent) | Attributes Needing Improvement for the Perfect Cup of Coffee (Percent) |
|---|---|---|
| Flavor/taste | 62 | 37 |
| Freshness | 46 | 24 |
| Good aroma | 44 | 21 |
| Gives you a lift | 37 | 18 |
| Relaxing | 35 | 16 |
| Strength without bitterness | 30 | 22 |

Most consumers described their optimum cup of coffee as slightly sweet, rich yet smooth, with a minimum of calories.

Because coffee played so many roles so often, a major concern with regard to ground coffee was the bother of preparation—that is, the time consumed in preparation and the bother of cleaning the pot and disposing of the grounds. Also cited by consumers was their inability to achieve a consistently good cup of coffee, whether ground or soluble.

## Size and Growth of Coffee Market

During the late fifties and early sixties, the combined instant and ground coffee market saw a period of consecutive increases well in excess of the 1.5 percent growth rate of the coffee drinking population (e.g., 14 years old and over). This growth can be traced to the introduction of a high quality soluble coffee in the early 1950's—Instant Maxwell House, and subsequently, to a general improvement in product quality for other soluble coffees, plus a limited amount of price elasticity.

Soluble coffees provided ease of preparation and made it convenient for people to serve coffee more frequently during the day. From 1950 to 1963, between meal coffee drinking doubled while meal-time coffee drinking showed small change (see Exhibit 5). Even though the between-meal convenience of soluble coffee came at some expense of flavor and aroma, its ease of preparation apparently weighed heavily enough to lead to its rapid adoption.

By 1962 instant coffee had added 0.67 cups per day to the average coffee intake while regular coffee had gained 0.14 cups per day (see Exhibits 5–7). Figures also show that the rapid growth of soluble consumption abetted the growth of the total industry until the soluble ratio[3] stood at 30.0 percent in 1964 (see Exhibit 8). This soluble ratio represented a slight decrease from the high of 31.6 percent in 1964.

## Market Segmentation

Associated with the complexity of coffee buying and consumption were significant variations from the population norm in the behavior patterns of coffee drinking consumers. Maxwell House marketing executives divided the coffee market as follows:

| | |
|---|---|
| By *user type*...................... | Predominantly ground<br>predominantly soluble<br>dual users |
| By *geographic area*.................. | East<br>West |
| By *size of urban area*............... | Over 1,000,000 TV homes<br>250,000 to 1,000,000 TV homes<br>75,000 to 250,000 TV homes<br>under 75,000 TV homes |

---

[3] The *soluble ratio* was the percent of total coffee volume (in units) accounted for by soluble coffee. This ratio is broken down by areas in Exhibit 16.

The usefulness of this analysis came from the very different patterns of coffee drinking displayed in the East and West. Traditionally, Westerners drank more cups per day than Easterners. Consequently, since light coffee users had converted to instant coffee most readily, the Eastern soluble ratio (i.e., soluble/regular units purchased) greatly exceeded that in the West. The East, more populous by half, accounted for half again as many unit sales of soluble. Correspondingly, it contained more densely settled urban areas; cities with over 250,000 *TV* homes made up 75 percent of its population, while, in the more thinly settled West, they composed 64 percent of the populace. This was important for the introduction of new General Foods' products since high-quality food innovations seemed to be adopted more readily in the larger urban areas. Exhibits 9 through 13 present the data which Maxwell House had collected to illuminate this market segmentation.

## COMPETITIVE POSITION OF THE MAXWELL HOUSE DIVISION AND THE POSITIONING OF ITS BRANDS

In 1964, General Foods had a substantial share of the coffee market. Maxwell House Division marketed Sanka, Yuban and Maxwell Coffees nationally in both instant and regular form, consciously aiming each brand at a distinct consumer need to avoid "cannibalizing" sales to the extent possible.

Exhibits 14 through 16 indicate the strength of the Division's competitive position. Its soluble offerings commanded approximately 50 percent market share in both the East and the West and Instant Maxwell House sold more than three times as well as its nearest competitor. General Foods regular coffees enjoyed a 36 percent share of the Eastern market and a 13.5 percent share of the "low soluble" West, where they encountered strong competition from well-established regional brands.

Sanka was marketed to consumers who sought a coffee that could claim to let them sleep by virtue of its low caffeine content—a selling point that sharply distinguished Sanka from Yuban and Maxwell House. Since Sanka's share of the total coffee market was about 4 percent, and research indicated that about one coffee drinker in three was "concerned" about his caffein intake, there remained a considerable potential market for the Sanka brand. The major barrier to increased usage was the belief by most prospects that it was not real coffee and did not taste as good as "real" coffee. Thus Sanka tended to be used as a supplement to the usual coffee consumed, rather than as the primary coffee.

Yuban Coffee had been developed and introduced as a premium coffee differing from other brands in flavor and price. Ground Yuban had a flavor judged by consumers to be richer and more full-bodied than other ground coffees; Instant Yuban's flavor was judged to be "bitter/burnt" and more like that of ground coffee than competitive soluble brands. Ground Yuban sold at about a 10 percent premium at retail over most manufacturers' brands and Instant Yuban sold at about a 20 percent premium over most other soluble brands. Ground Yuban had been on the market for some years and in 1964 held 1.2 percent of the total coffee market, or about 1.8 percent of the ground coffee market. Instant Yuban had been introduced in 1959 in selected areas and expansion of its geographical coverage had been continuing since then. By 1964, Instant Yuban had achieved a 1.5 percent share of the total coffee market or 4.2 percent of the soluble coffee market.

In 1964, attempts were underway to reposition Yuban to replace its exotic and sophisticated, but apparently unsociable and strange, image with a warm and personable approach designed to establish it as a friendly coffee. The new plan aimed Yuban at the market segment that desired a coffee to please discriminating tastes and could (or would) afford to pay premium prices. Its product planners expected Yuban to attract older (30–50 years), better educated people in the higher income groups (upper 50 percent). Instant Yuban achieved its greatest franchise in the West and Northeast by claiming to be more ground-like than other instants (see Exhibit 16).

Regular Maxwell House, designed to appeal to the majority of ground coffee users, was sold at popular prices. A promotional goal was to achieve maximum loyalty through intensely competitive promotional programs, including strong consumer advertising. For this brand, the Division wished to develop a stronger franchise in the low soluble West where it faced stiff competition from regional brands like Hills and Folger's that had captured strong loyalty. It also sought a way to attract more young users (aged 18–25) to insure its long range market position.

Instant Maxwell House paralleled Regular Maxwell House by offering quality at a popular price and by claiming greater value than any other soluble coffee. As a foil to the potentially devastating effects of price dealing, Instant Maxwell House continually sought an improved blend which would increase consumer loyalty. The Division had also introduced a new 14-ounce jar in an effort to maintain consumer interest and to increase time between purchases so that the consumer might be less responsive to competitive promotion. To increase the number of Instant Maxwell House users in the West, the Division used heavy sampling and represented Instant Maxwell House as offering the "optimum coffee experience."

Price deals were used by Maxwell House management primarily as a defensive measure to prevent competitive retail prices from getting so far below Instant Maxwell House that previously loyal users would be lost. They were used less frequently to provide extra value inducements to encourage switching to Instant Maxwell House.

In general, soluble coffee marketers were putting more emphasis on promotions and less emphasis on media advertising (see Exhibit 17). The majority of the promotional dollars were going to off-label deals.[4] By 1964, sales on off-label promotions accounted for an estimated 50 percent of Folger's soluble sales, 80 percent of Nescafé's soluble sales and 30 percent of Maxwell House soluble sales.

## DEVELOPMENT OF FREEZE-DRIED COFFEE

Through the middle and late 1950's, the Maxwell House Division had experimented with the use of a special freeze-drying process to produce a new type of soluble coffee. The Division's product planners began to focus increased attention on the still embryonic project in 1960, assigning it a top priority spot.

The freeze-drying process, the heart of the new development, closely resembled a technology long used by pharmaceutical firms. It produced a soluble coffee with a unique set of product characteristics. More concentrated than conventional instant coffee, crystalline in appearance, and soluble even in cold water, it offered flavor which rivalled that of regular ground coffee in consumer appeal.

The freeze-drying process began much like other techniques for manufacturing coffee: The manufacturer roasted and ground a carefully selected blend of green coffee beans. Then, as in the preparation of other soluble coffee, he brewed a strong coffee solution at a pressure and temperature somewhat higher than those found in normal home preparation. The next step differed radically from all other coffee-making techniques. At this point, the manufacturer flash-froze the solution. He subjected the resulting solid to a vacuum, and into this vacuum he suddenly introduced just enough local warmth to cause "sublimation" of the frozen solution's liquid content. "Sublimation," a kind of super-evaporation, resulted in a solid (ice) becoming a gas (water vapor) without passing through the liquid state. After this dehydration of the frozen coffee solution, the remaining sponge-like solids were ground up to ready them for packaging as soluble coffee.

This process departed entirely from the two more traditional techniques. The home-brewed method, used to prepare regular ground coffee, required only the first stages of the manufacturing process (blending, roasting and grinding) after which the user brewed the coffee himself in a percolator or dripolator at standard atmospheric pressure, with water heated to the boiling point (212° F.). Consumers have long regarded coffee prepared in this manner as the standard for good taste and aroma.

The spray-dried method, formerly used to manufacture all instant coffees, required similar initial preparation. But the sealed brewing system

---

[4] The term "off-label" referred to special tags or over-printing on labels, offering a special price reduction. In promotions of this type the manufacturers absorbed the drop in price and retailers received their regular dollar profit margin.

worked at super-normal pressure and temperature to make the solution dense enough to afford a profitable yield. When this liquid was sprayed into a column of hot air in a drying tower, its coffee content fell to the bottom in a fine soluble powder ready for packaging. The spray-drying process reduced the coffee's flavor and aroma somewhat.

Freeze-dried coffee suffered from the first of these disadvantages less than did spray-dried, since its brewing did not require such intense heat. And there its flavor loss ended. The freeze-drying process saved the coffee from further flavor loss that occurred when spray-dried coffee entered the drying tower. Freeze-dried coffee, therefore, closely resembled ground coffee in flavor and aroma. The following chart summarizes these and other differences that resulted from the freeze-drying process:

|  | Spray-Dried Coffee | Freeze-Dried Coffee |
|---|---|---|
| Flavor | Less quality than regular, no astringency or "mouth feel" | Comparable to regular, some astringency, but less than regular |
| Aroma | Very little in cup aroma | Resembles regular in cup |
| Appearance | Powder | Irregular crystals |
| Solubility | Fair in cold water, foam in cup (due to air trapped in drying) | Good even in cold water little foam in cup |
| Concentration (weight per unit volume) | Index = 100 | Index = 125 |
| Cost per ounce | Index = 100 | Index = 135 |

Freeze-dried coffee performed well when subjected to blind cup taste tests. The following figures show disguised, but representative figures from two blind taste tests:[5]

Percent Preferring Maxim Versus . . .

| Instant Maxwell House (Sample of 400 Soluble Users) (Percent) | Ground Maxwell House (Sample of 340 Ground Users) (Percent) |
|---|---|
| 47 | 44 |

## DEVELOPMENT OF A MARKETING STRATEGY

To make the planning task more manageable the new products group assigned to freeze-dry coffee first identified the following basic operating assumptions:

1. That the finished product would possess the flavor of regular coffee and the convenience of instant,

---

[5] In both these tests about 14 percent of the sample expressed no preference.

2. That its advertising could make this claim credible,
3. That it would receive backing from advertising expenditures comparable to those invested in other new General Foods products and that these would insure its domination of coffee advertising media,
4. That the product would succeed in maintaining the margin set for it.

These assumptions were necessary to provide a starting point for the setting of goals, put some constraints on the development of feasible price, advertising, promotion and position alternatives, and guide the consumer research program.

Secondly, Mr. Carter arranged a series of meetings with senior division and corporate executives to review these operating assumptions and to clarify what was expected of the new product. For the most part these performance expectations were based on requirements for a recognizable success. But success in this context was not merely achieving designated financial goals for the product itself; it also required that the new product should not prosper at the expense of other company brands.

The operating assumptions and the following performance expectations guided the thinking of the new product group during most of 1963. However, as the time came to solidify the marketing plan, some of these guides looked to be in conflict with others, or obsolete in terms of new evidence collected during 1963. Any changes made would have to be justified since the modified form would serve as the operating goal and performance criteria for the new product. Mr. Carter also suspected that it would be quite hard to have the expectations scaled down if subsequent research, planning and market experience showed them to be unreasonable.

### Performance Expectations

The following are the expectations that guided the initial planning of the freeze-dry coffee strategy:

A. The franchise would be built outside that currently held by other Division products.
B. The gross margin would be at least equal to that on comparable products and better than that on cannibalized business. This was necessary to help pay for the enormous investment in new plant and equipment.
C. The product should endeavor to increase the soluble ratio, particularly in the West.
D. The benefits of the freeze-dried process would be exploited before competition broadly marketed a comparable product.

Underlying these explicit expectations was a basic requirement that the new coffee achieve a going year franchise (expressed in terms of share of the soluble coffee market plus people converted from ground to freeze-dried) that would generate enough volume to meet corporate return on funds employed criteria for new products—and still support a campaign that would dominate coffee advertising media.

The product manager's estimate of the going year franchise, and ultimately its acceptance as a reasonable performance objective, required some very difficult judgments with respect to:

1. The probable rate at which regular and instant users would convert to the new product. A major question concerned the degree to which the "soluble stigma" would make ground users more difficult to convert.
2. The variation in the franchise by market size. The range of the variation would depend somewhat on the extent to which the product was perceived as a premium coffee. Experience with premium priced coffees such as Yuban showed that the larger urban markets would be more receptive to such an innovation. The question was: how much more receptive? The answer to this question would also weigh heavily in deciding media allocations by market size and type.
3. The effect of the various performance expectations, which are discussed in more detail below:

***Build a Franchise Outside That Currently Held by Other Division Products.*** Because the Division already commanded about half of the instant coffee market in both East and West, a sizeable share of the Eastern business would inevitably come from *other* Maxwell House Brands. Nevertheless, the greatest profits obviously lay in attracting those who had not previously used a General Foods coffee, since this new franchise would directly expand the company's volume and market share. Conversion of customers from other brands was, therefore, of primary importance.

In projecting profit figures for various marketing plans, Mr. Carter needed a device to predict the comparative likelihood of gains in company franchise as opposed to mere cannibalization. The simplest model considered was one which assumed that the new coffee's usage would come from all other brands in exact proportion to their previously existing market share (in units). Thus if Brand X currently held a 12 percent share of the Eastern soluble market, the new coffee would gain 12 percent of its Eastern soluble target from this brand. Other more complex "cannibalization" models were also considered. Their usefulness was limited because of the lack of evidence that they were any improvement over the simple model.

***Maintain a Gross Margin Higher Than That on Cannibalized Business.*** The logic of the simple model determined that if Instant Maxwell House commanded 38 percent of the Eastern soluble market, the new product would steal 38 percent of its Eastern soluble target from Instant Maxwell House. So, in order to insure the Division an incremental profit to help pay for the tremendous investment required to produce freeze-dried coffee, Mr. Carter suggested establishing a requirement that the gross margin on the new coffee must exceed that on Instant Maxwell House ($2.50 per unit) which in turn already exceeded that on Instant Maxwell House ($2.00 per unit). The higher margin on IMH over RMH reflected the greater cost for plant and equipment required to produce this form of coffee and the need to develop a reasonable return on this investment. This meant that, within reasonable limits which did not distort the scale of production on the Division's other offering, incremental profits would result even from stealing Maxwell House customers.

*Increase the Soluble Ratio, Particularly in the West.* The conversion of regular coffee buyers to use of the new soluble coffee was a more profitable prospect than the conversion of instant users for two reasons:

1.  The Division commanded a lower market share among regular users, particularly in the West, so that conversion of regular users produced cannibalization with fewer drawbacks than did the conversion of instant users (see Exhibit 14).
2.  Even where the Division's new product cannibalized its own brands, the margin on instant coffee ($2.50 per unit) exceeded that on regular ($2.00 per unit), making conversion of the latter the more profitable prospect (by $0.50 per unit).

*Exploit the Freeze-drying Process before the Competition Broadly Markets a Comparable Product.* Since the Division had spent years developing its new coffee product at a time when the question of its eventual practicability remained uncertain, it had necessarily borne the expense of such exploratory research which competitors would not need to repeat. Naturally, the Division wished to reap the rewards of its advantage by establishing a strongly loyal franchise before competitors could enter the market.

Mr. Carter estimated that it would take at least two years for any company to develop an offering of comparable quality and make it operational. Following that, it would be at least another year before the competitor had acquired enough production capacity to be able to go national. He reported that while anyone could produce limited quantities of freeze-dried coffee in the laboratory, transferring the technique to a mass production scale posed difficult problems that required at least two years to solve. He added that, even then, only a major coffee producer could handle such an operation.

Nevertheless, the manufacturing process, having served pharmaceutical firms for years, remained unpatentable. The situation, therefore, presented the danger that, after cannibalizing some of the Division's share, the new brand might then lose share to some especially successful and aggressive freeze-dried competitor with the net result that the Maxwell House Division's total share could actually decline.

Rumors in the trade indicated that one major international competitor

(Nestlé) and a very few small, North American firms were experimenting with—and were about ready to test, on a limited scale—freeze-dried, concentrated coffees. The quantity and quality of these possible competitive coffees were unknown. Of the firms in question it seemed highly probable that only the Nestlé company had the technical skill and financial resources necessary to market successfully a freeze-dried concentrated coffee. An interesting aspect of the rumors was the purported Nestlé strategy—to direct its freeze-dried coffee entirely against the soluble market. It would then cannibalize from Nescafé as well as attempt to take a share from all other solubles.

On a national level, the competitive position of General Foods' innovation depended on the company's ability to achieve enough capacity to serve a national market. Mr. Carter estimated that new plants could achieve additional volume at the rate of 2 million annual units per $10 million investment at an operating cost of $5.72 per 48-ounce unit[6] (this cost does not include depreciation). Each plant would take at least a year to build, plus several months to reach capacity volume. While the minimum plant size was two million units, plants could be built to any capacity up to a maximum of four million units. The operating cost per unit was expected to be the same regardless of the capacity.

## ACHIEVING THE GOALS

Mr. Carter recognized that the stringent performance expectations could only be met if the Division's marketing efforts found an effective set of appeals to give Maxim a favorable market "position." This meant that he had to decide first what image to seek for the new product, then he had to select a name, a label, a package, and other product features that would successfully conjure up this image in the public eye, and finally he had to decide how to allocate advertising and promotional funds for efficient attainment of these positioning goals.

### Positioning

The initial expectations of the new product suggested that it meet the following positioning requirements:

1. That it be assigned to a unique position, clearly different from the positions of the Division's existing brands, so as to minimize cannibalization.

---

[6] A unit is a fractional composite made up of:

6 — four-ounce jars
4.8 — two-ounce jars
1.8 — eight-ounce jars

which equals 48 ounces of Maxim. This is the basic unit of analysis.

2. That it be differentiated from both other types of coffee so as to establish it as a new *form* of coffee; a third type which offers ground users their customary flavor with new convenience and which allows instant users to retain ease of preparation while improving the taste of their brew.

3. That it be an extension to the Maxwell House line rather than a completely new brand name.

Mr. Carter recognized, however, that the threefold objectives of assigning the coffee a unique position, differentiating it from all others, and registering its association with Maxwell House, while difficult enough to achieve in themselves, complicated the situation still further by conflicting with each other at several points. For example, the more the package emphasized the connection between the new coffee and Maxwell House (a fulfillment of the third goal), the more it encouraged the probability of substitution between the two (a violation of the first). And so, Mr. Carter had to handle several dilemmas to achieve the best possible balance among these three goals.

### Name

To balance these positioning requirements Mr. Carter sought a name which would provide an optimum association with Maxwell House without producing so close an identity that substitution would occur to an undesirable degree. Before making his recommendation, he considered two concepts:[7]

1. Using the Maxwell House name directly with some modifier attached,
2. Using a separate brand name that implied its parentage with only minor emphasis.

For the second concept he considered several alternatives, finally narrowing the choice to three—Prima, Nova, and Maxim. A study, asking 463 women respondents to report their association with these names and rate them on various scales, produced the results given in Exhibit 19.

Alternatives based on the first concept included Maxwell House Coffee Concentrate, Maxwell House Concentrated Soluble Coffee, and Maxwell House Concentrated Instant Coffee. Of these, Mr. Carter preferred the first or second for their distinctiveness since research had shown them to be relatively unfamiliar to the consumer (see Exhibit 20). Mr. Carter rejected the first concept altogether because he felt that use of the Maxwell House name under these circumstances would merely attract current Division patrons rather than new users. He disliked the second concept because of

---

[7] These two basic concepts were subject to some further modifications according to the kind of descriptive designation associated with the chosen brand name (see Exhibits 18–21).

consumer unfamiliarity with the term soluble. Moreover, reassuring evidence came from a study which indicated that a separate brand name could generate almost as much consumer interest as the familiar "Maxwell House." Subjects who were offered a choice between three gifts—(1) Instant Maxwell House, (2) Regular Maxwell House, or (3) one of four competing alternative names—chose Maxim or Prima over 50% of the time, an acceptable frequency in Mr. Carter's judgment (see Exhibit 20).

Mr. Carter tentatively chose "Maxim" because of its easy association with coffee (22%) and favorable connotations,[8] pointing out that "Maxim": (1) Implies concentration and strength (index = 132), (2) connotates quality and superiority (37% and index = 135), (3) relates to Maxwell House (33%), and (4) is short, memorable and euphonious. However, not everyone was equally convinced that Maxim was the best choice, particularly because of the association with Maxwell House.

### Jar Size and Design

Mr. Carter recommended packing Maxim in 2-ounce, 4-ounce and 8-ounce sizes. He expected the 2-ounce size to encourage purchase on a trial basis, to expand Maxim's shelf facings, and to return a higher margin than other sizes. He selected the 4-ounce size to enable Maxim to offer the consumer a middle-sized jar with price and cup yield comparable to a pound of ground coffee (about 50 cups at under a dollar). He counted on the 8-ounce size to offer convenience and economy to heavy users and to attain a price comparable to other brands' large sizes.

As a further aid in distinguishing Maxim from all other brands, the packaging department designed a jar that differed markedly from everything else on the market. Oval instead of round, it faced the buyer with a shouldered, rectangular shape, topped by a special lug-screw cap with separate label panels instead of the customary wrap-around labeling. Tests showed that this shape was superior to either a square or a round alternative in generating product interest (see Exhibit 22).

### Copy Strategy

Mr. Carter proposed a copy strategy which grew out of his conviction that Maxim did indeed present an inherently superior product, combining the best features of traditional regular and instant coffees and eliminating many of the defects of both. He and his subordinates believed that Maxim's advertising must be directed to (1) convince ground users that they could continue to enjoy fine coffee flavor with new convenience, and (2) to persuade instant users that they could now make a soluble brew that tasted like regular ground coffee.

---

[8] See Exhibit 19.

To assign Maxim a position as a new type of coffee with the taste of regular and the convenience of instant, he planned to present the new entry as *being* real percolated coffee, the result of a scientific breakthrough which enabled freeze-dried coffee literally to *become* fresh perked coffee in the buyer's cup.

To overcome the slightly incredible aura of this claim, the copy strategy called for several reinforcing features. It counted on the freeze-dried process story as its "reason-why." Tangibly, the coffee's granular form would help establish it as a new type of coffee; and hopefully, the newness suggested by this crystalline shape would help reduce the "soluble stigma" that might otherwise contradict the claim to superior flavor. At the same time, the messages would offer the buyer reassurance through emphasis on the coffee's high quality and by alluding to its connection with Maxwell House—an association which would strengthen the suggestion of quality and lend an atmosphere of authority. Finally, the copy strategy proposed to reinforce Maxim's singular position by pointing to its concentration, i.e., the greater weight per unit volume. The buyer needed to use less, a characteristic which should connote both quality and economy (moreover, the consumer must recognize this fact when preparing his cupful to avoid excessively strong taste).

Assuming this was the best copy strategy to follow Mr. Carter then faced the problem of selecting the best means of translating it into complete advertisements. Two executions of the copy strategy submitted by the advertising agency for consideration by Mr. Carter are shown in Appendix I along with associated testing.

### Advertising Budget

Mr. Carter felt that the adoption of the operating assumption that Maxim should dominate coffee advertising logically implied the following media objectives:

1. *To direct weight against all coffee users 18 and over, especially housewives in households with incomes above $3,500.*

Experience with other products had suggested that those with incomes below $3,500 would hesitate to accept a premium-priced, high quality food product like Maxim. In a test conducted to determine the chief source of coffee buying decisions, the housewife proved to have made the choice entirely on her own in at least 65 percent of the instant-using homes and in at least 61 percent of the ground-using homes (see Exhibit 23).

2. *To provide weight sufficient to stimulate maximum trial and repeat usage.*
3. *To achieve media dominance within the soluble coffee category.*

In this respect, the plan "aimed to insure the consumer's attention and awareness of Maxim's introduction by saturating coffee-promoting media in each area in an effort to make Maxim the most salient new food product in the public consciousness."

New product advertising was typically divided into three periods—a two-week *stocking* period (to stimulate consumer—and trade—interest so as to insure adequate distribution), a 26-week *introductory* period (to create awareness, encourage trial, and provide reinforcement to secure repurchase), a 20-week *sustaining* period to retain initial triers and extend brand awareness over introductory goals).

The final advertising budget, for the first year, had to be built from these general considerations in a step-by-step process:

1.  Since it was assumed that no product trial would come without consumer awareness of the new brand, an awareness objective had to be set for each advertising period. Experience with other comparable new products showed that an overall awareness of at least 60 percent had to be achieved, by the end of the introductory period, if the product was to be successful.

2.  The awareness goals needed to be scaled by market size and by shares expected in those areas. Since bigger shares were expected to come from larger urban markets, the awareness objectives should be correspondingly higher. A reasonable range of awareness objectives is shown below.[9]

3.  A critical step would be the conversion of awareness goals into estimates of reach and frequency (that is, the cumulative audience, and the number of repeated messages being delivered to the cumulative audience). Sufficient impact during the introductory period could probably be generated in the largest markets with a reach of 80–90 percent and a frequency of once per week. During the sustaining period the frequency usually was cut by half or more. Also a budget at this sustaining level could probably suffice for the second year. Some adjustments might have to be made during the campaign to combat competitive advertising efforts. Usually this meant out-spending the competition by shifting funds into the period of heaviest competitive advertising.

---

[9] Reasonable share and awareness objectives during introductory period:

| Market Size (TV Homes) | Estimated Maximum and Minimum Feasible Awareness (Percent of TV Homes) |
|---|---|
| Over 1,000,000 | 65–75% |
| 250,000 to 1,000,000 | 60–70 |
| 75,000 to 250,000 | 50–60 |
| 0–75,000 | 40–60 |

4. There was little question that spot television would be the basic medium to be used. It was already the common media practice in the coffee industry; absorbing an estimated 59 percent of the industry's 1963 budget. Another 20 percent of the industry budget went to network television expenditures.

5. A final problem, resulting from the desire to increase the soluble ratio, was the relative allotment to the high and low soluble areas. The expenditure of the same number of dollars per capita in both areas would certainly result in regional disproportions in terms of dollars per units sold. The question was how far out of line was the extra expenditure per unit sold in the low soluble area?

Adherence to the initial assumptions of awareness, reach, frequency and media for the purpose of an "order of magnitude" estimate of the advertising investment produced an expenditure range of $9,500,000 to $12,500,000 in the first year and $6,000,000 to $7,000,000 in the second year. This clearly ensured media dominance (see Exhibit 24) but did not answer questions of adequacy or inadequacy.

### Promotions

As a general policy for Maxim, Mr. Carter urged the principle that wherever possible the brand should direct promotion at the consumer rather than the dealer. He believed that the industry had subscribed to too many trade incentives, many of which proved ineffective, and preferred promotional offers such as free containers, free jars for two innerseals, free enclosed premiums, and so on—offers which exerted "pull-through" by establishing direct contact with the consumer. This, of course, ruled out off-label dealing, which often lost its impact before reaching the consumer. However, some sort of introductory trade allowance and display offer would be necessary in order to ensure rapid distribution. Based on past experience, a trade promotion budget of at least $3,500,000 would be needed to ensure 80 to 85 percent distribution by the end of the 26 week introductory period.

A great deal of emphasis was placed on a promotional plan that would secure broad product trial. There was a strong belief that a buyer's experience with Maxim would result in a high level of satisfaction and that this was the best way to overcome inhibitions resulting from Maxim's premium price, or the "soluble stigma."

To obtain cost estimates Mr. Carter asked several large promotion houses to quote on the following promotional alternatives:

1. Two-ounce samples with 25 cent repurchase coupon delivered door-to-door

2. Mailed coupons redeemable for free jar

3.  Mailed packets of six individually measured servings with a 25 cent
    repurchase coupon.

The restriction placed on the quotes was that only urban homes with incomes over $3,500[10] be considered, in accord with the basic media objec-
tives. One quotation, based on sending just a coupon to the smaller urban
areas (which had an eligible population of 9,000,000 households), is shown
in Exhibit 25. This left Mr. Carter with the problem of deciding what
combination of samples, coupons and populations should be adopted. For
example, if a coupon (redeemable for a free jar) were sent to all 34,000,000
households the cost would be $12,400,000, but a 2-ounce jar and 25 cent
coupon would cost $16,050,000 if sent to all households. Other combina-
tions of samples and coupons were also possible.

## Pricing

Pricing presented particularly sticky problems. In the first place, Mr.
Carter could not hope to set a definite or permanent price for Maxim before actually entering the market, simply because the price of coffee imports had long showed a confirmed tendency to fluctuate violently—by as
much as 10 to 20 percent a year—and retail prices for the entire coffee
market reflected these fluctuations. Consequently, Mr. Carter tended to
view the Maxim pricing decision in terms of (a) Maxim's premium over
Instant Maxwell House and other Division brands and (b) the margin
generated after accounting for the retailer's mark-up.

Several other difficulties already mentioned above made the decision
for pricing Maxim particularly tough. First, freeze-dried coffee cost about
35 percent more to make than the equivalent weight of spray-dried. Secondly, pricing had to reflect a result of business it took away from the
Division's other brands. Thirdly, Maxim's concentrated form made the
per cup premium apply to a smaller total volume per ounce. This meant
that a smaller jar could be used for 2-ounce, 4-ounce and 8-ounce sizes, a
confusion which might affect the consumer's perception—either favorably
or unfavorably.

Indeed, Mr. Carter faced what he felt to be a sharply-pronged dilemma,
for he realized that with the coffee market's high price elasticity Maxim
might not realize its market share goals (especially for ground user conversion) if it were priced at a differential high enough to bring an incremental profit on cannibalized business.

To aid in clarifying the problem, several alternative price structures
were drawn up—each with a different margin and a different premium

---

[10] This was a total of 34 million homes, of which 25 million were in major urban
areas. This excluded 23 million homes that were either in rural areas or had incomes
less than $3,500.

relationship to Instant Maxwell House and other Division brands. Discussion was not limited to the price structure shown in Exhibits 26 and 27; nor was everyone willing to consider these two prices to be the extremes that were possible. Those who were more concerned with the market's price elasticity generally favored the price structure shown in Exhibit 26. This structure would establish a premium relationship to Instant Maxwell House of 12.2 percent/28.8 percent/43.0 percent for the 2-, 4-, and 8-ounce sizes respectively, and would yield a higher margin to reflect high investment in plant and equipment. The per cup cost to the consumer would be close to that of Regular Maxwell House.[11]

A second alternative with a great deal of support was based on the feeling that a higher premium such as 16.3 percent/40 percent/51.9 percent (see Exhibit 27) would not injure consumer acceptance of Maxim. This prediction came from the view that Maxim, as an inherently superior product, might show less price sensitivity than other coffees. On the other hand, the Yuban experience showed that it was harder to gain trade support for premium priced coffees. This was in spite of the fact that retailers would require a margin of 13 percent of the retail price, regardless of the price level chosen.

A further alternative, with some potential legal drawbacks, was to price Maxim lower in the West. The desired result was to lure a larger number of ground users, since the Division had less to fear from cannibalization.

## Choice of Alternatives

The final decision on the price level was bound up with the concurrent decisions on positioning, advertising and promotion. The approach used to consider the logical combinations of these elements was to create a "pro forma" share, budget and profit projection for each combination.

However, before these projections could be made, a number of problem areas had to be resolved:

1.  The gross margin and cost projections could be tentatively established from the requirement that Maxim demand a margin greater than that of other Maxwell House coffees.
2.  A more difficult problem concerned the state of the market to be expected in the three years following the introduction. Three years was a typical planning horizon for the financial evaluation of a new food product. But even this period was long when it came to estimating future sales trends and competitive responses.
3.  A broader policy question concerned the effect of the reduced sales volume of other Division brands (because of Maxim cannibalization) on the advertising and promotion budgets of these brands. If these

---

[11] Per cup costs were computed on the assumption that both spray-dried and freeze-dried coffee would yield the same number of cups per ounce. However, since Maxim was more concentrated the volume per cup would be smaller.

budgets were fixed at 1963 levels the rest of the Division would lose its
entire margin on each unit cannibalized. This loss would have to be
charged to Maxim profits. On the other hand, if these advertising and
promotion budgets were reduced in proportion to the decrease in
sales, the incremental loss to the rest of the Division would be limited
to the customary net profit per unit.

## APPENDIX I: ALTERNATIVE EXECUTIONS
## OF THE COPY STRATEGY

Ogilvy, Benson & Mather prepared two television commercials embody-
ing the general copy points outlined above, each with a somewhat different emphasis. The "Freeze-dried Announcement" stressed the effectiveness of the innovative manufacturing discovery; the "Perfect Percolator
Cup" concentrated on the claim that Maxim tastes even better than
ground coffee because it has no bitter aftertaste. The agency tested each
ad with forced in-home trials. O. B & M also submitted two newspaper
advertisements (one of which included a 10 cent coupon) stressing the
theme that freeze-drying produces a crystalline coffee with the power to
turn every cup into a percolator. The agency further suggested outdoor
and transit displays proclaiming first "Maxim Is Coming" and then "Maxim
Is Here."

### (A)  Freeze-dried Announcement

ANNOUNCER: You are looking at an entirely new form of coffee. You are looking at freeze-dried coffee. Tiny, concentrated crystals that have the power
to turn every cup in your house into a percolator! This is Maxim, the entirely new form of coffee from Maxwell House. After years of research,
it was discovered that freshly brewed coffee could be frozen. The ice
could be drawn off in a vacuum, and you would have freeze-dried coffee,
concentrated crystals of real percolated coffee. That's Maxim. Rich, full
bodied, exactly like the finest coffee you ever brewed. Let Maxim turn
every cup in your house into a percolator! Get Maxim, the entirely new
form of coffee from Maxwell House.

(Accompanied by appropriate *sound effects:* crystals dropping into
cup, water pouring, coffee perking, vacuum being applied, more water
pouring and perking; and by appropriate *visual effects:* close-up of
crystals on spoon, cup changing into percolator, close-up of jar, perked
coffee being frozen and vacuumized, man savoring taste, close-up of
label.)

### (B)  Perfect Percolator Coffee

PRETTY YOUNG HOUSEWIFE: I make better coffee than you do. That's right.
I make better coffee than you do. Without a coffee pot. Without a

powdery instant coffee. (Slams cupboard door.) But *with* an entirely new kind of coffee! It's Maxim. (Close-up of jar.) And it's fantastic! Maxim turns every cup in your house into a percolator. (Cups turning into percolators.) Yes. Maxim makes better coffee right in the cup than you can brew in a coffee pot. Perfect percolator coffee with none of that harsh, bitter taste you sometimes get with ground.

ANNOUNCER: Maxim's secret? A totally new process from Maxwell House turns real percolated coffee into crystals. Tiny concentrated crystals with the power to turn every cup in your house into a percolator. (Repeat visual sequence of cups turning into percolators.)

PRETTY YOUNG HOUSEWIFE: That's why I make better coffee than you do. Unless you've discovered Maxim too.

ANNOUNCER: Maxim, the entirely new form of coffee from Maxwell House.

### Test of "Freeze-dried Announcement" vs. "Perfect Percolator Cup"

|  | Freeze-dried Announcement | | Perfect Percolator Cup | |
|---|---|---|---|---|
|  | Immediate (Percent) | 24-Hour (Percent) | Immediate (Percent) | 24-Hour (Percent) |
| *Recall:* | | | | |
| It's Frozen | 63 | 72 | — | — |
| It's Dehydrated, Dried | 36 | 42 | — | — |
| It's Perked, Brewed | 26 | 22 | 4 | 4 |
| It's Crystallized | 18 | 14 | 40 | 40 |
| 8 Pots in One Jar | 36 | 15 | — | — |
| It's Concentrated | 15 | 10 | 10 | 10 |
| Tastes Like Real Perked | 20 | 14 | 16 | 14 |
| Can Make Better Coffee Than You | — | — | 20 | 12 |
| Turns Every Cup Into a Percolator | 16 | 7 | 24 | 18 |
| An Instant Coffee | 18 | 8 | 24 | 26 |
| *Connotation:* | | | | |
| Maxim Different | 84% | | 74% | |
| Reference to Process | 46 | | 23 | |
| Reference to Flavor | 20 | | 41 | |
| Reference to New, Different | 35 | | 19 | |
| About the Same | 14 | | 22 | |

## EXHIBIT 1

### General Foods Financial Statistics, Fiscal Years*

(all dollar amounts in millions, except assets per employee and figures on a share basis)

| | 1964 (Est.) | 1963 | 1962 | 1961 | 1960 | 1959 | 1958 |
|---|---|---|---|---|---|---|---|
| **INCOME** | | | | | | | |
| Sales to customers (net) | $1,338 | $1,216 | $1,189 | $1,160 | $1,087 | $1,053 | $1,009 |
| Cost of sales | 838 | 774 | 769 | 764 | 725 | 734 | 724 |
| Marketing, administrative and general expenses | 322 | 274 | 267 | 261 | 236 | 205 | 181 |
| Earnings before income taxes | 179 | 170 | 156 | 138 | 130 | 115 | 105 |
| Taxes on income | 95 | 91 | 84 | 71 | 69 | 61 | 57 |
| Net earnings | 84 | 79 | 72 | 67 | 61 | 54 | 48 |
| Net earnings per common share | 3.33 | 3.14 | 2.90 | 2.69 | 2.48 | 2.21 | 1.99 |
| Dividends on common shares | 50 | 45 | 40 | 35 | 32 | 28 | 24 |
| Dividends per common share | 2.00 | 1.80 | 1.60 | 1.40 | 1.30 | 1.15 | 1.00 |
| Earnings retained in business each year | 34 | 34 | 32 | 32 | 29 | 26 | 24 |
| **ASSETS, LIABILITIES, AND STOCKHOLDERS' EQUITY** | | | | | | | |
| Current assets | $ 436 | $ 411 | $ 387 | $ 360 | $ 357 | $ 329 | $ 313 |
| Current liabilities | 202 | 162 | 142 | 123 | 126 | 107 | 107 |
| Working capital | 234 | 249 | 245 | 237 | 230 | 222 | 206 |
| Land, buildings, equipment, gross | 436 | 375 | 328 | 289 | 247 | 221 | 203 |
| Land, buildings, equipment, net | 264 | 223 | 193 | 173 | 148 | 132 | 125 |
| Long-term debt | 23 | 34 | 35 | 37 | 40 | 44 | 49 |
| Stockholders' equity | 490 | 454 | 419 | 384 | 347 | 315 | 287 |
| Book value per common share | 19.53 | 18.17 | 16.80 | 15.46 | 14.07 | 12.87 | 11.78 |
| **OPERATING STATISTICS** | | | | | | | |
| Inventories | $ 256 | $ 205 | $ 183 | $ 189 | $ 157 | $ 149 | $ 169 |
| Capital additions | 70 | 57 | 42 | 40 | 35 | 24 | 28 |
| Depreciation | 26 | 24 | 21 | 18 | 15 | 14 | 11 |
| Wages, salaries, and benefits | 195 | 180 | 171 | 162 | 147 | 138 | 128 |
| Number of employees (in thousands) | 30 | 28 | 28 | 25 | 22 | 22 | 21 |
| Assets per employee (in thousands) | 24 | 23 | 22 | 22 | 23 | 22 | 21 |

* Fiscal 1964 ended April 2, 1964. Other fiscal years ended March 31.

## EXHIBIT 2

### Organizational Chart for Maxwell House Division

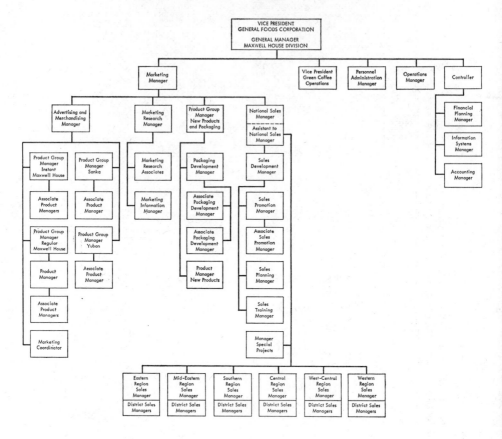

## EXHIBIT 3

### Consumption of Coffee and Other Beverages
### (percentage of persons 10 years of age and over)

|  | 1950 | 1962 | 1963 |
|---|---|---|---|
| Coffee | 74.7 | 74.7 | 73.2 |
| Milk and milk drinks | 51.0 | 52.6 | 52.3 |
| Fruit and vegetable juices | 32.8 | 41.4 | 38.3 |
| Soft drinks | 29.1 | 32.6 | 34.0 |
| Tea | 24.0 | 24.7 | 24.7 |
| Cocoa, hot chocolate | 5.4 | 4.5 | 4.0 |

**EXHIBIT 4**
**Coffee's Share of Beverage Market**
**(Index 1961 = 100)**

|  | Consumer $ Bases | Liquid Consumption Basis |
|---|---|---|
| 1961.............. | 100 | 100 |
| 1962.............. | 95 | 98 |
| 1963.............. | 90 | 97 |

SOURCE: Maxwell House Market Research Department.

**EXHIBIT 5**

**Trends in Coffee Drinking**
**(cups per person per day)**

|  | Fiscal Year | | | | | | |
|---|---|---|---|---|---|---|---|
|  | 1950 | 1953 | 1960 | 1961 | 1962 | 1963 | 1964 (Est.) |
| Regular: |  |  |  |  |  |  |  |
| At home.......... | N.A. | N.A. | 1.78 | 1.90 | 1.95 | 1.93 | 1.86 |
| At eating places..... | N.A. | N.A. | 0.25 | 0.26 | 0.28 | 0.22 | 0.24 |
| At work.......... | N.A. | N.A. | 0.18 | 0.17 | 0.22 | 0.21 | 0.19 |
| Total Regular........ |  | 2.31 | 2.21 | 2.33 | 2.45 | 2.36 | 2.29 |
| Instant: |  |  |  |  |  |  |  |
| At home.......... | N.A. | N.A. | 0.52 | 0.59 | 0.62 | 0.60 | 0.56 |
| At eating places..... | N.A. | N.A. | 0.00 | 0.01 | 0.01 | 0.00 | 0.00 |
| At work.......... | N.A. | N.A. | 0.04 | 0.04 | 0.04 | 0.05 | 0.05 |
| Total Instant......... |  | 0.56 | 0.56 | 0.64 | 0.67 | 0.65 | 0.61 |
| Breakfast............. | 1.03 | N.A. | 1.11 | 1.18 | 1.17 | 1.18 | 1.14 |
| Other meals.......... | 0.91 | N.A. | 0.89 | 0.92 | 0.98 | 0.90 | 0.85 |
| Between meals........ | 0.44 | N.A. | 0.77 | 0.87 | 0.97 | 0.93 | 0.91 |
| Total for day......... | 2.38 | 2.57 | 2.77 | 2.97 | 3.12 | 3.01 | 2.90 |

## EXHIBIT 6

### Coffee Drinking by Age Groups
(cups per person per day; percentage of age group drinking coffee)

| | | | Fiscal Year | | | | | | % Change 1950–64 | |
| --- | --- | --- | --- | --- | --- | --- | --- | --- | --- | --- |
| | 1950 | | 1962 | | 1963 | | 1964 (Est.) | | | |
| Age | Cups | Percent | Cups | Percent | Cups | Percent | Cups | Percent | Cups | Percent |
| 10–14......... | 0.21 | (16.0) | 0.18 | (13.4) | 0.18 | (13.1) | 0.18 | (12.2) | −14.3 | − 3.8 |
| 15–19......... | 1.13 | (53.8) | 1.09 | (40.2) | 0.89 | (37.1) | 0.71 | (31.7) | −37.2 | −22.1 |
| 20–24......... | 2.34 | (75.2) | 2.99 | (76.6) | 2.70 | (69.1) | 2.30 | (68.4) | − 1.7 | − 6.8 |
| 25–29......... | 2.78 | (83.3) | 3.88 | (85.2) | 3.76 | (81.4) | 3.64 | (84.3) | +30.9 | + 1.0 |
| 30–39......... | 3.02 | (87.4) | 4.50 | (88.8) | 4.38 | (89.7) | 4.14 | (85.8) | +37.1 | − 1.6 |
| 40–49......... | 2.98 | (88.0) | 4.44 | (91.4) | 4.27 | (90.7) | 4.33 | (89.6) | +45.3 | + 1.6 |
| 50–59......... | 2.85 | (91.2) | 3.83 | (92.9) | 3.75 | (89.3) | 3.68 | (88.2) | +29.1 | − 3.0 |
| 60–69......... | *2.22 | (86.0) | 3.01 | (89.8) | 3.17 | (89.8) | 3.06 | (90.6) | — | — |
| 70 and over... | | | 2.39 | (85.8) | 2.40 | (86.8) | 2.47 | (88.7) | — | — |

* Figures include all persons 60 years of age and older.
Source: Pan-American Coffee Bureau, based on a national probability sample survey of 6,000 civilians over 10 years of age, taken at midwinter.

**EXHIBIT 7**

**U.S. Per Capita Coffee Consumption, 1946–1964**
**(pounds per capita)**

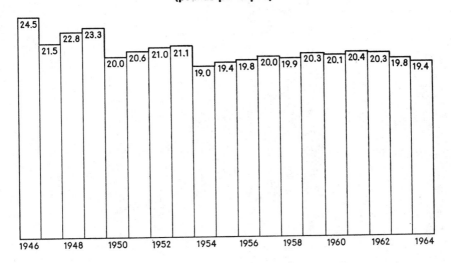

## EXHIBIT 8

### Coffee Consumption Trends, Fiscal 1955–1964

| Fiscal Years | Total Coffee (000,000 lbs.) | Equivalent Units (000,000) | Soluble Ratio | Growth of Soluble Sales vs. Year Ago (Percent) | High Sol. East (000,000) | | Low Sol. West (000,000) | |
|---|---|---|---|---|---|---|---|---|
| | | | | | Reg. Units | Sol. Units | Reg. Units | Sol. Units |
| 1964 (est.) | 2,102 | 174.5 | 30.0 | −2.1 | 63.0 | 38.2 | 59.1 | 14.2 |
| 1963 | 2,171 | 170.9 | 31.3 | 0.2 | 59.9 | 38.8 | 57.5 | 14.7 |
| 1962 | 2,163 | 168.8 | 31.6 | 5.6 | 58.4 | 38.9 | 57.0 | 14.5 |
| 1961 | 2,080 | 163.2 | 30.9 | 7.4 | 57.7 | 36.6 | 55.0 | 13.9 |
| 1960 | 1,984 | 155.9 | 30.1 | 5.3 | 55.4 | 33.6 | 53.5 | 13.4 |
| 1959 | 1,955 | 154.1 | 29.0 | 9.3 | 55.7 | 32.0 | 53.7 | 12.7 |
| 1958 | 1,863 | 147.5 | 27.7 | 19.4 | 54.3 | 29.3 | 52.3 | 11.6 |
| 1957 | 1,738 | 138.6 | 24.7 | 20.8 | 54.1 | 25.4 | 50.2 | 8.9 |
| 1956 | 1,654 | 131.5 | 21.6 | 21.5 | 54.8 | 21.2 | 48.3 | 7.2 |
| 1955 | 1,500 | 120.4 | 19.4 | — | 52.0 | 17.4 | 45.1 | 5.9 |

## EXHIBIT 9

### Coffee Drinking by Region
### (cups per person per day)

|  | 1950 | 1962 | 1963 | (Est.) 1964 | Percentage Change 1950–64 |
|---|---|---|---|---|---|
| East................ | 2.27 | 2.91 | 2.76 | 2.54 | +11.9 |
| Midwest............. | 2.72 | 3.34 | 3.30 | 3.20 | +17.6 |
| South.............. | 1.91 | 2.78 | 2.54 | 2.61 | +36.6 |
| West............... | 2.79 | 3.52 | 3.56 | 3.38 | +21.1 |
| U.S.A.............. | 2.38 | 3.12 | 3.01 | 2.90 | +21.8 |

SOURCE: Pan-American Coffee Bureau Annual Study.

## EXHIBIT 10

### Sales and Soluble Ratio by Area—Fiscal 1964 (Est.)

|  | East | West | Total U.S. |
|---|---|---|---|
| Population over 14 (000,000)....... | 81.0 | 53.0 | 134.0 |
| Total coffee market *(000,000 units)................ | 101.2 | 73.3 | 174.5 |
| Soluble ratio (Soluble/Total units)......................... | 42.9 | 22.9 | 30.0 |

* (Unit = 48-ounce soluble or 12-pounds ground)

## EXHIBIT 11

### Geographical Distribution of Coffee User Types

| Type of Coffee | Total U.S. (Percent) | North-east (Percent) | South (Percent) | Mid-west (Percent) | West Central (Percent) | Pacific (Percent) |
|---|---|---|---|---|---|---|
| Ground only users.............. | 37 | 24 | 40 | 34 | 49 | 51 |
| Users of both.................. | 48 | 57 | 35 | 52 | 42 | 32 |
| Instant only users............... | 15 | 19 | 25 | 14 | 9 | 7 |

**EXHIBIT 12**

**Composition of the Coffee Market by User Type**

| | Percentage of Families (Percent) | Percentage of Coffee Volume (Percent) | Percentage of Regular Coffee Volume (Percent) | Percentage of Instant Coffee Volume (Percent) |
|---|---|---|---|---|
| Exclusively Regular | 48 | 54 | 76 | 2 |
| Predominantly Regular (60–89 percent) | 14 | 15 | 17 | 12 |
| Instant and Regular (40–59 percent) | 5 | 5 | 4 | 8 |
| Predominantly Instant (60–89 percent) | 10 | 8 | 3 | 20 |
| Exclusively Instant | 23 | 18 | — | 58 |

SOURCE: Maxwell House Market Research Department.

**EXHIBIT 13**

**Population by Size of Urban Area (in 000s)**

| Number of TV Homes | East | West |
|---|---|---|
| Over 1 million | 42,896 | 20,454 |
| 250,000–1,000,000 | 41,348 | 27,071 |
| 75,000–250,000 | 22,520 | 18,116 |
| 0–75,000 | 5,481 | 8,483 |
| Total | 112,245 | 74,124 |

**EXHIBIT 14**

**Competitive Position—Fiscal 1964 (Est.)**

| | Percentage | | |
|---|---|---|---|
| | East | West | Total U.S. |
| *Division Share:* | | | |
| Regular | 36.0 | 13.5 | 24.9 |
| Instant | 50.7 | 47.1 | 50.3 |
| Volume | 76 | 24 | 100 |
| Gross Profit | 77 | 23 | 100 |
| Advertising and Promotion | 62 | 38 | 100 |
| Merchandising Profit | 84 | 16 | 100 |

## EXHIBIT 15

### Competitive Position—Fiscal 1964 (Est.)
### (brand share)

| Soluble Market | Percent | Ground Market | Percent |
|---|---|---|---|
| Instant Maxwell House | 36.8 | Regular Maxwell House | 21.4 |
| Nescafé | 12.2 | Folger's | 15.1 |
| Sanka | 9.3 | Hills | 9.7 |
| Chase and Sanborn | 6.6 | Chase and Sanborn | 6.5 |
| Folger's | 5.9 | | |
| Yuban | 4.2 | | |

## EXHIBIT 16

### Soluble Ratio and Market Share by Region

| | East | Mid-East | South | Central | West Central | West |
|---|---|---|---|---|---|---|
| **Fiscal 1963** | | | | | | |
| Maxwell House: | | | | | | |
| Instant | 39.2 | 40.2 | 43.1 | 37.4 | 39.4 | 28.1 |
| Regular | 32.1 | 35.9 | 32.7 | 16.1 | 7.6 | 8.9 |
| Yuban: | | | | | | |
| Instant | 7.6 | 3.3 | 2.6 | 2.4 | 0.8 | 7.9 |
| Regular | 2.2 | 1.2 | 0.8 | 0.5 | 0.1 | 4.8 |
| Soluble Ratio | 39.3 | 40.2 | 38.4 | 27.8 | 18.9 | 20.4 |
| **Fiscal 964 (Est.)** | | | | | | |
| Maxwell House: | | | | | | |
| Instant | 37.9 | 38.4 | 41.1 | 36.9 | 36.4 | 24.4 |
| Regular | 33.1 | 36.9 | 31.4 | 16.1 | 8.8 | 8.9 |
| Yuban: | | | | | | |
| Instant | 6.7 | 3.3 | 2.3 | 2.5 | 0.9 | 8.2 |
| Regular | 2.1 | 1.1 | 0.7 | 0.5 | 0.1 | 5.1 |
| Soluble Ratio | 39.5 | 39.2 | 37.0 | 21.1 | 18.2 | 19.7 |

## EXHIBIT 17

### A Comparison of the Trend for Estimated Advertising Expenditures

| Year | Total Coffee | 20 Leading Grocery Product Manu- facturers | $ Coffee Expenditures |
|---|---|---|---|
| 1958 = index | 100 | 100 | $43 million |
| 1959 | 88 | 109 | 37 |
| 1960 | 117 | 109 | 50 |
| 1961 | 119 | 117 | 51 |
| 1962 | 106 | 120 | 45 |
| 1963 | 104 | 130 | 44 |

## EXHIBIT 18

### Research on Eight Product Descriptions for Freeze-Dried Coffee
### (February 27, 1963)

| Description | Percentage Rating As "One of Best" on Attributes | | | | | Would Buy (Percent) |
|---|---|---|---|---|---|---|
| | Flavor | Aroma | Strength | Quality | Freshness | |
| Extract of coffee.............. 14 | | 16 | 37 | 20 | 29 | 43 |
| Freeze-dried coffee............ 17 | | 16 | 17 | 19 | 49 | 48 |
| Dry frozen coffee.............. 10 | | 7 | 25 | 17 | 46 | 52 |
| Crystal coffee................. 14 | | 14 | 6 | 21 | 40 | 45 |
| Groundless coffee.............. 12 | | 13 | 21 | 21 | 38 | 45 |
| Coffee concentrate............ 11 | | 8 | 39 | 18 | 30 | 51 |
| Whole coffee without grounds.................... 26 | | 27 | 30 | 26 | 42 | 52 |
| Concentrated Crystals of Real Coffee..................... 22 | | 23 | 25 | 23 | 44 | 55 |

| | Spontaneous Associations | |
|---|---|---|
| | Instant Coffee (Percent) | (Other) |
| Extract of coffee.............. 22 | | (Flavoring agent, 19 percent) |
| Freeze-dried coffee............ 18 | | (Frozen, 32 percent) |
| Dry frozen coffee............. 17 | | (Frozen, 34 percent) |
| Crystal coffee................ 19 | | (Crystal clear, 47 percent) |
| Groundless coffee.............. 29 | | (No sediment left in cup, 16 percent) |
| Coffee concentrate............ 42 | | (Stronger—won't need as much, 25 percent) |
| Whole coffee without grounds.................... 41 | | (Whole coffee beans, 26 percent) |
| Concentrated Crystals of Real Coffee..................... 44 | | (Grains/beads of coffee, 10 percent; Concentrated, 10 percent) |

## EXHIBIT 19

### A Study of Four Candidate Names
### (May, 1963)

Base: 463 respondents (women "heads of households")

| | MAXIM (Percent) | PRIMA (Percent) | NOVA (Percent) | KAABA (Control) (Percent) |
|---|---|---|---|---|
| *Spontaneous Association* | | | | |
| With coffee.................... | 22 | 5 | 4 | 14 |
| With Maxwell House........... | 7 | — | — | — |
| *Spontaneous Association When Identified as Coffee* | | | | |
| Major association............... | Best/Maximum (37) Maxwell House (33) | High Quality (43) | New (24) | Foreign (45) |
| Not a suitable name............. | 5 | 6 | 12 | 15 |
| *Anticipated Likes* | | | | |
| Will like nothing about it........ | 12 | 13 | 25 | 32 |
| Will dislike nothing about it...... | 37 | 31 | 24 | 18 |
| *Expected Type* | | | | |
| Instant coffee................... | 34 | 39 | 44 | 26 |
| Regular coffee.................. | 51 | 35 | 22 | 34 |
| New third type coffee........... | 15 | 21 | 38 | 40 |
| *Rating Index by Characteristics* (7 point scale: 4 = 100 index) | | | | |
| Fresh......................... | 148 | 148 | 132 | 130 |
| Fine aroma.................... | 135 | 132 | 112 | 118 |
| Highest quality................ | 135 | 135 | 110 | 112 |
| Strong........................ | 132 | 115 | 100 | 130 |
| Dark.......................... | 125 | 110 | 102 | 132 |
| Expensive..................... | 118 | 120 | 100 | 112 |
| Modern....................... | 112 | 122 | 122 | 112 |
| For men...................... | 106 | 90 | 90 | 112 |

## EXHIBIT 20

### Name Test—Choice of Gift Product from Three Alternatives*
#### (June, 1963)

| | Percent of Users of | | | | | | | | |
|---|---|---|---|---|---|---|---|---|---|
| Chose | Total | Regular Ground | Instant | Both | Maxwell House | Regular Maxwell House | Instant Maxwell House | Both Maxwell House | Not Maxwell House |
| MAXIM | 53 | 41 | 63 | 56 | 52 | 47 | 56 | 53 | 55 |
| Nova | 57 | 45 | 67 | 57 | 53 | 42 | 64 | 55 | 60 |
| Maxwell House concentrated soluble | 62 | 52 | 71 | 62 | 60 | 53 | 69 | 60 | 63 |
| Maxwell House concentrated instant | 62 | 48 | 73 | 64 | 59 | 47 | 73 | 55 | 64 |
| Regular Maxwell House (average four tests) | 28 | 50 | 4 | 29 | 28 | 50 | 5 | 29 | 28 |
| Instant Maxwell House (average four tests) | 14 | 3 | 27 | 8 | 16 | 3 | 24 | 15 | 12 |
| Base: (average) | (300) | (100) | (100) | (100) | (150) | (56) | (56) | (38) | (150) |

* In four matched tests the respondent was offered one of three products as a gift; namely, Regular Maxwell House, Instant Maxwell House, or one of the four descriptions for freeze-dried coffee. The table should be read as follows: Among all coffee drinkers (i.e., the total sample), who were given a choice of a description MAXIM versus IMH or RMH, 53 percent chose IMH. Similarly if Nova was the description it was chosen 57 percent of the time over either IMH or RMH. Similarly if Nova was the description it was chosen 57 percent of the time over either IMH or RMH.

## EXHIBIT 21

### Telephone Study on the
### Awareness, Association, and Connotations of "Soluble"
### (April 6–7, 1963)

| Association | Instant Coffee | Other | None Don't Know |
|---|---|---|---|
| Soluble coffee................... | 36% | 24% | 40% |
| Concentrated soluble coffee........ | 50 | 19 | 31 |
| Soluble coffee concentrate.......... | 52 | 18 | 30 |

| Awareness | Heard of Before | NOT Heard of Before |
|---|---|---|
| Soluble coffee.................... | 14% | 86% |
| Concentrated soluble coffee........ | 7 | 93 |
| Soluble coffee concentrate.......... | 8 | 92 |

| Definition (unaided) | Heard of Synonym | (Instant) | (Other) | Not Heard | Don't Know |
|---|---|---|---|---|---|
| Soluble coffee.................... | 16% | (14%) | (2%) | 44% | (40%) |
| Concentrated soluble coffee......... | 19 | (18 ) | (1 ) | 38 | (43 ) |
| Soluble coffee concentrate.......... | 15 | (15 ) | — | 43 | (42 ) |

| Definition (aided) | Regular Ground | Instant | Neither— 3rd Type |
|---|---|---|---|
| Soluble coffee.................... | 34% | 37% | 29% |
| Concentrated soluble coffee........ | 20 | 53 | 27 |
| Soluble coffee concentrate.......... | 2 | 61 | 37 |

| Connotation | Better Than Instant | Same as Instant | Not as Good as Instant |
|---|---|---|---|
| Soluble coffee.................... | 7% | 12% | 10% |
| Concentrated soluble coffee........ | 10 | 8 | 10 |
| Soluble coffee concentrate........ | 18 | 14 | 14 |

**EXHIBIT 22**

**Test of Consumer Reaction to Maxim Square, Round, and Rectangular Jars
(January, 1964)**

| | Shown Square and Round | | Shown Square and Rectangular | |
|---|---|---|---|---|
| | Square (Percent) | Round (Percent) | Square (Percent) | Rectangular (Percent) |
| *Interest in Buying*........................ 59 | | 58 | 55 | 64 |
| Use instant only.................... 62 | | 70 | 62 | 78 |
| Use only ground.................. 40 | | 38 | 40 | 40 |
| Use both........................ 72 | | 66 | 64 | 74 |
| *Consider Different from Other Coffees*........ 77 | | 57 | 85 | 79 |
| *Favorable Product Evaluations* | | | | |
| Flavor........................... 71 | | 81 | 80 | 80 |
| Aroma........................... 69 | | 79 | 82 | 84 |
| Color............................ 83 | | 87 | 86 | 89 |
| Strength......................... 75 | | 80 | 83 | 85 |
| Overall quality................... 77 | | 78 | 83 | 84 |
| Improvement over other products........................ 80 | | 81 | 88 | 88 |
| *Favorable Packaging Evaluation* | | | | |
| Ease of handling.................... 77 | | 88 | 87 | 91 |
| Ease of removing coffee.............. 80 | | 88 | 86 | 91 |
| Ease of storage..................... 82 | | 86 | 92 | 94 |
| Attractiveness..................... 72 | | 75 | 72 | 81 |
| Cap style......................... 87 | | 90 | 88 | 88 |
| Base: Female Heads of Households........ | (150) | | (150) | |

EXHIBIT 23

**Male Influence in Coffee Brand Buying Decision Study (1962)**

| Household Coffee Usage | Instant | | | Ground | | |
|---|---|---|---|---|---|---|
| | Total (Percent) | Use Instant Only (Percent) | Use Instant and Ground (Percent) | Total (Percent) | Use Ground Only (Percent) | Use Ground and Instant (Percent) |
| Husband asked directly for a brand, and wife bought it.............. | 18 | 18 | 18 | 16 | 15 | 17 |
| (Wife did not buy it)...... | (1) | (—)* | (1) | (—) | (—) | (1) |
| Husband mentioned a brand, and wife bought it..................... | 8 | 5 | 8 | 9 | 7 | 10 |
| Husband indicated dissatisfaction, and wife bought another brand.... | 15 | 14 | 16 | 20 | 17 | 22 |
| Husband bought a different brand........... | 7 | 8 | 7 | 7 | 6 | 8 |
| Husband shopped with wife and suggested a different brand, and wife bought it.......... | 8 | 10 | 8 | 9 | 8 | 10 |
| (Wife did not buy it)...... | (—) | (—) | (—) | (1) | (2) | (—) |
| Husband did none of the above................ | 65% | 66% | 65% | 61% | 61% | 61% |
| *Base:* Total housewives in each group (no male interviews)....... | (753) | (96) | (657) | (200) | (88) | (112) |

* Less than 0.05 percent.

EXHIBIT 24

**Soluble Coffee Brand Expenditures on Media Advertising (Estimated 1963)**

| Total Dollars*—By Region | Total | East | Mid-East | Central | West | South | West Central |
|---|---|---|---|---|---|---|---|
| IMH.................. | $6,490 | $1,710 | $1,153 | $1,048 | $821 | $1,053 | $705 |
| Nescafé.............. | 4,673 | 1,286 | 829 | 748 | 673 | 669 | 468 |
| Sanka................ | 2,981 | 675 | 448 | 462 | 520 | 464 | 412 |
| Chase & Sanborn........ | 3,243 | 946 | 582 | 574 | 267 | 611 | 263 |
| Folger's.............. | 1,627 | — | 143 | 192 | 732 | 194 | 366 |
| Yuban................ | 2,440 | 1,221 | 433 | 255 | 352 | 162 | 17 |

| *Dollars per Thousand Population—By Region* | Total | East | Mid-East | Central | West | South | West Central |
|---|---|---|---|---|---|---|---|
| IMH.................. | $34.33 | $40.83 | $43.09 | $34.01 | $25.63 | $32.26 | $28.29 |
| Nescafé.............. | 24.72 | 30.71 | 30.98 | 24.28 | 21.01 | 20.49 | 18.78 |
| Sanka................ | 15.77 | 16.12 | 16.74 | 14.99 | 16.24 | 14.21 | 16.53 |
| Chase & Sanborn........ | 17.16 | 22.59 | 21.75 | 18.63 | 8.34 | 18.72 | 10.55 |
| Folger's.............. | 8.61 | — | 5.34 | 6.23 | 22.85 | 5.94 | 14.69 |
| Yuban................ | 12.91 | 29.16 | 16.18 | 8.28 | 10.99 | 4.96 | 0.68 |
| 1/1/64 Population (000) . | 189,039.3 | 41,878.6 | 26,755.1 | 30,813.4 | 32,028.3 | 32,645.2 | 24,918.7 |

## EXHIBIT 25

### Comparative Projected National Costs of Alternative Promotional Techniques

|  | Cost Per Thousand | Extension |
|---|---|---|
| **2-Ounce Jar and 25-Cent Coupon** (Base: 25,000,000 homes) | | |
| Product and package................. | $241.00 | $ 6,025,000 |
| Distribution....................... | 120.00 | 3,000,000 |
| Carrier........................... | 13.00 | 325,000 |
| Freeze-dry leaflets.................. | 6.00 | 150,000 |
| 25-cent coupon..................... | 5.00 | 125,000 |
| Coupon redemption (25 percent)........ | 67.50 | 1,687,500 |
| Scoop............................ | 10.00 | 250,000 |
| Transportation..................... | 6.00 | 150,000 |
| Warehousing....................... | 5.00 | 125,000 |
|  | $473.50 | $11,837,500 |
| **Free Coupon** (Base: 9,000,000 homes) | | |
| Coupon........................... | $ 6.00 | $ 54,000 |
| Freeze-dry leaflets.................. | 6.00 | 54,000 |
| Distribution....................... | 10.50 | 94,500 |
| Postage........................... | 27.50 | 247,500 |
| Coupon redemption (50 percent)........ | 315.00 | 2,835,000 |
|  | $365.00 | $ 3,285,000 |
| **6 Single Serving Packets and a 25-Cent Coupon** (Base: 34,000,000 homes) | | |
| Product........................... | $130.50 | $ 4,437,000 |
| Container and top................... | 4.50 | 153,000 |
| Package........................... | 26.50 | 901,000 |
| Handling.......................... | 25.00 | 850,000 |
| Postage........................... | 39.00 | 1,326,000 |
| Leaflets........................... | 6.00 | 204,000 |
| 25-cent coupon..................... | 5.00 | 170,000 |
| Redemption (25 percent)............. | 67.50 | 2,295,000 |
| Mailing carton..................... | 10.00 | 340,000 |
|  | $314.00 | $10,676,000 |

**EXHIBIT 26**

**Pricing Alternatives—Maxim**

| Brand | Size | Retail Price | Retail Price per Ounce | Retail Economy vs. Next Smaller Size | Cost* per Cup | Maxim per Ounce Premium |
|-------|------|-------------|------------------------|--------------------------------------|--------------|-------------------------|
| Maxim | 2-oz. | $0.55 | $0.2750 | —% | 2.12¢ | —% |
|       | 4-oz. | 0.85 | 0.2125 | 29.4 | 1.63 | — |
|       | 8-oz. | 1.59 | 0.1988 | 6.9 | 1.53 | — |
| IMH   | 2-oz. | 0.49 | 0.2450 | — | 1.88 | 12.2 |
|       | 6-oz. | 0.99 | 0.1650 | 48.5 | 1.27 | 28.8 |
|       | 10-oz. | 1.39† | 0.1390 | 18.7 | 1.07 | 43.0 |
|       | 14-oz. | 1.89† | 0.1350 | 3.0 | 1.04 | 47.3 |
| IY    | 2-oz. | 0.53 | 0.2650 | — | 2.04 | 3.8 |
|       | 5-oz. | 0.99 | 0.1980 | 33.8 | 1.52 | 7.3 |
|       | 9-oz. | 1.39† | 0.1544 | 28.2 | 1.19 | 28.8 |
| IS    | 2-oz. | 0.53 | 0.2650 | — | 2.04 | 3.8 |
|       | 5-oz. | 1.09 | 0.2180 | 21.6 | 1.68 | (7.5) |
|       | 8-oz. | 1.49† | 0.1862 | 17.1 | 1.43 | 6.8 |
| RMH   | 1-lb. | 0.87 | — | — | 1.74 | (2.3) A |
|       | 2-lb. | 1.71 | — | — | 1.71 | (7.0) B |

* Soluble—13 cups per ounce.    (A) versus 4-ounce.
  Ground—50 cups per pound.    (B) versus 8-ounce.
† Reflects retail shelf price when label packs of the following values are in distribution:

|  |  |  |
|------|-----------|----------|
| IMH | 10-ounce | 20 cents |
| IMH | 14-ounce | 30 cents |
| IY | 9-ounce | 20 cents |
| IS | 8-ounce | 10 cents |

## EXHIBIT 27

### Pricing Alternatives—Maxim

| Brand | Size | Retail Price | Retail Price per Ounce | Retail Economy vs. Next Smaller Size | Cost* per Cup | Maxim per Ounce Premium |
|-------|------|-------------|----------------------|--------------------------------------|---------------|------------------------|
| Maxim | 2-oz. | $0.57 | $0.2850 | —% | 2.19¢ | —% |
|       | 4-oz. | 0.99 | 0.2475 | 15.1 | 1.90 | — |
|       | 8-oz. | 1.69 | 0.2112 | 17.2 | 1.63 | — |
| IMH   | 2-oz. | 0.49 | 0.2450 | — | 1.88 | 16.3 |
|       | 6-oz. | 0.99 | 0.1650 | 48.5 | 1.27 | 50.0 |
|       | 10-oz. | 1.39† | 0.1390 | 18.7 | 1.07 | 51.9 |
|       | 14-oz. | 1.89† | 0.1350 | 3.0 | 1.04 | 56.4 |
| IY    | 2-oz. | 0.53 | 0.2650 | — | 2.04 | 7.5 |
|       | 5-oz. | 0.99 | 0.1980 | 33.8 | 1.52 | 25.0 |
|       | 9-oz. | 1.39† | 0.1544 | 12.8 | 1.19 | 36.8 |
| IS    | 2-oz. | 0.53 | 0.2650 | — | 2.04 | 7.5 |
|       | 5-oz. | 1.09 | 0.2180 | 21.6 | 1.68 | 13.5 |
|       | 8-oz. | 1.49† | 0.1862 | 17.1 | 1.43 | 13.4 |
| RMH   | 1-lb. | 0.87 | — | — | 1.74 | 13.8 A |
|       | 2-lb. | 1.71 | — | — | 1.71 | 4.7 B |

\* Soluble—13 cups per ounce    (A) versus 4-ounce
   Ground—50 cups per pound    (B) versus 8-ounce
† Reflects retail shelf price when label packs of the following values are in distribution:

|  |  |  |
|--|--|--|
| IMH | 10-ounce | 20 cents |
| IMH | 14-ounce | 30 cents |
| IY  | 9-ounce  | 20 cents |
| IS  | 8-ounce  | 10 cents |

# Global Semiconductors, Inc.

Global Semiconductors, Inc., produces and sells a line of semi-conductors worldwide. In 1972 total company sales exceeded $100 million of which over half was made in the United States. Company sales have increased in recent years at a faster rate than those of the industry. This was due to an expansion in the company's line as well as rapid penetration of the fast-growing European market which the company entered in the late 1960's. Profits were considered to be above the in-dustry average, and despite low earnings in 1971 due to the recession the outlook for 1972 and beyond was considered favorable due to the rapid growth of relatively new markets. One such market, the U.S. automotive industry, was considered to represent an unusually good opportunity for the company.

The semiconductor industry is only about 20 years old. During the first decade of its existence industry sales grew at an unusually high rate —often exceeding 100% per year. Even so, its absolute size was not great, and emphasis was essentially on production. During the 1960's overall unit demand grew at an annual rate of 25–30%, and new firms continued to enter the industry; indeed, between 1966–1970 some 30 new firms entered. By 1972 total free worldwide industry sales were estimated to exceed $2.5 billion.

The recession of 1970–71 caused a decrease in demand for the first time in the industry's history. To compound the difficulties, large pro-duction units which were started in response to the 1968–1969 boom started coming on line. The resultant overcapacity led to unprecedented price cutting and losses for the industry as a whole. The industry broke even in 1971, but only after Sylvania, Union Carbide, and Philco Ford dropped out. Further, Motorola, RCA, General Instrument, Raytheon, Fairchild Cameras, and Texas Instruments de-emphasized or phased out portions of their lines. Strong growth reappeared in 1972, and capacity expenditures appeared to be more carefully rationalized than in the past.

Solid state electronics is the generic term used to describe the semi-conductor product line because all circuitry is compressed within a few thousandths of an inch on the silicon wafer surface. There is no glass covering and no moving parts; thus, unlike tubes, semiconductors can be easily miniaturized. The major trend throughout the 1960's was to build more complex integrated circuits which, in turn, became more difficult to fabricate and required more customization.

The economics of the semiconductor industry are closely related to experience curves. The latter describe an inverse relationship between accumulated volume (expressed in units produced) and average unit costs. In semiconductors the cost reduction per unit on value added for each doubling of accumulated experience was estimated as being between 20 and 30%.

Given this phenomenon, and the presence of strong competitors, per unit prices (expressed in real dollars) dropped substantially during the 1960's. Further, there was a strong tendency to build capacity and price low to gain market share. The industry is also characterized by high capital intensity with every dollar of sales requiring an investment of about 50 cents.

Products sold to four major end-user groups comprise the semi-conductor market—government/military communications, industrial/communications, computer, and household consumer. The government market which represented about 30% of total sales in 1970 was expected to decline to 19% by 1974. This change in relative importance is a result of a small demand growth in contrast to much stronger demand trends in the commercial sector. This was particularly the case with consumer products which were expected to grow from a share of 11% of total industry sales in 1970 to 25% in 1974. The shares held by the other two major markets—industrial/communications and computer—were expected to hold about the same over the next several years; i.e., at 27–28% and 24–26%, respectfully.

Global had always held a strong share of the government/military market. Its share of the industrial/communications and computer market was, according to management, "only fair," while its franchise in consumer products was considered "weak." Overall the company faced strong competition from such companies as Texas Instruments, Motorola, and Fairchild, all of which had considerably larger shares of the total market. Competition varied substantially from one market sector to another.

The fast-growing consumer products market segment was considered to have considerable appeal to Global mainly because of new applications. The motor vehicle market, in particular, was thought to have substantial potential due primarily to government requirements for safety and anti-pollution items which contain semiconductors. These included seat belt interlock systems, solid state ignitions, and antiskid braking systems for trucks. By 1975 vehicle semiconductor sales were forecasted at some $60 million versus about $50 million in 1972. By 1980 the total could well exceed $300 million.

In early 1973 the marketing director of the U.S. company was requested by corporate management to prepare a five-year marketing plan designed to "grow share" in the automotive market. He, in turn, set up a task force composed of five persons to complete the plan within 120 days. The highlights of their plan are shown in Exhibit 1.

After reading the proposed plan, the marketing director felt both frustrated and let down. He had hoped for a more precise statement of what company strategy and tactics should be implemented, in order to obtain a high share of this growing market, as well as a rough budget. After discussing his feelings with the group, however, he recognized that in retrospect his expectations were unreasonable and that very little in the way of planning could be done until corporate management decided which strategy option they would follow. What strategy guidelines should the company adopt with respect to the automotive market? How will these guidelines impact on the development of a marketing plan?

## EXHIBIT 1
### Five-Year Marketing Plan—Automotive

1.  *Assumptions*
1.1.  *Economic*
      "Consumption Expenditures for Durable Goods" are assumed to provide an economic "climate" for both the automotive and appliance markets. Figures 1 and 2 show the cumulative and year-by-year growth in this sector of the GNP. "Apparent Growth" includes the effect of inflation while "Real Growth" does not. Data are the latest published by Chase Econometrics.

## FIGURE 1
### Durable Goods—Cumulative Growth

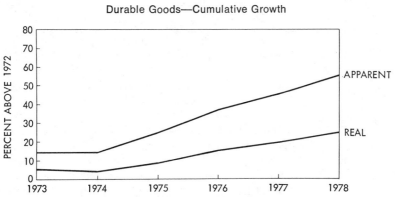

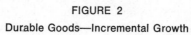

FIGURE 2

Durable Goods—Incremental Growth

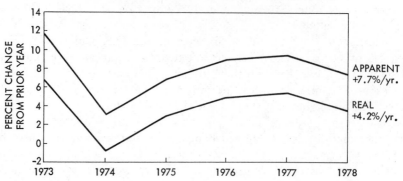

## 1.2    *Market*

### 1.2.1.    *Semiconductors*

Prices of mature semiconductor lines will remain relatively constant over the 1973 through 1978 period. However, this implies a steady attrition in real value because of the continued inflation depicted in Section 1.1 above.

Prices of new semiconductor lines will follow typical learning curve theory as high volume and design maturity are achieved.

### 1.2.2.    *Passenger Cars and Light Trucks*

North American production is projected in Figure 3.

FIGURE 3

Vehicle Production

|  | *Passenger Cars* | *Trucks* | *Total* |
|---|---|---|---|
| 1973 | 9,720,652 | 2,897,893 | 12,618,545 |
| 1974 | 9,026,597 | 2,690,983 | 11,717,580 |
| 1975 | 9,230,598 | 2,751,800 | 11,982,398 |
| 1976 | 9,769,665 | 2,912,505 | 12,682,170 |
| 1977 | 10,438,887 | 3,112,012 | 13,550,899 |
| 1978 | 10,789,633 | 3,216,576 | 14,006,209 |

Imports will continue to hold from 12% to 15% of the U.S. market. North American production will continue to be about ⅓ of the world total. Japanese growth in percentage of the world production will level off sharply during the next five years.

The strong trend toward smaller vehicles will not produce a corresponding decrease in average selling price. The penetration of deluxe features and options will not decline significantly with the shift to smaller vehicles although some historical growth trends will flatten.

Regulatory influence on vehicle design will continue as will resulting technical turmoil. However, two important relaxations are expected. First, the NOX portion of the 1977 emission standard will be changed, probably to coincide with the 1975 California standard. Second, the requirement for air bags will be dropped or postponed indefinitely. Some version of the seat belt interlock rule will continue through 1978.

### 1.2.3. *Medium and Heavy Trucks*

North American production for 1972 was 989,829. Growth in unit sales will closely approximate the real growth rates for durable goods as shown in Figures 1 and 2 of Section 1.1.

### 1.2.4. *Small Engines*

North American production for 1972 was 9.7 million. Annual growth through 1978 should average about 6% per year. This is greater than the 4.2% per year for durable goods because of rapid U.S. penetration of the snowmobile during 1974 and 1976.

### 2. *Automotive, Nonentertainment Market Definition*

The market includes all semiconductors used in the following applications:

A. Passenger cars and light truck OEM systems.
B. Medium and heavy truck OEM systems (including truck trailer systems).
C. Small engine systems for boats, motorcycles, snowmobiles, lawnmowers, garden tractors, etc.
D. Miscellaneous vehicles such as golf carts, farm tractors, recreational vehicles, etc.
E. After-market and replacement systems and components for the above categories.

The market *does not* include the following applications:

A. Aircraft systems.
B. Commercial, off-road equipment such as earthmovers, forklifts, etc.
C. Automotive test or service equipment.
D. Highway equipment such as signal systems, traffic monitoring, or guidance systems, etc.
E. Entertainment systems.

#### Semiconductor Market Size in $ \times 10^6$ and Projected Growth

| Five-Year Indexes Segment | Actual 1972 | Forecast 1973 | Five-Year Indexes | | | | |
|---|---|---|---|---|---|---|---|
| | | | 1974 | 1975 | 1976 | 1977 | 1978 |
| Industry ($ \times 10^6$)............ | $47.5 | $63.3 | $98.8 | $164.6 | $197.6 | $205.5 | $217.4 |
| Global sales ($ \times 10^6$)........ | $19.0 | $25.2 | $39.7 | $62.6 | $78.7 | $79.8 | $83.4 |
| Global share of market (%).......... | 10 | 8 | 10 | 15 | 20 | 20 | 20 |
| Total market growth rate (%)...... | — | 33 | 10.0 | 25.0 | 39.0 | 41.0 | 44.0 |

Only North American production of systems is considered. No separate breakout of Canadian versus U.S. production is attempted because of the complex nature of the reimportation situation.

4. *Automotive, Nonentertainment Market Trends*

4.1. *Where Is the Market Going?*

All sectors of the market are undergoing explosive growth that will accelerate during the plan period. This growth is largely independent of the usual economic factors.

No precise planning is possible. Many inventions must be scheduled. Every vehicle maker is operating with a wide variety of contingency plans. During the five-year plan period, many new programs will arise which are utterly unpredictable. Some programs which now have great urgency will simply stop. In all cases our customers' definitions of future systems requirements are extremely hazy or nonexistent.

The projections contained in this plan are believed to be generally very conservative—particularly when compared to projections from other sources and widely publicized in the electronics press.

4.2. *What Part of the Market Is Increasing? Why?*

All parts are increasing rapidly. The reasons for this vary from sector to sector.

A.  Passenger Car and Light Truck OEM Systems

Acceptance of electronic alternatives to existing electromechanical systems is growing rapidly both at the consumer and OEM levels. Freedom from maintenance and greatly improved reliability (real or imagined) are the bases of this acceptance. Also, federal and state regulations regarding safety and emissions have, in some cases, generated new system requirements which are highly compatible with electronic approaches. By 1978 total nonentertainment electronics per vehicle *may* reach $100. This is a billion dollar market in the United States alone.

B.  Medium and Heavy Trucks

The immediate growth factor in this market sector is the new braking standard which becomes effective for all air-braked trucks and trailers produced after September 1, 1974. All manufacturers have been committed to the use of electronic antiskid to meet the standard. Present market is 1.2 million systems per year. End-user reaction to antiskid can be expected to be so favorable that a temporary, retrofit market—much larger than the OEM equipment market—may materialize.

C.  Small Engines

There has been a continuing trend toward wider usage of electronic ignition and alternators in all small engine applications. This will continue during the plan period. The anticipated conversion of many engine applications to the Wankel engine will, if anything, extend the usage of engine electronics.

4.3. *What Part of the Market Is Decreasing? Why?*

No part of the market is, or will be, decreasing during the plan period. However, two negative factors should be considered.

A. The involvement of automotive corporations in semiconductor manufacture may increase. This is already a very serious limitation in the case of General Motors.

B. Foreign semiconductor sources may increase their penetration of the U.S. market. This is particularly possible in the automotive market because foreign automakers have established a clear lead in the design and manufacture of advanced engine types, and, consequently, their electronics designers are already working on supportive systems for these engines while their U.S. counterparts are groping for definitions of the tasks to be performed. This probable technology gap should give the foreign semiconductor industries a real advantage in developing appropriate device capabilities.

5. *Customers in the Nonentertainment Automotive Market Ranked in Order of Semiconductor Requirements (1973)*

| | |
|---|---|
| Chrysler | 14.5M |
| Ford | 12.5M |
| G.M. | 9.0M |

Note: Figures do not include usage by contractors to these OEM's or the chips internally sourced by G. M.

6. *Competition to the Nonentertainment Automotive Market*

There are three major semiconductor firms supplying this market. A has a 30% share, B has 15%, and C has 10%. Company A can be characterized as a reliable, large-volume, broad line producer with a strong full-coverage sales force and a strong distributor network. It is one of the largest in the overall semiconductor industry. This company is very aggressive in its pricing. They appear at times not to be totally committed to this industry since their new product development goes in "fits and starts," their quality control is not always the best, and their attention to various customers varies over time.

Competitor B dominates a major section of the automotive market and has priced their products aggressively over the years. They have consistently done a good job of working with their large customers and in holding to their delivery promises. Their major limitation is that they do not have a full semiconductor line; further, that the superiority of their specialized line has been eroded substantially over time. It is a relatively small company in the overall industry and has not been too profitable. It is possible that corporate funds may not be forthcoming to support the outlay necessary to tap this fast-growing market.

Competitor C (one of the largest firms in the overall industry) has a strong leadership reputation as a quality producer of a long line of products. In recent years they have not shown any strong evidence of committing R&D and sales resources to the automotive market—perhaps because of their large expenditures in other sectors in the industry. Their attitude seems to be one of "wait and see." It is rumored in the trade, however, that they are working on a new production technology which, if successful, could change their production economics to give them a substantial advantage in the automobile market.

7. *Strengths and Weaknesses of Global in the Nonentertainment Automotive Market*

We hold a relatively weak share of the market, and, although we have nearly all of the currently viable device technologies in our hands, we have not had much exposure to the technological needs of the market. We do hold some important patents—both the device and applications areas—but are not as strong here as competitors A and B. We have a weak distributor organization—especially when compared to competitor A. Our application sales group is good but small.

Global has several strategy options as follows:

A. Selling across the board a large line of products, stressing their reliability, and quoting competitive prices.
B. Attempting to develop new technology to obsolete conventional approaches in selected areas.
C. Following (reacting) quickly to developments pioneered by competitors and stressing their applications.
D. Some combination of the above.

In evaluating these alternatives the reader should keep in mind that large expenditures will be required to expense the R&D, build facilities, hire strong sales and application personnel, and finance inventories and accounts receivable. Further, it should be noted that there is a strong interdependency between many, if not most, of the semiconductor items demanded by the automotive industry as regards joint costs including R&D, production, and marketing. An earlier report on this subject requested of higher level management an evaluation of existing products to determine their inherent capability of surviving the automotive environment on a high confidence basis for a minimum of ten years of service. This report also indicated that as best we can predict our present line covers only about 40% of what will be required over the next three–five years. We have been advised that the remaining 60% of the required line can be developed, but the time and financial requirements are not known at this time. Nor do we know the costs and risks associated with attempting to assume a leadership position vis-à-vis new products using new technology.

It seems clear, however, that each of the aforementioned strategic options carries different risks and financial consequences. It also seems clear that the successful execution of the chosen strategy will require large sums of money. We will certainly need to hire "experience" at a variety of management levels including, of course, in the sales and application areas. We will probably have to do more direct selling to compensate for our relatively weak distributor organization.

Time is absolutely critical, especially so with regards to R&D product development projects. We need to "go" to the industry as soon as possible with a statement of our intentions and invite large potential customers to work with us in our development activities. If necessary we should, in the short run, seek to supply "missing items" in our line by outside purchase even where this means accepting a smaller margin. Delivery commitments must be honored at all costs, and our quality control must be near perfect. Inevitably a project group should be formed to finalize plans for implementing whatever strategy we choose to select.

In order to grow share we will have to concentrate on the largest customers and also on selected smaller customers involved with advanced concepts. Price will have to be used as a strong weapon, but reliability cannot be overlooked. The customer's basic requirements are to have needed components in the right place at the right time and to have them work during inspection, after assembly into systems, and for a reasonable time thereafter in the field. Less important, but still vital, his end products must be competitive in cost and performance, and the components he selected must help achieve this.

# Concorn Kitchens

Mr. Conrad, marketing director of the Packaged Foods Division of the Concorn Kitchens expressed reservations about the planning process used in his division. Previously, brand managers had prepared a document containing a review of the performance of each product and a pro forma profit and loss statement which implicitly contained a recommended price, promotion and advertising strategy for the following year. It was viewed by most brand managers as a "commitment" for sales and profits that would be forthcoming from the product.

Mr. Conrad felt that these documents were "ploys" used by his subordinates to obtain as many marketing resources as possible. He felt that the plans often had little relation to historical performance and that generally no clear meaning could be assigned to the sales and profit numbers included in the plan. He was frequently not sure if these numbers represented goals or predictions. It was never clear how the sales figures were related to the marketing inputs nor what would be the consequences of certain resource allocations.

As an example he cited the lack of relationship between the 1969 plan and actual performance, particularly for one of the company's products—instant puddings. He noted that because sales did not develop as anticipated during the first part of the year he had been forced to cut advertising budgets for subsequent quarters. He stated, "If the original projections had been better this would not have happened and we would not be in the profit squeeze we now face."

The Operations Research Manager, Mr. Kendall, suggested that the preparation of the marketing plan could be expedited by the development of some computer models. He recommended that he be authorized to de-

This case is based on one prepared by Gerald J. Eskin. Reprinted from *Stanford Business Cases 1973* with the permission of the publisher, Graduate School of Business, Stanford University. Copyright © 1973 by the Board of Trustees of the Leland Stanford Junior University.

velop such models. An Operations Research project was approved and undertaken, the results of which were summarized in a report to Mr. Conrad from Mr. Kendall (see Appendix A). Based on this report, Mr. Conrad decided to try the system out on two products—instant puddings and instant breakfasts. The marketing research staff was requested to get together the necessary information to use the models. The result of this effort is reported in Appendix B. Mr. Conrad issued orders to the applicable product managers to, first, develop a planning base which would typically require modifying the straight line projections made by the computer. He requested that all changes be supported with a "logical explanation." Once a base plan had been accomplished his instructions were to get quantified goals for the period 1970–1974 with respect to the company's case sales, dollar sales, total dollar gross margin contribution, and profits before taxes.

He reminded all concerned that these goals should be consistent one with another. Once the goals were set then the individual managers were to determine how they should be obtained. This required set annual expenditures with respect to advertising and promotion and possible changes in the list price of a case. All strategy decisions were to be supported logically.

In setting forth the new strategic planning method Mr. Conrad noted that it might be that the goals which were set were unobtainable in which case the manager would explain "why" and then proceed to set up new goals. If the goals were attainable then the manager would be asked to determine whether higher goals were possible. "In this way," stated Mr. Conrad, "we hope to come reasonably close to an optimization scheme through interactions which match inputs with outputs. While I'm very interested in the numbers which emerge from this planning exercise I am more interested in how they were derived. In this connection a man's thinking will be on display—starting with the magnitude of the planning gap; i.e., the difference between his goals and the planning base. To repeat, each product manager should do the following:

1. Analyse the past data on his brand and evaluate the complete projected data for 1970–1974. (See Appendix B for data on instant puddings and instant breakfasts.)
2. Make any changes in the projected data thought necessary based only, however, on historical trends.
3. Set goals for his brand; i.e., sales in cases, market share, and profit goals for the period 1970–1974.
4. Determine the "gap" between goals and the corrected projections.
5. Strategize expenditures to accomplish these goals.
6. Change goals up or down to optimize expenditures (as best possible)."

## APPENDIX A

To:       Mr. Conrad
From:     Mr. Kendall
Subject:  Computer Planning Model (PLAN)

We believe that a planning process should include the following steps:

1.  Data on past performance should be stored in an easily accessible
    way and these data should form the basis of a first projection of fu-
    ture outcomes.
2.  Projections of key components of the plan should be made assum-
    ing continuation of past trends and strategies. These component
    projections should then be combined into a pro forma profit and
    loss statement for each product. (We call this a *Planning Base.*)
3.  Alternate plans should then be developed which explicitly take into
    account the relationships between changes in spending, prices, and
    resulting levels of sales and profits. These alternate plans *should be*
    evaluated by comparison to the Planning Base.

These ideas have been incorporated into a model called PLAN. It
should be possible for your staff to use the model simply by making either
manual or machine changes in the sample output.

The model has made linear extrapolations of key planning components.
These extrapolations are purely mechanical in nature and will not always
be appropriate. Provisions for overriding the projections have been made
so that when you feel market share or costs can be better projected sub-
jectively this can be done—again manually or by the computer. In the
case of costs we have projected totals, but as you can see from the print-
out, you can consider cost a function of sales, rather than fixed in total.

Given that these first projections are intended to show the results of
*continuing historical strategies* any changes or overrides should not be
used to indicate new trends that might develop *from a shift in strategy.*
Such effects are considered in the next stage of analysis.

The remainder of the effort is designed to allow experimentation with
alternate marketing plans in order to improve on the base projection—i.e.,
obtain any goals which have been set. To use this section, the individual
involved must know something about the responsiveness of sales to various
marketing tools. This knowledge is summarized in the form of response
coefficients to be supplied by the user. These are defined as:

$$\frac{\% \text{ change in sales}}{\% \text{ change in inputs}} \text{ (e.g., price, adv., etc.)}$$

The way in which these coefficients affect sales is illustrated in the following tables:

| Change in Advertising (Percent Change from Planning Base) | Percent Change in Sales for an Advertising Response Coefficient of: | |
| --- | --- | --- |
| | .2 | .4 |
| +20% | +4% | +8% |
| +10% | +2% | +4% |
| Same Adv. as in Planning Base | Same Sales as PB | Same Sales as PB |
| −10% | −2% | −4% |
| −20% | −4% | −8% |

| Change in Price (as % of Price Planning Base) | Percent Change in Sales for a Price Response Coefficient of: | |
| --- | --- | --- |
| | −1 | −2 |
| +10% | −10% | −20% |
| No change | No change | No change |
| −10% | +10% | +20% |

We realize that complete knowledge is not always available on response coefficients but believe that your years of marketing experience and past research efforts should allow reasonable estimates to be made. When you are unsure of the exact value you may wish to use sensitivity testing through trying the same plan with different response coefficients.

When attempting to test the sensitivity of response coefficients remember that the coefficients are defined in terms of *changes* from the Planning Base; hence a sensitivity test can only be performed on a plan that is *different* from the base plan.

The following technical notes are provided on the program:

A. *Units of Measure*
   (1) Market and sales are measured in thousands of cases (12 units to the case).
   (2) All dollar values are in thousands.
   (3) Price is the case price charged by Concorn. Retail prices are roughly 30% higher.
B. *Accounting Conventions*
   (1) Gross Contribution Margin = Price − Variable Production Cost
   (2) Overhead includes only manufacturing expense. General and administrative expenses are not included in product level profit and loss statements at Concorn (sales force expense is considered G & A).
   (3) Promotional includes expenditures on:
       (a) Trade allowances (temporary price reductions)

    (b)   Cents-off packs and coupons
    (c)   Point-of-sale material
C.   A sample output is attached.


Which product do you want to consider
$ *"test product"*
HISTORICAL FILE


|                              | 1965      | 1966      | 1967      | 1968      | 1969       |
|------------------------------|-----------|-----------|-----------|-----------|------------|
| Market—total cases.......... | 1,000,000 | 2,000,000 | 3,000,000 | 4,000,000 | 5,000,000  |
| Share......................  | .20       | .20       | .20       | .20       | .20        |
| Price per case $............ | 2.50      | 2.50      | 2.25      | 2.25      | 2.25       |
| Gross C margin $........... | 1.00      | 1.00      | .80       | .80       | .80        |
| Sales volume in cases........ | 200,000   | 400,000   | 600,000   | 800,000   | 1,000,000  |
| Sales $.................... | 500,000   | 1,000,000 | 1,350,000 | 1,800,000 | 2,250,000  |
| Gross C margin $........... | 200,000   | 400,000   | 480,000   | 640,000   | 800,000    |
| Overhead $................ | 100,000   | 100,000   | 100,000   | 150,000   | 150,000    |
| Gross margin $............ | 100,000   | 300,000   | 380,000   | 490,000   | 650,000    |
| Advertising $.............. | 20,000    | 20,000    | 20,000    | 20,000    | 20,000     |
| Promotion $............... | 30,000    | 30,000    | 30,000    | 30,000    | 30,000     |
| Net operating profit $....... | 50,000    | 250,000   | 330,000   | 440,000   | 600,000    |


|                              | 1970      | 1971      | 1972      | 1973      | 1974       |
|------------------------------|-----------|-----------|-----------|-----------|------------|
| Market—total cases........ | 6,000,000 | 7,000,000 | 8,000,000 | 9,000,000 | 10,000,000 |
| Share...................... | .20       | .20       | .20       | .20       | .20        |
| Price per case.............. | 2.125     | 2.05      | 1.98      | 1.90      | 1.825      |
| Gross C margin $........... | .70       | .64       | .58       | .52       | .46        |
| Overhead $................ | 165,000   | 180,000   | 195,000   | 210,000   | 225,000    |
| Advertising $.............. | 20,000    | 20,000    | 20,000    | 20,000    | 20,000     |
| Promotion $............... | 30,000    | 30,000    | 30,000    | 30,000    | 30,000     |


Do you wish to override any projections "yes"
Which line 3
Input new values for line   2.25, 2.25, 2.25, 2.25, 2.25
Any others "yes"
Which line 4
Input new values for line   .8, .8, .8, .8, .8,
Any others "yes"
Illegal use of tabs, please retype
Any others "yes"
Which line 6
Input new values for line   150, 200, 200, 200, 250
Any others "no"

## PLANNING BASE P/L

|  | 1970 | 1971 | 1972 | 1973 | 1974 |
|---|---|---|---|---|---|
| Sales volume—cases.......... | 1,200,000 | 1,400,000 | 1,600,000 | 1,800,000 | 2,000,000 |
| Sales $...................... | 2,700,000 | 3,150,000 | 3,600,000 | 4,050,000 | 4,500,000 |
| Gross C margin $............ | 960,000 | 1,120,000 | 1,280,000 | 1,440,000 | 1,600,000 |
| Overhead $.................. | 150,000 | 200,000 | 200,000 | 200,000 | 250,000 |
| Gross margin $.............. | 810,000 | 920,000 | 1,080,000 | 1,240,000 | 1,350,000 |
| Advertising $............... | 20,000 | 20,000 | 20,000 | 20,000 | 20,000 |
| Promotion $................. | 30,000 | 30,000 | 30,000 | 30,000 | 30,000 |
| Net operating profit $........ | 760,000 | 870,000 | 1,030,000 | 1,190,000 | 1,300,000 |

Specify response coefficient to be used for each of 5 yrs.
Price                         $-2,-2,-2,-2,-2$
Advertising                   .2, .2, .2, .2, .2
Promotion                     .4, .4, .4, .4, .4
Time dependency
# 0,0,0,0,0
Which marketing variable do you wish to change "advertising"
Specify new levels by year 30, 40, 50, 60, 70
Any others "no"

|  | 1970 | 1971 | 1972 | 1973 | 1974 |
|---|---|---|---|---|---|
| Sales volume................ | 1,301,000 | 1,608,000 | 1,922,000 | 2,242,000 | 2,569,000 |
| Sales $...................... | 2,928,000 | 3,618,000 | 4,324,000 | 5,045,000 | 5,781,000 |
| Gross C margin.............. | 1,041,000 | 1,287,000 | 1,537,000 | 1,794,000 | 2,056,000 |
| Overhead................... | 150,000 | 200,000 | 200,000 | 200,000 | 250,000 |
| Gross margin............... | 891,000 | 1,087,000 | 1,337,000 | 1,594,000 | 1,806,000 |
| Advertising................. | 30,000 | 40,000 | 50,000 | 60,000 | 70,000 |
| Promotion.................. | 30,000 | 30,000 | 30,000 | 30,000 | 30,000 |
| Net operating profit......... | 831,000 | 1,017,000 | 1,257,000 | 1,504,000 | 1,706,000 |

Do you wish to try another plan "yes"
Which marketing variable do you wish to change "price"
Specify new levels by year 2,2,2,2,2
Any others "no"

|                      | 1970      | 1971      | 1972      | 1973      | 1974      |
|----------------------|-----------|-----------|-----------|-----------|-----------|
| Sales volume.................. | 1,647,000 | 2,035,000 | 2,432,000 | 2,838,000 | 3,252,000 |
| Sales $....................... | 3,294,000 | 4,071,000 | 4,865,000 | 5,676,000 | 6,504,000 |
| Gross C margin.............. | 906,000   | 1,119,000 | 1,338,000 | 1,561,000 | 1,789,000 |
| Overhead................... | 150,000   | 200,000   | 200,000   | 200,000   | 250,000   |
| Gross margin............... | 756,000   | 919,000   | 1,138,000 | 1,361,000 | 1,539,000 |
| Advertising................. | 30,000    | 40,000    | 50,000    | 60,000    | 70,000    |
| Promotion.................. | 30,000    | 30,000    | 30,000    | 30,000    | 30,000    |
| Net operating profit......... | 696,000   | 849,000   | 1,058,000 | 1,271,000 | 1,439,000 |

Do you wish to try another plan "no"
Do you wish to change a response coefficient "yes"
Which one "price"
New values –2.5, –2.5, –2.5, –2.5, –2.5
Any others "no"

|                      | 1970      | 1971      | 1972      | 1973      | 1974      |
|----------------------|-----------|-----------|-----------|-----------|-----------|
| Sales volume.................. | 1,747,000 | 2,159,000 | 2,580,000 | 3,010,000 | 3,449,000 |
| Sales $....................... | 3,494,000 | 4,318,000 | 5,160,000 | 6,020,000 | 6,898,000 |
| Gross C margin.............. | 961,000   | 1,187,000 | 1,419,000 | 1,656,000 | 1,897,000 |
| Overhead................... | 150,000   | 200,000   | 200,000   | 200,000   | 250,000   |
| Gross margin............... | 811,000   | 987,000   | 1,219,000 | 1,456,000 | 1,647,000 |
| Advertising................. | 30,000    | 40,000    | 50,000    | 60,000    | 70,000    |
| Promotion.................. | 30,000    | 30,000    | 30,000    | 30,000    | 30,000    |
| Net operating profit......... | 751,000   | 917,000   | 1,139,000 | 1,366,000 | 1,547,000 |

Do you wish to try another plan "no"
Do you wish to change a response coefficient "no"

## APPENDIX B

To:      Mr. Conrad
From:    Marketing Research Staff
Subject: Data for PLAN Computer Model

Per Mr. Kendall's request we have provided historical data on instant breakfasts and instant puddings for inclusion in the computer data base.[1] This information will be updated as it becomes available.

The request for response coefficient information is more difficult to satisfy. A controlled experiment was conducted on these products two years ago which provides some information on this product. The results of that test were:

---

[1] No effort was made in the initial plan to detail the sales of the product in question by subproducts. Thus, with regard to puddings, no plans were to be formulated by type or flavor of mix. Such detailing would be accomplished later.

price coefficient.................. −1.6
advertising coefficient.............    .1

We suspect that over time the price elasticity coefficient is rising (larger negative values) while the advertising coefficient is falling although we cannot prove this assertion.

There are no data available on instant breakfasts, but we do have some estimates on some other products which may have similar values to those of instant breakfasts in that they are also *new* package foods in our line.

They are:

|  | Price Coef. | Adv. |
|---|---|---|
| Corn muffin mix........ | −1.2 | .3 |
| Soy Snacks........... | −1.4 | .4 |

There does not exist any hard data on the promotions question although our sales manager feels that the response to cents off promotions is rather large for all our products. He feels that doubling promotional allowance might increase sales by 50 to 70% (he is unable to say which of our products are most responsive to promotion). We feel that his estimates represent a short run view and that such promotion may not be nearly as effective in the long run.

## INSTANT PUDDINGS

### Product History

The instant pudding market started in the early 1950's as a commercialization of some processing methods that were developed as part of World War II technology. Concorn was one of the first national brands in the market, and, for a number of years was the leading brand.

As the market grew, several other major companies entered the market. These companies had the advantage of having major sources of revenue in other higher margin industries plus experience in technologies important to the instant pudding market.

By 1965, the market had slowed and Concorn was tied for second place with Julia Childs at about 20% of the market. Gambles Deluxe had become the leading brand with 27% of the market following many years during which they dominated the market in terms of spending, primarily on advertising.

During the past five years, sales promotion has become an increasingly important marketing tool. In 1969, 90% of Concorn's volume moves at a dealing rate of 50 cents per case. There are no clear data about whether as high a percentage of competitor tonnage moves under a deal. About 40 cents per case is spent on cents off promotions which are not typically supported by media advertising.

There is some indication that Concorn technology has not kept pace with the industry and that Concorn may have a marginal product disadvantage.

Ingredient costs have been rising causing a deterioration in our margin. In the past Concorn has felt that these rising costs could not be passed on to the consumer given the highly competitive nature of the market.

While ad tests show Concorn advertising to be of equal quality to competition and perhaps marginally superior, awareness studies show the leading brand to be getting credit with consumers for the principal product benefits claimed by Concorn.

The following are the 1969 share of market and media expenditure data:

|  | Share (Percent) | Media $ Million |
| --- | --- | --- |
| Concorn | 16 | 1.5 |
| Gambles Deluxe | 30 | 3.5 |
| Julia Child | 20 | 2.5 |
| Private label | 25 | — |
| All others | 9 | — |

| Plan vs. Actual | Plan (000) | Actual (000) |
| --- | --- | --- |
| Market | 41,000 | 40,800 |
| Share | .17 | .157 |
| Sales volume | 6,970 | 6,406 |
| Sales $ | 36,592 | 33,629 |
| price 5.25 case (.55 per pkg. retail) | | |
| Gross contribution margin unit | 12,615 | 11,466 |
| | (1.81) | (1.79) |
| Overhead | 2,000 | 2,000 |
| Gross margin | 10,615 | 9,466 |
| Advertising | 2,000 | 1,500 |
| Promotion | 5,500 | 5,783 |
| Net operating profit | 3,115 | 2,183 |

Which product do you want to consider
$ Instant Puddings*
HISTORICAL FILE

|  | 1965 | 1966 | 1967 | 1968 | 1969 |
|---|---|---|---|---|---|
| Market (cases)......... | 39,000 | 40,000 | 40,600 | 40,800 | 40,800 |
| Share................. | .192 | .1849999 | .16 | .165 | .1569999 |
| Price................. | 5.25 | 5.25 | 5.25 | 5.25 | 5.25 |
| Gross C margin......... | 1.9 | 1.87 | 1.839999 | 1.809999 | 1.79 |
| Sales volume (cases)...... | 7,488 | 7,400 | 6,496 | 6,732 | 6,406 |
| Sales $................. | 39,312 | 38,850 | 34,104 | 35,343 | 33,629 |
| Gross C margin......... | 14,227 | 13,838 | 11,953 | 12,185 | 11,466 |
| Overhead.............. | 2,160 | 2,160 | 2,100 | 2,100 | 2,000 |
| Gross margin........... | 12,067 | 11,678 | 9,853 | 10,085 | 9,466 |
| Advertising............. | 2,114 | 2,105 | 1,561 | 1,610 | 1,500 |
| Promotion.............. | 5,028 | 5,032 | 5,101 | 5,500 | 5,783 |
| Net operating profit...... | 4,925 | 4,541 | 3,191 | 2,975 | 2,183 |

|  | 1970 | 1971 | 1972 | 1973 | 1974 |
|---|---|---|---|---|---|
| Market................. | 41,559.98 | 41,999.98 | 42,439,98 | 42,879.98 | 43,319.98 |
| Share................. | .145 | .136 | .127 | .118 | .109 |
| Price................. | 5.25 | 5.25 | 5.25 | 5.25 | 5.25 |
| Gross C margin......... | 1.757999 | 1.73 | 1.702 | 1.674 | 1.646 |
| Overhead/constant....... | 1,990 | 1,952 | 1,914 | 1,876 | 1.838 |
| Advertising constant...... | 1,261.1 | 1,088.8 | 916.5 | 744.2 | 571.8999 |
| Promotion constant....... | 5,882.191 | 6,079.992 | 6,277.789 | 6,475.59 | 6,673.391 |

## PLANNING BASE P/L

|  | 1970 | 1971 | 1972 | 1973 | 1974 |
|---|---|---|---|---|---|
| Sales volume.................. | 6,018 | 5,704 | 5,381 | 5,051 | 4,713 |
| Sales $........................ | 31,594 | 29,944 | 28,252 | 26,519 | 24,744 |
| Gross C margin................ | 10,579 | 9,867 | 9,159 | 8,456 | 7,758 |
| Overhead..................... | 1,990 | 1,952 | 1,914 | 1,876 | 1,838 |
| Gross margin.................. | 8,589 | 7,915 | 7,245 | 6,580 | 5,920 |
| Advertising................... | 1,261 | 1,089 | 917 | 744 | 572 |
| Promotion.................... | 5,882 | 6,080 | 6,278 | 6,476 | 6,673 |
| Net operating profit........... | 1,446 | 746 | 51 | −640 | −1,325 |

NOTE: To all figures except those in dollars and percentages add 000.

## INSTANT BREAKFASTS

### Product History

Concorn entered the instant breakfast market in 1964, correctly anticipating the growth trend in that segment of the food market. At that time,
the major competitors in the market were the first national brands—

Paulicci's Best with 40%, Obrien with 20% and a number of local or regional brands concentrated in major metropolitan areas—New York, Miami Beach, Los Angeles, Chicago, and Philadelphia.

By 1967, the growth trend in the market and the attractive margins had led the major chains to introduce private labels (store brand) with strong local advertising and shelf space support. Paulicci's Best initiated a price cut—which the other brands followed—in an effort to reduce the price spread between the advertised and private label brands.

In addition, each brand reacted to the 1967 market situation in different ways. Paulicci's Best de-emphasized sales promotion, and increased its advertising. Obrien held to its historical pattern of promotion and advertising spending.

Concorn's response to the situation is reflected in the historical file— a strong emphasis on sales promotion and sales execution efforts to get in-store trade support.

The following are the 1969 share of market and media expenditure data:

|  | Share (Percent) | Media $ Million |
|---|---|---|
| Concorn | 10.0 | 2.0 |
| Paulicci's | 42.5 | 7.5 |
| Obrien | 18.0 | 4.0 |
| Private label | 21.0 | |
| All others | 8.5 | |

Product quality and advertising claims are effectively equal for all brands.

| | 1969 | |
|---|---|---|
| Plan vs. Actual | Plan (000) | Actual (000) |
| Market | 36,500 | 36,500 |
| Share | .105 | .10 |
| Sales volume | 3,832 | 3,650 |
| Sales $ | 15,711 | 14,945 |
| price 4.59 case (.49 retail) | | |
| Gross cont. margin | 8,430 | 8,030 |
| unit | (2.20) | (2.20) |
| Overhead | 1,500 | 1,500 |
| Gross margin | 6,930 | 6,530 |
| Advertising | 2,000 | 2,000 |
| Promotion | 3,400 | 3,600 |
| Net operating profit | 1,530 | 930 |

Which product do you want to consider
$ Instant Puddings
HISTORICAL FILE

|  | 1965 | 1966 | 1967 | 1968 | 1969 |
|---|---|---|---|---|---|
| Market.................. | 21,000 | 24,500 | 28,900 | 32,700 | 36,500 |
| Share................... | 8.999997E–02 | .105 | .105 | 9.999996E–02 | 9.999996E–02 |
| Price................... | 4.599999 | 4.599999 | 4.099999 | 4.099999 | 4.099999 |
| Gross C margin.......... | 2.599999 | 2.599999 | 2.2 | 2.2 | 2.2 |
| Sales volume............ | 1,890 | 2,572 | 3,034 | 3,270 | 3,650 |
| Sales $................. | 8,694 | 11,833 | 12,441 | 13,407 | 14,965 |
| Gross C margin.......... | 4,914 | 6,688 | 6,676 | 7,194 | 8,030 |
| Overhead................ | 1,500 | 1,500 | 1,500 | 1,500 | 1,500 |
| Gross margin............ | 3,414 | 5,188 | 5,176 | 5,694 | 6,530 |
| Advertising............. | 2,000 | 2,000 | 2,000 | 2,000 | 2,000 |
| Promotion............... | 1,420 | 1,700 | 3,030 | 3,200 | 3,600 |
| Net operating profit.... | − 5 | 1,488 | 146 | 494 | 930 |

## INPUT PROJECTIONS FOR USE IN BASE PLAN

|  | Line Number | 1970 | 1971 | 1972 | 1973 | 1974 |
|---|---|---|---|---|---|---|
| Market.................. | 1 | 40,479.93 | 44,399.98 | 48,319.98 | 52,239.98 | 56,159.98 |
| Share................... | 2 | .10399997 | .1059999 | .107 | .109 | .11 |
| Price................... | 3 | 3.849999 | 3.7 | 3.549999 | 3.4 | 3.25 |
| Gross C margin.......... | 4 | 2 | 1.879999 | 1.759999 | 1.639999 | 1.52 |
| Overhead/unit........... | 5 | 0 | 0 | 0 | 0 | 0 |
| Overhead/constant....... | 6 | 1,500 | 1,500 | 1,500 | 1,500 | 1,500 |
| Advertising/unit........ | 7 | 0 | 0 | 0 | 0 | 0 |
| Advertising constant.... | 8 | 2,000 | 2,000 | 2,000 | 2,000 | 2,000 |
| Promotion/unit.......... | 9 | 0 | 0 | 0 | 0 | 0 |
| Promotion constant...... | 10 | 4,347.992 | 4,933.992 | 5,519.992 | 6,105.992 | 6,691.988 |

Do you wish to override any projections "no"

## PLANNING BASE P/L

|  | 1970 | 1971 | 1972 | 1973 | 1974 |
|---|---|---|---|---|---|
| Sales volume............ | 4,230 | 4,706 | 5,194 | 5,694 | 6,206 |
| Sales $................. | 16,286 | 17,414 | 18,440 | 19,360 | 20,168 |
| Gross C margin.......... | 8,460 | 8,848 | 9,142 | 9,338 | 9,433 |
| Overhead................ | 1,500 | 1,500 | 1,500 | 1,500 | 1,500 |
| Gross margin............ | 6,960 | 7,348 | 7,642 | 7,838 | 7,933 |
| Advertising............. | 2,000 | 2,000 | 2,000 | 2,000 | 2,000 |
| Promotion............... | 4,348 | 4,934 | 5,520 | 6,106 | 6,692 |
| Net operating profit.... | 612 | 414 | 122 | −268 | −759 |

Specify response coefficient to be used for each of 5 years.

# Far West Laboratory

John Hemphill, director of the Far West Laboratory for Educational Research and Development, stated in the introduction of the laboratory's 1972 annual report:

In 1972, more than in any other year of its brief history, the laboratory experienced its own "great upheaval" as the staff prepared for the long-anticipated move to a new facility in San Francisco and as the National Institute of Education (NIE) assumed a major role in determining the future direction of federally funded educational research and development activities. To cope with this accelerated and intensified change tempo, the laboratory must avoid "fixed ideas" yet still maintain its long-term goal of meeting the constant demand for renewal.

He went on to state that the laboratory had to find answers to a variety of questions concerning laboratory governance, objectives, and organization as a result of the formation of the new federal institute (NIE). Such questions included, "Could the laboratory remain sufficiently 'inner-directed' to carry out work . . . believed vital for children? Could the laboratory influence federal policy so that it might remain capable of acting, rather than simply reacting? Could the laboratory cope reasonably successfully with the value structures of the various review panels that were instrumental in determining NIE's 'program-buying' priorities? Could the laboratory shape effective and programmatic efforts of its own by fitting together funding from disparate sources?"

The Far West Laboratory for Educational Research and Development was created in the spring of 1966 through a joint powers agreement to which major educational agencies within California and Nevada were signatories. It was one of 20 regional educational laboratories established by the Elementary and Secondary Education Act (Title IV, Public Law 89–10) to form a national network. Each of the laboratories shared the

Reprinted from *Stanford Business Cases 1973* with the permission of the publisher, Graduate School of Business, Stanford University. Copyright © 1973 by the Board of Trustees of the Leland Stanford Junior University.

general objective of bringing the benefits derived from educational research and development into school classrooms as soon as possible.

At the time of its founding the lab's primary mission was stated as ". . . the rapid development of *viable educational alternatives* for improving classroom learning, based on the expanding knowledge generated by educational research." The "viable educational alternatives" meant "a practice or procedure . . . known to be of value for the achievement of an educational objective that differs in some significant way from a practice or procedure currently being employed."

The laboratory founders went on to state that:

Educational development entails two major phases in the creation of an end product: (1) *fully ready for operational use,* and (2) proven effective by an appropriate program of field testing. In the past, institutions engaged chiefly in research have rarely developed products ready for operational use and are concerned with development only to the point required to test research hypotheses. By analogy to industrial organizations the laboratory is a "product development laboratory." Its major directive is not to conduct original basic research but to synthesize research findings toward the innovation design, development, and field testing of products useful in education. Thus, the laboratory, working from promising new ideas derived from educational research, will complete a wide variety of tasks required to produce *educational alternatives* for use within the school setting.

A second, but less important, objective was that of dissemination. Thus, the laboratory committed itself to assist in the implementation and adoption of educational alternatives in schools. Its role was viewed as necessarily limited to providing objective information about alternatives.

## RATIONALE FOR GOVERNMENT ACTION IN SETTING UP THE LABORATORY SYSTEM

A major reason for creating the laboratory system was the increasing cost of education and the concern for improvement and efficiency. In 1962 the United States spent approximately $30.4 billion on education; expenditures in 1975 were projected at $82.1 billion in terms of 1962 dollars. Educational R&D was conceived of as a major strategy for improving the rate of return on educational investments. But despite the spending of many hundreds of millions of dollars during the 1950's and early 1960's, only a small fraction of the output had found its way into practice.

The utilization of the findings from educational research during the 1950's and 1960's was minuscule and to many observers not surprising, given the highly fragmented nature of the education industry. The several hundred universities performing research were typically concerned with testing highly specific learning hypotheses and not with the development of packaged learning systems. Indeed, universities did not profess to do otherwise, nor did they have the resources to do so. On the market side there were over 19,000 local school boards, tens of thousands of school administrators, and over 2 million teachers. The problem of linking fragmentary—often esoteric—research findings with a market of this size and complexity was overwhelming.

## FUNDING AND PRODUCT DEVELOPMENT
## AT FAR WEST LABORATORY

Over the years the organization of the laboratory had evolved to a point where in 1972 it was comprised of five relatively autonomous divisions and an administrative unit. Each division was headed by an associate laboratory director who typically had received his or her doctorate in education. With but few exceptions their staffs consisted of persons with graduate degrees in the behavioral sciences; many had backgrounds which included classroom teaching and school administration. Few had any experience in programmatic research or development before joining the laboratory.

The projects undertaken by each division depended largely on the initiative and aggressiveness of its associate director. The amount of money available to each was largely a function of the project requests developed, the documentation supporting the request for funds, and the division's past record of productivity. A problem which was faced by all of the divisions was the need to learn how to engineer prototype learning packages. Typically such work was carried out by divisional staff personnel.

Annually the laboratory compacted its funding requests (by projects) into an overall document which was presented to the U.S. Office of Education—a major organizational unit within the Department of Health, Education and Welfare. An override of 27 percent was added to the total project funds requested to pay for laboratory overhead. Once approved, these funds became available to the laboratory and were administered by the director. While he could—and often did—make some changes in the allocation of funds among divisions from what was contained in the request, he typically made only minor changes.

In addition to this basic fund the laboratory also received specific project funding from a variety of sources. In 1972 the laboratory's budget was $5,985,000 of which the Office of Education provided $4,696,000; the National Institute of Health, $569,000; the Carnegie Corporation, $254,000; the Office of Child Development, $226,000; and "other," $240,000. The funding by divisions for the years 1971–72 is shown below.

Major projects typically extended over several years. Most products developed by the laboratory went through the following prescribed steps: (1) collection of research and information; (2) planning the specific objectives or behavioral changes to be achieved and developing

| Division | 1972 | 1971 |
|---|---|---|
| Teacher education............... | $ 889,000 | $ 953,000 |
| Education systems............... | 1,750,000 | 1,733,000 |
| Early childhood.................. | 1,538,000 | 1,306,000 |
| Renewing home-school linkage...... | 320,000 | 221,000 |
| Information/utilization............ | 1,201,000 | 383,000 |
| Administration unit.............. | 287,000 | 505,000 |

a tentative course sequence; (3) developing preliminary product form including, for example, scripts, teacher handbooks, evaluation forms, instructional tapes, etc.; (4) preliminary field testing and evaluation of results; (5) product revision; (6) main field testing; (7) operational product revision; (8) operational field testing; (9) final product revision; (10) dissemination and distribution; (11) report preparation; and (12) implementation and monitoring of results.

By the end of 1972 the laboratory had produced approximately 200 developmental and knowledge products since its inception. One of the most important was a series of minicourses developed by the teacher education division at a cost well in excess of $1.5 million. Minicourses utilized microteaching—an adaption of videotape recording technology to teacher preparation developed by professors Robert Bush and Dwight Allen of Stanford University. A single minicourse provided all the instructional material which was required for a teacher to learn a specific set of teaching skills; e.g., how to use questions effectively in a discussion lesson. Some seven "courses" had been developed and field tested with good results.

Each such course consisted of filmed instructional materials and co-ordination handbooks containing evaluation forms and follow-up lessons. A minicourse required a teacher to devote 55 to 75 minutes a day for seven to nine days to microteaching with small groups of students, practicing the skills he had seen demonstrated on film. In this way the teacher could practice his skills under a simpler and less demanding situation than prevails in the full classroom. In each session he would videotape his performance and later evaluate it. Three main steps were involved:

1. The trainee views a filmed instructional lesson in which one to three specific teaching skills are described and illustrated. The trainee then views the practice model lesson which shows a model teacher conducting a lesson in which each technique is demonstrated several times.

2. The trainee prepares a lesson and uses it with five or six of his own pupils in a microteaching situation. The trainee records this lesson on videotape and upon completion replays it and evaluates the replay using special evaluation forms.

3. The trainee replans the microtech lesson and reteaches this lesson to another group of pupils. This is also recorded on videotape and again the trainee evaluates his performance.

Over the years Washington had not funded the development of the laboratory manufacturing and distribution resources required to make the minicourses (and any other lab products) available to schools that would use them. Thus, it was necessary to seek a commercial publisher to undertake the job of manufacturing, distributing, and installing the finished tested products. Although the course series was made generally available to publishers, only one proposal was received—from Macmillan Educational Services. The contract provided for Macmillan to sell the "system" under a 10% royalty agreement.

Film prices ranged from $1,145 to $1,575 per minicourse, but all could be rented for a six-week period for about $200 per course. The teacher's handbook cost $1.90 each and a coordinator's handbook, $3.80. To use the minicourse system required a complete videotape recording system that ranged in cost from $1,400 to $1,800 depending on the number of microphones and type of equipment used. In its publicity releases about the minicourses the laboratory suggested that state departments of education, extension divisions of universities, and local school districts buy the system and use it on a cooperative basis, thereby substantially reducing the costs per teacher trained. By the end of 1972 Macmillan reported selling 326 minicourse films, renting 102 films, and selling 15,702 handbooks.

During parts of 1971 and 1972 the utilization division of the laboratory established and operated a number of demonstration sites for minicourses in such major population centers as Los Angeles, New York, Pennsylvania, Chicago, Wisconsin, Massachusetts, and Washington, D.C. A grant of $305,000 from the National Center for Educational Communication made such work possible. It was estimated that the seven demonstration sites reached a total of 4,638 individuals. Minicourse centers sponsored by the Teacher Corps were established in 1972 at three teacher-training institutions: Livingston University (Alabama), Kansas State Teachers College (Emporia, Kansas), and State University College at Buffalo (New York).

### Other Products

A feeling for the types of other products developed by the laboratory can be obtained by referring to the laboratory's 1972 annual report which describes accomplishments by divisions.

Division I—Teacher Education ($889,000)

In addition to continuing work on the minicourses described above, the division conducted operational field tests on a variety of additional products including "Content Analysis of Textbooks for Black Students," "Interaction Analysis," and "Discussing Controversial Issues." A third set of teacher-training "Protocol Materials" began its development cycle.

The Dental Health Center of San Francisco provided funds to adapt Minicourse I into a new training course for instructors and dental schools. The staff began its own divisional publication series by collecting, cataloging, and making available reports, evaluation manuals, and research papers. Several senior staff members attended meetings in Europe at which the "transformation" of minicourses into new cultures and languages was begun. Work also continued at home on a framework of basic class skills that appear to constitute the irreducible minimum for any beginning teacher.

Division II—Educational Systems ($1,750,000)

This division is organized into three individual programmatic efforts: educational management; instructional and training systems; and employer-based career education. The educational management program completed its first training unit for middle-echelon administrator training. "Determining Instructional Purposes" (the "purposing" training package) includes three units: "Setting Goals," "Analyzing Problems," and "Deriving Objectives." The training time per unit ranges from 10 to 18 hours. Each unit is self-contained so training can be carried out wherever participants can gather in small teams. Additional training packages, covering "Planning" and "Evaluation," continued under development in this program.

The first released product of the training systems program was completed with funds provided by the National Center for Educational Communication, after original support from the research training branch of the National Center for Educational Research and Development. This instructional package, "The Educational Information Consultant: Skills in Disseminating Education Information," has already been widely used in workshops, institutes, graduate courses, and extension programs. This program is also responsible for the planning, management, development, and evaluation work that undergirds the Far West Development, Dissemination, and Evaluation (DD&E) Consortium, a group of Bay Area agencies including American Institutes for Research, California State University (San Francisco), Educational Testing Service, the Human Resources Research Organization, Technicon, Inc., the San Mateo Community Colleges, Stanford Research Institute, and the laboratory. With funds provided by the Researcher Training Task Force (NIE), the consortium has been developing, field-testing, and evaluating a functional competence training system for professional and preprofessional R&D personnel. In addition, an experimental doctoral program was about to begin at the University of California, Berkeley, for a handful of students already experienced in DD&E practices.

The division began the design of an R&D training information system and issued its first prototype newsletter to practitioners of this specialized field. The staff also designed a DD&E manpower survey for the Office of Education and provided support for DD&E management development for the National Institute of Education.

The laboratory's Employer-Based Career Education Program, headquartered in a downtown Oakland office building, enrolled its first pilot group of

14 high school students in the fall of the year. Arrangements were made with a widely varied group of East Bay employers so that the youngsters would be able to sample a broad number of occupations in close conjunction with their other educational experiences. More than 50 resource people, working in a variety of positions, have volunteered to guide individual students as they sample the world of work. At the learning center a team of curriculum experts, student advisors, and coordinators help the students with their individualized learning programs.

## Division III—Early Childhood Education ($1,538,000)

The Responsive Program continued to train program advisors, teachers, and teaching assistants in Head Start and Follow Through communities from coast to coast. Teacher training notebooks were released on an interim basis for national distribution, along with most of the other in-service training materials, after several years of successful field testing. Simultaneously the staff moved ahead with development of self-contained competency units for early childhood personnel. When completed, these units will constitute a flexible training system for all participants in the Responsive Education Program and for those in other early childhood model programs who wish to adopt them.

The Head Start program, funded by the Office of Child Development, and the Follow Through program, funded by the U.S. Office of Education, began to look toward national dissemination and utilization stages in accord with federal priorities. The staff visited a number of states to explain the Responsive Program's requirements and implications if and when adopted statewide.

A report on the evaluation of five planned variation communities was completed at the end of the year, and work began on the editing of a collection of readings dealing with the improvement of educational opportunities for ethnic minority children.

With national release of the preschool Parent/Child Toy-Lending Library, the division shifted its efforts to field testing of additional parent/child program materials for children of ages five to nine. Funding for toy library development work was provided by the Carnegie Corporation of New York. *A Guide to Securing and Installing the Parent/Child Toy-Lending Library* was published by the Superintendent of Documents.

At year's end a proposal was being negotiated for the production of filmed training materials to be used by the satellite project of the Federation of Rocky Mountain States and the Education Commission of the States in Denver. In May the laboratory had withdrawn from operation of the National Demonstration Day-Care Center at the U.S. Office of Education building in Washington, D.C.

## Division IV—Renewing Home–School Linkage ($320,000)

The division shifted its major emphasis from development to basic research, after being encouraged by the National Institute of Education to generate an entirely new overall program plan. The programmatic thrust will henceforth focus on research into communicative competence, as perceived through theoretical approaches to language development and their implications for the learning of reading skills by ethnic minority children.

In cooperation with Division III the staff devoted some of its efforts to studying parent-school relations in a number of planned variation communities. Additionally, the division prepared a report on parental preferences and criteria to be used in the evaluation of educational products and processes.

Also, in the course of determining the validity of locus of control scales, the staff began to develop diagnostic instruments that could help to assess the life-control beliefs of low-income urban black children. Preliminary development of a prototype social studies core curriculum ensemble, with accompanying teacher-training manual, was interrupted by the necessity of reformulating the long-range goals of the renewing home-school linkage program.

## THE UTILIZATION DIVISION

This division was formed in mid-1971. Its origins, however, went back several years, and, to understand fully its mission and strategy, one would have to review a certain amount of laboratory history, as well as changing attitudes among administrators in Washington.

As was noted earlier, the laboratory initially operated on the premise that its dissemination role was limited to providing objective information —both descriptive and evaluative—about the products it developed. Over time it became increasingly clear that such an awareness model was not succeeding; i.e., it was not obtaining utilization of its products.

During the late 1960's and early 1970's the signals from Washington on the role of the laboratories in diffusion and implementation were confusing and contradictory. Increasingly Washington was saying to the labs, "Get more utilization," but, in the next breath, "Dissemination is not your job." But regardless of the latter the labs felt they were evaluated largely on the impact their programs had on the real world. As one lab director summed up the situation:

Damn it! They tell us not to do so much implementation . . . it is not our job. They won't give us money for it, at least not through the direct budgets. But then when they come around to check up, the first question out of the evaluator's mouth is how much direct impact we are having on kids in schools. It's crazy; the budgets and the policies don't match the evaluation.[1]

Any discussion by laboratory staff members regarding increasing utilization of its products inevitably raised a number of questions such as, "How much should the lab be concerned about how its products were used?" and "How much control should be exercised over users of the product?" The major goal of the utilization program was to develop systems that deliver educational research and development products to full utilization by the intended users. This general goal can be described in terms of specific goals:

---

[1] J. Victor Baldridge and Rudolph Johnson, "The Impact of Educational R&D Centers and Laboratories: An Analysis of Effective Organizational Strategies" (Stanford, Calif.: Stanford University, May 1972), p. 23.

1. The program will invent, test, and implement systems that deliver the tested products of the laboratory to a national market.
2. The program will extend these delivery systems to insure utilization of other tested products (nonlaboratory products).
3. The program will provide others with the knowledge, methods and systems of delivery developed by the laboratory so that the utilization of all R&D products can be improved.
4. The program will provide a utilization planning service that will facilitate the preparation of educational products so as to maximize their utilization potential.

Dr. Hutchins, the director of the new division, noted that it was necessary to translate the mission of the utilization program into more specific terms than those used above. He felt that it was essential that the *functions* of the development-dissemination-utilization *process* be understood. Not all of these functions would be assigned to his division; some would be the province of the other divisions (the product-development programs). The more essential functions he cited were market analysis and projection, finalizing the final product, dissemination of information to create awareness about the product and its functions, distribution, installation, postpurchase servicing, and control and monitoring.

Hutchins proposed three models as alternative ways of structuring the relationships between the new division and other programs within the laboratory. He summarized his views on these as follows:

Three alternatives, "pure" models, are proposed to describe the relationship between the utilization program and the rest of the laboratory. One would be the "inventor" model, another the "market" model, a third the "service" or "developer" model. Mixed models can be derived from combinations of these three ways of projecting the relationship between utilization and the rest of the laboratory.

*1. The Inventor Model.* The strength of this model is the inventor's freedom to explore and perfect his ideas to the fullest without heavy concern for the ambiguities of an everchanging marketplace. The researchers and creators would not need to be market analysts, communicators, or salesmen. The weakness of the model is brought about by the high risk that an inventor's product could never be marketed: because the initial target was never there, because the market changed as the product developed, or because the product itself was not designed in a way that permitted full utilization.

*2. The Marketing Model.* From the inventor's point of view, the marketing model is a case of the tail wagging the dog. It is based upon the idea that no product should be undertaken until a successful marketing effort can be envisioned. This model places the initiative for starting a product in the hands of a market analyst rather than in the hands of a product developer.

It is easy to overdraw this model to the point of ludicrousness. However, it has virtues and a practical point of view that are appealing: It minimizes the risk of developing products that are ill-conceived from a utilization point of view. It separates the talents required for marketing from those demanded for development. Under this model the utilization program would be responsible for defining a need and monitoring the development to insure conformity to the realities of the user.

3. *The Service or Developer Model.* The approach suggested by this model is to assign all of the functions to a single, all-encompassing management system responsible for all aspects of development. The utilization program would be a service agency providing the information and technology required for delivery. The nature of all services would be specified and controlled by the development system. The appeal of this model is great. It certainly represents a "systems view" of the development process. If properly and efficiently executed, it could result in a very powerful plan. There are also drawbacks to this model, however. First, there are few—if any—who now possess the capability of organizing and managing such a system. Considerable training, as well as a new management model for development programs, would be required. Furthermore, the "developer" model does not provide comfortably for the concept of independent audit or accountability. The other models are, to some extent, "conflict" or "counter-advocate" models that possess an inherent kind of independent auditing. The developer model would require a carefully delineated set of objective check points that would detect errors in the early stages of a product's development.

*The Recommended Plan: A Mixed Model.* The recommended plan is a mixed one. It is based upon some of the strongest features of each model but attempts to deal realistically with the most powerful of the existing constraints. These constraints include the following: the pressure of strong, highly motivated program personnel who would be reluctant to lose control of the conceptualization and development of products; the lack of utilization experience with R&D products; and the need to remain somewhat flexible to account for differences in the focus and style of the laboratory's products. In terms of the laboratory's development cycle the following model is the recommended one.

During the initial conceptualization, planning, preliminary development and testing, the "service" models will be used. The product development programs will be responsible for all the planning for utilization. The utilization program will provide market analysis and product formulation services when requested, although the programs will not be required to use these services. The only constraint upon the programs comes from the laboratory's management. It is recommended that the nature of this control be as follows:

The laboratory's management *must* hold the product development programs responsible for the development of a utilization plan *prior to the initiation of main form development.* This plan should be reviewed by someone whom the program director feels is competent in the area of utilization. At the discretion of the product development program's director this planning or critiquing can involve the product utilization program. The plan and critique should be made available to the laboratory's management, including the director of utilization. The decision to accept the plan and to be main product development rests with the director of the product development program—subject, of course, to review by the laboratory director or those to whom he would delegate responsibility.

By the conclusion of the main field test the dissemination plan should be revised and agreed to by *both* the product development and the utilization programs—if the product development program anticipates turning the product over to utilization at any future point in the product's life. Stated more directly, the utilization program shall have a determining voice in the final preparation of a utilization plan for each product. The plan shall be developed before any operational development and field testing begin—unless the product development program wishes to assume full responsibility for ultimate use of the product by its target audience.

If a plan cannot be developed to insure the utilization of a product, then development work will be terminated in a manner that will capitalize on the experience and contribute to the state of the art of development.

Operational development and field testing require participation of the utilization program. In fact, at the product developer's discretion the utilization program can actually carry out this field test.

The final development of the product and the selection of agents for later states of utilization shall be the responsibility of the utilization program. If not assigned sooner, the product officially becomes the responsibility of the utilization program at the time it completes its operational testing and is accepted for release by laboratory management. (Unless, of course, the utilization program has not been involved in the preparation of the utilization plan; in this case, the product development program retains responsibility.)

During the remainder of 1971 Hutchin's division spent $383,000. The 1971 annual report reported on the division's activities as follows:

To encourage and support national installation and utilization of minicourses, the laboratory obtained a one-year grant from the National Center for Educational Communication to establish and operate a number of demonstration sites in major population centers such as Los Angeles, New York, Pennsylvania, Chicago, Wisconsin, Massachusetts, and Washington, D.C.

In conjunction with CEMREL, Inc., and Northwest Regional Educational Laboratory, staff members formed a joint dissemination program that enables field representatives of the three agencies to provide information about and to demonstrate each other's products for educators anywhere in the nation.

A demonstration project for division II's information products carried staff members to Seattle, Chicago, New York, and Florida. Funding was supplied by the National Center for Educational Communication.

For the Office of Civil Defense the division is investigating the best means of introducing "survival" concepts into the curricula of grades 7–9 of the nation's public schools. This work dovetails with the building of an alternative utilization model program that is to develop new techniques, alliances, and channels for full utilization of R&D output.

Product presentations were made at a number of major national professional meetings: AASA, AERA, ASCD, NEA, NCTE, etc. A computer program was written and tested which will monitor the effectiveness of utilization of laboratory products; at the same time it will produce on a regular schedule a guide to selected users of those products and will integrate all the various types of feedback needed to maintain close communication between the laboratory and its various publics.

The division assisted in negotiations for the manufacture and distribution of completed laboratory products. As educational development becomes more sophisticated, the tasks of making available to educators the various new actionable options have increased in both magnitude and complexity. Such proliferation and diversity have already caused the laboratory to budget significant resources and talent for its fledgling utilization division.

By early 1972 the division had grown to more than 30 people, chiefly because the information component of division II (educational systems) was transferred to Hutchins. At that time the division was renamed the information/utilization division. In March 1972 the division produced a manual describing its basic plan for the next five years. The estimated costs for this plan were $11 million of which $3,207,500 was to be spent in 1972. The plan called for all of these funds to be obtained from the federal government—about half from the Office of Education and half from other federal agencies. The plan was to be accomplished by taking on three major projects—information, installation, and product planning. (See Exhibits 1–4.) Hutchins felt that if these requests were funded his unit would be able to demonstrate to the other divisions and to other labs the viability of a well-reasoned utilization program.

### EXHIBIT 1
#### Program Resume

Program Code: R   3   6   F   3

Institution: Far West Laboratory          Date Prepared: March 1972

Program title: Information/Utilization

Begin and end dates of (proposed) program: 1972–1977

Staff member in charge: C. L. Hutchins

Resume:

This program is designed to get existing R&D products out and used. We believe people need more and better information than they have about these products. They need more access to the products and associated training, and we all need better information on how extensively these products are now being used and what techniques have been most effective in getting them used. Thus, the program has two primary goals:

To help people *know* more about educational development and research (R&D) and exemplary practice in education.

To help increase the use of R&D and evaluated exemplary practice.

In order to carry out the work of the program, three major components will be used: (1) the *information component* which focuses on specific information products and systems and the technology to develop them, (2) the *installation component* to provide demonstrations and installation support for selected R&D products through a cooperative network of R&D agencies and regional service agencies, and (3) the *product planning, production and monitoring component* to provide market analyses, utilization planning, and monitoring reports of feedback from users of R&D products. Each of these components will produce a series of products that will impact on the problems of getting R&D into the "pipeline" of use by schools, teachers, and children.

## EXHIBIT 2

### Component Resume

Component Code: R   3   6   F   3   C

Institution: Far West Laboratory                Date Prepared: March 1972

Program title: Information/Utilization

Component title: Information

Begin and end dates of (proposed) component: 1972–1977

Staff member in charge: S. Glovinsky

Resume:

The information component is targeted for user-based information centers, educational linking agents, and educational practitioners, and its objective is to generate knowledge about R&D programs and validated exemplary practices.

The need for practitioner-oriented information on R&D innovations has been well-documented in the literature on information science and educational change. Our experience in development and testing of a number of information products concurred with findings from the literature. In addition, we found that the products developed by the information component have been successful in generating a level of awareness and knowledge about R&D innovations and in facilitating decision making regarding the adoption of innovations.

The major activities of the information component are:

To engineer practitioner-oriented information software about R&D programs and other validated, exemplary practices.

To create support for linking agents and information centers in improving educational practice.

To develop the technology for input, processing, and output of practitioner-oriented R&D information and to deliver that technological capability to other information processing agencies. The outcomes from the efforts of this component will be products that provide awareness about R&D alternatives and aid in rational decision making about these alternatives. Examples of these products are: newsletters, brochures, state of the art documents, manipulatives, information units, simulation units, transportable awareness workshops, selective profile systems, user guides, curriculum catalogs, and compilations for information centers.

## EXHIBIT 3

### Component Resume

Component code: R   3   6   F   3   D

Institution: Far West Laboratory          Date prepared: March 1972

Program title: Information/Utilization

Component title: Installation

Begin and end dates of (proposed) component: 1972–1977

Staff member in charge: R. Bateman

Resume:

The objective of this component is to provide demonstration, distribution, training, and installation support for selected R&D products to be used in a cooperative network of R&D agencies and intermediate service agencies. It is essential that more efficient and effective means of communications between R&D product producers and users be established. More productive working relationships with various linking agencies seems to be the most viable alternative. Keeping this in mind, the component will play a major role in establishing such a cooperative network based on the dissemination consortium currently existing between FWL, CEMREL, Inc., NWREL, and Wisconsin R&D Center. The number of such developmental agencies contributing to the network is projected for 30 by November 1977. Starting with 20 selected intermediate linking agencies to be working in the network in 1973, the number of such agencies projected for 1977 will be 500.

The component will engage in a number of activities in support of the network. It will:

Help train network members in developing effective publication and distribution technologies.

Help devise training programs for linking agents in the product dissemination and installation area.

Develop and test role definitions for people who will serve as product specialists or "manufacturer's representatives" for R&D products to linking agencies.

Help devise and implement a management technology for operating and maintaining the network.

The component perceives that several outcomes and/or products will result from the above listed activities. They are:

1. Tested packages for use in training linking agents and/or agencies in developing dissemination and installation skills.
2. Training programs for product specialists or "manufacturer's representatives" for R&D products.
3. The establishment of as many as 30 showcase schools whose curriculum is based on R&D products.
4. The production of printed and audiovisual materials for use by linking agents and agencies for dissemination and installation purposes.
5. A telephone network used to connect R&D agencies with users and linking agents.
6. A model of an information center which can be used by R&D agencies and/or linking agencies to provide visitors with viable descriptions of R&D products and programs.

The component's involvement in these activities will serve to provide those dissemination procedures and materials necessary for in-house purposes as well as service to the emerging network.

### EXHIBIT 4
#### Component Resume

Component code: R   3   6   F   3   E

Institution: Far West Laboratory            Date prepared: March 1972

Program title: Information/Utilization

Component title: Product Planning, Production, and Monitoring

Begin and end dates of (proposed) component: 1972–1977

Staff member in charge: C. L. Hutchins

Resume:

The objective of this component is to maximize the effectiveness of the R&D utilization process. Few resources have been allocated to date to overseeing the utilization of finished products. Now, however, products are increasingly ready for distribution. To accomplish the task of maximizing the utilization process, this component will carry on the following levels of activities:

Provide assistance upon request to product developers to assist in their early planning of products to be developed.

Provide information and technical production advice to developers whose products are ready for production for testing or final release.

Secure information on the use of completed R&D products and feed this information to developers in a form that will assist them in planning for new educational products. A national survey of the use of R&D products will be conducted.

The outcome of the efforts of this component will provide invaluable information to improve the utilization of R&D products. This information will be continued in a variety of studies in the areas of product monitoring, general utilization, cost analysis, data gathering, quality control, and marketing research.

# Institutional Services, Inc.

Institutional Services, Inc. (ISI), a subsidiary of Saga Administrative Corporation (Saga), is headquartered in Menlo Park, California. In early July, 1969, David Reeves, Vice President and General Manager of ISI, was reviewing the progress of this company's first six months of operations. Mr. Reeves was scheduled to report to the Board of Directors at their end of July meeting on progress to date, ISI's prospects for future development, and to recommend, for the Board's approval, a strategy for the company to follow over the next several years.

## Saga's Background

In the spring of 1948 the cafeteria at Hobart College in Geneva, New York, went out of business. Three enterprising Hobart students who were supplementing their G.I. bill with various part time jobs presented a proposal to the dean to reopen and operate the dining hall themselves. Permission was granted and success followed quickly. Based on their record, a neighboring girls' college asked them the following year to take over their food service operation on a contract basis. Further growth and expansion brought the firm's annual sales to over $1 million by 1956. The partnership was dissolved and the business incorporated in 1957, with the three original partners serving as the principal officers of the corporation.

As the firm entered the 1960's, diversification was planned in either or both of two directions. Saga had, by this time, gained considerable expertise—as well as reputation—in institutional food service, but had restricted its operations to colleges and universities. Expansion into other institutional markets was thought feasible, and thus, in 1963 a hospital division was started with the objective of coordinating and channeling the firm's food service expertise into hospitals and other health care

Reprinted from *Stanford Business Cases 1970* with the permission of the publisher, Graduate School of Business, Stanford University. Copyright © 1970 by the Board of Trustees of the Leland Stanford Junior University.

facilities including retirement homes. Because a successful college food service operation required close familiarity with both college financial administration and changing student attitudes, it was thought that Saga could also enter the college market in fields other than food service. Thus, in 1965 a subsidiary company, Scope, was formed to specialize in the design, construction and operation of off-campus student dormitories and residences. In 1968, Saga provided a food service program for 244 colleges and universities in 41 states, the District of Columbia, Canada, and Puerto Rico. In these schools, Saga served about 200,000 students out of a boarding student potential of about 2.5 million.

In early 1967 a Venture Committee, later set up as a development division, was organized to facilitate the carrying out of expansion opportunities. The first completed project was the formation of Le Fromage, a chain of specialty cheeses and gourmet cooking supplies shops, which opened its first store in October, 1967. In November, 1968, Institutional Services was organized as a subsidiary, followed in April, 1969, by the acquisition of Harding-Williams, a Midwestern food service operator specializing in corporate cafeterias and catering. The Harding-Williams acquisition was to provide the organizational nuclei for a horizontal expansion of Saga's food service expertise into the corporate food market. A preliminary step toward vertical integration of food service was taken by entering into a joint venture agreement with General Foods Corporation to manufacture preprepared frozen food products.

In fiscal 1968 the College Division accounted for 92% of Saga's $89.9 million in sales. Scope Corporation was carried on an equity basis, so its minor losses to that date entered the income statement only at the earnings level and did not contribute to the sales figure. The remaining 8% of sales came from the Hospital Division. Harding-Williams was to be accounted for as a purchase rather than pooling of interests, so the fiscal 1969 results would reflect its contribution only from the April acquisition date through the end of the fiscal year in June. An investment advisory service estimated fiscal 1969 Saga sales at $105 million. Their report also forecasted that fiscal 1970 sales would rise to $135 million, with the Harding-Williams and other acquisitions contributing $20 million of this total (see Exhibits 1 and 2 for 1968 income and asset/liability data).

### Formation of ISI

During discussions of diversification possibilities, a consultant to Saga in the fields of materials management and procurement suggested that college purchasing practices were commonly outmoded and inefficient, and were often extremely costly to the institutions in terms of lost opportunities for large savings through modern procurement methods. The consultant argued that better purchasing methods were urgently needed by the institutions Saga served, and the potential savings were great enough to provide a reasonable profit to Saga, as well as to significantly reduce materials costs for the institutions. In preliminary contracts with college financial and purchasing managers, this idea was favorably received, and further discussion and examination of the potential market led to the formation of ISI in October, 1968.

The consultant who initially proposed the idea agreed to devote approximately half of his time to the new company to guide development of its policies and operating plans. The full-time staff was to consist, initially, of a Vice President/General Manager, selected for his knowledge and experience in purchasing management, and a secretary. ISI's initial capital was 1,000 shares of one dollar par value, with Saga holding 85% and the principal officers and Board members holding the remainder. Additional financing was provided by Saga through a line of credit, at one quarter point above the prime rate, for up to $150,000 over the first two years of operation. The corporate charter declared, "the primary business in which this corporation intends to engage is the provision of a service to colleges, universities, hospitals, and other institutions in the area of organized cooperative purchasing."

Beneath these formalities was a simple set of ground rules established for ISI by Saga. ISI was to begin business on November 1, 1968 "as a single product company (consolidated purchasing services) serving two classes of customers: colleges and hospitals." The $150,000 in loan funds could be used over the two-year period to develop that product with either one or both of the customer classes, but ISI was expected to establish a base sufficient to finance operations beyond the two-year period from its own retained earnings. Because of the greater familiarity of the officers with the college market, ISI devoted its initial efforts to this area.

*Consolidated Purchasing.*  Current college purchasing practices suffer from three major problems: lack of standardization, effective negotiation, and size. The standardization problem stems, in part, from the characteristic independence of the academic community and the absence of strong, centralized control over such administrative functions as procurement. For example, each departmental secretary is generally allowed to use the particular mimeograph paper she likes best, while each building superintendent uses the brand of floor wax he considers easiest to apply, etc. A leading purchasing text[1] calls the solution to this problem "simplification" —reducing the number of standard items carried in inventory—and cites the example of a company which saved $67,000 yearly from having standardized the paper towels used throughout its multiplant operations.

Simplification savings come primarily from reduced inventory investment, greater quantity discounts, better competitive prices because of greater unit volume, and reduced clerical and handling costs resulting from the fact that

---

[1] Lamar Lee, Jr., and Donald W. Dobler, *Purchasing and Materials* (New York: McGraw Hill Book Co., 1965).

fewer different items have to be recorded, controlled, received, inspected, and delivered."[2]

If standardization is difficult on a single college campus, the problem would seem hopelessly multiplied in trying to serve a multi-college customer class, but ISI had some hope of resolution. Because brand differences are often minute or nonexistent, brand preference can be attacked in a simplification program by taking samples of "preferred" products, and promising exact duplication under private brand labeling. Actual quality differences must, of course, be recognized, but this can still be done through standardization within each grade level, and through attempting to minimize the number of different levels carried and used. Impetus can be given to this effort by obtaining prices on the desired "standard" products so attractive that the cost differential becomes too great to justify a small quality differential.

The negotiation problem is at least partially due to the inability, or unwillingness, of colleges to pay the salary of really first-rate purchasing personnel. A glance through the classified sections of the *Wall Street Journal* during early 1969 would have revealed salaries offered to purchasing managers of between $15,000–22,000 per year. A survey of 1968–69 college operating practices noted in *College and University Business*[3] reported the average annual salary for purchasing agents in public institutions was $10,604, while private colleges paid only $9,301. Skill in conducting effective negotiations can only be acquired through experience, and negotiating strength is increased by thorough knowledge of the suppliers with whom the bargaining is done. It is only natural to expect that the men with this knowledge and experience will seek the more lucrative industrial positions, resulting too often in a college purchasing manager poorly equipped to do an effective job of negotiating. ISI, with the guidance of its consultant, and with an experienced purchasing manager as its Vice President/General Manager, had, it was thought, the necessary knowledge and experience to offer colleges who participated in the ISI program a savings alternative to "negotiating" skills. Two strategies, in particular, were expected to add greatly to the effectiveness of ISI's negotiations. First, suppliers would be sought who had not previously participated in the college market. ISI could offer such suppliers entrance to a large market with substantially no marketing cost to them. ISI expected to be able to negotiate these marketing cost savings into price reductions for ISI customers. The second approach would be to seek out suppliers with current overcapacity. By operating at full capacity the supplier could allocate his fixed costs over a larger number of units and, therefore, could improve his profits even if he sold the incremental units

---

[2] *Ibid.,* pp. 58–59.

[3] Dennis W. Binning, "1968–69 College Operating Practices Analysis, Part 2," *College and University Business,* Vol. 44, No. 10 (October, 1968).

at a price which covered less than the full cost. ISI planned to utilize this rationale in negotiating for marginal cost pricing from such suppliers.

The third major problem is size, or lack of sufficient purchasing volume to be able to take advantage of quantity discounts. The small college is by far the dominant type of higher educational institution in the U.S.: in the 1965–66 school year 53.2% of all colleges had enrollments of less than 1,000, and another 24.9% fell in the enrollment range of 1,000 to 2,500.[4] Lack of standardization accentuates this problem of low purchasing volume, and the two factors combined virtually preclude the kind of purchasing "muscle" necessary for establishing a strong negotiating position. Although some larger universities have been relatively successful in overcoming these problems, their purchasing effectiveness could be improved upon through buying in still larger quantities. Thus, purchasing of standardized products by an experienced and capable purchasing staff in the large quantities made possible by consolidation of many schools' demands, combine to provide unusual opportunities for reduction of materials costs.

The mechanism which makes consolidated purchasing possible is master purchasing contracts. As practiced by many of the largest corporations (GE, RCA, IBM, for example), a central corporate purchasing office negotiates a large volume order with a supplier of a single item or class of items. These contracts provide four primary benefits to the purchaser.[5] The supplier will usually agree to keep the materials on hand and available for shipment on request from the buyer, thus reducing the buyer's inventory problems. Second, because the supplier is assured of a sizeable volume of business and knows approximate delivery schedules, he can more efficiently schedule his production and marketing efforts thereby reducing his costs in these areas. Through negotiation and competitive bidding, the buyer benefits from these savings through lower costs. A third advantage can be protection against price increases during the term of the contract. Finally, since contracts are negotiated for longer periods of time than if the purchases were made as needed, the buyer spends less time negotiating separate agreements for recurring requirements. The combination of better service and better price obtained through the master contract is generally so dramatic that even though the individual divisions and subsidiaries are not bound to buy against the master contract, they can find no better deal elsewhere. Thus, the volume promised in the contract can be fulfilled even without centralized control over the purchasing functions of the divisions.

In the corporate setting, the operating costs of the central purchasing organization are simply included in the total corporate overhead. Be-

---

[4] U.S. Department of Health, Education and Welfare, Office of Education, *Digest of Educational Statistics, 1967* (Washington, D.C.: U.S. Government Printing Office, 1968).

[5] Lee and Dobler, *op. cit.*, p. 44.

cause ISI would operate as a financially distinct enterprise from the colleges it served, its master contracts would be drawn up differently; i.e., the colleges would pay a nominal membership fee to become affiliated with ISI, and would thereby become entitled to purchase against the master contracts at the contract price. The master contract would not only provide for the lower price to the ISI affiliated colleges, but also for a payment from the supplier to ISI proportional to the volume actually purchased against the contract.[6]

*Competition.* The idea of a buyers' co-operative was not a new one; co-ops have been an especially common device for improving the economic leverage of farmers and individual consumers. Generally these co-ops, rather than pass on their purchasing savings through reduced prices, accumulate the benefits from quantity buying and distribute them periodically in a lump-sum rebate proportional to each member's purchases during the period. When such co-operatives become large enough to require full-time management and staff, the savings often disappear into operating overheads and the co-op members receive neither lower prices nor their rebate. In such an organization there is often very little incentive to cut operating costs and manage efficiently, because any excess costs come out of member's rebates and not the manager's pocket. ISI's founders believed that by reducing prices to the customer so that a relatively small margin was left to ISI, the profit incentive would enable them to operate more efficiently than the traditional co-ops.

The major competitor of ISI in the college market was Educational and Institutional Co-op (E & I Co-op), organized as a nonprofit buyer's co-op. Formed by the National Association of Educational Buyers (NAEB), its services were available only to NAEB member schools. The 1968 annual report of E & I Co-op showed that they had processed $18.2 million of purchasing volume for 1,189 member schools, down from $19.5 million in 1967. Their fees had totaled 5.5% of this volume in 1968, and with a staff of approximately 80 (including a ten-man field service staff) their operating costs were nearly 4.4% of total volume. The remaining 1.1% of volume distributed as rebates would, if spread equally among all 1,189 members, total less than $170 per school. This annual report and other sources known to Saga indicated that E & I had several problems. First, the NAEB tend to be dominated by its big school members, who need the services of E & I Co-op least because of their own economic strength. Second, attractiveness of some of E & I's contracts has been diminished by the fact that they had not dealt with major brand-name producers. Also, it was thought that the size of their staff was excessive. Saga found much sentiment in favor of the certainty of lower prices and no rebate rather than the vagaries of an uncertain and relatively small rebate.

---

[6] The Robinson-Patman Act, which prohibits discriminatory pricing by a seller under certain conditions, specifically excludes educational institutions.

The hospital market was not dominated by any one major factor. Of twenty-some existing purchasing organizations serving this market, the largest was the Hospital Bureau. Organized as an association of local New York hospitals more than 60 years earlier, by 1968, the Hospital Bureau had 750 members in roughly half of the U.S. Their staff of 27 (including one field representative) processed $9–10 million of purchasing volume in 1968. There had been a change in top management a few years earlier, and the Bureau's Board of Directors had begun to include professional businessmen as well as hospital administrators and doctors. These changes seemed to have infused a better management climate and the Hospital Bureau seemed poised for expansion. It was, however, hampered by a lack of capital, and was attempting to finance growth by giving up any form of dividend or rebate distribution and using all retained earnings for expansion.

**The College Market for ISI Services.** College enrollment trends provided a rough measure of the potential for ISI services (see Exhibits 3 and 4 for detailed figures). Total degree credit enrollment increased from 3.05 million students at the beginning of the 1957–58 school year to an estimated 6.35 million in Fall 1967. Recent statistical projections of the Office of Education indicated further increases to 9.7 million by 1977. A significant trend in this growth has been a shift in enrollment toward public institutions. In the 1957–58 school year, 58% of the total enrollment was found in publicly controlled schools, and 42% in private colleges and universities. By 1967 this ratio had changed to 68%–32%, and the corresponding projection for 1977 was 73%–27%. Another marked change has been the growth of the two year colleges. Enrollment in four year schools doubled during the decade 1957 to 1967, while in that period two year enrollment nearly trebled. The projections for 1967–77 show a further 73% increase in enrollment in the two-year colleges, while four-year enrollment is expected to rise by only another third. Although comparable trend and projection data were not available for categorizing enrollment by size of institution, 63.1% of total enrollment in the 1965–66 school year was in schools with more than 5,000 students. The trend away from private colleges, and the rapid growth of the two-year schools both suggest that this concentration of enrollment in the larger schools is likely to become even more pronounced.

The same type of institutional differentiation provides another measure of the potential for institutional marketing, although projections are not available and the information is neither as current nor complete (Exhibits 4 and 5). The two enrollment trends of explosive growth in two-year schools and a shift away from private colleges appear to be reflected in the number of comparable types of institutions as well. During the period 1961–67 the total number of institutions of higher education increased by 16.5%, from 2,044 to 2,382. However, the number of four-year colleges increased by only 9%, while there were 35% more two-year schools in 1967. No breakdown of public versus private control was available for 1967, but for 1961 to 1965 the rate of growth in the number of public schools (14%) was twice that of private colleges (7%), and the marked increase of two-year schools from 1965 to 1967 suggests that the public schools had accelerated their growth rate even more. The 1965 breakdown by institutional size revealed that 53.2% of all colleges had enrollments below 1,000, and the next 24.9% were in the 1,000–2,499 range. This, only 21.9% of U.S. institutions of higher education had enrollments greater than 2,500. Although statistical projections had not been made, it seemed that these figures might change, since many of the rapidly growing two-year colleges currently fell in the 1,000–2,499 range and could not be expected to remain that small, while the increasing financial difficulties of the small private colleges threatened the demise of many of the schools in the under 2,500 groups.

The attempt to estimate the potential for institutional marketing in terms of dollar volume of purchases made by the schools proved even more difficult. ISI began by dividing purchasing volume into three broad categories:

Assets:   furniture and equipment for offices, laboratories, classrooms; maintenance equipment; vehicles; etc.
Supplies: stationery, forms and other office supplies; laboratory supplies; maintenance and housekeeping supplies; automotive supplies and petroleum products; etc.
Services: food service and housing for students and faculty; insurance; janitorial; medical; policy/security; etc.

These categories proved hard to track down because the typical college accounting system records expenditures by user or by source of funds used rather than by the type of goods and services purchased. For example, all expenditures for library operation are recorded together, including salaries, microfilm equipment, books, checkout forms, etc. Appendix A describes this accounting system in greater detail and presents aggregate data for the 1963–64 school year, and historical data for alternate years in the previous decade.

Using the aggregate data from Appendix A and Office of Education projections of expenditures (see Exhibits 6 and 7), a rough measure of overall potential can be made. Approximately 55% of current fund expenditures in 1963–64 were for payrolls. Applying this as an assumed constant ratio of projections of future current fund expenditures reveals that the 45% spent on goods and services would have been $7.16 billion in 1967–68, and can be expected to rise to $12.74 billion (in constant 1967–68 dollars) by 1977–78. Subtracting out the amount of current fund expenditures for plant leaves an approximation of the total purchasing volume in ISI's categories of "supplies" and "services." In order to plan specific marketing strategies these estimates should be broken down further, but they do provide a starting point. Similar analysis yields an approximation of ISI's "asset" category based on plant expenditures for "equipment." Roughly 75% of the current fund expenditures for plant and 7% of the total plant fund expenditure, in 1963–64, were specifically identified as equipment expense. Because some of the "building (including fixed equipment)" group of expenses also includes some assets ISI could provide purchasing services for, the portion of plant fund expenditures that might be considered market potential for ISI was assumed to be 10%. Combining these calculations, the total market potential for providing purchasing services for assets, supplies, and services in the college market can be approximated as follows:

**(figures in billions of 1967–68 dollars)**

| School Year | Supplies & Services | Assets | Total |
|---|---|---|---|
| 1969–70 | $ 7.60 | $0.67 | $ 8.27 |
| 1970–71 | 8.05 | 0.66 | 8.71 |
| 1971–72 | 8.69 | 0.57 | 9.26 |
| 1972–73 | 9.32 | 0.57 | 9.89 |
| 1973–74 | 9.90 | 0.67 | 10.57 |
| 1974–75 | 10.48 | 0.67 | 11.15 |
| 1975–76 | 11.11 | 0.66 | 11.77 |
| 1976–77 | 11.70 | 0.64 | 12.34 |
| 1977–78 | 12.24 | 0.63 | 12.87 |

## ISI'S FIRST SIX MONTHS

During this initial organization period, ISI activities were somewhat diffuse. Some effort was initiated to sign up colleges and universities as potential customers, and 28 had become ISI Associates by early June.

The process of contract negotiation had started with areas familiar to ISI personnel. While Special Assistant to the Director of Purchasing at Stanford University, Mr. Reeves had conducted a survey of the purchase and use of campus cars among 152 colleges and universities.[7] Mr. Reeves was convinced by this experience that leasing provided a valuable alternative to purchase in many circumstances and he sought to negotiate a master contract for vehicle leasing. The contract awaiting signature in early June called for the leasing company to provide a complete range of

[7] David E. Reeves, "How Colleges Manage the Purchase and Use of Official Campus Cars," *College and University Business*, Vol. 37, No. 5 (1964). The effort consisted of a letter signed by the president of Saga, which was sent to all Saga schools reporting the founding of ISI and offering membership which entitled the "buyer" the opportunity to use all master contracts negotiated by ISI. An associate paid a membership fee of $50.00 for five years. Generally, schools were enthusiastic about the new Saga venture and urged Mr. Reeves to move as quickly as possible to obtain useful master contracts. Mr. Reeves was reluctant to spend much time in the field signing up new members since this prevented him from doing the work necessary to screen potential suppliers and negotiate contracts.

services for ISI customers at a price to be kept competitive with any other leasing firm. ISI agreed to actively advertise and promote the lease contract, to add a staff member to coordinate vehicle leasing, and to provide credit screening for current Saga customers. Mr. Reeves estimated the cost of these activities at $42,000 the first year, with 10% annual increases thereafter. ISI would receive from the leasing company $3 per car per month for every vehicle leased under the contract, and Mr. Reeves was confident that 1,000 cars could be leased in 1969–70, 2,000 in 1970–71 and 3,000 by 1971–72. The question of whether Saga personnel could or should be used to market this and subsequent contracts was a matter of concern to all involved. It was decided not to attempt to use any such personnel to sell the car leasing service and instead to rely on direct mail solicitation.

One quite unforeseen development was that several opportunities had arisen for possible ISI participation that did not really fall within the charter of the company. The first such occurrence was an agreement entered into with Scope Corporation (Saga's dormitory construction and management subsidiary) to provide purchasing services for their projects. Scope agreed to pay a fixed 5% of purchasing volume for this service, and ISI hired an additional staff member, Mr. George Rawson, plus a secretary to coordinate Scope purchasing and to assist in the regular purchasing activities of ISI. It was anticipated that Scope would spend about $800,000 on furniture during the next year. This, in turn, led to another development. When Mr. Rawson began soliciting bids on beds for the Scope projects, it was revealed that there were only two institutional-bed manufacturers in the U.S., one of which dominated the market with a superior product. Thus, price negotiations were understandably stiff and one-sided. Contacts were initiated with the major institutional-bed manufacturer in Europe, and the opportunity was presented to ISI to become the exclusive U.S. market agent for that firm. The manufacturer would pay all transportation, warehousing, and distribution costs, guarantee to keep his price competitive with the leading U.S. bed, even though his product was thought to be better than the U.S.-made product. At current levels this price was expected to be $22.50, and ISI was to receive 10% of this amount for their efforts in advertising and marketing the beds. The ten-year agreement was made contingent upon ISI's meeting sales quotas of 2,000 beds in 1969, and 20% annual increases thereafter to a total of 10,000 beds in 1978.

Two other projects had come to the notice of ISI which, though outside the corporate charter, were thought to have such a substantial potential that preliminary negotiations had been conducted. The first of these was a proposal from an established foreign study and travel organization that had operated primarily in the high school market, but was now seeking an entry into the college market. It offered the opportunity for a 50% joint venture with a $40,000 initial investment from ISI. The ultimate market potential was thought to be substantial because of the expanding college population and the fact that college student travel to Europe had been growing at a 20% annual rate in recent years. In 1969, 250,000 college students were expected to go to Europe, and this figure was projected to rise to 432,000 in 1972. By forming the joint venture at this time, 1% (3,000 students) of the 1970 market was considered within reach, with added experience yielding 2% in 1971 and 3% in 1972. The anticipated pricing structure would provide $50 per student to ISI, before tax and expenses. Aside from the initial $40,000 investment the capital requirements would be minimal, because the students would pay prior to departure, thus providing the funds for flight reservations and accommodations in advance. The only expense to ISI would be marketing and overhead costs. It was planned to hire two salesmen (total costs, including travel per salesman, were estimated at $30,000 per year), and further, to have Mr. Reeves devote about one-half of his time to the new venture for at least the first year. Saga was to use its 244 resident college managers to help sell the travel service. The Foreign Study League, a subsidiary of the Transamerica Corporation, offered such courses as French language and civilization, German language and civilization, and Russian language and civilization; such courses lasted between five and six weeks and typically cost about $850 (all inclusive). High school students were solicited largely by offering a high school faculty member a "free" trip if he could attract seven or so students. Contacts with the faculty were made largely by direct mail although the League did have a sales force of about seven men who contacted various school organizations such as the Archdiocese of Chicago. They also did a certain amount of promotion work with larger schools.

There was some question as to how the Saga resident food managers would respond to this extra assignment. It was thought that they should be given an incentive to sell the program and tentatively it was planned to offer them a free trip with every ten reservations they obtained. They could take another member of their family if they sold another ten. If they did not wish to accept the trip as their reward they could accept money in the amount of $50 per student enrolled. In either case the cost would be paid by the joint venture and therefore was not charged against ISI's commission.

The foreign study proposal seemed to Mr. Reeves to represent a substantial opportunity since ISI could contract with universities and colleges to conduct their programs abroad. The school could provide faculty which would permit the granting of academic credit. It was thought that this market segment would expand substantially over time and that ISI could help the originating schools market their credit courses to students located on other campuses.

The marketing of the service to non-Saga schools could possibly be handled by the Saga District Managers. There were such managers and it was thought that they would visit non-Saga campuses for the purpose of locating a student "representative" who would then assume responsibility for selling the tours. He would be paid the same as the Saga resident food manager. It had not yet been decided how the Saga District Manager should be rewarded for his "extra" assignment.

The remaining project discussed during these first six months was comprehensive insurance service for the institutional markets ISI served. Important savings, greater convenience, and better service all seemed possible through consolidating the insurance needs of the institution into a single package or portfolio of policies in which the institutional customers might be considered as a distinct risk (and rate) class. An insurance broker was found who was sufficiently enthusiastic about the prospects for such a package that he volunteered to organize, capitalize, and devote 18 months of his time independently operating and building up a corporation designed to provide such coverage to ISI's markets. After the initial 18 months, ISI would have an option to purchase 49% of the corporation for $100,000, of a price to be determined on the basis of an independent evaluation of the worth of such an interest. After an additional seven years, the original entrepreneur would trade the remaining 51% to ISI for an equal value of public stock in Saga.

Evaluate ISI's progress to date. What recommendations should Mr. Reeves make to his board?

## EXHIBIT 1

### SAGA ADMINISTRATIVE CORPORATION AND WHOLLY-OWNED SUBSIDIARIES
### CONSOLIDATED STATEMENT OF INCOME AND EARNINGS
### RETAINED FOR USE IN THE BUSINESS

| | Fiscal year ended | |
|---|---|---|
| | June 29, 1968 (53 weeks) | June 24, 1967 (52 weeks) |
| Net revenues . . . . . . . . . . . . . . . | $85,919,000 | $71,732,000 |
| Costs and expenses: | | |
| Cost of food sold . . . . . . . . . . . . . . | 42,203,000 | 36,651,000 |
| Salaries and wages . . . . . . . . . . . . . | 28,187,000 | 23,080,000 |
| Other operating, general and administrative expenses, including provision for depreciation and amortization of $298,000 in 1968 and $312,000 in 1967 . . . . . . . | 11,887,000 | 9,673,000 |
| | 82,277,000 | 69,404,000 |
| Income before federal income taxes . . . . . . . . . | 3,642,000 | 2,328,000 |
| Provision for federal income taxes . . . . . . . . | 1,740,000 | 1,045,000 |
| Net income for the year . . . . . . . . | 1,902,000 | 1,283,000 |
| Earnings retained for use in the business, beginning of year . . . | 5,278,000 | 3,995,000 |
| Transfer to common stock in connection with 3 for 1 stock split (Note 3) . . . . . . . . . . | (1,107,000) | |
| Earnings retained for use in the business, end of year . . . . | $ 6,073,000 | $ 5,278,000 |
| Net income per share, after giving retroactive effect to 3 for 1 stock split (Note 3) . . . . . . . . . . | $1.18 | $.78 |
| Pro forma net income per share, assuming issuance of shares under employee stock plans (Note 4) . . . . . . . | $1.09 | |

### CONSOLIDATED STATEMENT OF SOURCE AND APPLICATION OF FUNDS

| | Fiscal year ended | |
|---|---|---|
| | June 29, 1968 (53 weeks) | June 24, 1967 (52 weeks) |
| Funds provided: | | |
| From operations: | | |
| Net income for the year . . . . . . . . . . | $1,902,000 | $1,283,000 |
| Expenses which did not require cash outlay: | | |
| Depreciation and amortization . . . . . . . . . | 298,000 | 312,000 |
| Other . . . . . . . . . . . . . . | 241,000 | 148,000 |
| | 2,441,000 | 1,743,000 |
| Proceeds from sale of stock . . . . . . . . . . | 60,000 | |
| | 2,501,000 | 1,743,000 |
| Funds applied: | | |
| Additions to property and equipment, net . . . . . . . | 2,920,000 | 203,000 |
| Less—long-term obligation assumed in connection therewith . . . | 1,938,000 | |
| | 982,000 | 203,000 |
| Increases in investments and deferred charges . . . . . . | 282,000 | 253,000 |
| Reduction in long-term obligations . . . . . . . . | 110,000 | 107,000 |
| Purchase of treasury stock . . . . . . . . . . | 23,000 | 14,000 |
| | 1,397,000 | 577,000 |
| Net increase in working capital . . . . . . . . . | 1,104,000 | 1,166,000 |
| Working capital, beginning of year . . . . . . . . . | 2,403,000 | 1,237,000 |
| Working capital, end of year . . . . . . . . . | $3,507,000 | $2,403,000 |

## EXHIBIT 2

### SAGA ADMINISTRATIVE CORPORATION AND WHOLLY-OWNED SUBSIDIARIES
### CONSOLIDATED BALANCE SHEET

| ASSETS | June 29, 1968 | June 24, 1967 |
|---|---|---|
| Current assets: | | |
| Cash (including time deposits of | | |
| $2,500,000 in 1968 and $1,000,000 in 1967) . . . . . . | $ 4,963,000 | $ 2,759,000 |
| Trade accounts receivable, less allowance for doubtful accounts | | |
| of $106,000 in 1968 and $23,000 in 1967 . . . . . . | 4,470,000 | 4,576,000 |
| Advances to officers and employees and other miscellaneous receivables . | 328,000 | 198,000 |
| Inventories of food and supplies, at actual cost, not in excess of market . | 1,210,000 | 1,053,000 |
| Prepaid expenses . . . . . . . . . . . . . | 97,000 | 53,000 |
| Total current assets . . . . . . . . . | 11,068,000 | 8,639,000 |
| Property and equipment, at cost (Note 2): | | |
| Land and land improvements . . . . . . . . . | 1,518,000 | 920,000 |
| Buildings . . . . . . . . . . . . . | 3,503,000 | 1,520,000 |
| Fixtures and equipment . . . . . . . . . . | 1,809,000 | 1,625,000 |
| | 6,830,000 | 4,065,000 |
| Less—Accumulated depreciation . . . . . . . . | 1,095,000 | 952,000 |
| | 5,735,000 | 3,113,000 |
| Investments: | | |
| Cash surrender value of life insurance . . . . . . | 339,000 | 260,000 |
| Investments in affiliate and associated companies (Note 1) . . . | 179,000 | 292,000 |
| Other . . . . . . . . . . . . . . | 131,000 | 108,000 |
| | 649,000 | 660,000 |
| Deferred charges . . . . . . . . . . . . | 648,000 | 595,000 |
| | $18,100,000 | $13,007,000 |

| LIABILITIES AND SHAREHOLDERS' EQUITY | | |
|---|---|---|
| Current liabilities: | | |
| Note payable . . . . . . . . . . . . | $ 429,000 | |
| Current portion of long-term obligations . . . . . . | 147,000 | $ 107,000 |
| Trade accounts payable . . . . . . . . . . | 2,431,000 | 2,778,000 |
| Accrued salaries, wages and bonuses . . . . . . . | 1,300,000 | 1,066,000 |
| Other accounts payable and accrued expenses . . . . . | 1,416,000 | 1,214,000 |
| Estimated federal income taxes . . . . . . . . | 1,838,000 | 1,070,000 |
| Total current liabilities . . . . . . . | 7,561,000 | 6,235,000 |
| Long-term obligations (Note 2): | | |
| 7% mortgage note, payable $175,000 annually, | | |
| including interest, through 1990 . . . . . | 1,938,000 | |
| 5½% mortgage note, payable $66,000 annually, | | |
| including interest, through 1980 . . . . . . . | 563,000 | 598,000 |
| Instalment contract, payable $75,000 annually to 1973 . . . . | 287,000 | 362,000 |
| | 2,788,000 | 960,000 |
| Shareholders' equity (Notes 3 and 4): | | |
| Common stock, par value $1: | | |

| | Shares | | | | |
|---|---|---|---|---|---|
| | 1968 | 1967 | | | |
| Authorized . . . . | 5,000,000 | 2,000,000 | . . | | |
| Issued . . . . . | 1,661,127 | 552,296 | . . . | 1,661,000 | 552,000 |
| Held in treasury . . . | 45,486 | 6,379 | . . | | |
| Outstanding . . . | 1,615,641 | 545,917 | . . . | | |
| Capital in excess of par value . . . . . . . . | | | | 144,000 | 103,000 |
| Earnings retained for use in the business . . . . . . | | | | 6,073,000 | 5,278,000 |
| | | | | 7,878,000 | 5,933,000 |
| Less—cost of treasury shares . . . . . . . . | | | | 127,000 | 121,000 |
| | | | | 7,751,000 | 5,812,000 |
| Contingent liabilities (Note 5) | | | | | |
| | | | | $18,100,000 | $13,007,000 |

## EXHIBIT 3

### U.S. Degree—Credit Enrollment in Higher Education Institution
### (figures in thousands of students)

| Year | Total | Type of Institution | | Type of Control | |
|---|---|---|---|---|---|
| | | 4 Year | 2 Year | Public | Private |
| 1957............ | 3,047 | 2,678 | 369 | 1,763 | 1,284 |
| 1958............ | 3,236 | 2,851 | 386 | 1,894 | 1,342 |
| 1959............ | 3,377 | 2,968 | 410 | 1,984 | 1,393 |
| 1960............ | 3,583 | 3,131 | 451 | 2,116 | 1,467 |
| 1961............ | 3,861 | 3,343 | 518 | 2,329 | 1,532 |
| 1962............ | 4,175 | 3,585 | 590 | 2,574 | 1,601 |
| 1963............ | 4,495 | 3,870 | 625 | 2,848 | 1,646 |
| 1964............ | 4,950 | 4,239 | 711 | 3,179 | 1,771 |
| 1965............ | 5,526 | 4,685 | 841 | 3,624 | 1,902 |
| 1966............ | 5,885* | 4,941* | 945* | 3,897* | 1,988* |
| 1967............ | 6,348* | 5,272* | 1,075* | 4,305* | 2,043* |
| Projected | | | | | |
| 1968............ | 6,758 | 5,595 | 1,164 | 4,629 | 2,129 |
| 1969............ | 6,906 | 4,698 | 1,207 | 4,775 | 2,131 |
| 1970............ | 7,181 | 5,908 | 1,273 | 5,009 | 2,172 |
| 1971............ | 7,530 | 6,177 | 1,353 | 5,297 | 2,233 |
| 1972............ | 7,925 | 6,483 | 1,442 | 5,619 | 2,306 |
| 1973............ | 8,322 | 6,789 | 1,533 | 5,944 | 2,377 |
| 1974............ | 8,645 | 7,075 | 1,619 | 6,255 | 2,440 |
| 1975............ | 9,056 | 7,351 | 1,705 | 6,559 | 2,497 |
| 1976............ | 9,388 | 7,603 | 1,785 | 6,843 | 2,545 |
| 1977............ | 9,684 | 7,825 | 1,859 | 7,102 | 2,581 |

* Estimated on basis of aggregated degree-credit and non-degree-credit data collected from *Opening Fall Enrollment* in 1966 and 1967.
SOURCE: Compiled from U.S. Department of Health, Education and Welfare, Office of Education, Projections of Educational Statistics to 1977–78 (1968 edition); (Washington, D.C.: U.S. Government Printing Office, 1969).

## EXHIBIT 4

### Enrollment and Number of Institutions, by Size of Institution, 1965–66

| No. of Students | Enrollment | | Number of Institutions | |
|---|---|---|---|---|
| | Number | Percent | Number | Percent |
| Under 200............. | 31,419 | 0.5 | 310 | 14.1 |
| 200–499............... | 132,239 | 2.4 | 377 | 17.2 |
| 500–999............... | 343,922 | 6.2 | 479 | 21.9 |
| 1,000–2,499............ | 840,196 | 15.1 | 545 | 24.9 |
| 2,500–4,999............ | 705,041 | 12.7 | 202 | 9.2 |
| 5,000–9,999............ | 1,147,283 | 20.6 | 159 | 7.2 |
| 10,000–19,999.......... | 1,115,631 | 20.0 | 80 | 3.7 |
| 20,000 or more......... | 1,254,540 | 22.5 | 40 | 1.8 |
| Total............. | 5,570,271 | 100.0 | 2,192 | 100.0 |

SOURCE: U.S. Department of Health, Education and Welfare, Office of Education, *Digest of Educational Statistics, 1967* (Washington, D.C.: U.S. Government Printing Office, 1968).

**EXHIBIT 5**

**Enrollment and Number of Institutions, by Size of Institution, 1965–66**

| Type and Control | Number of Institutions | | | |
|---|---|---|---|---|
| | *1961–62* | *1963–64* | *1965–66* | *1967–68* |
| Total.......................... | 2,044 | 2,140 | 2,238 | 2,382 |
| 4 Year Total.................. | 1,458 | 1,503 | 1,556 | 1,593 |
| Public................... | 376 | 387 | 403 | * |
| Private.................. | 1,082 | 1,116 | 1,153 | * |
| University Total............ | 143 | 146 | 155 | 157 |
| Public................... | 83 | 88 | 90 | * |
| Private.................. | 60 | 58 | 65 | * |
| Other 4 Year Total.......... | 1,315 | 1,357 | 1,401 | 1,436 |
| Public................... | 293 | 299 | 313 | * |
| Private.................. | 1,022 | 1,058 | 1,088 | * |
| 2 Year Total................. | 586 | 637 | 682 | 789 |
| Public................... | 348 | 378 | 422 | * |
| Private.................. | 238 | 259 | 260 | * |
| Public Total................. | 724 | 765 | 825 | * |
| Private Total................ | 1,320 | 1,375 | 1,413 | * |

* Data not available.

SOURCE: Compiled from U.S. Department of Health, Education and Welfare, Office of Education (Washington, D.C.: U.S. Government Printing Office); *Higher Education Finances* (1968); *Digest of Educational Statistics, 1967* (1968); *Opening Fall Enrollment in Higher Education, 1967–68* (1968).

## EXHIBIT 6

**Expenditures from Current Funds and Total Current Expenditures (1967–68 Dollars) by Institutions of Higher Education: United States, 1957–58 to 1977–78 (amounts in billions of 1967–68 dollars)**

| Year and control | Expenditure for educational and general purposes | | | | Expenditure for auxiliary enterprises and student aid [a] | Total expenditures from current funds | Capital outlay from current funds only | Total current expenditures [a] |
| | Student education [a] | Organized research | Related activities [a] | Total | | | | |
| (1) | (2) | (3) | (4) | (5) | (6) | (7) | (8) | (9) |
| **1957–58:** | | | | | | | | |
| Total | $3.1 | $0.9 | $0.3 | $4.3 | $1.0 | $5.3 | $0.2 | $5.1 |
| Public | 1.8 | .5 | .2 | 2.5 | .5 | 3.0 | .1 | 2.9 |
| Nonpublic | 1.3 | .4 | .1 | 1.8 | .5 | 2.3 | .1 | 2.2 |
| **1958–59:** [a] | | | | | | | | |
| Total | 3.4 | 1.0 | .3 | 4.7 | 1.2 | 5.9 | .2 | 5.7 |
| Public | 2.0 | .5 | .2 | 2.7 | .6 | 3.3 | .1 | 3.2 |
| Nonpublic | 1.4 | .5 | .1 | 2.0 | .6 | 2.6 | .1 | 2.5 |
| **1959–60:** | | | | | | | | |
| Total | 3.7 | 1.2 | .4 | 5.3 | 1.2 | 6.5 | .3 | 6.2 |
| Public | 2.2 | .6 | .2 | 3.0 | .6 | 3.6 | .2 | 3.4 |
| Nonpublic | 1.5 | .6 | .2 | 2.3 | .6 | 2.9 | .1 | 2.8 |
| **1960–61:** [a] | | | | | | | | |
| Total | 4.1 | 1.4 | .4 | 5.9 | 1.4 | 7.3 | .3 | 7.0 |
| Public | 2.4 | .7 | .2 | 3.3 | .7 | 4.0 | .2 | 3.8 |
| Nonpublic | 1.7 | .7 | .2 | 2.6 | .7 | 3.3 | .1 | 3.2 |
| **1961–62:** | | | | | | | | |
| Total | 4.4 | 1.6 | .5 | 6.5 | 1.6 | 8.1 | .3 | 7.8 |
| Public | 2.6 | .8 | .3 | 3.7 | .8 | 4.5 | .2 | 4.3 |
| Nonpublic | 1.8 | .8 | .2 | 2.8 | .8 | 3.6 | .1 | 3.5 |
| **1962–63:** [a] | | | | | | | | |
| Total | 4.9 | 1.9 | .5 | 7.3 | 1.8 | 9.1 | .5 | 8.6 |
| Public | 2.9 | .9 | .3 | 4.1 | .9 | 5.0 | .3 | 4.7 |
| Nonpublic | 2.0 | 1.0 | .2 | 3.2 | .9 | 4.1 | .2 | 3.9 |
| **1963–64:** | | | | | | | | |
| Total | 5.5 | 2.2 | .5 | 8.2 | 1.9 | 10.1 | .5 | 9.6 |
| Public | 3.3 | 1.0 | .3 | 4.6 | 1.0 | 5.6 | .3 | 5.3 |
| Nonpublic | 2.2 | 1.2 | .2 | 3.6 | .9 | 4.5 | .2 | 4.3 |
| **1964–65:** [a] | | | | | | | | |
| Total | 6.2 | 2.4 | .6 | 9.2 | 2.2 | 11.4 | .6 | 10.8 |
| Public | 3.7 | 1.1 | .4 | 5.2 | 1.2 | 6.4 | .4 | 6.0 |
| Nonpublic | 2.5 | 1.3 | .2 | 4.0 | 1.0 | 5.0 | .2 | 4.8 |
| **1965–66:** [a] | | | | | | | | |
| Total | 7.2 | 2.6 | .7 | 10.5 | 2.6 | 13.1 | .6 | 12.5 |
| Public | 4.4 | 1.2 | .4 | 6.0 | 1.4 | 7.4 | .4 | 7.0 |
| Nonpublic | 2.3 | 1.4 | .3 | 4.5 | 1.2 | 5.7 | .2 | 5.5 |
| **1966–67:** [a] | | | | | | | | |
| Total | 8.0 | 2.8 | .8 | 11.6 | 2.8 | 14.4 | .6 | 13.8 |
| Public | 4.9 | 1.3 | .5 | 6.7 | 1.5 | 8.2 | .4 | 7.8 |
| Nonpublic | 3.1 | 1.5 | .3 | 4.9 | 1.3 | 6.2 | .2 | 6.0 |
| **1967–68:** [a] | | | | | | | | |
| Total | 8.8 | 3.1 | .8 | 12.7 | 3.2 | 15.9 | .6 | 15.3 |
| Public | 5.5 | 1.4 | .5 | 7.4 | 1.8 | 9.2 | .4 | 8.8 |
| Nonpublic | 3.3 | 1.7 | .3 | 5.3 | 1.4 | 6.7 | .2 | 6.5 |

## EXHIBIT 6 (Continued)

| Year and control | Expenditure for educational and general purposes | | | | Expenditure for auxiliary enterprises and student aid [3] | Total expenditures from current funds | Capital outlay from current funds only | Total current expenditures [4] |
| | Student education [1] | Organized research | Related activities [2] | Total | | | | |
| (1) | (2) | (3) | (4) | (5) | (6) | (7) | (8) | (9) |

### PROJECTED [7]

| Year and control | | | | | | | | |
|---|---|---|---|---|---|---|---|---|
| **1968–69:** | | | | | | | | |
| Total | $9.6 | $3.3 | $0.9 | $13.8 | $3.4 | $17.2 | $0.6 | $16.6 |
| Public | 6.0 | 1.5 | .6 | 8.1 | 1.9 | 10.0 | .4 | 9.6 |
| Nonpublic | 3.6 | 1.8 | .3 | 5.7 | 1.5 | 7.2 | .2 | 7.0 |
| **1969–70:** | | | | | | | | |
| Total | 9.9 | 3.5 | .9 | 14.3 | 3.7 | 18.0 | .5 | 17.5 |
| Public | 6.2 | 1.6 | .6 | 8.4 | 2.1 | 10.5 | .4 | 10.1 |
| Nonpublic | 3.7 | 1.9 | .3 | 5.9 | 1.6 | 7.5 | .1 | 7.4 |
| **1970–71:** | | | | | | | | |
| Total | 10.5 | 3.7 | 1.0 | 15.2 | 3.8 | 19.0 | .5 | 18.5 |
| Public | 6.6 | 1.7 | .6 | 8.9 | 2.2 | 11.1 | .4 | 10.7 |
| Nonpublic | 3.9 | 2.0 | .4 | 6.3 | 1.6 | 7.9 | .1 | 7.8 |
| **1971–72:** | | | | | | | | |
| Total | 11.1 | 4.0 | 1.1 | 16.2 | 4.0 | 20.2 | .4 | 19.8 |
| Public | 7.0 | 1.8 | .7 | 9.5 | 2.3 | 11.8 | .3 | 11.5 |
| Nonpublic | 4.1 | 2.2 | .4 | 6.7 | 1.7 | 8.4 | .1 | 8.3 |
| **1972–73:** | | | | | | | | |
| Total | 11.9 | 4.2 | 1.2 | 17.3 | 4.3 | 21.6 | .4 | 21.2 |
| Public | 7.5 | 1.9 | .8 | 10.2 | 2.5 | 12.7 | .3 | 12.4 |
| Nonpublic | 4.4 | 2.3 | .4 | 7.1 | 1.8 | 8.9 | .1 | 8.8 |
| **1973–74:** | | | | | | | | |
| Total | 12.8 | 4.4 | 1.2 | 18.4 | 4.7 | 23.1 | .5 | 22.6 |
| Public | 8.1 | 2.0 | .8 | 10.9 | 2.7 | 13.6 | .4 | 13.2 |
| Nonpublic | 4.7 | 2.4 | .4 | 7.5 | 2.0 | 9.5 | .1 | 9.4 |
| **1974–75:** | | | | | | | | |
| Total | 13.4 | 4.6 | 1.4 | 19.4 | 5.0 | 24.4 | .5 | 23.9 |
| Public | 8.5 | 2.1 | .9 | 11.5 | 2.9 | 14.4 | .4 | 14.0 |
| Nonpublic | 4.9 | 2.5 | .5 | 7.9 | 2.1 | 10.0 | .1 | 9.9 |
| **1975–76:** | | | | | | | | |
| Total | 14.3 | 4.8 | 1.4 | 20.5 | 5.3 | 25.8 | .5 | 25.3 |
| Public | 9.1 | 2.2 | .9 | 12.2 | 3.1 | 15.3 | .4 | 14.9 |
| Nonpublic | 5.2 | 2.6 | .5 | 8.3 | 2.2 | 10.5 | .1 | 10.4 |
| **1976–77:** | | | | | | | | |
| Total | 15.0 | 5.0 | 1.5 | 21.5 | 5.6 | 27.1 | .5 | 26.6 |
| Public | 9.6 | 2.2 | 1.0 | 12.8 | 3.3 | 16.1 | .4 | 15.7 |
| Nonpublic | 5.4 | 2.8 | .5 | 8.7 | 2.3 | 11.0 | .1 | 10.9 |
| **1977–78:** | | | | | | | | |
| Total | 15.7 | 5.2 | 1.5 | 22.4 | 5.9 | 28.3 | .5 | 27.8 |
| Public | 10.1 | 2.3 | 1.0 | 13.4 | 3.5 | 16.9 | .4 | 16.5 |
| Nonpublic | 5.6 | 2.9 | .5 | 9.0 | 2.4 | 11.4 | .1 | 11.3 |

NOTES:
1. Includes general administration, instruction and departmental research, extension and public services, libraries, and operation and maintenance of the physical plant.
2. Includes expenditures for such items as laboratory schools, medical school hospitals, dental clinics, home economics cafeterias, agricultural college creameries, college-operated industrial plants connected with instructional programs but not actually integral parts of it, etc.

## EXHIBIT 6 (Continued)

3. Auxiliary enterprises include student dormitories, dining halls, cafeterias, student unions, bookstores, faculty housing, athletic programs not part of the instructional program, lectures, concerts, etc.

Student aid consists of scholarships, fellowships, and prizes and includes remission of fees.

4. Current-fund expenditures less capital outlay from current funds.

5. Interpolated.

6. Estimated.

7. The projection of expenditures from current funds is based on assumption that: (1) Expenditure per student and the percent of college-age persons attending college, on which expenditures for student education depend, will continue to increase as they did during the years 1957–58 to 1967–68; (2) expenditures for organized research will follow the 1957–58 to 1967–68 trend; (3) the relationship to student education of expenditures for related activities, for auxiliary enterprises, and for student aid will each continue the 1957–58 to 1967–68 trend; and (4) the 1967–68 to 1977–78 expenditures from current funds for capital outlay will approximate 16 percent of total capital outlay.

Data are for 50 States and the District of Columbia for all years.

Conversion to 1967–68 dollars was based on the Consumer Price Index published by the Bureau of Labor Statistics, U.S. Department of Labor and (for capital outlay) on the American Appraisal Company Construction Cost Index.

SOURCE: U.S. Department of Health, Education and Welfare, Office of Education, *Projections of Educational Statistics to 1977–78* (1968 edition; Washington, D.C.: U.S. Government Printing Office, 1969).

## EXHIBIT 7

### Capital Outlay of Institutions of Higher Education: United States, 1957–58 to 1977–78

| Year | Total | | Public | | Nonpublic | |
|------|-------|---|--------|---|-----------|---|
| | Billions of current dollars | Billions of 1967–68 dollars | Billions of current dollars | Billions of 1967–68 dollars | Billions of current dollars | Billions of 1967–68 dollars |
| (1) | (2) | (3) | (4) | (5) | (6) | (7) |
| 1957–58 | $1. 161 | $1. 610 | $0. 732 | $1. 015 | $0. 429 | $0. 595 |
| 1958–59 [1] | 1. 304 | 1. 754 | . 721 | . 970 | . 583 | . 784 |
| 1959–60 | 1. 354 | 1. 768 | . 807 | 1. 054 | . 547 | . 714 |
| 1960–61 [1] | 1. 737 | 2. 216 | . 932 | 1. 189 | . 805 | 1. 027 |
| 1961–62 | 1. 714 | 2. 137 | 1. 010 | 1. 259 | . 704 | . 878 |
| 1962–63 [1] | 2. 534 | 3. 074 | 1. 596 | 1. 936 | . 938 | 1. 138 |
| 1958–59 to 1961–62 | 8. 643 | 10. 949 | 5. 066 | 6. 408 | 3. 577 | 4. 541 |
| 1963–64 | 2. 466 | 2. 906 | 1. 518 | 1. 789 | . 948 | 1. 117 |
| 1964–65 [2] | 3. 089 | 3. 549 | 2. 064 | 2. 371 | 1. 025 | 1. 178 |
| 1965–66 [2] | 3. 323 | 3. 687 | 2. 233 | 2. 478 | 1. 090 | 1. 209 |
| 1966–67 [2] | 3. 293 | 3. 462 | 2. 279 | 2. 396 | 1. 014 | 1. 066 |
| 1967–68 [2] | 3. 462 | 3. 462 | 2. 396 | 2. 396 | 1. 066 | 1. 066 |
| 1963–64 to 1967–68 | 15. 633 | 17. 066 | 10. 490 | 11. 430 | 5. 143 | 5. 636 |

### PROJECTED [3]

| Year | Total | | Public | | Nonpublic | |
|------|-------|---|--------|---|-----------|---|
| 1968–69 | 3. 409 | 3. 268 | 2. 413 | 2. 313 | 0. 996 | 0. 955 |
| 1969–70 | 3. 191 | 2. 935 | 2. 326 | 2. 139 | . 865 | . 796 |
| 1970–71 | | 2. 838 | | 2. 106 | | . 732 |
| 1971–72 | | 2. 731 | | 1. 999 | | . 732 |
| 1972–73 | | 2. 658 | | 1. 974 | | . 684 |
| 1968–69 to 1972–73 | | 14. 430 | | 10. 531 | | 3. 899 |
| 1973–74 | | 2. 879 | | 2. 115 | | . 764 |
| 1974–75 | | 2. 903 | | 2. 139 | | . 764 |
| 1975–76 | | 2. 831 | | 2. 115 | | . 716 |
| 1976–77 | | 2. 637 | | 2. 016 | | . 621 |
| 1977–78 | | 2. 490 | | 1. 933 | | . 557 |
| 1973–74 to 1977–78 | | 13. 740 | | 10. 318 | | 3. 422 |

NOTES:
1. Interpolated.
2. Estimated.
3. The projection of capital outlay is based on assumption that: (1) capital outlay per additional full-time equivalent of total opening fall enrollment will follow the 1957–58 to 1967–68 trend insofar as capital outlay resulting in increased value of plant is concerned; (2) capital outlay for replacement and rehabilitation will remain constant at the level of 1% of value of plant each year through 1977–78; and (3) since capital outlay related to increased numbers of students over a number of years rather than annually, a moving average would more reasonably reflect annual capital outlay.
SOURCE: See Exhibit 6.

## APPENDIX A: ACCOUNTING FOR EXPENDITURES IN INSTITUTIONS OF HIGHER EDUCATION

The financial statistics maintained by the Office of Education are both shaped by, and help to standardize, the type of accounting systems in use in higher educational institutions. This appendix describes and presents the expenditure portion of those statistics as they relate to ISI's attempts to estimate the potential dollar volume of the institutional market they serve.

An initial distinction is made in this system between funds used for the day-to-day operation of the institution (Current-Fund), and funds used for capital improvements and expansion (Plant-Fund). Each of these funds is further divided into categories by the end-use of the expenditure. The Plant-Fund broad division is between disbursements for additions to plant assets (including renewals, replacements, major repairs, and building materials as well as finished construction), and the interest expense on borrowed capital. The Current-Fund divides initially into three broad categories: (1) Educational and General Expenditures, which are the daily expenses of operating the educational activities of the institution; (2) Auxiliary Enterprise Expenditures, consisting of the administration, operation and maintenance expense of cafeterias and dining halls, student residence halls, bookstores, student unions, student health care facilities, intercollegiate athletics, concerts, university presses, etc.; and (3) Student Financial Aid Expenditures.

The Educational and General Expenditures are further divided into seven categories of expense:

1. *General Administration and General Expense.* General executive and administrative offices serving the institution as a whole, and expenditures of a general character. Includes student personnel services such as admissions, counseling and guidance, dean's office, placement, registrar, student activities, etc.

2. *Instruction and Departmental Research.* All current expenditures of instructional departments, colleges and schools, *including* expenditures for research not separately budgeted or funded. Includes office expense and equipment, laboratory expense and equipment, salaries of instructional staff, secretaries, technicians, etc.

3. *Extension and Public Service.* Includes nondegree courses, public lectures and institutes, public television and radio programs, etc.

4. *Libraries.* Includes salaries, books, operating expenses, binding, etc.

5. *Operation and Maintenance of Physical Plant.* Includes salaries, supplies, equipment and other maintenance expenses, but *not*, however, maintenance of auxiliary facilities like dormitories and dining halls, or activities related to educational departments (see item 7).

6. *Organized Research.* Separately budgeted or financed research

either from outside contracts and grants or from the institution's regular funds.

**7. *Organized Activities Related to Educational Departments.*** Administration, operation and maintenance of such activities as experimental agricultural farms, medical school hospitals, materials testing laboratories, etc.

Within the Plant-Fund, the broad group of expenditures for Additions to Plant Assets are further divided into: (1) Land; (2) Buildings—including fixed equipment; (3) Improvements Other Than Buildings—roads, landscaping, etc.; and (4) Equipment—laboratory and office machinery and equipment, furniture and furnishings, library books, vehicles, farm implements, nonlaboratory livestock, etc.

The tables which follow present pertinent expenditure data.

### APPENDIX A—TABLE 1

### Current-Fund Expenditures of U.S. Higher Educational Institutions by Category of Expense, Biennial from 1953–54 to 1963–64
### (figures in millions of dollars)

|  | 1953–54 | 1955–56 | 1957–58 | 1959–60 | 1961–62 | 1963–64 |
|---|---|---|---|---|---|---|
| Total Current Fund Expenditures | 2,902 | 3,525 | 4,544 | 5,628 | 7,190 | 9,225 |
| Educational and General | 2,288 | 2,789 | 3,634 | 4,536 | 5,789 | 7,466 |
| Gen. Administration & Gen. Expense | 291 | 358 | 478 | 587 | 736 | 964 |
| Instruction & Dept'l Research | 467 | 1,149 | 1,477 | 1,803 | 2,216 | 2,821 |
| Extension & Public Services | 115 | 141 | 179 | 208 | 245 | 298 |
| Libraries | 73 | 86 | 111 | 136 | 178 | 238 |
| Plant Operation & Maintenance | 280 | 326 | 409 | 474 | 566 | 689 |
| Organized Research | 375 | 506 | 734 | 1,024 | 1,481 | 1,983 |
| Related Activities | 181 | 222 | 246 | 303 | 375 | 473 |
| Auxiliary Enterprises | 539 | 640 | 778 | 918 | 1,161 | 1,455 |
| Student Aid | 75 | 96 | 131 | 174 | 231 | 303 |

SOURCE: U.S. Department of Health, Education and Welfare, Office of Education, *Higher Education Finances* (Washington D.C.: U.S. Government Printing Office, 1968).

# APPENDIX A—TABLE 2

## Expenditures of U.S. Higher Educational Institutions, by Type and Control of Institution, 1963–64
### (figures in millions of dollars)

| | Current Expenditures | Educational & General | Gen'l Admin. & Gen. Exp. | Instruction & Departmental Research | Extension & Public Service | Libraries | Plant Operation & Maintenance | Organized Research | Related Activities | Auxiliary Enterprises | Student Aid | Plant-Fund Expenditures | Addition to Plant |
|---|---|---|---|---|---|---|---|---|---|---|---|---|---|
| Total | 9,225 | 7,466 | 964 | 2,821 | 298 | 238 | 689 | 1,983 | 473 | 1,455 | 303 | 2,295 | 1,408 |
| 4 Year Total | 8,739 | 7,063 | 892 | 2,567 | 293 | 225 | 634 | 1,982 | 469 | 1,376 | 300 | 2,119 | 1,760 |
| Public | 4,750 | 3,884 | 410 | 1,503 | 270 | 123 | 351 | 936 | 291 | 757 | 109 | 1,279 | 1,064 |
| Private | 3,989 | 3,179 | 482 | 1,064 | 23 | 102 | 283 | 1,046 | 178 | 619 | 191 | 840 | 696 |
| Univ. Total | 5,435 | 4,539 | 436 | 1,484 | 270 | 129 | 337 | 1,499 | 384 | 721 | 175 | 1,199 | 966 |
| Public | 3,543 | 2,958 | 263 | 981 | 257 | 81 | 219 | 899 | 258 | 504 | 81 | 825 | 660 |
| Private | 1,892 | 1,581 | 173 | 503 | 13 | 48 | 118 | 600 | 126 | 217 | 94 | 374 | 306 |
| Other 4 Yr. | 3,304 | 2,524 | 456 | 1,083 | 23 | 96 | 297 | 483 | 85 | 655 | 125 | 920 | 794 |
| Public | 1,207 | 926 | 147 | 522 | 13 | 42 | 132 | 37 | 33 | 253 | 28 | 454 | 404 |
| Private | 2,097 | 1,598 | 309 | 561 | 10 | 54 | 165 | 446 | 52 | 402 | 97 | 466 | 390 |
| 2 Yr. Total | 485.5 | 403 | 71.5 | 253 | 6 | 13.5 | 55 | 1 | 3 | 79 | 3 | 176 | 147 |
| Public | 364 | 315 | 46 | 210 | 5 | 10.5 | 41 | * | 2 | 48 | 1 | 140 | 118 |
| Private | 121.5 | 88 | 25.5 | 43 | 1 | 3 | 14 | 1 | 1 | 31 | 2 | 36 | 31 |
| Public Total | 5,114 | 4,199 | 456 | 1,713 | 275 | 134 | 392 | 936 | 293 | 805 | 110 | 1,419 | 1,182 |
| Private Total | 4,111 | 3,267 | 508 | 1,107 | 24 | 105 | 297 | 1,047 | 179 | 650 | 193 | 876 | 727 |

Note: * less than $100,000.
Source: U.S. Department of Health, Education and Welfare, Office of Education, *Higher Education Finances* (Washington, D.C.: U.S. Government Printing Office, 1968).

## APPENDIX A—TABLE 3

### Supplemental Data on 1963–64 Expenditures of U.S. Higher Educational Institutions, by Control of Institution
### (figures in millions of dollars)

|  | *Total* | *Public* | *Private* |
|---|---|---|---|
| Current-Fund Expenditures for Payroll: |  |  |  |
| Total................................ | 5,068 | 3,060 | 2,009 |
| Instruction & Dept'l Research |  |  |  |
| Professional........................ | 2,023 | 1,250 | 773 |
| Nonprofessional.................... | 230 | 147 | 83 |
| Organized Research.................... | 985 | 526 | 458 |
| Auxiliary Enterprises.................. | 406 | 242 | 164 |
| All Other............................ | 1,424 | 893 | 531 |
| Current-Fund Expenditures for Plant: |  |  |  |
| Total................................ | 371 | 218 | 152 |
| Equipment........................... | 278 | 186 | 92 |
| Plant Expansion & Improvement.......... | 93 | 32 | 60 |
| Plant-Fund Expenditures |  |  |  |
| Total................................ | 2,295 | 1,419 | 876 |
| Addition to Plant: Total............... | 1,908 | 1,182 | 727 |
| Land............................... | 88 | 62 | 26 |
| Buildings (incl. fixed equipment) ....... | 1,588 | 979 | 609 |
| Improvements other than building...... | 67 | 51 | 15 |

SOURCE: U.S. Department of Health, Education and Welfare, Office of Education, *Higher Education Finances*, Selected Trend and Summary Data (Washington, D.C.: U.S. Government Printing Office, 1968).

SECTION **IX**

## CONTROL AND REAPPRAISAL

# Tasty Foods Company

## AUDITING A SALES REGION

Mr. Charles Magnes, the Vice-President of Marketing for Tasty Foods Company (TFC), a large national manufacturer of packaged grocery products, was concerned about the Boston Region because its sales had been considerably below the Company's market share objectives. Mr. Magnes wanted to explore the forces influencing TFC's market position in the Boston Region by auditing the region, but he wondered what the best way was to go about making such an audit.

During the summer of 1966, Montgomery Joy, an MBA student between his first and second year in Business School, participated in a special summer program at Tasty Foods Company. The dual objectives of the program were to allow the student to take a good look at the Company and the industry, and to allow the Company to reciprocate with a good look at the student. To effect these objectives, a great deal of flexibility was incorporated into the program.

Since Monty's interest was in marketing, Mr. Charles Magnes assigned the study of the Boston market area to Monty and provided him with the latitude to approach this investigation as he wished. Essentially, Monty's task was to: "Find out why Tasty Foods Company is not the Number One company in share of the Boston market and recommend a course of action which will help Tasty Foods Company attain that position."

## Background

The Tasty Foods Company processed and sold a wide product line including cereals, baking mix products, snacks, coffee, salad dressings, margarine, mayonnaise, pancakes, and dehydrated potatoes. Company sales of consumer products had increased substantially over the past several years due primarily to new product introductions. Sales in 1966

Reprinted from *Stanford Business Cases 1970* with the permission of the publisher, Graduate School of Business, Stanford University. Copyright © 1970 by the Board of Trustees of the Leland Stanford Junior University.

reached $397 million. In that year, the Company successfully introduced 26 new consumer products. About three-quarters of the total sales dollar volume was generated by eight product categories: cereals, cake mixes, puddings, pancake mixes, coffee, mayonnaise, salad dressings, and de-hydrated potatoes. (See Exhibit 1 for a per capita consumption index of these products in Boston.) Because of its wide range of products, TFC was in competition with many of the larger companies in the food processing industry. TFC's products competed with those of Corn Products Company, General Foods, General Mills, National Biscuit Company, Pillsbury, Procter and Gamble (Duncan Hines' and Folger's Divisions), Quaker Oats, Standard Brands, and others.

Tasty Foods Company subscribed to industry market data from an outside market research organization which provided statistics on total consumer sales by brand within product class within sales region over time. Although these statistics indicated that TFC had improved its market position in Boston in many products over the past five years, Mr. Magnes expressed concern that some of the major product categories not only failed to meet share objectives but also had shown a decline in market share in 1966: cake mixes ($-5.5$ share points), pancakes ($-1.0$), cereals ($-1.3$), coffee ($-3.7$), and mayonnaise ($-1.0$). At the same time, other lines that were not meeting share objectives did show some improvement: puddings ($+0.7$), dehydrated potatoes ($+3.0$), and salad dressings ($+2.1$). (See Exhibit 2 for graphs of market size and of TFC's share of market in the Boston Region.)

### The Boston Market

After first familiarizing himself with Tasty Foods' relative market position, Monty examined the characteristics of the Boston market. The Boston Region, including all of metropolitan Boston, the North Shore, Worcester, and Rhode Island, had a population of about 5.5 million. Monty found that the demographic profile of this segment appeared to differ markedly from what might be called an American "norm." One out of two persons in the region was Roman Catholic, compared to one out of four nationally. Immigrant groups were strong: 42% of metropolitan Boston's 1960 population were either immigrants or born of immigrant parents, compared to 19% for the U.S. as a whole. The major ethnic groups were Canadian, Italian, Irish, Russian, English, and Polish. Three percent of the SMSA[1] population was Negro compared to 10.5% in the U.S. as a whole; 9% of the Boston City population was Negro. Coexisting with the immigrant population in Boston was an older, higher-income, and more established group—the Back Bay Brahmins—which tended to inhabit the suburban areas. (See Exhibit 3.)

---

[1] Standard Metropolitan Statistical Area.

When Monty tried to view the Boston Region as a socioeconomic entity, he found some interesting contrasts. Across the nation, 46% of family incomes exceeded $6,000 in 1960 while 58% of Boston's families exceeded that figure. The median family income in Boston was $6,687. Bostonians annually spent more per person ($103 each in 1963) on dining out than consumers in most other major cities; similarly, Bostonians spent more for retail bakery goods than did consumers of other major cities. (See Exhibit 4.) In addition, the lower per capita consumption of flour (see Exhibit 5) indicated that baking from "scratch" was not popular in Boston.

Age and social class characteristics provided further insights into the Boston area. The median age in Boston was 32 years; the median age for women was 33.7 years; 38.1% of all women over 14 were in the labor force in Boston compared to only 34.5% nationally.

In the Boston Region there were approximately 6,000 retail food stores. The major chains were Stop & Shop (S & S), First National, and A & P; smaller chains included Elm Farm, Buy Rite, and Star. According to a newspaper report, leadership in retail sales dollar volume had recently passed from First National to Stop & Shop because of the latter's discount operations; however, profits of all three major chains were said to be hurt by S & S's move. Some of the principal wholesalers were New England, Cressy-Dockham, Roger Williams, Almacs, C & S Wholesale, and A.G. The top 12 retail and wholesale accounts accounted for 75% of the TFC's branch retail dollar volume.

While the retail chain stores constituted the single largest distribution network for consumer food products in the Boston Region as a whole, their influence varied markedly in the different cities. For example, independents and voluntary cooperatives accounted for 34% of sales in metropolitan Boston, 67% in Worcester, and 20% in Providence [according to *Supermarket News*]. The corresponding figure for independents and voluntary cooperatives in the U.S. in 1965 was 58.6%.

**Marketing Organization**

Monty also studied the operation of the marketing department at Tasty Foods. The TFC Marketing Managers, under the general guidance of the Vice-President of Marketing, were responsible and accountable for the sales and profits of their products. The functions of the Marketing Manager were defined in a memo regarding organizational structure.

The Marketing Manager . . . ties together all company activities connected with his product(s) to build volume and profits. He plans, implements, maintains administrative control, and evaluates results for replanning.

To do this he must have the proven ability to motivate people of diverse interests and functions.

*Planning.* The Marketing Manager shapes a broad 5-year plan for his products and prepares a comprehensive annual plan within that framework. Plans are written, specific, and contain supporting detail; they are both a plan for action and a standard for measurement. They contain,

a statement of current positions, strengths, and weaknesses of a product, and assumptions of expected market trends.

a statement of objectives, to include share, volume, revenue, spending and contribution and subobjectives such as geographical penetration and distribution penetration.

a recommended marketing program based on evaluation of alternatives, and experimentation to achieve objectives set forth.

*Implementing.* The ongoing activity of the Marketing Manager is directed largely to implementation of the programs outlined in the annual plan. His participation in the decision making that this involves is shown in . . . advertising, promotion, product improvement, and pricing.

The Marketing Managers focused their attention on the 25 major population centers which accounted for well over half of Company sales. The sales effort within each area was allocated to the key wholesale and retail accounts by a weighting of present and potential sales. Actual allocation of the sales effort was the responsibility of each Regional Sales Manager. (See Exhibit 6 for an organizational chart.)

Monty talked with some of the Marketing Managers in an attempt to determine the nature of the problem in Boston. He first contacted the pancake manager, Harry Bremmer:

HARRY: I don't know whether you can say there's a "corporate" problem in Boston. I think you ought to tackle your assignment in terms of the various categories of products we market there. The problem for pancakes, I would say, is considerably different from that for coffee. Our share in two-pound pancakes (#2) increased steadily for five years until this year when we tried to stop offering deals on our products. This attempt to eliminate price cutting hurt us across the nation. But that doesn't tell you anything about brownies or cereals. Regular cereals declined, for example, because of the introduction of Instant Breakfast. My chief concern right now in Boston is the loss of distribution for one-pound pancakes (#1) in the S & S chain which accounts for over 20% of the Boston Region retail dollar volume. S & S even turned us down recently when we offered them a big promotional allowance. Maybe *you* can tell *me* the problem after you've been in Boston a while.

Monty next called on the cereal manager, Arthur Gordon, and asked him if he could offer any suggestions as to the problems in Boston.

ART: I don't know how much I can help you, Monty. Although I've personally never been in Boston, I don't think that Boston's problems are any different from those in any other key marketing area. All our cereal products have the same trouble; the "franchise," or brand loyalty, is weak.

MONTY: You make it *sound* really bad, but the record shows you've increased your share of cereal sales in Boston over the past five years. Isn't that your chief objective in any city?

ART: Well, we've isolated some variables which we think will increase long run sales, and we have the salesmen working on them. For example, the more shelf fronts we get, the more visual impact the product should have on the buying consumer. Also, getting products positioned next to the leading brands provides a higher probability of the consumer seeing and buying them.

The increase in the number of trade and consumer promotions offered has probably contributed to our share increase, too. When a consumer buys our product at a reduced price, we hope she will buy it again later at full price. But where we don't have strong brand loyalty, we *have* to deal to keep the product moving off the retailer's shelves. For example, when we adopted a policy to stop dealing for awhile, some sales dropped off. The consumer may be buying our products on price rather than on brand preference.

The big questions, Monty, are, of course, where to deal and what type of deal to offer. We can promote either nationally or in selected areas. If the latter, should it be in strong or weak areas? Should we offer trade money or consumer money?

Frankly, I don't know what type of deal would go best in Boston or whether there is some sort of general promotion we could use. What makes Bostonians tick? Maybe they're different from people in the rest of the country. Should we try a green St. Patrick's Day cereal—you let me know. . . .

Monty also talked briefly to the Marketing Manager for puddings who attributed his brand problems to the allocation of the sales effort. He complained to Monty that the Boston sales manager, Parris Shaw, was "always pushing cakes."

## Sales Organization

The TFC sales organization, headed by the Vice President of Sales, consisted of 6 Divisional Sales Managers in charge of the 6 geographical divisions, 45 Regional Sales Managers, and approximately 700 salesmen. The chief responsibility of the sales organization was to obtain and maintain distribution of the Company's brands, and to reach the sales goals set in the annual marketing plans. The sales executive groups also advised the Marketing Managers about certain elements of the marketing plans, particularly the use of various types of trade and consumer promotions. All planning and coordinating of plans at the local level were based on discussions between the Divisional Sales Managers and the Marketing Managers, although some informal contact existed between the Marketing Managers and the Regional Sales Managers.

Parris Shaw had been the Regional Sales Manager in Boston for six years, having risen from the ranks of the salesmen. There were 20 full-time salesmen under his direction: 6 were assigned to the key accounts (the largest retail chains); 3 were "sales merchandisers" for these salesmen; 11 covered the smaller chains and independents. The sales force was unique in the Eastern Division because no salesman had left the force in over two years; this record was attributed to the morale established under Parris Shaw.

When Monty arrived at Branch Headquarters in Boston, he introduced himself to Parris.

PARRIS: You picked a good day to arrive! Take a look at this letter I got this morning. It confirms the rumors that have been flying for the past week. First National has decided to cut out what they call "slow moving" products. Some of our competitors have lost up to ten pounds apiece, but it looks like we're going to lose more than that. Most of these products don't account for a lot of sales, but. . . .

MONTY: How come they're so anxious to trim the shelves?

PARRIS: Personally, I think it's a belated reaction to the profit squeeze created when Stop & Shop turned to discount supermarketing. Instead of dropping prices when S & S adopted "mini-pricing" and discontinued trading stamps, First National increased the number of trading stamps given. According to a newspaper report, both stores have been hurt; First National's sales and profits dropped and S & S's sales didn't increase enough to offset its lower margins.

MONTY: What about offering more deals? Would that help to keep things on the shelves?

PARRIS: We've tried trade money, Monty, and it doesn't seem to hit home. Take the buyer from S & S—he probably wouldn't take our salad dressings even if we gave them away. I'm not sure trade money is the answer: last month we offered a deal on cake mixes, and one of the chains just kept the money. We could go for some consumer packs maybe, but there are other problems there. The independents won't take the price-off packs because they can't make anything on them. They'll take trade money, but that doesn't solve the problem with the chains. And since the independents are pretty strong in the branch—especially in Worcester—we often suggest trade promotions when regional management asks for recommendations on the type of deals to offer. The trade always asks us for deals on dehydrated potatoes because they sell well, but it doesn't do *us* any good because the consumers of those products are relatively price insensitive. I think advertising's the answer on something like that. On the other hand, I thought we should offer a deal on mayonnaise to meet our competition, but the head office doesn't agree, I guess.

MONTY: Which product categories do you think should be pushed in Boston to improve TFC's position?

PARRIS: Well, we usually can tell which products the head office feels are most important by the number of salesman bonus points assigned to each product category. This list ranks products according to sales bonus points: cake mix, pancakes, dehydrated potatoes, salad dressing, cereal, coffee, mayonnaise, pudding. I have another list which ranks the product categories by quantity consumed per capita in Boston: cereal, coffee, cake mix, mayonnaise, puddings, dehydrated potatoes, salad dressings, and pancakes. By consolidating these two, I came up with a list of specific products I think we ought to push: pancakes (#2), instant coffee, chocolate and butterscotch pudding, Berry Bran, and Yellow Cake. Since Bostonians consume more of these specific products than people almost anywhere in the country, I think they ought to be pushed the hardest.

Parris discussed new product introductions with Monty since "Raisin Custard Puddin'," a new pudding mix, was scheduled for introduction the following week.

PARRIS: I'm not sure how the men should present "Raisin Custard Puddin'." Three weeks ago, when we presented the deal on one-pound pancakes to S & S, they did a total "movement" analysis of the whole pancake section and discovered that our buttermilk pancakes were the slowest moving; not only did they reject the offer to reintroduce one-pound, but they threw out buttermilk as well! I'm afraid with "Raisin Custard Puddin' " that they'll analyze our whole pudding and pie filling section. . . .

I don't really understand it, Monty. The deal we offered on one-pound pancakes would have earned them a $50,000 profit if it sold as predicted. And, that's not peanuts, even for S & S! But since margins on pancakes are relatively low, they want to use the space for other products. I can see their point, I guess, but it sure hurts.

MONTY: That doesn't sound too promising. How are you going to present "Raisin Custard Puddin' " to minimize the possibility of that happening to puddings?

PARRIS: Well, I've thought of presenting it first to the independents outside Boston. If it goes, the track record and consumer pull might help us gain distribution in Stop & Shop. Our brand image just isn't strong enough to get our new products in easily.

After spending several weeks in the Boston Region attempting to clearly visualize and understand its operations and problems, Monty concluded that he would have to limit the scope of his investigation; thus, he did not attempt to evaluate the effectiveness of the salesforce. He felt, however, that TFC's sales effort was not always directed toward the apparent wants of the trade because the Boston retail trade judged TFC's quality food products as *discount items:* buyers who were once food men had become businessmen who based their purchases on IBM stock sheets.

Monty also concluded that TFC's franchise, or brand loyalty, in the Boston area appeared to be relatively weak; there was a direct correlation between total sales and the number of deals offered on products. To strengthen TFC's franchise, the salesmen had been instructed to concentrate on getting both more shelf fronts for TFC products and better placement of TFC products next to the leading brand to increase the consumer's exposure to the product. In addition, TFC normally allocated about 60% of its advertising budget to national advertising (including print, radio, and TV) and about 40% for deals and other promotions.[2] The cost of the sales force was roughly half of that budgeted for advertising.

Monty also learned that, since 1960, three major events had revolu-

---

[2] Grocery products were often promoted by offering "deals" to either the consumer or the trade. A consumer deal might be a "cents-off" package; a trade deal might consist of a discount to the retailer of, say, $1/case.

tionized the market for packaged grocery products: first, the introduction of private label brands in leading supermarket chains across the nation; second, the trend toward committee buying; and third, the advent of discount supermarketing.

The growth of private label brands increased rapidly in New England in the early sixties. Private labels existed for cakes, bread, coffee, cheese, canned fruits and vegetables, frozen vegetables and juices, mayonnaise, and salad dressing. They were usually given the shelf position nearest the leading brand; thus, as the number of products and brands increased and floor space remained constant, the number three and four brands (in relative sales volume) in each product category were often eliminated when computerized stock sheets indicated they were not "moving."

The trend toward committee buying greatly influenced the purchasing function of many supermarkets. In evaluating new products, a supermarket's buying committee considered profitability, market factors, advertising, packaging, product characteristics, merchandising; no product could gain admission to a store's product line without the express consent of the buying committee.

The Boston grocery market was becoming increasingly discount oriented, especially with the advent of Stop & Shop's conversion to "mini-pricing." Discounting in supermarkets had effectively diminished the number of baking mix products which were carried. When Stop & Shop decided to allot space according to contribution to store profit, the areas of the baking mix departments generally were reduced. With less space available, S & S used "case movement from the warehouse" as the criterion for allotting space to the major brands—thus assuming that its margins on major brands were identical. As a consequence, TFC had lost its distribution of one-pound pancakes in the S & S stores. In addition to the new criterion for space allotment, increasing competition and the proliferation of new products were also squeezing out the slower moving items.

The trend toward discount supermarketing had placed the non-discount supermarkets in a profit squeeze; thus, these markets were accepting TFC's trade money without reflecting it in consumer prices. There were actually two separate attitudes held by discount supermarkets in Boston: one favored high-powered promotional programs; the other favored consistently low prices on the leading brand. The independents and smaller chains generally adopted the high-powered promotional approach to discounting. They were amenable to trade money and often featured TFC products on mass displays as loss leaders. They did not like cents-off packs because of the additional warehousing space required for the special product and because the cents-off packs were factory marked and had to be sold at the reduced price.

The larger discount supermarkets such as Stop & Shop favored consistently low prices on the leading brand. These supermarkets tended to stock only that portion of TFC's product line which were already best sellers. The aim of these markets was to increase profitability by a high turnover of goods and by reduced labor charges for stocking.

The small independent stores which practiced full pricing constituted about one-third of the metropolitan Boston retail trade. Many of these stores were in the tenement areas of Boston, and they usually carried only the leading brand of any product category. Eastern Division management felt it would be almost impossible to displace the leading brand and take over the business in these stores because they had either a brand conscious clientele or a pre-established relationship with the wholesaler.

When Monty returned to TFC headquarters near the end of summer, he had a massive amount of information on the industry, the Boston Market, and TFC's position in the Boston Market, which he had to consolidate into a meaningful report to Mr. Magnes. He concluded that the most critical general problems in Boston resulted from a lack of communication between the Marketing Managers and the Regional Sales Managers regarding the priorities which should be placed on the various products. He wanted to write a report to management which not only would show how TFC's position in Boston could be improved, but also would be helpful to him in approaching future studies in other marketing areas. Monty's final report to management follows.

September 1, 1966

TO:      Charles Magnes
FROM:   Montgomery Joy
RE:      *A Study of the Boston Revenue Opportunity*

My assignment was to make an analysis of the Boston market which would result in recommendations for improving TFC's corporate position in that market. The analysis was to serve both as an aid to decision-making for TFC, and as a meaningful learning experience about TFC and the food industry for me. This report centers on what I consider the first and most important step in improving TFC's market position—the establishment of priorities for TFC products. Hopefully, by providing the means for setting priorities, the different functions of TFC management will be able to arrive more easily at a consensus on the allocation of resources for any given branch.

The importance of good communications to the effective cooperation of sales and marketing organizations should not be underestimated. Although it is not intuitively obvious that "communications" is the answer to the general question of "How can TFC improve its position in Boston?," the effective solution of marketing problems *presupposes* that a system of priorities has been set up and agreed upon by the Regional and Marketing managers. I have thus tackled the strategic question, "Where do we go?," rather than the more operational question, "How do we get there?"

This report thus has a dual purpose: to establish a priority list for incremental investment of TFC's money and effort in Boston and, more generally, to provide a method for structuring the problems in any given region. On the basis of my analysis, I recommend that the "revenue reward" approach to setting priorities for incremental investment at regional level be used, and that the following product categories be emphasized for incremental investment in

Boston (in order of magnitude): cake mix, cereal, pudding, pancakes, dehydrated potatoes, mayonnaise, coffee, salad dressing.

I have chosen the concept of "revenue reward" as a foundation for approaching the question of how and where TFC should allocate its marketing resources. This concept is a composite of the two elements which are necessary to maximize the return on each investment dollar. The first element is "revenue after fixed." I measured TFC's opportunities in Boston with gross margin revenue dollars rather than sales dollars or tonnage because it provides an approximation of the dollar amount we can expect on our investment. For example, if the long run average return on product "A" is $50,000 per year, we would not want to spend more than $50,000 per year to get it. Revenue also measures the efficiency with which TFC uses its investment capital. For maximum efficiency, TFC should invest where the revenue return per case is the greatest. Based on this criterion alone, the product categories would be ranked in the following order: coffee, cereal, cake mix, pancakes, mayonnaise, dehydrated potatoes, salad dressing, pudding.

The second element in investment consideration is the absolute size of the potential market gain. As a measure of this, I have used the size of the gap between TFC and the chief competitor. Essentially, I take the competitor's level of retail distribution and case movement for each product as standards of what is possible for TFC in Boston and compute how much it would be worth to gain that sales level. The maximum reward for each product is calculated by measuring the gap in terms of the number of cases and then multiplying that figure by the revenue per case.[3]

The "revenue reward" is thus a composite which weights the absolute size of the potential market gain for a product by the revenue per case it returns to TFC. The list of such rewards provides a rough idea of the priorities for incremental investment in any given market. These rewards, in addition to trend and distribution analyses, and information about the Boston retail trade and consumer, should provide the Marketing Managers and Divisional or Regional Sales Managers with a solid basis for decisions on the allocation of resources. Moreover, although the Marketing Managers may have only limited use for the priority list of a given branch, the revenue reward concept applied to a whole region would enable them to spotlight their opportunities on a national scale.

If the revenue reward concept is adopted, it will provide a means of communication between the Marketing and Divisional Sales Managers. Since the Divisional Sales Manager must formulate and defend a division-wide strategy, this concept offers him a basis for planning and for discussing divisional differences. In thus facilitating consensus on priorities for incremental investment or for allocation of sales effort, TFC's over-all position in the market would be improved.

---

[3] A more rigorous financial analysis would probably disregard the absolute size of the reward (which might favor new products) for the relative contribution return each product makes. But if TFC were to disregard the absolute size of the gap for certain products (particularly where the gap was considerable), the Boston retail trade might discontinue additional products. TFC must, therefore, consider the hidden financial cost of discontinuance and reintroduction when deciding on incremental investment.

## SECTION I

### *Boston Branch*

In this study, I concentrated on the major product lines which had not met the Company's sales objectives. I measured each product against similar (in price and quality) products among the major brands because these competitors possessed roughly the same tools as TFC for generating marketing impact.

The revenue reward approach may be illustrated by taking Wheat Flakes cereal as an example. The two variables in this approach are the average number of distribution points (DP)[4] per product and the movement or number of cases sold through each distribution point (C/pt.). The top competitor for Wheat Flakes had 98 distribution points in the region with an average yearly movement of 498 cases per point. TFC, on the other hand, had only 73 DP's averaging only 371 cases per point. If TFC gained 25 DP's (to reach the level of the competitor) without increasing its movement, the gain would be worth $15,026, or 9,275 cases. Similarly, if TFC increased movement by 127 C/pt., the value of the gain (holding DP constant) would be $15,019, or 9,271 cases. Calculating the rewards for movement and distribution improvement separately provides a means to determine whether the Boston share problem is one of movement or distribution or both.

The total revenue reward to be gained from increasing both movement and distribution to the major competitor's level is greater than the sum of the revenues for improving each separately. Thus, to obtain the total revenue reward for Wheat Flakes (the competitor's current volume less TFC's current volume), TFC would have to sell 21,721 additional cases by increasing distribution and movement simultaneously. This would be worth $35,188.

The following matrix of the revenue opportunities for the Boston Region market by product shows how much revenue[5] TFC could generate by increasing either distribution or movement to the level of its chief competitor in Boston, or by increasing both distribution and movement to its chief competitor's level. (See Exhibit 7 of this report.) Based on these results, the product categories should be emphasized for incremental investment in Boston in the following order:

Cake Mix
Cereal
Pudding
Pancakes
Dehydrated Potatoes
Mayonnaise
Coffee
Salad Dressing

---

[4] DP (Distribution Point) is a measurement established by an outside marketing research organization for comparing market penetration. The total number of DP's for a given product is computed by weighting the actual number of outlets for that product by the sales volumes of the outlets.

[5] Revenue after fixed, but before advertising, sales promotion, and general administrative expenses.

The "revenue reward" method can also be used to spotlight and compare opportunities between regions. To illustrate this, I have compared the revenue opportunities for pancakes *within* the Eastern Division and *between* the Eastern Division as a whole and the Los Angeles Region. By this method, the Los Angeles revenue opportunity exceeds that of the whole Eastern Division. (See Exhibit 8 of this report.) These results suggest that TFC *consider* taking some action in the Los Angeles market.

Should the proposed revenue reward be accepted?

## EXHIBIT 1

### Boston Per Capita Consumption Index
### (U.S. = 100)

| | | | | |
|---|---|---|---|---|
| *Cereals* | | 112 | *Pancakes* | 63 |
| Wheat Flakes | 102 | | 1 Pound (#1) | 54 |
| Corn Puffs | 98 | | 2 Pound (#2) | 212 |
| Choc-Bits | 113 | | Buttermilk | 59 |
| Rice Crunchies | 96 | | | |
| Toasted Oats | 112 | | *Mayonnaise* | 102 |
| Sugar Snaks | 107 | | *Coffee* | 111 |
| Berry Bran | 131 | | Regular | 89 |
| *Cake Mixes* | | 110 | Instant | 127 |
| White | 85 | | *Puddings and Pie Fillings* | 100 |
| Yellow | 125 | | Vanilla | 99 |
| Chocolate | 113 | | Chocolate | 136 |
| Spice | 113 | | Butterscotch | 114 |
| Angel Food | 103 | | Lemon | 74 |
| *Salad Dressings* | | 89 | *Potato Products* | 93 |
| Italian | 62 | | Instant Mashed | 47 |
| Garlic | 73 | | Au Gratin | 98 |
| Blue Cheese | 97 | | | |

**EXHIBIT 2**

**Graphical Presentation of Size of Total Market
and TFC's Share of Market in the Boston Region
for Eight Product Categories**

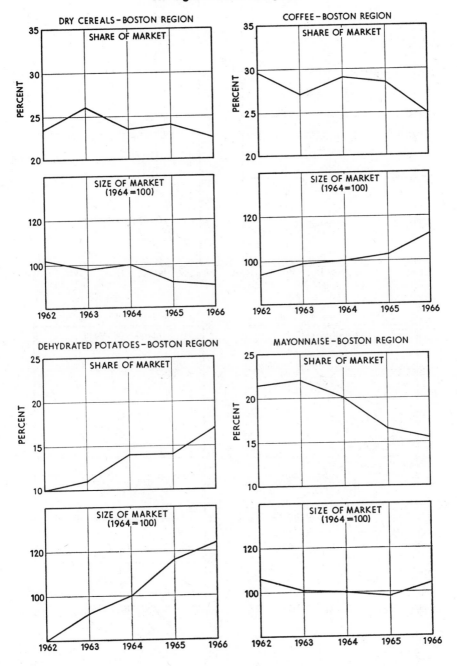

## EXHIBIT 2 (Continued)

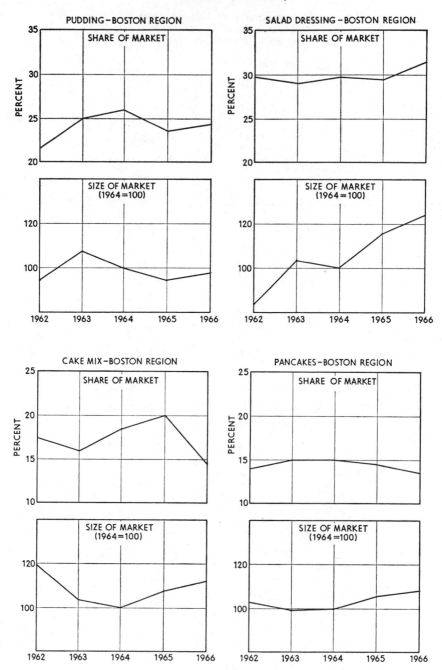

# EXHIBIT 3

## Socioeconomic Data on Selected SMSA's*

| SMSA | Population of SMSA | Age | | | | Annual Family Income | | | Women over 14 in Labor Force | Foreign Stock | |
|---|---|---|---|---|---|---|---|---|---|---|---|
| | | Median Age | <18 | >65 | Median Age —Women— | <$6,000 | >$10,000 | Median | | Foreign Born | Second Generation |
| Boston | 2,595,481 | 32.0 yrs. | 32.5% | 10.9% | 33.7 yrs. | 41.7% | 21.3% | $6,687 | 38.1% | 12.4% | 29.4% |
| Buffalo | 1,306,957 | 30.9 | 35.0 | 9.0 | 31.4 | 43.8 | 17.3 | 6,455 | 33.3 | 8.8 | 23.7 |
| Chicago | 6,220,913 | 31.3 | 33.8 | 8.6 | 31.8 | 34.9 | 25.9 | 7,342 | 39.0 | 9.7 | 22.7 |
| Cleveland | 1,909,483 | 31.4 | 34.3 | 8.9 | 31.9 | 37.8 | 22.4 | 6,962 | 36.3 | 9.7 | 23.0 |
| Dallas | 1,083,601 | 28.2 | 36.1 | 7.1 | 28.8 | 50.8 | 17.7 | 5,925 | 41.2 | 1.5 | 4.3 |
| Detroit | 3,762,360 | 29.3 | 37.3 | 7.2 | 29.5 | 40.1 | 22.0 | 6,825 | 32.9 | 9.7 | 20.4 |
| Los Angeles | 10,687,367 | 30.9 | 33.8 | 8.9 | 31.8 | 37.9 | 24.6 | 7,066 | 37.6 | 9.1 | 17.4 |
| Milwaukee | 1,706,994 | 30.0 | 34.9 | 8.8 | 30.5 | 35.6 | 20.7 | 6,995 | 37.2 | 6.7 | 21.5 |
| New Orleans | 1,123,033 | 26.1 | 37.1 | 7.3 | 29.4 | 59.6 | 13.4 | 5,195 | 33.8 | 2.1 | 6.0 |
| New York | 15,646,307 | 34.0 | 30.2 | 9.7 | 34.8 | 43.9 | 22.2 | 6,548 | 37.9 | 17.4 | 28.4 |
| Philadelphia | 5,737,442 | 31.5 | 33.5 | 9.1 | 32.6 | 44.8 | 19.2 | 6,433 | 35.8 | 6.8 | 18.2 |
| Pittsburgh | 2,878,235 | 32.1 | 33.9 | 9.5 | 32.5 | 50.7 | 15.8 | 5,954 | 28.4 | 6.5 | 22.3 |
| St. Louis | 2,104,669 | 30.5 | 35.3 | 9.3 | 31.3 | 46.6 | 16.9 | 6,275 | 34.7 | 2.8 | 10.0 |
| San Francisco | 2,648,762 | 31.8 | 32.6 | 9.0 | 32.5 | 37.0 | 24.3 | 7,092 | 38.9 | 10.8 | 19.6 |
| Seattle | 1,107,213 | 30.2 | 35.3 | 9.6 | 30.5 | 38.6 | 21.9 | 6,896 | 36.9 | 8.1 | 18.7 |
| Washington, D.C. | 2,001,897 | 28.9 | 34.9 | 6.2 | 30.2 | 35.0 | 30.5 | 7,577 | 44.5 | 4.2 | 9.3 |
| U.S. | 179,272,920 | 29.5 | 38.5 | 9.0 | 30.4 | 54.2 | 14.1 | 5,660 | 34.5 | 5.4 | 13.6 |

* Data based on Standard Metropolitan Statistical Areas (SMSA) designated by the U.S. Bureau of the Budget.
SOURCE: *1960 U.S. Census.*

## EXHIBIT 4

### Per Capita Expenditures on Bakery Goods and Dining out in Selected Areas

| SMSA* | Per Capita Expenditures on Bakery Goods | Per Capita Expenditures on Dining out |
|---|---|---|
| Boston | $9.12 | $103.12 |
| Buffalo | 5.99 | 71.75 |
| Chicago | 7.66 | 102.11 |
| Cleveland | 4.99 | 84.88 |
| Dallas | 1.92 | 97.70 |
| Detroit | 4.57 | 70.49 |
| Los Angeles | 3.34 | 71.93 |
| Milwaukee | 5.50 | 51.90 |
| New Orleans | 3.41 | 64.59 |
| New York | 8.66 | 97.72 |
| Philadelphia | 4.18 | 62.94 |
| Pittsburgh | 6.08 | 47.18 |
| St. Louis | 5.36 | 72.65 |
| San Francisco | 7.56 | 132.05 |
| Seattle | 3.68 | 98.32 |
| Washington, D.C. | 3.48 | 128.38 |
| U.S. | 4.64 | 77.64 |

* Data based on Standard Metropolitan Statistical Areas (SMSA) designated by the U.S. Bureau of the Budget.
Source: *1963 Census of Business.*

## EXHIBIT 5

### Flour Consumption Index for TFC's Eastern Division and Selected Regions (U.S. = 100)

| | |
|---|---|
| Eastern Division | 49 |
| Boston Region | 40 |
| Buffalo Region | 76 |
| Chicago Region | 60 |
| Jacksonville Region | 91 |
| Minneapolis Region | 81 |
| New York Region | 32 |
| Philadelphia Region | 44 |
| Portland Region | 71 |

**EXHIBIT 6**

**Organizational Chart**

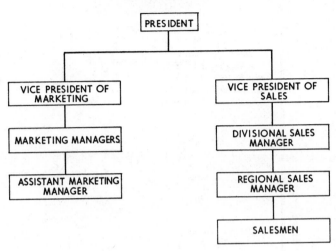

## EXHIBIT 7

### Boston Region Revenue Opportunity for Selected Products

| | TFC's Average Level of Distribution (DP)* | Chief Competitor's Average Level of Distribution (DP) | TFC's Average Annual Movement (C/pt.)† | Chief Competitor's Average Annual Movement (C/pt.) | Revenue Reward for Increasing Distribution (DP) to Chief Competitor's Level | Revenue Reward for Increasing Movement (C/pt.) to Chief Competitor's Level | Total Revenue Reward for Increasing Both Distribution and Movement to Chief Competitor's Level |
|---|---|---|---|---|---|---|---|
| **Cereals‡** | | | | | | | |
| Wheat Flakes | 73 | 98 | 371 | 498 | 15,026 | 15,019 | 35,188 |
| Corn Puffs | 66 | 81 | 213 | 386 | 5,176 | 18,497 | 27,877 |
| Choc-Bits | 31 | 78 | 43 | 116 | 3,395 | 3,802 | 12,961 |
| Rice Crunchies | 74 | 89 | 176 | 244 | 4,250 | 8,102 | 13,994 |
| Toasted Oats | 47 | 42 | 84 | 88 | ... | 301 | ... |
| Sugar Snaks | 79 | 84 | 254 | 196 | 2,108 | ... | ... |
| Berry Bran | 75 | 76 | 79 | 93 | 133 | 1,764 | 1,920 |
| TOTAL | | | | | 30,088 | 47,485 | 91,940 |
| **Cake Mixes** | | | | | | | |
| White | 68 | 97 | 214 | 273 | 8,564 | 5,537 | 16,462 |
| Yellow | 79 | 98 | 296 | 532 | 8,099 | 26,847 | 41,403 |
| Chocolate | 72 | 86 | 138 | 391 | 2,724 | 25,685 | 33,403 |
| Spice | 44 | 79 | 176 | 198 | 8,870 | 1,394 | 11,373 |
| Angel Food | 69 | 98 | 250 | 316 | 10,150 | 6,376 | 19,205 |
| TOTAL | | | | | 38,407 | 65,839 | 121,846 |

| | | | | | | | |
|---|---|---|---|---|---|---|---|
| **Salad Dressings** | | | | | | | |
| Italian | 87 | 95 | 86 | 128 | 482 | 2,558 | 3,275 |
| Garlic | 79 | 79 | 51 | 101 | ... | 2,765 | 2,765 |
| Blue Cheese | 23 | 63 | 36 | 84 | 1,008 | 773 | 3,125 |
| TOTAL | | | | | 1,490 | 6,096 | 9,165 |
| **Pancakes** | | | | | | | |
| #1 (one pound) | 42 | 87 | 177 | 211 | 8,363 | 1,499 | 11,469 |
| #2 (two pound) | 64 | 88 | 605 | 719 | 14,084 | 7,077 | 23,815 |
| Buttermilk | 23 | 25 | 154 | 154 | 339 | ... | 339 |
| TOTAL | | | | | 22,786 | 8,576 | 35,623 |
| Mayonnaise | 73 | 86 | 636 | 754 | 7,110 | 7,408 | 15,838 |
| **Coffee** | | | | | | | |
| Regular | 98 | 99 | 531 | 593 | 1,062 | 12,152 | 13,338 |
| Instant | 98 | 98 | 476 | 505 | ... | 5,997 | 5,997 |
| TOTAL | | | | | 1,062 | 18,149 | 19,335 |
| **Puddings & Pie Fillings** | | | | | | | |
| Vanilla | 77 | 88 | 76 | 243 | 510 | 7,844 | 9,475 |
| Chocolate | 77 | 93 | 88 | 297 | 831 | 9,495 | 12,299 |
| Butterscotch | 39 | 81 | 36 | 201 | 922 | 3,925 | 9,075 |
| Lemon | 42 | 75 | 84 | 193 | 1,663 | 2,747 | 6,568 |
| TOTAL | | | | | 3,926 | 24,011 | 37,417 |
| **Potato Products** | | | | | | | |
| Mashed | 77 | 88 | 714 | 832 | 5,262 | 6,088 | 12,219 |
| Au Gratin | 65 | 69 | 56 | 298 | 199 | 14,000 | 15,061 |
| TOTAL | | | | | 5,461 | 20,088 | 27,280 |

* Distribution point.
† Cases per DP.
‡ Each cereal is measured against comparable ones, e.g., Choc-Bits with other chocolate flavored dry cereals.

**EXHIBIT 8**

**Pancake Revenue Opportunity**
**Eastern Division vs. Los Angeles Region**

| | TFC's Average Level of Distribution (DP) | Chief Competitor's Average Level of Distribution (DP) | TFC's Average Annual Movement (C/pt.) | Chief Competitor's Average Annual Movement (C/pt.) | Revenue Reward for Increasing Distribution (DP) to Chief Competitor's Level | Revenue Reward for Increasing Movement (C/pt.) to Chief Competitor's Level | Total Revenue Reward for Increasing Both Distribution and Movement to Chief Competitor's Level |
|---|---|---|---|---|---|---|---|
| *Eastern Division* | | | | | | | |
| **Boston Region** | | | | | | | |
| One pound (#1) | 42 | 87 | 177 | 211 | 8,363 | 1,499 | 11,469 |
| Two pound (#2) | 64 | 88 | 605 | 719 | 14,084 | 7,077 | 23,815 |
| Buttermilk | 23 | 25 | 154 | 154 | 339 | .... | 339 |
| Total | | | | | 22,786 | 8,576 | 35,623 |
| **Buffalo Region** | | | | | | | |
| #1 | 66 | 77 | 158 | 184 | 1,825 | 1,801 | 3,927 |
| #2 | 85 | 85 | 1,076 | 1,294 | .... | 17,974 | 17,974 |
| Buttermilk | 51 | 59 | 343 | 417 | 3,018 | 4,151 | 7,821 |
| Total | | | | | 4,843 | 23,926 | 29,722 |
| **Philadelphia Region** | | | | | | | |
| #1 | 75 | 90 | 209 | 458 | 3,292 | 19,609 | 26,822 |
| #2 | 77 | 91 | 509 | 1,153 | 6,912 | 48,100 | 63,758 |
| Buttermilk | 40 | 41 | 146 | 250 | 161 | 4,576 | 4,851 |
| Total | | | | | 10,365 | 72,285 | 95,431 |

| | | | | | | |
|---|--:|--:|--:|--:|--:|--:|
| **Portland Region** | | | | | | |
| #1 | 66 | 221 | 250 | 2,553 | 2,010 | 4,897 |
| #2 | 83 | 1,104 | 1,173 | 2,142 | 5,555 | 7,831 |
| Buttermilk | 38 | 407 | 448 | .... | 1,714 | 1,221 |
| Total | | | | 4,695 | 9,279 | 13,949 |
| **New York Region** | | | | | | |
| #1 | 69 | 400 | 737 | 8,400 | 24,416 | 39,893 |
| #2 | 73 | 833 | 1,489 | 10,504 | 46,451 | 65,228 |
| Buttermilk | 28 | 252 | 436 | 5,821 | 5,667 | 15,739 |
| Total | | | | 24,725 | 76,534 | 120,860 |
| Total Eastern Division | | | | 67,414 | 190,600 | 295,585 |
| **Los Angeles Region** | | | | | | |
| #1 | 37 | 224 | 757 | 12,230 | 20,707 | 62,039 |
| #2 | 78 | 1,242 | 3,271 | 16,866 | 153,514 | 197,934 |
| Buttermilk | 29 | 278 | 666 | 17,431 | 12,377 | 54,135 |
| Total Los Angeles Region | | | | 46,527 | 186,598 | 314,108 |

# North Star Shipping Company (B)

Further discussions between Mr. Kruger, his superior, and North Star executives in New York led to the conclusion that the new marketing approach for Germany, described in the (A) case, could well yield reasonable results in the short term. Moreover, despite earlier pessimistic forecasts for 1974, European exports to North America had reached an all-time high, and shipping capacity had become tight on the North Atlantic route. It was felt, however, that there still existed a need for more information to establish procedures for optimizing the allocation of marketing and operational resources to Germany. This was thought to be particularly true with respect to the activities of the sales force.

A logical starting point was what had been accomplished in the past, and, thus, a proposal was prepared dealing with an analysis of past and present accounts. In the process of preparing the specifications for this analysis, such questions as the following were raised:

What information could be gained this way?
How relevant would this information be? What other data are needed?
Would it facilitate the development of viable marketing sales strategy?
And, from the operational side would such a data collection system be feasible? How should it be implemented?

## The Proposal

The central thrust of the proposal was to analyze past and present accounts and to identify "important" *target* accounts and commodities on a geographical basis. Such an analysis would also reveal a good deal about the way in which the sales force operated and to what extent it was desirable to provide them with more guidance, as well as facilitate forward planning, including the preparation of sales forecasts and budgets. Before undertaking the analysis, it was decided to have the desired data specified through the construction of tabulation tables. (These appear in Exhibit 1.) After examining these tables, Mr. Kruger was not at all certain that some of the data required could be provided accurately by the sales force. And he was reluctant to request the Werther Agency to aid in the data gathering process since North Star was only one of their clients. Before deciding what to do with the proposal, he asked his assistant to evaluate it critically and make recommendations.

## Questions

1. What is the purpose/objective of the sales analysis system being proposed?
2. To what extent will the data generated by the proposed system accomplish the objectives you set forth in 1, above? In order to answer this question, you should evaluate the contribution made by each table *and* what is obtained by evaluating the data between tables—i.e., the interrelationships involved. And, finally, what data gap exists between your objective and the data generated internally? Can any part of this gap be filled from an analysis of any other internal data?
3. On an individual table basis would you suggest any changes in the way of deletions or additions? Are the measurement terms clear in all cases?
4. From the data provided, could you determine the frequency with which a sales call should be made? What data are required to determine such an activity?
5. From the data provided, could you determine whether any accounts are unprofitable? What data are required to do so?
6. There are no data on shipments from the United States coming into Germany. What kinds of data (and from what sources) are needed in order to take "appropriate" action on this "part" of the business? Be as specific as possible.

**EXHIBIT 1**

**Proposed Tabulation Tables**

TABLE 1

Number and Value of North Star Accounts by Geographical Subarea 1970–1973

| Subarea | Number of Active Accounts | | | | | | | | Value of Active Accounts | | | | | | | |
|---|---|---|---|---|---|---|---|---|---|---|---|---|---|---|---|---|
| | 1970 | | 1971 | | 1972 | | 1973 | | 1970 | | 1971 | | 1972 | | 1973 | |
| | No. | % | No. | % | No. | % | No. | % | $ | % | $ | % | $ | % | $ | % |
| 1 2 — — — | | | | | | | | | | | | | | | | |
| Total | 100 | | 100 | | 100 | | 100 | | 100 | | 100 | | 100 | | 100 | |

TABLE 2

Commodity Types by Subarea, 1970–1973, in TEUs, Tons, or Units

| Subarea | 1970 | | 1971 | | 1972 | | 1973 | |
|---|---|---|---|---|---|---|---|---|
| | Tons | % | Tons | % | Tons | % | Tons | % |
| 1 2 — — — | | | | | | | | |
| Total | | 100 | | 100 | | 100 | | 100 |

Note: One table for each major commodity and one for "all others."

TABLE 3

Repeat Table 2 in terms of $ revenue

TABLE 4

Repeat Table 2 in terms of TEUs

TABLE 5

Number and Size of Accounts in Revenue and in Tons or Units

| Account Size ($) (annual billing) | 1970 | | | | | | 1971 | 1972 | 1973 |
|---|---|---|---|---|---|---|---|---|---|
| | No. | % | % Cum. | Total $'s | % | % Cum. | | | |
| $ 0–$49 | | | | | | | Same as 1970 | Same as 1970 | Same as 1970 |
| $50–$99 | | | | | | | | | |
| — | | | | | | | | | |
| — | | | | | | | | | |
| — | | | | | | | | | |
| Total | | 100 | | | | 100 | | | |

TABLE 6

Repeat Table 5 in terms of individual shipments

TABLE 7

Number of Accounts by Commodity Type

| Commodity Type | 1970 | | 1971 | | 1972 | | 1973 | |
|---|---|---|---|---|---|---|---|---|
| | No. | % | No. | % | No. | % | No. | % |
| A | | | | | | | | |
| B | | | | | | | | |
| — | | | | | | | | |
| — | | | | | | | | |
| — | | | | | | | | |
| Total | | 100 | | 100 | | 100 | | 100 |

## TABLE 12

### Sales Calls by Size of Account—1970–1973

| Account Size | 1970 | | | | | | | 1971 | 1972 |
| | Accounts | | | | | Sales Calls | | | |
| $ | No. | % | $ | % | No. | % | | Same format | Same format |
| | | | | | | | | | |

# Foods Limited

In September 1974 Ms. Nancy Schulte had to decide whether to recommend further investment by Foods Limited (FL) in on-premise vending. In June top management had authorized a study whose purpose was to identify new profitable areas for FL's industrial division to pursue. Among the many possibilities was vending, and Ms. Schulte had been assigned the vending portion of the study.

## BACKGROUND

Foods Limited had been established in 1945 by two brothers, Jim and Neil Star, when they were both students at a midwestern university. In 1945 the student body of the university voted to rid the university catering service of its current management and place it under student control. Since both Neil and Jim had had previous experience in the food industry (short-order cooking at a home-town diner), they applied to be the joint managers of the catering service, which would place them in complete charge of all the food services on campus. They were subsequently awarded the jobs and formed Foods Limited.

FL was so successful that the Stars decided to continue to operate at the university after graduation and to try to sell new accounts at nearby universities, colleges, and schools. Little capital outlay was required. FL provided good staff, supervision, and meal plans. The schools provided the kitchens, appliances, and utensils. Dishes and the silverware were negotiable items—sometimes the school supplied them, other times FL did.

The business grew rapidly. By 1965 FL had sales of $200 million and was a well-known national name in the manual feeding segment of the

Reprinted from *Stanford Business Cases 1975* with the permission of the publisher, Graduate School of Business, Stanford University. Copyright © 1975 by the Board of Trustees of the Leland Stanford Junior University.

This case was prepared by Joan Haynes under the supervision of Professor Carlton A. Pederson.

food industry. (Manual feeding refers to food service where food is distributed by one or more attendants, i.e., a cafeteria line.) FL, which enjoyed a very healthy cash position, was ready to diversify. After many areas of investment were considered, FL bought two well-known restaurant groups. The main criterion for purchase was an expected future yearly ROI (after taxes) of 11% or better.

As a result of these acquisitions the company was divided into two major divisions—the foods division and the restaurant division. Originally, the foods division had only one type of account (institutional/school), but, shortly after the restaurants were acquired, FL bought up a well-known company which specialized in industrial food service. The foods division was then split into the institutional division and the industrial division.

## INDUSTRIAL DIVISION

The industrial division's plans and progress received much attention from top management. It did well for two years, but by the beginning of the third year the division head felt that the group could move much faster if it had a specific plan to follow. One way to improve on this situation, however, would be to target on certain segments which contained potentially profitable accounts, determine what it would take for FL to win these accounts, and then go after them. It was decided, therefore, that a study of the industrial division's opportunities should be conducted. The purpose of the study would be two-fold—(1) to identify potentially profitable accounts, and (2) to formulate ways to reach and win these accounts.

## THE STUDY

The study began in mid-June and was concluded in late September. Nine people were involved: four full-time employees of FL, three summer associates (including Ms. Schulte) who were working on their M.B.A.'s at a well known local business school, and two consultants from the consulting firm Price, Jones and Company. The two consultants headed up and organized the study.

There were, in fact, many potential opportunities for the industrial division. The problem was how to recognize these opportunities and then to make use of them. The consultants outlined the problem and assigned various sections of the outline to the individuals participating in the study. Vending was considered important enough to warrant an entire section.

### Vending

The vending industry enjoyed a market of nearly $8 billion dollars. Projections suggested that the market would exceed $10.5 billion by

1980. No one company had a dominant position in the industry—the five largest vendors combined accounted for only 8% of the total market. There were over 6,000 companies involved in vending of which only 600 had annual sales of $2–8 million or more.

The vending industry involved a large number of products. Any article which was small enough to fit in a vending machine and could be sold for a relatively small price was vendable. Among the vending product areas were:

Full-line food vending (beverages, sandwiches, fruit, dairy products, etc.).

Specialized food vending (only coffee, or only cigarettes, etc.).

Music and games vending.

Paperback book vending.

Cosmetic and drug vending.

All vending, regardless of the type of product sold, was organized as either *route vending* or *on-premise vending*. It was not known how the vending market was shared by these two types of operations. Both are described below.

*Route Vending.* Typically, a vending company contracted for a number of small accounts (generally fewer than 20 machines at one location) in a fairly concentrated geographic area. This was referred to as the route. The number of machines and the miles traveled in one route were determined by what one person or a team of two persons could reasonably handle in one day. A vending company would normally have control over a large number of such routes.

The supplies for the machines were kept in a centralized warehouse. Each day the route person/persons started out from the warehouse with supplies and made the rounds: filling the machines, clearing the coin jams, and reporting any broken machines.

Depending on its size, a company would have one or more mechanics who repaired the machines which had been reported broken. In the larger vending operations the mechanics kept in contact with a central office by two-way car radio and could be at the site of the breakdown very quickly.

Some of the more successful route vending companies enjoyed annual sales of $10 million or more, but there were few companies of this size.

*On-Premise Vending.* Generally the vending company contracted for a large account (ideally 100 machines or more) at one client location. Vending companies which were involved in this type of vending typically had many such accounts.

Supplies for the machines were sent directly to the client address and stored in a small warehousing facility generally loaned by or rented from the client. The machines were supplied and maintained by a staff which was under the control and employ of the vending company but which remained on location with the client on a full-time basis. Typically, this staff would be composed of at least one mechanic and one or more route persons, depending on the size of the account.

*Foods Limited's Current Position in Vending.* Before FL acquired the industrial feeding company in 1965, it had no vending accounts. As a result of the acquisition, however, FL gained one vending route in the Atlanta region and four on-premise accounts: two in Oklahoma City, one in Portland, Oregon, and one in Birmingham, Alabama. (The acquisition also brought FL feeding accounts.) FL's share of the total vending market with the new accounts was less than 1/20 of 1%.

At the time of the acquisition FL management had little or no expertise in the area of vending and soon learned that there was little carryover of techniques from manual feeding to vending. The only similarity between the two areas was that they both dealt with food.

*Economics of Vending.* Where a company vends is as important as what it vends. Certain locations offered greater sales potential than others (see Exhibit 1); plants and factories were clearly the volume leaders.

Product choice was the other important feature. There were four industry favorites among vendors—cigarettes, cold drinks, candy, and coffee (the four Cs). Their margins (see Exhibit 2) combined with volume sold (see Exhibit 3) put them way out in front as the top money makers (see Exhibit 4). In fact, they were so profitable, and, if it were left up to vendors, the four C's would be the only products vended; machines which vended other products (i.e., cold food, milk, and ice cream) would never be installed. Most clients, however, required a full line of vended products for their employees. So, in order to win an account, certain concessions were made by the vendors, and a minimum number of the less desirable machines were installed (see Exhibit 5). In general, however, machines which vended a product other than the four Cs were unprofitable, due either to high product spoilage rates or low customer volume.

The average vending machine cost was found to be $1,540. In addition, auxiliary equipment such as coin sorters ran approximately 10% of total machine costs. Average vending machine sales per client employee per year were $55.00. Generally, one machine per 50 employees was installed in an on-premise setup.

*The Economics of Food Limited's Vending.* Vending accounted for annual company sales of $1.4 million, 7% of the industrial division's sales for the fiscal year ending in June 1974. Of this 7%, 6% was accounted for by on-premise vending; the other 1% came from the route in Atlanta. The industrial division was dissatisfied by the performance of its route vending, which showed a net profit of 4% of sales. On-premise vending, however, showed an average net profit of 16%. The manual feeding accounts in the division brought in 6%.

Currently, FL had a total of 509 active vending machines—73 of them were used in the one route system, and 436 were located in on-premise accounts. On the vending equipment FL used a straightline depreciation method over a five-year life with zero salvage value. The company was taxed at a rate of 50%.

Contracts with clients were generally set up on a one-year basis and renegotiated upon expiration.

### Questions

1. Should Foods Limited maintain its vending accounts, phase them out, or expand vending by pursuing more vending accounts? More specifically, what profitability would result if on-premise accounted for 10% or 20% of the division's sales and route vending was phased out? What other factors should be considered before deciding to increase the vending business?

2. If the decision is made to go after more vending, how should FL go about it?

**EXHIBIT 1**

**Total Vended Volume Varies Greatly by Location**

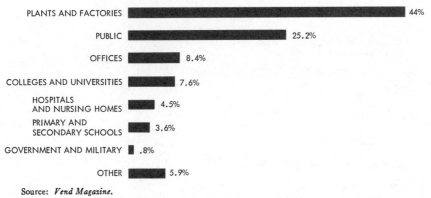

| | |
|---|---|
| PLANTS AND FACTORIES | 44% |
| PUBLIC | 25.2% |
| OFFICES | 8.4% |
| COLLEGES AND UNIVERSITIES | 7.6% |
| HOSPITALS AND NURSING HOMES | 4.5% |
| PRIMARY AND SECONDARY SCHOOLS | 3.6% |
| GOVERNMENT AND MILITARY | .8% |
| OTHER | 5.9% |

Source: *Vend Magazine.*

## EXHIBIT 2

### The Margins on the Products Vary Widely

| Products | Margin |
|---|---|
| Coffee*............................ | 67% |
| Cup cold drinks*.................... | 67 |
| Snacks............................. | 57 |
| Candy*............................ | 53 |
| Ice cream.......................... | 52 |
| Milk.............................. | 42 |
| Pastry............................. | 40 |
| Hot canned foods................... | 31 |
| Cigarettes*........................ | 25 |
| Canned cold drinks*................. | 16 |
| Cold bottled drinks*................ | 16 |

* The four C's.
SOURCE: *Vend Magazine.*

## EXHIBIT 3

### The Four C's Are Clear Leaders in Terms of Dollar Sales (000)

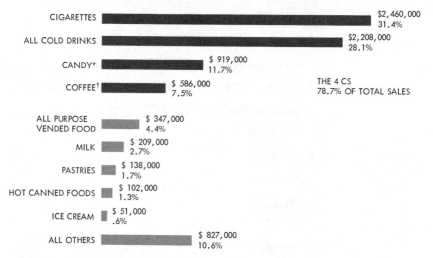

CIGARETTES — $2,460,000 / 31.4%
ALL COLD DRINKS — $2,208,000 / 28.1%
CANDY* — $ 919,000 / 11.7%
COFFEE† — $ 586,000 / 7.5%

THE 4 CS
78.7% OF TOTAL SALES

ALL PURPOSE VENDED FOOD — $ 347,000 / 4.4%
MILK — $ 209,000 / 2.7%
PASTRIES — $ 138,000 / 1.7%
HOT CANNED FOODS — $ 102,000 / 1.3%
ICE CREAM — $ 51,000 / .6%
ALL OTHERS — $ 827,000 / 10.6%

* The sales of candy are slightly inflated by including snacks.
† The sales of coffee are slightly inflated by including soup and hot chocolate.
SOURCE: *Vend Magazine.*

## EXHIBIT 4

### The Four C's Are the Leaders in Dollar Profits (000)

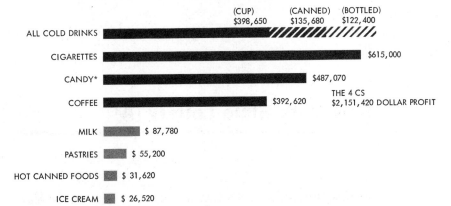

(CUP) $398,650  (CANNED) $135,680  (BOTTLED) $122,400

ALL COLD DRINKS

CIGARETTES — $615,000

CANDY* — $487,070

COFFEE — $392,620

THE 4 CS
$2,151,420 DOLLAR PROFIT

MILK — $ 87,780

PASTRIES — $ 55,200

HOT CANNED FOODS — $ 31,620

ICE CREAM — $ 26,520

* The dollar profit of candy is slightly inflated by including snacks.
† The dollar profit of coffee is slightly inflated by including soup and hot chocolate.
Source: *Vend Magazine.*

## EXHIBIT 5

### The High Volume and Profitability of the Four C's Are Reflected in the Number of Machines in Use Nationally

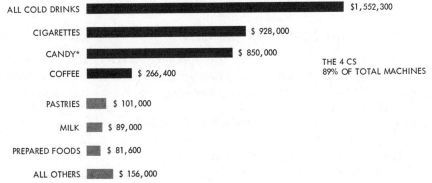

ALL COLD DRINKS — $1,552,300

CIGARETTES — $ 928,000

CANDY* — $ 850,000

COFFEE — $ 266,400

THE 4 CS
89% OF TOTAL MACHINES

PASTRIES — $ 101,000

MILK — $ 89,000

PREPARED FOODS — $ 81,600

ALL OTHERS — $ 156,000

* The number of candy machines is slightly inflated by the inclusion of snack machines.
Source: *Vend Magazine.*

# New York State Lottery (A)

In June, 1968, at the end of its first year of operation, the New York State Lottery seemed well established. A public survey, held in fall, 1967, indicated eight out of ten state residents were in favor of continuing the lottery, and the strident criticism of opponents of the lottery that had marked its early months seemed diminished. But lottery sales had continued to fall throughout the year, and there was considerable uncertainty among responsible officials as to what steps might be taken to increase sales.

## GENERAL BACKGROUND ON THE LOTTERY

The New York State Lottery was approved in referendum by New York State voters in November, 1966, by a vote of 2.46 million to 1.60 million. The State Lottery Law, required to put the lottery into operation, was passed during the 1967 session of the New York Legislature and was the result of a series of compromises between Governor Nelson A. Rockefeller and high legislative officials.

The first major compromise concerned the form the lottery was to take. Governor Rockefeller favored a simple, direct drawing to determine a winner. Anthony J. Travia, Speaker of the New York Assembly, wanted the winners to be determined by a horse race in part, because the addition of a horse race to the lottery meant New York State could avoid paying the U.S. Federal Gambling Tax of 10 percent on all gross gambling receipts, except receipts from horse racing. The form decided on was that winners would be determined in a two-stage process, the first stage separating winners from non-winners, the second deciding the dollar amount each winner would receive. Names of winners in the first stage would be drawn from a bowl. For each million tickets sold, fifteen names would be

This case was prepared by Professor David L. Rados of the Graduate School of Business, Columbia University. Reproduced by permission.

drawn and assigned numbers from one to fifteen, equivalent to fifteen post positions in a horse race already held at a specified track during the previous week. Then the horse race ticket was drawn from a second bowl. The winners' prizes would then be determined by the finish of the horse starting in the equivalent numbered post position. For example, in the first round a winner's name might be drawn and assigned post position No. 6. In the second round if the horse that ran from post position No. 6 finished first, the winner would receive the top prize. If the horse finished fifth, the fifth highest prize would be awarded. This process would be repeated for each million dollars in sales.

The total payout was to be $300,000 per million dollars of sales. The prize schedule was:

| | Number of Winners | Size of Prize |
|---|---|---|
| | 1 | $100,000 |
| | 1 | 75,000 |
| | 1 | 50,000 |
| | 1 | 20,000 |
| | 11 | 5,000 |
| Totals | 15 | $300,000 |

A second major compromise concerned the administration of the lottery. Governor Rockefeller wanted the lottery to be under the full control of the State Department of Taxation and Finance, while Speaker Travia wanted it controlled by an independent commission. The compromise solution resulted in a four-member, bipartisan commission within the Department of Taxation and Finance to advise the Commissioner of Taxation and Finance. Actual operation of the lottery was the responsibility of the Division of the Lottery within the Department of Taxation and Finance. The Division would be headed by a Director and three Deputy Directors of Sales and Administration, Prizes and Drawings, and Security and Accounting. A former agent for the Federal Bureau of Investigation, Ernest T. Bird, was hired as Director.

Even with these compromises, continued dispute between the Governor and Speaker Travia and various maneuvers by opponents of the lottery delayed passage of the legislation until the final day of the 1967 legislative session. The final bill specified that the lottery tickets be priced at one dollar, that drawings be held once a month, and that sales be allowed in hotels, motels, banks, Western Union offices, and some New York State offices. The ticket form was also decided on: the ticket was to be check sized, pale green, and consist of two portions separated by a piece of carbon paper. The buyer would write his name and address on the ticket and deposit half in a lottery box at the point of sale. The ticket design also included several features to help detect illegal tampering. Excerpts from the State Lottery Law are found in the Appendix.

Following passage of the State Lottery Law, State Tax Commissioner,

Joseph H. Murphy, had approximately eight weeks in which to prepare for the start of sales on June 1, 1967. After holding hearings on the size of commission to be paid sales outlets, he ruled that retail sales agents would be paid a commission of five cents on each dollar ticket. Commissioner Murphy announced that this ruling was subject to review and possible change at the end of six months' operation. Some prospective sellers had asked for commissions ranging from ten to twenty cents per ticket. Shortly after this decision Western Union announced that it would not sell lottery tickets, because 5 percent commission was insufficient to cover costs.

At this time a sales forecast of $360 million dollars was prepared for the first year's operation. Pro forma income statement for the year is found in Exhibit 1. The Lottery Law required that the payout in prizes not exceed 30 percent of sales and that 55 percent of sales be used for educational purposes in the state.

## OTHER FORMS OF GAMBLING

Competing with the new lottery were several other forms of gambling. The New Hampshire Sweepstakes, like New York's lottery, was designed to raise money for education. Until passage of the New York lottery, the New Hampshire Sweepstakes had been the only legal lottery in the United States. The winner of the New Hampshire Sweepstakes was determined by an annual horse race run at Rockingham Race Track in New Hampshire, a procedure modeled on the Irish Sweepstakes. Bettors bought tickets on the race for three dollars. There were approximately two thousand prizes; six first prizes of $100,000 each, six of $50,000, six of $25,000, and the remaining prizes of lesser amounts. Results for the first four years are given in Exhibit 2. Poor results in 1965 led the Sweepstakes Commission to give prizes on two Sweepstakes races; there were twice as many prizes, each worth half the amount given above. This prize schedule was still in effect in mid-1967. A survey of New Hampshire ticket buyers showed that most were purchased by middle class, out-of-state residents, including many residents of New York State. In 1967 New Hampshire's population was approximately 690,000.

A second form of gambling, illegal in the United States, was the "numbers" or "policy" game. The most popular form of this game was the three-digit number bet, in which payments were based on a three-digit random number published in the daily newspaper, such as the last three digits of the total number of shares traded on the New York Stock Exchange or the "mutual handle" at the Aqueduct (N.Y.) Race Track. The player chose any three-digit number, say 007, and bet as little as ten cents or as much as one hundred dollars, the limits depending on local conditions. He placed his bets with a local collector who followed a daily route or at neighborhood businesses. After a compulsory tip of 10 percent on all winnings, paid to the collector, net payoff odds were between 450:1 and 540:1. The numbers game was believed to thrive in low income neighborhoods, and the net amount bet in New York City alone was estimated at about $200 million per year.

As a form of gambling the numbers game seemed to offer residents of New York State several advantages. Distribution was widespread, making it easy to place a bet. There was flexibility in the amount wagered; the minimum bet in New York City was believed to be twenty-five cents. The bettor could play hunches and choose his own "lucky" number. Results of wagers were known the same day or the following day. There were frequent opportunities to play, usually six days per week. Finally while it was a criminal offense in New York State to receive bets it was not illegal to place them. Many numbers players were believed addicted to the game, as the following quote from a detective in the New York City Police Department illustrates:

> We made an arrest, and we took the collectors away, and people came in—you know, people from the street, housewives and such—and their eyes must have been glazed. They'd walk up to us and try to place bets. We'd show them the police shield, and they'd still try. They just *had* to get their numbers in that day.

Bingo[1] was widely played in New York State, being legal in almost seven hundred cities, towns and villages, and it appeared to be becoming an increasingly popular way of raising money for non-profit organizations such as churches, temples, fraternal organizations, hospitals and veterans posts (see Exhibit 3). In its annual report for 1966 the State Bingo Commission cited three factors in explaining the popularity of bingo: the large share of gross receipts returned as prizes, approximately 64 percent; the respectability of bingo as a way of raising funds; and the rigid supervision of bingo games and operators throughout the State by the Bingo Commission.

Tickets for the Irish Sweepstakes were also sold in the United States. Owned and operated by Hospitals' Trust Ltd., Dublin, Ireland, a private firm that had invested its sweepstakes profits in a number of industrial enterprises, the Irish Sweepstakes was one of the best known and most popular sweepstakes in the world. Estimates of United States sales varied from $21 million to $33 million per year, with sales in New York State estimated between 10 and 30 percent of the total. Each ticket cost three dollars; the odds against winning exceeded 500:1; and drawings, based on horse races, were held three times a year.

Prize money was divided into units, each containing a full set of prizes,

---

[1] Bingo, a variant of lotto, was played on boards divided into twenty-five numbered squares. Numbers selected by lot were called out and players covered the numbers on their boards with markers. The winner was the first player to cover the numbered squares on his board in any of several standard configurations.

i.e., one first prize, one second prize, and so on. Thus if the total prize money to be awarded on a race amounted to $2,940,000 and each unit contained $294,000 worth of prizes, there would be ten first prizes, ten second prizes, and so on. Usually over 50 percent of net proceeds was paid out in winnings. The approximate prize structure for a typical drawing was as follows:

### Approximate Prize Structure of The Irish Sweepstakes, Typical Drawing

| Size of Prize | Number of Winners | Totals |
|---|---|---|
| $119,500 | 17 | $2,031,500 |
| 47,800 | 17 | 812,600 |
| 23,900 | 17 | 406,300 |
| 1,280 | 952 | 1,218,560 |
| 97* | 5,600† | 543,160 |
| | 6,600 | $5,012,120 |

\* Average figure only.
† Approximate.
SOURCE: *New York Post.*

Sales for this particular drawing are not known.

Sales of Irish Sweepstakes tickets were illegal in most countries of the world, except Ireland, making it difficult to assess methods of distribution. In the United States tickets were apparently imported by a few "importers." These men sold to "distributors" who in turn sold to "retail" salesmen. These resold the tickets to friends and acquaintances, receiving thirty cents per ticket as commission. It was believed both the distributors and importers received gross commissions exceeding 10 percent. The buyer kept part of this ticket; the other part, the counterfoil, containing his name and address, was sent to Dublin to be placed in a drum for the drawing. The buyer was supposed to receive a receipt acknowledging that his ticket had been received in Dublin. This method of distribution offered little control over distributors, and because it was relatively easy to counterfeit both tickets and receipts, the vast majority of Sweepstakes tickets sold in the United States were believed to be forgeries.

There were also other opportunities to gamble in New York State. In 1967, for example, attendance at thoroughbred tracks was 6.7 million with $667 million bet; and harness racing attendance was 9.9 million with $745 million bet. There was believed to be substantial illegal off-track betting as well. In 1967 the U.S. Attorney Robert Morgenthau, on the basis of figures obtained from recent arrests, estimated that bookmakers in metropolitan New York handled more than $100 million per year in bets on horse races and sporting events. And it was also possible to engage in sports pools, private games of chance, and charitable gambling for prizes. Moreover it seemed likely in mid-1968 that several other states might adopt lotteries, among them New Jersey, Kentucky and Florida.

## RESTRICTIONS ON LOTTERY OPERATIONS

There were several important restrictions on the alternatives available to a lottery operator such as New York State. Many states in the United States had laws making purchase or possession of any type of lottery ticket a misdemeanor. Both New Jersey and Connecticut had had such laws until 1967, when they were repealed by their legislatures.

Advertising the lottery on radio was forbidden by Section 1304 of the U.S. Criminal Code:

Whoever broadcasts by means of any radio station for which a license is required by any law of the U.S., or whoever, operating any such station, knowingly permits the broadcasting of, any advertisement of or information concerning any lottery . . . offering prizes dependent in whole or in part upon lot or chance . . . shall be fined not more than $1,000 or imprisoned not more than one year, or both. Each day's broadcasting shall constitute a separate offense. Source: 18 U.S.C. 1304.

Federal Communications Commission rules had extended the reach of this section to television as well. In a declaratory ruling in September 1968 the Commission upheld the ban on use of radio and television for lottery advertising, but it indicated that reasonable, good faith news coverage was permissible:

. . . the phrase "any information" about lotteries, should not, in our view, be construed to bar ordinary news reports concerning legislation authorizing the institution of a State Lottery, or of public debate on the course State policy should take. Licensee editorials on public debate in this area are also not, in our view, proscribed by the statute, and our rules are not to be read as prohibiting them. In the category of news, any material broadcast in normal good faith coverage, which is reasonably related to the audience's right and desire to know and be informed of the day-to-day happenings within the community is permissible. Source: F.C.C. Declaratory Ruling, #68–976 (Sept. 25, 1968).

In addition federal law made it a crime to publish full lists of lottery winners, but not interviews with local winners or top prize winners as matters of general interest. U.S. Post Office regulations forbade mailing lottery tickets, full lists of names of winners, and any materials pertaining to the operation of a lottery. Publications not in interstate commerce and not using the mails could carry full names of winners; for example the *Manchester Union Leader* published full lists of New Hampshire Sweepstakes winners in editions not distributed by mail. Only such publications could carry advertising for any lottery. Federal law also forbade transporting lottery tickets across state lines for sale.

A different type of restriction was the political circumstances surrounding the lottery. The Governor and several powerful members of the State Legislature had not supported the lottery referendum but had reluctantly accepted its results. Criticism of the lottery had diminished during its first year, but if results remained poor criticism was likely to mount, including efforts to resubmit the entire question to the voters via another referendum. Moreover, major changes in the lottery such as enlarging the pool of prospective sales agents required approval by the State Legislature of an amendment to the State Lottery Law.

## FIRST YEAR SALES

Sales on the first day, June 1, 1967, were heavy, later estimated to be somewhat over one million tickets in New York City alone. Many distributors throughout the state had underestimated sales and doubled or tripled their first reorders. A spokesman for Manufacturers Hanover in New York City indicated that sales had been particularly heavy at branches in business districts of the city and in low-income residential areas. Sales for the month were approximately $6.5 million, far below the forecast of $30 million. Commissioner Murphy offered several explanations. The division of the Lottery was virtually unstaffed. Distribution was considered poor. By the end of June only 4,200 of the potential 10,000 sales agents had been licensed. Moreover the advertising campaign was not fully under way nor were adequate point-of-sale display and promotional materials available. For example, the official blue and yellow sign announcing "New York State Lottery Tickets For Sale Here" was unavailable in most outlets during June.

Criticism began to mount during the month, as it appeared sales would fall far short of the forecast. State Education Commissioner James D. Allen said that the Lottery was "completely inconsistent" with such objectives of education as teaching children that gambling was evil. *The New York Times* criticized the use of billboards to promote the lottery as "sad and ironic" because billboards tended to diminish scenic and esthetic values. It also said that the planned promotional budget of $1.5 million was too much, particularly as the lottery at that time, June 9, appeared to be selling itself.

In addition the lottery received poor news coverage during the month. Even on the first day not all three of New York's major television stations carried news stories. NBC carried no news of the lottery at all, neither on network or local news broadcasts. CBS gave a brief report on its local news report, as did ABC. All three were reported to be concerned about Section 1304 of the U.S. Criminal Code mentioned earlier.

*The New York Times* also published an interview during June with several operators of the numbers game. These anonymous operators reported that the lottery had not hurt their business, citing that the numbers game provided action six times per week, and that winners were not publicly announced, and thus not subject to "relatives moochin' around" or to taxes.

For the remainder of the year sales continued below initial forecasts. In September the forecast itself was revised. Initially the state had hoped to realize $198 million for education from the lottery. In September this was revised to $35 million for the first year. Monthly gross receipts were as follows:

| Month | Gross Receipts (millions) |
|---|---|
| June 1967 | $ 6.45 |
| July | 4.13 |
| August | 5.99 |
| September | 5.80 |
| October | 6.02 |
| November | 5.45 |
| December | 4.77 |
| January 1968 | 4.92 |
| February | 4.93 |
| March | 5.22 |
| April | 4.23 |
| May | 4.53 |
| | $62.44 |

Sixty-six percent of total sales for the year had been made in New York City, which contained 8 million of New York's 18 million residents. Surveys also indicated that about 30 percent of ticket sales were made by nonresidents of New York State.

## LICENSED SALES AGENTS

In the weeks immediately preceding June 1, considerable interest was shown by potential vendors in becoming sales agents, so that by June 1 some 3,800 hotels, motels, banks, and their branches had been licensed to sell lottery tickets. In addition some of the state's 1,700 offices were to be licensed. Not all possible distributors were licensed, however, due in part to the short time the Division of the Lottery had had to prepare for the beginning of sales. It is estimated that another 3,000 banks and bank branches and 4,500 hotels and motels were potentially available, although lottery officials felt some were of dubious size and stability.

Licensees were given a seventeen-page manual with instructions for obtaining and selling tickets and for preparing weekly and end-of-month sales reports, a kit containing advertising and promotional materials, a list of free point-of-sale materials available and instructions on the legal limitations on lottery advertising and promotion. A monthly newsletter for sales agents called "Profit Margin" was also distributed. It contained news of successful promotions by agents, pictures of agents selling winning tickets, and merchandising tips. Like all such promotional material,

"Profit Margin" had to be delivered by hand. In addition a bonus plan for agents selling winning tickets was put into effect during the year:

| Size of | | | | |
|---|---|---|---|---|
| winning ticket ($) . . . . . . . | 100,000 | 50,000 | 20,000 | 10,000 |
| Bonus to agent selling the | | | | |
| winning ticket ($) . . . . . . . | 500 | 250 | 100 | 50 |

The number of licensed sales agents varied between 4,100 and 4,400 during the first ten months of lottery operations. The number rose to over 9,000 by the beginning of May, 1968 and over 9,800 by the beginning of June.

Also on June 1, 1967, Representative Wright Patman, Chairman of the House Banking Committee, announced hearings to consider a bill banning participation by national banks and federally insured banks in the sale of lottery tickets. Action on this bill proceeded rapidly and on June 13, 1967, the House passed the bill. The Director of the New Hampshire Sweepstakes stated that the bill would not affect New Hampshire because no tickets were sold through banks. A spokesman for Commissioner Murphy estimated switching the bookkeeping done by the banks to the State would raise the administrative costs of the lottery from $500,000 to $1 million. At the time banks comprised approximately 2,400 of the total lottery outlets. The bill subsequently passed the Senate and on December 15 was signed into law by President Johnson without comment. It banned sales of lottery tickets or disbursing of prize winnings by federally insured banks, effective April 1, 1968.

As a result it became clear that new outlets for lottery tickets sales would have to be found. To this end a series of sales tests were conducted in five of the state's twelve tax districts in selected supermarkets, drugstores and department stores. Since none of these outlets was licensed to sell lottery tickets, state employees were used, thus making the test outlet a temporary state office, where sales were legal. The typical test ran two or three days. One, conducted at the Daitch-Shopwell supermarket, 90th street and Broadway, New York City, was typical of the results: In two days three state employees sold 705 tickets, 305 the first day, 400 on the second. The employees sat at a table near the exit of the supermarket from 10 A.M. to 6:45 P.M. Average daily sales of tickets were obtained from two nearby banks, one a branch of Chemical Bank New York Trust, one block to the north, the other a branch of the New York Bank for Savings, four blocks to the south. The Chemical Bank branch reported sales averaging 3,000 per month. The Bank for Savings reported average sales during the first four days of the week as 200 and on Friday, when it stayed open until 6 P.M., as 500. In another sales test, state employees sold 2,000 tickets in two days in a "poor" location in the lobby of the Pan American building in New York City. Buyer reaction at both test sites was favorable, with buyers citing the convenience of the purchase and the generally long lines at banks. It appeared that a majority of purchasers in the sales tests had not bought lottery tickets before. Overall test results showed an average sale of 221 tickets per day in the test outlets, versus 98 per day in banks.

As a result Commissioner Murphy recommended to the Governor that he propose new outlets to the Legislature, which the Governor did in his annual message to the Legislature. Senate Majority Leader Brydges stated at that time that while he still opposed the lottery he would reluctantly accept the Governor's recommendations. The Lottery Law was amended so that any store or place of business could be licensed to sell lottery tickets with the exception of bars, schools, banks, and religious, charitable, or scientific organizations. In voting for the bill Senator Brydges said the lottery deserved "one final fling." The bill took effect April 1. Until this time banks had accounted for approximately 75 percent of all ticket sales.

While this major change was taking place several minor developments occurred. Sales at racetracks in the state were good. At Yonkers Raceway sales averaged more than 10 percent of daily attendance, exceeding the expectations of lottery officials. As a result application was made to the State Racing Authority for permission to sell tickets at more tracks in the state. This permission was granted and by September 1967 tickets were being sold at Roosevelt, Yonkers, and Monticello Raceways, at Batavia Downs and at Finger Lakes Track, but not at Saratoga, which did not open until summer 1968. The New York Transit Authority considered selling lottery tickets in a few high traffic locations in the subway system but because of the insufficient manpower rejected the proposal. Selling tickets at all token booths in the system was not considered, apparently because of possible difficulties in the Transit Workers' Union.

In the spring 1968 the Lottery Commission entered into negotiations with the American News Company, which operated almost 500 retail newsstands in the state, mostly in New York City. A contract was ultimately reached and signed by July 30, 1968 providing a commission of $5\frac{3}{4}$ percent per ticket if sales exceeded 500,000 tickets per month and an additional $1\frac{3}{4}$ percent if the Company performed all distribution, accounting, administrative and promotional activities which otherwise would have been performed by the state.

## SALES REPRESENTATIVES

Licensed agents were to be visited by a force of eighteen sales representatives, most of whom had been hired by September, 1967. Each representative was assigned to a tax district—for example, there were eleven representatives in New York City—and was responsible for calling on sales agents within the district. Sales representatives were expected to answer questions, deliver promotional materials, assist the agent in merchandising the lottery, and enlist new sales agents. A sales meeting was held during the year at which sales techniques were discussed and future advertising plans were explained to the representatives.

Sales representatives reported to the local District Tax Supervisor for day-to-day supervision, and to the Supervising Lottery Sales Representative in Albany for policy matters. Efforts were begun during the year to establish hiring standards for sales representatives. The position of a lottery sales representative was a non-civil service job that paid about $9,000 per year. The Supervising Lottery Sales Representative received about $14,000 per year. Sales representatives received a travel allowance but no expense account.

## LOTTERY ADVERTISING

As indicated above, federal law forbade use of forms of advertising media, including broadcast media and direct mail. Initial media were limited to transit and outdoor advertising. A heavy schedule of transit advertising was employed. Each of the 7,000 cars in the New York subway system was double-carded and another 1,800 posters were placed in the stations. Bus advertising was used both in New York City and upstate, principally in Rochester, Buffalo, and the trading areas of Albany, Syracuse, and Niagara Falls. In all cases interior cards were used.

Outdoor advertising began on June 15, 1967 with the purchase of approximately 2,000 30-sheet boards throughout the state. After two months this was reduced to 1,000 boards. The amount of outdoor advertising declined during the year and the funds released went into newspaper advertising. In summer 1967, Commissioner Murphy, apparently concerned about criticism of lottery outdoor advertising, announced guidelines for its use. These included using only existing boards, erecting no new signs and concentrating outdoor advertising in the state's urban areas where the opportunity to spoil natural scenery was small.

Efforts made before the start of the lottery to purchase newspaper space had been unsuccessful. The principal difficulty had been the fact that all newspapers distributed at least part of their circulation by mail. But in July, 1967, two newspapers agreed to carry lottery advertisements. Editions going through the mails were replated so as not to carry lottery ads. By the end of the first year of operation, forty of the state's approximately seventy-five dailies were carrying lottery ads. (All materials were sent to newspapers by bus carrier or railway express.) The schedule was three weekly insertions in every four-week month and four weekly insertions in every five-week month. Each month there was no advertising in the week of the drawing because it was felt the drawing itself generated considerable publicity.

There were two principal copy themes. Initial copy stressed that purchase of a lottery ticket would help education. In mid-August, 1967, copy began to emphasize prize winnings. Both appeals continued to be used through the first year. Photographs of winners were also used in some ads.

The total budget, approximately $1.5 million, is given in Exhibit 4.

## PRIZE STRUCTURE AND DRAWINGS

Two changes were made in the form of the lottery during the first year. On May 24, 1967, one week before the first public ticket sale, Governor Rockefeller announced the addition of 225 prizes to the prize schedule. Prizes were now divided into two tiers: a Grand Prize Tier with an allocation of $240,000 and a Consolation Prize Tier with an allocation of $60,000. In the Grand Prize Tier the prizes were top, $100,000; second, $50,000; third, $25,000; fourth $10,000; the remaining eleven prizes being worth $5,000 each. In the Consolation Prize Tier there were fifteen prizes of $1,000 each; fifteen of $700 each, fifteen of $400 each, fifteen of $250 each, and one hundred and sixty-five of $150 each. As a result of these changes there were now 240 prizes for each million dollars in sales. Furthermore, the Governor announced an annual bonus drawing worth $250,000 to be held each March. Names of past winners were to be placed in a drum and one drawn. The prize would be $250,000, payable $25,000 per year for ten years, to reduce income taxes.

The second change dealt with the frequency of drawings. Legislation was passed by the New York State Legislature permitting prize drawings to be held as often as once a week. This was an apparent attempt to answer some of the lottery's critics who claimed that monthly drawings were too infrequent to stimulate interest among potential bettors. Upon passage of the bill, which became effective April 1, 1968, Commissioner Murphy announced he would start with two drawings a month, because the Department of Taxation and Finance did not have the necessary manpower to control weekly drawings. By June 1, 1968, semimonthly drawings had not yet begun.

## ACTIVITY IN OTHER STATES

In September, 1967, New Hampshire made the following changes in its sweepstakes. The number of drawings per year was doubled to four. The value of the top prize in each drawing was increased from $50,000 to $100,000. At the same time other changes in the prize schedule were announced. The result of these changes was that the proportion of prize money to total gross receipts was increased from 36 to 38 percent. The Sweepstakes Commission also began efforts to persuade corporations in New Hampshire to use sweepstakes tickets in various incentive schemes, such as a reward to an individual worker for low absenteeism or as an award in a sales contest.

After some changes in announced position, Governor Hughes of New

Jersey said he would support placing a lottery referendum on the New Jersey election slate for November, 1968.

## LOTTERY RESEARCH

A survey of New York State residents was conducted in September, 1967.[2] Ninety-six percent of the respondents were aware of the lottery's existence, and awareness of individual components of the lottery was generally high. For example, slightly more than one-half of the respondents came reasonably close (within $25,000) to being able to name the top monthly prize, and 86 percent knew that banks sold lottery tickets. But when classified as to awareness of three aspects of the lottery together —its purpose, prize structure, and ticket-selling locations—almost half were considered poorly informed.

Almost one-half of the sample had already bought lottery tickets by the time the interviewing was conducted, in late September, of which three-quarters were repeat buyers. Ninety-five percent of past buyers indicated they intended to purchase more in the future. (Exhibit 5 contains selected data on both buyers and nonbuyers.)

Number of tickets purchased was distributed as follows:

| Largest Number of Tickets Bought at Any One Time | Percent of Ticket Buyers |
|---|---|
| 1 | 35 |
| 2 | 30 |
| 3 | 13 |
| 4 or more | 21 |
| Did not specify | 1 |
| | 100 |

In response to a question dealing with the degree of planning in a purchase, one-third of the respondents said they purchased on "the spur of the moment," while the remainder indicated they decided to buy ahead of time. Respondents were also asked how often they had purchased tickets.

| Number of Times Purchased | Percent of Ticket Buyers | Percent of Total Sample |
|---|---|---|
| Once | 23.1 | 11.3 |
| Twice | 15.8 | 7.8 |
| Three times | 24.1 | 11.8 |
| Four times | 17.4 | 8.6 |
| More than four times | 13.9 | 6.8 |
| Other replies | 5.7 | 2.8 |
| | 100.0 | 49.1 |

---

[2] A stratified, random sample was used, designed to approximate the New York State population over eighteen years old. It contained 1,202 respondents.

The survey attempted to identify interest in gambling by asking how frequently respondents engaged in various types of gambling activities. Respondents were classified as Outright Gamblers if they frequently or occasionally engaged in any form of "hard" gambling such as playing the numbers, placing off-track bets (both illegal in New York State) or betting at the horse track; as Quasi-Gamblers if they frequently or occasionally engaged in "soft" gambling such as charitable chances with interest in a prize, product purchases with a prize chance, or games with a money chance; as Low-Interest Gamblers if they seldom engaged in "soft" gambling; and as Non-Gamblers if they never engaged in any gambling except for charitable chances without interest in a prize. Exhibit 6 classifies the total sample by these categories. The distribution of buyers and non-buyers by these classifications is found in Exhibit 7.

Respondents were also asked why people bought lottery tickets and shown a card listing "Help Education, Hope of Winning, Excitement and Suspense" as possible reasons. Sixty-one percent of respondents picked "Hope of Winning" and 23 percent picked "Help Education."

A number of questions dealt with factors inhibiting sales. Forty-two percent of respondents said they would be more likely to buy if purchases could be made at supermarkets, 38 percent at drugstores, and 29 percent at department stores. Two out of three thought they would become buyers if there were more winners and smaller prizes, while 15 percent felt sales would increase with fewer winners and bigger prizes. About 40 percent said more frequent drawings would increase sales. Many also felt that smaller, tax free prizes would increase sales.

Attempts were made to develop some measure of the lottery's potential by asking non-buyers if they planned to buy tickets in the future and how many; and if they might buy under certain conditions such as wider distribution of sales outlets. Those who said they would buy under certain conditions or who gave a specific number of tickets they planned to buy in the future were classified Likely New Buyers. This group comprised 55 percent of non-buyers.[3] The highest percentages of Likely New Buyers were found among women, the young (18–29 years of age), those with family incomes under $5,000 per year, Negroes, Puerto Ricans, and Protestants.

## PROPOSED CHANGES

As of June, 1968, lottery officials still did not feel they had the key to successful promotion of the lottery. Numerous options had been suggested by hostile and sympathetic critics. One legislator had introduced into the 1968 Legislature a bill that would have abolished the lottery. It had been

---

[3] The researchers estimated that 0.7 percent of the total sample could be classified as Low-Interest Gamblers *and* Likely New Buyers, and 13.2 percent of the total sample as Non-Gamblers *and* Likely New Buyers.

killed in committee. Some suggested doubling the number of prizes to 480 while keeping the total payout the same. Others suggested use of street vendors to sell tickets, a practice common in many foreign countries. Commissioner Murphy did not feel street vendors were appropriate, however, nor did he feel such a proposal could pass the Legislature. Many suggestions dealt with reducing or eliminating the state income tax on winnings, and the research on lottery buyers cited above indicated that many respondents were concerned about taxes on winnings. There were three arguments against such a course: it would entail considerable administrative difficulties; it would conflict with the income tax conformity agreement between state and federal tax authorities; and it would likely draw demands for similar treatment from parimutuel operators, a far more important source of tax revenues. Machine vending of tickets had also been proposed. But there was concern that machines would enable persons under eighteen years of age to buy tickets, in violation of the Lottery Bill. If machines were to be used, it was felt, they would require operators.

By mid-June the first preliminary estimate of June sales became available. It was $4.05 million, the lowest since the start of the lottery.

## EXHIBIT 1

### Pro Forma Income Statement, New York State Lottery
### (June 1967–May 1968)

|  |  | Millions of Dollars | Percent |
|---|---|---|---|
| Gross receipts |  | $360 | 100 |
| Expenses |  |  |  |
| Commissions | $ 18 |  | 5* |
| Administration | 36 |  | 10 |
| Prizes | 108 | 162 | 30† |
| Net receipts |  | $198 | 55† |

\* As determined by the State Tax Commissioner.
† As required by State Lottery Law.
SOURCE: *New York Times*, May 11, 1967.

**EXHIBIT 2**

**Operating Results, New Hampshire Sweepstakes, 1963–1967***
**(000 omitted)**

| | July 29,1963 to Sept. 30,1964 | | Oct.1,1964 to Sept. 30,1965 | | Oct.1,1965 to Sept. 30,1966 | | Oct.1,1966 to Sept. 30,1967 | |
|---|---|---|---|---|---|---|---|---|
| Gross ticket revenue........ | | $5,729 | | $3,901 | | $3,862 | | $2,567 |
| Gross operating expenses.... | 1,071† | | 478 | | 433 | | 377 | |
| Prizes: | | | | | | | | |
|   Sweepstakes purse...... | 100 | | 200 | | 200 | | 200 | |
|   Prizes................ | 1,800 | 2,971 | 1,400 | 2,078 | 1,415 | 2,048 | 944 | 1,521 |
| Net ticket revenue.......... | | 2,758 | | 1,823 | | 1,814 | | 1,046 |
| Other income.............. | | 10 | | 661‡ | | 26 | | 9 |
| Net income available for | | | | | | | | |
|   distribution.............. | | 2,768 | | 2,487 | | 1,841 | | 1,055 |

* Figures may not add, due to rounding.
† Includes Internal Revenue 10% tax and stamps ($588).
‡ Includes refund of 1964 Internal Revenue tax plus interest ($617).
SOURCE: New Hampshire Sweepstakes Commission.

**EXHIBIT 3**

**Bingo in New York State: Gross Receipts**
**Net Profit and Number of Conducting Organizations, 1953–1966***

| Year | Gross Receipts (millions) | Net Profit (millions) | Number of Organizations Conducting Bingo |
|---|---|---|---|
| 1959................. | $21.4 | $ 4.8 | 1,501 |
| 1960................. | 41.4 | 9.4 | 1,441 |
| 1961................. | 45.4 | 11.0 | 1,296 |
| 1962................. | 50.6 | 13.6 | 1,232 |
| 1963................. | 57.3 | 16.1 | 1,242 |
| 1964................. | 64.9 | 18.7 | 1,337 |
| 1965................. | 74.1 | 21.6 | 1,449 |
| 1966................. | 83.3 | 24.6 | 1,543 |

* Bingo was legalized in 1958 on a local option basis.
SOURCE: *Fifth Annual Report* (N.Y.), State Bingo Control Commission (1967).

## EXHIBIT 4

### Advertising and Promotional Budget by Media, June 1967–March 1968*

| | |
|---|---:|
| Transit......................................... | $ 255,000 |
| Newspaper..................................... | 214,000 |
| Matchbooks.................................... | 21,000 |
| Billboards..................................... | 745,000 |
| Other.......................................... | 8,000 |
| | $1,245,000 |
| Production..................................... | 150,000 |
| Total media and production budget.......... | $1,395,000 |

* Figures do not add because of rounding. Total budget for the period June, 1967 to May, 1968 was $1,500,000.
SOURCE: Fuller & Smith & Ross.

## EXHIBIT 5

### Selected Characteristics of Lottery Buyers and Non-Buyers, October, 1967

| | Total Sample (percent) | Non-Buyers* (percent) | Repeat Buyers (percent) | Non-Repeat Buyers (percent) |
|---|---|---|---|---|
| Total state........................... | 100 | 51.0 | 37.3 | 11.7 |
| *Age* | | | | |
| 18–29........................... | 19.2 | 65.8 | 25.5 | 8.7 |
| 30–49........................... | 39.6 | 46.0 | 41.0 | 13.0 |
| 50 and over..................... | 38.9 | 49.0 | 39.0 | 12.0 |
| *Income* | | | | |
| Under $5,000.................... | 26.2 | 64.0 | 26.0 | 10.0 |
| $5,000–$9,999................... | 46.3 | 44.5 | 44.0 | 11.5 |
| Over $10,000.................... | 25.1 | 49.6 | 36.1 | 14.3 |
| *Occupation* | | | | |
| Business & professional............ | 23.9 | 57.8 | 30.7 | 12.5 |
| Clerical & sales................. | 13.2 | 40.9 | 47.8 | 11.3 |
| Manual.......................... | 42.2 | 46.3 | 42.4 | 11.3 |
| *Religion* | | | | |
| Protestant....................... | 33.1 | 66.0 | 23.2 | 10.8 |
| Catholic......................... | 50.2 | 41.6 | 45.6 | 12.8 |
| Jewish.......................... | 11.9 | 47.3 | 42.4 | 10.3 |
| *Region* | | | | |
| New York City.................. | 50.9 | 41.4 | 46.3 | 12.3 |
| New York suburbs............... | 12.1 | 42.4 | 42.5 | 15.1 |
| Upstate cities................... | 21.3 | 64.5 | 24.6 | 10.9 |
| Upstate towns.................. | 15.7 | 70.7 | 21.3 | 8.0 |
| *Number of respondents*................. | 1,202 | 613 | 448 | 141 |

* Including "not heard of."
SOURCE: Division of the Lottery.

**EXHIBIT 6**

**Survey Respondents Classified by Interest in Gambling**

|  | Outright Gamblers (percent) | Quasi-Gamblers (percent) | Low-Interest Gamblers (percent) | Non-Gamblers (percent) |
|---|---|---|---|---|
| Total state................... | 17.2 | 31.9 | 2.3 | 48.6 |
| *Age* |  |  |  |  |
| 18–29................... | 17.7 | 28.6 | 4.3 | 49.4 |
| 30–49................... | 20.8 | 34.9 | 1.5 | 42.8 |
| 50 and over.............. | 13.7 | 30.2 | 2.4 | 53.7 |
| *Income* |  |  |  |  |
| Under $5,000............. | 14.0 | 23.5 | 3.8 | 58.7 |
| $5,000–$9,999............ | 18.8 | 35.4 | 1.8 | 44.0 |
| $10,000 and over.......... | 17.3 | 34.9 | 1.7 | 46.1 |
| *Occupation* |  |  |  |  |
| Business & professional..... | 13.9 | 28.2 | 1.8 | 56.1 |
| Clerical & sales........... | 20.8 | 37.7 | 1.9 | 39.6 |
| Manual.................. | 19.5 | 34.1 | 2.4 | 44.0 |
| *Religion* |  |  |  |  |
| Protestant............... | 12.6 | 27.4 | 2.5 | 57.5 |
| Catholic................. | 21.2 | 35.5 | 1.8 | 41.5 |
| Jewish.................. | 14.0 | 30.8 | 3.5 | 51.7 |
| *Region* |  |  |  |  |
| New York City............ | 20.6 | 31.7 | 3.3 | 44.4 |
| New York suburbs......... | 13.0 | 41.1 | .0 | 45.9 |
| Upstate cities............. | 16.8 | 27.3 | 2.0 | 53.9 |
| Upstate towns............ | 10.1 | 31.4 | 1.6 | 56.9 |
| *Number of respondents*.......... | 207 | 383 | 28 | 584 |

SOURCE: Division of the Lottery.

**EXHIBIT 7**

**Buyers and Non-Buyers Classified by Interest in Gambling**

|  | Total Sample (percent) | Outright Gamblers (percent) | Quasi-Gamblers (percent) | Low-Interest Gamblers (percent) | Non-Gamblers (percent) |
|---|---|---|---|---|---|
| Buyers............... | 49.0 | 72.0 | 63.5 | 35.7 | 32.2 |
| Repeat............ | 37.3 | 60.9 | 50.7 | 28.6 | 20.7 |
| Non-repeat........ | 11.7 | 11.1 | 12.8 | 7.1 | 11.5 |
| Non-buyers............ | 51.0* | 27.5 | 35.2 | 42.9 | 60.8 |
| Never heard of......... |  | 0.5 | 1.3 | 21.4 | 7.0 |
|  | 100.0 | 100.0 | 100.0 | 100.0 | 100.0 |
| Number of respondents. | 1,202 | 207 | 383 | 28 | 584 |

* Including "never heard of" category.
SOURCE: Division of the Lottery.

## APPENDIX: EXCERPTS FROM THE STATE LOTTERY LAW

Section 1305. Powers and duties of the commissioner of taxation and finance

[The commissioner shall have the power:]

1. (A) To establish the time and place of regular drawings of the state lottery, but limited to not more than one regular drawing in any week.

(B) To establish the time and place of special or bonus drawings.

4. To provide for compensation in . . . manner and amounts to . . . licensed sellers of lottery tickets only where the commissioner finds that such compensation is necessary to assure adequate availability of lottery tickets . . .

5. To decide . . . the price at which tickets are sold.

(b) . . . to determine the method . . . used in selling lottery tickets and . . . to purchase or lease machines through which tickets may be sold. Such machines may not be coin operated . . .

(d) . . . to license agents to sell tickets for the state lottery. The commissioner may require a bond from any licensed agent, in an amount to be determined by the commissioner.

Section 1306. Lottery sales agents

(a) The commissioner may license as agents to sell lottery tickets such persons as in his opinion will best serve public convenience, except that no license shall be issued to any person to engage in business exclusively as a lottery sales agent, nor shall any license be issued to any person for the sale of lottery tickets within . . . premises licensed to sell beer, liquor or wine. . . .

(c) . . . before issuing a license . . . the commissioner shall consider, with respect to each person:

1. Financial responsibility and security of the business or activity.
2. Accessibility of the place of business or activity to the public.
3. Sufficiency of existing licenses to serve public convenience.
4. Whether the place of business or activity is predominately frequented by minors.
5. Volume of expected sales.

Section 1310. Lottery tickets

The price at which tickets are sold shall not be less than one dollar for each ticket. . . . [E]ach ticket shall bear the name and address of the person entitled to receive any prize. . . . No ticket shall be sold at a price greater than that fixed by the commissioner nor shall a sale be made by any person other than a licensed lottery sales agent . . .

Section 1311. Sales to certain persons prohibited

(a) No ticket shall be sold to any person actually or apparently under eighteen years, but this shall not be deemed to prohibit . . . purchase . . . for the purpose of making a gift . . . to a person less than [eighteen].

(b) No ticket shall be sold to, and no prize paid to . . . : (i) any officer or employee of the department of taxation and finance, (ii) any member of the [state lottery] commission, or (iii) any spouse, child, brother, sister or parent residing as a member of the same household in the principal place of abode of any of the foregoing persons.

Section 1314. Disposition of revenues

All moneys received by the commissioner from the sale of lottery tickets . . . shall be used for the payment of lottery prizes, but the amount so used shall in no event exceed thirty percent of the total amount for which the tickets have been sold. On or before the twentieth day of each month, the commissioner shall pay into the state treasury . . . not less than fifty-five percent of the total amount . . . sold during the preceding month . . .

SOURCE: New York State Tax Law Sections 1300–1315, April, 1967, amended March, 1968.

# Index of Cases